BUS STOP
©2008 Eddie Campbell.

ALEC

"The Years Have Pants"

(A LIFE-SIZED OMNIBUS)

Eddie Campbell

Top Shelf Productions

For the real life versions of the three people in the sieve, without whom I would have had to make up most of the funny parts of this book.

Softcover ISBN 978-1-60309-025-4 / Hardcover ISBN 978-1-60309-047-6
1. Autobiographical Fiction / 2. Comics

Cover design by Eric Skillman. Interior design by Eddie Campbell. Production assistance by Emi Lenox.

Eddie Campbell

The years have pants.

Knee pants, long pants, baggy pants, as they say in the U.S. In Britain, 'pants' is more likely to make us think of the ones we wear underneath. Otherwise we say 'trousers.' But they fit much the same: *"I grow old, I wear the bottoms of my trousers rolled,"* (the words of TS Eliot's Alfred J Prufrock). And thus the years pass. The title quote at top is the first line in a poem by the buddy of Hoagy Carmichael's college pants, William Ernest Moenkhaus, and you'll find the whole piece away along on page 605. The blue-jean photo on the facing page is from 1979, making this a collection spanning thirty years. People are born, grow up and leave home in the course of these 640 pages. I used to wonder what that would be like, when, in the 1970s, I first delved into the old long-running daily newspaper strip *Gasoline Alley*, in which a cast of paper people grew up day by day, devised in the days before actors grew older by default before our eyes in long-running TV soap operas. Somebody once called that strip a 'great twentieth-century American novel.' Poet-critic of the funnies, Donald Phelps, begged to differ: *"The sustenance of the comic strip is sheer continuity, the endurance of its daily, hypnotic present tense. How can traditional form, itself dedicated to the illusion of finality through its own totality, be represented, much less honoured in the comic strip?"*

I also wondered if I'd live long enough and not get too sidetracked by life's practicalities, or disheartened by its disappointments, to continue the project to a point where the great shifts in a life could be mapped out. But at the same time I wanted to not lose sight of the everyday details that we tend to otherwise forget when we have our eye focused on a goal.

This is the first digital version of the so-called *Alec* books, and I guess it's too late to call them by another name. I've scanned and prepared all the pages myself from the original art. The collection includes all of the published books—six—with the exception of a seventh, *The Fate of the Artist* (2006), which is in colour and available from another publisher, First Second Books. Add to that a completely new book made just for the present compendium, titled *The Years Have Pants.* In the course of putting the package together, its title became the title for the whole thing. You will also find here a selection of my shorts and also my fragmentary and abandoned books, insofar as they are worth salvaging. For those who think they already have it all, there are forty-five pages of previously unpublished material and fifty-five more that are rare or a long time out of print. I can only hope there will be an old baggy version of this book in another twenty, but you should enjoy this neatly pressed one in the meantime.

Eddie Campbell, 2009

the King Canute Crowd

Picking the exact point at which to enter a big narrative is a matter of some importance to the author with the kind of ambition described opposite. It took me several attempts to arrive at page 1, which is why you'll see some older material being interpolated as I go along. In fact I had drawn hundreds of comic-book pages before it, but halfway through that page, it occurred to me that I had found an artistic voice. I am presuming it's mine until I find out differently.

Alec MacGarry was feeling that mental malaise that was going around in some circles at the time. Having in his mind condemned the world to wallow in its own stupidity, and wearing an old jacket he picked up for a quid at Oxfam, he had apathetically worked his way down the employment ladder to the position of unskilled factory hand...

One

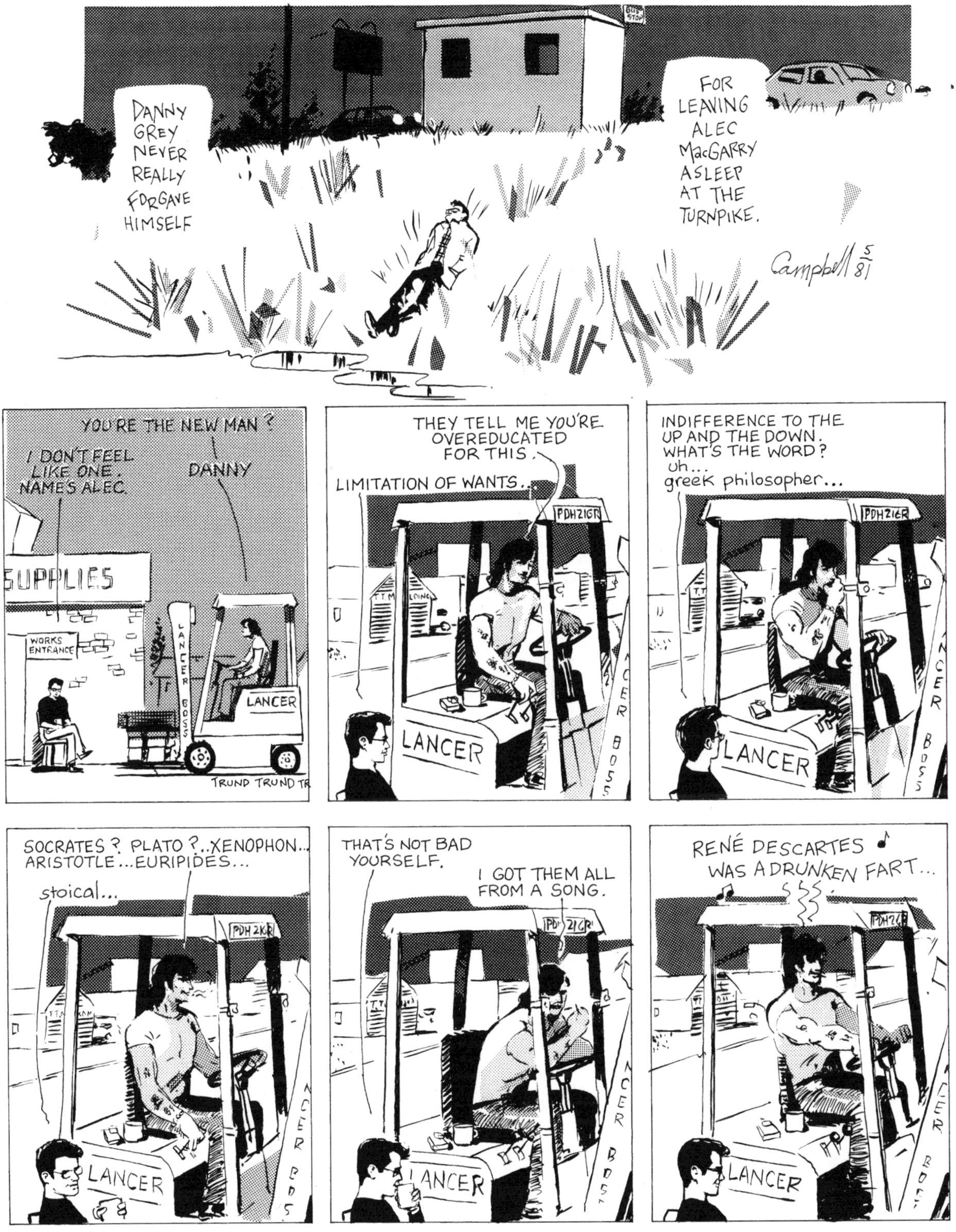

BUS STOP
DANNY GREY NEVER REALLY FORGAVE HIMSELF
FOR LEAVING ALEC MacGARRY ASLEEP AT THE TURNPIKE.
Campbell 5/81
YOU'RE THE NEW MAN?
I DON'T FEEL LIKE ONE. NAME'S ALEC.
DANNY
SUPPLIES
WORKS ENTRANCE
LANCER BOSS
LANCER
TRUND TRUND TR
THEY TELL ME YOU'RE OVEREDUCATED FOR THIS.
LIMITATION OF WANTS..
PDH216R
LANCER
INDIFFERENCE TO THE UP AND THE DOWN. WHAT'S THE WORD? uh... greek philosopher...
LANCER
SOCRATES? PLATO?..XENOPHON... ARISTOTLE...EURIPIDES...
stoical...
LANCER
THAT'S NOT BAD YOURSELF.
I GOT THEM ALL FROM A SONG.
LANCER
RENÉ DESCARTES WAS A DRUNKEN FART...
LANCER

I FIND IT A GOOD IDEA, WHEN DRINKING IN NEW COMPANY, TO NOTE DOWN SOME POSSIBLE CONVERSATION STARTERS BEFOREHAND.
SORT OF HELPS YOU OVER THE UNCOMFORTABLE PAUSES.
PREPARED NOTES, YOU MIGHT SAY.
shopping list. SHALL WE CHECK THEM OFF?
ACCORDING TO HIS BIOGRAPHER, JACK KEROUAC FELT THAT ONE OF THE MOST BEAUTIFUL IDEAS IN THE WORLD IS THE IDEA A CHILD HAS THAT HIS FATHER KNOWS EVERYTHING.
I PICKED UP THE WORD 'SYNCOPHANT' FROM MY FATHER. THE FIRST TIME I WENT INTO A PUB I CALLED THIS BLOKE A SYNCOPHANT.
"AND THE FELLOW REPLIED.. "uh.. YOU MEAN SYCOPHANT" OH NO, SAID I ... SYNCOPHANT.
Then I looked it up.
WHAT ELSE HAVE YOU GOT THERE?
"MAN, IT HAS BEEN SAID, DIFFERS FROM OTHER ANIMALS IN ONLY TWO RESPECTS... HE DRINKS WHEN HE IS NOT THIRSTY AND HE MAKES LOVE ALL YEAR ROUND."

LIGHT 'N' BITTER AND BROWN 'N' BITTER, PLEASE.
GLOP
ANYWAY, AFTER THE DIVORCE I WENT TO GREECE. GOT WORK WITH A RESTAURANT THAT HAD ME SITTING ON THE BEACH ALL DAY BASHING SQUIDS ON A ROCK. IT WAS LIKE BEING BACK ON THE LINE AT FORDS.
GALOOP
GALOOP
GALOOP
GAL
LET'S TALK ABOUT THE WEATHER- YOU KNOW HOW WHEN IT RAINS ALL THE SNAILS CRAWL OUT OF THE GARDENS ONTO THE PAVEMENTS AND YOU HAVE TO DO COMPLICATED BALLET-STEPS TO AVOID CRUSHING THEM.
yes, and
MY MOTHER'S IRISH. IN MY MOTOR-BIKE DAYS SHE ONCE SAID TO ME: "IF YOU FALL OFF THAT THING AND BREAK YOUR LEGS, DON'T COME RUNNING TO ME".
coincidence!! my mother too!
THE 'IRISH BULL'. IT'S CHARM LIES IN THE FACT THE SPEAKER IS UNAWARE IT DOESN'T MILK.
..TRYING TO EXPRESS THE NOCTURNAL NATURE OF CATS, SHE SAID THEY MUST BE NIGHT-BIRDS.
good way of putting it.
THAT GIRL OVER THERE... PLAYING DARTS. I FIND HER VERY ATTRACTIVE.
WHY?
oh no. you mean we... disagree.?

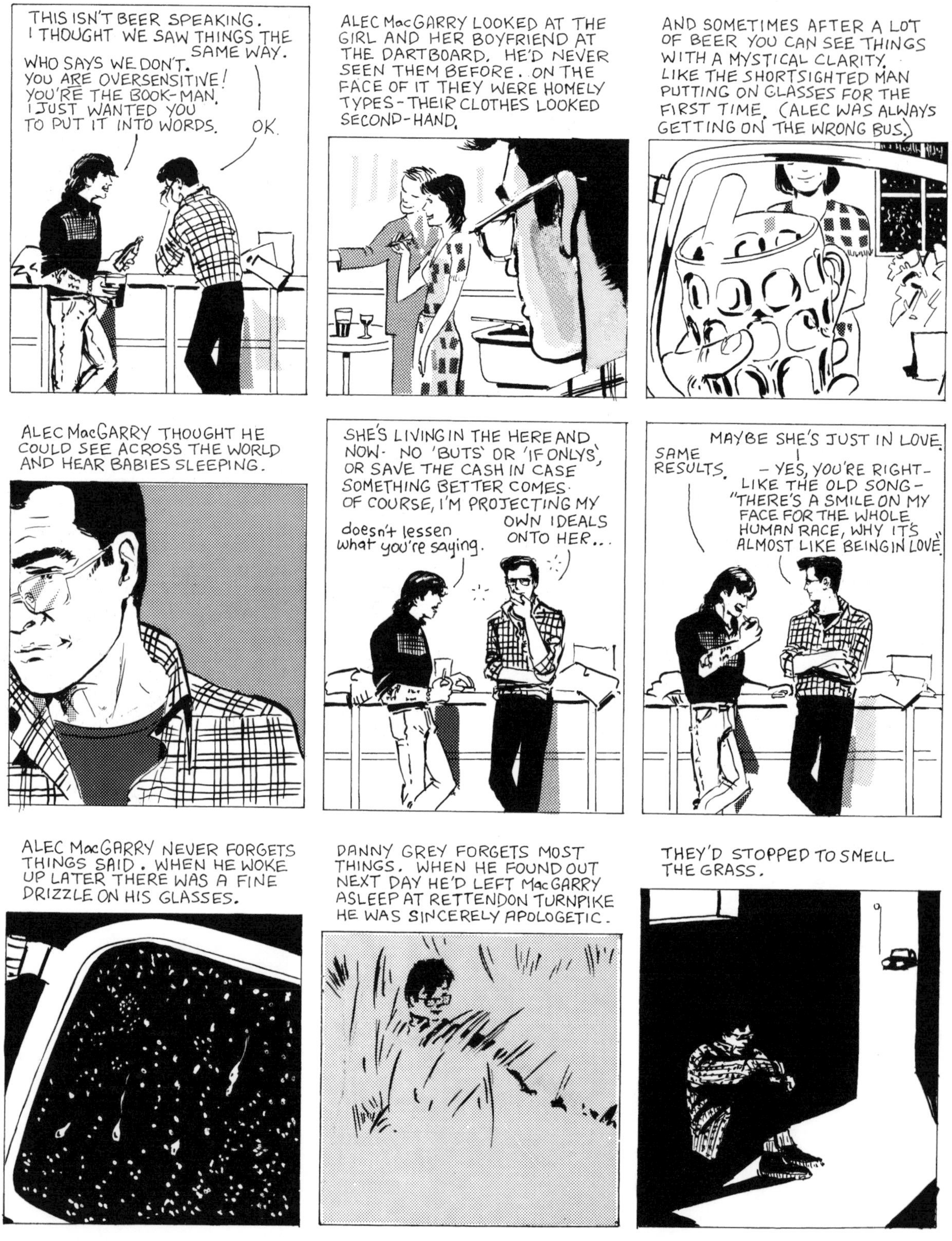
THIS ISN'T BEER SPEAKING. I THOUGHT WE SAW THINGS THE SAME WAY.
WHO SAYS WE DON'T. YOU ARE OVERSENSITIVE! YOU'RE THE BOOK-MAN. I JUST WANTED YOU TO PUT IT INTO WORDS.
OK.
ALEC MacGARRY LOOKED AT THE GIRL AND HER BOYFRIEND AT THE DARTBOARD. HE'D NEVER SEEN THEM BEFORE. ON THE FACE OF IT THEY WERE HOMELY TYPES - THEIR CLOTHES LOOKED SECOND-HAND.
AND SOMETIMES AFTER A LOT OF BEER YOU CAN SEE THINGS WITH A MYSTICAL CLARITY. LIKE THE SHORTSIGHTED MAN PUTTING ON GLASSES FOR THE FIRST TIME. (ALEC WAS ALWAYS GETTING ON THE WRONG BUS.)
ALEC MacGARRY THOUGHT HE COULD SEE ACROSS THE WORLD AND HEAR BABIES SLEEPING.
SHE'S LIVING IN THE HERE AND NOW- NO 'BUTS' OR 'IF ONLYS', OR SAVE THE CASH IN CASE SOMETHING BETTER COMES. OF COURSE, I'M PROJECTING MY OWN IDEALS ONTO HER...
doesn't lessen what you're saying.
MAYBE SHE'S JUST IN LOVE.
SAME RESULTS.
- YES, YOU'RE RIGHT- LIKE THE OLD SONG- "THERE'S A SMILE ON MY FACE FOR THE WHOLE HUMAN RACE, WHY IT'S ALMOST LIKE BEING IN LOVE".
ALEC MacGARRY NEVER FORGETS THINGS SAID. WHEN HE WOKE UP LATER THERE WAS A FINE DRIZZLE ON HIS GLASSES.
DANNY GREY FORGETS MOST THINGS. WHEN HE FOUND OUT NEXT DAY HE'D LEFT MacGARRY ASLEEP AT RETTENDON TURNPIKE HE WAS SINCERELY APOLOGETIC.
THEY'D STOPPED TO SMELL THE GRASS.

ALEC MacGARRY WALKED BACK INTO TOWN AND STOOD A LONG TIME IN FRONT OF A BUTCHER'S SHOP-WINDOW THINKING ABOUT THE POULTRY.

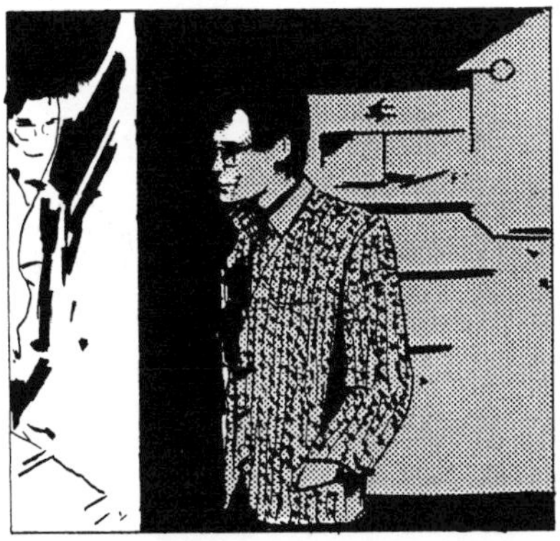

HE FELT NO INCLINATION TO GO HOME OR BACK THE WAY HE'D COME.

SQUISH
SQUISH

SQUISH!
SQUISH!
SQUISH!

LONELINESS, HE REMEMBERED READING, IS NOT SO MUCH A LONGING FOR COMPANY AS A LONGING FOR KIND.

Josephine

E Campbell 6/81

LEND US A QUID, YOU MEAN SCOTTISH BASTARD.
A REAL SCOT WOULDN'T STAND FOR BEING CALLED SCOTTISH.
WHERE DID YOU GET THAT IDEA?
MY DAUGHTER'S TUTOR IS SCOTS... THAT'S WHAT IT SHOULD BE ... SCOTS.
BUT I'M SCOTTISH, FOR HEAVEN'S SAKE... ISN'T IT LIKELY I WOULD KNOW?
IT MUST BE SCOTCH YOU'RE THINKING ABOUT...WHICH IS WHISKY.
NO, I'M SURE SHE SAID...
ANYWAY, WHAT ABOUT SCOTCH EGGS?

I DIDN'T KNOW THEY'D CHANGED THE LOGO ON THE NEW MUSICAL EXPRESS.
JUST THIS WEEK
WHERE DID IRENE GET A WORD LIKE 'LOGO'?
HER DAUGHTER'S AN ART STUDENT.
REMEMBER WE WERE DISCUSSING THE IDEA THAT A CHILD BELIEVES HIS FATHER KNOWS EVERYTHING? WELL IT'S SORT OF THE OTHER WAY ABOUT WITH IRENE.
IRENE'S IN HER SECOND CHILDHOOD AND LOOKS UP TO HER DAUGHTER JOSEPHINE FOR POINTERS.
YOU CAN MEET HER IF YOU LIKE.
LET'S SEE. SOUTHEND TECH. COMES OUT HALF PAST FOUR. mm... FIFTEEN MINUTES TO GET THERE.
YOU CAN'T DRIVE THERE IN 15 MINUTES!!
why not? MEET ME BY THE VAN AT 4.10
wh... WHAT ABOUT WORK?
oh, STOP WORRYING,

ALEC MacGARRY DIDN'T GET TO MEET JOSEPHINE THAT DAY, AND MANY THINGS HAPPENED BETWEEN THEN AND NOW. BUT A FEW MONTHS LATER WHEN ALEC HAS A RENTED BEDSIT IN SOUTHEND DANNY GREY IS BRINGING JOSEPHINE ROUND FOR EVENINGS.
AND DO YOU KNOW.. ALEC PAINTED THIS EIGHT YEARS AGO AT THE AGE OF FOURTEEN...
MacGARRY'S SELF-PORTRAIT OF VAN GOGH!
ARE YOU SURE IT WASN'T THE OTHER EAR HE CUT OFF?
NEVER GAVE IT A THOUGHT. mirror-image I suppose.
LET ME PUT THIS TO YOU AS A CONVERSATION-STARTER... DO YOU THINK JACKSON POLLOCK'S PAINTINGS CAN BE JUSTIFIED?
HE'S A DRIP.
YOU REALLY PUT THAT GUY ON A PEDESTAL.
DO YOU THINK SO?
I FIND HIM VERY HESITANT.. INDECISIVE... WHY'S HE WASTING HIS LIFE IN THAT FACTORY..?
ROD
ROD

IT SEEMED LIKE A GOOD IDEA, YOU BOTH BEING ARTISTIC. BUT YOU DIDN'T HIT IT OFF AT ALL.
ISN'T THAT LIKE EXPECTING DOGGIES TO GET ALONG BY DINT OF BEING MEMBERS OF THE UNIVERSAL FELLOWSHIP OF CANINES.
YOU PUT THE DOGGIES TOGETHER AND THEY RIP THE SHIT OUT OF EACH OTHER.
Point taken.
JOSEPHINE WOULDN'T THINK SO, SHE TOLD ME OFF FOR SAYING 'DOGGIE'. SAID IT'S CHILDISH.
sounds Glaswegian to me.
BUT YOU KNOW. I REALLY FANCY HER. THOSE EYES.
WHAT YOU DON'T WANT ME TO SAY IS "THERE'S PLENTY MORE FISH IN THE SEA"
THAT'S GOOD... VERY UNDERSTANDING ...HEY! I'M IMPRESSED WITH THAT...?
Mmmm...
HEY!!
ANYWAY, JOSEPHINE IS THE SORT WHO WILL GO PLACES, GET WHAT SHE WANTS.
YOU CAN SAY THAT AGAIN.
SHE GOT HOLD OF TWO TICKETS FOR BOB DYLAN'S BLACKBUSHE CONCERT.
you dawwg.
AND THAT I CAN'T RESIST.

HEY! HOW ARE YOU?
OKAY. YOURSELF?
HOW'S DANNY THESE DAYS. DO YOU SEE MUCH OF HIM?
DO YOU KNOW...
LAST WEEK ON THE TRAIN THERE WAS THIS TROUBLE AND DANNY SORTED IT OUT IN TWO MINUTES. AND THERE WERE THREE OF THEM. WOULD YOU BELIEVE IT?
YES. HE BROKE UP A FIGHT AT BLACKBUSHE AS WELL.
A REAL MAN OF ACTION.
YOU REALLY FEEL OVERSHADOWED BY HIM, DON'T YOU
YES.

EAT: BEING SPECIAL OCCASION OF BIRTHDAY, MRS. MacGARRY SERVES UP RAINBOW TROUT WITH ALMONDS, THEIR EYEBALLS, FOR THE SAKE OF DELICACY, BEING REPLACED BY BRIGHT GREEN PEAS.
Eat, drink, be merry.
Campbell 7/81
FOR ALL WE KNOW IT COULD BE STANDARD ETIQUETTE -
I SUPPOSE SO
DID YOU HEAR THE ONE MUM CAME OUT WITH YESTERDAY?
TELL.
STOP TALKING ABOUT ME
DAD WAS AT A CHEESE AND WINE PARTY, AND WHEN HE WAS LATE HOME SHE SAID "I THINK YOU'VE BEEN DRINKING MORE THAN CHEESE AND WINE!"
DRINK: ALEC MacGARRY AND DANNY GREY MEET AT 6:30 SHARP, THE USUAL EARLY START AND THEY SAMPLE THE ALE IN THE CASTLE.
THEN THE SWAN, THE QUART POT, RUNWELL HALL,
JIM BEAM
THE BELL, THE OASIS.

AND ON OTHER OCCASIONS IN THE SHEPHERD AND DOG, THE COACH AND HORSES, THE KING'S HEAD, THE CROWN.
THE PRINCE OF WALES FEATHERS, THE CARPENTERS ARMS, THE BLUE BOAR, THE QUEENS HOTEL, THE HALF MOON, THE
SPUTTER
RISING SUN, THE CHEQUERS, THE TRAVELLERS JOY, THE CHICHESTER ARMS... THE SPREADEAGLE.
WHERE THEY DRANK WATNEYS, TRUMANS, COURAGE, IND COOPE, GREENE KING, RIDLEYS, STONES, McEWANS, CHARRINGTONS, WILSON'S, JOHN SMITHS...
KLUP!
FROM MUGS AND GLASSES AND BOTTLES AND CANS.
THE KING CANUTE.. NOW THERE WAS A PUB.. BACK WHEN MARY WAS RUNNING IT. I REMEMBER ONE NIGHT WE SAT AT THE BAR DRINKING AFTER-HOURS.
AND MARY SAID SHE WAS GOING TO MAKE SOME BREAKFAST. I THOUGHT SHE WAS BEING SARCASTIC TO MAKE US GO HOME.
THEN SHE PULLED BACK THE CURTAINS AND THE SUN STREAMED IN.
SMOKE: ALEC MacGARRY PRODUCES HIS CONVERSATION PIECE FOR THE EVENING: TWO BROOMHANDLE CIGARS.

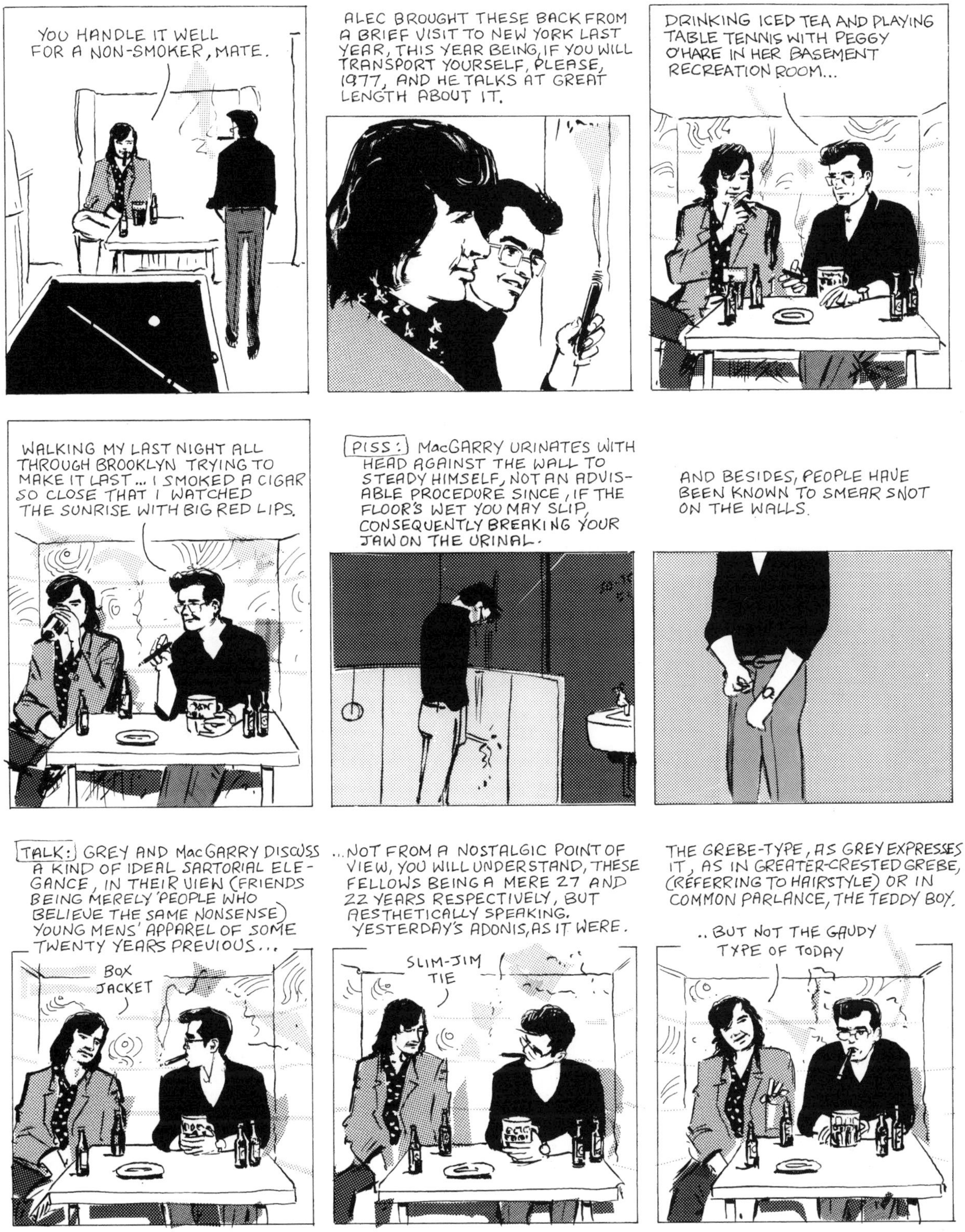
YOU HANDLE IT WELL FOR A NON-SMOKER, MATE.
ALEC BROUGHT THESE BACK FROM A BRIEF VISIT TO NEW YORK LAST YEAR, THIS YEAR BEING, IF YOU WILL TRANSPORT YOURSELF, PLEASE, 1977, AND HE TALKS AT GREAT LENGTH ABOUT IT.
DRINKING ICED TEA AND PLAYING TABLE TENNIS WITH PEGGY O'HARE IN HER BASEMENT RECREATION ROOM...
WALKING MY LAST NIGHT ALL THROUGH BROOKLYN TRYING TO MAKE IT LAST... I SMOKED A CIGAR SO CLOSE THAT I WATCHED THE SUNRISE WITH BIG RED LIPS.
PISS: MacGARRY URINATES WITH HEAD AGAINST THE WALL TO STEADY HIMSELF, NOT AN ADVISABLE PROCEDURE SINCE, IF THE FLOOR'S WET YOU MAY SLIP, CONSEQUENTLY BREAKING YOUR JAW ON THE URINAL.
AND BESIDES, PEOPLE HAVE BEEN KNOWN TO SMEAR SNOT ON THE WALLS.
TALK: GREY AND MacGARRY DISCUSS A KIND OF IDEAL SARTORIAL ELEGANCE, IN THEIR VIEW (FRIENDS BEING MERELY 'PEOPLE WHO BELIEVE THE SAME NONSENSE) YOUNG MENS' APPAREL OF SOME TWENTY YEARS PREVIOUS...
BOX JACKET
..NOT FROM A NOSTALGIC POINT OF VIEW, YOU WILL UNDERSTAND, THESE FELLOWS BEING A MERE 27 AND 22 YEARS RESPECTIVELY, BUT AESTHETICALLY SPEAKING. YESTERDAY'S ADONIS, AS IT WERE.
SLIM-JIM TIE
THE GREBE-TYPE, AS GREY EXPRESSES IT, AS IN GREATER-CRESTED GREBE, (REFERRING TO HAIRSTYLE) OR IN COMMON PARLANCE, THE TEDDY BOY.
.. BUT NOT THE GAUDY TYPE OF TODAY

AS AN EXERCISE IN FLATTERY AND HUMAN STUDIES, DANNY GREY SINGLES OUT AN EX-GREBE TYPE FROM AMONG THE PATRONS OF THE PUBLIC HOUSE.
AND MOOCHES A LIFT.
SAFELY INSTALLED IN THE VEHICLE, DANNY GREY JOGS THE ORIGINAL GREBE-TYPE'S MEMORY WITH REGARD TO AN ARTICLE OF DRESS WORN IN CLASSICAL ANTIQUITY.
YOU MUST HAVE A FEW SLIM-JIM TIES AT HOME, MATE.
WHAT DO YOU MEAN?
NATURALLY, THE FEMALE COMPANION IS NOT FLATTERED BY BEING TOO CLOSELY ASSOCIATED WITH FASHIONS THAT WALKED THE EARTH SO LONG AGO AND THE LADS ARE POLITELY LET OUT ONCE MORE AT THE TURNPIKE.
WALK: DANNY GREY FEELS DEEPLY MORTIFIED. ALEC MacGARRY, EXHALED ONCE MORE INTO THE COLD NIGHT AIR FEELS INSTANTANEOUSLY EMBALMED...
...WHICH IS TO SAY, BIBULOUS, FUZZLED, AND TO BE HONEST, SENTIMENT NOTWITHSTANDING, SICK AS A DOG.
wait a minute
GENUFLECTING TO THE PATRON SAINTS OF NOVICE CIGAR SMOKERS, HE LOWERS HIS HEAD AND INTONES THEIR NAMES.
RUTH! HUGHIE!!

SLEEP: WHO KILLED SUNDAY?

THE REDEEMING FACTOR OF THIS SORT OF SITUATION IS THAT YOU NEVER KNOW WHERE YOU ARE (YOU KNOW THE FEELING)-EAR NOTES THAT IT IS SANDWICHED COSILY BETWEEN HEAD AND CUSHION, BRAIN DEDUCES YOU ARE HORIZONTAL AND THEREFORE IN BED— A BED. YOU SINK A LITTLE.-BODY HEAT RISES - SOUR TASTE IN THE MOUTH.-...the tail-end of your dream has just sneaked off...

EAT: ALEC'S BEEN USING THE COUCH AT DANNY'S GIRL-FRIEND VALERIE'S PLACE REGULARLY FOR A FEW WEEKENDS NOW. EVENTUALLY THERE ARE SIGNS OF LIFE FROM THE BEDROOMS, AND TALK OF BREAKFAST, PLAYING OF RECORDS. AND IN NO TIME AT ALL, THE SLIGHTEST MENTION OF DINNER.

The dating game:
me versus you.
E Campbell
8/81

DAVE BARNES, ON HIS WAY TO WORK, COMES UP BEHIND ALEC MacGARRY AND OBSERVES HIM CONVERSING WITH A YOUNG LADY WHOM WE SHALL CALL BETTY BOOP.
BARNES FANCIES THE GIRLIE, AND BY PROCESSES CONVOLUTED AND CUNNING THE TWO ARRIVE IN ALL SERIOUSNESS AT THE NOVEL PROPOSITION OF SWAPPING GIRL-FRIENDS
DAVE BARNES IS AT THIS TIME GOING OUT WITH JOSEPHINE PRINGLE WHOM ALEC MacGARRY HAS NOT YET MET AND TO WHOM HE MOST DEARLY DESIRES AN INTRODUCTION.
A WEEK LATER, IT COMES ABOUT LIKE THIS: MONDAY, SEPTEMBER 12, DAVE BARNES ASKS FOR A RAISE UNSUCCESSFULLY. HE PHONES FOR ANOTHER JOB AND LEAVES.
SAFETY REGULATIO
HE PROMISES TO CALL MacGARRY THAT NIGHT TO MAKE A DEFINITE PLAN. MacGARRY BUMPS INTO BOOP AGAIN ON HIS WAY HOME FROM WORK.
POST OFFICE
I HAD TO SEE YOU, ALEC. I'M GOING INTO HOSPITAL FOR A BIG OPERATION. I'VE MADE A WILL.
I'M LEAVING YOU SOME MONEY AS WELL AS THAT PHOTO THE PRIVATE DETECTIVE TOOK OF US WHEN I WAS LIVING WITH PETER.
MacGARRY AGREES TO MEET HER THE FOLLOWING NIGHT FOR A SYMPATHETIC DRINK AND PHONES BARNES TO MAKE THE NECCESSARY ARRANGEMENTS.

WHY'S JOSEPHINE GOING OUT WITH THAT NIT ANYWAY. YOU KNOW I HAD TO EVEN WRITE HIS QUIT-NOTICE FOR HIM.
LANCER
IRENE PRINGLE ARRIVES AND PASSES ON A MESSAGE.
ALEC, DAVE SAID TO TELL YOU THE WHOLE THING'S OFF. HE SAID YOU'D KNOW WHAT THAT MEANS.
LANCER
AND WHEN MacGARRY GETS HOME.
SOMEONE CALLED DAVE PHONED TO SAY HE'D PICK YOU UP AT SEVEN.
DAVE BARNES TURNS UP IN HIS FATHER'S DOGGIE-VAN (runs greyhounds) BUT INSTEAD OF JOSEPHINE HE BRINGS ADAM, WHO WORKS AT THE FACTORY.
BARNES DECIDES TO PICK UP JOSEPHINE ANYWAY, AND LEAVES MacGARRY IN RAYLEIGH TO RENDEZVOUS WITH BETTY BOOP.
THEY ALL MEET UP IN THE MIDDLE OF THE ROAD. THE FIRST TIME MacGARRY SEES JOSEPHINE SHE'S WEARING A JUNGLE HAT AS SHE'D MEANT TO STAY IN AND WASH HER HAIR.
oh dear.. WAS THIS MEANT TO BE A DOUB— I'VE FUCKED IT UP.
AFTER MUCH DRINKING, MacGARRY, JOSEPHINE AND ADAM ARE IN THE SAWDUST ON THE HOME ROUTE.
STOP TO COMPARE NOTES.
I GAVE HER MY PHONE-NUMBER- HOW ABOUT YOU?
DON'T WORRY ABOUT ME, MATE.

SHE SAYS SHE'S GOING INTO HOSPITAL FOR FOUR DAYS. WHY DON'T WE VISIT HER?
I DONNO... I DON'T THINK IT'S A GOOD IDEA.
DID YOU HAVE A GOOD TIME? POOR JOSEPHINE. I THINK DAVE WAS IGNORING HER BECAUSE OF THAT SILLY HAT.
BOOP'S GONE INTO HOSPITAL TODAY.
SERIOUS OPERATION?
YES.
hmmm.
TELL ME ABOUT HER.
WELL, THERE WAS THE MARRIAGE WHICH WASN'T, THE PREGNANCY AND THE FALLING DOWN STAIRS, A PHOTO I'VE NEVER SEEN, AN UNCLE WITH A PRIVATE PLANE
THURSDAY: DAVE BARNES' TWELVE-YEAR-OLD SISTER IS KILLED IN A RIDING ACCIDENT AT THE BOTTOM OF THE LANE.
ALEC MacGARRY AND DANNY GREY COME ACROSS JOSEPHINE (and the sweetest lady of this entire period, by name of Julia) – SHE DOESN'T KNOW THAT BAD NEWS.
FRIDAY: ADAM IS LAID OFF FROM THE FACTORY.
I DON'T CARE ABOUT THAT. IT'S MY GIRL-FRIEND SARAH GOING OFF WITH BARNES' MATE.
TUESDAY: BOOP CALLS ALEC.
OK. IF YOU SAY SO. LET'S SEE THE PHOTO THEN. THE NEIGHBOUR'S KIDDY MUST HAVE TAKEN IT?
yeah

SUNDAY: DAVE BARNES PICKS ALEC UP. AROUND TO HIS PLACE. SEEMS OKAY BUT AVOIDS THE SPOT WHERE HIS SISTER WAS FOUND. HIS FOLKS ARE AWAY AND HE'S REDECORATING THE HOUSE.
MacGARRY MEETS SARAH, WHO LIES SLEEPING, SITS SNOGGING AND IN THE PUB ASKS FOR A PIMMS No. 1. AND EATS THREE TOASTED SANDWICHES.
AND KEITH, WHO PAYS FOR ALL THE AFOREMENTIONED.
THEY ALL PILE INTO KEITH'S CAR AND GO TO PICK UP JOSEPHINE. BARNES INSTRUCTS HIM TO AVOID THE SPOT.
BARNES AND JOSEPHINE ARE IN THE BEDROOM. THE OTHER TWO ARE IN THE CAR. THE GIRL IN THE GROUND WILL NEVER KNOW THE JOYS OF COURTSHIP.
FRIDAY: BETTY BOOP CALLS ALEC. HE DATES HER UP WITH BARNES MUCH AGAINST HER TOKEN RATHERNOTS.
BARNES TAKES BOOP OUT ON SATURDAY, SUNDAY AND MONDAY.
FRIDAY: (THIS BY NOW OCTOBER 7) MacGARRY SEES BOOP IN THE STREET AND THEY'RE TALKING WHEN JOSEPHINE AND JULIA COME ALONG.
For God's sake don't say anything.
Reported overheard on bus:
I WONDER WHAT THAT DAVE'S PLAYING AT ?

MONDAY: BOOP PHONES ALEC AND INFORMS HIM SHE HAD NOT CALLED DAVE ON SATURDAY, BUT HED COME ROUND ANYWAY AND APPEARS TO HAVE A CRUSH ON HER.
SHE TELLS HIM FURTHERMORE THAT DAVE BROUGHT WITH HIM A CHAP NAMED KEITH, AND SHE'D ATTEMPTED TO MATCH THIS CHAP WITH HER SISTER.
WEDNESDAY:
DAVE?.- I THINK HE'S TRYING TO GIVE ME THE GENTLE SHOVE -
COME OUT WITH ME THEN
maybe -
THURSDAY: MacGARRY CHOOSES TO PLAY HARD-TO-GET AND TAKES A DIFFERENT ROUTE HOME FROM WORK.
JOSEPHINE PHONED DAVE LAST NIGHT BUT HE WASN'T IN. HIS MOTHER SAID HE WAS GOING OUT WITH BETTY BOOP. JOSEPHINE NATURALLY WAS VERY UPSET
yeah.
SARAH CAME ROUND CRYING, BUT FUCK 'ER. ALSO, YOU MUST HAVE HEARD DAVE CHUCKED BOOP AND HE'S GETTING ENGAGED TO THE BARMAID FROM THE JOLLY CRICKETER.
yeah.
BETTY BOOP PHONES—
SO I THOUGHT, DAVE AND MY MOTHER HAD THE SAME SURNAME AND BOTH ORIGINATE FROM HORNCHURCH, SO DAVE COULD BE THE SON OF THE SON OF THE BROTHER OF MY MOTHER'S FATHER.
no, let me go back over that...
JOSEPHINE ASKS IF YOU CAN LEND HER A RECORD, PLEASE, DANNY: 'SYMPATHY FOR THE DEVIL' BY THE ROLLING STONES.
LANCER

THE COMPANY VAN
(Using it to go out in the evening)
12/80 5/81
158T

J. RODEN
RO
LIGHT
METAL
PRODUCT
HOLD ON, LOVE.
IT WON'T BE LONG.
HOW DO YOU FEEL?
broken leg..
YES
HAS SOMEONE CALLED AN AMBULANCE?
WILL SHE BE ALRIGHT?
I REALLY DON'T KNOW
YOU ARE A DOCTOR, AREN'T YOU?
NAH, I'M A FORKLIFT DRIVER.
SHOULDN'T YOU KEEP AWAY?

DANNY GREY YANKS THE WHEEL AROUND WHILE STATIONARY.
LANCER
AUTHORISED PERSONNEL ONLY
SO WHEN HE REVERSES, THE WHEEL SPINS AND KNOCKS HIS THUMB OUT.
THE MANAGER SENDS HIM TO THE HOSPITAL TO GET IT CHECKED.
WHILE HE'S WAITING HE CAN'T HELP NOTICING THE OLD LADY. SHE'S BEEN WAITING A LONG TIME TO BE PICKED UP.
ARE YOU SURE YOUR DAUGHTER'S COMING?
oh yes
MR. GREY, IT LOOKS LIKE JUST A BAD BRUISE.
BUT YOU'VE BEEN HERE FORTY-FIVE MINUTES ALREADY.
REST THE HAND FOR A DAY OR TWO AND YOU'LL BE FINE.
MAYBE I CAN HELP. WHERE DOES SHE LIVE?
RAYLEIGH RD.
IS THAT IN EASTWOOD?
YES, I THINK IT IS.
I'LL GIVE HER A LIFT, IF YOU LIKE.
WOULD YOU? THAT WOULD BE GREAT.
WAIT HERE. I'LL BRING ROUND THE... uh... WAGON.

RODEN
LIGHT METAL PRODUCTS
HE PUTS ONE OF HER MITTS ON THE GRAB-HANDLE AND HELPS HER IN.
IT'S NEAR A CHURCH. YOU'RE A NICE BOY. ARE YOU MARRIED?
FIAT
SHE KNOWS SHE LIVES IN RAYLEIGH ROAD BUT HASN'T A CLUE WHERE THAT IS. DANNY TRIES ASKING DIRECTIONS.
RAYLEIGH ROAD, MATE.
SORRY. NEVER HEARD OF IT.
HE WORKS HIS WAY AROUND CHALKWELL PARK WHERE HE SPIES SOMEONE HE KNOWS.
SORRY, DANNY. CAN'T HELP YOU.
IT'S TIME FOR A TEA-BREAK.
IT'S MANY A YEAR SINCE A HANDSOME FELLOW TOOK ME OUT TO TEA. DID YOU SAY YOU WERE MARRIED?
I'VE BEEN TRYING TO GET YOU HOME FOR AN HOUR. HAVE YOU NO IDEA AT ALL WHERE YOU LIVE?
THERE'S ONLY ONE THING FOR IT: DANNY GRABS HER HANDBAG.
SQUAWK.
FIAT
THE PENSION BOOK IS IN THERE.
RAYLEIGH ROAD, LEIGH. SHOULD HAVE DONE THIS IN THE FIRST PLACE.
FIAT
LEIGH POLICE STATION:
THERE IT IS. NOT FAR. IF YOU CAN'T SORT IT OUT, COME BACK AND LEAVE HER WITH US.

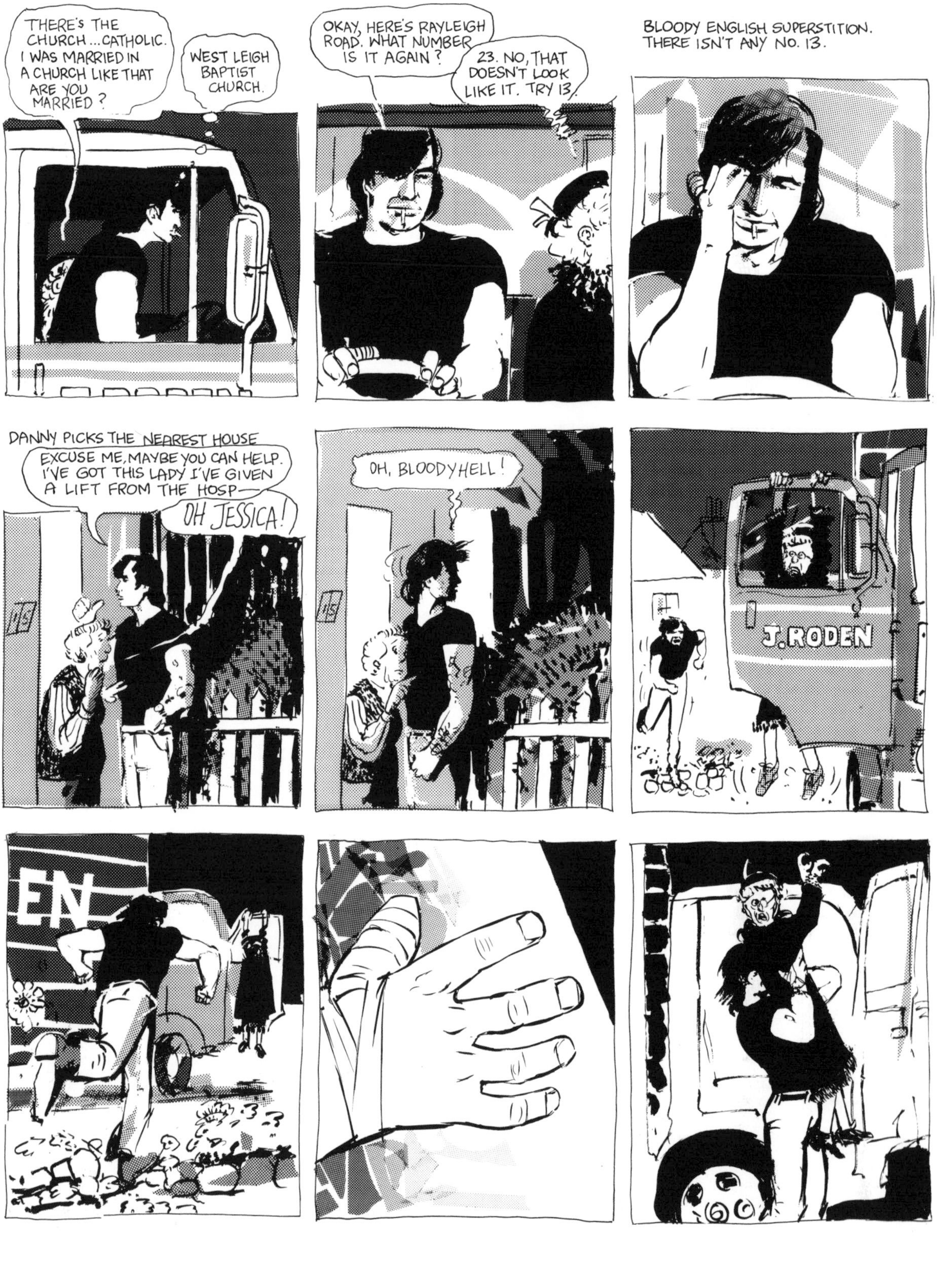
THERE'S THE CHURCH ... CATHOLIC. I WAS MARRIED IN A CHURCH LIKE THAT ARE YOU MARRIED ?
WEST LEIGH BAPTIST CHURCH.
OKAY, HERE'S RAYLEIGH ROAD. WHAT NUMBER IS IT AGAIN ?
23. NO, THAT DOESN'T LOOK LIKE IT. TRY 13.
BLOODY ENGLISH SUPERSTITION. THERE ISN'T ANY NO. 13.
DANNY PICKS THE NEAREST HOUSE
EXCUSE ME, MAYBE YOU CAN HELP. I'VE GOT THIS LADY I'VE GIVEN A LIFT FROM THE HOSP—
OH JESSICA!
OH, BLOODY HELL!
J. RODEN
EN

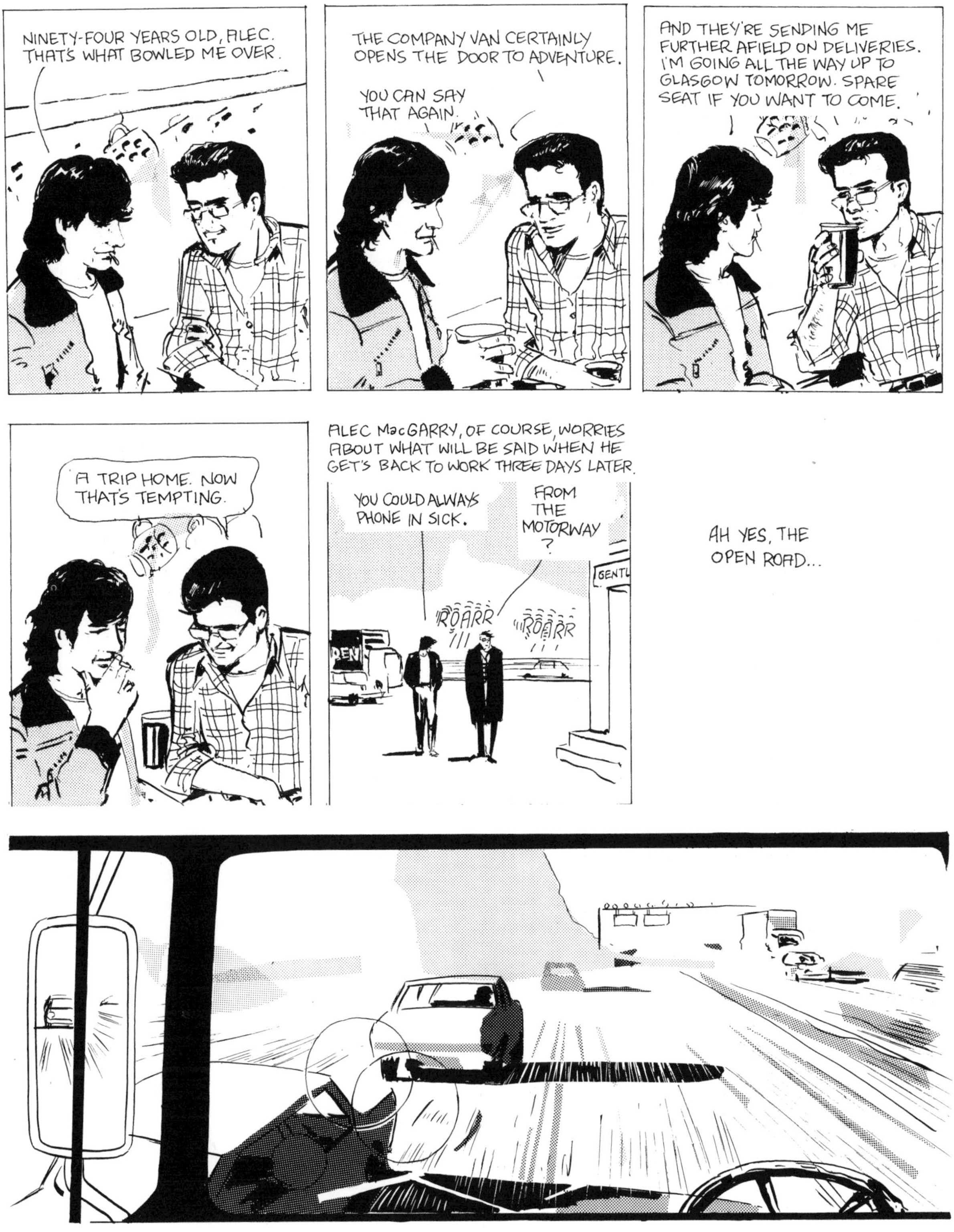
NINETY-FOUR YEARS OLD, ALEC. THAT'S WHAT BOWLED ME OVER.
THE COMPANY VAN CERTAINLY OPENS THE DOOR TO ADVENTURE.
YOU CAN SAY THAT AGAIN.
AND THEY'RE SENDING ME FURTHER AFIELD ON DELIVERIES. I'M GOING ALL THE WAY UP TO GLASGOW TOMORROW. SPARE SEAT IF YOU WANT TO COME.
A TRIP HOME. NOW THAT'S TEMPTING.
ALEC MacGARRY, OF COURSE, WORRIES ABOUT WHAT WILL BE SAID WHEN HE GET'S BACK TO WORK THREE DAYS LATER.
YOU COULD ALWAYS PHONE IN SICK.
FROM THE MOTORWAY ?
ROARR
ROARR
GENTL
AH YES, THE OPEN ROAD...

ALEC MacGARRY IS A MAMMOTH IN THE ICE.
ECampbell 9/81
SEND A REFUGEE-AIRLIFT OR THE VALKYRIE OR SOMETHING
UM..YEP.
BOTTLEOPEN HIM.

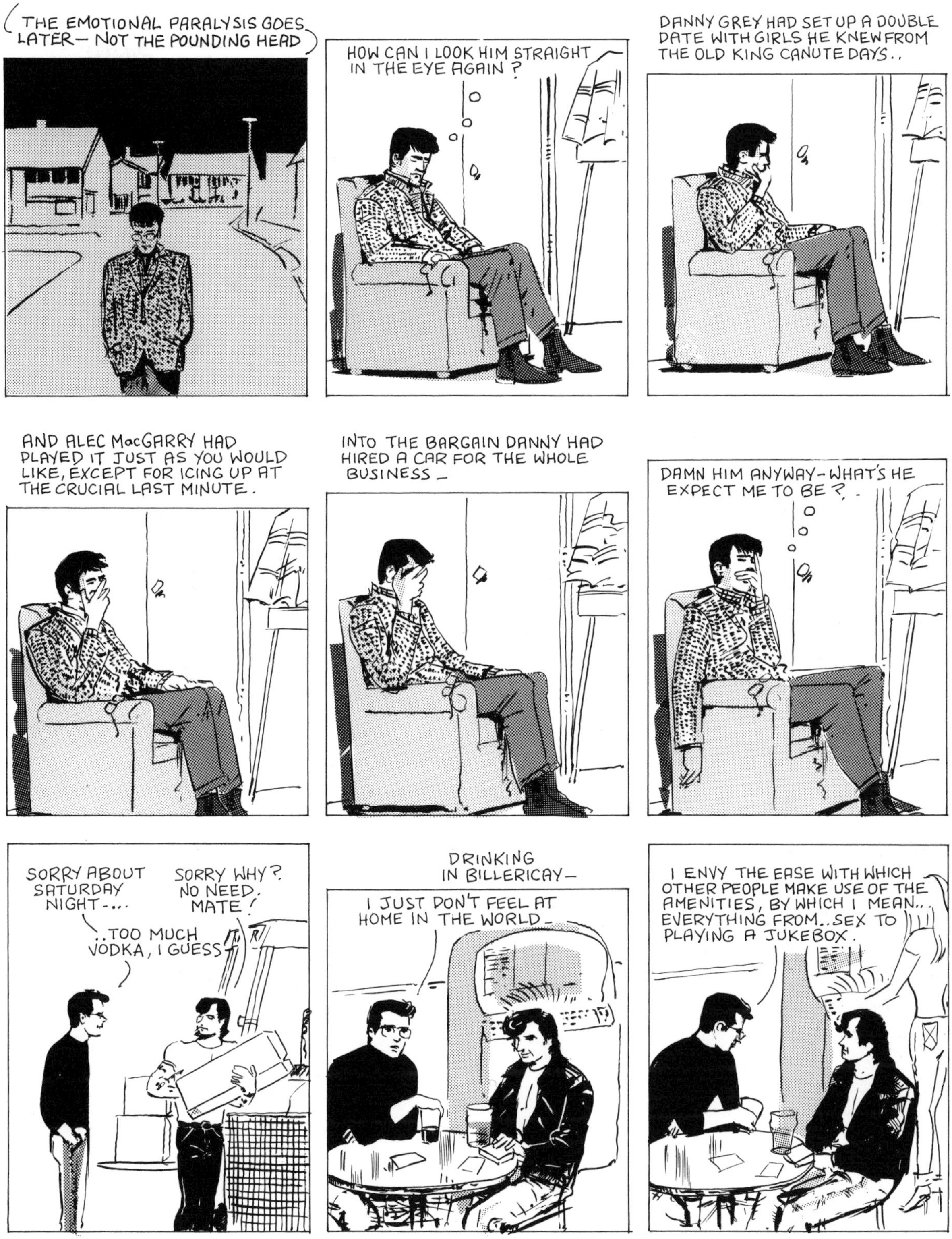
(THE EMOTIONAL PARALYSIS GOES LATER— NOT THE POUNDING HEAD)
HOW CAN I LOOK HIM STRAIGHT IN THE EYE AGAIN?
DANNY GREY HAD SET UP A DOUBLE DATE WITH GIRLS HE KNEW FROM THE OLD KING CANUTE DAYS..
AND ALEC MacGARRY HAD PLAYED IT JUST AS YOU WOULD LIKE, EXCEPT FOR ICING UP AT THE CRUCIAL LAST MINUTE.
INTO THE BARGAIN DANNY HAD HIRED A CAR FOR THE WHOLE BUSINESS_
DAMN HIM ANYWAY- WHAT'S HE EXPECT ME TO BE?_
SORRY ABOUT SATURDAY NIGHT-...
SORRY WHY? NO NEED, MATE!
..TOO MUCH VODKA, I GUESS
DRINKING IN BILLERICAY—
I JUST DON'T FEEL AT HOME IN THE WORLD_
I ENVY THE EASE WITH WHICH OTHER PEOPLE MAKE USE OF THE AMENITIES, BY WHICH I MEAN.. EVERYTHING FROM..SEX TO PLAYING A JUKEBOX.

I THINK YOU'RE ONE OF COLIN WILSON'S 'OUTSIDERS' - HAVE YOU READ THAT BOOK?
no -
ah! - ONE YOU HAVEN'T READ.
I IDENTIFIED WITH THAT BOOK MYSELF.. mm.. A FRIEND OF MINE ONCE SAID TO ME.."YOU KNOW WHAT I LIKE ABOUT YOU, DANNY? YOU'RE A WASTER.
yes... fits.
THE REASON FOR BEING IN BILLERICAY WAS THAT DANNY HAD USED THE COMPANY VAN TO TRANSPORT A PUNK ROCK GROUP TO THIS GIG -
ON THE HOME ROUTE ALEC MacGARRY PUTS ON A SPONTANEOUS DEMONSTRATION (OF CONFIDENCE)
YOU'RE NO' PUTTIN' HER IN THE BACK WI' THE JUNK ARE YE?!
?
is he coming too?
HIS PATTER IS FLUENT.
HIS WORDS COME OUT LIKE MAGICIANS' DOVES.
AND IT IS ALL, YOU UNDERSTAND OF COURSE, BY WAY OF MAKIN' UP.

ALEC SHORTLY OBSERVED THAT SOCIAL SKILL AND SEXUAL SKILL ARE NOT UNRELATED—
(RE-ENTER BETTY BOOP)
I WANT YOU TO COME TO PARIS WITH ME FOR A WEEKEND—
THERE WON'T BE ANY FUNNY BUSINESS, I HOPE...
Umm...YOU MEAN SEX ?
NO, OF COURSE NOT, SILLY— I MEAN YOU WON'T TRY TO SWOP ME AGAIN...
: hmmph :

PARIS — in short —

. . . flights promptly began calling Roissy tower, *Hullo Charlie! Hullo Airport Charlie!* . . . They received in reply the austere mouthful, *This is Roissy-Charles De Gaulle Airport*.
Official spokesmen explained smoothly that "use of the abbreviation 'C for Charlie' is natural as it is part of the international alphabet." But pilots were strictly forbidden to repeat this lèse-majesté in future in case 'Charlie' should be confused with 'Orly'."

Staying in Rue de la Republique
It's cold for January -
See you next week -

Betty

Two

WHEN ALEC MacGARRY'S FOLKS MOVED BACK UP NORTH HE DECIDED TO STAY IN THE AREA AND QUICKLY FOUND A BEDSIT ON WESTCLIFF SEAFRONT.
ECampbell 10/81

(SAME WEEKEND AS THE DAFT JANUARY FLIGHT TO PARIS I MENTIONED BEFORE) THE LANDLADY HAD ADVERTISED FOR A BUSINESSMAN TYPE AND WASN'T TOO SURE ABOUT MacG AT FIRST.

THE PREVIOUS TENANT HAD APPARENTLY DONE A BUNK, AMONG OTHER THINGS, BECAUSE ALEC MET ALL HIS NEW NEIGHBOURS AT ONCE OF A SATURDAY MORNING...

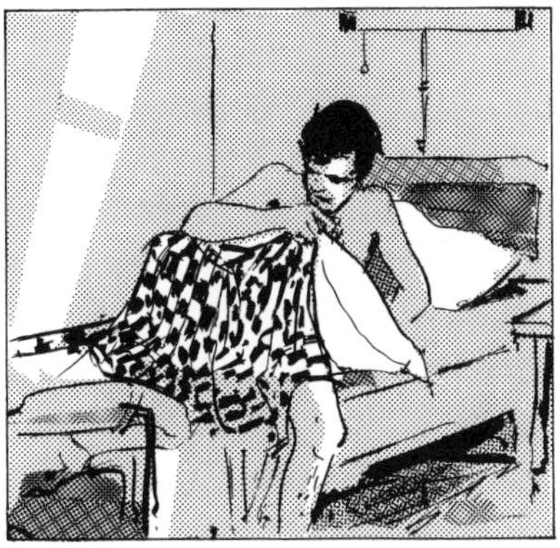

...WHEN ALL TEN BELLS IN THE HOUSE WERE RUNG BY A POLICEMAN AND THE POSTMAN (WITH MacGARRY'S NEW POSTOFFICE ACCOUNT BOOK - ALL OF TWENTY QUID IN IT)

A LAUREL AND HARDY SCENE WHICH INTRODUCED ONLY ONE CHARACTER OF NOTE; MALCOLM, A POET OF SORTS.

— ANYTHING FOR SIMPKINS?

...STANDING CONFUSED IN THE DOORWAY LOOKING LIKE NOEL COWARD OR SOMETHING,

(AND NEXT DAY MOST OF THE TENANTS GOT OUT AND PUT THEIR NAMES UNDER THEIR BELLS).

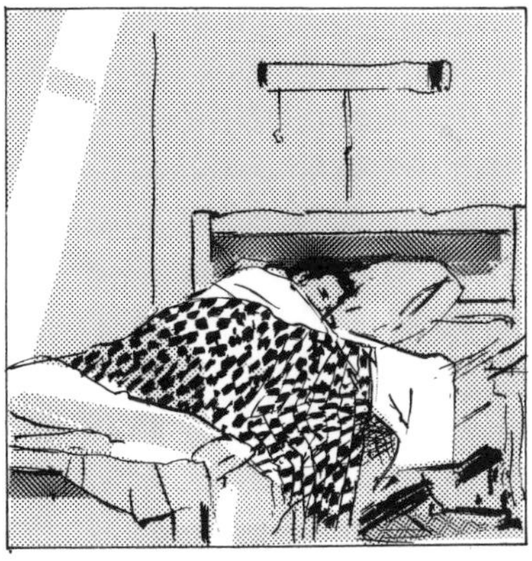

SOME WARM JUNE NIGHTS YOU UNCORK THE BOTTLE AND THE SITUATIONS TUMBLE OUT BACKFLIPPING AFTER EACH OTHER LIKE CIRCUS MIDGETS
E Campbell 11/81
ALEC MacGARRY WANDERS INTO A CERTAIN PUB AND ORDERS A PINT.
REALIZING AFTER A MINUTE THAT HE HAS INADVERTENTLY COME IN SOUTHEND'S GAY HAUNT HE BECOMES SWIFTLY INTOXICATED BY THE NOVELTY OF THE SITUATION
(AND THE BARMAID)
WOULD YOU LIKE THIS STOOL?
NO THANKS. A GENTLEMAN ALWAYS TAKES THE WEIGHT ON HIS ELBOWS.
HEH HAH
oh you
WHAT ARE YOU DRINKING?
THAT'S VERY GOOD OF YOU. ORANGE JUICE.
SET'EM UP JOE
ARE YOU DOING ANYTHING AFTERWARDS?
maybe.

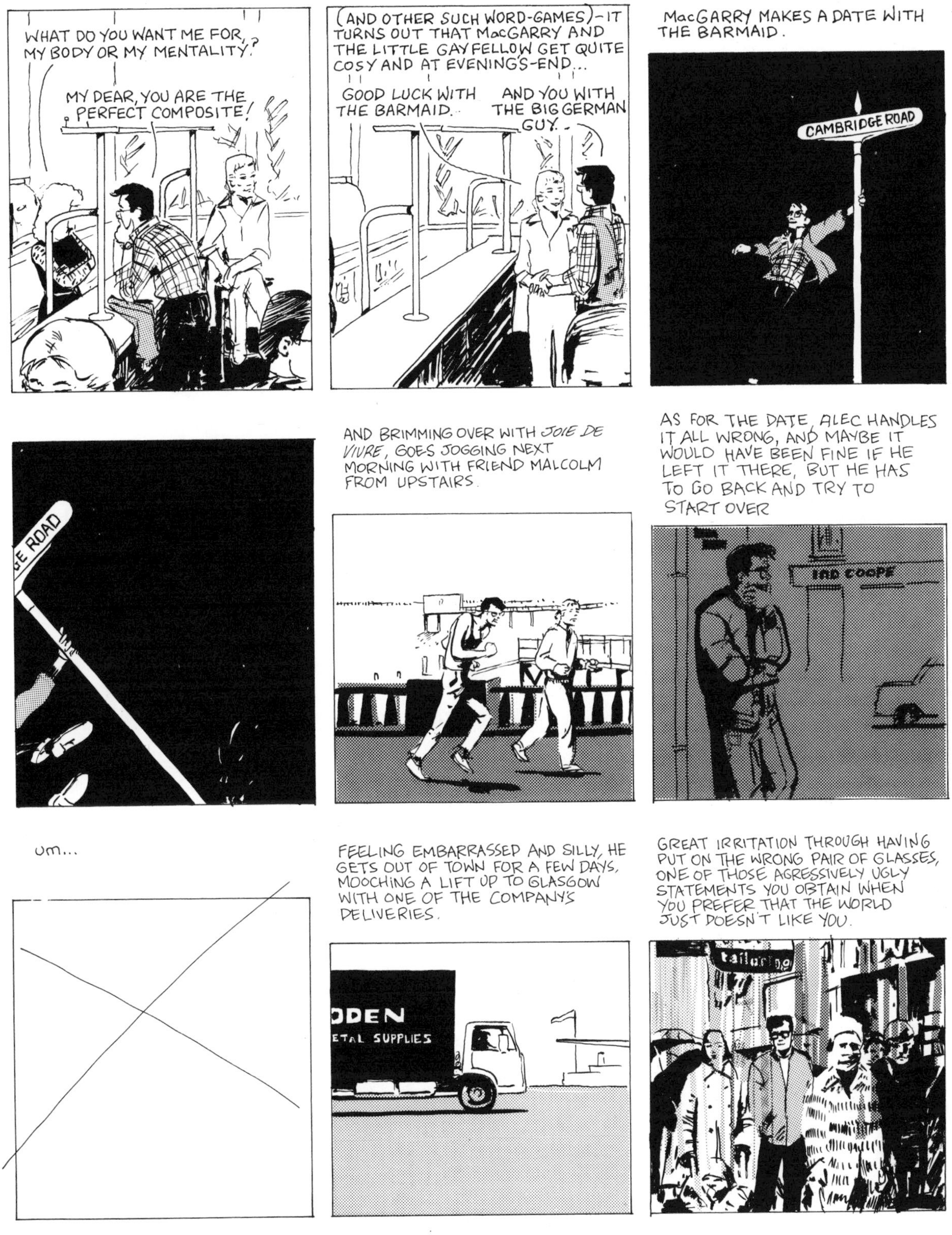
WHAT DO YOU WANT ME FOR, MY BODY OR MY MENTALITY?
MY DEAR, YOU ARE THE PERFECT COMPOSITE!
(AND OTHER SUCH WORD-GAMES)-IT TURNS OUT THAT MacGARRY AND THE LITTLE GAY FELLOW GET QUITE COSY AND AT EVENING'S-END...
GOOD LUCK WITH THE BARMAID.
AND YOU WITH THE BIG GERMAN GUY.
MacGARRY MAKES A DATE WITH THE BARMAID.
CAMBRIDGE ROAD
GE ROAD
AND BRIMMING OVER WITH JOIE DE VIVRE, GOES JOGGING NEXT MORNING WITH FRIEND MALCOLM FROM UPSTAIRS.
AS FOR THE DATE, ALEC HANDLES IT ALL WRONG, AND MAYBE IT WOULD HAVE BEEN FINE IF HE LEFT IT THERE, BUT HE HAS TO GO BACK AND TRY TO START OVER
IND COOPE
um...
FEELING EMBARRASSED AND SILLY, HE GETS OUT OF TOWN FOR A FEW DAYS, MOOCHING A LIFT UP TO GLASGOW WITH ONE OF THE COMPANY'S DELIVERIES.
ODEN
ETAL SUPPLIES
GREAT IRRITATION THROUGH HAVING PUT ON THE WRONG PAIR OF GLASSES, ONE OF THOSE AGRESSIVELY UGLY STATEMENTS YOU OBTAIN WHEN YOU PREFER THAT THE WORLD JUST DOESN'T LIKE YOU.
tailoring

MacGARRY BUYS A PAIR OF JEANS BEFORE NOTICING THEY'VE GOT NO FRONT POCKETS.
IT'S A BAD HAIR YEAR.
smoking
oh damn
MacGARRY AND THE TRUCK-DRIVER CRASH OUT AT ALEC'S AUNTIE'S FLAT, AND NEXT DAY GO THEIR SEPARATE WAYS.
ALEC WALKS INTO A SAUCHIEHALL STREET JAZZ CELLAR WITH HIS OLD SCHOOL CRONY, 'MEAN' JIM BEECH.
HERE'S THE AGREEABLE PART.
NO BAR SERVICE (common thing in these parts) - NO SPARE TABLE- ONE WITH TWO GIRLS —— OK
Beechy is trying to impress me by asking at the bar if Big Johnny is in tonight
NOW THIS STUFF I ALWAYS GET IF I CAN.
blether blether
IT'S A BIG BOTTLE FOR A WEE LASSIE
OH, YOU'VE MADE MY NIGHT, YOU REALLY HAVE.
GOOD LORD! LOOK AT THAT PHOTO.
jesus christ, man, I only use it for a gag
MIND YOUR ELB-
I'LL GET THESE
IT'S NOT THAT I DON'T TRUST THE BAR STAFF, BUT PUT YOUR WALLET IN YOUR FRONT POCKET AND BUTTON IT-
no pocket
you've just broken up with someone and it's affecting you deeply...
YOU'RE A CLAIRVOYANT?
THE SEVENTH CHILD OF A SEVENTH CHILD - MY NAME'S JEANIE-THIS IS VELMA.
Jim, Alec
TELL ME, DO YOU BELIEVE IN GOD?
NO, 'GOD' TOOK AWAY THE ONLY MAN WHO EVER MEANT ANY THING TO ME, SO IF THERE IS ONE HE'S NO' GOT MY SUPPORT.
been playing with cats? those scratches...
uh...

I WAS IN A ROAD ACCIDENT TWO MONTHS AGO.
CAN YOU DO THIS WITH ANYONE, LIKE ME ?
IT WOULDN'T WORK, ALEC. YOU'RE A SKEPTIC. YOU DON'T BELIEVE IN SUPERSTITION OR GOD-
DING DING
(they're ringing last orders.)
THAT HAS TO BE WORTH A ROUND OF DRINKS.
NO THANK YOU. I WILL NOT ACCEPT SILVER OR GOLD
oh..but..I'LL HAVE A VODKA AND LEMONADE.
well well
WAITRESS!
HOW DO YOU KNOW ALL ABOUT THIS FORTUNE STUFF ?
I'M A DIDECOI.-
MADAME GYPSY LEE, THE TRUE ROMANY-
MIND YOUR SHOULD-
I'M RELATED TO THAT FAMILY-
HA ! - LEAVE IT ! - IT'S GOOD LUCK !
OOPS
KLUNK
EXCUSE ME A MOMENT...
you'll talk about me now-
COME ON NOW DRINK UP!
I daren't say anything.
JEANIE CLEARS UP VELMA'S REMAINING LAGER AND WE ALL BUNDLE UPSTAIRS.

DOWN SAUCHIEHALL STREET GUYS ARE BUSTLING OUT OF SIDE-STREET BARS IN USUAL GLASGOW STYLE. VELMA SHUDDERS AND HER COMPOSURE RUNS OFF LIKE A NEST OF DISTURBED SPIDERS.
MMM
HEY
THAT SOUNDS OVERDRAMATIC, BUT THAT'S THE WAY IT SOMETIMES COMES AT YOU WHEN YOU'VE HAD A SNOUTFUL. AND LITTLE MYSTERIES WORK YOUR MIND. ABOUT THE SCRATCHES, I MEAN.
WELL, LOOK - I'VE GOT TO GET BACK TO THE HOSTEL - IT'S BEEN...NICE. SEE YOU AROUND - JIM, ALEC. SEE YOU LATER, VELMA.
OK, JAMES. VELMA'S WITH ME.
(this is not the big possessive act, but in case of any beef over who pays what - Beechy professes to be the meanest guy in Glasgow)
(BEECHY TAKES US BY THE SCENIC ROUTE)
YOU DON'T HAVE A GLASGOW ACCENT - COUNTRY?
I WAS BORN IN PARTICK - BUT MOVED WHEN I WAS EIGHT - TO ALLOA. HOW ABOUT YOU, ALEC?
ALEC.
WHEN A GIRL OF YOUR FANCY REMEMBERS YOUR NAME IT'S MUSIC.
BUT THE ACCENT —— mm — NOT GLASGOW, LIKE SPITTING OUT PLAYING CARDS, OR ROLLED SOUTHEND VOWELS (GARLIC)
TRANSLUCENT —— A (RAINDROP IN THE) LAKE.
AND HALF-POUNDER SALAD AND ALL THE TRIMMINGS.
MY FRIEND, JIM BEECH, HERE...

...CAME INTO THIS RESTAURANT WITH A JEWISH AQUAINTANCE OF HIS AND JIM OFFERED TO PAY THE BILL. THE NEXT DAY'S HEADLINE READ:- JEWISH VENTRILOQUIST FOUND MURDERED
HEE HEE
SO WE ALL TELL A JOKE BEECHY TELLS ONE ABOUT CONDOMS, MacGARRY KICKS HIM UNDER THE TABLE.
IT'S MY TURN.
THERE WAS THIS BEAR- GALLUMPHING THROUGH THE FOREST- gallumph gallumph gallUMPH
MacGARRY IS GALLUMPHED ON SOME UNIVERSAL MATERNAL LAP.
THEN HE SPOILS IT.
DOES THIS JOKE HAVE A RABBIT IN IT?
oh you've heard it before...
THE KIDDY WHO KNOWS THE STORY BUT WANTS THE GALLUMPHING BIT ALL OVER AGAIN.
WHAT'S THE NEXT MOVE? SEE HER HOME? AND DO THE BUSINESS? AT SOME PREARRANGED SPOT A GUY JUMPS OUT FROM BEHIND A WALL AND HITS YOU WI' A BOTTLE? DON'T ASK ME.
WHERE'S VELMA?
GONE TO PHONE HER LANDLORD AND TELL HIM TO LEAVE THE DOOR OPEN.
CANCEL ALL PREVIOUS PLANS AND I'LL SEE YOU IN A FEW DAYS?
NO, I DON'T THINK SHE'LL BE BACK
reckon?
I can't figure her out at all - she didn't even eat her salad-

BEECHY KICKS UP A FUSS ABOUT THE BILL- CLAIMS THERE WAS NO SALAD DRESSING AND GETS A FEW PENNIES KNOCKED OFF (BUT DOESN'T QUESTION SPLITTING THE BILL HALF AND HALF) — (Pal of mine) -
WE WAKE UP NEXT MORNING IN BEECHY'S BED -
JAMES!! HAVE YOU GOT SOMEONE IN THERE?
Groaann.
THAT NIGHT WE HAVE A DRINK IN BURNSIDE AND GO OVER THE WHOLE THING, WHEN IN WALKS A FELLOW CALLED 'NED' KELLY, WITH HIS WIFE AND A CAMERA -
I NEED A COUPLE OF GUYS FOR SOME PHOTIES -
BEECH AND MacGARRY PRETEND TO LIKE SOME AWFUL WOMEN FOR THE SAKE OF A FEW PICTURES.
mum didn't bring me up to be no gigolo -
AND AFTERWARDS SOMEONE DRIVES KELLY AND HIS MRS. BACK TO THEIR ROOM IN POLLOCKSHAWS (MAYBE IT WAS KELLY HIMSELF. I'M LONG PAST REMEMBERING.)
AND MacGARRY HAS A COFFEE THERE -
WELL, I'M OFF .. REMEMBER TO SEND ME A PHOTO.
sure.
HE DIDN'T, OF COURSE, BUT THAT'S HOW IT GOES -
TAXI
WE'RE ONLY PASSING THROUGH.....

E Campbell 8/82.
THE FINEST THING IN THIS LIFE IS JUST TO BE WITH YOUR FRIENDS.
IF I ASKED FOR A PINT OF GUINNESS AND THE BARMAID GAVE ME BITTER BY MISTAKE- I'D BE TOO SHY AND SILLY TO ASK HER TO CHANGE IT.
YOU'RE A GENTLEMAN, JIM.. A GENTLE MAN.
SNUFSH
NOW ME - I'M SHY AND SILLY_ I REMEMBER THIS TAXI-DRIVER WHO GOT ANNOYED WITH ME BECAUSE I DIDN'T SAY PLEASE AND THANK YOU.. WHEN I GOT OUT AT MY DESTINATION HE TRIED TO RUN ME OVER -
I WAS SO BLOODY ANGRY I NEARLY DIDN'T TIP HIM.
FURTHER ON.. SAME THEME -
REMEMBER THAT TIME I FOUND MYSELF ASLEEP ONE SUNDAY MORNING ROUND YOUR PLACE AND I DIDN'T RECOGNISE IT, NOT HAVING BEEN THERE BEFORE -
- SO I GRABBED MY COAT AND RAN FOR MY LIFE -
I KEEP MEANING TO ASK YOU WHERE YOU GOT ALL THESE PINK HANKIES, DANNY -
SNUFSH
THEY WERE WHITE T-SHIRTS- REMEMBER THAT RED ONE WITH THE PICTURE OF DYLAN.?
oh dear

...GOING BY TRAIN ACROSS GERMANY. I WAS IN A COMPARTMENT WITH SEVERAL TURKISH BUSINESSMEN.
IT WASN'T A SLEEPING COMPARTMENT. I WAS TRYING TO SLEEP UPRIGHT IN MY COAT AND THE TURKS... AFTER A BIG SPREAD WHICH THEY ATE WITH VICIOUS LONG KNIVES...
...ALL GOT UP AND CHANGED INTO PYJAMAS.
THE MAN WHO GIVES ME A LIFT TO WORK FROM CHALKWELL PARK EVERY MORNING... TOM HIS NAME IS. HE FORGOT TO TELL ME HE WAS HAVING MONDAY OFF...
SO ON MONDAY I WALKED ROUND TO HIS PLACE JUST THE SAME...
TOM WAS TOO POLITE TO MENTION THAT HE'D ARRANGED TO STAY HOME. SO HE PUT ON HIS WORK-CLOTHES AND DROVE ME THE TEN MILES.
come on, Tom-
we're late
I DIDN'T GIVE IT A THOUGHT TILL THE AFTERNOON WHEN I REALIZED THERE WAS NO LIFT HOME.
CHRISTMAS DAY AT BIG JIM BATEMAN'S HOUSE. GOD BLESS THE TURKEY. BOXING DAY AT VALERIE'S
POOR LITTLE VALERIE, I ALWAYS HAD A DEEP SYMPATHY FOR HER. TWICE MARRIED, NEARLY THREE EXCEPT DANNY DROPPED OUT AT THE LAST MINUTE. ONLY TWO MONTHS AGO.

I WENT ROUND WHILE SHE WAS AT WORK TO PICK UP MY CLOTHES. SHE HAD A NEW BLUE DRESS IN THE WARDROBE ... for her big day.
I ALMOST STAYED JUST ON THE STRENGTH OF IT.
BUT YOU MUSTN'T THINK I'M INSENSITIVE. CALLOUS, YES BUT NEVER INSENSITIVE.
THIS SOUNDED LIKE SPLITTING HAIRS TO ME, LIKE OTHER DISCUSSIONS WE'D HAD.
'IMPRESSIONISM' IS WHERE YOU PAINT WHAT'S IN YOUR HEAD AS OPPOSED TO WHAT YOU SEE
no, no, no.
INSIST ON DEFINING IT THAT WAY IF YOU LIKE, BUT YOU'RE IN DANGER OF LOSING AN IDEA, WHICH IS MORE IMPORTANT THAN A WORD; THE CAPTURING IN PAINT OF EFFECTS OF LIGHT, AIR, TIME OF DAY.
BUT I SEE WHAT HE MEANT- AFTER ALL, HE WAS SENSITIVE TO ALL MY OWN ANXIETIES IN A WAY.
I'VE BEEN THROUGH IT MYSELF, MATE.
LANCET
LANCET
AT THE SAME TIME, AND THIS IS WHAT IMPRESSED ME MOST, HE HAD AN INTRINSIC GRASP OF JUNGLE-TYPE CONFRONTATIONS. (AT THE PREVIOUS YEAR'S WORKS XMAS PARTY.)
OUTSIDE, ALEC !!
What's up?
BETTY SAYS YOU TOLD HER TO BE WARY OF ME -
(DANNY SAID I SHOULD HAVE KNOWN BETTER, WHICH STRIKES ME NOW AS A PRETTY FAIR OBSERVATION) —
DAVE, YOU SHOULD BELIEVE NONE OF WHAT YOU HEAR AND HALF OF WHAT YOU SEE -

AND SMILING VALERIE TURNS UP BEHIND THE BAR AT GATOR'S, THE NEW DISCO. EVERYONE TURNS UP AGAIN SOONER OR LATER.
LIKE JOSEPHINE PRINGLE SENDING CRYPTIC MESSAGES THROUGH HER MOTHER.
...ASKED ME TO ASK IF YOU CAN REMEMBER THE TITLE OF THE FILM LED ZEPPELIN MADE.
sorry, can't stop now, Irene _
KEN - YOU'RE A LED ZEPPELIN NUT - WHAT WAS THE FILM THEY MADE?
'THE SONG REMAINS THE SAME -'
_ hhmm _
ARSENAL
ONCE WHEN HE LET HER DOWN.
JOSEPHINE WOULD LIKE TO BORROW THE 10cc ALBUM 'HOW DARE YOU'
LANCE
LANCER
THE NICEST THING IN THIS LIFE IS JUST TO BE WITH YOUR FRIENDS. NO BIG STORY NEED COME OF IT. THE ADRENALIN MAY NOT FLOW.
REN
BUT THOSE THINGS ARE NECESSARY TOO. ENERGY BUILDS UP AND YOU BECOME RESTLESS IN THAT FINE COMPANY AND IT'S TIME TO GO.
GO BOOMERANGING ACROSS THE COUNTRY AND GET IT OUT OF YOUR SYSTEM.
PREST
THERE'S AN EXPRESSION DANNY USES SOMETIMES, WHICH HE GOT FROM HIS FATHER, WARTIME R.A.F. MAN.
"THE MEN CAN'T WAIT TO GET ASHORE AND GET SOME DIRTY WATER OFF THEIR CHESTS"

GIRLS. I HAD AN ON-OFF THING WITH A TALL BLONDE GIRL THAT DIDN'T HAVE MANY DAYS AS PLEASANT AS THIS CHRISTMAS.

NO SMOKING

I'D VISIT ONE NIGHT A LARGE LADY NAMED PAM, WITH TWO BOTTLES OF WINE, AND HAVE ALL THE PAINT SCRAPED OFF MY BACK.

...KISS HER GOODBYE IN THE MORNING LIKE SHE'S MY WIFEY AND GO TO WORK OBLIVIOUS OF THE RAIN-

...GET LITTLE LEAPS OF PLEASURE EVERY TIME I BUMP INTO HER AGAIN... BUY HER A DRINK.

YEAH, I'LL AMOUNT TO SOMETHING-

I'M SHARPENING MY CLAWS

NEW YEAR'S EVE MY BROTHER AND I ARE STUCK 30 MILES NORTH OF BIRMINGHAM HEADED BACK TO LONDON WHEN THE SNOW STARTS.

WE COME ACROSS THE STRAND
LIKE A LOG ON A DUCK-POND...
E Campbell 9/82
CITIBANK
WE, THAT IS, ALEC MacGARRY AND BRENDAN MacGARRY ON HAZARDOUS RETURN TRIP FROM CHRISTMAS VISIT TO THE FOLKS IN BLACKPOOL —ARE STRANDED IN LAMBETH FOR HOGMANAY.
AND MEANWHILE THE BIG SCENE AT THE KING CANUTE HAS ALREADY STARTED.
FOR AULD LANG SYNE
JOHN!
DA DA DA DA DA DAA—
SQUISH!
DA DA DA DA DA DA
SQUISH!

BLACK ICE ~ Four Wickford men die in car that goes off road on A130 and finishes upside down in water-filled ditch-

CAR BURSTS INTO FLAMES ~ on Pitsea flyover causing pile-up of twenty-five cars and two coaches

POLICE MAN ~ breaks pelvis and youth breaks back jumping 30ft. from flyover to avoid skidding car - eighteen other people treated in hospital - A13 closed for 6 hours-

TANKER AND LORRY DRIVERS STRIKE ~ and at the works we run out of heating fuel - getting some through later but in the meantime they decide to pipe diesel fuel into the heating tank, diesel at 90p gal. costing three times as much-

20 HULLBRIDGE

SNOWED UNDER ~ the weather comes out in sympathy with the striking railmen and council workers today ~.

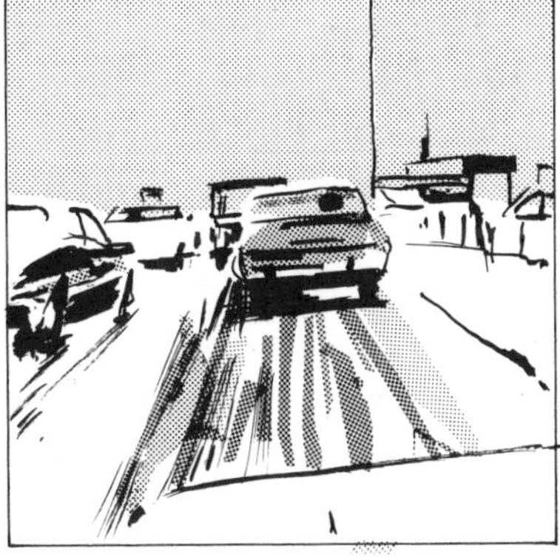

COMING HOME FROM WORK ONE NIGHT, ALEC MacGARRY GETTING LIFT FROM TOM AND FALLING ASLEEP IN THE FRONT SEAT...
...COMES AWAKE TO FIND TOM HAS GOT CAUGHT IN DRIFT AND ASKED BUNCH OF PASSERS-BY TO HELP PUSH THE CAR...
...BUT TOO POLITE TO WAKE UP MacGARRY.
ONE NIGHT AT THE KING CANUTE:-
THIS IS THE WINTER OF MY DISCONTENT-..AS THE CHAP SAID
uh ~ . .
SHOULDN'T THAT BE OUR DISCONTENT?
I THINK YOU'LL FIND IT'S THE ROYAL 'WE'-RICHARD III SPEAKING THEREFORE 'OUR' DISCONTENT-
I SAY! - ARE YOU A FELLOW THESPIAN?
WHAT STRATA ARE YOU IN?
ACTUALLY I'M A FORKLIFT DRIVER
ONE SWEET NIGHT IN JANUARY DANNY GREY COMES IN THE MINERVA WITH LITTLE PENNY MOORE.
WHO GIVES ME A PERSONAL BIG SMILE
AFTERWARDS TAKES DANNY TO WHERE SHE STABLES HER HORSE-
BEST NOT GO TOO NEAR- HE DOESN'T LIKE PEOPLE MUCH.

THEN OTHER GIRLS OCCUPIED HIS TIME AND I THOUGHT MORE AND MORE ABOUT PENNY. ONCE DRIVING TO SOUTHEND FROM THE CANUTE HE REMARKS THAT A LITTLE GIRL WE'VE JUST PASSED LOOKS LIKE PENNY'S DAUGHTER.
I DIDN'T KNOW SHE HAS ONE, DIDN'T SEE, ASK WHAT SHE'S LIKE AND SO ON.
IN MARCH IT'S PENNY'S BIRTHDAY PARTY AND SHE TELLS HER SISTER JEN TO BRING DANNY ALONG... "AND HIS FRIEND ALEC."
PLEASED TO HAVE BEEN REMEMBERED AND DECIDE I WILL MAKE SOME KIND OF PLAY FOR PENNY TONIGHT.
PARTY'S OFF, MATE.
WHAT'S UP THEN?
SOME BLACK ICE ON ASHINGDON HILL, APPARENTLY. SHE HIT THE FRONT OF A LORRY AND THEY SAY THE CAR'S A WRITE-OFF.
JOHN SAID SHE LOOKED QUITE BASHED ABOUT. LOST A COUPLE OF TEETH...

ALL ABOUT THE FIGHT AT GATOR'S, THE NIGHT-SPOT WHOSE GIMMICK IS A LIVE ALLIGATOR IN A GLASS ENCLOSURE. IT NEVER BATS AN EYE.
Eddie Campbell 10/3/83.
ALEC MacGARRY AND DANNY GREY ARE THERE WITH SMIFFY AND A GUY THEY CALL THE VIKING.
MONICA'S THERE. HER BOYFRIEND'S IN AUSTRALIA FOR THREE MONTHS AND SHE'S HOBNOBBING WITH DANNY MEANWHILE.
MONICA'S ON THE DANCEFLOOR PINCHING ARSES.
SHE DRINKS LAGER LIKE A SQUIRREL WITH A NUT.
STEPHANIE'S THERE TOO. THE GIRLS ARE DOING IMPRESSIONS OF TV COMEDIANS WHEN THE PUNCH-UP STARTS.
YOU AIN'T APOLOGISED FOR TALKING TO MY WIFE LAST WEEK
I DON'T REMEMBER MEETING YOUR WIFE? IS SHE ...?

THIS WOULD BE A NON-INCIDENT EXCEPT THAT AT THE FIRST HINT OF AGGRAVATION A NUT DROOLING LIKE PAVLOV'S DOG RUSHES UP.
ARSE
FROM MacGARRY'S POINT OF VIEW A GLIMPSE OF WHITE SHIRT AT THREE O'CLOCK.
LEAVE THAT ONE TO DANNY.
DON'T TAKE EYES OFF THIS ONE.
DANNY GREY STEAMS IN.
THE CLUB BOUNCER TRIES TO NIP IT IN THE BUD.
AS DANNY GOES DOWN HE SEES MacGARRY STILL BENDING AN EAR.
SMIFFY PINS A HEAD TO THE GROUND. THE ALLIGATOR'S SEEN IT ALL BEFORE.
STAY!
THE VIKING IS CORALLING THE GIRLS AROUND THE CORNER OF THE BAR.

WHILE THE BOUNCER THREATENS MacGARRY'S AMIGOS WITH THE BIG HEAVE, PAVLOV'S DOG THROWS A RABID FIT IN THE BACKGROUND.
IN THE NAME OF–
IT ENDS WITH THIS RIPPED-SHIRT WHIRLIGIG — TRUE.
HEY!
WHEN YOU TELL AND RETELL A STORY YOU TEND TO STREAMLINE IT, GIVE IT A DRAMATIC SHAPE-LEAVE OUT NICE LITTLE TOUCHES LIKE MY PAL PAM WAITING TO NOBBLE THE NEXT WHITE SHIRT THAT COMES UP——————.
ME, FULL OF REMORSE 'CAUSE EVERYONE'S FIGHTING MY FIGHT AND I DON'T ACTUALLY HIT ANYONE.
BLESS ALL MY FRIENDS.
KISS THEM GOODNIGHT AT THE STATION.
ABSENTMINDEDLY WALK IN THE PARCELS ROOM.
STAFF ONLY
TRAINS
OI

HAY FEVER
HELLO. I'M YOUR NEW NEIGHBOUR. MY NAME'S EVE.
COULD YOU SPARE A MOMENT TO SHOW ME HOW TO USE THE BATH BOILER, PLEASE?
ON WAY TO PUB
E. Campbell 1/81 6/83
IT SAYS FIVES OR TENS ON THE METER, BUT IT ONLY TAKES TENS
THAT'S THAT THEN.. I'VE JUST MADE A POT OF TEA- WILL YOU JOIN ME?
WHAT SORT OF WORK DO YOU DO?
OH, THIS AND THAT.. AT THE MOMENT I'M CUTTING SHEET-METAL.
AN INTELLIGENT FELLOW LIKE YOU?
hmmmm.... why, thank you.
HOW ABOUT YOU?
POLICE
WHILE ALEC MacGARRY TREADS THE FINE LINE BETWEEN GOOD NEIGHBOUR AND PRANCING DON JUAN...
... A SIMILAR CONFRONTATION TAKES PLACE AT THE KING CANUTE
LET'S TAKE SOME CARRY-OOTS, AS MacGARRY CALLS THEM UP INTO THE HAYBARN
WHERE IS ALEC ANYWAY?

THE CASE OF THE GREAT HAY ROBBERY _
EXHIBIT C HOUSE OF MRS. WILLIAMS
I'M GOING HOME - YOU KNOW I CAN'T STAND HEIGHTS
EXHIBIT A THE PUB.
EXHIBIT B THE HAYBARN
AFTER ABOUT AN HOUR UP THERE DANNY GREY REALIZES HE MUST HAVE DROPPED HIS WATCH AND STARTS LOOKING FOR IT
WHOSE BOOTS ARE THOSE ?
HE CAN'T BREATHE! GET HIM OUT OF THERE!!
HE'S SLIPPING! SHIFT SOME HAY!!
NEIGHBOURING MRS. WILLIAMS BLOWS THE WHISTLE
PEEP
THE GENDARMES ARRIVE IN DUE COURSE
BEEOOP
BEEOOP
I'LL RACE YOU.
O.K.

ALL RIGHT! WE KNOW YOU'RE UP THERE - WE KNOW THERE WERE FOUR OF YOU!!
SMIFFY IS ARRESTED IN JAMES CAGNEY FASHION
HAHA! HE ONLY TRIED TO OUTRUN THE ESSEX SPRINT CHAMPION!
IF YOU'RE GOING TO LOCK ME UP ALL NIGHT YOU'LL HAVE TO GET IN TOUCH WITH MY WIFE - SHE'S NOT ON THE PHONE .. MY NAME'S JOHN GODFREY.. the caravan etc -
EMPTY POCKETS!
sigh .. I WONDER IF THEY'LL LET US OUT ON BALE ..
SHUT UP AND GO TO SLEEP!
HA HA HA HA
NEXT DOOR
I COULD UNLOAD A CRAP BUT I DON'T FANCY SNIFFING IT ALL NIGHT .. GUESS I BETTER HOLD ON TO IT .. THERE WAS THIS BLOKE IN MY CLASS AT SCHOOL USED TO HOLD ON TO IT -
TOM THE TURD THEY CALLED 'IM.
.. HE'D GO TO THE TOILET ONCE A FORTNIGHT AND IT WOULD COME OUT TWO FEET LONG .. THE FRONT END WOULD CURL AROUND THE U-BEND AND THE BACK END WOULD STICK OUT OF THE WATER LIKE BEACHY HEAD LIGHTHOUSE ..
THEY ALWAYS HAD TO GET THE JANITOR IN TO BREAK IT UP WITH A SHOVEL -
DO YOU KNOW THE [redacted]
A SOUTHEND PUB
NOT REALLY
WELL WE WENT UP THERE AND SEARCHED ALL THE PROSTITUTES FOR THE £300
SOUNDS LIKE A HORRID PLACE .. I WONDER IF STEGGY STILL DRINKS IN THERE

JOHN GODFREY'S GOOD LADY WIFE GETS THE NEWS
BLEEB
MORNINK, MATE- WHAT YOU IN FOR ?
KICKIN' HAYSTACKS !
MOVE ALONG
A WEEK LATER EVERYONE IS STILL TALKING ABOUT IT—
ALL THAT STRAW... WITH A COUPLE OF ANIMALS MY FRONT PORCH WOULD HAVE LOOKED LIKE A NATIVITY PLAY !
WHAT WE'LL NEED IS A CHARACTER WITNESS.
I'D LIKE TO. BUT I'M IN COURT MYSELF NEXT WEEK FOR HOLDING THE ST. VALENTINE'S DISCO WITHOUT A LICENSE.
HEY, YOU'LL NEVER BELIEVE IT ! WHILE I WAS DRINKING TEA WITH YOU LAST WEEK ALL MY FRIENDS GOT ARRESTED ON A HAYSTACK ! ISN'T THAT HILARIOUS !
THEY SHOULDN'T HAVE BEEN THERE.
THE FARMER WITHDRAWS ALL COMPLAINTS - BUT THE POLICE PUSH THE CASE THROUGH ANYWAY-
JAMES SMITH, GEORGE WAITE, JOHN GODFREY, AND DANIEL GREY.. WOULD YOU STAND IN THAT ORDER PLEASE...
DANNY SAVES A BON MOT FOR THE SUM-UP
AS FOR MRS WILLIAMS. IN THE WORDS OF AN AMERICAN COMEDIAN. THEY COULD HAVE USED HER AT PEARL HARBOUR.
THEY WERE FINED TWELVE QUID EACH FOR DAMAGES AND COURT COSTS
THE VAN IS STILL FULL OF STRAW FROM THE FIASCO. SEVERAL NIGHTS LATER, IN THE WEE HOURS :
BrrrrrRR - FUCK THE HOMOSEXUALITY - WE'LL HAVE TO GET CLOSER-

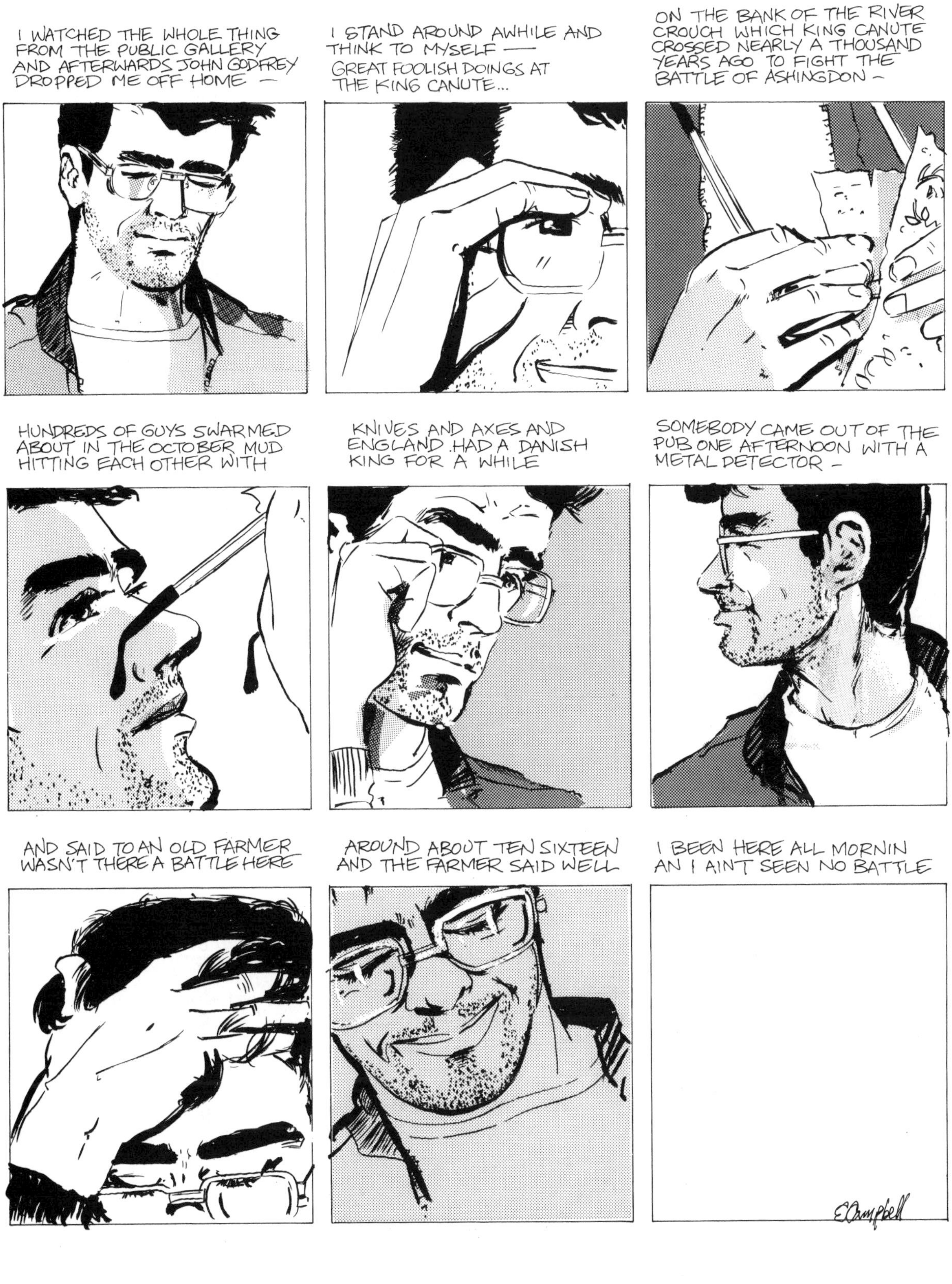
I WATCHED THE WHOLE THING FROM THE PUBLIC GALLERY AND AFTERWARDS JOHN GODFREY DROPPED ME OFF HOME –
I STAND AROUND AWHILE AND THINK TO MYSELF —— GREAT FOOLISH DOINGS AT THE KING CANUTE...
ON THE BANK OF THE RIVER CROUCH WHICH KING CANUTE CROSSED NEARLY A THOUSAND YEARS AGO TO FIGHT THE BATTLE OF ASHINGDON –
HUNDREDS OF GUYS SWARMED ABOUT IN THE OCTOBER MUD HITTING EACH OTHER WITH
KNIVES AND AXES AND ENGLAND HAD A DANISH KING FOR A WHILE
SOMEBODY CAME OUT OF THE PUB ONE AFTERNOON WITH A METAL DETECTOR –
AND SAID TO AN OLD FARMER WASN'T THERE A BATTLE HERE
AROUND ABOUT TEN SIXTEEN AND THE FARMER SAID WELL
I BEEN HERE ALL MORNIN AN I AIN'T SEEN NO BATTLE

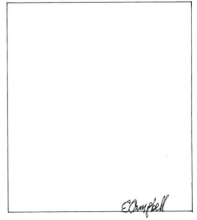

THE KING CANUTE SITS WELL OFF THE BEATEN TRACK.
YOU NEED A CAR
E Campbell 12/81

DGJ 312T
THE KING
CANUTE

I SAW MY AIMLESSNESS SUMMED UP ONE MORNING IN THE KING CANUTE WHEN GEORGE WAITE LEFT HIS CLOGS BY THE COAL FIRE, WENT TO THE PIANO AND PLONKED OUT 'KNEES UP MOTHER BROWN' IN THE STYLE OF WAGNER...

ECampbell
7/83

I'D JUST SPENT THE EASTER WEEKEND WITH MY FOLKS IN BLACKPOOL, AND WE'D HAD SAD ARGUMENTS LIKE THIS ONE –

HOW CAN YOU HAVE NO OPINION AT ALL ABOUT SOMETHING THIS SERIOUS ?!

IT HAD STARTED WITH A PHOTO IN THE CATHOLIC WEEKLY OF A DUSTBIN-LINER FULL OF ABORTED BABIES — HERE'S SOMETHING SIMILAR –

off!

YOU CAN'T HAVE HALF AN ABORTION... YOU HAVE TO BE ON ONE SIDE OR THE OTHER– YOU CAN'T GO THROUGH LIFE WITH YOUR EYES CLOSED!

DANNY GREY'S MOTHER USED TO BE THE DISTRICT NURSE IN HOCKLEY AND DANNY OFTEN ESCORTED HER THROUGH THE WOODS TO LAY OUT A DEAD PERSON IN SOME HOUSE OR OTHER.

DANNY SAYS HE'D SEEN MORE CORPSES BEFORE HE WAS SIXTEEN THAN MOST OF US SEE IN A LIFETIME.

HAVING NO INFLUENCE ONE WAY OR THE OTHER IN MATTERS OF LIFE; THAT IS, NOT BEING FATHER, MIDWIFE, MURDERER, GOVERNMENT FIRE-SAFETY INSPECTOR, I'M GOING ALONG VOICING EFFETE PHILOSOPHIES ON THE SUBJECT.
LIFE IS JUST PASSING TIME TILL THE TRAIN COMES IN -
AH, BUT WHICH WAY IS THE TRAIN GOING? - AND CAN YOU LET IT GO AND WAIT FOR A LATER ONE?
IT'S ONLY A METAPHOR... ANYWAY, I WAS TRYING TO BE FUNNY, NOT PASS A BLOODY PARLIAMENTARY BILL -
AS A PHILOSOPHER YOU'RE HUMOROUS.
AS IT HAPPENED I DIDN'T VISIT MY PARENTS AGAIN FOR OVER A YEAR, AND NOT BECAUSE OF THOSE DISAGREEMENTS, MINISCULE THINGS IN FACT,
...BUT BECAUSE OF A NEW PREOCCUPATION IN MY LIFE, WHICH CAME ALONG AT THE END OF THE MAYDAY BANK HOLIDAY WEEKEND. BEAR WITH ME A COUPLE OF CHAPTERS; IT BEGINS LIKE THIS...
AND THEN WE HAD A HELL OF A CONVERSATION ABOUT THE ABORTION QUESTION.
...AND I WOKE UP THE OTHER DAY WITH A PIECE OF ALMOST GOLDBERGIAN WISDOM IN MY HEAD
... WHATEVER WAY YOU BOUNCE IT, IT'S STILL A BABY
HELLO, DARLINGS... I NEED YOUR HELP, DANNY.
HI LOUISE
TRUMAN

REMEMBER MY UNCLE ART?
uh...
EASTER WEEKEND. HE WAS HERE, CAMPED OUTSIDE WITH HIS SPACE APPRENTICES
Air Training Cadets
YES, WELL REMEMBER THE LITTLE PLAQUE HE AWARDED US FOR LETTING THEM USE THE FIELD AND YOU PROMISED HIM IT WOULD BE HUNG OVER THE BAR THE VERY NEXT DAY...
oh, I see
WELL HE'S COMING TONIGHT!
WE BETTER GET A HAMMER AND NAIL THEN. HAVE YOU GOT ANY?
no, darling
AT JOHN GODFREY'S PLACE WE GET A HAMMER AND A CURTAIN-HOOK.
BUT THE PUB'S BUSTLING WHEN WE WALK BACK IN. ART'S ARRIVED AND HE'S LOOKING GLUM.
HI ART.
KEEP 'IM BUSY VIKKI!
IF I'M HONEST, I MUST RECORD THIS BIT.
I HOPE YOU'RE RECORDING ALL THIS, MacGARRY: 'IN THE DAYS OF THE KING CANUTE'
...IN EFFECT, CASTING A GLANCE AT THE FUTURE TO SAY "WHAT DO YOU THINK OF THIS, EH?" - PICTURE OF A MAN PICTURING HIS PICTURE.
- YUP, I WAS JUST THINKING THE COMPOSITION REMINDS ME OF GERICAULT'S 'RAFT OF THE MEDUSA'-
SELF-CONSCIOUS, YES, BUT NOT AS IN PEOPLE'S "I COULD WRITE A BOOK ABOUT THIS PLACE" (BUT NEVER DO). DANNY NEVER KIDS HIMSELF THAT THE WRITING OF BOOKS REQUIRES ONLY THAT ONE HAS SEEN SOMETHING MEMORABLE.

HE LIVES HIS LIFE TO THE FULL. NO PART IS SAVED LIKE A SLICE OF BIRTHDAY CAKE GOING STALE.
HE'S SELF-CONSCIOUS, BUT NOT AS IN PEOPLE'S GOING AND SEEING THE WORLD WITH THEIR INEVITABLE RECORD OF IT; PHOTO OF ME IN FRONT OF THE STATUE OF LIBERTY...
...ME IN FRONT OF THE ARC DE TRIOMPHE, ME BESIDE THE GUARD AT BUCKINGHAM PALACE, NOT SEEING THAT THE COMMON DENOMINATOR IS THE ME...
...ME IN THE KITCHEN SINK.
CHEMICO
I USED TO SIT IN THE GARDEN PAINTING OILS OF RHUBARB PATCHES AND FULL DUSTBINS AND MY AUNT ASKED "WHY DON'T YOU PAINT NICE SCENES?"
TO ME, THESE ARE THE 'NICE SCENES'. I MADE MENTAL PICTURES, AND SOMETIMES PHOTOS WHEN I TOOK TO HAVING A SMALL CAMERA HANDY. THE GANG GOT USED TO IT AND AFTER A WHILE FORGOT TO POSE.
I HAD NO AMBITION BEYOND LIFE'S DAILY ROUND AND THE WEEKEND CELEBRATION OF IT.
THAT NIGHT LOUISE LETS DANNY AND ME SLEEP IN THE ROOM THAT USED TO BE THE RESTAURANT.
BEDDING DOWN WARM I ALMOST MAKE LOVE TO BELLA.
AND IN THE MORNING IN COMES THE MORNING-COFFEE NYMPH.
© Campbell

THE KING CANUTE
FREE HOUSE

IS THIS A BOTTLE IN FRONT O' ME OR A FRONTAL LOBOTOMY?
YAWN
A FAMOUS INTELLECTUAL WROTE THAT THE POWER OF ALCOHOL OVER MANKIND LIES IN ITS STIMULATION OF THE MYSTICAL FACULTIES OF HUMAN NATURE.
A FAMOUS GLASGOW DRUNK..(MY UNCLE GEORGE) SAID 'YOU WAKE UP THE NEXT MORNING WITH A SORE HEID AND A POCKET FULL OF STICKY PENNIES.
MY FATHER, ON THE OTHER HAND,.. ENCOURAGED ME TO DRINK IN AN "EDUCATED" MANNER..I GUESS THAT'S WHY I'M AN EDUCATED DRUNK.
humm... It's going to be another good day
HEY, WHERE DID ALL THESE BLANKETS COME FROM.?
LOUISE BROUGHT THEM DOWN.
OH OH...IT'S JUST COME BACK TO ME
huh.?
I WANDERED OUT TO THE LOO ABOUT FOUR O'CLOCK, I DIDN'T EVEN NOTICE THE LIGHT WAS ON.
OOPS

SORRY UH. OH, I EXPECT YOU'VE SEEN ONE BEFORE.
HOW CAN I FACE HER AGAIN? OH WELL, LET'S GET IT OVER WITH.
GOOD MORNING, LOUISE.
hmmm.. DANNY! NOW I KNOW WHAT YOU'VE GOT. hee hee...
I'LL MAKE THE BREAKFAST. YOU HOOVER THE FLOOR AND GET A FIRE GOING.
WELL IT'S G.W. EARLY FOR YOU IS IT NOT?
GOOD MORNING, ALEC. TIMES CROSSWORD: FIVE, TWO, FOUR, FOUR: LISTEN INTENTLY TO SEXUAL DEVIATION...
GIVE IN.
PRICK UP ONE'S EARS
YOU MADE THAT UP!
HA HA HA
THAT'S IN THE SAME LEAGUE AS THE ONE SMIFFY CAME OUT WITH A WHILE AGO ON THIS VERY SPOT.
ALAS POOR YORLIK, I KNEW HIM BACKWARDS.
KILROY WAS HERE!
Well, well. DO I SMELL EGGS FRYING?

YOU REALLY OUGHT TO LET US PAY FOR THIS LOT.
DON'T BE SILLY,
BUT...UH...LET ME BORROW YOUR HAT.
MAKES YOU LOOK LIKE ISADORA DUNCAN,
hmmm.... WELL I'LL OPEN UP IN TEN MINUTES IF YOU WANT TO GO IN AND WAIT.
oh well,, what'll we do?
I'VE GOT AN IDEA.. LET'S SEE HOW LONG IT TAKES US TO REMEMBER THE FIFTY STATES OF THE USA.
half hour I would think.
I'LL GET SOME PAPER.
SHALL WE PUT THE OBVIOUS ONES OUT OF THE WAY. CALIFORNIA, NEW YORK, WASHINGTON, TEXAS, KANSAS, NOT TO MENTION ARKANSAS -
ARIZONA, NEW MEXICO.
SLOW UP! LET ME GET THEM DOWN.
WHAT'S NEXT GOING WEST, COLORADO?
GO WEST YOUNG MAN.
GO SOUTH: VIRGINIA, GEORGIA, KENTUCKY, NORTH AND SOUTH CAROLINA, ALABAMA.
HEY, THERE'S THE ORDERLY APPROACH. WHAT ARE THE OTHER SOUTHERN STATES-LOUISIANA, MISSOURI -
AND THE NEW ENGLAND STATES-CONNECTICUT, MASSACHUSSETTS.
I think it's your round, Al.
THERE'S ILLINOIS, NORTH AND SOUTH DAKOTA, NEVADA ...uh... WISCONSIN.
THE MORMON STATE ...UTAH !!
begins with a W - plains Indians...
HOW MANY'S THAT?
ONLY TWENTY-FIVE - NOT BAD FOR FIFTEEN MINUTES PERHAPS.
Little Big Horn,,
Sitting Bull.

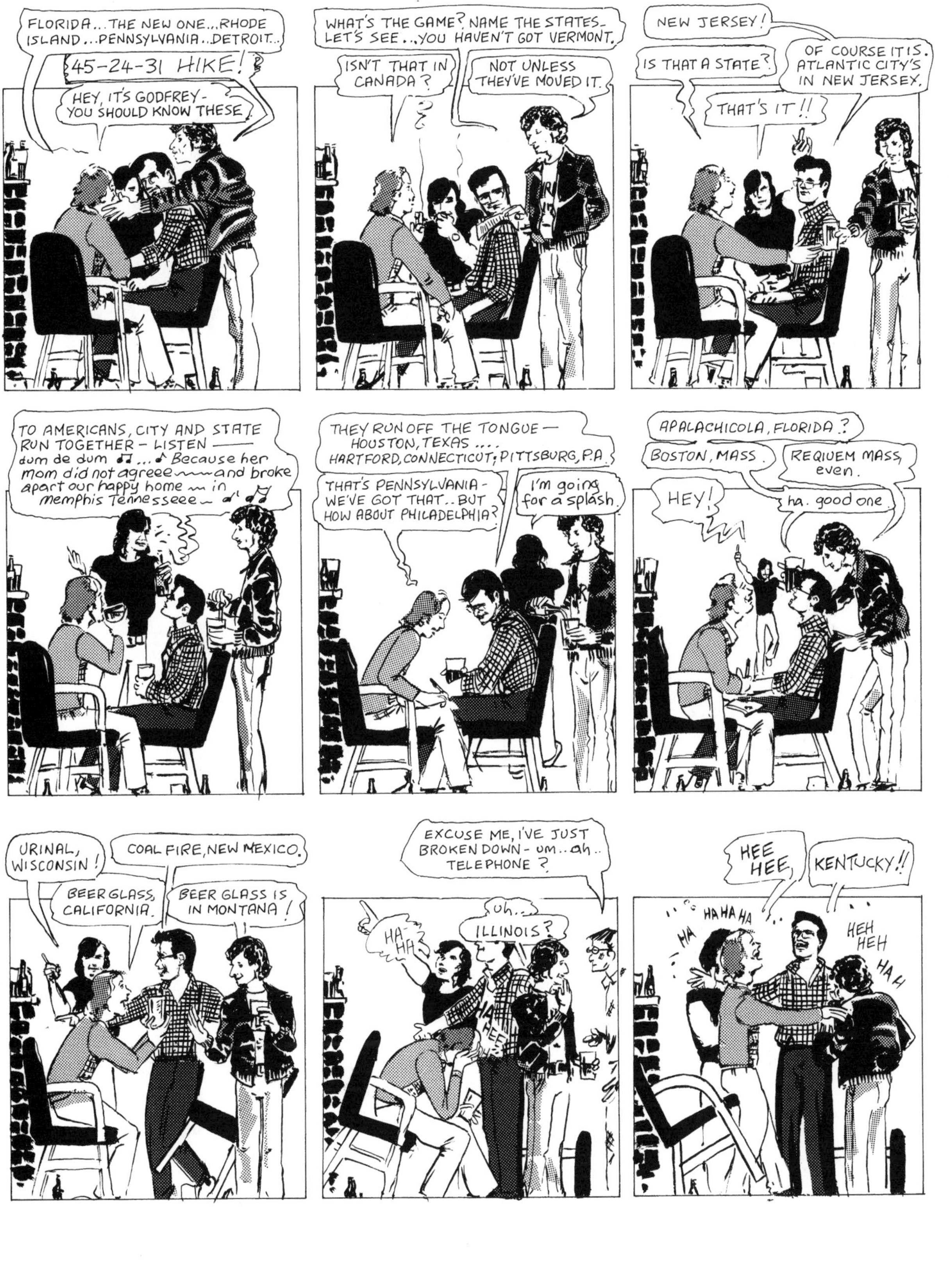

FLORIDA... THE NEW ONE... RHODE ISLAND... PENNSYLVANIA... DETROIT...
45-24-31 HIKE!
HEY, IT'S GODFREY- YOU SHOULD KNOW THESE.
WHAT'S THE GAME? NAME THE STATES- LET'S SEE... YOU HAVEN'T GOT VERMONT.
ISN'T THAT IN CANADA?
NOT UNLESS THEY'VE MOVED IT.
NEW JERSEY!
IS THAT A STATE?
OF COURSE IT IS. ATLANTIC CITY'S IN NEW JERSEY.
THAT'S IT!!
TO AMERICANS, CITY AND STATE RUN TOGETHER - LISTEN — dum de dum ... Because her mom did not agreee — and broke apart our happy home — in memphis Tennesseee —
THEY RUN OFF THE TONGUE— HOUSTON, TEXAS.... HARTFORD, CONNECTICUT; PITTSBURG, P.A.
THAT'S PENNSYLVANIA- WE'VE GOT THAT.. BUT HOW ABOUT PHILADELPHIA?
I'm going for a splash.
APALACHICOLA, FLORIDA?
BOSTON, MASS.
REQUIEM MASS, even.
HEY!
ha. good one.
URINAL, WISCONSIN!
COAL FIRE, NEW MEXICO.
BEER GLASS, CALIFORNIA.
BEER GLASS IS IN MONTANA!
EXCUSE ME, I'VE JUST BROKEN DOWN - um.. ah.. TELEPHONE?
HA-HA
oh..
ILLINOIS?
HEE HEE,
KENTUCKY!!
HA HA HA HA
HEH HEH

HI, RICHIE.
WHAT'S GOING ON HERE THEN?
cheers, mate
I WONDER IF THERE'S A BUNCH OF GUYS IN A BAR IN, SAY PHILADELPHIA AT THIS VERY MOMENT TRYING TO REMEMBER ALL THE ENGLISH COUNTIES.
cheers
cns
Cheers Rich
CHIPPING, SODBURY.
LIKE MAIDSTONE, KENT
PRATTS, BOTTOM. HA HA HA HA HA.
COME ON, NOW, DARLINGS! I LOVE YOU BUT GETT OUTT!!! TIME'S UP.
HERE, YOU BETTER TAKE YOUR HAT BACK ... WHO IS THIS GLORIA DUNCAN ANYWAY?
EH?
oh, never mind.

ah. happy days... NOTHING TO THINK ABOUT BUT THE BON MOT, THE WITTY RIPOSTE AND THE PINT IN YOUR HAND...
LONG LIVE THE KING!
THE KING CANUTE
FREE HOUS

COLORADO SPRINGS, COLORADO
URINAL, WISCONSIN
WASHINGTON, D.C.
EL SEGUNDO, CALIFORNIA
HAMPTON, VIRGINIA
NORCO, CALIFORNIA
COD, ALABAMA
TWOBLONDES, ARIZONA
HUNTSVILLE, ALABAMA

C. Campbell

A PERMANENT FEATURE OF THE KING CANUTE IS A BUNCH OF GUYS WHO PARK THEIR BIKES ON THE PORCH.
AND LEAVE THEIR 'SKID-LIDS' ON THE MANTLEPIECE.
AND SAY THINGS I DON'T UNDERSTAND LIKE -
THE 900 CRANK IS FASTER -
YOU HAVE TO DRILL HOLES IN THE PINS -
Dave Pooles been building bikes for as long as I remember
THERE'S NICK LAING, JUST BACK FROM AUSTRALIA, AND HIS LONG-TIME GIRL-FRIEND MONICA; THERE'S THE VIKING AND OTHER CHARACTERS -
TRIUMPH
PARTY IN HOCKLEY - YOU MUST ALL COME.
MY PALS ARE DIVIDED ON THE MATTER OF GOING TO THIS PARTY AND WANDER IN AND OUT OF DAVE TIMMINS' ROOM -
- WE COULDN'T GET A TAXI -
KEN JUST PHONED US TO COME ALONG TO THE PARTY? WHO'S GAME?
I'M NOT TOO HEAVY, ALEC?
LIKE WEARING A THICK VEST.
hmm - oh, he's got a good grip on the curves.
(le printemps)
picasso

I DON'T THINK HE IS ASLEEP - HE'S STUDYING THE CAT FOR A DRAWING - YOU KNOW HOW HE IS -
BEER!
BEER!
GLUCK
GLUCK
GLUCK
WENCH! WHERE ARE YOU?
ARE YOU LAUGHING AT ME? - YOU! OUTSIDE!!
I DON'T BELIEVE IT! - WE'RE ALL LAUGHING BUT HE PICKS ON THE PACIFIST -
YOU WERE ALL LAUGHING AT ME! YES YOU WERE.
gulp
LOOK, JOHN, ARE YOU SAYING YOU'VE NEVER SAID ANYTHING THAT MADE US LAUGH?

I HAVE ENTERED INTO A TWILIGHT WORLD OF DRUNKENNESS NOW, A LAND OF FAERIE THAT STILL SPARKLES IN THE LIGHT OF DAY.
A HOLY FEW HOURS IN WHICH I WILL FALL IN LOVE, AMONG OTHER THINGS.
YOU HAVE BELITTLED ME!!
I'D GONE TO SLEEP BECAUSE I'D HAD MY FILL, AND MORE - I WAS FED UP, READY TO CHANGE MY LIFESTYLE IF I COULD JUST GET HOME FOR 12 HOURS KIP.
BUT AS I PRESSED AHEAD ONE SENSATION PILED ON ANOTHER WITHOUT ANY LOGICAL PROGRESSION AND I AM 'DRUNK' ON THESE-
THE VIKING, RATTLER OF WHOLE GARAGE WITH HIS NUT; SMIFFY, DICER WITH DOGSHIT; DANNY GREY, ROUNDER UP OF TWO HUNDRED AND FIFTY SHEEP-
AND KNOWER OF COUNTRY THINGS—
IT'S GOING TO BE A FINE DAY.
HOW CAN YOU TELL?
THERE HAS TO BE HEAT TO BRING ALL THIS MIST UP-
FIVE O'CLOCK BACK IN TIMMINS' ROOM—LOOKING AT TEETH, POTENTIAL NO-TEETH IN BOOZY NEGLIGENCE (I EXAGGERATE BUT IT'S MY PARTICULAR ANXIETY)
GO TO SLEEP FR FKSAKE
..SORT OF LITTLE-GETHSEMANE GRIEF WITH DANNY GREY LOATHSOME DRUNK ASLEEP WITH HIS UGLY HAT ON - I WANT TO STEP ON HIS HEAD.
HOURS LATER, GEORGE AND VICKI
SO I SAID WHAT ABOUT THE REST?
AND I REPLIED WHAT ABOUT A REST?

GEORGE TRANSPORTS THE RITUAL GLASS OF BEER UPSTAIRS
OH WHAT A FART-LOOKING SMELLER.
HO HUM
LOUISE COMES IN FROM THE GARDEN WITH A BABY WRAPPED IN SPRING TREES..
AND IN THIS FIRST SUNDAY DINNER MOMENT I, RECORDER AND REMEMBERER OF THESE THINGS, TAKE A PHOTO –
THE FIRST AND UNEQUALLED, OF DANNY GREY - GABRIEL TOUSLED CLEANSHAVEN SHEPHERD FACE -
AND SPEAKING OF BABES, IN WALKS MINE - (ACTUALLY NOT QUITE LIKE THAT, AMERICAN TOUGH GUY PRIVATE-EYE SORT OF INTRODUCTION)
PENNY AND ANGELINE IN FACT ARRIVED A LITTLE EARLIER, SAW US FROM THE LOUNGE BAR AND CAME THROUGH –
TWO BLONDES, ARIZONA
EH?
PENNY MOORE, HOCKLEYWOOD RIDING FACED, MIDNIGHT WINK EYELASHES, THE SUN ALL CAUGHT UP IN HER HEAD –
AND THERE MUST HAVE BEEN SQUIRRELS IN BROWN GLASS BOTTLE BRANCHES UP BEHIND THE BAR.

Three

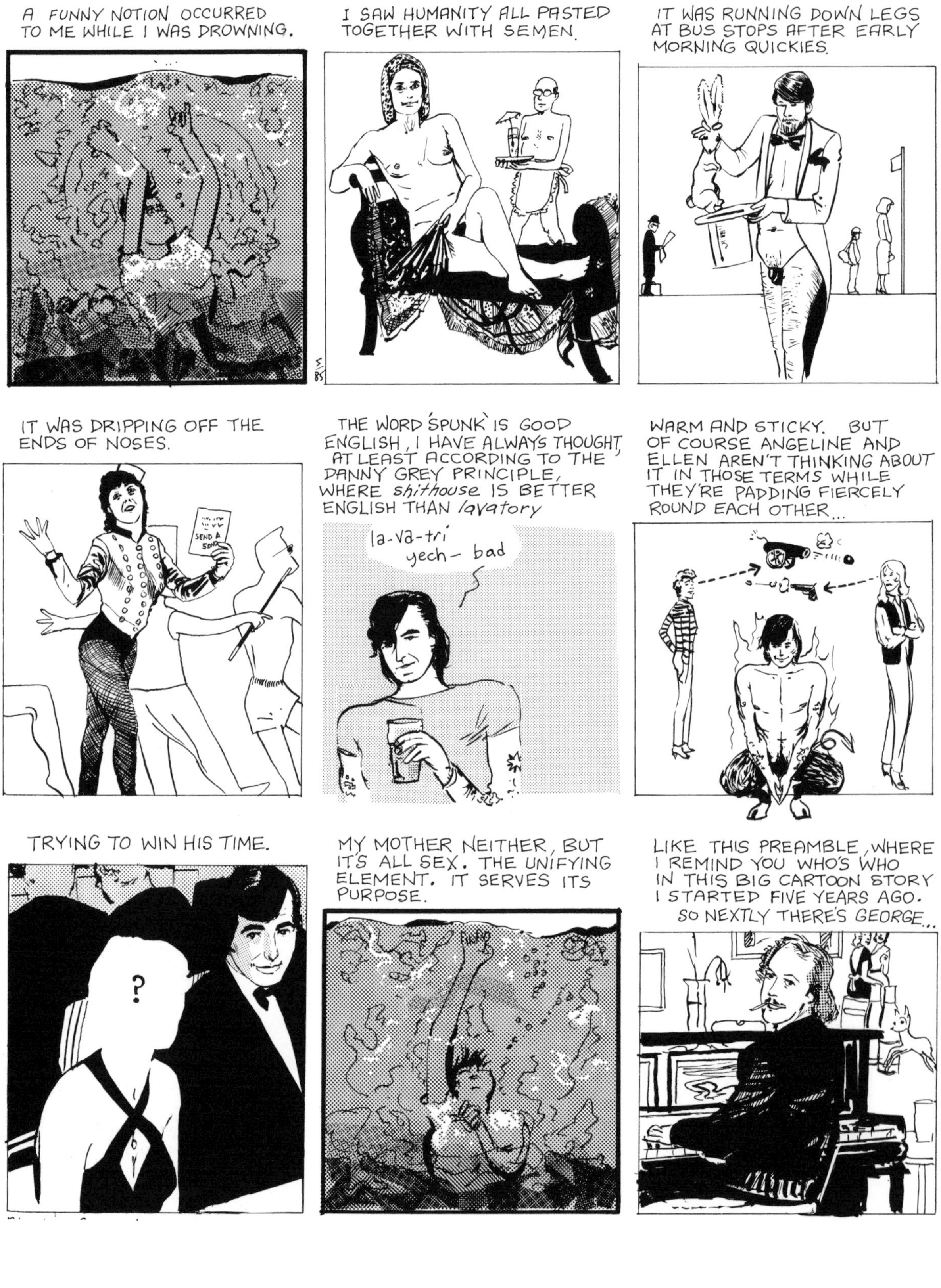
A FUNNY NOTION OCCURRED TO ME WHILE I WAS DROWNING.
I SAW HUMANITY ALL PASTED TOGETHER WITH SEMEN.
IT WAS RUNNING DOWN LEGS AT BUS STOPS AFTER EARLY MORNING QUICKIES.
IT WAS DRIPPING OFF THE ENDS OF NOSES.
THE WORD 'SPUNK' IS GOOD ENGLISH, I HAVE ALWAYS THOUGHT, AT LEAST ACCORDING TO THE DANNY GREY PRINCIPLE, WHERE *shithouse* IS BETTER ENGLISH THAN *lavatory*
la-va-tri yech- bad
WARM AND STICKY. BUT OF COURSE ANGELINE AND ELLEN AREN'T THINKING ABOUT IT IN THOSE TERMS WHILE THEY'RE PADDING FIERCELY ROUND EACH OTHER...
TRYING TO WIN HIS TIME.
?
MY MOTHER NEITHER, BUT IT'S ALL SEX. THE UNIFYING ELEMENT. IT SERVES ITS PURPOSE.
LIKE THIS PREAMBLE, WHERE I REMIND YOU WHO'S WHO IN THIS BIG CARTOON STORY I STARTED FIVE YEARS AGO.
SO NEXTLY THERE'S *GEORGE*...

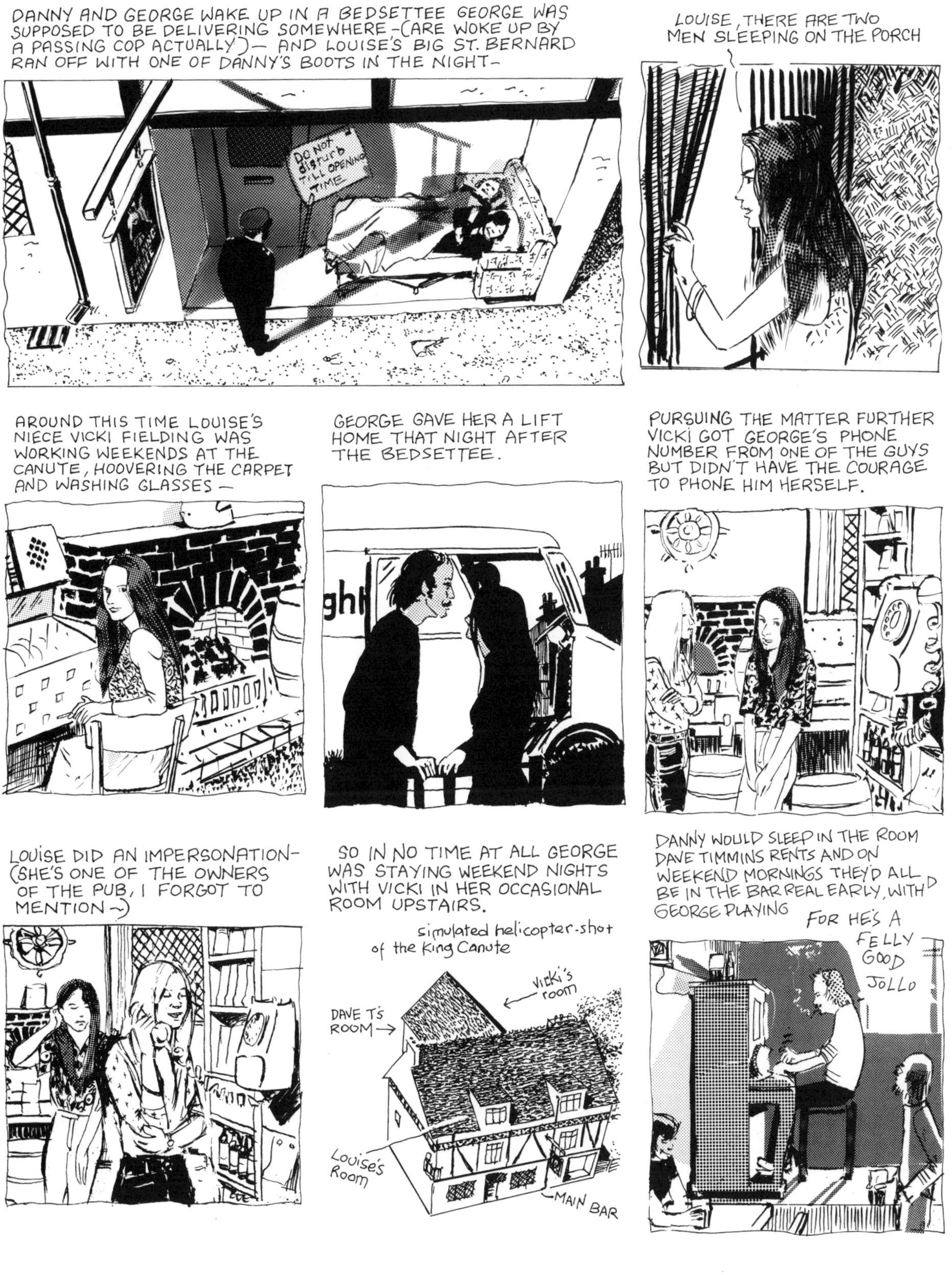
DANNY AND GEORGE WAKE UP IN A BEDSETTEE GEORGE WAS SUPPOSED TO BE DELIVERING SOMEWHERE -(ARE WOKE UP BY A PASSING COP ACTUALLY)— AND LOUISE'S BIG ST. BERNARD RAN OFF WITH ONE OF DANNY'S BOOTS IN THE NIGHT-
DO NOT DISTURB TILL OPENING TIME
LOUISE, THERE ARE TWO MEN SLEEPING ON THE PORCH
AROUND THIS TIME LOUISE'S NIECE VICKI FIELDING WAS WORKING WEEKENDS AT THE CANUTE, HOOVERING THE CARPET AND WASHING GLASSES —
GEORGE GAVE HER A LIFT HOME THAT NIGHT AFTER THE BEDSETTEE.
PURSUING THE MATTER FURTHER VICKI GOT GEORGE'S PHONE NUMBER FROM ONE OF THE GUYS BUT DIDN'T HAVE THE COURAGE TO PHONE HIM HERSELF.
LOUISE DID AN IMPERSONATION-(SHE'S ONE OF THE OWNERS OF THE PUB, I FORGOT TO MENTION ~)
SO IN NO TIME AT ALL GEORGE WAS STAYING WEEKEND NIGHTS WITH VICKI IN HER OCCASIONAL ROOM UPSTAIRS.
simulated helicopter-shot of the King Canute
Vicki's room
DAVE T'S ROOM
Louise's Room
MAIN BAR
DANNY WOULD SLEEP IN THE ROOM DAVE TIMMINS RENTS AND ON WEEKEND MORNINGS THEY'D ALL BE IN THE BAR REAL EARLY, WITH GEORGE PLAYING
FOR HE'S A FELLY GOOD JOLLO

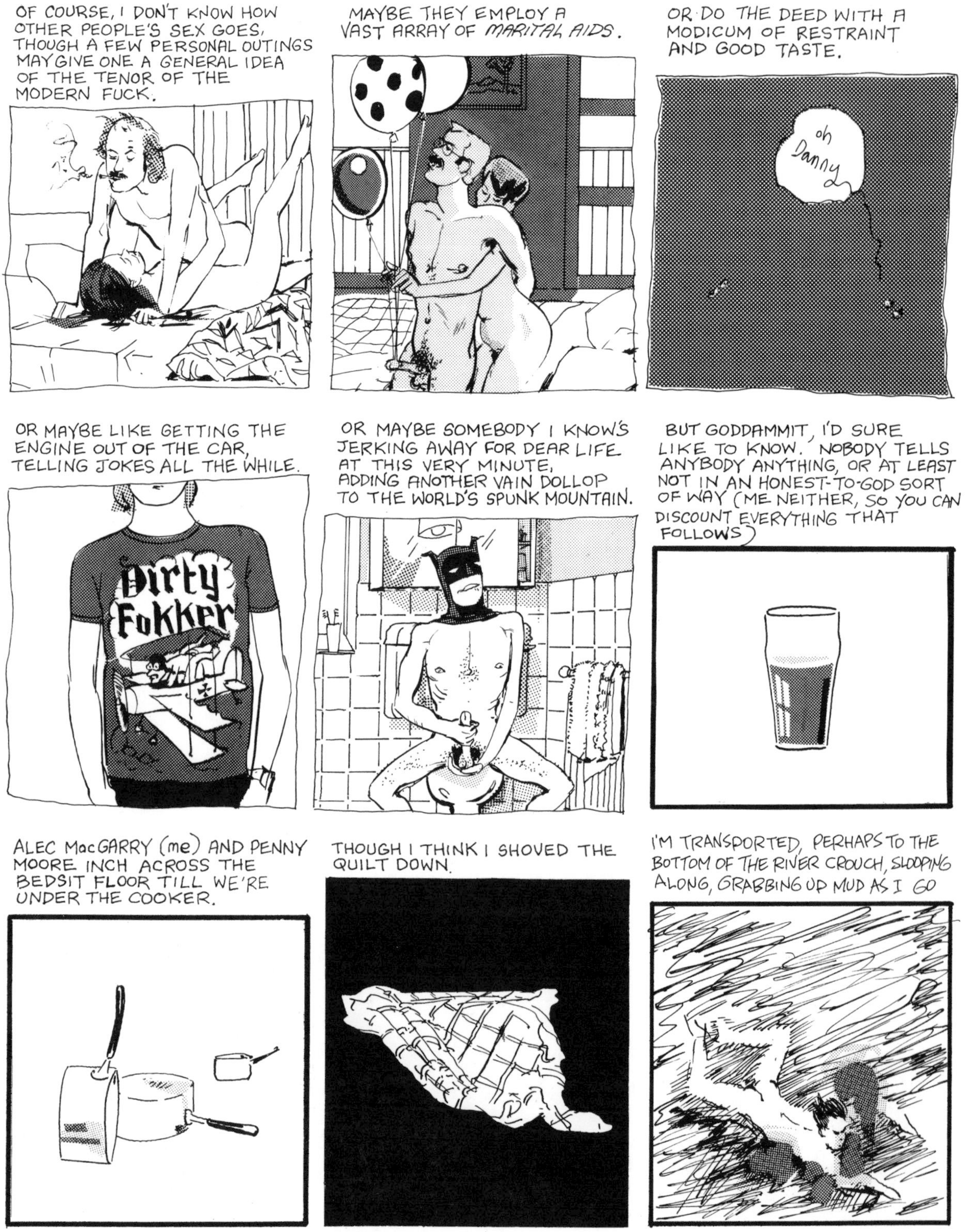
OF COURSE, I DON'T KNOW HOW OTHER PEOPLE'S SEX GOES, THOUGH A FEW PERSONAL OUTINGS MAY GIVE ONE A GENERAL IDEA OF THE TENOR OF THE MODERN FUCK.
MAYBE THEY EMPLOY A VAST ARRAY OF MARITAL AIDS.
OR DO THE DEED WITH A MODICUM OF RESTRAINT AND GOOD TASTE.
oh Danny
OR MAYBE LIKE GETTING THE ENGINE OUT OF THE CAR, TELLING JOKES ALL THE WHILE.
Dirty Fokker
OR MAYBE SOMEBODY I KNOW'S JERKING AWAY FOR DEAR LIFE AT THIS VERY MINUTE, ADDING ANOTHER VAIN DOLLOP TO THE WORLD'S SPUNK MOUNTAIN.
BUT GODDAMMIT, I'D SURE LIKE TO KNOW. NOBODY TELLS ANYBODY ANYTHING, OR AT LEAST NOT IN AN HONEST-TO-GOD SORT OF WAY (ME NEITHER, SO YOU CAN DISCOUNT EVERYTHING THAT FOLLOWS)
ALEC MacGARRY (me) AND PENNY MOORE INCH ACROSS THE BEDSIT FLOOR TILL WE'RE UNDER THE COOKER.
THOUGH I THINK I SHOVED THE QUILT DOWN.
I'M TRANSPORTED, PERHAPS TO THE BOTTOM OF THE RIVER CROUCH, SLOOPING ALONG, GRABBING UP MUD AS I GO

NEXT DAY, THE DAY OF THE HAT PARTY, SHE COMES INTO THE CANUTE AND HESITATES TO APPROACH.
THINKING PERHAPS NOW WE'VE DONE THE BUSINESS I'M MOVING ON (ME THINKING LIKEWISE SHE...)
Carlsberg
LATER IN THE WEEK WE GET ALL DRESSED UP FOR EACH OTHER WITH A COYNESS WE BOTH LATER FIND FUNNY.
(LOOKING BACK AT ALL THIS) I SEE PENNY IN CHANGES; IN AN OLD PHOTO AGE SEVENTEEN LIKE GREEK ATHENA.-
CENSORIOUS SEVERE MOTHER.
BUBBLING AUNT GIBBERISH.
blub
OUTDOORS TYPE RIDING.
MIDNIGHT SCHEMING.
(IN THE ALEXANDRA THAT NIGHT I COME FROM THE GENTS ROOM TO FIND A BIG IRISH DRUNK MOPPING HIS BROW WITH HER LITTLE MITT.)

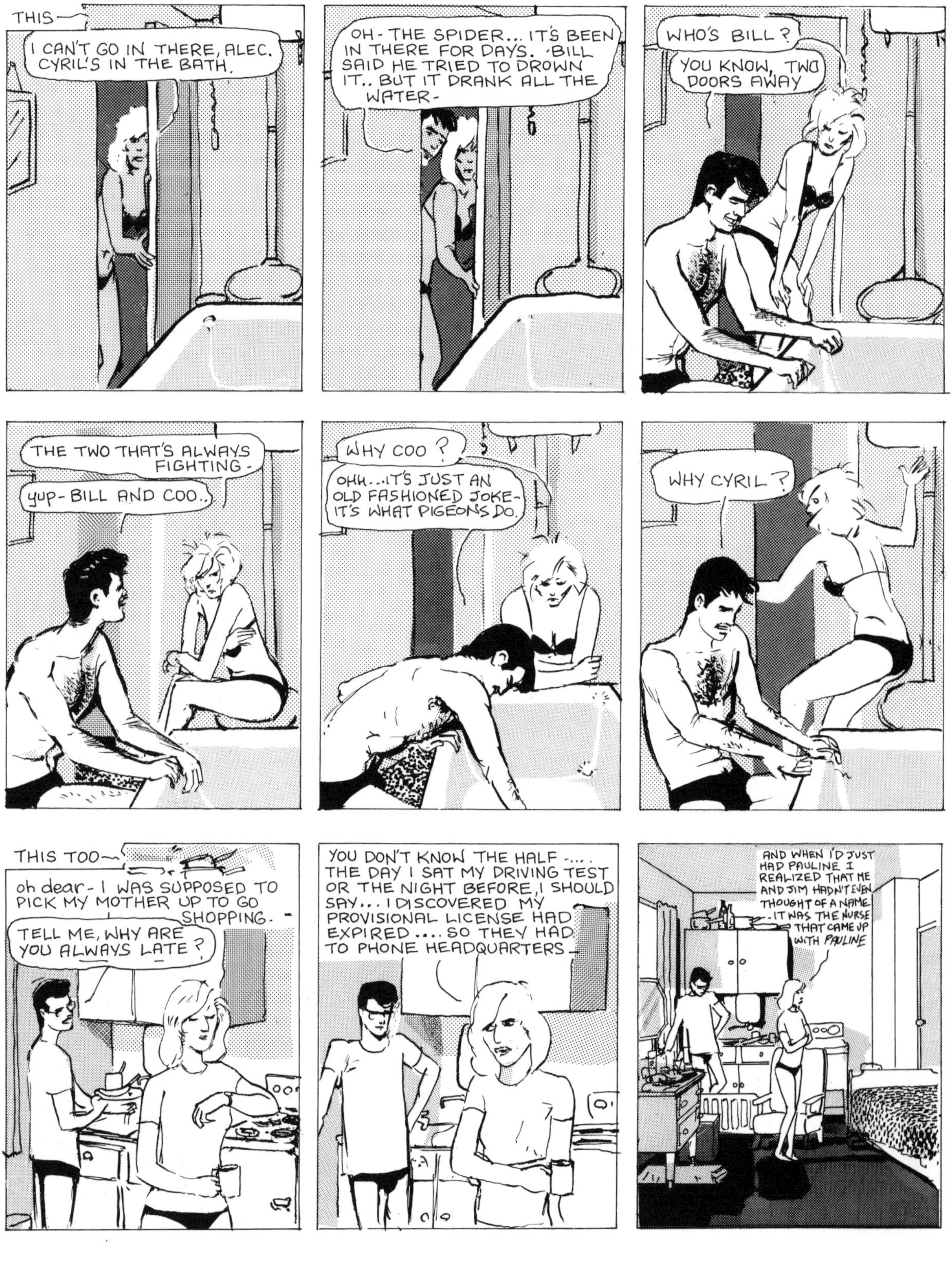
THIS
I CAN'T GO IN THERE, ALEC. CYRIL'S IN THE BATH.
OH - THE SPIDER... IT'S BEEN IN THERE FOR DAYS. BILL SAID HE TRIED TO DROWN IT.. BUT IT DRANK ALL THE WATER -
WHO'S BILL?
YOU KNOW, TWO DOORS AWAY
THE TWO THAT'S ALWAYS FIGHTING -
yup - BILL AND COO..
WHY COO?
OHH...IT'S JUST AN OLD FASHIONED JOKE - IT'S WHAT PIGEONS DO.
WHY CYRIL?
THIS TOO
oh dear - I WAS SUPPOSED TO PICK MY MOTHER UP TO GO SHOPPING.
TELL ME, WHY ARE YOU ALWAYS LATE?
YOU DON'T KNOW THE HALF.... THE DAY I SAT MY DRIVING TEST OR THE NIGHT BEFORE, I SHOULD SAY... I DISCOVERED MY PROVISIONAL LICENSE HAD EXPIRED.... SO THEY HAD TO PHONE HEADQUARTERS
AND WHEN I'D JUST HAD PAULINE I REALIZED THAT ME AND JIM HADN'T EVEN THOUGHT OF A NAME. IT WAS THE NURSE THAT CAME UP WITH PAULINE

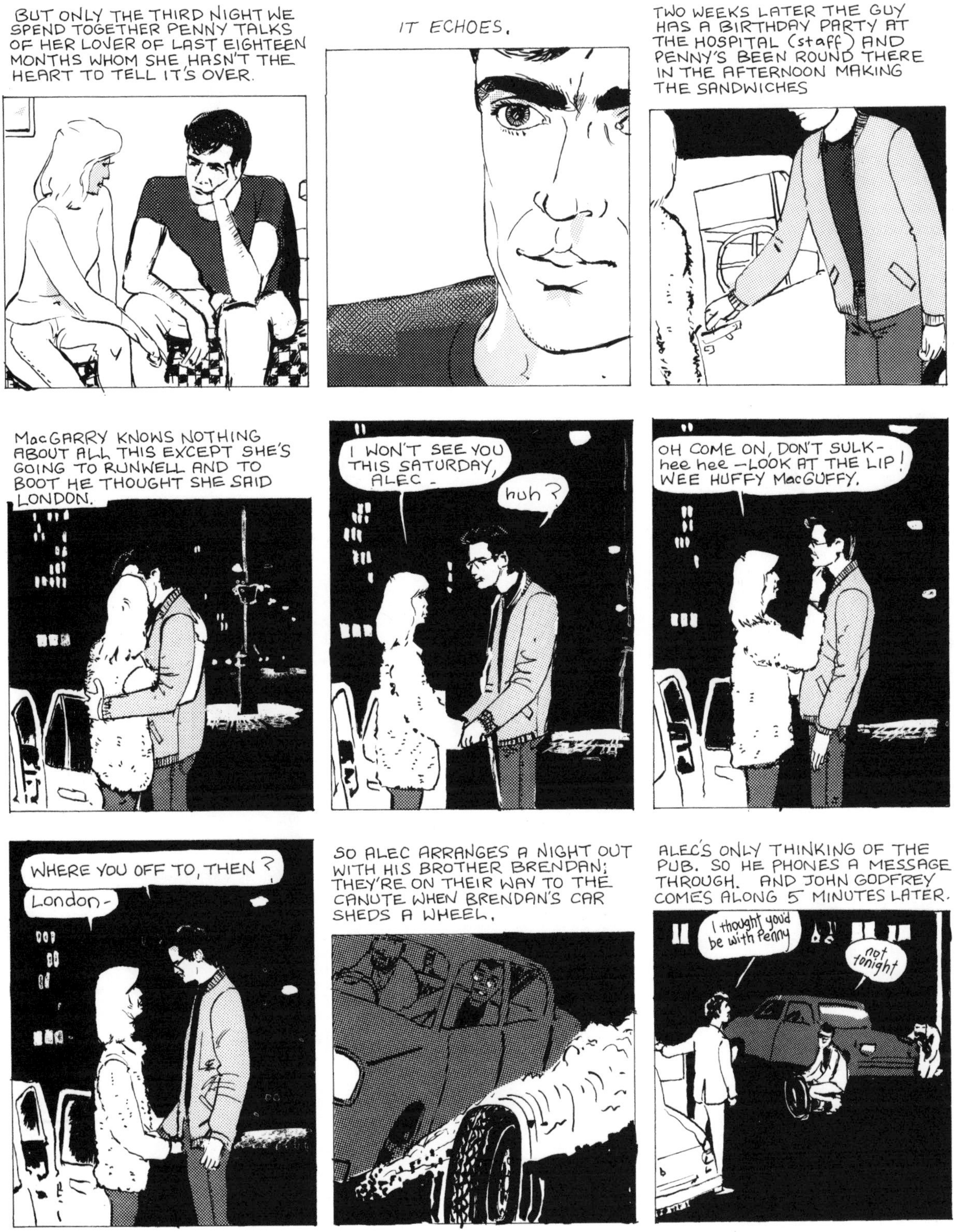
BUT ONLY THE THIRD NIGHT WE SPEND TOGETHER PENNY TALKS OF HER LOVER OF LAST EIGHTEEN MONTHS WHOM SHE HASN'T THE HEART TO TELL IT'S OVER.
IT ECHOES.
TWO WEEKS LATER THE GUY HAS A BIRTHDAY PARTY AT THE HOSPITAL (staff) AND PENNY'S BEEN ROUND THERE IN THE AFTERNOON MAKING THE SANDWICHES
MacGARRY KNOWS NOTHING ABOUT ALL THIS EXCEPT SHE'S GOING TO RUNWELL AND TO BOOT HE THOUGHT SHE SAID LONDON.
I WON'T SEE YOU THIS SATURDAY, ALEC.
huh?
OH COME ON, DON'T SULK- hee hee -LOOK AT THE LIP! WEE HUFFY MacGUFFY.
WHERE YOU OFF TO, THEN?
London-
SO ALEC ARRANGES A NIGHT OUT WITH HIS BROTHER BRENDAN; THEY'RE ON THEIR WAY TO THE CANUTE WHEN BRENDAN'S CAR SHEDS A WHEEL.
ALEC'S ONLY THINKING OF THE PUB. SO HE PHONES A MESSAGE THROUGH. AND JOHN GODFREY COMES ALONG 5 MINUTES LATER.
I thought you'd be with Penny
not tonight

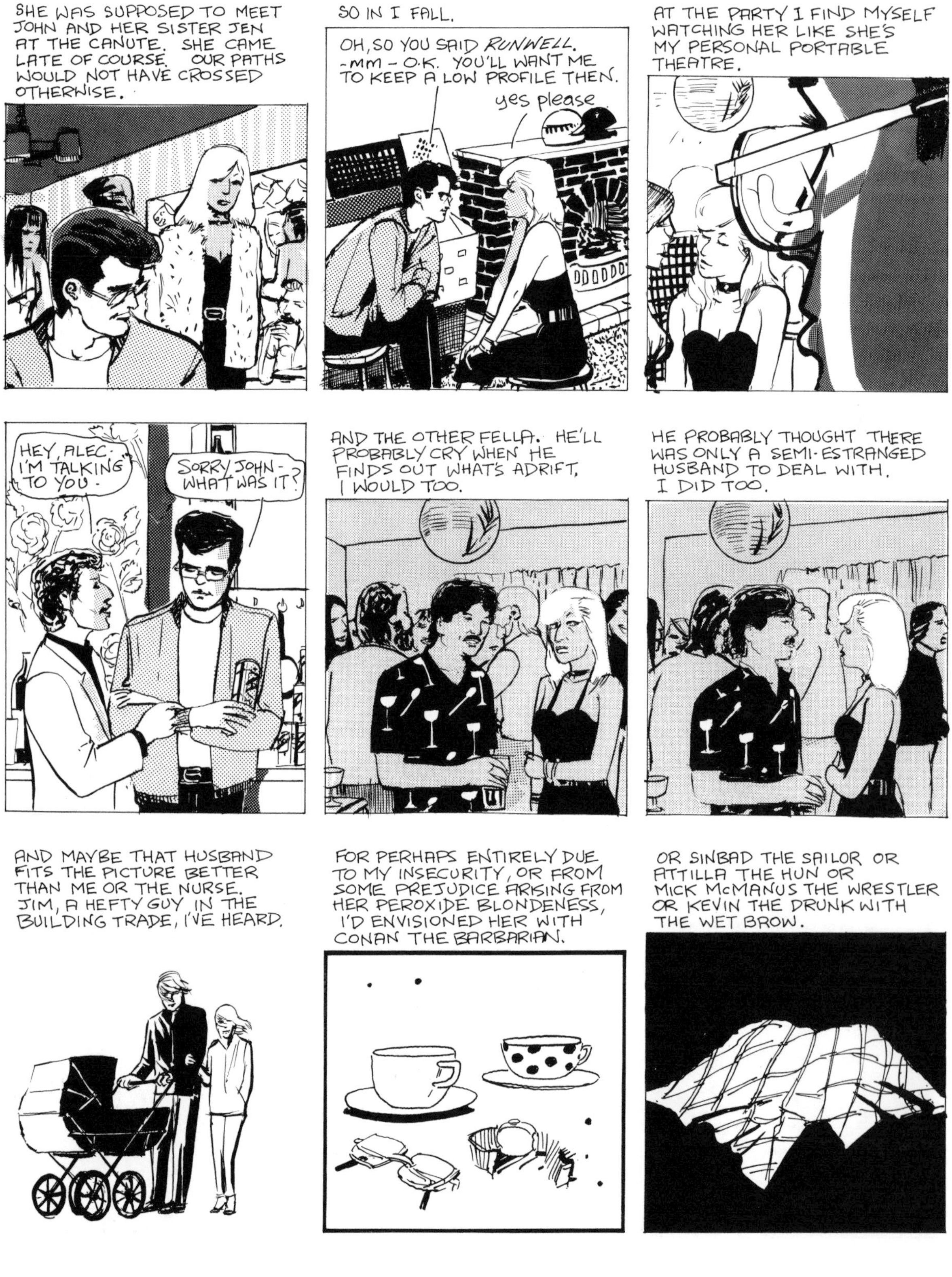
SHE WAS SUPPOSED TO MEET JOHN AND HER SISTER JEN AT THE CANUTE. SHE CAME LATE OF COURSE. OUR PATHS WOULD NOT HAVE CROSSED OTHERWISE.
SO IN I FALL.
OH, SO YOU SAID RUNWELL. -MM - O.K. YOU'LL WANT ME TO KEEP A LOW PROFILE THEN.
yes please
AT THE PARTY I FIND MYSELF WATCHING HER LIKE SHE'S MY PERSONAL PORTABLE THEATRE.
HEY, ALEC. I'M TALKING TO YOU -
SORRY JOHN - WHAT WAS IT?
AND THE OTHER FELLA. HE'LL PROBABLY CRY WHEN HE FINDS OUT WHAT'S ADRIFT, I WOULD TOO.
HE PROBABLY THOUGHT THERE WAS ONLY A SEMI-ESTRANGED HUSBAND TO DEAL WITH. I DID TOO.
AND MAYBE THAT HUSBAND FITS THE PICTURE BETTER THAN ME OR THE NURSE. JIM, A HEFTY GUY IN THE BUILDING TRADE, I'VE HEARD.
FOR PERHAPS ENTIRELY DUE TO MY INSECURITY, OR FROM SOME PREJUDICE ARISING FROM HER PEROXIDE BLONDENESS, I'D ENVISIONED HER WITH CONAN THE BARBARIAN.
OR SINBAD THE SAILOR OR ATTILLA THE HUN OR MICK McMANUS THE WRESTLER OR KEVIN THE DRUNK WITH THE WET BROW.

HOLLY SHERIDAN STARTED COMING INTO THE KING CANUTE WITH DAVE TIMMINS AROUND THE TIME OF THE HAT PARTY.
AND WAS PRESENT AT THE PECULIAR FALLING-OVER INCIDENT
IN WHICH TIMMINS AND DANNY GREY DRANK AROUND THE CLOCK.
DANNY WENT HOME AND DECANTED HIMSELF INTO THE BATH.
ZZ
TIMMINS MADE A DASH FOR THE FINISH-LINE.
GAA

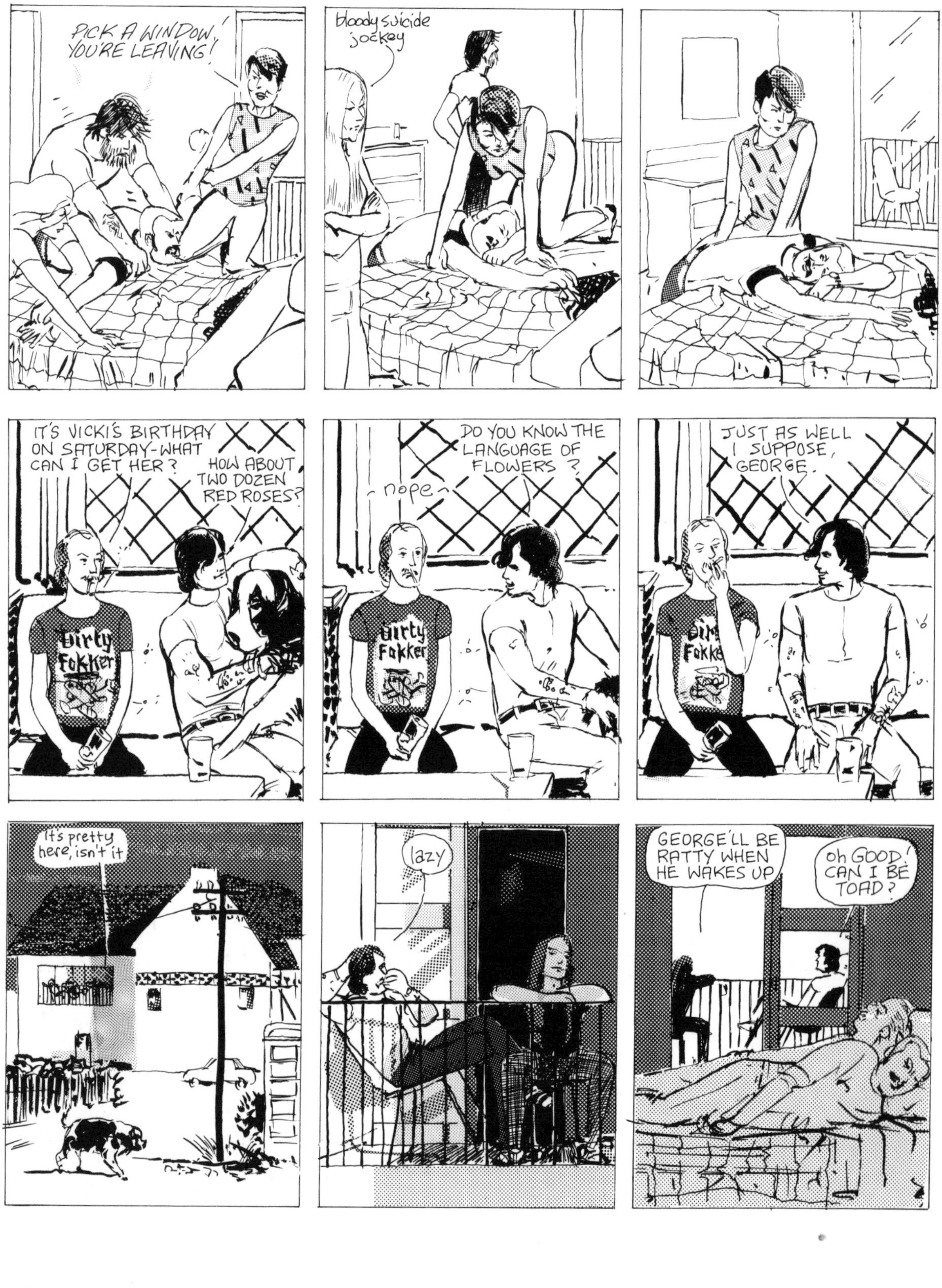
PICK A WINDOW, YOU'RE LEAVING!
bloody suicide jockey
IT'S VICKI'S BIRTHDAY ON SATURDAY-WHAT CAN I GET HER?
HOW ABOUT TWO DOZEN RED ROSES?
Dirty Fokker
DO YOU KNOW THE LANGUAGE OF FLOWERS?
-nope-
Dirty Fokker
JUST AS WELL I SUPPOSE, GEORGE.
It's pretty here, isn't it
lazy
GEORGE'LL BE RATTY WHEN HE WAKES UP
oh GOOD! CAN I BE TOAD?

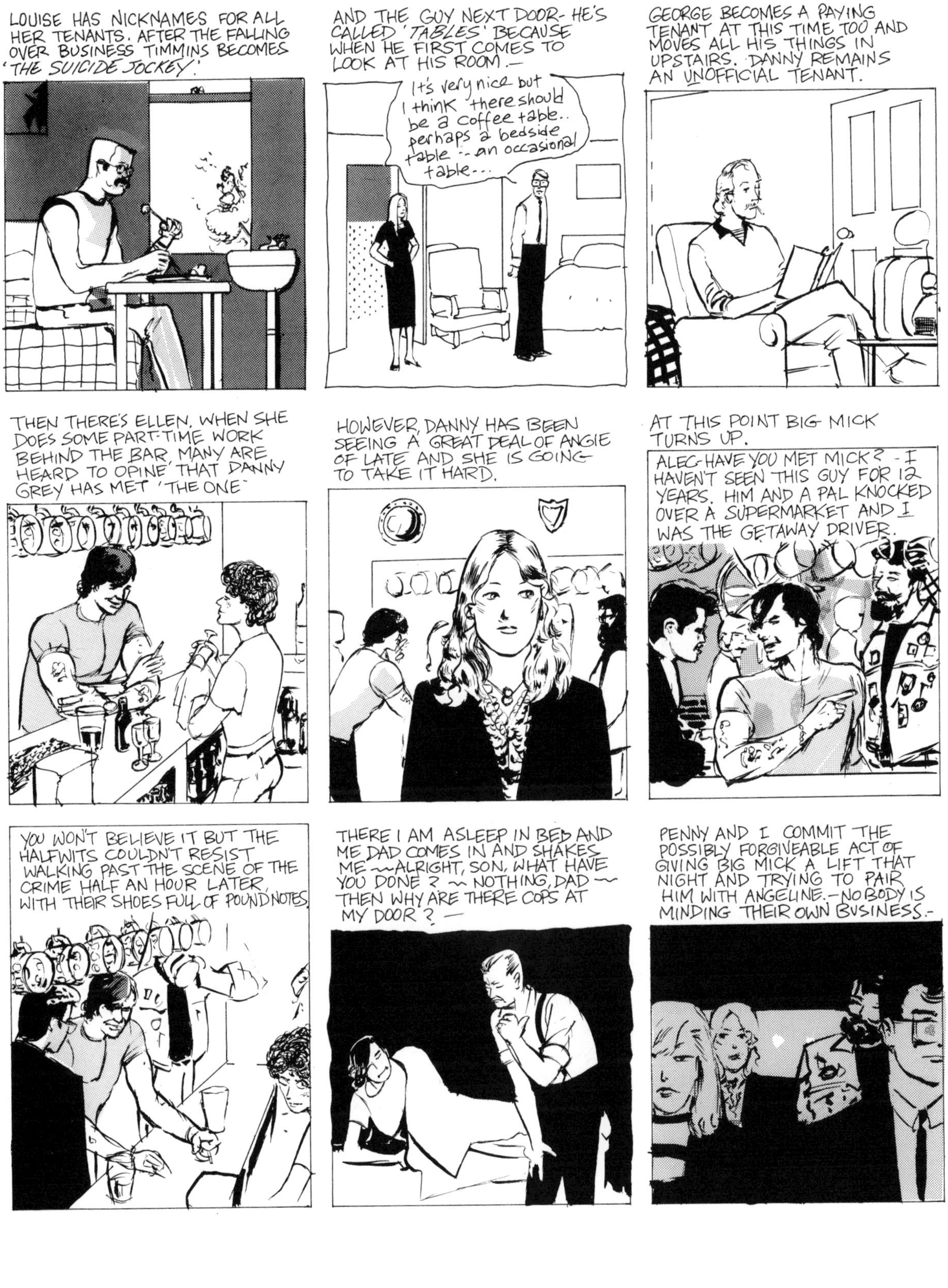
LOUISE HAS NICKNAMES FOR ALL HER TENANTS. AFTER THE FALLING OVER BUSINESS TIMMINS BECOMES 'THE SUICIDE JOCKEY'.
AND THE GUY NEXT DOOR- HE'S CALLED 'TABLES' BECAUSE WHEN HE FIRST COMES TO LOOK AT HIS ROOM.—
It's very nice but I think there should be a coffee table.. perhaps a bedside table -- an occasional table...
GEORGE BECOMES A PAYING TENANT AT THIS TIME TOO AND MOVES ALL HIS THINGS IN UPSTAIRS. DANNY REMAINS AN UNOFFICIAL TENANT.
THEN THERE'S ELLEN. WHEN SHE DOES SOME PART-TIME WORK BEHIND THE BAR, MANY ARE HEARD TO OPINE THAT DANNY GREY HAS MET 'THE ONE'
HOWEVER, DANNY HAS BEEN SEEING A GREAT DEAL OF ANGIE OF LATE AND SHE IS GOING TO TAKE IT HARD.
AT THIS POINT BIG MICK TURNS UP.
ALEC- HAVE YOU MET MICK? - I HAVEN'T SEEN THIS GUY FOR 12 YEARS. HIM AND A PAL KNOCKED OVER A SUPERMARKET AND I WAS THE GETAWAY DRIVER.
YOU WON'T BELIEVE IT BUT THE HALFWITS COULDN'T RESIST WALKING PAST THE SCENE OF THE CRIME HALF AN HOUR LATER, WITH THEIR SHOES FULL OF POUND NOTES.
THERE I AM ASLEEP IN BED AND ME DAD COMES IN AND SHAKES ME ~ ALRIGHT, SON, WHAT HAVE YOU DONE? ~ NOTHING, DAD ~ THEN WHY ARE THERE COPS AT MY DOOR? —
PENNY AND I COMMIT THE POSSIBLY FORGIVEABLE ACT OF GIVING BIG MICK A LIFT THAT NIGHT AND TRYING TO PAIR HIM WITH ANGELINE.—NOBODY IS MINDING THEIR OWN BUSINESS.-

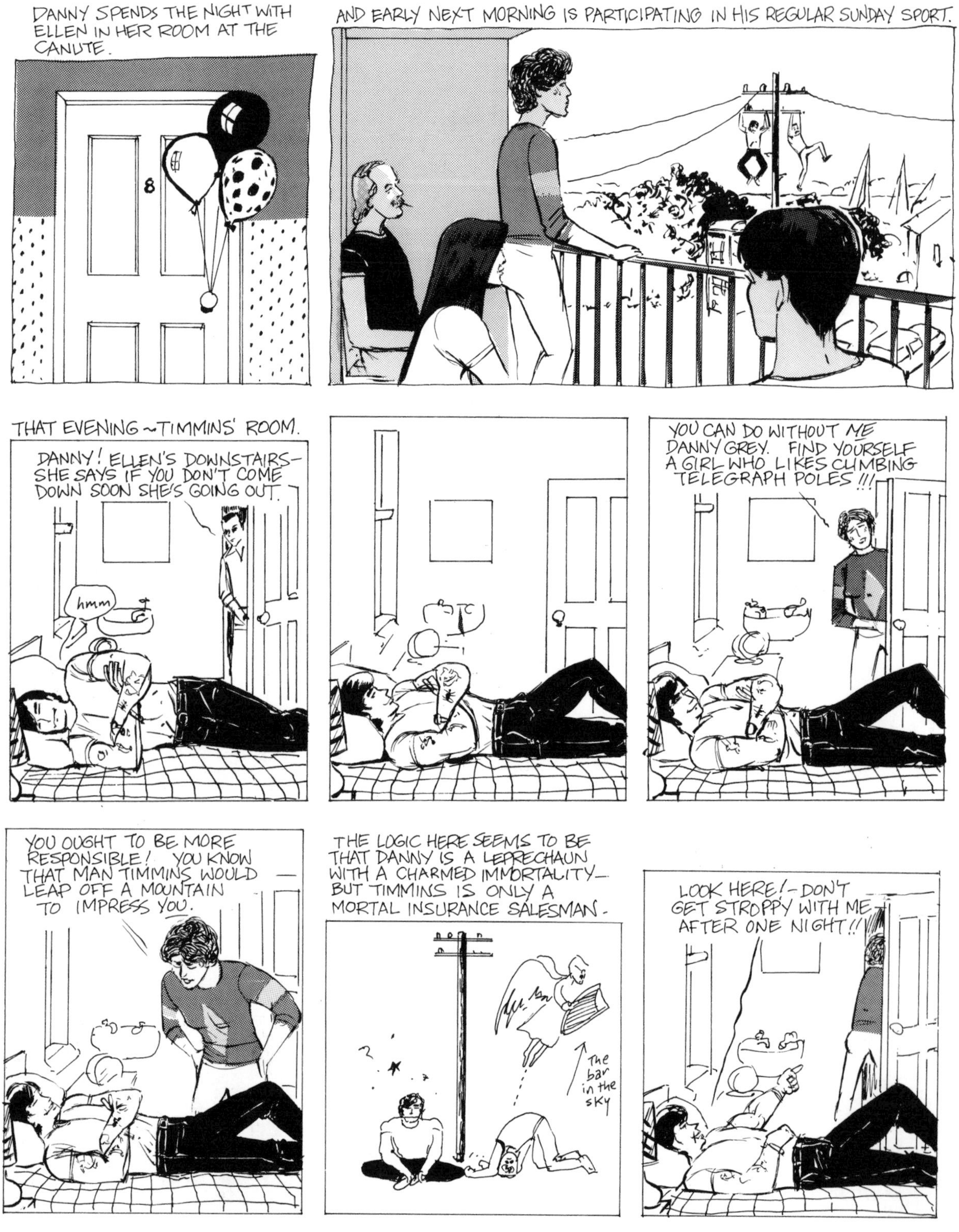
DANNY SPENDS THE NIGHT WITH ELLEN IN HER ROOM AT THE CANUTE.
8
AND EARLY NEXT MORNING IS PARTICIPATING IN HIS REGULAR SUNDAY SPORT.
THAT EVENING ~ TIMMINS' ROOM.
DANNY! ELLEN'S DOWNSTAIRS- SHE SAYS IF YOU DON'T COME DOWN SOON SHE'S GOING OUT.
hmm
YOU CAN DO WITHOUT ME DANNY GREY. FIND YOURSELF A GIRL WHO LIKES CLIMBING TELEGRAPH POLES!!!
YOU OUGHT TO BE MORE RESPONSIBLE! YOU KNOW THAT MAN TIMMINS WOULD LEAP OFF A MOUNTAIN TO IMPRESS YOU.
THE LOGIC HERE SEEMS TO BE THAT DANNY IS A LEPRECHAUN WITH A CHARMED IMMORTALITY — BUT TIMMINS IS ONLY A MORTAL INSURANCE SALESMAN.
The bar in the sky
LOOK HERE! - DON'T GET STROPPY WITH ME AFTER ONE NIGHT!!

LET HIM IN, I'LL VOUCH FOR HIM.
NO, DANNY THE GEEZER'S DRUNK.
YOU CAN'T BRING HIM UPSTAIRS AND THAT'S THE END OF IT!!
HELL WITH IT I'M FINISHED WITH THIS PUB!
WHERE'S DANNY?
I SAW HIM HEADING FOR THE RIVER- ERIC WON'T LET HIM UP-
I'VE GOT TO FIND HIM- HE'S PROBABLY GOING TO HIS MOTHER'S-
eh?
SEE HOLLY'S O.K. FOR ME, WILL YOU, ALEC?
sure
Dirty FoKKer
HOW WILL YOU GET HOME, HOLLY?
IT'S O.K. I LIVE HERE WITH DAVE NOW.

DOES HE MEAN IT? NO MORE CANUTE?
LOOKS LIKE IT.
FAYRE
BEE
LOOK AT IT THIS WAY, DANNY: WHAT WILL BELLA DO WITHOUT YOU?
I'VE KNOCKED MY JOB ON THE HEAD — I'M NOT CUT OUT TO BE AN INSURANCE SALESMAN.
Too bad.
GEORGE, CAN YOU LEND ME A FIVER?
NO, NOT THAT PATCH, DARLING. IT'S JUST BEEN SEEDED.
£
LET ME ASK YOU SOMETHING, DANNY: WHOSE FRIENDSHIP DO YOU VALUE MORE, MINE OR DAVE'S?
HOW WOULD HE FEEL IF YOU AND I WERE TO GO OUT TOGETHER?
NO POINT IN DISCUSSING IT.—THE SITUATION WON'T ARISE.—

RODEN

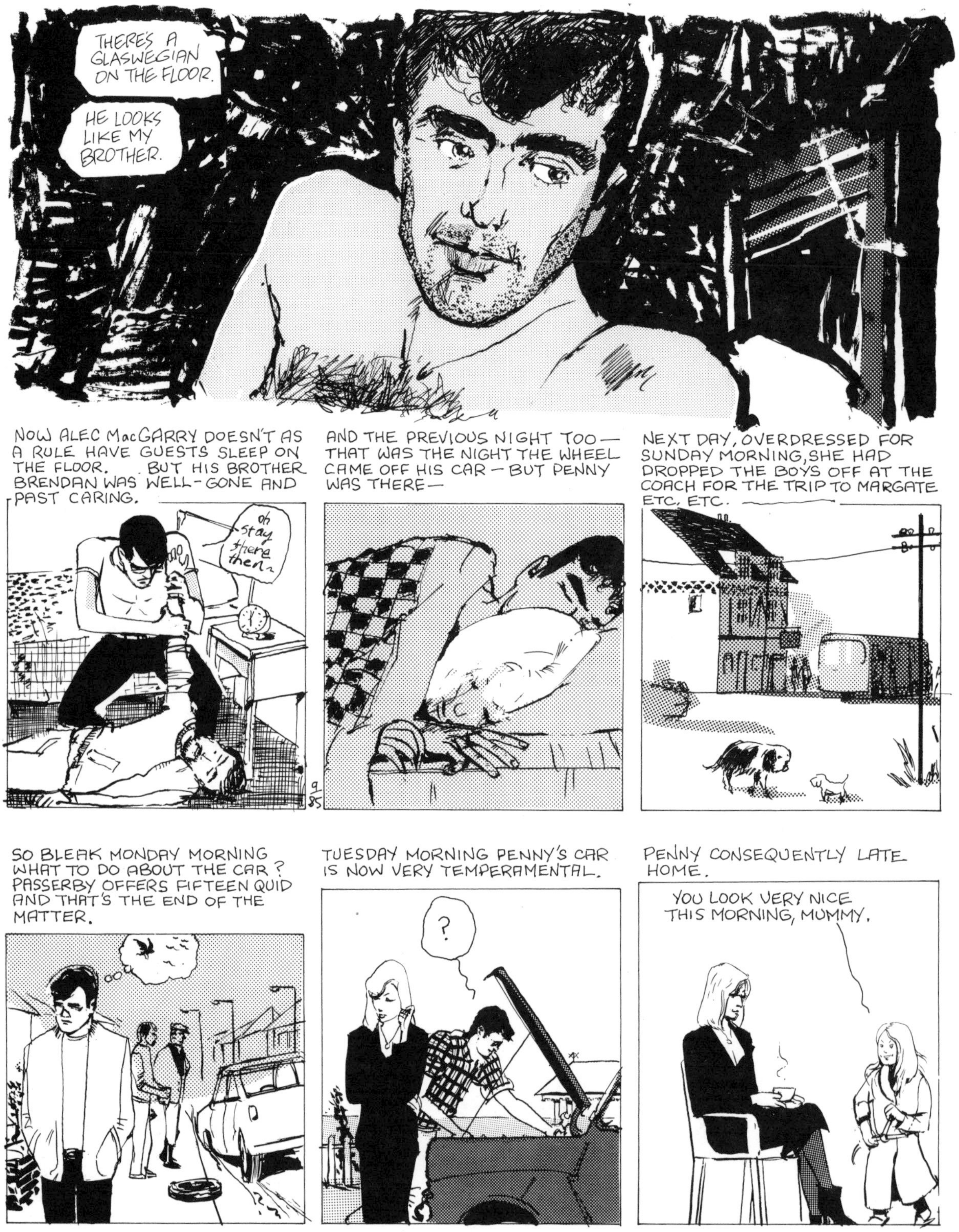
THERE'S A GLASWEGIAN ON THE FLOOR.
HE LOOKS LIKE MY BROTHER.
NOW ALEC MacGARRY DOESN'T AS A RULE HAVE GUESTS SLEEP ON THE FLOOR. BUT HIS BROTHER BRENDAN WAS WELL-GONE AND PAST CARING.
oh stay there then..
AND THE PREVIOUS NIGHT TOO— THAT WAS THE NIGHT THE WHEEL CAME OFF HIS CAR — BUT PENNY WAS THERE—
NEXT DAY, OVERDRESSED FOR SUNDAY MORNING, SHE HAD DROPPED THE BOYS OFF AT THE COACH FOR THE TRIP TO MARGATE ETC, ETC.
SO BLEAK MONDAY MORNING WHAT TO DO ABOUT THE CAR? PASSERBY OFFERS FIFTEEN QUID AND THAT'S THE END OF THE MATTER.
TUESDAY MORNING PENNY'S CAR IS NOW VERY TEMPERAMENTAL.
?
PENNY CONSEQUENTLY LATE HOME.
YOU LOOK VERY NICE THIS MORNING, MUMMY.

d o m e s t i c   I n t e r l u d e

WHAT'S THE MATTER WITH YOU TODAY?
nucunt.
WHAT DID YOU SAY THEN?
NUCUNT,
WHERE DID YOU GET THAT WORD?
SHARON AND ME INVENTED IT... IT MEANS 'NOTHING' ...nucunt!
WELL DON'T SAY IT! IT SOUNDS LIKE SOMETHING ELSE!
WHAT SOMETHING ELSE?
IT SOUNDS LIKE A RUDE WORD. SO DON'T LET ME HEAR YOU SAYING IT AGAIN ALRIGHT??
WHAT RUDE WORD DOES IT SOUND LIKE?- TELL ME!! TELL ME! WHAT WORD?
I'LL SMACK YOU HARD!
MUMMY- DOESN'T ALEC'S HOUSE SMELL-
IT'S THE DAMP.
DO YOU LIVE HERE WITH YOUR MUMMY?
MUMMY?- DO YOU STILL LOVE DADDY?
That's enough of that now, Pauline.

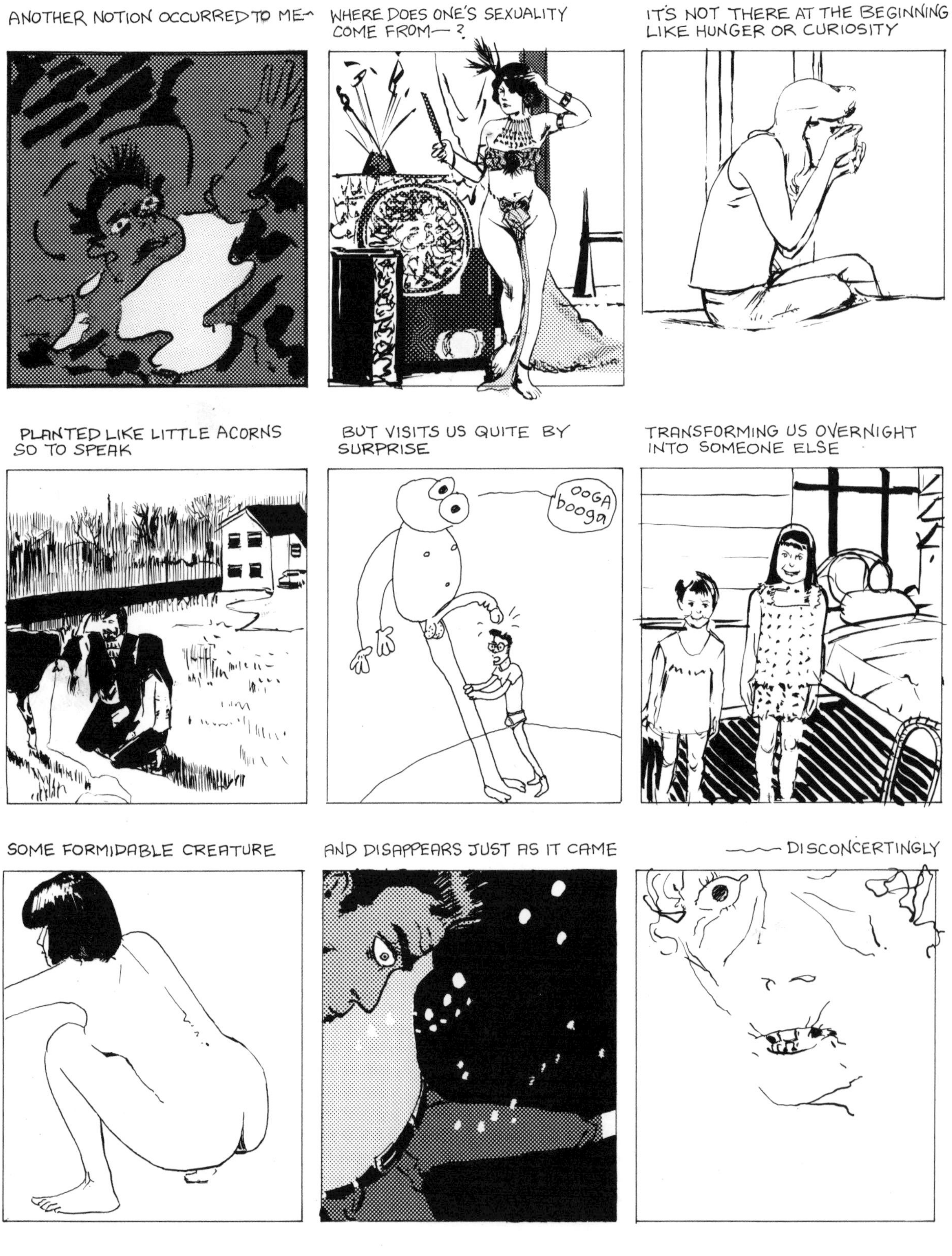
ANOTHER NOTION OCCURRED TO ME—
WHERE DOES ONE'S SEXUALITY COME FROM— ?
IT'S NOT THERE AT THE BEGINNING LIKE HUNGER OR CURIOSITY
PLANTED LIKE LITTLE ACORNS SO TO SPEAK
BUT VISITS US QUITE BY SURPRISE
OOGA booga
TRANSFORMING US OVERNIGHT INTO SOMEONE ELSE
SOME FORMIDABLE CREATURE
AND DISAPPEARS JUST AS IT CAME
—— DISCONCERTINGLY

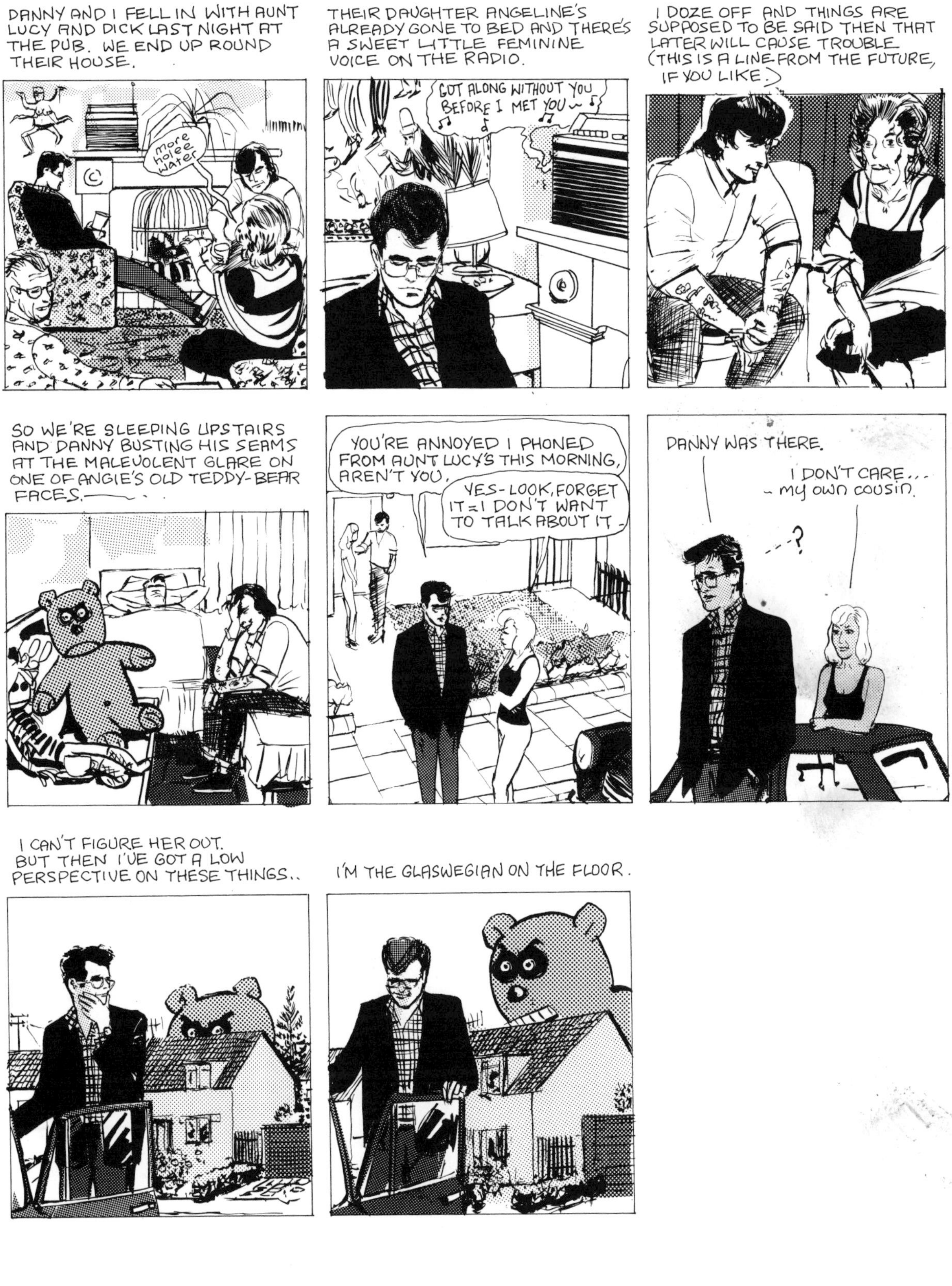
DANNY AND I FELL IN WITH AUNT LUCY AND DICK LAST NIGHT AT THE PUB. WE END UP ROUND THEIR HOUSE.
more holee water
THEIR DAUGHTER ANGELINE'S ALREADY GONE TO BED AND THERE'S A SWEET LITTLE FEMININE VOICE ON THE RADIO.
GOT ALONG WITHOUT YOU BEFORE I MET YOU ~
I DOZE OFF AND THINGS ARE SUPPOSED TO BE SAID THEN THAT LATER WILL CAUSE TROUBLE (THIS IS A LINE FROM THE FUTURE, IF YOU LIKE.)
SO WE'RE SLEEPING UPSTAIRS AND DANNY BUSTING HIS SEAMS AT THE MALEVOLENT GLARE ON ONE OF ANGIE'S OLD TEDDY-BEAR FACES.
YOU'RE ANNOYED I PHONED FROM AUNT LUCY'S THIS MORNING, AREN'T YOU.
YES- LOOK, FORGET IT = I DON'T WANT TO TALK ABOUT IT -
DANNY WAS THERE.
I DON'T CARE... - MY OWN COUSIN.
- - ?
I CAN'T FIGURE HER OUT. BUT THEN I'VE GOT A LOW PERSPECTIVE ON THESE THINGS..
I'M THE GLASWEGIAN ON THE FLOOR.

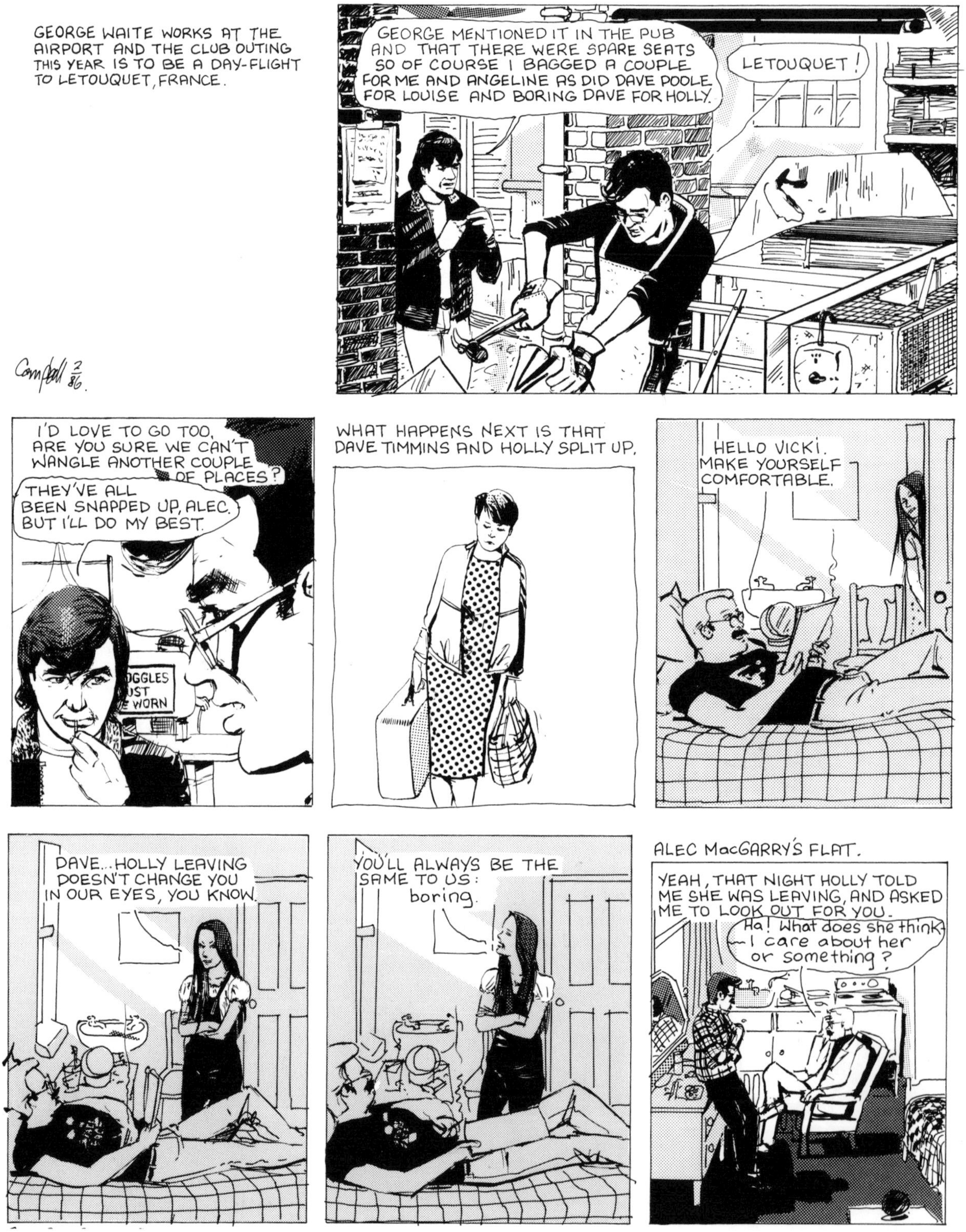
GEORGE WAITE WORKS AT THE AIRPORT AND THE CLUB OUTING THIS YEAR IS TO BE A DAY-FLIGHT TO LETOUQUET, FRANCE.
GEORGE MENTIONED IT IN THE PUB AND THAT THERE WERE SPARE SEATS SO OF COURSE I BAGGED A COUPLE FOR ME AND ANGELINE AS DID DAVE POOLE FOR LOUISE AND BORING DAVE FOR HOLLY.
LETOUQUET!
I'D LOVE TO GO TOO, ARE YOU SURE WE CAN'T WANGLE ANOTHER COUPLE OF PLACES?
THEY'VE ALL BEEN SNAPPED UP, ALEC. BUT I'LL DO MY BEST.
GOGGLES MUST BE WORN
WHAT HAPPENS NEXT IS THAT DAVE TIMMINS AND HOLLY SPLIT UP.
HELLO VICKI. MAKE YOURSELF COMFORTABLE.
DAVE... HOLLY LEAVING DOESN'T CHANGE YOU IN OUR EYES, YOU KNOW.
YOU'LL ALWAYS BE THE SAME TO US: boring.
ALEC MacGARRY'S FLAT.
YEAH, THAT NIGHT HOLLY TOLD ME SHE WAS LEAVING, AND ASKED ME TO LOOK OUT FOR YOU.
Ha! What does she think I care about her or something?

DAVE TIMMINS ROOM AT THE KING CANUTE.
IT'S NOT GOING TO LOOK TOO GOOD TO LOUISE, DAVE YOU GOING TO LETOUQUET AS THOUGH YOU CAN AFFORD THAT BUT NOT THE LAST THREE WEEKS' RENT.
YES, BUT I HATE TO LET GEORGE DOWN.
I THINK I MIGHT BE ABLE TO INTEREST ALEC AND PENNY IN GOING
YOU COULD?! THANKS!!
SAVE YOUR PENNIES, ALEC. LOOKS LIKE YOU'RE GOING. PENNY TOO. WE'LL POP UP TO THE CANUTE AFTER WORK AND SORT OUT THE DETAILS.
HEY, DANNY! I'M SORRY IF THIS SCREWS THINGS UP, BUT HOLLY SAYS WE'RE GOING AND SHE'S PAYING.
!!!
it's alright. I wasn't banking on it.
NO, NO. HOLD ON NOW, FOLKS.. THERE MUST BE A SOLUTION TO THIS ...um... yup... WHAT WE NEED IS A LARGE BOX... no, only kidding. TWO OF US WILL HAVE TO TAKE THE FERRY AND THUMB FROM CALAIS.
..MYSELF AND ONE OF YOU.
I'M HAPPY TO THUMB.
NO! I'LL DO IT!!
YOU CAN BORROW MY ESCORT VAN.
TOO EXPENSIVE ON THE FERRY, LOUISE.
oh for heavens sake!!
I JUST PHONED HOLLY. WE'RE NOT GOING AND THAT'S THE END OF IT.
COME, COME, NOW.

WHAT DO YOU THINK, GEORGE?
I DON'T GIVE A SHIT WHO WALKS OR SWIMS. I JUST WANT YOU THREE TO ALL NOD IN AGREEMENT WHO'S GOING ON THE BLOODY PLANE!
HOLLY YOU'RE GOING !!
THE NEXT PROBLEM-
I THINK YOU CAN GO TO HELL, MISTER MacGARRY-
OH COME ON NOW-WHAT CAN I GET UP TO ON A HITCHIKING ADVENTURE?
THAT'S NOT IT!!
WHAT IS IT THEN?!
I've never flown before. I'm not going on my own O.K.?
THIS DEADLOCK RESOLVES ITSELF IN A PERFECTLY NATURAL MANNER AT THE CANUTE. DANNY DRIVES HOLLY UP THERE.
SHE'S UPSTAIRS DISCUSSING THE SITUATION WITH DAVE.
I'M GOING TO FERRY OVER THERE WITH MY FRIEND SHARON AND HITCH-HIKE LIKE DANNY AND ALEC.-
WHILST IN THE LOUNGE BAR ANGELINE'S MOTHER, 'AUNT' LUCY, EXPRESSES A MORTAL FEAR OF FLYING.
I DON'T SEE WHY ALL OF YOU CAN'T HITCH-HIKE.
FURTHERMORE, SHE HAS ARRANGED TO HAVE A BIG PARTY ON THE SAME NIGHT AS THE TRIP AND WE'RE ALL INTENDING TO RUSH BACK TO IT.
only £8-60 for foot travellers on Thorsen-
IN THE MIDDLE OF ALL THIS, IN WALKS DAVE TIMMINS.
DANNY, COULD YOU RUN HOLLY HOME AGAIN?

DANNY DISAPPEARS FOR HALF AN HOUR OR SO AND ALL THE MAPS AND LEAFLETS ARE TEMPORARILY FORGOTTEN. THEN!—
OH DEAR! DAVE
what?
DANNY'S BEATING UP THE SUICIDE JOCKEY!!
who?
TIMMINS
your jokin'!
CRAZY, EH? (ACCORDING TO DANNY..) THEY JUST GOT BACK FROM DRIVING HOLLY HOME... TIMMINS SEEMED TO BE SHAPING UP FOR ONE OF HIS RAMPAGES—
THE KING CANUTE
GAA
PUBLIC BAR
HEY COME BACK HERE
GAA

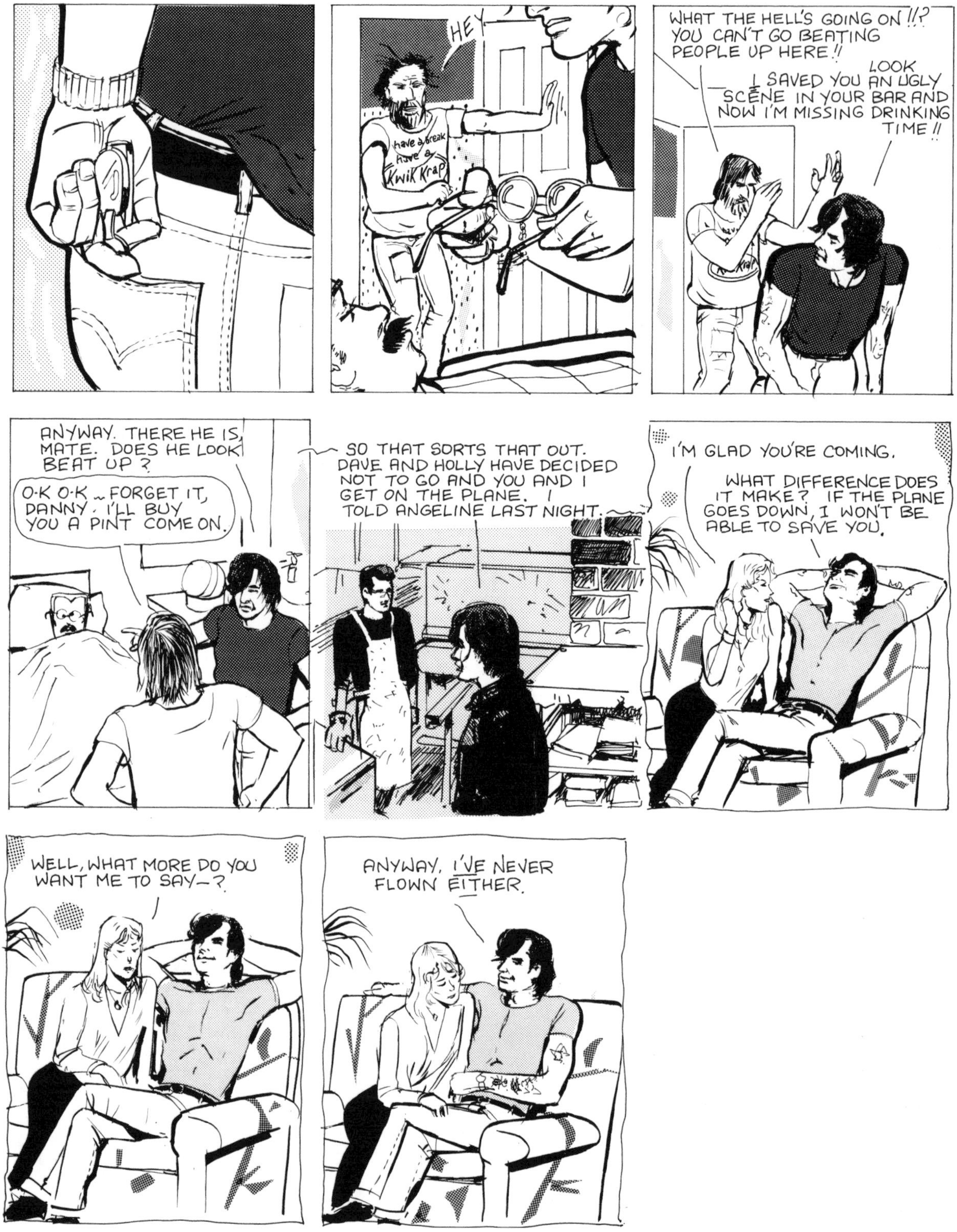
HEY
have a break have a Kwik Krap
WHAT THE HELL'S GOING ON !!? YOU CAN'T GO BEATING PEOPLE UP HERE !!
LOOK I SAVED YOU AN UGLY SCENE IN YOUR BAR AND NOW I'M MISSING DRINKING TIME !!
ANYWAY. THERE HE IS, MATE. DOES HE LOOK BEAT UP ?
O.K O.K ~ FORGET IT, DANNY. I'LL BUY YOU A PINT COME ON.
SO THAT SORTS THAT OUT. DAVE AND HOLLY HAVE DECIDED NOT TO GO AND YOU AND I GET ON THE PLANE. I TOLD ANGELINE LAST NIGHT.
I'M GLAD YOU'RE COMING.
WHAT DIFFERENCE DOES IT MAKE? IF THE PLANE GOES DOWN, I WON'T BE ABLE TO SAVE YOU.
WELL, WHAT MORE DO YOU WANT ME TO SAY—?
ANYWAY, I'VE NEVER FLOWN EITHER.

England
france
DESCRIPTION SIGNALEMENT
Bearer
wife
Photo
DERNIER CRI
SOLDES
BAR de la PISCINE

VIC
BUREAU DE LOCATION
TENTES CABINES

wha
viens
Anaïs Nin in 1946, writing in her diary about an American suburb while longing for France —
"Everyone was at home with bottles from which they hoped to extract a gaiety bottled elsewhere"

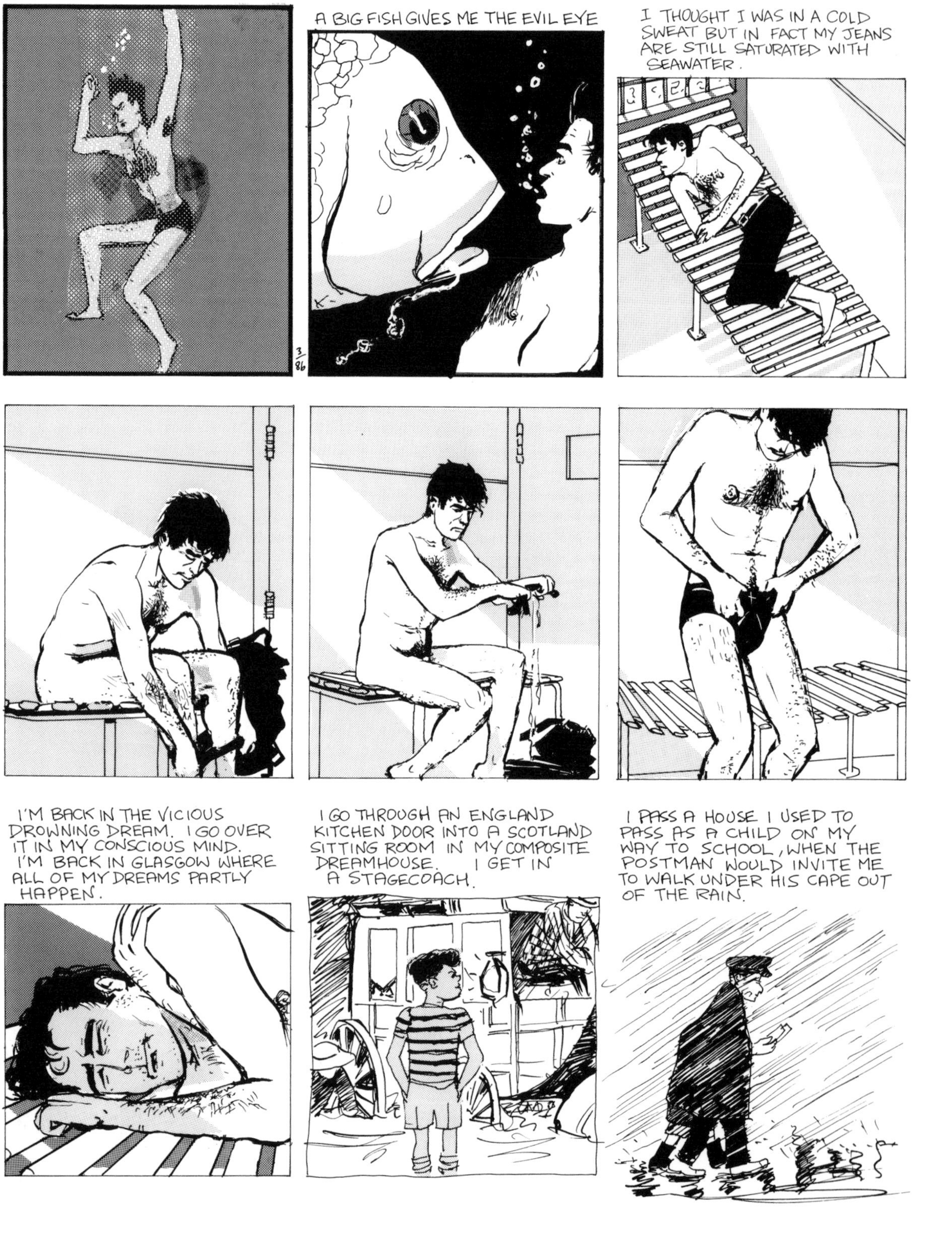

A BIG FISH GIVES ME THE EVIL EYE
3/86
I THOUGHT I WAS IN A COLD SWEAT BUT IN FACT MY JEANS ARE STILL SATURATED WITH SEAWATER.
I'M BACK IN THE VICIOUS DROWNING DREAM. I GO OVER IT IN MY CONSCIOUS MIND. I'M BACK IN GLASGOW WHERE ALL OF MY DREAMS PARTLY HAPPEN.
I GO THROUGH AN ENGLAND KITCHEN DOOR INTO A SCOTLAND SITTING ROOM IN MY COMPOSITE DREAMHOUSE. I GET IN A STAGECOACH.
I PASS A HOUSE I USED TO PASS AS A CHILD ON MY WAY TO SCHOOL, WHEN THE POSTMAN WOULD INVITE ME TO WALK UNDER HIS CAPE OUT OF THE RAIN.

I REMEMBER A BIG DOG WAS ALWAYS AT THE WINDOW, WATCHING ME GO OFF DOWN THE ROAD OF MY LIFE.
I HAVE OFTEN EXPECTED TO SEE HIM EVEN NOW, AT OTHER WINDOWS.
I'M WITH ELIZABETH BONNATTI MY CHILDHOOD SWEETHEART, SHOWING OFF JUST BEFORE A MATCH.
THOSE MATCHES — I REMEMBER THE WHOLE TEAM, IN LINES AND STANZAS (FILL IN YOUR OWN ELEVEN).
PETER HUDDLESTON WITH HIS PUDDING BOWL RAZORED HAIRCUT. JIM IRELAND PUSHING THEM OUT DEPENDABLY.
HUGH MacDONALD, MY BOSOM PAL, WAS CAPTAIN AND LATER, IT IS SAID, A PRIEST.
JOHNNY MURPHY, PADDY DOYLE ME, CENTRE-FORWARD, COMPLETELY IN THE WRONG PLACE, BUT INTUITIVELY RIGHT FOR THE MOST INGENIOUS SHOT AGAINST THE BRICKWALLS.
THE THOMASSOS WERE CLAPPING THEIR HANDS OFF.
AH ME, I WAKE UP IN MY LITTLE ROOM IN SOUTHEND.

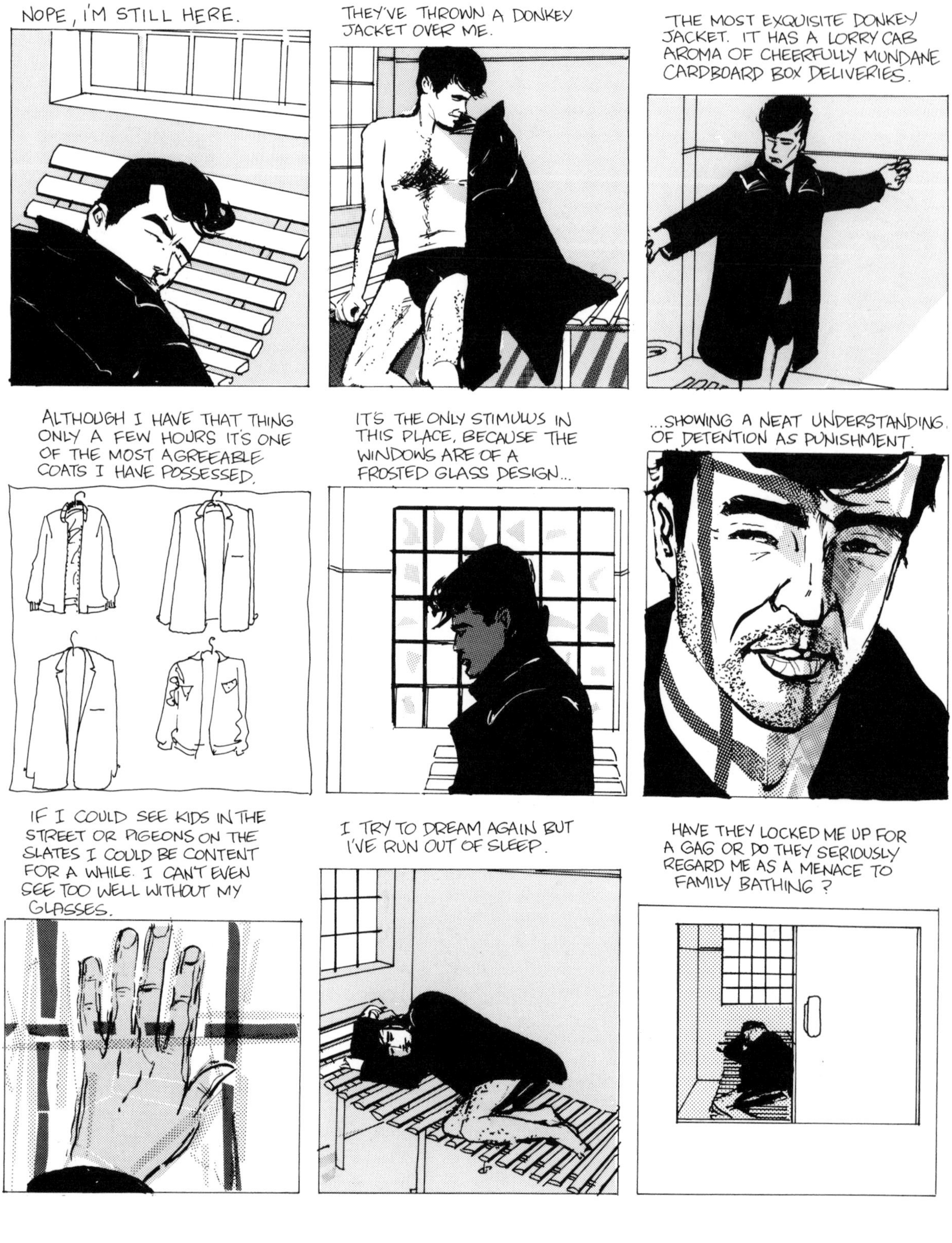
NOPE, I'M STILL HERE.
THEY'VE THROWN A DONKEY JACKET OVER ME.
THE MOST EXQUISITE DONKEY JACKET. IT HAS A LORRY CAB AROMA OF CHEERFULLY MUNDANE CARDBOARD BOX DELIVERIES.
ALTHOUGH I HAVE THAT THING ONLY A FEW HOURS IT'S ONE OF THE MOST AGREEABLE COATS I HAVE POSSESSED.
IT'S THE ONLY STIMULUS IN THIS PLACE, BECAUSE THE WINDOWS ARE OF A FROSTED GLASS DESIGN...
...SHOWING A NEAT UNDERSTANDING OF DETENTION AS PUNISHMENT.
IF I COULD SEE KIDS IN THE STREET OR PIGEONS ON THE SLATES I COULD BE CONTENT FOR A WHILE. I CAN'T EVEN SEE TOO WELL WITHOUT MY GLASSES.
I TRY TO DREAM AGAIN BUT I'VE RUN OUT OF SLEEP.
HAVE THEY LOCKED ME UP FOR A GAG OR DO THEY SERIOUSLY REGARD ME AS A MENACE TO FAMILY BATHING ?

I NOTICE MY CLOTHES ARE SPREAD OVER A RADIATOR.
EXCUSÉ MOI S'IL VOUS PLAIT
TU ES blindé
THE NEXT HOUR (TWO? FOUR?) IS PAINFUL. EITHER THE SUN'S OVER THE OTHER SIDE OF THE BUILDING OR IT'S GETTING LATE. MAYBE I'VE MISSED THE PLANE HOME.
IT DAWNS ON ME THAT PENNY HAS MY PASSPORT IN HER HANDBAG AND IF I DON'T GET TO THE AIRPORT BY SEVEN I'LL BE IN AN EVEN BIGGER FIX.
MA GIRL-FRIEND A MON PASSEPORE
SOON AS I GET OUT OF THERE AGG THE RADIATORS AREN'T ON.!!
BRR.
OH DAMNIT! ANYWAY THE BOOTS ARE ON
I'M A BIG GUY AGAIN.- NOBODY'S GONNA STEP ON MY SKELETON FEET.
I'LL MARCH ACROSS EUROPE.
LOSE MYSELF IN A THOUSAND ADVENTURES.
ALEC!! HERE!!

PENNY IS PEEVED.
WHERE THE HELL HAVE YOU BEEN? —SEVEN HOURS – SEVEN BLOODY HOURS !!
BAR TABAC
Stella Artois
LE PUB
THE FISH IS INTACT.
LE PUB
BAR
THERE'S NO PLANE BACK. REPLACEMENT TRANSPORT IS PROVIDED ONLY AFTER PROTEST.
a coach will take you to the ferry
AIR-Z
GEORGE IS UNRULY.
IT SAYS HERE CONTRACTED TO CARRY PASSENGERS BY ALL AIR CARRIERS - IT DOES NOT SAY ANYTHING ABOUT FUCKIN BOATS.
George!
AIR-
HIS CLUB MEMBERSHIP IS LATER SUSPENDED
DRIVER WHY ARE WE WAITING SO LONG?
cos he won't let us on with fish n chips you stupid cow.
DANNY SMUGGLES THE COD ONTO THE FERRY.
COD OH COD – IT'S JUST LOST ALL ITS FLUIDS –
HE HAD HALF A PLAN TO TAKE IT TO AUNT LUCY'S PARTY.
THE PLANE'S GONE DOWN! I KNEW IT!!
DANNY MOVES INTO A FLAT WITH HOLLY.
THEY GET MARRIED A FEW MONTHS LATER.

AS FOR ALL THIS DROWNING STUFF. I FELL IN THE THAMES WHILE STANDING UP IN GEORGE WAITE'S DINGHY.
I LIED EARLIER ABOUT THE FUNNY NOTIONS,
IN FACT THE IMAGINATION MUST CEASE TO FUNCTION -
ONE MUST BECOME MACHINE-LIKE
FLIP
... AUTOMATIC.
FWAP!
~ chomp! ~
FWONK
ARE YOU COMING TO BED EARLY TONIGHT? - YOU CAN DO THOSE LAST THREE PICTURES TOMORROW -
YEH.. ANYWAY THERE'S NOTHING MORE TO SAY —
chookie chicken !!
TRIO IN AN IMPROMPTU PUB SINGSONG EASTER SUNDAY, BRIGHTON, 1986 ~~.
Eddie Campbell

OH NO! OH NO!
OH BLOODY BLATHERIN' POO!

four

ONE NIGHT SIX YEARS AFTER THE END OF THIS BOOK, DANNY GREY GETS THE TWO OF US INTO A FIGHT.
RAR B Coy
WHICH DOESN'T HAVE ANY OF THE BALLETIC PERFECTION OF THE GATOR'S RUMPUS. INDEED, A YOUNG TURK WIPES THE FLOOR WITH OUR BOY.
DANNY SMOULDERS FOR AN HOUR THEN DISAPPEARS BACK TO THE SCENE OF THE INCIDENT.
ON HIS RETURN, HE AND HOLLY HIGH-TAIL IT OUT OF THE TOWN WHERE I'M LIVING. SHE LATER TELLS ME A SCREW DRIVER IS MISSING FROM THE TOOL BOX.
DANNY CAN REMEMBER NOTHING ABOUT IT, AND THIS BUSINESS LINGERS IN MY MIND AS A DISQUIETING EXAMPLE OF HIS FIERCE VANITY...
...ONE OF THE MAN'S DARKER CORNERS THAT BECAME REVEALED TO ME NEAR THE END OF THE KING CANUTE DAYS.
THERE WERE NIGHTS BACK THEN WHEN WE HAD LOUD DISAGREEMENTS
I never won sherry in any raffle — I remember these things
You're a supercilious bastard!!
AND TIMES ON THE WORKING HIGHWAY WHEN HIS TEMPER EXPLODED.
I'll fukkin' teach you to make signs at me!!
WAIT!
--I'm only trying to tell you that you've been dropping your load for two miles!!
oh my God

I PREFER TO REMEMBER OTHER TIMES, DIFFERENT ENTIRELY MOMENTS OF CHILDLIKE WONDER- A LOVE OF SIMPLE THINGS.
I wonder what causes that little noise.
It's the bleedin' fag-paper aint it.
crinkle crinkle
EVEN WHEN HE'S NOT IN THE PICTURE, HE'S THE TOUCHSTONE FOR THE SPECIAL GAEITY OF THE KING CANUTE. WITHOUT HIM IT WILL, AND DOES, DISSIPATE.
EVEN AFTER HE MARRIES HOLLY, THE CAVALCADE OF INCIDENTS AND ADVENTURES CONTINUES.
WHEN HE INHERITS SOME MONEY (TO COME) HE WASTES IT IN A GRAND AND MEMORABLE STYLE.
WISCONSIN URINALS
AND IN THE MEANTIME, WHEN PAYDAY IS SLOW IN COMING, THERE IS THAT SUBTERRANEAN ECONOMICS.
LANCER BOSS
LANCER
A LARGE DRUM OF DIESEL MIGHT GO MISSING AND BE SOLD TO FINANCE HIS EVENING AT THE CANUTE,
The spanish fly
OR GETTING AWAY FROM MONEY AND PROFIT ALTOGETHER TOWARDS A MORE PERFECT BALANCE OF EXCHANGES WHERE ONLY PROVIDENCE KEEPS THE BOOKS.
RODEN
PRODUCTS
WHERE ONE GUY MIGHT HAVE A LOAD OF BROKEN CONCRETE TO GET RID OF FROM HIS HOUSE RENOVATIONS AND DANNY GREY CHEERFULLY ASSISTS.
THEN ANOTHER GUY WILL IMMEDIATELY ANNOUNCE HIS NEED OF "CRAZY PAVING" FOR HIS FRONT GARDEN.
RODEN

THERE WAS A COUPLE WHO LIVED NEAR THE KING CANUTE - SHEP AND JEAN - WE SPENT A WHOLE SUMMER CONVENING IN THEIR HOUSE AFTER PUB-CLOSING,
uh.. I've just moved in daorwoon the road and I've got this concrete to shift
WITH BEER FROM THE PUB, AND WE'D TALK AND SING AND DANCE TILL LATE AND SLEEP ON THE FLOOR TILL MORNING.
THEY HAD COME FROM BUCKINGHAMSHIRE AND TOOK US BACK THAT WAY ON THREE OCCASIONS TO A SMALL COUNTRY PLACE WHOSE NAME I FORGET (IT WAS ON ONE OF THESE JAUNTS THAT I FELL IN THE RIVER).
WE'D SLEEP ON THE BACK OF THE TRUCK OUTSIDE THIS PICTURESQUE PUB— THE LANDLORD'S NAME WAS BERT.
It was a hot foggy day in Julember
ON ONE OCCASION LITTLE PAULINE WAS WITH US AND BERT HAD GIVEN ME AND PENNY A SMALL UPSTAIRS ROOM FOR THE NIGHT.
IN THE MORNING THE CHILD WOULD NOT SPEAK TO ME AND NATURALLY I FIGURED I'D DONE SOMETHING BAD— BUT
She wet herself in the night- don't say anthing about it.
IT GOT ME THINKING ABOUT THE PECULIAR PHENOMENON OF NOCTURNAL URINARY ADVENTURES, PARTICULARLY WITH REGARD TO DANNY GREY.
DRUNKENNESS WOULD NEVER SHOW ON MY FRIEND BUT HE WOULD GO TO BED CONTENTEDLY AND WAKE UP AN HOUR LATER AS A CRAZED PISSING SOMNAMBULIST.
WARDROBES WOULD BE CAREFULLY LOCKED AND SEALED THE PREVIOUS EVENING BY HIS NEAREST AND DEAREST. ARMCHAIRS WOULD BE CAUTIOUSLY PUSHED AGAINST SIDEBOARD DOORS.

THE FINAL OCCASION THAT WE DROVE THE SEVENTY MILES TO BERT'S PUB WAS TO CELEBRATE HIS RETIREMENT. THAT NIGHT WE WERE SLEEPING IN THE HOUSE OF AMERICAN FRIENDS OF SHEP AND JEAN.
KING SIZ
I WAS NOT PRESENT MYSELF AT THE TIME IN QUESTION — HAVING HAD ONE OF MY INCREASINGLY REGULAR FLARE-UPS WITH PENNY MOORE.
I WAS IN FACT SLEEPING IN OUR CAR AFTER STORMING AROUND FOR FOUR HOURS IN THE COUNTRY NIGHT BEFORE DISCOVERING A REMARKABLE, ALMOST SPIRITUAL CALM.
PENNY SAID SHE WAS WAKENED BY THE SOUND OF RAIN ON THE ROOF, BUT ON COCKING HER EAR BECAME DISTURBED BY THE APPARENT NEARNESS OF IT.
SHE SAT BOLT UPRIGHT IN TIME TO SEE DANNY GREY URINATING ON LEN WAITE IN HIS SLEEPING BAG.
pitta patta pitta
Shep Help!
Heh heh
THE POOR GUY SLEPT THROUGH IT AND THEY TOLD HIM THE FISH TANK HAD LEAKED.
Maybe it came out here Roger.
DANNY, OF COURSE, KNEW NOTHING OF THE INCIDENT.
raoyoond the raoyoondaboot
SPEAKING OF PECULIAR BEHAVIOUR - HERE'S DAVE TIMMINS — I HAD STARTED TO THINK HE WAS BECOMING A BETTER ADJUSTED INDIVIDUAL - AT LEAST, HE HAD STARTED TO GRASP THAT SUBLIME PHILOSOPHY OF THE TRUE WASTER.
It's just the realization that nothing matters - whatever you do is basically pointless.
THAT EVENING, SHEP AND JEAN'S PLACE - THERE WERE MORE THAN 17 PEOPLE INSIDE, SO I WAS OUTSIDE WITH TIMMINS —
Observe, Alec... In light of what we were discussing earlier - this twig which I now put in my wallet .. lateral thinking
Uh- you're broke so your wallet's in a splint
No, No.

JUST LIKE THIS, HE STARTS FALLING OVER.
Oh for God's sake.
TIMMINS' HUMILITY ISN'T REALISTIC, -WHICH IS NOT TO SAY THAT IT ISN'T REAL- HERE'S PENNY ASKING HIM TO MOVE HER CAR- NOT "BE A DEAR, DAVE, I CAN'T SEEM TO FIND MY SHOES," BUT OUTRIGHT.
BRING THE CAR, DAVE
SHE RECOGNISED WHAT MUST HAVE BEEN SERVILE TRAITS -IT GRATED WITH ME THAT SHE HAD THE POOR GUY RUNNING AROUND CHIVALROUSLY WHILE AT THE SAME TIME SEEMED ONLY TO HATE HIM BECAUSE OF IT.
Bring my overnight bag off the front seat...
THEN SHE'D LOVE HIM FOR SOMETHING ELSE- LIKE HIS BRASH CONFIDENCE IN TELLING FUNNY STORIES- I GUESS THESE THINGS FIND THEIR OWN BALANCE.
you can't criticize a humble man — you either bow to him or crucify him - Dr. Eric Berne.
BACK TO SHEP AND JEAN, IT'S THE NIGHT OF ONE OF OUR FANCY-DRESS PARTIES AT THE KING CANUTE.
AFTERWARDS JEAN DISAPPEARS INTO THE DARK WANDERING THE STREET IN SEMI-DRESS AND IS PICKED UP BY THE POLICE WHO DELIVER HER HOME.
come on now— we'll see you home —here's a bunch of flowers—
Steve was right — you get them ALL on this patch
SHEP UNEXPECTEDLY HAS A FIT OF THUNDEROUS ANGER.
Where these BLUDDY Flowers come frowm?

DRINK BRINGS US TOGETHER IN WIT, LAUGHTER, FELLOWSHIP AND PLEASANT FOLLY.
THEN CHURNS UP ALL THE MUDDIER ECSTASIES – THE NOCTURNAL URINARY ADVENTURES, THE FITS OF THUNDEROUS ANGER.
TODAY IF WE WANT WE CAN GET THROUGH OUR LIVES ON A PROSAIC MEAT-AND-TWO-VEG.
oggy oggy
OR FROM TIME TO TIME WE CAN PARTAKE OF SOME SWEET COMMUNAL POETIC FRUIT.
get dawroon shep
AND RISK FLEXING THE DARKENED MUSCLES OF OUR PSYCHOLOGICAL BACK-PASSAGE — DO A BEHAVIOURAL POOPOO, SO TO SPEAK.
I BUMPED INTO TIMMINS A COUPLE OF YEARS AFTER THE KING CANUTE PERIOD. HE WAS A BOUNCER AT A CLUB DOOR. OR APPEARED TO BE.
Hello Alec.
HE PULLED ME IN FOR A BEER.
I'll never forgive Danny. He played me for a fool
SAID HE WAS ACTUALLY ON A WEEKEND OFF FROM THE ARMY AND THAT HE WAS HOPEFULLY OFF TO THE FALKLANDS WAR NEXT WEEK — SO THERE YOU GO.
ONE MORE OF SHEP'S BELLY BUTTON THEN PRETEND YOU'RE AT THE MOVIES.
snowr

LOOK OUT, JEREMY. SHOOT!!
BOOF!
AAAAAA
SCOOSH!
foam
THAT SPRAY WAS SCENTED!!
YOU BASTARD
COME ON NOW. LET'S HAVE YOUR TICKETS

TICKETS PLEASE
It was scented
WHAT DIFFERENCE DOES IT MAKE
SCENTED STINGS.
YOU DIDN'T HAVE TO THROW IT IN THE OTHER FIELD — THAT COST ME 80p
DANNY
FOR GOD'S SAKE — IT ISN'T SUPPOSED TO BE LIKE THIS
THERE'S PANDEMONIUM AT THE STREAM.. AS FOR THE SECOND WAVE — THEY'VE GONE IN THE WRONG DIRECTION
Wish Penny and I hadn't had that fight today
MIGHT AS WELL GO TO THE RENDEZVOUS POINT -. BETTER UNTIE THE WIRE FIRST, HAN -
WAIT- FOOTSTEPS
GAAA
suburban guerillas.

Must phone Penny
IT'S BEEN REALLY GOOD SO FAR—WE STAGED A BATTLE MANOEUVRE TONIGHT —
WELL, THE MEN FROM THE PUB ARRANGED IT REALLY... THEY PHOTOCOPIED A MAP AND THEY HID IN THE WOODS, AND SOME OF US WENT WITH THEM AND THE REST OF US HAD TO GET THROUGH
TELEPHONE
TO REACH THE MOUND ON THE HILL.... WE'RE BACK AT BASE NOW AND WE'RE JUST ABOUT TO HAVE SOME SOUP AND BED DOWN FOR THE NIGHT.. YES, UH, DAD? — YES, PUT HIM ON.
TELEPHONE
HELLO, DAD—YES, WELL THE MEN FROM THE PUB ARRANGED IT ALL.. THEY PHOTOCOPIED MAPS AND THEY HID IN THE WOODS.. SOME OF US WENT WITH THEM AND THE REST HAD TO GET
TELEPHONE
THROUGH.. WE'RE BACK AT BASE AND WE'RE JUST GOING TO HAVE SOME SOUP AND BED DOWN FOR THE NIGHT... YES.. HELLO... MUM!! IS THAT YOU.. YES, WELL THE MEN FROM THE PUB
TELEPHONE
THEY HID IN THE WOODS AND THE REST OF US HAD TO GET THROUGH... NO.. IT WASN'T DANGEROUS.
TELEPHONE
WE'RE BACK AT BASE CAMP AND WE'RE JUST ABOUT TO HAVE SOME SOUP AND BED DOWN FOR THE NIGHT.
TELEPHONE
EH? ... UM ... OXTAIL.
TELEPHONE

IT WAS LOUISE'S UNCLE ART- HE COMES CAMPING EVERY EASTER WITH HIS AIR CADET TROOP- ...OR SPACE APPRENTICES AS LOUISE CALLS THEM
HOW DID IT GO?
DANNY WAS REALLY INTO IT! I THINK THAT MAN MISSED HIS CALLING ... I ALWAYS FEEL AN AIR OF SUPPRESSED VIOLENCE ABOUT HIM... HE SHOULD HAVE BEEN A WAR-HERO OR SOMETHING-
ALEC! Have you got clothes on?
PAULINE! NOW YOU GO UPSTAIRS AND GET DRESSED AND I'LL COME UP AND DO YOUR HAIR!!
SO WHAT HAVE YOU GOT LINED UP FOR TODAY?
WELL, JOHN- ALEC'S GOING TO HELP ME MEND SOME FENCING AT THE STABLES.
WHO?
ALEC
HA HA HA HA HA HA HA
FIRST WE'VE GOT TO CLEAR THIS DOORWAY
YOU'LL NEVER DO IT LIKE THAT!
STAND BACK.

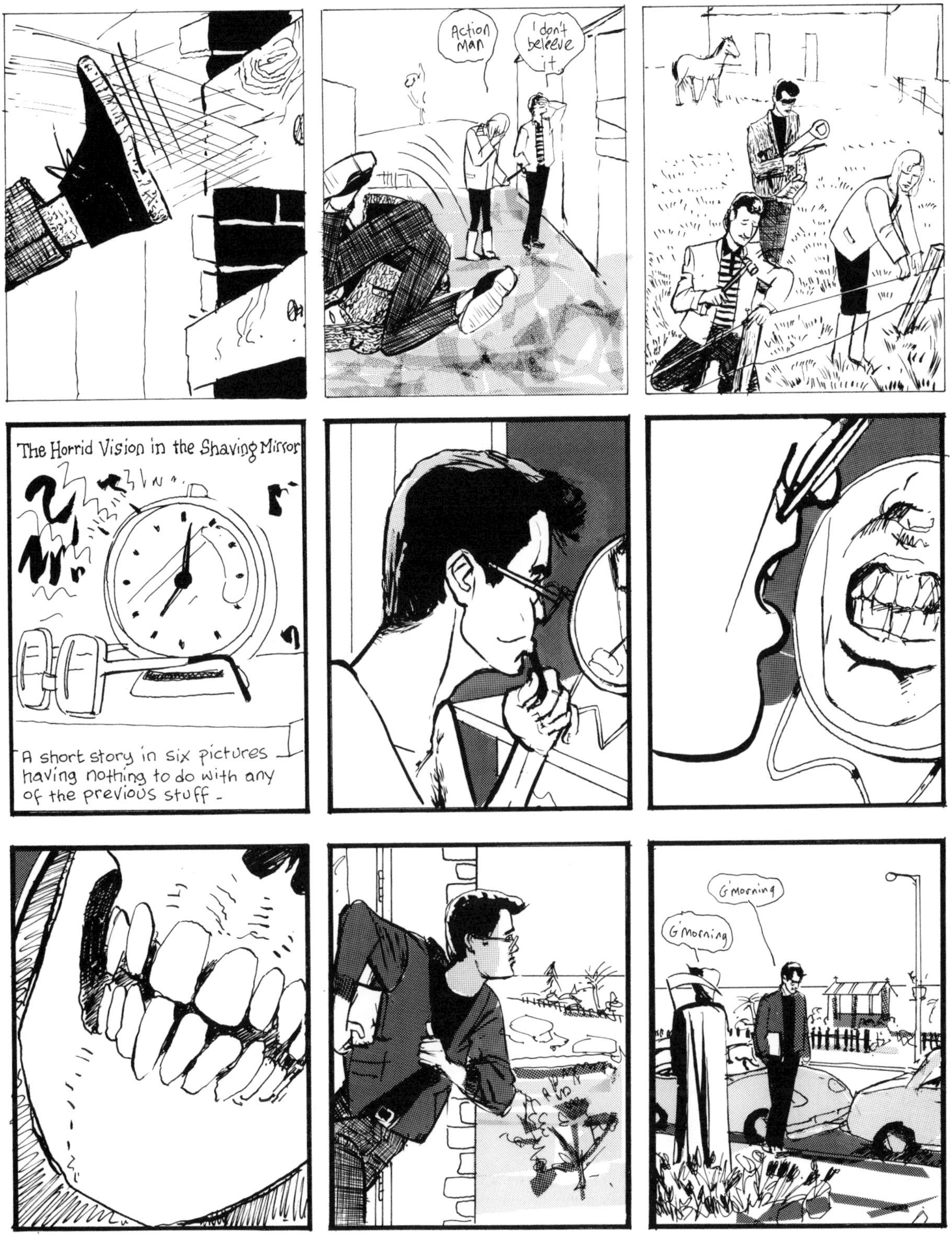
Action Man
I don't beleeve it.
The Horrid Vision in the Shaving Mirror
A short story in six pictures having nothing to do with any of the previous stuff -
G'Morning
G'Morning

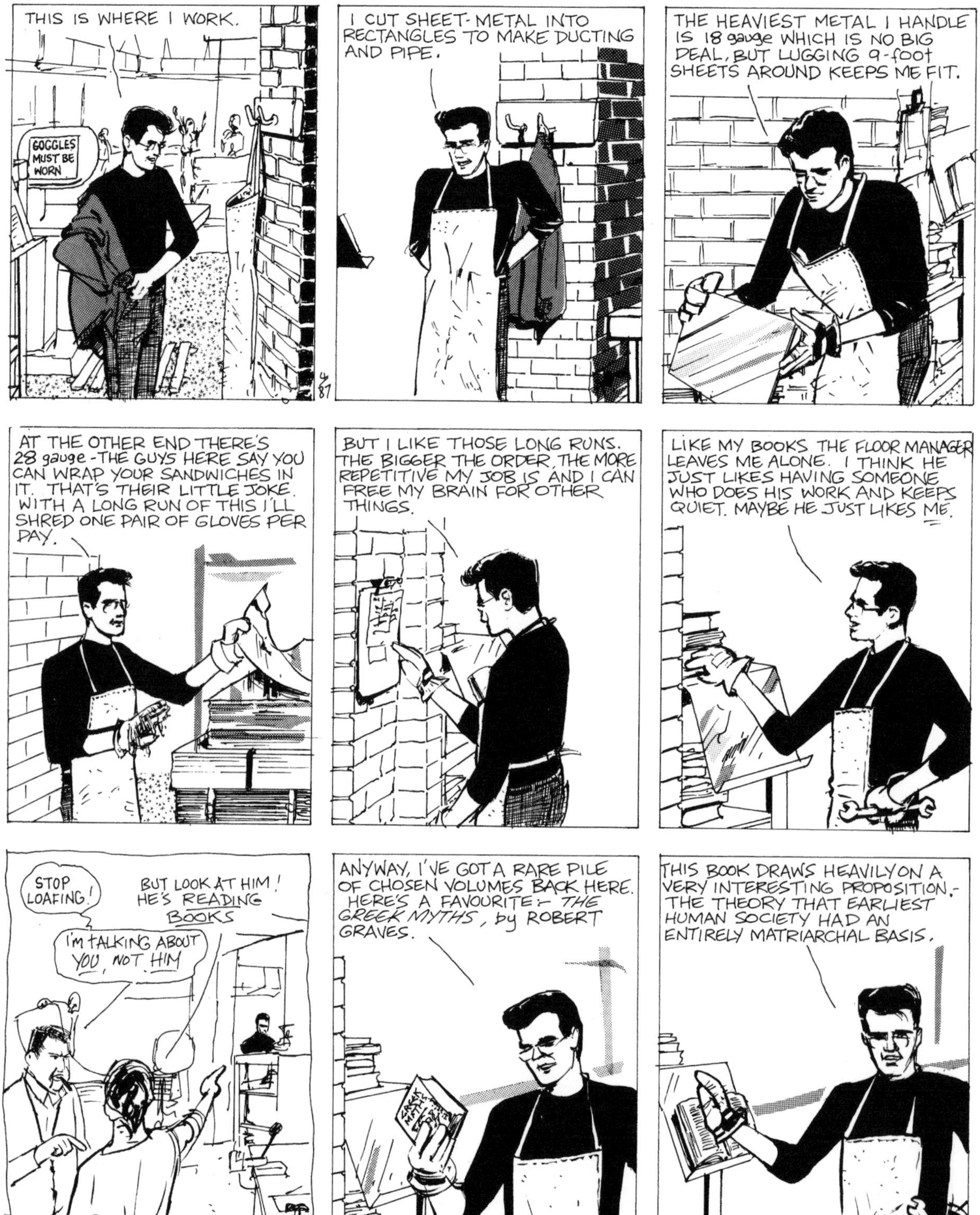
THIS IS WHERE I WORK.
GOGGLES MUST BE WORN
I CUT SHEET-METAL INTO RECTANGLES TO MAKE DUCTING AND PIPE.
THE HEAVIEST METAL I HANDLE IS 18 gauge WHICH IS NO BIG DEAL, BUT LUGGING 9-foot SHEETS AROUND KEEPS ME FIT.
AT THE OTHER END THERE'S 28 gauge - THE GUYS HERE SAY YOU CAN WRAP YOUR SANDWICHES IN IT. THAT'S THEIR LITTLE JOKE. WITH A LONG RUN OF THIS I'LL SHRED ONE PAIR OF GLOVES PER DAY.
BUT I LIKE THOSE LONG RUNS. THE BIGGER THE ORDER, THE MORE REPETITIVE MY JOB IS AND I CAN FREE MY BRAIN FOR OTHER THINGS.
LIKE MY BOOKS. THE FLOOR MANAGER LEAVES ME ALONE. I THINK HE JUST LIKES HAVING SOMEONE WHO DOES HIS WORK AND KEEPS QUIET. MAYBE HE JUST LIKES ME.
STOP LOAFING!
BUT LOOK AT HIM! HE'S READING BOOKS
I'M TALKING ABOUT YOU, NOT HIM
ANYWAY, I'VE GOT A RARE PILE OF CHOSEN VOLUMES BACK HERE. HERE'S A FAVOURITE:- THE GREEK MYTHS, by ROBERT GRAVES.
THIS BOOK DRAWS HEAVILY ON A VERY INTERESTING PROPOSITION,- THE THEORY THAT EARLIEST HUMAN SOCIETY HAD AN ENTIRELY MATRIARCHAL BASIS.

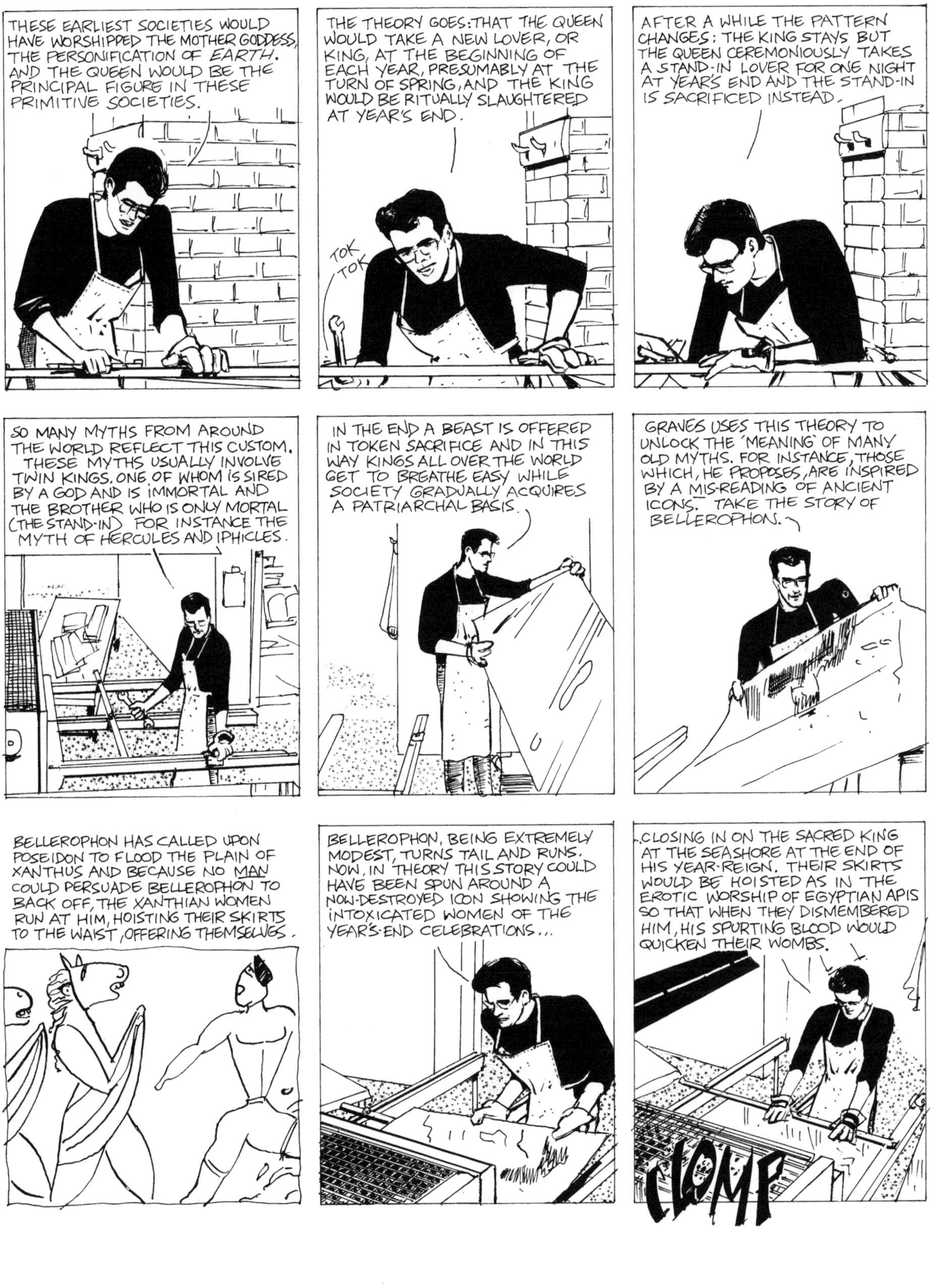
THESE EARLIEST SOCIETIES WOULD HAVE WORSHIPPED THE MOTHER GODDESS, THE PERSONIFICATION OF EARTH. AND THE QUEEN WOULD BE THE PRINCIPAL FIGURE IN THESE PRIMITIVE SOCIETIES.
THE THEORY GOES: THAT THE QUEEN WOULD TAKE A NEW LOVER, OR KING, AT THE BEGINNING OF EACH YEAR, PRESUMABLY AT THE TURN OF SPRING, AND THE KING WOULD BE RITUALLY SLAUGHTERED AT YEAR'S END.
TOK TOK
AFTER A WHILE THE PATTERN CHANGES: THE KING STAYS BUT THE QUEEN CEREMONIOUSLY TAKES A STAND-IN LOVER FOR ONE NIGHT AT YEAR'S END AND THE STAND-IN IS SACRIFICED INSTEAD.
SO MANY MYTHS FROM AROUND THE WORLD REFLECT THIS CUSTOM. THESE MYTHS USUALLY INVOLVE TWIN KINGS, ONE OF WHOM IS SIRED BY A GOD AND IS IMMORTAL AND THE BROTHER WHO IS ONLY MORTAL (THE STAND-IN) FOR INSTANCE THE MYTH OF HERCULES AND IPHICLES.
IN THE END A BEAST IS OFFERED IN TOKEN SACRIFICE AND IN THIS WAY KINGS ALL OVER THE WORLD GET TO BREATHE EASY WHILE SOCIETY GRADUALLY ACQUIRES A PATRIARCHAL BASIS.
GRAVES USES THIS THEORY TO UNLOCK THE 'MEANING' OF MANY OLD MYTHS. FOR INSTANCE, THOSE WHICH, HE PROPOSES, ARE INSPIRED BY A MIS-READING OF ANCIENT ICONS. TAKE THE STORY OF BELLEROPHON.
BELLEROPHON HAS CALLED UPON POSEIDON TO FLOOD THE PLAIN OF XANTHUS AND BECAUSE NO MAN COULD PERSUADE BELLEROPHON TO BACK OFF, THE XANTHIAN WOMEN RUN AT HIM, HOISTING THEIR SKIRTS TO THE WAIST, OFFERING THEMSELVES.
BELLEROPHON, BEING EXTREMELY MODEST, TURNS TAIL AND RUNS. NOW, IN THEORY THIS STORY COULD HAVE BEEN SPUN AROUND A NOW-DESTROYED ICON SHOWING THE INTOXICATED WOMEN OF THE YEAR'S-END CELEBRATIONS...
..CLOSING IN ON THE SACRED KING AT THE SEASHORE AT THE END OF HIS YEAR-REIGN. THEIR SKIRTS WOULD BE HOISTED AS IN THE EROTIC WORSHIP OF EGYPTIAN APIS SO THAT WHEN THEY DISMEMBERED HIM, HIS SPURTING BLOOD WOULD QUICKEN THEIR WOMBS.
CLOMP

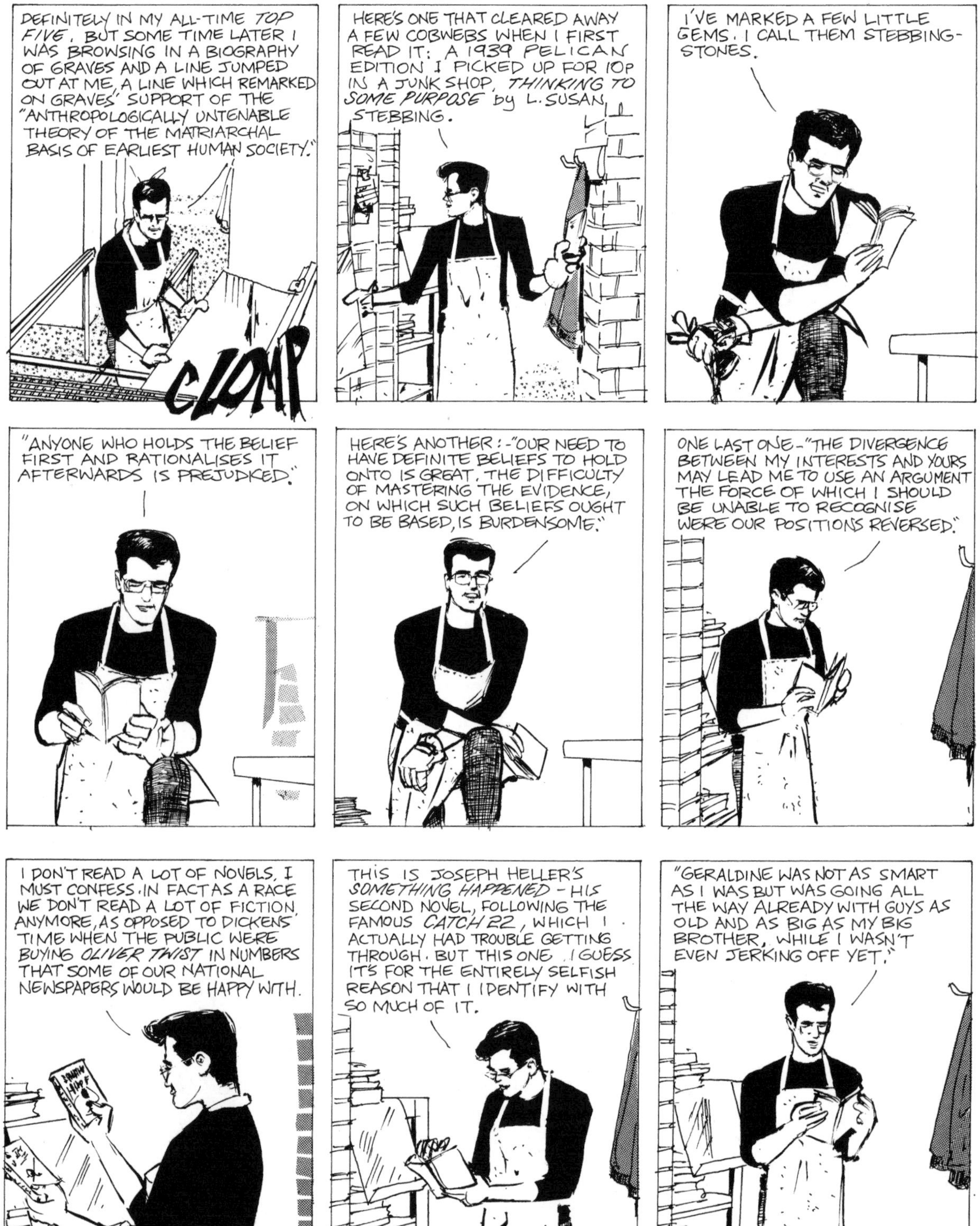
DEFINITELY IN MY ALL-TIME *TOP FIVE*. BUT SOME TIME LATER I WAS BROWSING IN A BIOGRAPHY OF GRAVES AND A LINE JUMPED OUT AT ME, A LINE WHICH REMARKED ON GRAVES' SUPPORT OF THE "ANTHROPOLOGICALLY UNTENABLE THEORY OF THE MATRIARCHAL BASIS OF EARLIEST HUMAN SOCIETY."
CLOMP
HERE'S ONE THAT CLEARED AWAY A FEW COBWEBS WHEN I FIRST READ IT: A 1939 PELICAN EDITION I PICKED UP FOR 10P IN A JUNK SHOP, *THINKING TO SOME PURPOSE* by L. SUSAN STEBBING.
I'VE MARKED A FEW LITTLE GEMS. I CALL THEM STEBBING-STONES.
"ANYONE WHO HOLDS THE BELIEF FIRST AND RATIONALISES IT AFTERWARDS IS PREJUDICED."
HERE'S ANOTHER: -"OUR NEED TO HAVE DEFINITE BELIEFS TO HOLD ONTO IS GREAT. THE DIFFICULTY OF MASTERING THE EVIDENCE, ON WHICH SUCH BELIEFS OUGHT TO BE BASED, IS BURDENSOME."
ONE LAST ONE -"THE DIVERGENCE BETWEEN MY INTERESTS AND YOURS MAY LEAD ME TO USE AN ARGUMENT THE FORCE OF WHICH I SHOULD BE UNABLE TO RECOGNISE WERE OUR POSITIONS REVERSED."
I DON'T READ A LOT OF NOVELS, I MUST CONFESS. IN FACT AS A RACE WE DON'T READ A LOT OF FICTION ANYMORE, AS OPPOSED TO DICKENS' TIME WHEN THE PUBLIC WERE BUYING *OLIVER TWIST* IN NUMBERS THAT SOME OF OUR NATIONAL NEWSPAPERS WOULD BE HAPPY WITH.
THIS IS JOSEPH HELLER'S *SOMETHING HAPPENED* - HIS SECOND NOVEL, FOLLOWING THE FAMOUS *CATCH 22*, WHICH I ACTUALLY HAD TROUBLE GETTING THROUGH. BUT THIS ONE, I GUESS IT'S FOR THE ENTIRELY SELFISH REASON THAT I IDENTIFY WITH SO MUCH OF IT.
"GERALDINE WAS NOT AS SMART AS I WAS BUT WAS GOING ALL THE WAY ALREADY WITH GUYS AS OLD AND AS BIG AS MY BIG BROTHER, WHILE I WASN'T EVEN JERKING OFF YET."

LATER, THIS BIT.."PRETTY AS SHE WAS, SHE COULD TURN AS GRISLY TO ME ALL AT ONCE AS THAT SEPARATED HEAD OF MEDUSA, THAT EVIL, HAIRY, PERISTALTIC NEST OF COUNTLESS CRAWLING
VIPERS ARCHING OUT TO FANG ME."
HI ALEC
HOW'S IT GOIN', DANNY! Y'KNOW, I'M DEEP IN THIS BOOK HERE, I KEEP SEEING MY RELATIONSHIP WITH PENNY IN IT.
YEH, HEY, I'VE GOT AN IDEA -
LIKE THIS BIT.."PRETTY AS SHE WAS..
FOR HEAVEN'S SAKE!! YOU READ ALL THESE BOOKS AND YOU SEE PENNY IN THEM ALL!!
THEY WROTE ALL THOSE BOOKS JUST FOR YOU AND PENNY. PENNY. PENNY. YOU'RE BESOTTED WITH THE GIRL. YOU'VE GOT NO TIME FOR ANYONE ELSE SINCE PENNY!!!
I WAS GOING TO SAY LET'S GO OUT FOR A DRINK. BUT YOU WOULDN'T COME, WOULD YOU?!!
NOW!!? BLOODY NO, I WOULDN'T -
F-
AH!
"IT HIT ME WITH THE FORCE OF A FUTURE RECOLLECTION." THAT'S FROM NABOKOV'S LOLITA
IS THAT A BOOK?
YOU ONLY KNOW BOOKS. YOU DON'T KNOW ANYTHING FOR YOURSELF, DO YOU? WHY DON'T YOU GO OUT AND LEARN SOMETHING FOR YOURSELF?
Eh?

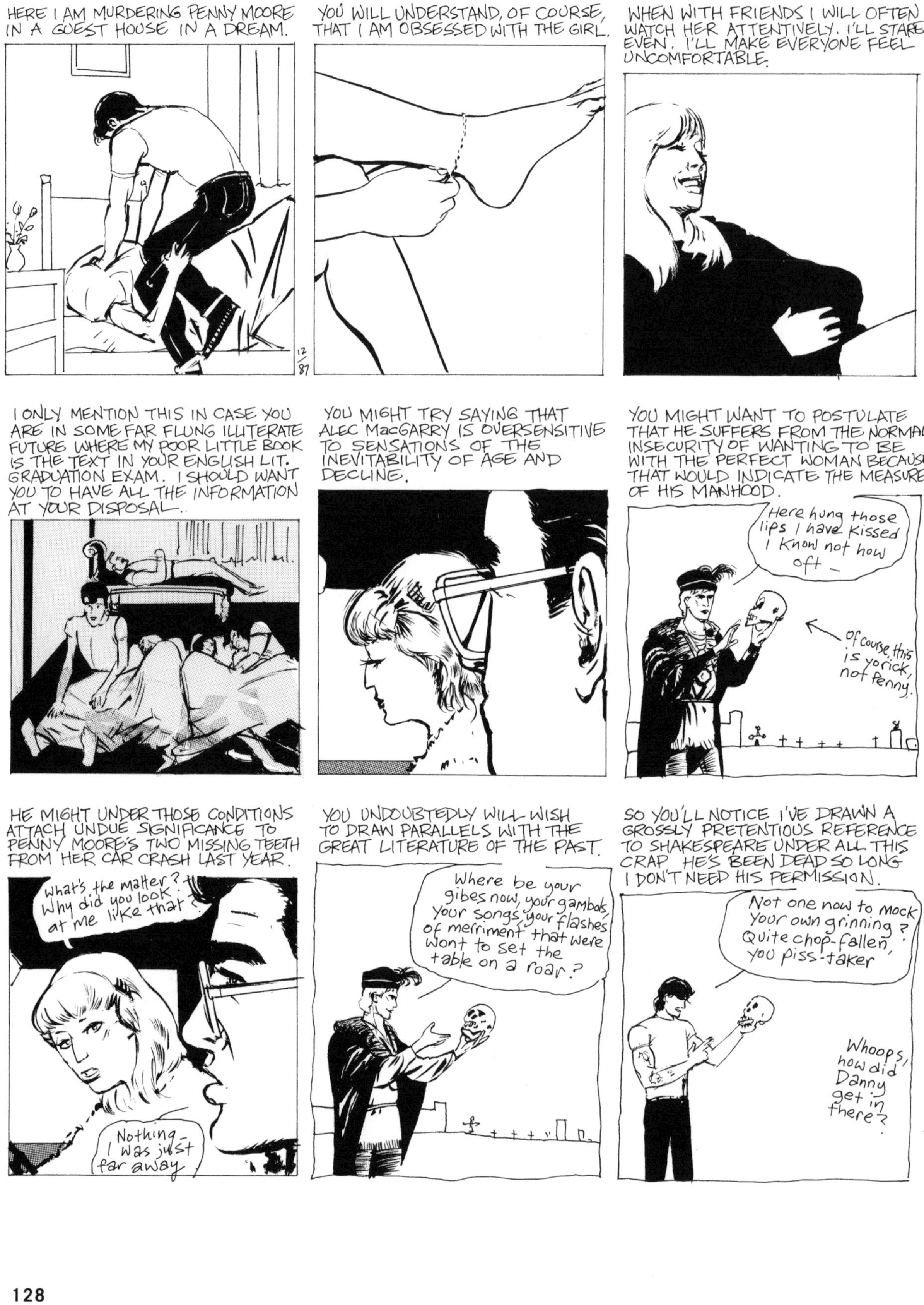
HERE I AM MURDERING PENNY MOORE IN A GUEST HOUSE IN A DREAM.
YOU WILL UNDERSTAND, OF COURSE, THAT I AM OBSESSED WITH THE GIRL.
WHEN WITH FRIENDS I WILL OFTEN WATCH HER ATTENTIVELY. I'LL STARE EVEN. I'LL MAKE EVERYONE FEEL UNCOMFORTABLE.
I ONLY MENTION THIS IN CASE YOU ARE IN SOME FAR FLUNG ILLITERATE FUTURE WHERE MY POOR LITTLE BOOK IS THE TEXT IN YOUR ENGLISH LIT. GRADUATION EXAM. I SHOULD WANT YOU TO HAVE ALL THE INFORMATION AT YOUR DISPOSAL..
YOU MIGHT TRY SAYING THAT ALEC MacGARRY IS OVERSENSITIVE TO SENSATIONS OF THE INEVITABILITY OF AGE AND DECLINE.
YOU MIGHT WANT TO POSTULATE THAT HE SUFFERS FROM THE NORMAL INSECURITY OF WANTING TO BE WITH THE PERFECT WOMAN BECAUSE THAT WOULD INDICATE THE MEASURE OF HIS MANHOOD.
Here hung those lips I have kissed I know not how oft –
Of course, this is yorick, not Penny.
HE MIGHT UNDER THOSE CONDITIONS ATTACH UNDUE SIGNIFICANCE TO PENNY MOORE'S TWO MISSING TEETH FROM HER CAR CRASH LAST YEAR.
What's the matter? Why did you look at me like that?
Nothing. I was just far away.
YOU UNDOUBTEDLY WILL WISH TO DRAW PARALLELS WITH THE GREAT LITERATURE OF THE PAST.
Where be your gibes now, your gambols, your songs, your flashes of merriment that were wont to set the table on a roar?
SO YOU'LL NOTICE I'VE DRAWN A GROSSLY PRETENTIOUS REFERENCE TO SHAKESPEARE UNDER ALL THIS CRAP. HE'S BEEN DEAD SO LONG I DON'T NEED HIS PERMISSION.
Not one now to mock your own grinning? Quite chop-fallen, you piss-taker
Whoops, how did Danny get in there?

WHAT DO WE LEAVE AFTER WE GO? A FEW DULL AND CHIPPED ARTEFACTS? HERE'S A SCENE AFTER JOHN GODFREY'S BROTHER-IN-LAW COMES INTO THE PUB CARRYING HIS METAL-DETECTOR. HE'S STILL ON THE TRAIL OF THE REAL KING CANUTE.
Let's hear it again, mick.
The Irishman was on the digger when they cleared the way for the flyover - He said he buried this thing two feet from the old church wall
Even if we find the gold chalice there probably won't be anything in it.
OR PERHAPS SOME EERIE SPIRITUAL AFTER-EFFECT; AUNT LUCY IS THE MOST SUPERSTITIOUS PERSON I KNOW; THIS IS A MONDAY, THE NIGHT AFTER WE GET BACK FROM LETOUQUET.
I closed my eyes and saw bars.. I knew one of you was locked up
It's true
SHE'S AT THE PUB THAT NIGHT EN ROUTE TO LOOKING AT AN UNATTENDED HOUSE WHICH SHE IS CONSIDERING BUYING. NATURALLY WE ALL GO ALONG TO OFFER OUR PROFESSIONAL OPINIONS AS REALTORS.
Up a ladder, down a well, on a bicycle, Raorwoond straight corners
THE OMENS, HOWEVER, ARE NOT GOOD. ORION IS IN THE CONFLUENCE OF MICKEY MOUSE AND PLUTO IS IN A TIFF.
SOMEBODY COMMITS THE CALAMITOUS ERROR OF LIGHTING A CANDLE WHOSE COLOUR IS THE PORTENTOUS COLOUR GREEN.
FURTHERMORE, SHEP, WHO IS BY TRADE A PLUMBER, FINDS SEVERAL LENGTHS OF COPPER PIPE IN THE HALL AND BLOWS DOWN ONE OF THEM.
hoooooooo.
AAAAH
Get Daoown Shep

AUNT LUCY THROWS A FANCY DRESS PARTY. THE THEME IS INDIA. MAKE OF THIS PICTURE WHAT YOU WILL.
Oggy Oggy
LUCY, IN FACT, WAS BORN AND GREW UP IN INDIA IN THE TIME WHEN IT WAS STILL UNDER ENGLISH RULE. SHE TELLS A RATHER TOUCHING STORY ABOUT WHEN SHE WAS A CHILD AND HER LITTLE DOG DIED.
IN 1920s INDIA NOBODY IS LIKELY TO WEEP MUCH OVER A POOR DEAD DOG, BUT A LITTLE SERVANT BOY INTUITIVELY IMPROVISES A FUNERAL PROCESSION AND MOCK BURIAL.
LUCY, LIKE TIMMINS, IS NOT A GREAT FAN OF DANNY GREY AT THIS TIME, FOR REASONS MADE OBVIOUS SOME PAGES BACK. INDEED, ANGELINE WAS QUITE HEARTBROKEN FOR A WHILE.
CLOSED.
There's plenty more fish in the sea.
LUCY'S O-K BY ME. I'LL EVEN FORGIVE THIS SINCE IT IS QUITE TRUE.
ALEC? - WHAT FUTURE DOES HE HAVE - HE HASN'T GOT A TRADE - YOU HAVE LITTLE PAULINE TO THINK OF.
SHEP AND JEAN SEEM TO FALL OUT WITH DANNY TOO. BUT I DON'T KNOW WHY FOR SURE. JEAN IS QUITE PARANOID AFTER SHEP'S FIT OF DOMESTIC VIOLENCE.
THE KING CANUTE
NOW THERE'S A GREATLY MISUSED WORD. PARANOID. IN COMMON CURRENCY IT MEANS JUST ABOUT ANY SORT OF DISQUIET OR MENTAL DISCOMFORT.
He said the wrong thing to Penny and he's paranoid about it.
HERE'S ANOTHER: PEOPLE SAY ENORMITY WHEN THEY MEAN ENORMOUSNESS. IT'S A LIVE LANGUAGE, SO WE CAN DEFORM IT AS MUCH AS WE LIKE. DICTIONARIES WILL IN THE END SIDE WITH THE MAJORITY, AND IN THIS CASE THEY ALREADY GIVE THE WORDS AS INTERCHANGEABLE.
and that is the real enormity, your honour.
ON THE OTHER HAND, LATIN, BEING A DEAD LANGUAGE, IS FOREVER PERFECT.
Nil sine labore MacGarry, that does not mean NO SIGN OF WORK

HERE'S THE SLIPPERY SLOPE TO THE LAST PAGE. DANNY GREY INHERITS A BIT OF MONEY.
THE OLD BOY FINALLY DIED. MY GRANDMOTHER'S SECOND HUSBAND. SO MY BROTHER AND I GET THE BUNGALOW.
"IT WAS SOLD OFF PRETTY QUICKLY 15 THOU. WE ARRANGED WITH THE ESTATE AGENT TO GET FIVE OF THAT CASH-IN-HAND BECAUSE WE THOUGHT THAT WOULD LET US OUT TAX-WISE."
95 96 97
FRRIP
I HOPE THIS ISN'T GOING TO AFFECT OUR RELATIONSHIP, ME HAVING A BIT OF MONEY.
WELL, I KNOW I WON'T BE TALKING TO YOU AGAIN.
I'LL TELL YOU WHAT! TWO WEEKS FROM NOW WE'LL ALL GO UP TO HARWICH..DO ALL THE PUBS, STAY THE NIGHT.
ACCORDING TO DANNY, HARWICH HAS THE GREATEST CONCENTRATION OF PUBS PER SQUARE MILE IN ALL OF BRITAIN.
ME, HOLLY, YOU AND PENNY GEORGE AND VICKI
TWO DAYS BEFORE WE GO TO HARWICH. IT'S THE EASTER SCHOOL HOLIDAY AND THE GUY IN CHARGE OF LOADING HAS HIS KID HELPING OUT.
RODEN
THE KID IS LARKING ABOUT AND HAS A BAD ACCIDENT.
WAIT
WA HEY
DANNY!

(My god - MUST keep him from getting excited)
- SPIT!
SIT STILL, MATE. THE AMBULANCE WILL BE ALONG IN A MINUTE
(Let's put this piece back in there ... yes.)
THAT WAS A SILLY THING TO DO, EH?
WHO WANTS TO BE WORKING ON A DAY LIKE THIS. LISTEN TO THOSE BIRDS SING.
HOW ARE YOU FEELING?
WELL I'M O.K. NOW. I DON'T KNOW ABOUT HIM.
THAT ALL STRIKES ME AS IMPORTANT FOR SOME REASON. FINISH THE BOOK AND MAKE YOUR OWN CONNECTIONS.
can't even see the joins
HARWICH. AS THE EVENING PROGRESSES I FEEL THE ATMOSPHERE GOING ALL WRONG. DANNY'S TALKING ABOUT A SEXUAL INCIDENT INVOLVING HIS FIRST WIFE IN FRONT OF HOLLY. FAILING TO SENSE HER INSECURE AURA.
AND SO IT GOES.
DANNY, YOU WERE DRESSED JUST AS YOU ARE TONIGHT ONE OTHER NIGHT AT THE MINERVA
WHAT NIGHT WOULD THAT BE? WHO WERE YOU WITH?
BLOODY MR. MEMORY WILL ATTEMPT TO DAZZLE EVERYONE IN A MINUTE BY TELLING WHAT DAY OF THE YEAR IT WAS.
A GIRL NAMED FRANCES.
OH YES I WAS WITH PENNY.
PENNY- YOU NEVER TOLD ME YOU USED TO GO OUT WITH PENNY.
OH IT WAS.
I CAN'T STAND IT ANY MORE, ALEC. THIS ISN'T JEALOUSY. I HAVE STRONG FEELINGS AGAINST THAT BUT HE CRITICISES EVERY SINGLE THING I DO. YOU DON'T KNOW HOW IT IS. I WANT OUT-

WHERE IS HE, ALEC? WHERE HAS HE GONE? I'VE GOT TO GO AND LOOK FOR HIM.
HE'S JUST GETTING YOUR BAGS FROM THE CAR THEN WE'RE STAYING IN A COUPLE OF ROOMS UPSTAIRS
DANNY
COME AWAY. DON'T YOU SEE YOU'RE AGGRAVATING A LOUSY SITUATION I'D EVEN GUESS YOU'RE DOING IT DELIBERATELY.
WHAT'S THAT SUPPOSED TO MEAN. YOU'VE ALWAYS GOT TO BE THE GOOD FUCKIN' SAMARITAN —!!
SNAP!
COME ON!
WHERE?
WE'LL WALK ALL NIGHT IF WE HAVE TO!!
PUT ME DOWN
YOU CAN'T DO THAT!
It's alright! we're together!
GIVE ME THAT!

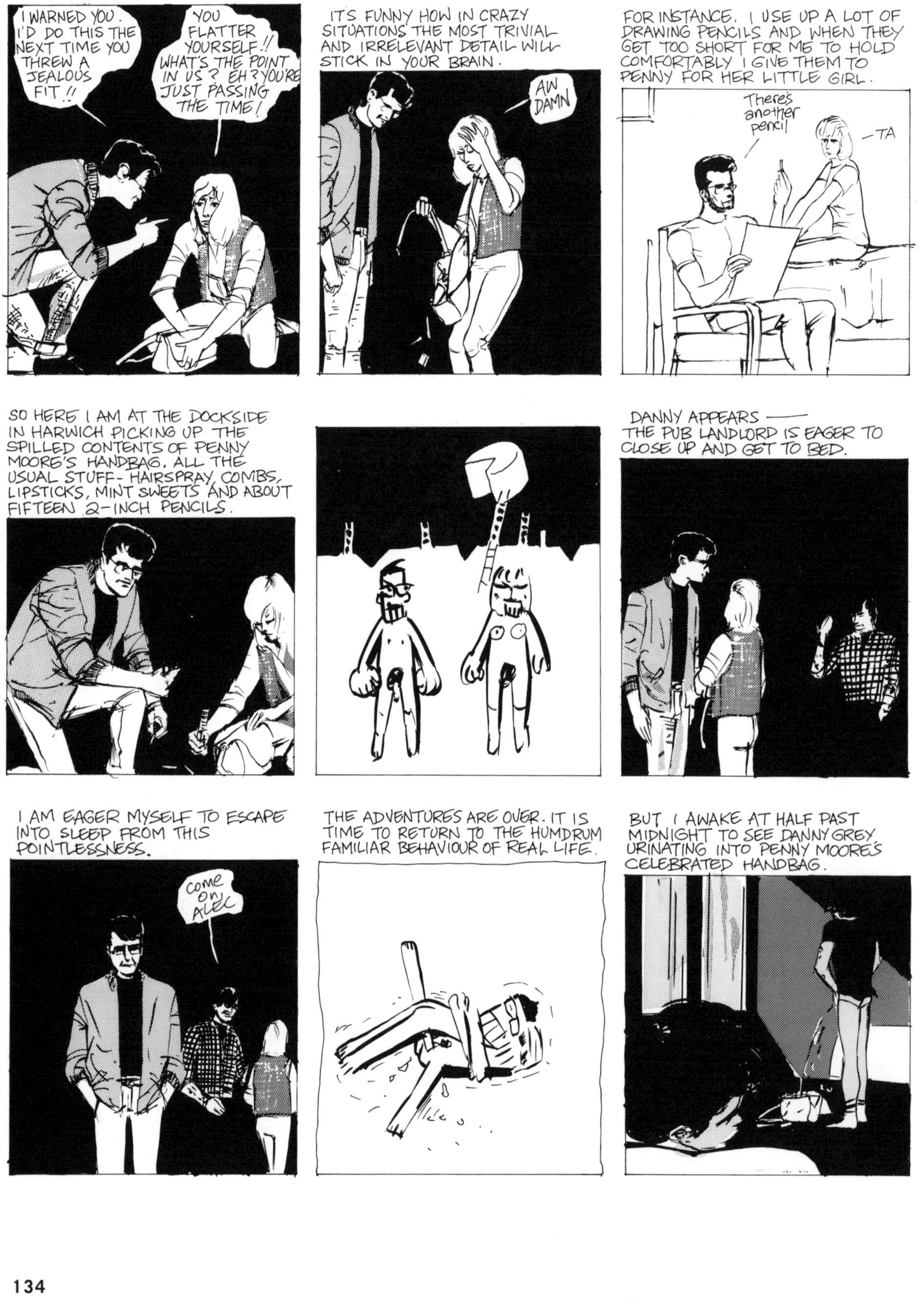
I WARNED YOU. I'D DO THIS THE NEXT TIME YOU THREW A JEALOUS FIT!!
YOU FLATTER YOURSELF!! WHAT'S THE POINT IN US? EH? YOU'RE JUST PASSING THE TIME!
IT'S FUNNY HOW IN CRAZY SITUATIONS THE MOST TRIVIAL AND IRRELEVANT DETAIL WILL STICK IN YOUR BRAIN.
AW DAMN
FOR INSTANCE. I USE UP A LOT OF DRAWING PENCILS AND WHEN THEY GET TOO SHORT FOR ME TO HOLD COMFORTABLY I GIVE THEM TO PENNY FOR HER LITTLE GIRL.
There's another pencil
—TA
SO HERE I AM AT THE DOCKSIDE IN HARWICH PICKING UP THE SPILLED CONTENTS OF PENNY MOORE'S HANDBAG. ALL THE USUAL STUFF- HAIRSPRAY, COMBS, LIPSTICKS, MINT SWEETS AND ABOUT FIFTEEN 2-INCH PENCILS.
DANNY APPEARS — THE PUB LANDLORD IS EAGER TO CLOSE UP AND GET TO BED.
I AM EAGER MYSELF TO ESCAPE INTO SLEEP FROM THIS POINTLESSNESS.
come on ALEC
THE ADVENTURES ARE OVER. IT IS TIME TO RETURN TO THE HUMDRUM FAMILIAR BEHAVIOUR OF REAL LIFE.
BUT I AWAKE AT HALF PAST MIDNIGHT TO SEE DANNY GREY URINATING INTO PENNY MOORE'S CELEBRATED HANDBAG.

L-O-V-E.
DANNY.. WHY DON'T YOU TAKE PENNY'S BAG TO THE SINK AND EMPTY IT - HA HA HA HA
IT'S A BIG JOKE TO YOU! EVERYTHING'S A BIG JOKE TO YOU! - YOU'VE GONE TOO FAR THIS TIME, SMART-ARSE! NOW YOU'VE COOKED YOUR GOOSE!
COME OUT OF THERE
My God!
NO, DANNY, DON'T HIT HIM AGAIN!
No, Danny please - I've got no clothes on
Lemme out dammit Penny
I'M GETTING OUT!
YOU NEEDN'T BOTHER - I'M GOING
Where's my Jeans
AW F—
Damn Pisstaker
YOU'RE SO SMUG - YOU THINK YOU'RE SO SECURE!

STOP HIM ALEC
GRRR
ALEC?
YOU'RE HURTING HIM ALEC! LET GO! -I'LL TALK TO HIM!!
DANNY. WE'RE YOUR FRIENDS
NO WAY!!
-Friends huh! You're just a bunch of piss-takers
WHAT IN HEAVEN'S NAME ARE YOU DOING?
GET GEORGE FROM THE OTHER ROOM
WHAT'S THE MATTER?
Eh? Oh- Forget it.
bloody idiots
WHY DID YOU WAKE GEORGE UP IF YOU DON'T NEED HIM?
WHAT DO YOU WANT WITH HIM AT THIS TIME OF NIGHT?

SKREEE
Tom hasn't noticed the piss on the floor
Bloody Roman orgy
Poor Danny
I HOPE HE PAID YOU IN ADVANCE
IN THE MORNING IT'S A BIG SHARED HANGOVER. GEORGE REGRETS BEING RATTY.
I'll get it
ALEC- can you go back for my watch
DANNY AND ALEC DON'T SPEAK TO EACH OTHER FOR A WHOLE YEAR, MAINLY DUE TO EMBARRASSMENT.
AH, IF WE COULD SEE THE FUTURE. FIVE YEARS AFTER THIS, GEORGE WAITE AND PENNY MOORE GET MARRIED FOR A WHILE.
ME, TODAY.. I'M ON THE OTHER SIDE OF THE WORLD RIDING A GREYHOUND DOWN TO BRISBANE TO TRY TO FIND WORK. A FORD FAIRLANE PASSES WITH A DOGGIE IN THE BACK SEAT-. WATCHING ME THROUGH THE WINDOW-

SHOULD I LAY ME DOWN FOR KEEPS, BEFORE WHAT'S GRIM MY SPIRIT REAPS,
HOLD FOR ME A LITTLE WAKE AND DROWN IN WHAT THE BREWERS MAKE.
THE BEST ALE
WHEN MY TIME COMES, WHEN I RATTLE MY CLACK.
UGH Y'got me!
BADDA BADDA
WHEN I KICK THE BUCKET,
In the name of the father and of the son and into the hole he goes
FALL INTO THE CRACK,
ALAS, POOR ALEC.
SAY SOME WORDS BUT KEEP IT BRIEF.
He Never did a good Likeness of me, Danny, why was that?
dunno, Dave
CAPTAIN TIMMINS
THEN ALL SING ALONG TO MY FAVOURITE TRACK ("I CAN'T GET STARTED" by BUNNY BERIGAN and his orchestra, 1938.)
I've got a house, a show-place, but I can't get no place, with you
CAPTAIN TIMMINS
Life goes on ... the book stops here
Eddie Campbell NTH. Queensland 2/87

graffiti Kitchen

In which I have delusions of being a mythical beast. And would that I could again.

This one demanded a different style, a more spontaneous one, but also intimate, if somewhat mad. I found that style by borrowing the working method of my fellow cartoonist, Glenn Dakin, who pops up in person in a later book in this compendium. The first 16 pages (not counting page 5, which was inserted during the second sitting) were drawn four years ahead of the rest (1988 and 1992, respectively). I had trouble getting the style completely right and had to put it aside and come back to it; the short story on page 195 of this volume was drawn between the two, and you can see me still trying to work it out. I also stalled because I thought a publisher would have to be crazy to take on this book. A crazy publisher turned up (Tundra). He and his crazy story also pop up later in this compendium of tail-chasing beasts.

Watch me. I'm the Most important guy in this bestiary.
I walk with a forward tilt and cut through brick walls with my beak! But here I am adopting the human position to listen to a drunk named Jimmy Fulton.
GAROOGA.
All's for the best in the best of all possible worlds
Thats from Candide - an' ye know what it means?
"It means the situation ye're in's the one ye deserve te be in," he says while two kids make off with his coat.
Penny said she'd come to dinner Sunday, me thinking she might bring something - we argue about it. She's for hamburgers - I'm for cooking up something.
We compromise by getting in a heap of chips. In the car I moan about the dripping grease.
I think about those scratches on her back.
The paw-mark on her shoulder - not one of mine.
GAROOGA.
Today I'm reading a book that tells me to move on to new adventures. Tomorrow I'm reading another book.
ONE

I Stop Keeping a diary. Cue the Dark Ages.
I step out of this one evening at Harwood's place.
when he tells me
Georgette's just been round here looking for you.
George is another important mythical creature
I brush my teeth right there. I've taken to carrying a brush. Walking along I have to figure hard where this started.
It was way before my two-year bout with Penny Moore. I met Jane Maison, fortyish, with her boyfriend in the Westcliff Hotel.
He was a writer. They invited me along to a poetry reading, or work-shop, Jane had just got custody of her daughter at that time.
Dark Pull of the Stranger's child...
TWO.
George was thirteen then. She quite deliberately captivated me and I laughed, Knowing in my heart she would never be pinned down and never should be.
That was then.

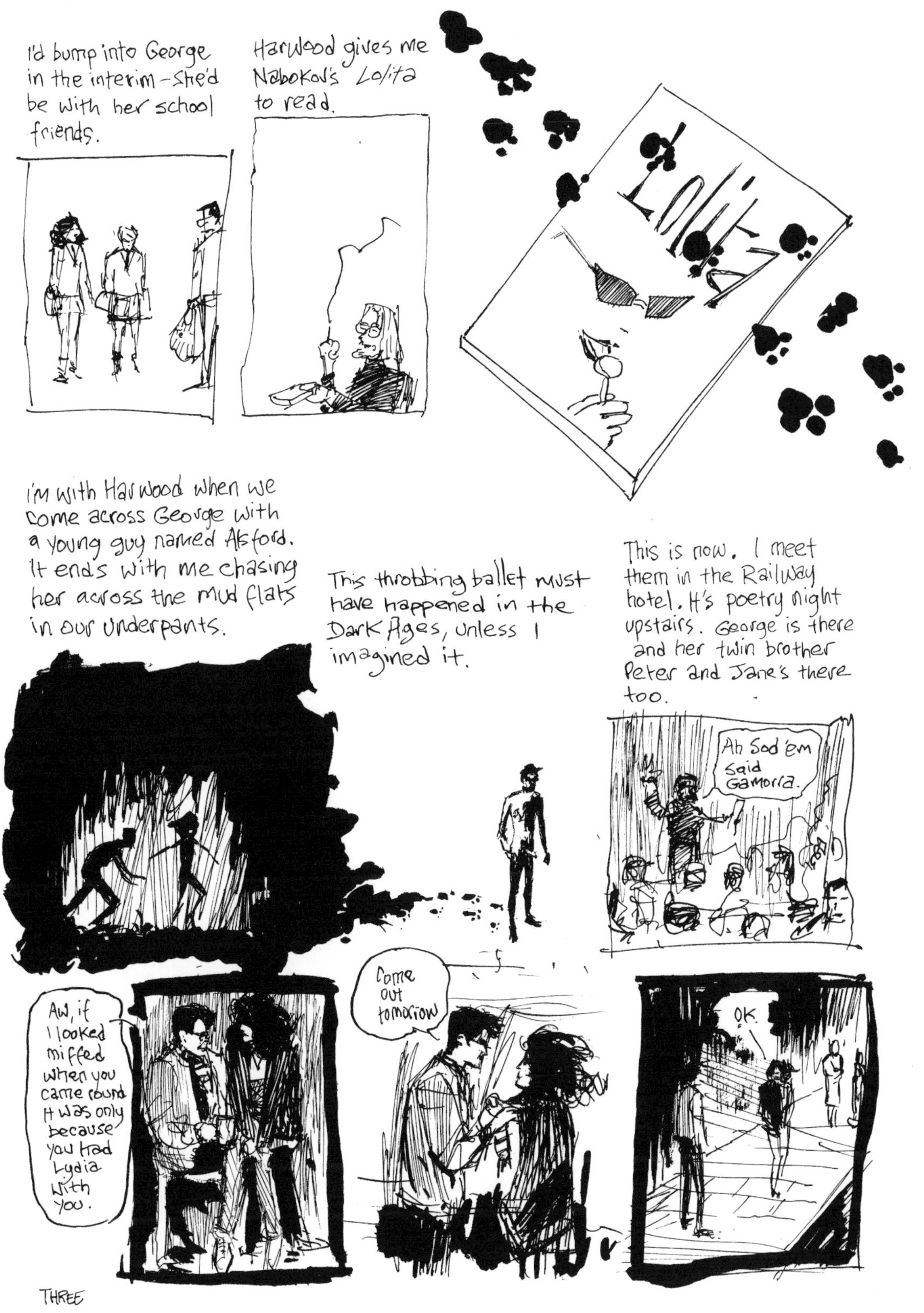

I'd bump into George in the interim - she'd be with her school friends.
Harwood gives me Nabokov's Lolita to read.
Lolita
I'm with Harwood when we come across George with a young guy named Alsford. It ends with me chasing her across the mud flats in our underpants.
This throbbing ballet must have happened in the Dark Ages, unless I imagined it.
This is now. I meet them in the Railway hotel. It's poetry night upstairs. George is there and her twin brother Peter and Jane's there too.
Ah Sod 'em said Gamorra.
Aw, if I looked miffed when you came round it was only because you had Lydia with you.
Come out tomorrow
OK.
THREE

It's half eleven when I get back to my flat. On my doorstep there's a Dark-Age ghost.
Hello Alec- Do you remember me from yesterday? It's not too late is it?
This fellow had handed me a leaflet which had led me to venture into an Easter celebration at the local Baptist centre.
IMPLOSION
DRAMA, MUSIC ACTION, HUMOUR
A new experience for young people
EASTER SATURDAY
One thing led to another and I slept among the young people in the church to greet the holy dawn. I gave off such a rich spiritual aroma that faces from that night keep seeking me out to talk some more
The ghost of the Dark Ages asks if its OK to bring in another guy from the car who'd like to meet me - let's call him the ghost of the Dark pages.
In among speaking in tongues he gives me his life story and a fine one it is too.
In the army - deserted - across France to England - caught - deserted again - locked up for 108 days - Born again
Tomorrow I go round for George. Jane's just heading out with a guy less than half her age.
Jane and the Writer had parted company quite a while back — after about seven years of domestic bliss.
You don't know the real me - we suppress so much of ourselves in a relationship.
The writer moved out of the house up to London and wrote a foosty old historical novel. Actually I don't know that, but I never bumped into him again at those bloody poetry nights.
I wonder what part George played in all of that —
FOUR

I say "Now let's have a drink," and she says:
I'd like a beer, Mr. McGollygosh
But when it reaches my ears it goes something like "I'd like you to win Havana in a card game and turn it back into a romantic resort."
We're doing Shakespeare. God, he's a gasbag that ol' woggledagger.
To me this is no more or less than the first spark of a new literary movement.
Georgette's magical voice is telling the planets to all change places.
But there is something amiss in the spirit of Alec MacGarry tonight.
And in the spirits of so many poor bastards walking abroad dangerously with the unfucked blues.
The time is all wrong.
garoog
Mezozoic man nips down to the Renaissance for a beer.
what was that?
Beep
Five.

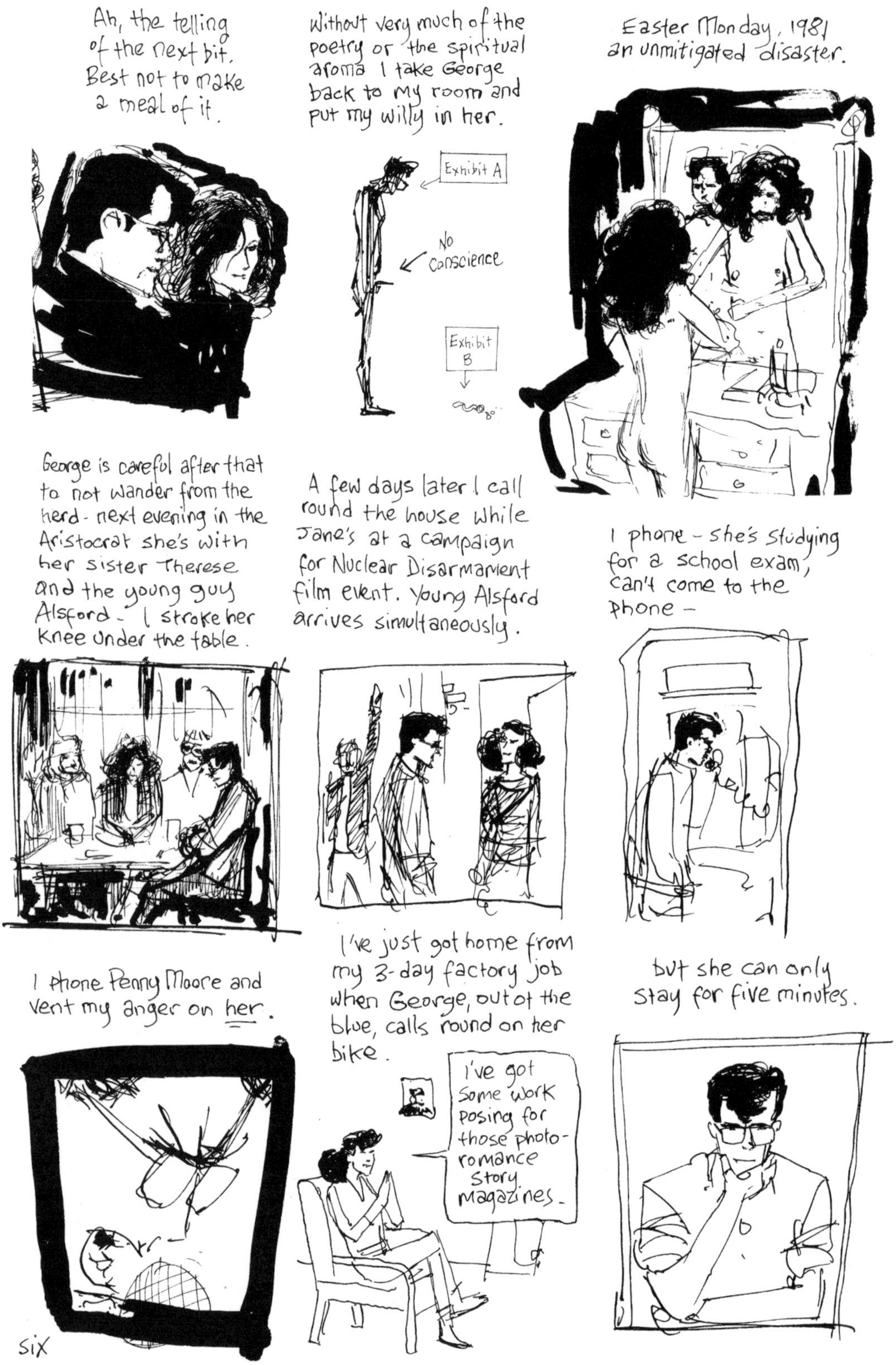
Ah, the telling of the next bit. Best not to make a meal of it.
Without very much of the poetry or the spiritual aroma I take George back to my room and put my willy in her.
Exhibit A
No Conscience
Exhibit B
Easter Monday, 1981 an unmitigated disaster.
George is careful after that to not wander from the herd - next evening in the Aristocrat she's with her sister Therese and the young guy Alsford - I stroke her knee under the table.
A few days later I call round the house while Jane's at a campaign for Nuclear Disarmament film event. Young Alsford arrives simultaneously.
I phone - she's studying for a school exam, can't come to the phone -
I phone Penny Moore and vent my anger on her.
SIX
I've just got home from my 3-day factory job when George, out of the blue, calls round on her bike.
I've got some work posing for those photo-romance story magazines.
but she can only stay for five minutes.

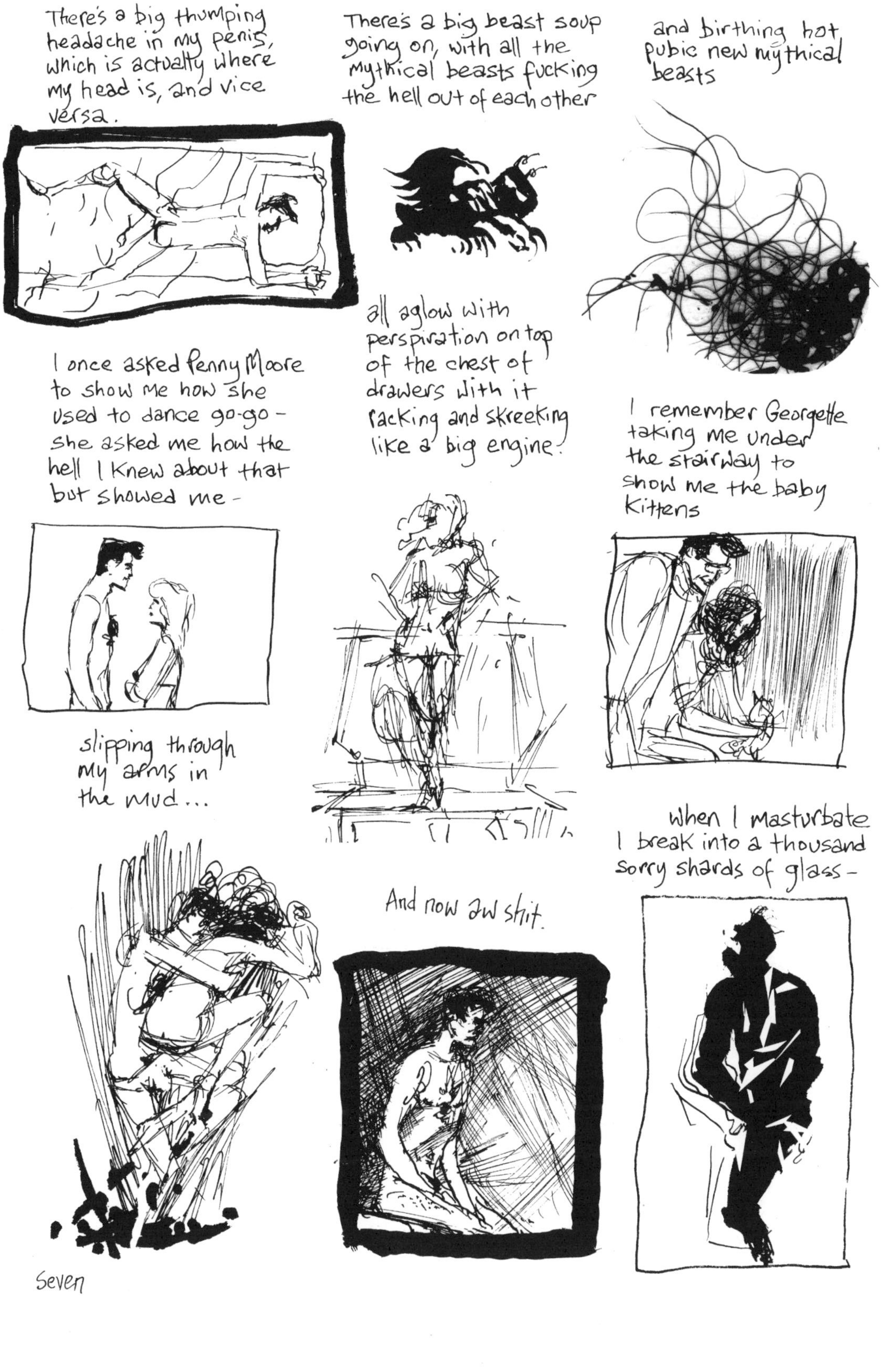
There's a big thumping headache in my penis, which is actually where my head is, and vice versa.
There's a big beast soup going on, with all the mythical beasts fucking the hell out of each other
and birthing hot pubic new mythical beasts
all aglow with perspiration on top of the chest of drawers with it racking and skreeking like a big engine.
I once asked Penny Moore to show me how she used to dance go-go - she asked me how the hell I knew about that but showed me -
I remember Georgette taking me under the stairway to show me the baby kittens
slipping through my arms in the mud...
when I masturbate I break into a thousand sorry shards of glass -
And now aw shit.
Seven

The alarm clock wakes me.. it's 11 a.m. Strange. Anyway it's Tuesday, a no-work day. Hey it wasn't the clock, it was the doorbell -
It's another ghost - was in town to sign for his dole money.
The ghost of the dole-cheque tells me his life story and this is also a fine one too —
Drove without a license — caused death of girl-friend - two years in Hell - born again
I paint a sign for some money.
BEST OF BREED
I go out alone for a drink and end up in front of the Armada where Penny Moore used to dance go-go on a little ledge, or so I was told - I peer in to see it.
I wander up behind the Esplanade, looking down on the sea and the big black sky and I am the adrenalin rushing through the streets —
I have an insight:
I am the only element of continuity in my own life
Excited I rouse Harwood and we have a few beers.
I smile at a girl in The Fishermans - She tells me to piss off. I laugh -
ARF
ARF
Eight

I don't usually get Harwood out more than twice a week as he's generally short on money. He's on the dole - been there for years —
But he's an artist, 3 or 4 nights a week I'll happily sit in his room and we talk about our art and everybody else's till late.
He gives me Joyce's Ulysses to read.
ULYSSES.
JAMES JOYCE
I make a Sunday lunch-time date with two girls I meet in the Aristocrat and get Harwood in on it.
Later, I've lost interest in the whole thing and I'm absentmindedly baying at the moon while he sets up another outing —
I go, silent, destructive. One of the girls starts to panic and buy the drinks. Harwood says she looked embarrassed.
GIGGLE
GIGGLE
GIGGLE
ARISTOCRAT
GIGGLE
I give 10 pence to a hobo I tell him it's my last -
He argues and tries to give it back —
I'm stung by his humanity.
nine

The ghost of the Pages reappears and I call him that because I'm working on something of enormous importance when he reappears.

ALEC- IT'S ME, ANDREW- I SO ENJOYED OUR PREVIOUS MEETING

You see, for the previous couple of years I'd been struggling with the Artistic problem of embodying the simplest kind of Truth in the lowly form of the comic strip —

That, is the world's challenge to me as an Artist — I show Pages the pages - .

It's sheer poetry, ALEC.

Let me take the speaker's chair —

Spent a year at Art School, next seven becoming a nothing. rejected by lover- born again.

At work my former pal Danny Grey talks to me — We've only spoken twice since the Harwich punch-up a year ago.

I hear you and Penny split up.

We have a drink in the Westcliff Hotel and I show him the five pages —

"Danny Grey never forgave himself for leaving ALEC MacGarry asleep at the turnpike."

And who's to say we're not all important characters in somebody else's book, a bleak one or a full one, or maybe even just ghosts milling around in the back of somebody's head imagining ourselves to be more or less crucial to the plot, yet written or not, eh, Danny?

But tonight he seems only to want to remind me of past arguments and bitterness — I stay the night with him and Holly, his wife, in Basildon.

Arriving back in Southend the next midday, Saturday, I realise how there has come to be a vitality to this town and that in my anonymous way I am a part of it. I stop to watch a group of women folk-dancers in the shopping mall —

ten

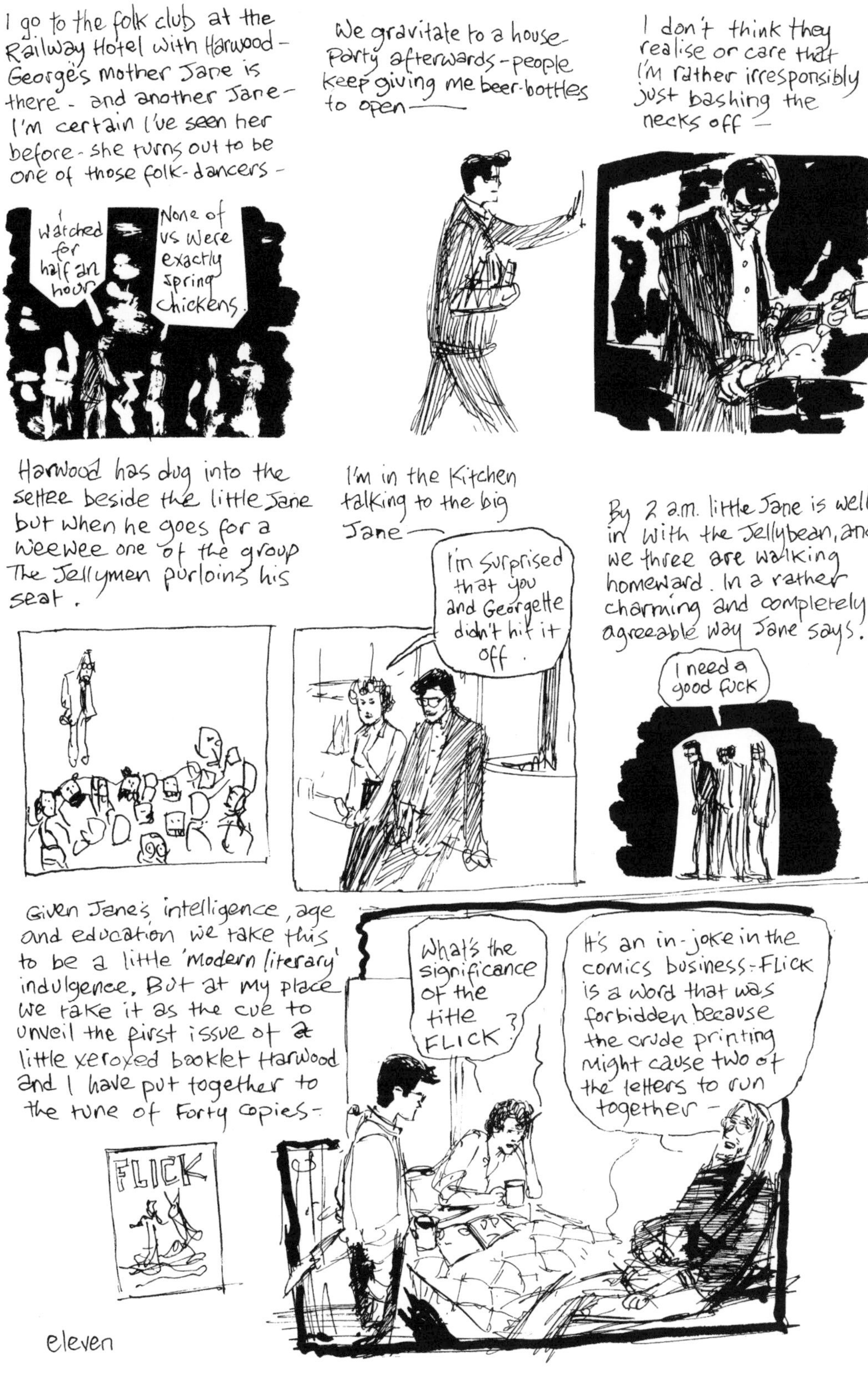
I go to the folk club at the Railway Hotel with Harwood - George's mother Jane is there - and another Jane - I'm certain I've seen her before - she turns out to be one of those folk-dancers -
I watched for half an hour
None of us were exactly spring chickens.
We gravitate to a house-party afterwards - people keep giving me beer-bottles to open —
I don't think they realise or care that I'm rather irresponsibly just bashing the necks off —
Harwood has dug into the settee beside the little Jane but when he goes for a weewee one of the group The Jellymen purloins his seat.
I'm in the kitchen talking to the big Jane —
I'm surprised that you and Georgette didn't hit it off.
By 2 a.m. little Jane is well in with the Jellybean, and we three are walking homeward. In a rather charming and completely agreeable way Jane says:
I need a good fuck
Given Jane's intelligence, age and education we take this to be a little 'modern literary' indulgence. But at my place we take it as the cue to unveil the first issue of a little xeroxed booklet Harwood and I have put together to the tune of forty copies -
FLICK
What's the significance of the title FLICK?
It's an in-joke in the comics business - FLICK is a word that was forbidden because the crude printing might cause two of the letters to run together -
eleven

Jane is an artist too of course - she's going to a University up north in September to start her Art Degree course.
I'm going to sell up the house here and buy one up there.
she loves Art with a passion. Harwood and I tell her we only draw to pass the time
you're a pair of nihilists
We explain that in an absolute sense we believe anything people contrive for the purpose of keeping their minds busy is ultimately just vanity, and god knows we're saying it all just for effect -
Another thing that is beyond the mortal sphere of knowledge is what time it is when I see Jane to her door - Must be Four A.M.
we start in on her home-made beer - she brings up Georgette again -
It'll be strange if she arrives home from her Dad's place tomorrow morning to find me wandering about.
oh, I'm sorry, that's a bit presumptious
yes, it IS, Alec.
Then it's a good job you didn't see the toothbrush.
FLICK
twelve.

An hour or so later a memorable quietude is resting on me, The cool sea breeze is blowing across a bedroom whose aesthetic sparseness inclines one towards a spiritual frame of mind. My willy is sniffing all the wet pollinated smells of the spring dawn –

We have breakfast and I'm certain it was my intention to get going before her family turned up. Therese is the first to arrive –

hello, Alec - have you just arrived, or did you stay the night ?

That remark comes completely innocently – I did nearly stay a night once in this house – I sat up late talking to a professional tea-taster and George tried to persuade me to stay over in the front room –

Uh .. he stayed the night - with ME.
Oh sorree .. How embarrassing

In the ensuing conversation Jane comes out with this line.

Alec's such a nihilist – But his pal Dave – he's even worse.

thirteen

Therese doesn't actually live here – she's at University doing medicine – comes home for holidays and stuff – This is the May Whitsun bank-holiday Monday

My spiritual frame of mind has been spirited away. I can hear George's raucous tones coming up the garden path –

In come the rest of them - Nicole, who lives with a guy nearby - they have a little boy of two which of course makes Jane a grandmother.
Add to the three sisters, Nicole, Therese and Georgette, two brothers - The 'Moose' and Peter, George's twin - Of the five only George lives here -
On the theme of family complexity Jane also has a sister of five from when her father remarried in his sixties -
With all of that to keep her busy and more importantly, with University coming up soon, the last thing Jane needs is a stray to look after - here comes one now -
Jane had been up to London to discuss with the writer the 'tragedy' of their separation -
She came back to find another tragedy - One of George's school pals, Amy Bodmin asleep on the couch in the front room. -
Amy had been molested by her stepfather and ran away from home -
Fourteen.
She's been with George for a couple of weeks now - The two go everywhere together.
('Dunno, Elizabethan bed-gowns or something)
I greet them warmly on my way out -

I sleep for 14 hours - next day Jane cycles round for a talk -
She tells me that after I left yesterday Georgette was going to come round to see me, so Jane had to come clean -
What can he possibly see in you?
He's a BASTARD!
And you're a BITCH
etc -
Anyway, I don't care - Alec's a CRANK -
He's like all the rest - only interested in himself - and all he talks about is Penny Moore.
next day we drive in her car to the Plough & Sail, where I hog the microphone -
b-b
The one after that I get a letter —
"I had a ghastly hour with Amy's welfare officer - he's a filthy capitalist. Also I felt intellectually frustrated, being superior (yes - I'm an intellectual snob - I hate myself (lies))" -
Jane's working in the office of a jeans factory at this time, only a temporary measure of course - she gets me some cut-rate clothes -
At the weekend she takes me to a workers' Rights Rally in Brixton - All day open air concert and other fund raising stuff.
Fifteen.

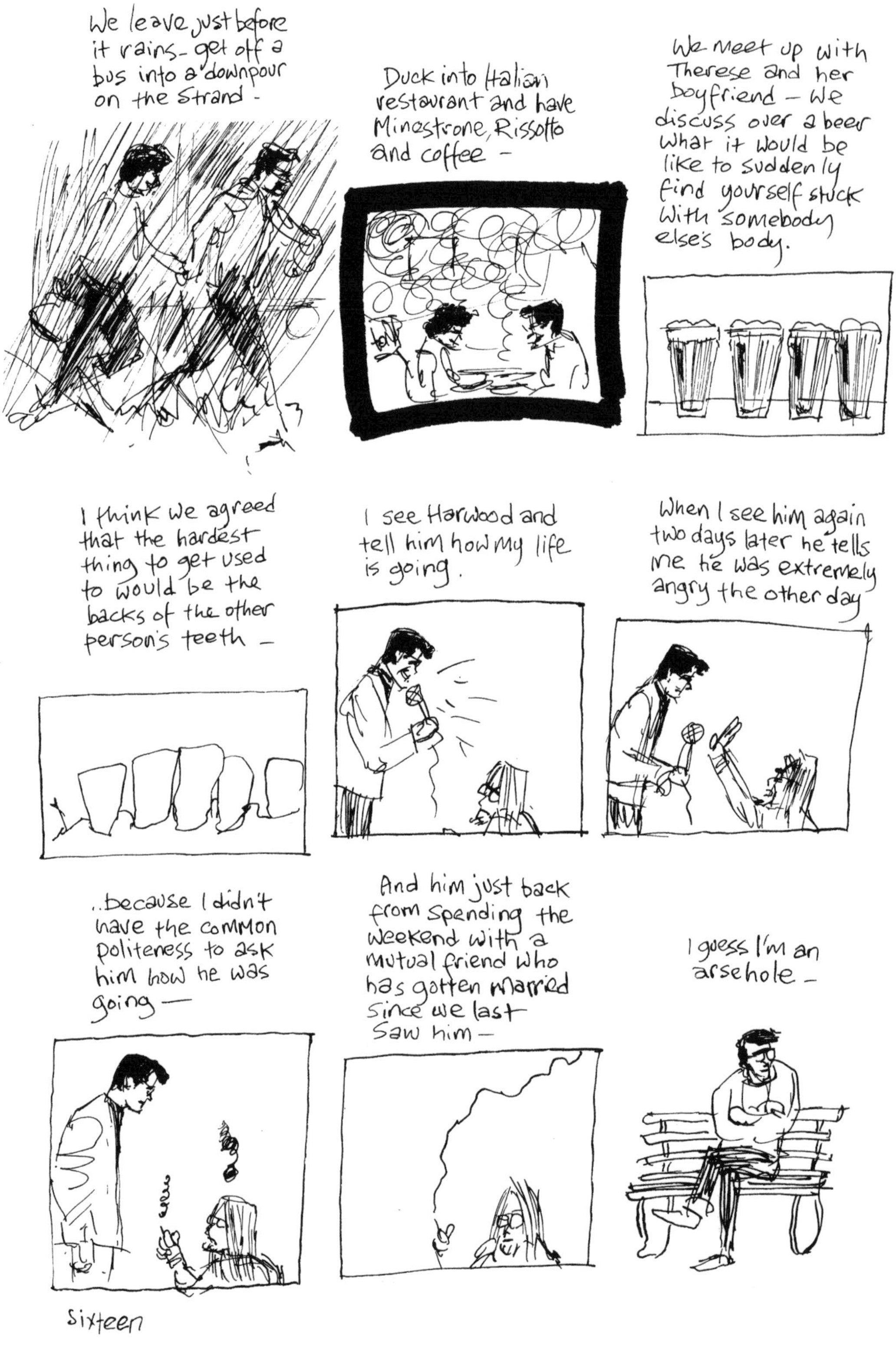
We leave just before it rains - get off a bus into a downpour on the Strand -
Duck into Italian restaurant and have Minestrone, Rissotto and coffee -
We meet up with Therese and her boyfriend - We discuss over a beer what it would be like to suddenly find yourself stuck with somebody else's body.
I think we agreed that the hardest thing to get used to would be the backs of the other person's teeth -
I see Harwood and tell him how my life is going.
When I see him again two days later he tells me he was extremely angry the other day
..because I didn't have the common politeness to ask him how he was going —
And him just back from spending the weekend with a mutual friend who has gotten married since we last saw him -
I guess I'm an arsehole -
Sixteen

Letter from Jane:
"My dear Surprising talkative cynical dark + handsome not to mention sexy, Alec... etc.
she has to give Nicole's bloke Joe some readies for work on the car and pick up the jalopy while she's there —
Nicole gets the kiddy out of bed to see Grandma and life is all kind of fruity and warm and sweet
Now it's late and she's reading her poems at my insistence and she is happy and the home brew is hoppy
I try to be quiet going up the stairs lest Georgette should hear ——
The bed is deliciously fucky —
In the Morning she drives to where a bloke named Tom gives me a lift to work —
Rattle rattle
Her little titties are all agog as I fondle them under her tracksuit.
Seventeen
Tom comes over and gives her a budding rose. He's about Jane's age —
In the womb it must be like this, all mushy and tweety —
BRRUM

At work I'm on a 3-day week. I seem to spend more of the '80s out of work than in it.
I'm drawing close to five years of cutting big sheets of metal into rectangles. It takes one who has seen the absurdity of modern life to enjoy something like this
Ah yes! perfect
(A little bit down the line they hand me my redundancy payment. 300 quid; An invit-ation to go forth and find my destiny)
(When Danny Grey gets his he goes out for a lunchtime drink then goes into the office and breaks the executive manager's hooter)
OH MY GOD DANNY NO!!
POP!
(It's not that he loves the job; he just doesn't care to have his life organised by somebody else)
So everybody's in a strange mood. Prendergast, one of the newer bench hands is trying to wind me up.
I don't remember making a decision to do this. It just came about. It's the only trick I've got in a confrontation, but I once pinned Danny Grey down with it. It goes like this-
MY BACK! YOU'R KILLIN ME
And then you tap the guy's head on the floor like this except this daft coot keeps on laughing the most uproarious hooting howl I've ever heard.
AH HA HOO HO HA OH LORDY YA HOO HA.
To laugh so in the face of adversity; What a Virtue! I must practise it. I go out that night and laugh at the moon just like the guy with his head on the floor.
YEE HOO HA!
Eighteen.

I'm round there next night fixing a plug. I take the opportunity, out of curiosity, to play a disc of Holy music the Ghost of the Pages gave me. I never could be bothered owning a record player.
And I'm watching her have a bath.
It occurs to me to put little blobs of soap on the ends of her nipples.
That night she accuses me of being selfish in "not trying to discover her sexuality"
Women obviously have more aspects of this than men.
Is that so?
And I wonder just what she thinks "men" get out of it anyway. We'll next morning we're off to the Cambridge Poetry Festival.
We've never been in this town together before but each independently pre-selects the same Greek restaurant as obligatory first port of call.
We check out the program at the Corn Exchange and take a cursory glance at the Small Press offerings. There are all these weedy people moving around like loose bones in a box.
Let's go to a pub.
We didn't come here to sit in pubs.
I'm Blodwin. I'm reading in the Hudson Gallery tomorrow blah blah.
We'll be there blah blah
nineteen

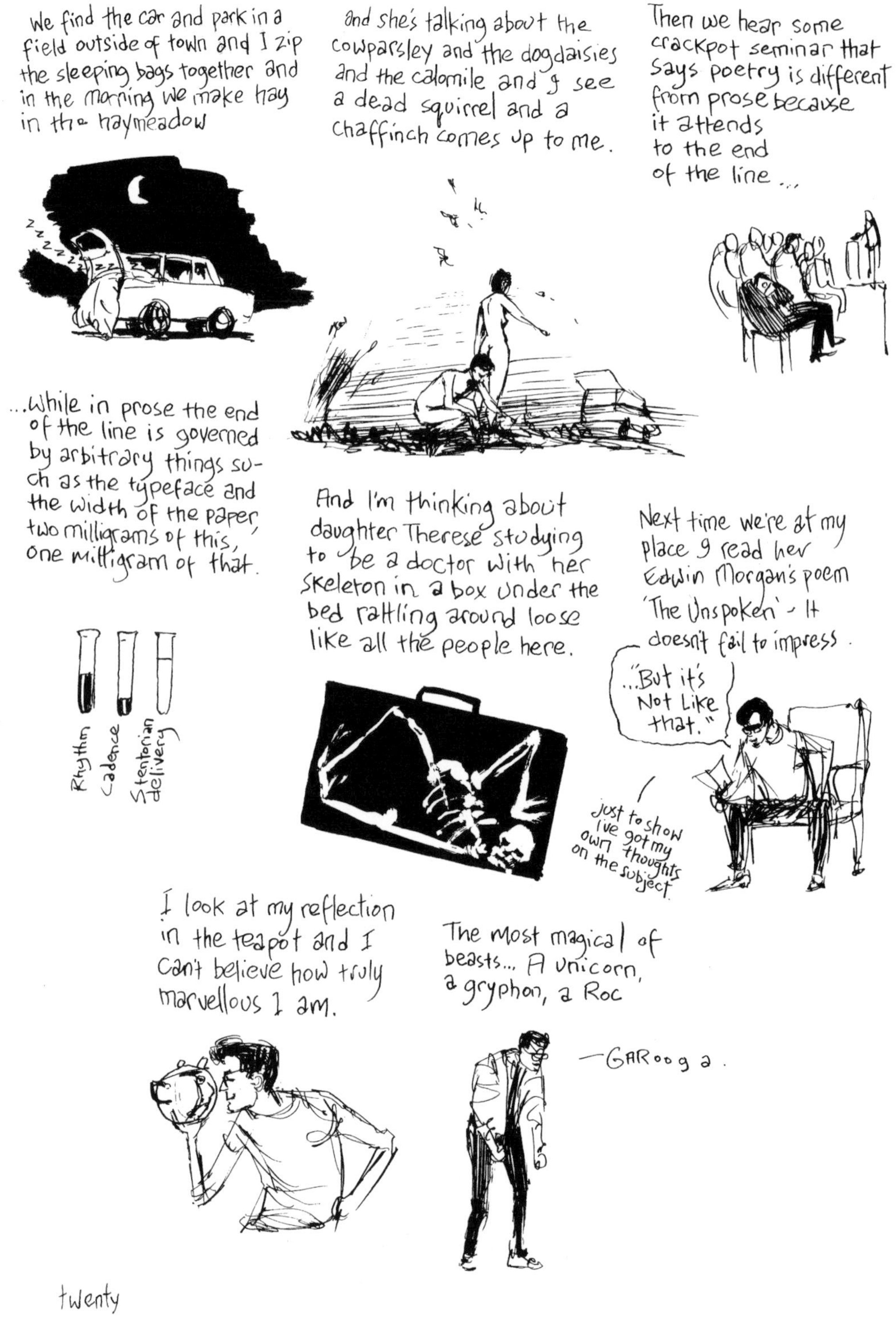
We find the car and park in a field outside of town and I zip the sleeping bags together and in the morning we make hay in the haymeadow
and she's talking about the cowparsley and the dogdaisies and the calomile and I see a dead squirrel and a chaffinch comes up to me.
Then we hear some crackpot seminar that says poetry is different from prose because it attends to the end of the line...
...while in prose the end of the line is governed by arbitrary things such as the typeface and the width of the paper, two milligrams of this, one milligram of that.
Rhythm
Cadence
Stentorian delivery
And I'm thinking about daughter Therese studying to be a doctor with her skeleton in a box under the bed rattling around loose like all the people here.
Next time we're at my place I read her Edwin Morgan's poem 'The Unspoken' - It doesn't fail to impress.
..."But it's Not like that."
just to show I've got my own thoughts on the subject.
I look at my reflection in the teapot and I can't believe how truly marvellous I am.
The most magical of beasts... A unicorn, a gryphon, a Roc
—GARooga.
twenty

Once you have given Fate the nod to indicate that you are ready, it starts marking out your path for you.
ggarooga!
So I exit my abode the next evening to find the dragon's tail flopped onto the porch and I just have to follow it right up its back to where the hot part is.
I'm on my way to visit my old pals George and Vicki and I'm lost when I see this guy fixing his Triumph Spitfire.
He gets his road-map out and then gives me a lift. I forget about my pals and Woofy and me end up in the pub.
I blew all my dosh in Cambridge so Janey gave me a quid to buy a pint of beer, so I get Woofy and me a half-pint each.
The guy's a news-photographer. Now we're at his place drinking his homemade wine and looking at his work. His coverage of the Brentwood Siege is impressive. Guns'n'all.
Then he drives me home and looks at my work and tells me how to be an artist, because it is widely assumed that artists always need advice
do this do that then I could do a story on you.
He takes the Truthful Chair for a moment of honesty.
All those models in the Bikinis- I've never been able to get off with any of them.
Well that was a peculiar evening, thinks I to myself as he gets into his car still trying to look like Philip Marlowe.
twenty-one

Next night, Fate sends round a big bottom to pick me up.
It drops me at a pub where Janey is.
Georgette walks in with her hair all sticking out one side of her head and everything starts going awry
Here's Georgette waiting across the road from my place.
Here she is lying awake listening-
I have to get out of here— Janey follows.
I hail another bottom. It's a big flobbery one.
We politely copulate in the dark.
And in the morning I make bacon and eggs with my clothes on.
twenty-two.

Events enter a new phase. I'm having dinner with Janey and her family. The Moose is sulking on account of his girl friend Kate wearing make-up and being tipsy.
George gets pissed off
You're not going to let him ruin the evening just because he wants to behave like a spoiled child
I'll speak to him
Kate sticks her finger up in the air every time she speaks. It occurs to me to bite it.
Amy Bodmin sits there like a marble sphinx, never more than two feet away from George.
Jane gets sentimental
How lovely you all are, and we're all going to split up soon... Moose and Kate... Georgette and Amy... Alec and I.
And in spite of all this wishywashy nonsense I'm so stimulated I do the business
with Jane, but mentally tossing it into the mainstream of all sex.
We all put on silly hats one night and go and sing silent night in a pub in the middle of summer. It's terrible but nobody throws us out.
I trim the hedges.
And in the dark in the middle of the night I bump into Georgette and kiss her and she kisses me.
twenty-three.

Janey's Kitchen walls are covered with graffiti
Men are like some women
I AM WHAT I AM A FOOD PERSON NOTHING MORE NOTHING LESS
OGGI OGGI OGGI OI OI OI
THIS IS THE HAPPY HOUSE
George thanks for the omelette
I told somebody about this recently who said 'she's obviously only renting the place', like people renting a house can't wait to be wrecking it or something
Bizarre steaks are cool
But not so; She just places the creativity of her children above wallpaper in scale of importance.
STOP WRITING ON THE WALLS!
Jane
I think the ancestors of the comic strip are to be found in the facetious scribbles on ancient walls such as those preserved in Pompeii and Rome.
...rather than in the more formal artefacts from which the comic-strip's self-appointed spokesmen would claim descent for it, such as the Bayeux Tapestry.
There was a highly developed variant of graffiti in 16th century Rome where the wits of the town would sneak out in the night and paste their satirical epigrams onto the ruin of an antique heroic torso they nicknamed 'Pasquino'
Words
pictures
2 mg of this 1 mg of that.
Pancakes. I said, would you like pancakes for breakfast?
I most certainly would, my dear.
King Bing proves his importance by having the Royal Mythographer rewrite his genealogy so that one of the Gods was a great grand-father.
GOD.
Joe Blow does it half as intelligibly but more honestly on the outhouse wall
UGGI UGGI OI OI
GARNOGA
MOOSE
twenty-four.

I eat fish and chips on the way home from work and get round there to find another 'tragedy' underway.
We can't afford to have Amy stay any longer
Why don't you get a weekend job then?
Oh, you! I'll kill you!
For God's sake, decide one way or the other then stop moaning about it.
Jane on the phone, to the headmistress or someone:
It's been decided that Amy's part of the family from now on and no more 'moaning about it'. If we have to 'sell the silver', that's just too bad.
So they tell Amy they can keep her and they all cry on each other's shoulders
I have a bath there, as is my wont, then parade around in front of the mirror doing famous Greek sculptures before turning up at the table just in time for the fruit salad.
Belvedere Apollo
They've already cooked up a plan for Jane to go see Amy's wicked stepfather and lean on him for some dosh. I'm to go along to lean on the door-jamb and look threatening.
The fat slob has buried his wallet in the garden or stuck it up his arse or something because it all amounts to bugger all and we're back the way the world was when we all got out of bed this morning.
oh yeh?
I empty out my pocket at day's end and get Janey and me a couple of beers.
twenty-five

I pick up a wage packet then we're off to Cornwall on bikes. I'm riding the moose's and we're up at 4.A.M. in the rain.
This was all cunningly planned in advance of course, saving up Persil box tops for one of those two-for-the-price-of-one ticket deals and we might as well go a long distance on the freebie.
To London and accross it, train from Paddington, still ahead of the rush hour
There's a Scots girl named Natasha on the train on the way to a Southern harbour where her husband works, diving to retrieve old leftover wartime unexploded mines-
At St. Erth we ask if there's a train to St. Ives.
Well that depends on whether there are any passenjurs
He phones the train and when it trundles up he gets in and he's the guard.
And the other end he's at the gate and he's the ticket-collector.
ticket please sir
We have a chicken dinner in a pub with a free juke-box. Ah, life in the slow-lane.
twenty-six

We look up an old friend of mine in St. Ives called Malc and have a poetry shouting in a pub...
"Dark pull of the stranger's child..."
Balasingham was a dancing man...
I even wrote one myself because I had an idea this would come up.
"Penny Moore danced go-go on my chest of drawers one night, wearing just a gold anklechain..."
"...and her eyelashes curved out like aerofoils"
Janey and I go find our tent on the cliff-top.
If I was with a guy we'd probably have left the tent til dark, tried hopelessly to put it up then just crawled inside and used it as a big sleeping bag.
But with women sleep is an enjoyable pastime that must be carefully planned.
On the way up the hill it is dark except for the stars in the sky, their reflections in the sea and the glow-worms in the grass.
I pick one up and hold it in the palm of my hand.
twenty-seven

I'm doing a dance to the sun next morning when I spy a wee boat
And I'll be damned if Georgette isn't in it.
Janey's got a bee in her bonnet about the whole world this morning. She wants to change it.
You don't care about anything you're selfish!
Malcolm's poetry was "too orderly" for her. I think of an orderly snack he once served.
Well yours is probably too openly emotional for his taste.
I recall a reader at Cambridge not omitting to remind us a few times of 'the cool taste of coins'
Yes, that's what we do; repeat a potent phrase like that.
"That's what we do..." like wearing one earring or shaking hands with the fingers in funny places, Ellway atway ooday ooyay owknay.
Give me Georgette's childlike jabberings:
Often he is standing there, the rain drizzling overboard his hat...
Some people are coming along. It occurs to me to put on some clobber.
twenty eight

The way she's got the bikes packed they look like horses. I smack mine on the rump and off we go
Janey stops to sketch St. Michael's Mount.
Then Penzance and a feeling of having gotten somewhere. It's so different from the retirement village of St. Ives.
Even Malcolm went there to withdraw, suffering from a chronic inability to be interested in the rigmarole of 'making a living' in the modern world.
Now another argument. Janey's scoffing at the 'artists' painting old galleys washed up on sunset beaches for the tourist.
It's so painfully disappointing! This isn't Art!
This guy's doing pictures, that guy's doing stained pine chairs, that guy's making sandals... what's your problem with that - it's just 'making a living'.
Why do you expect the spirit of Art to always dwell in painting or poetry?
All the arguments we've ever had pop up from behind the fence saying 'there's going to be a fight' - The nude-girls-in-the-newspapers is there, also the inadequacies-of-the-Social-Services
You can't change the whole world history by ranting and raving - you've got to just concentrate on here and now.
Look, Alec, you'll see it all differently when you've got my years.
Something comes to a halt right here.
twenty nine

Back home I can't find an opportunity to get George alone to talk -
"our budgie died last week/no more will we hear his gibbering tweet/"
It's so romantic to be depressed
Amy's always beside her or behind her or in front of her.
I'm having a drink with Harwood when they come in. Janey's gone to London to sort out some business for Therese. I'd said to George if she was around I'd buy her a hamburger.
So she stomps in and says:
Buy me a hamburger then... Amy too.
NGH
Buy me the damn hamburger.
The Russian Scriabin or somebody was criticising the emotional simplism of Tchaikovsky's opera: "Romeo loved Juliet so he gave her an ice-cream"
So I buy Georgette a hamburger - and everybody else too.
Aren't you having one too?
Then I bugger off home and go to bed
thirty

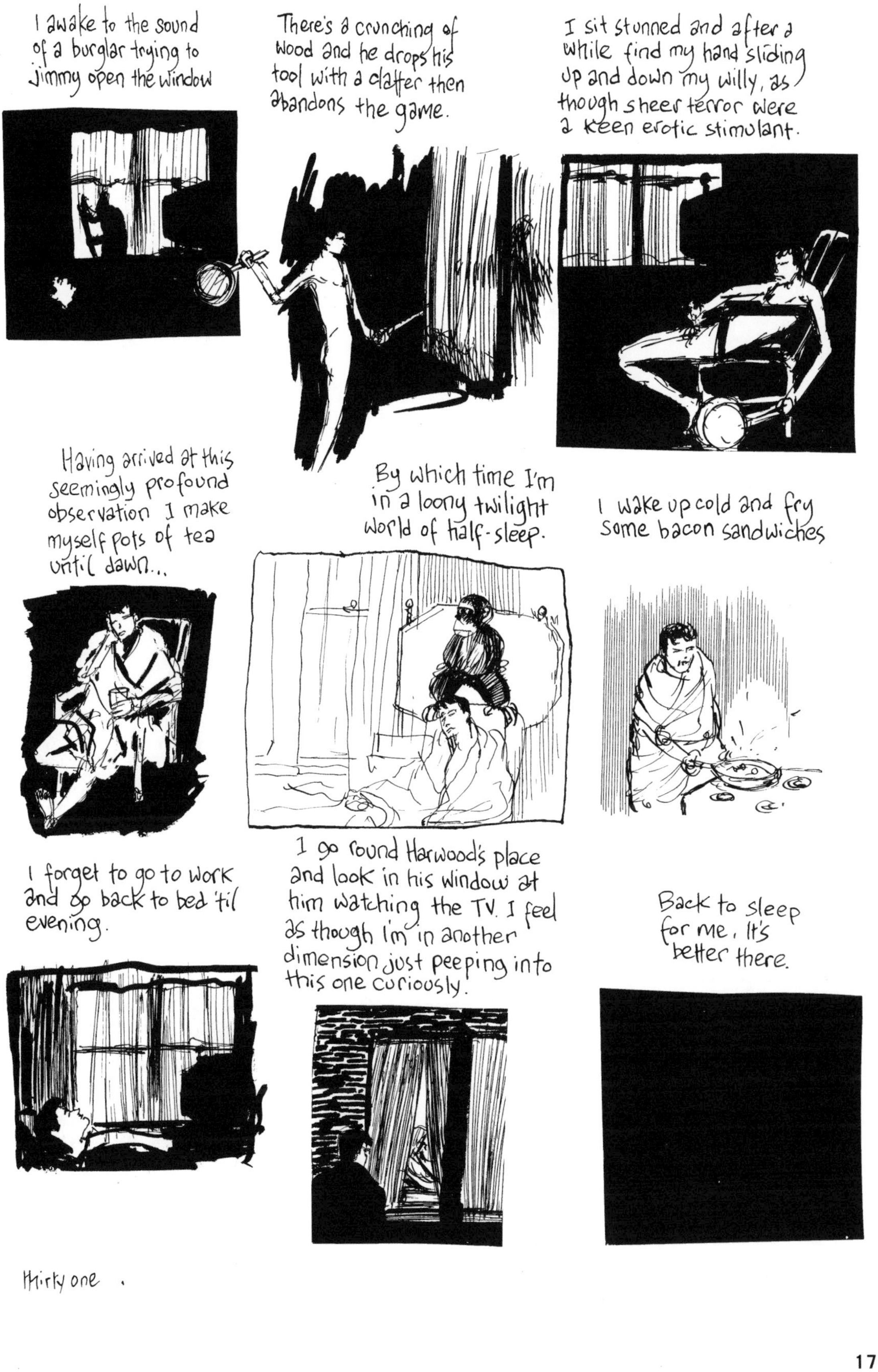
I awake to the sound of a burglar trying to jimmy open the window
There's a crunching of wood and he drops his tool with a clatter then abandons the game.
I sit stunned and after a while find my hand sliding up and down my willy, as though sheer terror were a keen erotic stimulant.
Having arrived at this seemingly profound observation I make myself pots of tea until dawn...
By which time I'm in a loony twilight world of half-sleep.
I wake up cold and fry some bacon sandwiches
I forget to go to work and go back to bed 'til evening.
I go round Harwood's place and look in his window at him watching the TV. I feel as though I'm in another dimension just peeping into this one curiously.
Back to sleep for me. It's better there.
thirty one.

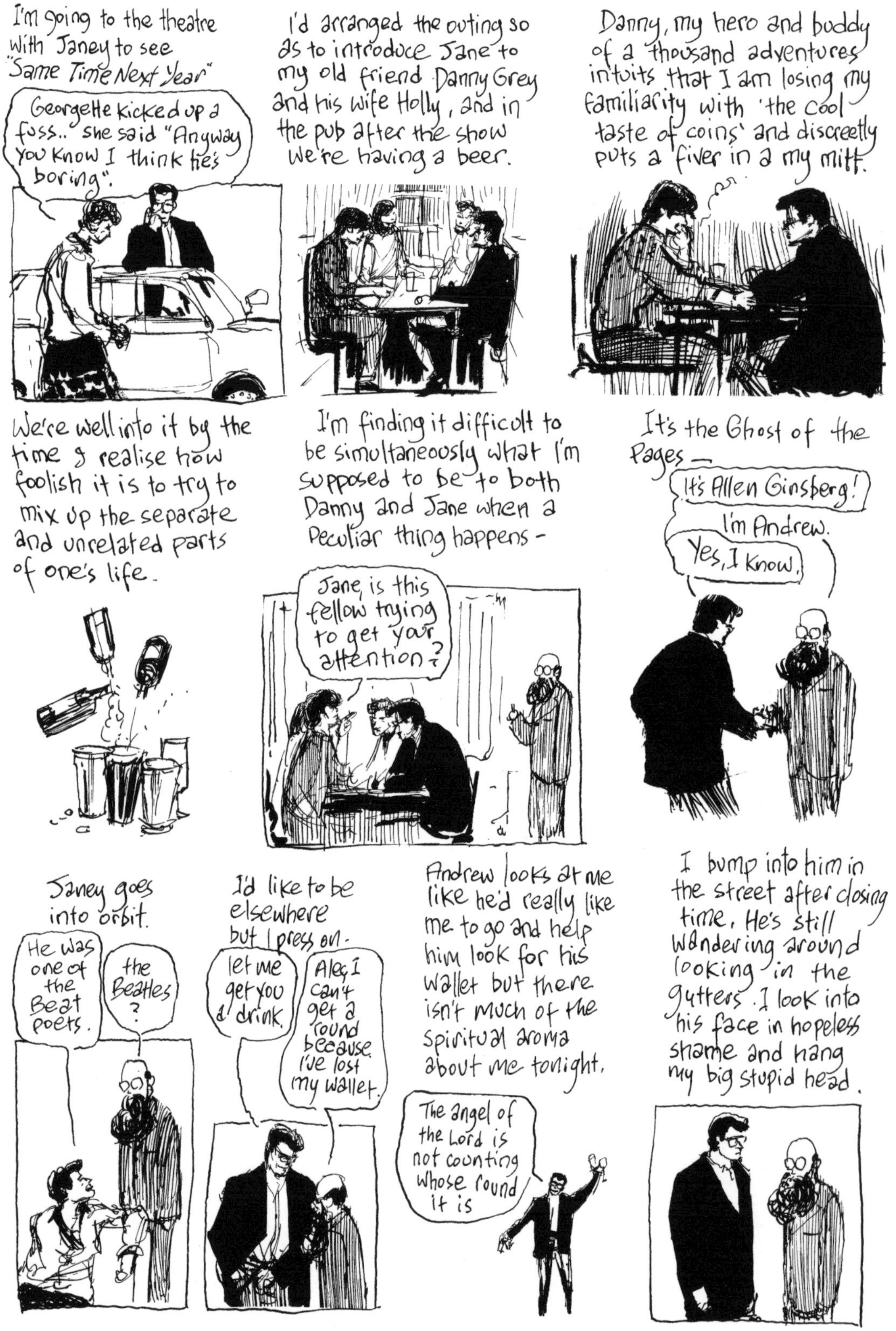
I'm going to the theatre with Janey to see "Same Time Next Year"
Georgette kicked up a fuss.. she said "Anyway you know I think he's boring".
I'd arranged the outing so as to introduce Jane to my old friend Danny Grey and his wife Holly, and in the pub after the show we're having a beer.
Danny, my hero and buddy of a thousand adventures intuits that I am losing my familiarity with 'the cool taste of coins' and discreetly puts a fiver in a my mitt.
We're well into it by the time I realise how foolish it is to try to mix up the separate and unrelated parts of one's life.
I'm finding it difficult to be simultaneously what I'm supposed to be to both Danny and Jane when a peculiar thing happens -
Jane, is this fellow trying to get your attention?
It's the Ghost of the Pages —
It's Allen Ginsberg!
I'm Andrew.
Yes, I know.
Janey goes into orbit.
He was one of the Beat poets.
the Beatles?
I'd like to be elsewhere but I press on.
let me get you a drink.
Alec, I can't get a round because I've lost my wallet.
Andrew looks at me like he'd really like me to go and help him look for his wallet but there isn't much of the spiritual aroma about me tonight.
The angel of the Lord is not counting whose round it is
I bump into him in the street after closing time. He's still wandering around looking in the gutters. I look into his face in hopeless shame and hang my big stupid head.

thirty two

Back in my little room I am only half aware of Jane telling Danny about my pal Harwood being a nihilist and they're disagreeing about the pronunciation.
Nee
Nigh
Pages turning up like that has caused a sublimely mischievous idea to form in my noodle...
Next day I find that Georgette has become even more unreachable. She has an entourage now.
Alec come in
This young guy Gerald is a budding photographer and is now on the scene.
George has become his muse or something.
It is clear to me that rampant foolishness is to be the order of the day.
I will empty all the separate jars and bottles of my life into one big pot and cook them all up into a stew.
I'll take all the characters from my other book and put them into this one. It'll be a great big cross-over.
It's time to reintroduce the KING CANUTE CROWD.
thirty three

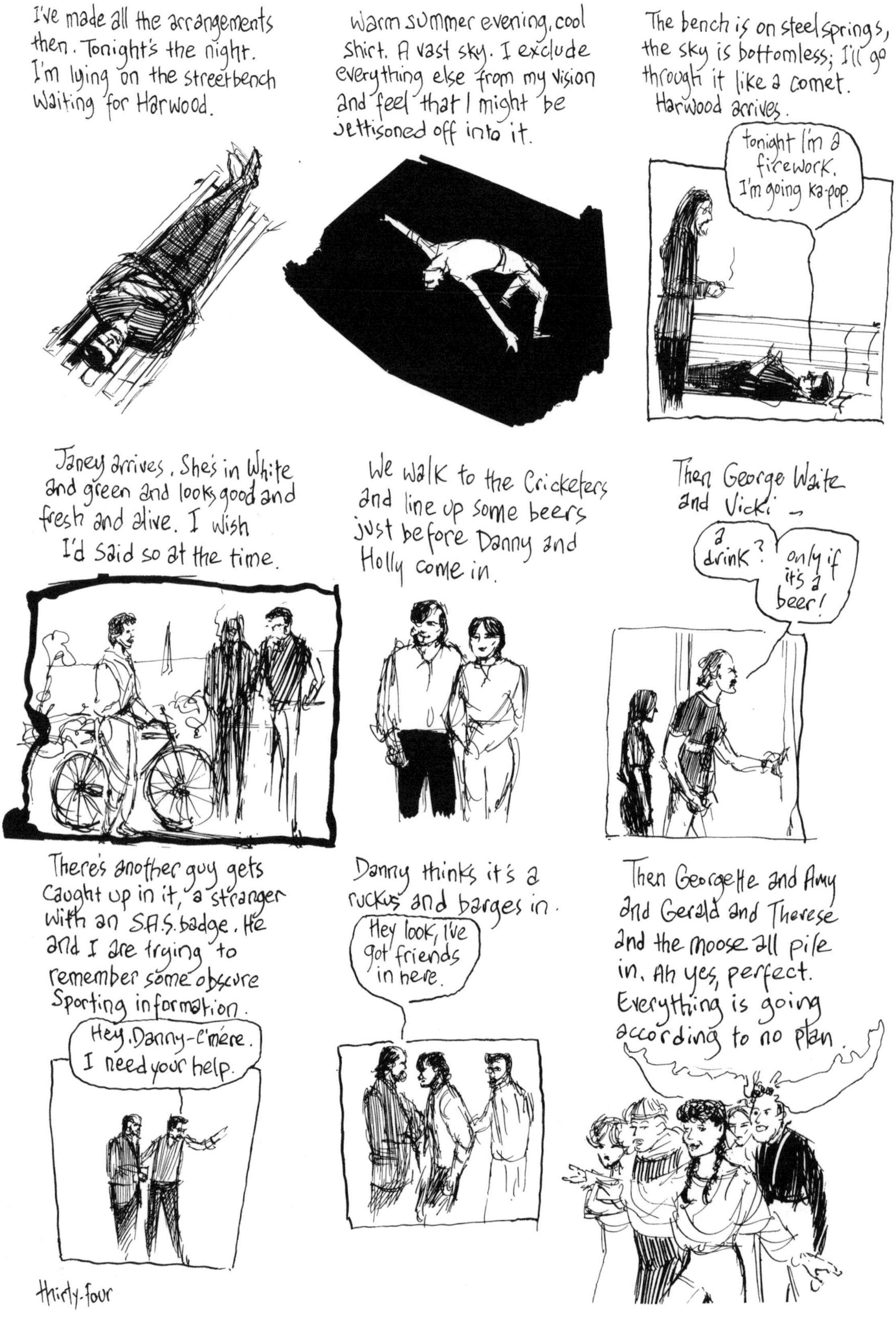
I've made all the arrangements then. Tonight's the night. I'm lying on the streetbench waiting for Harwood.
Warm summer evening, cool shirt. A vast sky. I exclude everything else from my vision and feel that I might be jettisoned off into it.
The bench is on steel springs, the sky is bottomless; I'll go through it like a comet. Harwood arrives.
tonight I'm a firework. I'm going ka-pop.
Janey arrives. She's in white and green and looks good and fresh and alive. I wish I'd said so at the time.
We walk to the Cricketers and line up some beers just before Danny and Holly come in.
Then George Waite and Vicki -
a drink?
only if it's a beer!
There's another guy gets caught up in it, a stranger with an S.A.S. badge. He and I are trying to remember some obscure sporting information.
Hey, Danny-c'mere. I need your help.
Danny thinks it's a ruckus and barges in.
Hey look, I've got friends in here.
Then Georgette and Amy and Gerald and Therese and the moose all pile in. Ah yes, perfect. Everything is going according to no plan
thirty-four

And so the night progresses swiftly to the last bell, at which point...
Everyone to my house for home made beer then?
Let's get some take-aways too.
My perception is confused. I have got it into my noodle to take care of Janey's bike while she gets a ride ahead with Danny -
George - can you give me a lift round my place to get the bike
And the guy with the S.A.S. badge is coming too, trying to keep tabs on me, thinking I'm the key to the whole barmy episode, but I lose him -
In fact, when I clamber in the back of Waite's van, it's Georgette that hops in after me.
She's barking directions to her own place.
What about the bike?
It was outside the pub - Janey's already taken it, you idiot.
And at the other end
Janey won't be here yet - I'll go and look for her
Alec, come out of there.
come on... let's go.
thirty-five

Georgette has a voice like a landslide, or a projectile, and when she calls you from the other side of the street your first impulse is to duck rather than turn. She goes
Alec, you shithead!
And when it reaches my ears it goes "Alec, you are the King of Persia"
When she tells a story she says "So he goes bla bla bla and I go woo woo woo" and Janey says "For god's sake stop saying "he goes"; it's bad English, say "he says."" But for me what Georgette says goes.
And if Georgette wants to fart, well that's music to my ears too.
George, tell me what.
I'll tell you what! I think you really fucked it up!
what did you want to go and sleep with my mother for?
Well, you didn't want to know... all those times I phoned you and you made excuses.
oh can't you see?
No, what?
I just didn't have the confidence... You know how I feel about you.
Well what do I do now? For want of any better idea I vault a six-foot wall -
thirty-six

we better not go back together.
okay
I go looning off around the block and when I come in everyone's writing more stuff on the walls, all my pals too, and Danny Grey's rubbishing Gerald's photos.
These are rubbish. I've never seen Alec look like that.
HAPPY
And I don't notice it at the time but Danny and George Waite are eagle-eyeing Harwood because they figure he's chasing Janey behind my back. ah yes! wonderful!
Alec, would you take these sandwiches into the other room, please.
Sure, Janey.
SOME
In the other room people are in sleeping bags sipping mugs of coffee. It occurs to me to haul Therese out and bite her foot.
ALEC!
Then Georgette's running out the front door to go for a moonlight swim in the sea half a mile away, and the party bursts into stars all over the night—
YAHOOOOOO..
Danny comes across me.
Get in and come home with us, Alec.
No, Danny. I'm going to walk awhile.
What the Hell's going on, mate?
Can't you see I've become a mythical beast?
Only in your own head, mate. But you have been running around at a fortyfive degree angle like you're trying to take off.
garooga
thirty-seven.

I bump into the guy with the S.A.S. badge. He was at the party at Janey's place, must have tagged along with someone else
Alec!
Is that young Georgette attached?
Isn't Jane more your age?
You've got to be kidding.
Funny, but Janey said the same thing -
Wouldn't you say that guy with the SAS badge cuts a fine figure
ugh, He's too old.
Ah, it's all nuts, the world of sex.
bedlam bedlam bedlam
what?
Well I created the night's confusion with my majiks and now I step into its slipstream and am carried along.
I have been adopting the human position for too long
I have missed the feeling of the wind in my feathers.
I flex my claws and fly home to bed.
thirty-eight.

I should have left it right there but there is something in my nature that likes to poke among the innards of the carcass.
I write my first letter to Jane, discussing the demise of our relationship in tender terms.
Of course you will not see the son and the moon discussing their relationship. Such is only for fools.
Janey replies in a sensible and orderly manner: "... You will only be hurt if you go on trying to 'touch' Georgette, I assure you. You are chasing a shadow and ignoring me as a real caring person in so doing."
I should have been on the next bus to Dimension X, but I find myself walking round to Janey's house when I spy Georgette.
George!
Have you decided what you're going to do?
Yes, I'm just going to get out.
oh no, I'm going to get the blame for this
I'll maybe come round for a cup of tea in a week or two before you all go away.
You don't sound very enthusiastic.
thirty-nine.

At the house there's a new entourage and they're all going off to a Campaign for Nuclear Disarmament meeting.
Georgette gets changed
won't you be too warm?
One has to suffer for these things.
Why so glum, Alec? Help yourself to some beer.
If we left you any.
Janey's making more beer. I feel that I've behaved badly so I run home some 3 or 4 miles to get the extra sugar that's needed.
So now we're in the pub.
Your letter made me angry
Alec, if you pursue Georgette you're headed for heart-break
You're underestimating me. I know I'll get nothing from Georgette. Alec loves Georgette, so he bought her a hamburger.
That's not love. I don't think you know what love is
You don't even know me. You've never tried to "touch" me..
I love Monet's Waterlilies but I know I can't take them out of the Tate Gallery.
FORTY

Georgette doesn't CARE about you, can't you see that?
If you think she does, why don't you ask her out. Why don't you?
Jane...
ASK GEORGETTE OUT!
I don't want to "go out" with anyone, It's too late for that. Y'know, one night I went steaming out on my own and fetched up in front of the Armada looking in the window...
...and I saw that night that the only true element of continuity in my life is me.
What a selfish attitude! You only ever think of yourself. That's why you haven't got any friends!
For some reason I become mesmerized by these statements as though my boiler's being stoked.
If you think you and Georgette have got something between you...
Far from being abashed, I feel a new head of steam coming on:-
ASK HER OUT!
Forty-one.

As we leave the pub I'm warming to the absurdity of it: that huge and noble concept, Love, is reduced in the modern world to 'going out', and Romeo is stuck indoors with his ice-cream melting.

Fate sticks its oar in right at this point. As we walk unevenly past Gerry's Nosh hamburger stall, a drunk separates himself from the throng and punches me in the gut.

Yes, fate has its messengers waiting on life's street corners to deliver their life-changing instructions, Drunks like this bozo and Jimmy Fulton, and dogs too, and cats and packing cases and god knows what.

GERRYS NOSH
TAKE AWAY FOOD

Well that's it. I start to laugh the most raucous fearsome howling hooting laugh.

YEE Hoo HA.

Janey lays into the dumb bastard.

Then she turns, crying, while I'm laughing to the moon:

I'll come round for my books
Hoo

She runs off.

IT JUST GETS YA HERE EH

And I find myself in the quiet cold dark night. I really am alone now.

The wind stirs my feathers a little

Forty-two.

Immediately I get back to my room I round up Janey's books, throw in some of my own and take them round to her.
Therese is consoling her when I come in. Her theory is that Janey's too intense
Ah, don't change
And there we sit, among the graffiti
IS THE HAPPY HOUSE FALLING DOWN THE HILL
Janey's sold the house and got a new one up north and made only a tiny profit on the deal, not enough to get her through university with comfort –
HEY JANEY
A couple of weeks after this and summer's on its last legs.
HOW ARE THINGS?
Life's always tough, Janey, I said stupidly, not knowing the half of it then.
You'll need some help then
So I'm helping clean the place before they move out of my life.
AND I'M ON THE BOTTOM
I'm scraping the paper in the kitchen when I find myself immersed in a little poem.
Forty three.

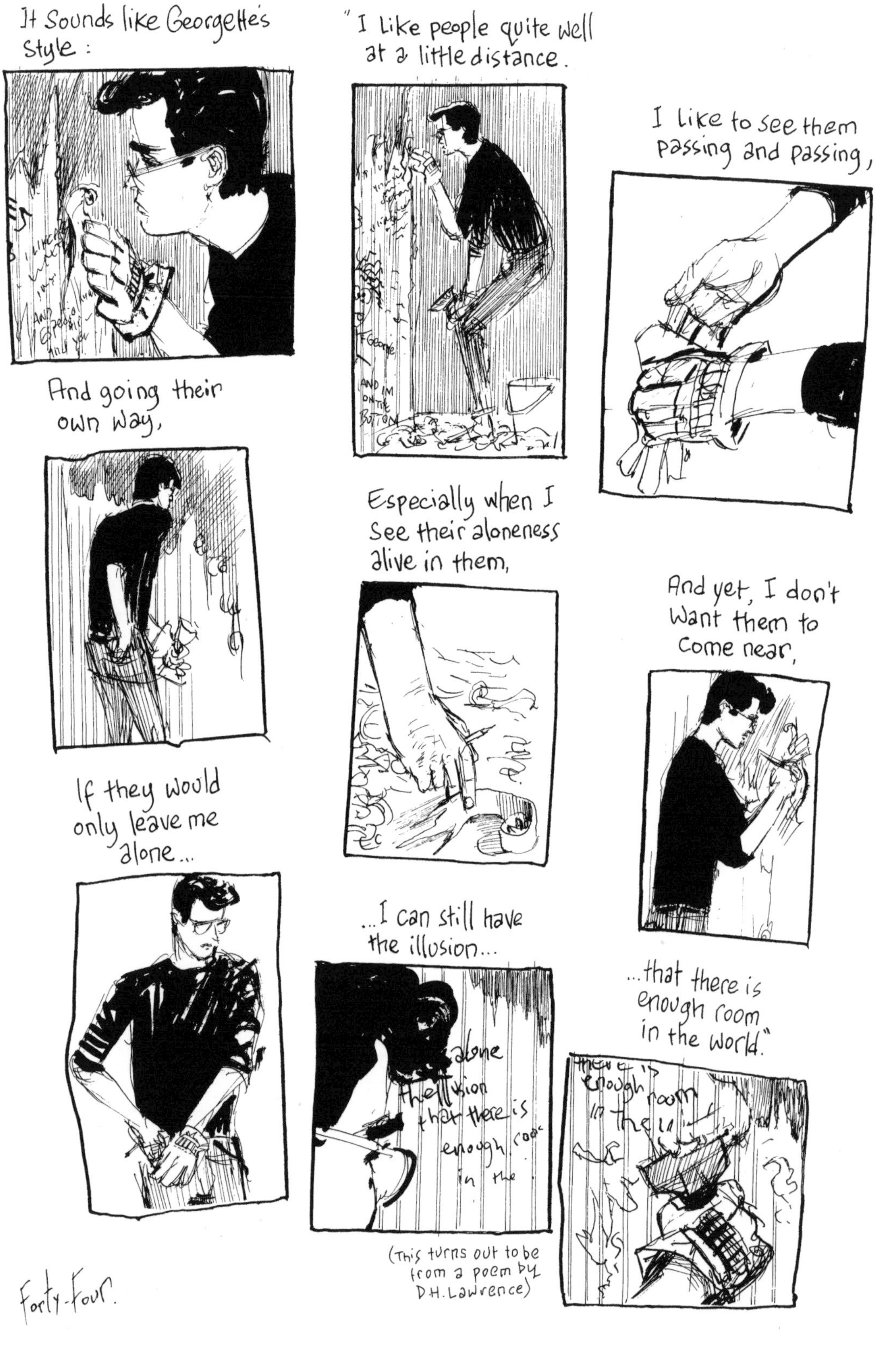
It Sounds like Georgette's Style :
"I like people quite well at a little distance.
I like to see them passing and passing,
And going their own way,
Especially when I See their aloneness alive in them,
And yet, I don't Want them to come near,
If they would only leave me alone...
...I can still have the illusion...
...that there is enough room in the world."
(This turns out to be from a poem by D.H. Lawrence)
Forty-Four.

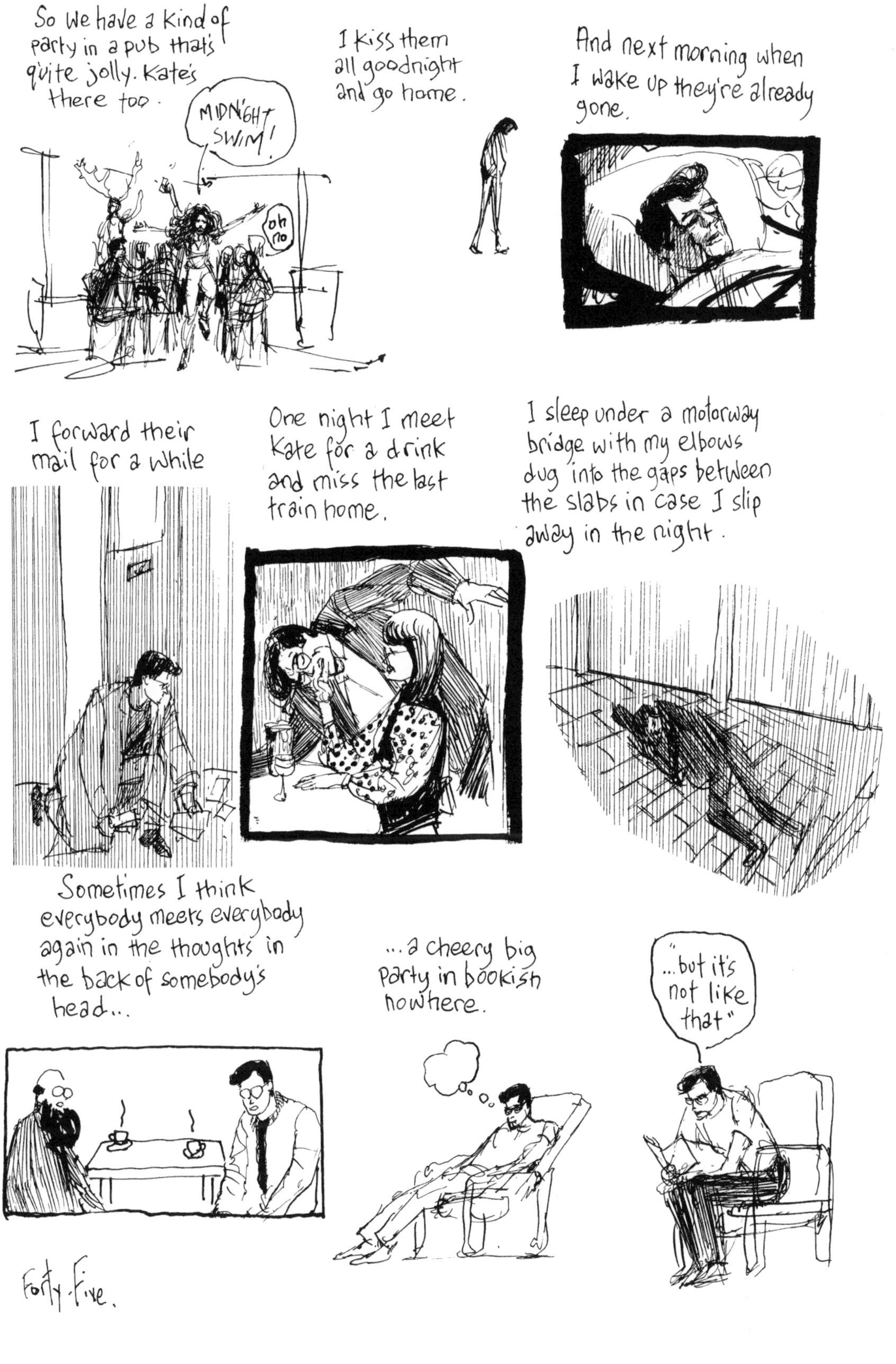
So we have a kind of party in a pub that's quite jolly. Kate's there too.
MIDNIGHT SWIM!
oh no
I kiss them all goodnight and go home.
And next morning when I wake up they're already gone.
I forward their mail for a while
One night I meet Kate for a drink and miss the last train home.
I sleep under a motorway bridge with my elbows dug into the gaps between the slabs in case I slip away in the night.
Sometimes I think everybody meets everybody again in the thoughts in the back of somebody's head...
...a cheery big party in bookish nowhere.
"...but it's not like that"
Forty-Five.

"And sometimes I remember grey English weather when the rain beat on the bus shelter and you leaned against me."
"And sometimes I caught a glimpse of your face and knew that I would never see it again."
(Edwin Morgan)
I go see Danny and I've got no money and no work.
He takes me to the Bullocks and orders beer.
And when I come back from the toilet, a steak dinner has turned up too
Get stuck in, mate.
Aw man
I go see Harwood and we plan great artistic works
I hope you put Danny right about Jane and me.
Can you imagine trying to put Danny right about something?
But one night I sit in my room and just burst into tears.
Forty Six.

I don't want to be getting into a sentimental slough so I phone Penny Moore. It's about four months since we broke up.
Meeting her again is stupid, because she's off with another guy now and her mind is set on that course
But a little incident takes place that must be told here.
PUBLIC BAR
I turn up at the pub where she's working and chat with her over the bar when she's not serving customers.
I really don't know if I seriously wanted to "re-open the wound" as she puts it but here I stand.
After they close she'll have a coffee with me, just to be agreeable.
So I'm waiting outside in the car-park when a bozo comes up and says:
Are you waiting for Joanne?
I said are you waitin..
Forty-Seven.

Hey, Fuckface, I said are you waitin—
c'mere.
I bang the daft bugger's head on the ground a couple of times then people start rushing out.
I bang his head again and laugh about it.
Alec! Don't hurt him.
HA!
HAHA- but I fully intend to hurt him.
Well give me your glasses in case they get broken.
That little moment makes me laugh all the harder and I bang the idiot's head again for good measure.
DONK.
Mythical
HOO HA.
BU-DONK.
Truly mythical
GARROOGAA!.
Forty-Eight

E.C.
FliCK

Shorts

CHARLIE
©
E Campbell

There exist in my archives a number of short pieces that relate to the main body of the 'Alec' work. Usually they didn't make it into one of the books because they were superfluous, but sometimes it was just because they were too stylistically odd. Here are a couple of those orphans. *The Crow* was drawn for a magazine that never came about, and it was subsequently adopted by Escape magazine. *How To Avoid Sex* was made for an anthology whose purpose was a healthy open discussion of sex for fourteen-year-olds. The editors rejected it (in horror). I used it somewhere else but can no longer recall where.

The Crow
Eddie Campbell © 3.86.
I HOPE YOU GET ALONG WITH MY FATHER CHARLIE
OH, I DONT SEE WHY WE SHOULDN'T GET ALONG LIKE THE COLORADO RAPIDS
HE LOOKS LIKE MY KIND OF MAN - WE'RE CHIPS OUT OF THE SAME PAN -
RIGHT, LET'S GO THEN!
AH, YOU'VE ARRIVED, SUZIE.
HELLO, MUM - THIS IS CHARLIE
HELLO, SUZIE'S MUM.. OH FRABJOUS JOY
GO ON THROUGH AND MEET SUZIE'S DAD
?
FLUTTER
FLUTTER
DAD, THIS IS CHARLIE
HELLO, MR. CAMPBELL - WE HAVE SO MUCH IN COMMON -
.. MAY I CALL YOU CAMBO
DRAP DEAD.

I'LL SHOW YOU TO YOUR ROOM CHARLIE
ODEER, THIS IS BAD
YOU MUST TRY TO BE FRIENDLY WITH DAD AT DINNER, CHARLIE
CERTAINLY MY SWEET- IF IT WILL MAKE YOU HAPPY
HERE'S THE CHEESE BOARD
AH! STILTON! OH, BRIE ~ MY SWEET AUNT ETHEL - IT'S DANISH BLUE!
OH, MRS CAMPBELL, YOU KNOW HOW TO MAKE HAPPY TUMMIES
SLICE IT CHARLIE SLICE IT
PSST
OH, LIEBFRAUMILCH! HOW EXQUISITE
WHO'S BEEN SWIPIN BLUDDY LUMPS AFF THE CHEESE?

DAD - YOU MUST MAKE THE EFFORT TO LIKE CHARLIE - I MANAGED IT
WHY DON'T YOU ASK HIM OUT FOR A DRINK
CHARRRULS - HOW WOULD YOU LIKE TO GO OUT FOR A DRINK?
OH, MR CAMPBELL - I KNEW YOU'D LIKE ME REALLY - I KNEW WE'D GET ALONG JUST FINE -
I'D LOVE TO GO OUT FOR A DRINK
GOOD - CUZ AH'M STAYIN' IN
LATER
YOUR MOVE MR CAMPBELL
Daily Telegraph
CHECKMATE
Daily Telegraph
SOOZIE - COME AND HELP ME LAY THE TABLE
MRS CAMPBELL! WHAT CAN I DO? WHAT CAN I DO?
YOU CAN BOIL YER HEAD!

SNAP
SNAP
GOODBYE, MR CAMPBELL
GOODBYE, MRS CAMPBELL
THANKS FOR HAVING ME.
CAW
END

How to Avoid SEX
by Eddie Campbell 5/90.
In the days before AIDS confused the issue, the most frightening thing about sex...
...was SEX ITSELF.
In a sophisticated mode we might describe it as a fear of losing control of a situation after submitting to INTIMACY...
...a fear of leaving oneself vulnerable.
Perhaps we should call it STAGE FRIGHT- the result of a natural shyness only blushing virgins should rightly possess.
And we don't want anyone to know, of course.
But the bottom line is...
Sometimes sex is just...
spooky

There are many legitimate subterfuges in which one might engage in order to avoid the awful moment of truth.
The simplest is of course TELEPHONUS INTERRUPTUS-
It's uncanny how you can depend on hearing that ugly jangle...
... just as you were about to nervously put...it...in.
Closely related is DOORBELL.. in which a friend turns up with two litres of wine and you curse him volubly later when alone with your lover...
...even though you breathed an inaudible sigh of relief at the time.
The lady need never know that your ejaculation was imminent.
OUCH! MY HERNIA. requires considerable dramatic talent_
But I will attempt it for THY sake.
I wouldst not hear of it, my sweet.
...while more complex and challenging black-belt manoeuvres include:-
I've received a telepathic communication saying my mother just died.

That is all fine and good when the subject is operating in his own territory
On the other hand, when he is...uh...as they say...stepping out...
He must depend upon multifarious unrelated threads of fate to extricate him from his predicament-
This throws the whole game into MIND OVER MATTER levels beyond the range of the novice.
The subject of today's case history is one Alec MacGarry.
...who along with his bosom companion of many comic strip adventures, Danny Grey, is entertained in the female lair by two young ladies.
Danny Grey must go to the bathroom...
...where he finds himself, as one often does, performing an unscheduled bowel movement.
Seeing strength in numbers, the girls become more aggressive.

Tempus fidgets, if you will permit me a little bon mot.
Alec wonders what has happened to Danny Grey.
And what happened is as follows...
Having deposited his excrements in the porcelain...
He notices the disturbing absence of toilet paper.
oh bugger
He searches here...
...there...
...scratches here...
...Resolves to use face flannel.

He uses said flannel to near satisfaction...
...but is horrified to find that it WILL NOT FLUSH AWAY!
After three or four attempts he decides to just hoy it out the window—
He strides back into the main room...
Alec was by this time in an advanced state of nervous confusion.
Liberato est sum tomato.
Come on Alec- we're leaving
He departs the scene knowing that he has played this one on a truly transcendental level.
Next week on PSYCHOLOGY TODAY we examine why whales beach themselves..
Thank you and good night from me, Professor Bean—
puff puff puff

how to be an artist

I took a notion to try writing the next book in the second person singular, future perfect tense, and see how far I could get before screwing up. I think I made it all the way. I took up the idea, first tried in *The Dead Muse* (which comes later in the chronology), of weaving pictorial 'quotes' from the work of my contemporaries into the argument, which is as tricky as you'd think. The chapters were drawn consecutively for appearance in the quarterly (then bi-monthly) anthology titled *Deevee*, between June 1997 and April 2000, usually close to publication date (see notes at end of this volume).

I remain fond of the back cover blurb that Mick Evans and I composed for the original publication in book form in 2001: *"Campbell has created a graphic novel about the rise and fall of the graphic novel itself... It is about making your way in the world as an artist. The narrative teems with figures who are or would be artists. Many are briefly examined while a few have been made the subjects of penetrating case histories in this cavalcade of dreamers, fools and sudden millionaires."*

Having come by a couple of new incidents and insights since the previous publication of the book, I wanted to add them into the narrative but have restrained myself and settled for a two-page post-script in the same style.

You might want to observe that several notable individuals of the comic strip art, who make an appearance in this book, have since died, including Will Eisner, Stan Drake, Hugo Pratt, Harvey Kurtzman, Don Lawrence, Claude Moliterni, Dennis Gifford and Alan Gaulton, who was the unnamed driver on page 204.

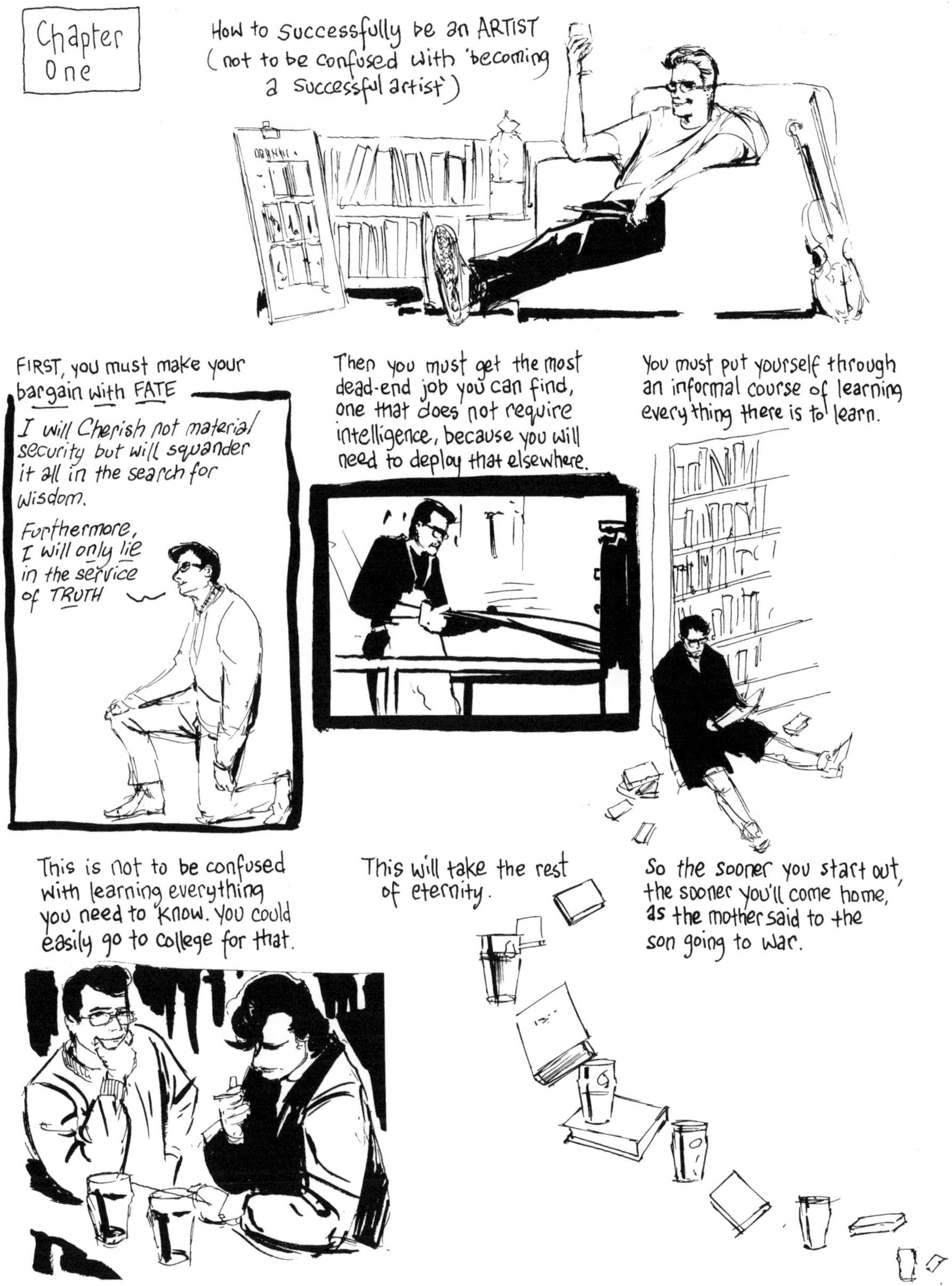
Chapter One
How to successfully be an ARTIST (not to be confused with 'becoming a successful artist')
FIRST, you must make your bargain with FATE
I will Cherish not material security but will squander it all in the search for wisdom.
Furthermore, I will only lie in the service of TRUTH
Then you must get the most dead-end job you can find, one that does not require intelligence, because you will need to deploy that elsewhere.
You must put yourself through an informal course of learning everything there is to learn.
This is not to be confused with learning everything you need to know. You could easily go to college for that.
This will take the rest of eternity.
So the sooner you start out, the sooner you'll come home, as the mother said to the son going to war.

Once you have made your decision you may wait a while for the change to fall upon you from heaven.
However, your cue to step out onto the stage will be clear and precise. One day the pointless job will finish. The factory will close down
From that moment you may confidently describe yourself as an ARTIST Do not be deterred.
You. mean an unemployed one!
HA HA HA.
At your own small expense put your work where it will be seen and continue to be seen. It's the age of the photocopier. Quality reproduction is available to all.
FLICK
FLICK
In direct consequence, one day a letter will arrive in the mail.
Alec MacGarry Westcliff Parade Southend-on-Sea Essex
This will be your communication from The Man at the Crossroads.
He will not be a practitioner, but an 'amateur'. If you expected someone experienced and with a sphere of influence, you obviously don't know how these things work. If you get someone like that, you can't be very deep.
He need not be aware that FATE has already assigned him a title, nor need you for that matter. Like yourself he has been freed up for his purpose. That's all that matters.
TELEPHONE
TELEPHONE
He will be the purest, most fresh-faced wee fellow you have ever met. His ingenuous enthusiasm will beam from his cheery countenance.

The man at the Crossroads will open the next door.
You see, I run a table at the bi-monthly comic marts in Westminster. I invite anybody to put their homemade comic on it, all takings to the producer.
You will undoubtedly ask what he gets out of it. such cynicism should be considered a lapse of faith in the bargain you made with FATE. You will only be permitted three such lapses.
sorry
You'll reach a bigger audience than the thirty people who are reading you in the Amateur Press Association
Furthermore, you'll meet other artists whom you see to be on a similar mission of TRUTH, and you'll tell them so.
Hey, can you do me a two pager for my comic, Phil?
yeh, great! can you do me one?
Once started, things will move faster than you expected. your little show will get a write-up in the hip music press.
Page 32 — New Musical Express 29th May, 1982
FINE PRINT, Cafeteria-Style
NME
NEW MUSICAL EXPRESS
The "birds of the air" will fly in from north, south east, west. A veritable small press movement will be underway.
Dear Alec
I am thrilled that you liked my little comic. In fact, it was your story in Fast Fiction #2 which inspired me to print it myself...
You will have no trouble separating the innovators from the novelty-hunters.
I don't want Alec in our comic after this issue. He's too conservative, all his pictures in neat little boxes.
That will be a recurrent theme; Guys with one eye on the coolometer And myopic guys, diletantes, pretenders, complete wankers, sweethearts, boy geniuses. They'll all traffic past you.
FAST FICTION

Ilya, the entrepreneur in this realm of D.I.Y. publishing: every nihilist young pencil's connected and he's the wiring.

Biff, role model, antecedent: he's manufacturing his cartoons onto t-shirts, drinking mugs and postcards and hawking them from a street-market stall at Camden Lock.

A mysterious, nameless religious nut's pamphlet tells us vitamins are an alien invasion from outer space.

Get schoolmasterish Lock to review your comic in his fanzine. He writes it all under pseudonyms like Christine Padgett, and his masterpiece, Reg Uspatoff.

Myra will turn up with her venomous little punky vicious characters. She's the opposite.

Miss March
© Myra Hancock

The guy who can't draw but is in great demand because he can drive and pick up boxes from the printer. (Real artists are useless in that department). He'll do a comic called CRIME with a micro-comic freebie insert called PETTY CRIME. Everybody's got at least one good idea.

People you never meet but whose work you keep an eye on over the years, like Helen Cusack, who's always being lumped in with the feminist crowd: you'll come across one of her books in a remainder-shop years later in Australia.

© Cusack
INCENSED NUDES (AFTER PICASSO)
Helen Cusack

"What's she doing now?" you'll ask.

Mail Art will be in for a while. An entity designating himself BU TO SA HO sends out postcard-sized cuttings from huge billboards.

Somebody will use a highlighter pen to attract eyes to a cover blurb and suddenly hand-coloured covers are the thing. Ilya will help you do a run of 350 copies, several colours plus strokes of tippex correction white. You're an artist. Things are flying this way and that. Every month you've got at least one story in print. You won't even remember half of it.

It is essential that in the middle of all this you meet your future wife.

FATE will land her from Australia in the middle of the London tube strike.

You can impress her by jumping on and off buses in a system that no visitor can ever comprehend.

Wind up at the WORLD'S END in Chelsea and play the juke box. Whatever's on there will have to be "our song" forever. So choose quickly, but wisely.

ONLY YOU

Life is sure to get very ramshackle from here on. Annie will be sleeping on a friend's floor in Earl's Court. (your brother's girl friend's)

Then she'll be sharing a bedsit room with a cousin of that friend, a bloke.

Three of his pals will arrive from Australia and they'll all sleep on the floor of the single room. Merry Christmas.

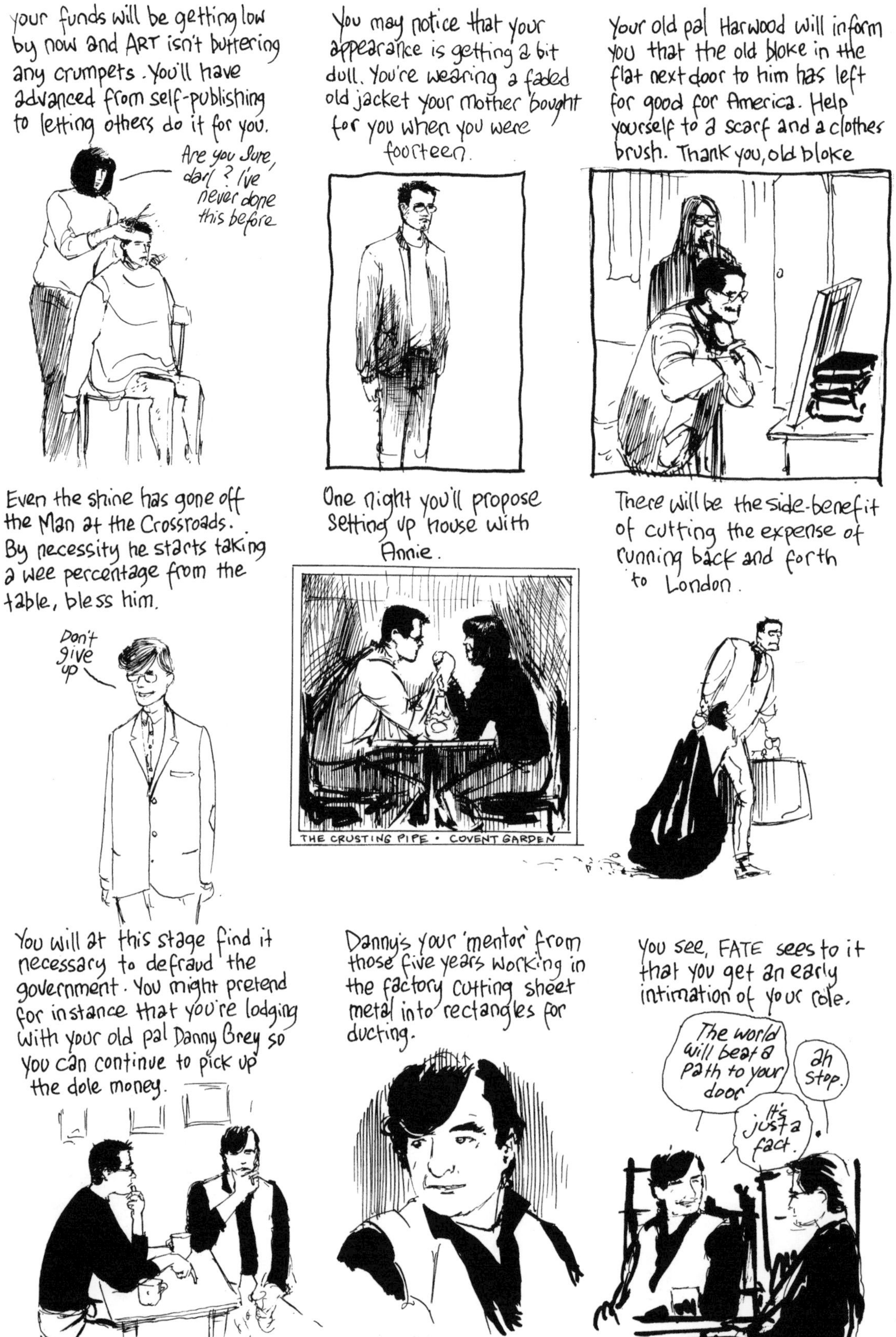
your funds will be getting low by now and ART isn't buttering any crumpets. You'll have advanced from self-publishing to letting others do it for you.
Are you sure, darl? I've never done this before
You may notice that your appearance is getting a bit dull. You're wearing a faded old jacket your mother bought for you when you were fourteen.
Your old pal Harwood will inform you that the old bloke in the flat next door to him has left for good for America. Help yourself to a scarf and a clothes brush. Thank you, old bloke
Even the shine has gone off the Man at the Crossroads. By necessity he starts taking a wee percentage from the table, bless him.
Don't give up
One night you'll propose setting up house with Annie.
THE CRUSTING PIPE • COVENT GARDEN
There will be the side-benefit of cutting the expense of running back and forth to London.
You will at this stage find it necessary to defraud the government. You might pretend for instance that you're lodging with your old pal Danny Grey so you can continue to pick up the dole money.
Danny's your 'mentor' from those five years working in the factory cutting sheet metal into rectangles for ducting.
You see, FATE sees to it that you get an early intimation of your role.
The world will beat a path to your door
ah stop.
It's just a fact.

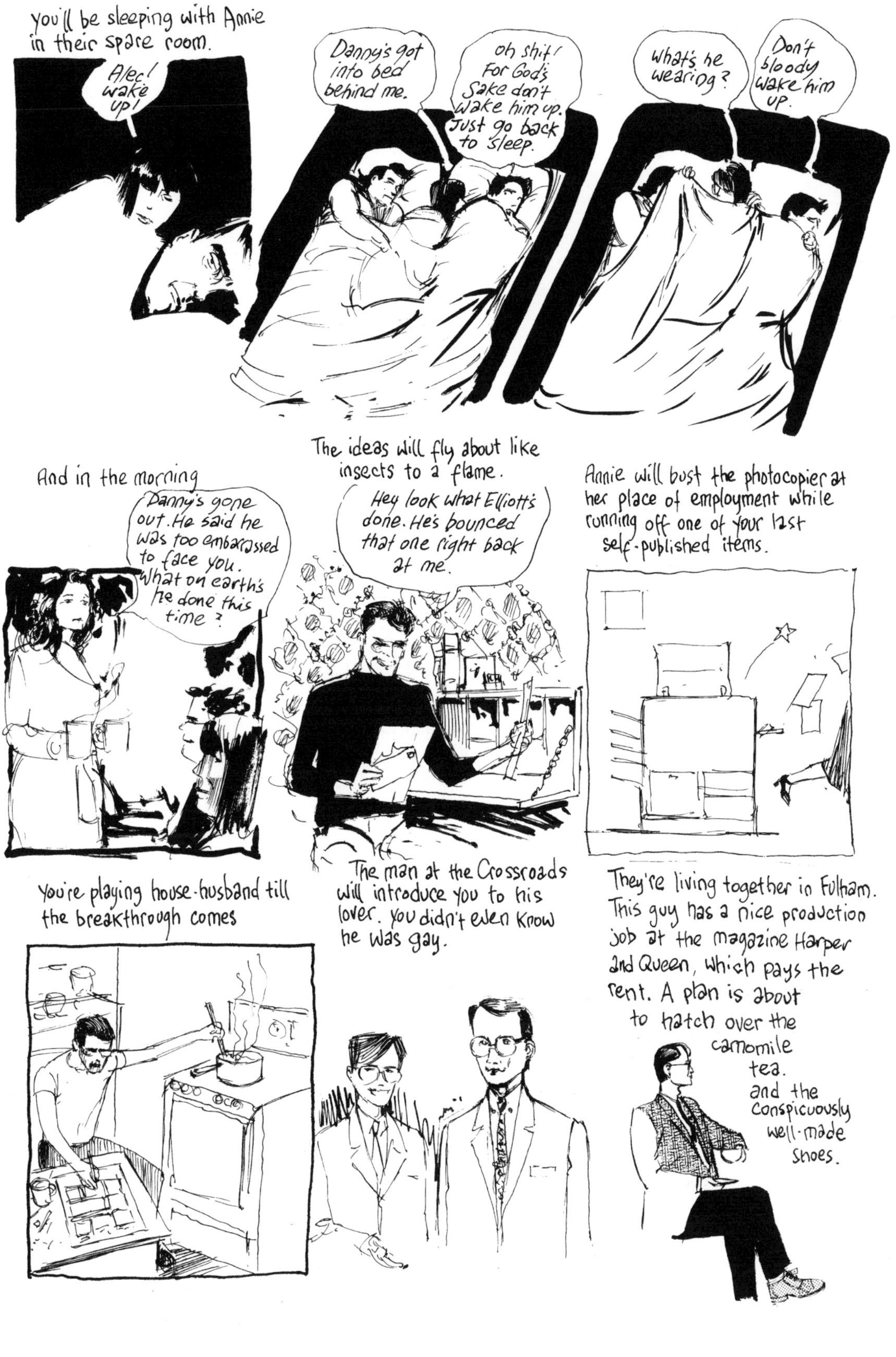

You'll be sleeping with Annie in their spare room.
Alec! wake up!
Danny's got into bed behind me.
oh shit! For God's sake don't wake him up. Just go back to sleep.
What's he wearing?
Don't bloody wake him up.
And in the morning
Danny's gone out. He said he was too embarrassed to face you. What on earth's he done this time?
The ideas will fly about like insects to a flame.
Hey look what Elliott's done. He's bounced that one right back at me.
Annie will bust the photocopier at her place of employment while running off one of your last self-published items.
You're playing house-husband till the breakthrough comes
The man at the Crossroads will introduce you to his lover. you didn't even know he was gay.
They're living together in Fulham. This guy has a nice production job at the magazine Harper and Queen, which pays the rent. A plan is about to hatch over the camomile tea.
and the conspicuously well-made shoes.

It will be an ambitious plan, to be sure.
We'll publish a magazine
From right here in our rented bedsit.
They will corral all the talent and promise of the Fast Fiction table and put it in a magazine which they will launch in the new year.
A showcase for yourself, Elliott... those who are doing work of real value
They're rounding it up from hither and yon. You didn't know so much was happening...
And others I haven't had time to introduce to you yet. I'm meeting new people every week. I'm certain that we're on the verge of something important.
Designy typography stuff like Rian Hughes is doing...
© R. Hughes
...or Shaky Kane's hip funny stuff...
WILD BILL BURROUGHS
by Shaky Kane
SINCE THE FINAL ACADEMY, I'M GETTING THE RECOGNITION I DESERVE!
I THOUGHT JACK BENNY WAS DEAD...
© Shaky Kane
...or Savage Pencil's graphic spittle
MY FAVORIT TOO. A TONIC FOR ONES BOWELLS! ALWAYS...
LOOK MATE I THINK YOU OUGHT TO KNOW THAT I THINK YOU'RE A BIG JAKOFF A POSIN' PILLUK. AN' I'M A FRAUD I AINT VORTY AT ALL I'M JUST A REGULAR INSECURE KINDA GUY WITH NOTHIN' BETTA TO DO THAN FOLLA FASHION!!
© Pencil
It's the early '80s It's Thatcher's Britain
YAHOO
You run through Epping Forest in the nude (after Annie)
You're an artist, after all

So what in blazes is it anyway ?
Chapter Two
Art.
I don't mean: is this Art ?
THE EXHAUSTED SOLDIERS, SLEEPLESS FOR FIVE AND SIX DAYS AT A TIME, ALWAYS HUNGRY FOR DECENT CHOW, SUFFERING FROM THE TROPICAL FUNGUS INFECTIONS, KEPT FIGHTING!
TAKKA TAKKA
© Roy Lichtenstein.
And is this not ?
ON GUADALCANAL, THE EXHAUSTED MARINES, SLEEPLESS FOR FIVE AND SIX DAYS AT A TIME, ALWAYS HUNGRY FOR DECENT CHOW, SUFFERING FROM THE TROPICAL FUNGUS INFECTIONS, KEPT ON FIGHTING!
TAKKA TAKKA
© prob. D.C. Comics
It's all bloody aRt as far as you're concerned, Alec MacGarry
And the question is a semantic splitting of hairs, as mighty Alan Moore will say, more or less
Whether he will speak it or write it is not likely to be later recalled.
But what is it made of ? How does it happen ? A person, the artist, sees or hears a thing in his or her brain and strives to make it exist outside of there. simple.
?
But how did it get in there and arrange itself just so, the stuff in his or her noggin, presuming it wasn't lifted wholesale from somebody else like with that writer who had to give her prize back.

You will have cultivated your own chosen little plants on the great plains of the past and present, little shoots among the grass and the big world hardly even knows the grass is there
The shoots connect by fragile root systems one to another and then to yourself, informing a particular vision of the world.
Astonishing. Why does nobody else see it just so.?
One day you will spy somebody else watering the same wee shoots.
HEY, YOU!
And all your youthful idealism will burst out in a great big lovely messy salad.
Status Quo will raise objection to the sloppy lack of discipline among ye young opstarts, as tho the small press were a matter for consumer debate, like bus timetables. (How perceptive to see a threat so far off)
I don't agree with the proposition that if a story is true there is no need to make it convincing
He'll probably be only at the beginning of his own career, otherwise he wouldn't even be aware of your existence, but at this stage of your life, anyone who's made a living at it for a year and a half is an old pro.
But somebody's got to play Darth Vader.
It will strike you as odd, his unflinching willingness to adopt the reactionary point of view, artistic suicide in this Age of the neurosis of innovation.
This guy's a larf.
Doesn't he know that posterity pillories such types indiscriminately. Better to read your grocery list on stage,
He obviously doesn't know you like I do.
or go down Main Street chained back to back with three other people. The Frat initiation has hijacked art.
ART
For the love of Beta Zeta Pi
HU

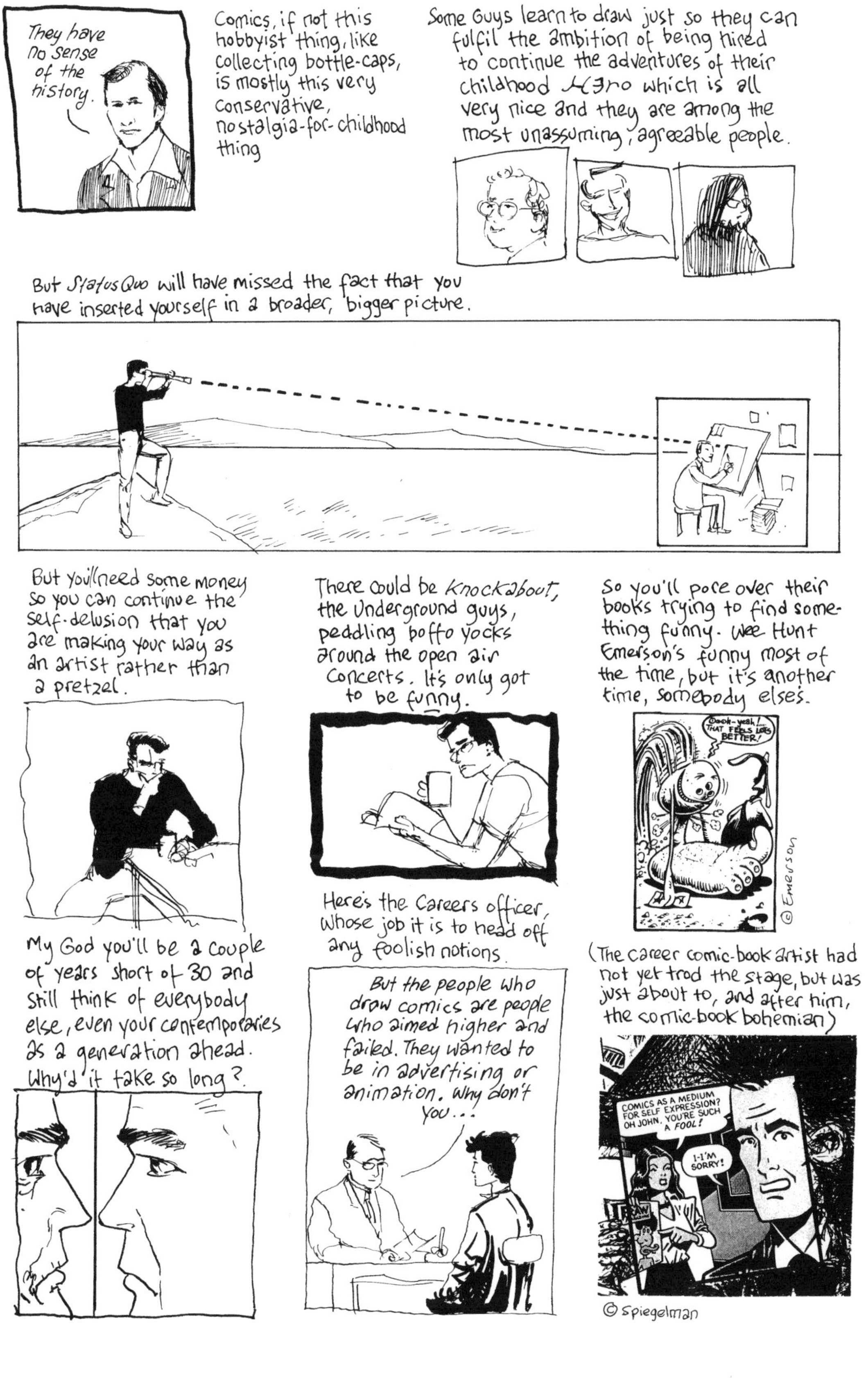
They have no sense of the history.
Comics, if not this hobbyist thing, like collecting bottle-caps, is mostly this very conservative, nostalgia-for-childhood thing
Some Guys learn to draw just so they can fulfil the ambition of being hired to continue the adventures of their childhood Hero which is all very nice and they are among the most unassuming, agreeable people.
But Status Quo will have missed the fact that you have inserted yourself in a broader, bigger picture.
But you'll need some money so you can continue the self-delusion that you are making your way as an artist rather than a pretzel.
There could be Knockabout, the Underground guys, peddling boffo yocks around the open air concerts. It's only got to be funny.
So you'll pore over their books trying to find something funny. Wee Hunt Emerson's funny most of the time, but it's another time, somebody else's.
Oooh-yeah!... THAT FEELS LOTS BETTER!
© Emerson
My God you'll be a couple of years short of 30 and still think of everybody else, even your contemporaries as a generation ahead. Why'd it take so long?
Here's the Careers officer, whose job it is to head off any foolish notions.
But the people who draw comics are people who aimed higher and failed. They wanted to be in advertising or animation. Why don't you...
(The career comic-book artist had not yet trod the stage, but was just about to, and after him, the comic-book bohemian)
COMICS AS A MEDIUM FOR SELF EXPRESSION? OH JOHN, YOU'RE SUCH A FOOL!
I-I'M SORRY!
© Spiegelman

Arch bohemian Spiegelman will have just started serializing his Maus in the U.S.A., after spending most of the seventies editing novelties for a bubble-gum co. The Man at the Crossroads will compel you to read it.
Alec, when I got home the other day I realized you paid for the lunch, so I got you the new RAW.
HA! you're a man with a mission
RAW
Alan Moore will be the great anomaly. He'll be caught up with the HƎro boys at this stage.
I'M BACK
© Moore-Leach
But he is to be an artist of high merit. He will have started by selling the weekly Maxwell the Magic Cat to his local paper, the Northants Post, under the name Jill de Ray, a 'frustrated bitch' according to one reader.
YOU THINK IT NEEDS MORE SEX, THEN?
YEAH.
© Moore
As Curt Vile he will have added to that a half-page spot in the weekly national rock paper SOUNDS, sharing the page with Savage Pencil
I HATE IT! I GET SICK JUST THINKING ABOUT IT!
I REALLY, REALLY HATE IT! YOU DON'T KNOW HOW MUCH I HATE IT!!
THIS IS THE BIT I HATE...
THE IMMOLATO TOMATO IS RELEASED!!
© Moore
For a laugh Vile and Pencil will have swapped places for one week. Pencil will have continued Vile's characters admirably but Vile will have killed off all the charges entrusted to him.
CYARK!! ALL MY WONDERFUL LITTLE CARIKTURS...DEAD!! I DON'T BELIEVE IT! I'M RUINED! SAY IT ISN'T TRUE!!
HEH HEH... UH... CHEER UP, SAVS!! OL' NYARLATHOTEP THE CRAWLING CHAOS HERE JUST TOLD ME A GREAT RECIPE FOR "SHOGGOTH VOL-AU-VENTS"!!
TH-TH-THAT'S ARR FOL NOW, FORKS!!
© Moore
Savage will thereafter have put down his pencil and drawn no more comic strips in Sounds
more or less
or so legend will have it.
Everybody will be wanting Moore. He'll be simultaneously writing for all 3 of the publishers of American-style HƎroic comics. He'll get big fat Marvel UK, in the interests of fanning local flames, to run small-press reviews.
INE REVIEWS
by alan moore
fanzine space is given over entirely to the not inconsiderable outpourings
T GEN, a multi-media empire making an attempt at global domination!
EA BEHIND PRO-IS ... is to arrive at ated entirely by its ce. So, if you're an mic strip writer who artist, or an artist in writer, or a poet, or r musician, or a pre- tatooist or indeed else that's interesting legal, get in touch with ple at GEN by dropping a
HILLYER, 13 FRESHFIELD TRENT GARDENS, HGATE, LONDON N14
GEN 2
34 loose-leaf pages, £1.00 inc. postage from Ed Hillyer, address left
I saw the first issue of Gen a few months ago and must admit to not being terribly impressed. It
With this second issue, most of my initial doubts have gone the way of all flesh. This is a remarkably entertaining package containing strips, poetry, illustration, music reviews, handy home hints, eight free postcards and a liberal smattering of fear, loathing and boffo yoks.
That's not to say that there weren't bits I enjoyed more than
There's a sort of foaming-at-the-mouth brain-damaged energy at play here, and I find that entirely commendable. I shall be watching out for this one in the months to come. Then, I can rip off all the good, original ideas that come up and get paid vast sums of money for them while the creators languish in squalor and obscurity. I'm sorry. That's just the sort of person I am . . .
ACES No.1
A four page broadsheet-cum-scrapbook of deranged oddities, available for 10p and a first class stamp from Ed Hillyer, address above.
© Moore
Here he will write a piece on one of the books you will have done with Ilya and through Ilya you'll receive a very important communication.
The guy who will hand you your travelling ticket for the next leg; you will not even be aware he's been watching you.
ALEC
ALAN MOORE DROPPING SOUNDS. RING HIM IMMEDIATELY ON 0604-7198.
ILYA

You'll have been watching him too, an unmistakable figure in the Westminster Arms, unofficial creative H.Q. of the bi-monthly comic marts, especially after his photo was in the first issue of Skinn's ambitious WARRIOR magazine. Oddly, a lager drinker.
You'll exchange a great many thoughts with this creative juggernaut, insofar as anyone is able, in that melee, and this before anybody was a 'star'.
You'll visit with him at his home in Northants a month later, mooching a lift from truck driver Danny Grey on one of his far-flung deliveries.
Danny Grey, Alan Moore
Good Grief, It's Danny Grey
JUST FOR AN INSTANT I HAVE THE SENSE OF PANEL BORDERS LOOMING ON THE PERIPHERY OF MY VISION
..FRAMING ME, the LORRY, THE HANDSHAKE, THE SAINSBURY'S CARRIER BAG IN MY OTHER HAND, The INFANTS SCHOOL OVER THE ROAD...
The Moore household will be a chaotic thing.
At the end of every night Alan and Phyllis will round up all the tiles of the fireplace and put them back where they belong.
Never cement them or glue them down or anything, just arrange them loosely back in their places.
Doesn't that broken bit go with that other broken bit?

Another person will turn up to share the living room floor...
...which means you'll have to keep going outside to fart.
You will feel on the doorstep of an important revelation.
And will consequently append your contract with Fate:
I will create around me my own brand of gibbering chaos in order to be a genius like big hairy Alan Moore.
But meanwhile, you'll prepare a set of samples and go up to Sounds.
Security will be high in London in these days. Metal doors will open, but not until you've sweated a bit.
Down through busy magazine production offices, feeling very self-conscious.
into the inner Sanctum
No, this isn't what I expected.
Getting out will seem an even longer hike.

It's a bit squirmy to go and miss a wide open goal in full view of people whose opinion matters.

Never mind, we'll find other strategies
(And when they're so damn nice about it)

Bryan Talbot will get the *Sounds* spot. He'll call it *Scumworld* and go under the alias *Bryan Talbot and the crabs from Uranus*. You will observe that the requirement here is a raffish quality which is not your metier. To hell with art, you will resolve, and bugger the metier while you're at it.

You'll finish off one set of samples into a readable story and send them to a small press publisher named Sharp up in Manchester, one of Ilya's multifarious connections.

There's a second set of samples you composed after the initial rejection but these will fail to elicit any kind of response. Yesterday you were being turned down, now you're beneath notice.

These ones will not even be funny. You'll send them to *Knockabout* where they'll be immediately accepted, to appear December.

You are one of those animals of which nothing goes to waste. Your hooves go to the glue factory and your head makes margarine.

Never mind, honey. You'll get there.

The Man at the Crossroads will have got the first issue of *Escape* magazine printed. It will be well received all over the place.

It will be reviewed in an Arts magazine on a big tabloid page split equally among reviews of: a new translation of Cellini, a study of the architect who designed the Oxo Stock Cube building like an Oxo Stock cube, and Escape magazine, with a reproduction of one of your pieces.

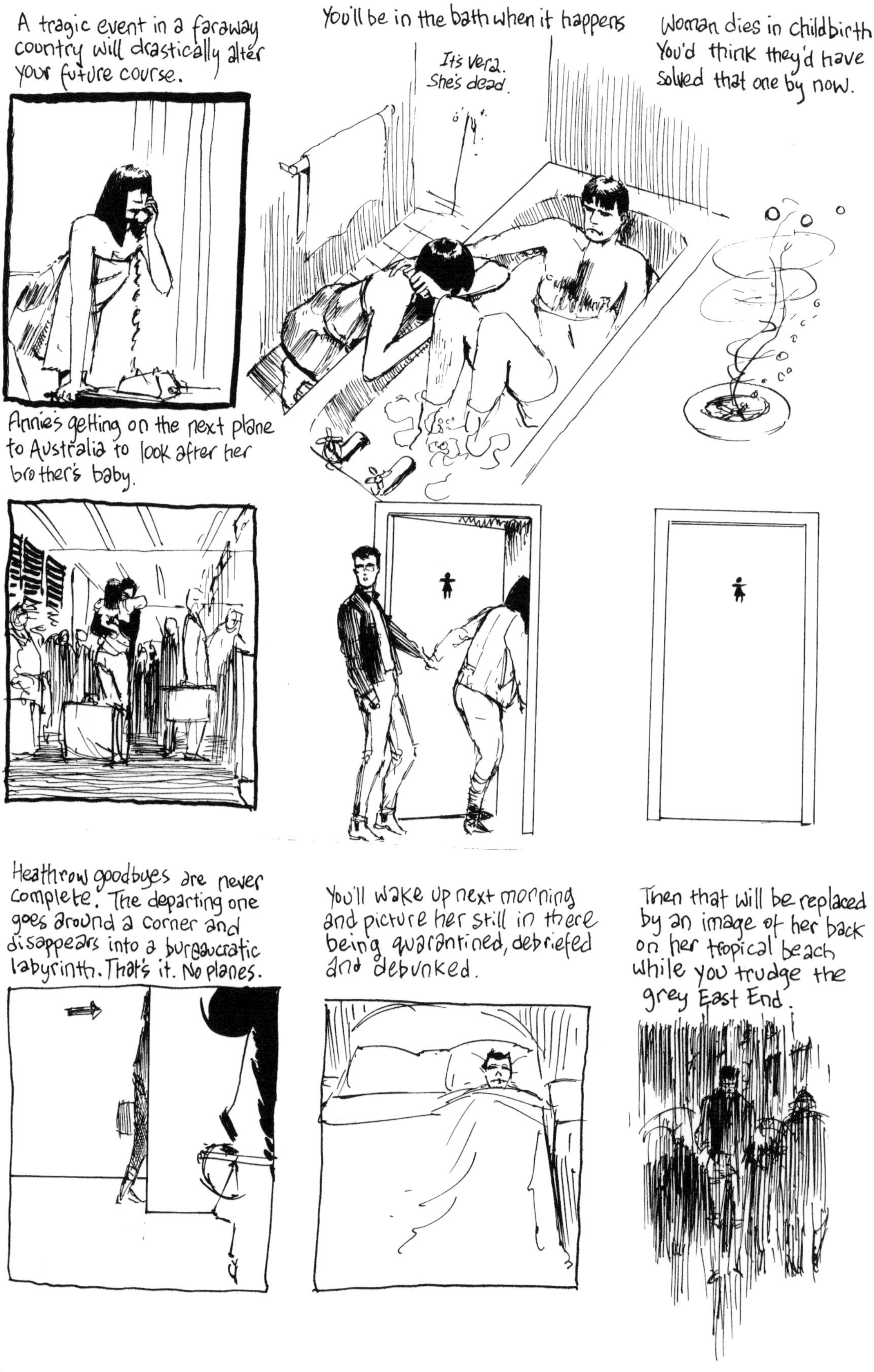

A tragic event in a faraway country will drastically alter your future course.
You'll be in the bath when it happens
It's Vera. She's dead.
Woman dies in childbirth. You'd think they'd have solved that one by now.
Annie's getting on the next plane to Australia to look after her brother's baby.
Heathrow goodbyes are never complete. The departing one goes around a corner and disappears into a bureaucratic labyrinth. That's it. No planes.
You'll wake up next morning and picture her still in there being quarantined, debriefed and debunked.
Then that will be replaced by an image of her back on her tropical beach while you trudge the grey East End.

Chapter Three
The resolve to be, to the exclusion of all else, an artist, will be a difficult one to maintain.
You will have immediately gone into free-fall, with the ground rushing up at an alarming speed.
You may find that you start to lose patience with the bargain you made with FATE.
ya bastard! ya forgot me! Just give me one sign, let me hold the cash from one sale of my work! Just one!
This will be your second lapse of faith, Alec MacGarry.
Sorry.
Then Annie's unscheduled return to Australia will have precipitated an hour of crisis.
You can't pay the rent on your own so you'll call the landlord and try to wrap it up without pain.
I rented this to Anne as a favour. You're not even supposed to be here.
Come on, man, this is difficult enough.
You'll go up north to Blackpool and live with your parents again after all this time.
You'll get a job in a seafront nightclub and save some money.
Did anybody hand in a set of false teeth last night? this is so embarrassing.

The Escape Summer issue will arrive late in the mail: 3-D section, spectacles and everything. Yourself, Elliott, Kane, Emerson, Hughes, Myra. The gang's all here. But your mind will be elsewhere.
The night sky will be calling you across the sea.
I'll go round the world and bring her back.
But to leave when I'm so close to cracking it. Is life intimidating Art or is Art intimidating Life?
I've never borrowed money from my father before.
Dad, I want to go to Australia but I haven't got enough money.
Do they still do the "Assisted passage"
Eh? the "£10 assisted passage" that finished in the 'sixties. I envision my Dad saying:
Here's twenty. Take Danny with you.
You'll meet up with Ilya in a hilltop cottage in Derbyshire.
We've covered so much ground over the last year... Now I'm off to college and you're going abroad.
...sniff... To a hot place.
Have you got any of the hand-coloured Xmas cards left? We could get 'em out again this year.
Those bloody cards. They'd have been alright if you hadn't put them in cling-wrap.
fghlubb
How was I to know the pictures would peel off? Selling photocopied Art is a new game altogether.

You'll be on your way to Australia, Alec MacGarry...
...But it will be a good idea to stop over in London for the first official meeting of *Escape* magazine, publishers and contributors.
They will have hired an upstairs room at a pub.
You and I would just go in the bar, Alec MacGarry, but factionalism will have already taken its hold.
They don't want every Tom, Dick and Harry getting mixed up in it.
A guy named Dakin's here.
HEY YOU!
He will be surprised that everyone will know his stuff. But that's how it is when your stuff's the right stuff. He'll pull his first photocopied comic out of a plastic bag.
Humour Extractor.
© Dakin.
Portfolio Cases? Nobody here uses one. That must be another faction you're thinking of.

Dakin will have appeared in a crap glossy expensive comic called *pssst!* which will have had the Man at the Crossroads for a sub-editorial gopher at the time when he first sent out his various communications.

Isn't it wonderful how circumstances change values!
in credible
© Dakin

pssst! will have systematically rejected everything of value that came its way (except Dakin, curiously) including yourself. Almost too uncanny to be coincidental. Fate will have placed it there to test everybody's patience.

AHH! KILL! DESTROY THE BASTARDS.

There will always be a *pssst!* though it may go by another name in your own epoch, preaching the 'Art' of comics while squandering the potential of the market on its foolish inanities before collapsing under the weight of expensive folly.

It was a year ago. How can you still be angry?
Don't get me started.

It will also have *psssd off* the hoary old pros at the *Society of Strip Illustrators* by inviting them to compete for the prize of designing the *pssst* logo, instead of hiring someone to do it, treating them like a mob of young hopefuls.

Naturally one of the hoary old pros will have rubbished the magazine in their own monthly SSI Journal.

The Man at the Crossroads will have obtained for you a copy to peruse. There's a member in the correspondence columns beefing about coming all the way down from the Orkneys with his good lady wife for the annual dinner and some of the members haven't even bothered to hire tuxedos.

...offence to the dignity of his good lady and all that.

The SSI is an association of professionals. Acceptance to membership will require that the applicant have made a living from comics for one year. *Status Quo* is the new chairman. They meet upstairs at a pub.

From the other side of the planet you can't see it.

Even at night, Darwin airport will be a steam bath. It may cause you to consider how climate would influence national temperament, or it may not.
At Townsville Annie will meet you and ensconce you in the Travelodge for the afternoon.
(It will have been six months after all)
Then in Ingham you will meet her charge, the motherless child.
And there will be many beers at the house on the beach under the tropical sun with your future father-in-law and his remarkable fund of anecdotes
And there will be islands with nobody on them.
Can you be an artist not connected with any 'Art World'? Can you be one if nobody ever knows it?
Here's one of those anecdotes:
Among several poems by one Dan Sheahan, sugar cane farmer, published in the *North Queensland Register* was, in 1944, one titled *The Pub Without Beer*.
It is lonely away from your kindred and all, In the bushland at night when the warrigals call

In 1957, one Gordon Parsons, timber man and country singer, comes upon the basis of the poem aurally, and, believing it to be public domain 'folk' material, sets about constructing it into a workable song.

Get this down:
Oh, it's lonesome away from your kindred and all, By the campfire at night, where the wild dingoes call...

That year it is recorded by his mate Slim Dusty when he's a song short of his quota at a session. It becomes a million seller, his first hit, and a big surprise to himself. It does well in Britain too but probably remains unheard in America.

But there's nothing so lonesome, morbid or drear...

The story goes that Sheahan's boys took the matter up with Dusty when he toured through Ingham. For half an hour the story is a cause celebre in musical circles and for slightly longer than that in the town of Ingham.

Than to stand in the bar of a pub with no beer.

Plagiarism? Artists adapt stuff all the time. It's just a bit embarrassing if it becomes a runaway hit. (It didn't seem to matter to anyone that the tune Parsons set the poem to was essentially *Beautiful Dreamer* with a country gait.)

Register
There's a faraway look on the face of the bum, While the barmaid glares down at the paint on her thumb.

But that's just copping a feel in comparison to the triumphal loss of virginity that will accompany the sale of your first story.

So send out your messages in bottles, one and all. Who knows what may come of it? *Caveat emptor.*

Right at this time, however, you will be working on the problem of raising a mere hundred. You'll have enough to get you through the three months but it'd be nice to have a bit more.

or strip, as Elliott calls them.

Alec can you do us another strip?

Years previously you will have painted some designs on some leather jackets for five quid a pop.

By now your "virginity" will weigh heavily upon your soul, and here is how you will set about losing it:...

The British Comics "Small Press thing" will be starting to make international connections. There are some guys in Canada doing their own thing and a girl in Tokyo. Elliott will have sold some sticker designs to Fiorucci in Italy.
He's very nervous
Well he's never met the guy
An Australian guy, Beardy Bentley of Melbourne, will have been in London, heard the word and taken it back with him.
He will have been corresponding with you for a year now. You'll call him up North.
Are all Alec's mates a bit funny?
Are you suggesting that Alec isn't?
You're a guest here, so he'll be a guest of a guest. You will watch, with amazement at his adeptness, his dismantlement of a quiche into its encyclopedic components.
He'll be one of a team putting out a comics mag called INKSPOTS which, if truth be told, will be nearer the pssst model than any other.
Let's go down the beach
You'll put it to him that in his, uh, editorial capacity, he might like to patronise a worthy artist to the tune of one hundred frogskins.
...and take away with him the originals of a four-pager you'll have been busy drawing about 'The Pyjama Girl', an infamous Australian murder.
© Campbell · 84 · Pyjama Girl.
And there you'll do the deal. You'll make your first ever sale. On a tropical beach.
I haven't got a hundred on me right at this minute. You'll have to wait till we get back to the house
Full of yourself, you will then drink too many beers and put your head through the fluorescent tube in the garage.
All over Dad's new Volvo—how will I explain it?

With the taste of impending celebrity in your saliva you'll be eager to get back to London.
It'll be the pull of gravity.
Annie will cry though she leaves the baby in competent hands.
You'll propose marriage at Darwin airport.
In London you'll drop in on the Escape boys and have showers. Dakin will be visiting.
You'll confess to him that you feel you shouldn't have been away from the hub of things for so long
If you weren't here you were somewhere else.
That remarkable thought will splash through your brain.
If I wasn't here I was somewhere else.
What a deliciously egocentric notion.
The most interesting place is where you are.
The Society of Alec MacGarry.

In the days when you had to make your own entertainment.
Chapter Four
it's funny how the people on the top deck of the bus go past our second storey window like that
I'm going to show them your bum.
Not if I show them yours first.
GERROF
DON'T!
AAG STOPPIT
You're killing time waiting for your book to come out.
ALEC
With an introduction by Alan Moore
(c) Campbell · Escape.
The Escape boys are being fussy and finicky in their publishing of it.
We can reverse this out and burn off that and uh...
Let's have another cup of nettle tea.

It'll be an Ice-Age of waiting. Take your mind off it.
You'll be down on the South Coast at Easter with Danny Grey and co.
Annie will say:
To think that France is just across that water. A whole other country. In Australia we're so isolated
Shut up.
Wouldn't it be so easy...
Shut up for god's sake they'll do it.
So next thing you've got day-return passports, virtually all your cash is gone and you're looking into the steely grey of the English channel
Prendergast's hanging off the rail for a photo.
Danny Grey's romancing it up with the waitress in a late café-bar. Annie, who started the whole thing, is asleep in a corner and they keep rousing her because sleep isn't on the menu.
I'm the English Pilot and you're Mamzel Marie of the rayzeestawnce~
You'll miss the last ferry and have to crash in the transit depot.
You'll wake up only thinking of the book: "Danny Grey never really forgave himself for leaving Alec MacGarry asleep at the turnpike."

It'll be an Ice Age waiting for a candle to flicker.
For a shining moment you'll be a novelty and you can only be that once.
Your first feeling upon seeing your first proper book will be disappointment. Getting beyond the hand-made photocopied things turns out to be no big deal.
FAST FICTION
From that moment the concept of "book" will hold no value and you will often buy expensively bound books and think nothing of cutting them up. If an idiot like you can be published, there can't be any inherent authority in the form.
But hardly anybody ever looking at it will think of the sum of the experiences that will crowd around it, your "first book."
You'll be on a London Radio Arts program, stuck in behind playwright Alan Ayckbourn. They'll ask him about his themes; they'll ask you what made you want to draw a comic.
Worse than that, they'll play you in with Queen's theme to Flash Gordon, the most audible contemporary example of comicstripiana.
bzz War-rocket Ajax approaching
Fizz buzzz bzzz
AW SHIT
Even if you were to know that it would be at least another thirteen years before you'd make a penny out of the material in that book...
Annie and your sister sitting on top of the Sussex Downs trying to catch it on the car radio.
... you'd still laugh so hard.
HA HA HA

A Mayfair gallery wakes up one morning with the idea that comic books are the next page in the story of ART.
An assemblage of the new comics and some paintings influenced by comics. They'll get hold of the Man at the Crossroads for the 'New Comics'.
Comics?
Comics
I couldn't help overhearing...
GIMPEL FILS GALLE
Don't ask how he always pops up when he's needed, or descends from a passing cloud
I rather fancy reading a comic, Jeremy.
I was in the neighbourhood...
So it'll be the real McCoy, all the right people. From the Comics camp at any rate.
Spiegelman will be on that wall...
I WAS EXPECTED TO COMFORT HIM!
MOTHER... MOTHER...
© Spiegelman.
And Biff,
LATER, I TRAVELLED WIDELY..
IN AFRICA, THEY USED TO CALL ME "THE WHITE NEGRO". I'LL TAKE THE FRIED EGG SANDWICH PLEASE.
NOT ANOTHER CULTURAL IMPERIALIST!
© Biff
And Oscar Zarate, Savage Pencil, Myra, Anarchist Cliff Harper...
3 WHAT IS GOVERNMENT?
© Harper.
I DECLARE THEM TO BE MY ENEMY...
© Harper
ZZZ
And Alec MacGarry will be asleep again at the turnpike.
"When the neurotics appropriated the strip cartoon," says the Arts Correspondent in The Guardian, Waldemar Januscak, "we witnessed an ideal marriage of form and content. They subverted its innocence and filled its thought balloons with their wretched, guilt-sodden soliloquies."
ZZZ
The Guardian
THATCHER
In another time and place and with a different bunch of people there would now be a group proclaiming themselves The Neurotics but this lot are too busy agonizing about whether it's hip to be in a posh Mayfair gallery.
THE NEWROTIC

The *New Musical Express* man Watson's at the opening party too. He tapes a chat with you. For a couple of years Comics will be a hip sub-culture.

Big Argentinian Oscar Zarate tags along on that one.

It's all International. Waiting to happen in a lot of places all at once.

Oscar's the illustrator on one of Anne Tauté's Comicbook Shakespeare Volumes: the *Othello*.

—O, CURSE OF MARRIAGE, THAT WE CAN CALL THESE DELICATE CREATURES OURS AND NOT THEIR APPETITES! I HAD RATHER BE A TOAD, AND LIVE UPON THE VAPOUR OF A DUNGEON, THAN KEEP A CORNER IN THE THING I LOVE FOR OTHERS' USES.
© Zarate.

The valiant lady re-mortgaged her house to raise 90,000 quid to set herself up as a publisher and do this series.

At the opening party she has a bandage on her face. The only time you ever meet her she has a bust nose.

You and Annie will be lodging with your sister in Brighton. You'll have got yourself a short-term job filing soldiers' medical records.

Then the floodgates open. You land a weekly spot in *Sounds*.

SOUNDS
NME
MELODY MAKER

You won't even have to go up there this time. Savage Pencil in his everyday on-staff guise of Edwin Pouncey will send word via the *Man at the Crossroads* that the spot's open again.

Every time there's a new editor the first thing he does is toss out the cartoons. They like to mark their territory and this will offend the least people. That's a double-edged sword but never mind.

© Elliott

So you'll get Elliott on the phone and lay out a plan. He'll have had a spot in the *Melody Maker* for four weeks while you were in Australia. He knows these things aren't easy to hold onto.

FABBO-DINKUMS!

BUSBY'S
ROCK & POP FACTS
THE RECENT DISCO DANCE CRAZE OF 'BODY-POPPING' WAS IN FACT INITIATED BY L.P. LIME OF THE JACKSON VILLE ASYLUM. "HE SPENDS HOURS DANCING AND TWITCHING IN HIS ROOM" SAYS L.P.'S NURSE.
© Elliott

So rather than be in competition for the gig, you'll create a phony cartoonist, Charlie Trumper and take turns in ghosting for him.

I'll do all the lettering and sign them, so nobody'll be any the wiser.

The Wonders of Science. It's in a Music Paper and its got nothing to do with music. What a joy.

Which came first? The bacon or the egg
How should I Know
© Charlie 84 Trumper

It's got nothing to do with Science either, for that matter.

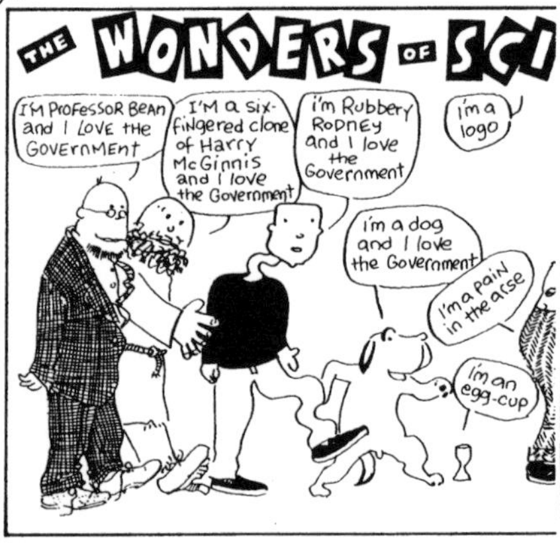
THE WONDERS OF SCI
I'm Professor Bean and I love the Government
I'm a six-fingered clone of Harry McGinnis and I love the Government
I'm Rubbery Rodney and I love the Government
I'm a logo
I'm a dog and I love the Government
I'm a pain in the arse
I'm an egg-cup

With your interview in the NME you'll get invited to fill up the 'THRILLS', or guest cartoonist spot for a month with your autobiographical nonsense. They've been running some hot new American Cartoonists in there like Seattle's Lynda Barry.

IS THERE SOMETHING YOU'RE TRYING TO TELL ME MYRNA?
ED BREAD
© Barry.

And Mark Beyer, of RAW

LATER AT A HOSPITAL
THE PILLS MUST HAVE BEEN CONTAMINATED!
© Beyer.

Punk pamphleteer Holmstrom, J.D. King, Bagge,.. What a rich variety of voices is in the air.

HONEST! I WANNA DANCE WITH YOU!
I WOULDN'T DANCE WITH YOU IF YOU PUT A GUN TO MY HEAD!
© Holmstrom.

Dakin will be visiting. You'll get him in on it and bang out a half dozen pieces.

And there, with a testament to your brilliance, will be his drawings.

"If MacGarry's quirky line-drawings seem primitive at first, they soon establish a charm of their own."

AT THE EURYTHMICS CONCERT I MET THIS INCREDIBLE GIRL.. SHE WAS UNBELIEVABLE ~ IT WAS THE SWEETEST NIGHT OF MY LIFE !!
BENNET'S
© Dakin

They say these oh-so perceptive things but they can't tell the difference
Charlie Trumper © 91

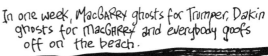

In one week, MacGARRY ghosts for Trumper, Dakin ghosts for MacGARRY and everybody goofs off on the beach.

Goofing off. You know, one of the things America has given the world along with the endless coffee refill, is a colourful bunch of expressions for doing nothing.

Like 'hanging out' and 'goofing off'.

Big Hairy Alan Moore's now writing for the Americans and taking them by storm.

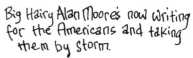

Alright, here goes

They were probably all goofing off and hanging about when he landed among them like a hungry wolf...

...doing violence to their cosy concepts of the mud-monster and the earnest super-being.

© D.C. Comics INC.

The Man at the Crossroads gets you to hook up with him to tape a conversation for Escape.

THOMAS PYNCHON!
HENRY MILLER!
© Escape

It'll happen at the Princess Louise. As you arrive you see a peculiar thing. There's a guy assessing the pub in his "*Real Ale Guide*".

Weighing up how many 'traditionally brewed' beers are on tap, how many stars awarded, etc. etc.

A strange way indeed to measure the quality of a pub. Surely you should put your ear to the door and listen for sounds of jollity.

Everywhere you turn a door opens. Your sister will need a display for the *Electronic Point of Sale Expo* for which she's part of the organising team.

Susie

Your drawing gets blown up to eleven feet high in the foyer of the Hammersmith Exhibition Centre. In one month you're regular in two national rock weeklies and hanging in two choice spots in the capital.

CORN FLAKES
BEAM UP
CORN FLAKES
SUGAR

You're not getting rich or anything though. Life goes on much the same.

The five fifteen goes past in ten seconds

Your favourite types of young artist will be social creatures, too often swopping their work with their fellows instead of selling it and 'getting ahead' or working all day flogging it and glogging down the takings with a hot pie.

One day, Alec, you'll be seeing your confreres grinning back at you from glossy magazines.

BLITZ
SOUNDS
NME

Chapter Five

The media makes no differentiation between the national daily leftwing cartoonist Steve Bell...

I WANT TO VOTE FOR MARGARET THATCHER!! HONK TWEET YIBYIB!! GURBLE GURBLE!!
FLAP
CLAP
© Bell

...and anarchic vicious sometimes-cartoonist Savage Pencil, looking like Dracula's nephew.

...And Myra, selling her photocopied pamphlets at Camden Lock market in the manner of the Little Match Girl.

It's all shades of a colourful story to them.

Myra lands a spot in proximity to Bell in London's *City Limits* magazine doing her punk agony aunt *Miss March* on the letters page...

Miss March
gives advice
© myra
DEAR MISS MARCH,
I've been in LONDON for 7 mths now and I really can't see what people see in it. I haven't even seen anyone famous.

...dispensing anti-wisdom into the atmosphere.

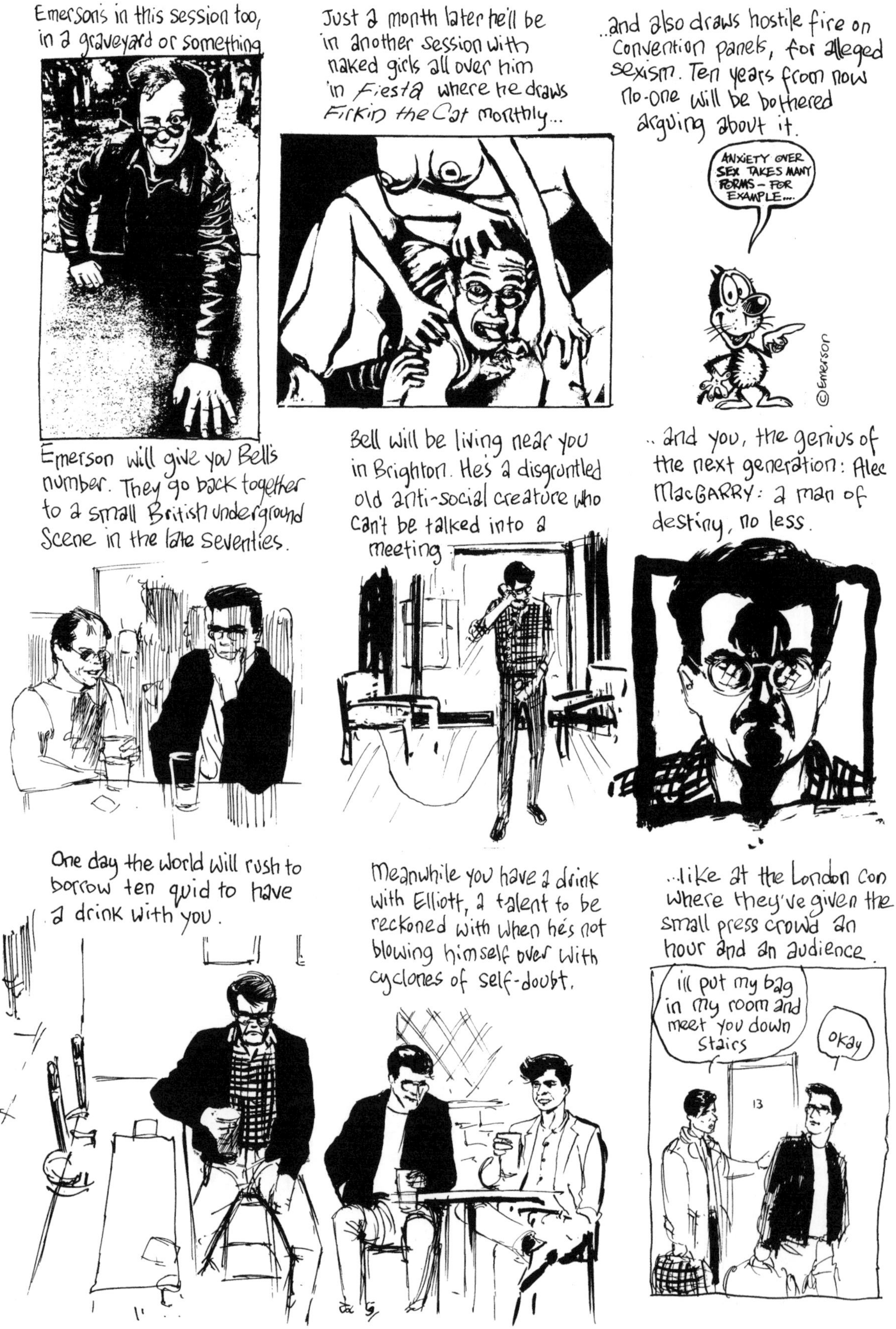
Emerson's in this session too, in a graveyard or something
Just a month later he'll be in another session with naked girls all over him in *Fiesta* where he draws *Firkin the Cat* monthly...
...and also draws hostile fire on Convention panels, for alleged sexism. Ten years from now no-one will be bothered arguing about it.
ANXIETY OVER SEX TAKES MANY FORMS – FOR EXAMPLE....
©Emerson
Emerson will give you Bell's number. They go back together to a small British underground Scene in the late seventies.
Bell will be living near you in Brighton. He's a disgruntled old anti-social creature who can't be talked into a meeting
..and you, the genius of the next generation: Alec MacGARRY: a man of destiny, no less.
One day the world will rush to borrow ten quid to have a drink with you.
Meanwhile you have a drink with Elliott, a talent to be reckoned with when he's not blowing himself over with cyclones of self-doubt.
..like at the London con where they've given the small press crowd an hour and an audience.
ill put my bag in my room and meet you down stairs
okay
13

while you're throwing your bag in your hotel room, Elliott's done a runner back to Maidstone
AW NO...no...
Elliott gets an arty gig creating slide images for some performance artist in Dublin.
He has to go over there and do the work in situ.
ill put my bag in my room
OKay
By daybreak he's on a boat back again...
AW no
...envisioning himself putting his bags in Davy Jones' locker.
© Elliott
He'll make a comic of it, using his character Gimbley, shaking it up in a cocktail with metaphors and other discursive techniques.
Hughes doesn't borrow ten quid to drink with anyone, or at least he slips the tenner away for more important matters. Which is not to say he isn't a social creature.
where's the beer?
He lands a harmless pussycat spot at the back of Seventeen magazine.
MIOW
MIOW
MIOW MIOW
MIOW
MI OW
MIOW
MIOW MIOW
MI OW
MIOW
© Hughes
Produces his wee pamphlets at art-school's expense, like his mini-comic, ZIT. The man who names his work thus will years later design a typeface called:
FF Knobcheese™!
© Hughes.

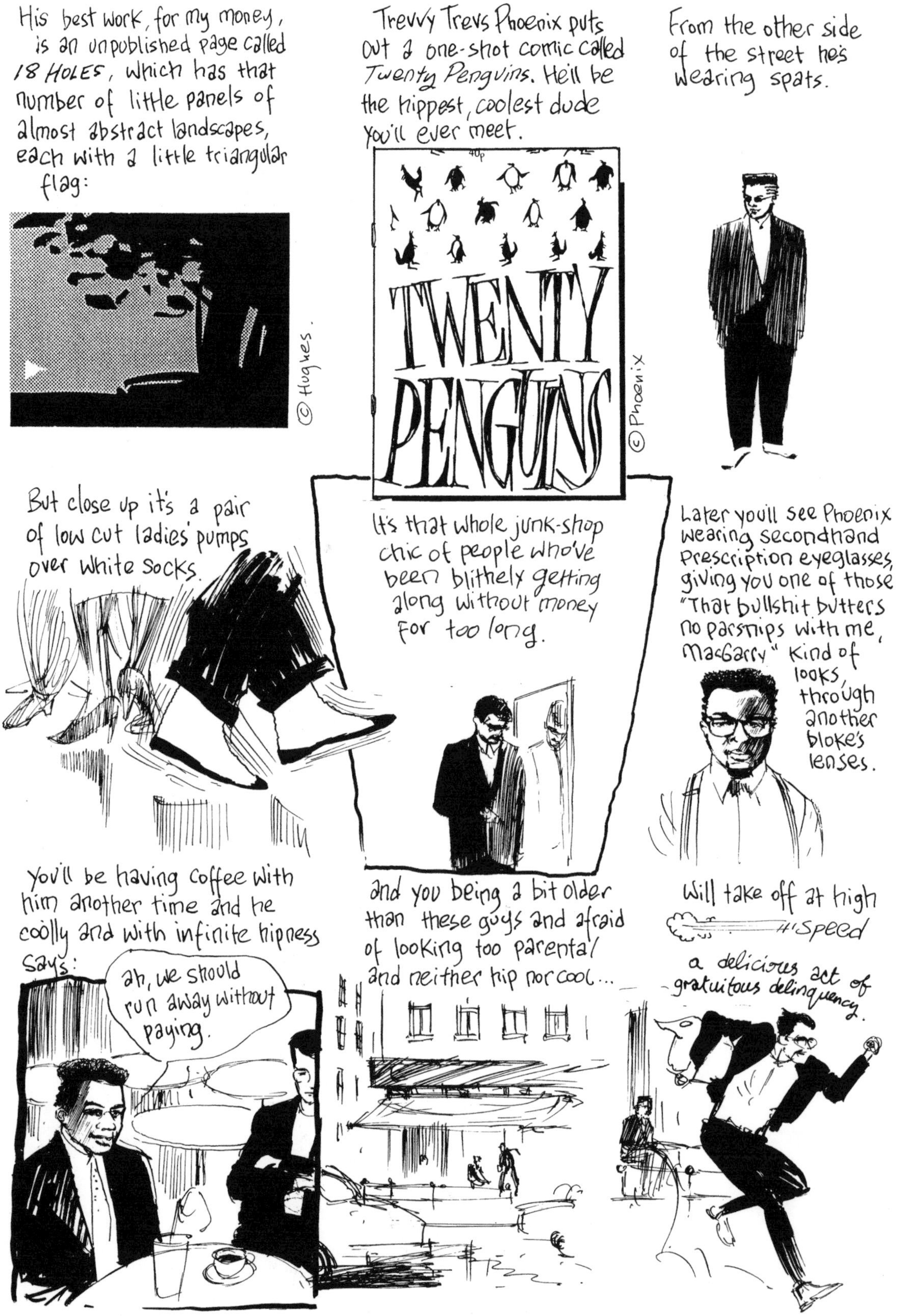
His best work, for my money, is an unpublished page called 18 HOLES, which has that number of little panels of almost abstract landscapes, each with a little triangular flag:
© Hughes.
Trevvy Trevs Phoenix puts out a one-shot comic called Twenty Penguins. He'll be the hippest, coolest dude you'll ever meet.
40p
TWENTY PENGUINS
© Phoenix
From the other side of the street he's wearing spats.
But close up it's a pair of low cut ladies' pumps over white socks.
It's that whole junk-shop chic of people who've been blithely getting along without money for too long.
Later you'll see Phoenix wearing secondhand prescription eyeglasses, giving you one of those "That bullshit butters no parsnips with me, MacGarry" kind of looks, through another bloke's lenses.
You'll be having coffee with him another time and he coolly and with infinite hipness says:
ah, we should run away without paying.
and you being a bit older than these guys and afraid of looking too parental and neither hip nor cool...
Will take off at high speed
a delicious act of gratuitous delinquency.

You'll look back and, in spite of the distance, see him blush to the very roots of his being.

You'll have to go back and pick up the parsnips.

Dakin does a comic about flamenco buskers Forcione and Niebla.

The Musical Adventures of
EDUARDO NIEBLA
ANTONIO FORCIONE
© Dakin.

They sell it out of their guitar cases.

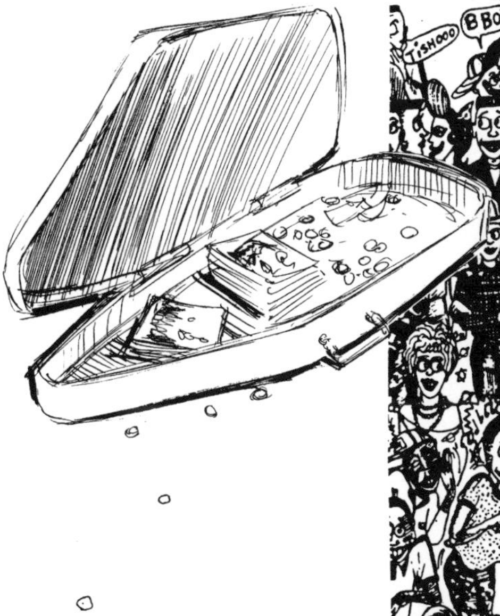

In I-D magazine there's a guy signing himself 'Wigan' draws big crowded cartoons where everybody's saying stuff.

TISHOOO
B BOYS
DON'T BE SO SEXIST!
YOU FAKIN CANT!
KNOCK IT ON THE EAD WIW YA!
WE'RE MADE FOR ONE ANOTHER YOU AND I
WOMEN ARE ANGRY!
WATCHA DADDY-O
LIFE!
DONT TELL ME "LIFE IN THIS CRAZY CITY UN NERVES YOU!
DONT LAY ANY HEAVY NUMBERS ON ME MAN
YOU SWEET SEXY THING
MAN AM I TRIPING?
PLAY THAT FUNKY MUSIC
I'M JUST A SUCKER FOR YOUR LOVE
TUNE IN TURN ON DROP OUT
FREEBIRD!
TAKE A TRIP!
THERE'S A KILLER ON THE ROAD HIS BRAIN IS SQUIRMIN LIKE A TOAD
I'M A LIVING SICKNESS
BLACK NIGHT AND A
DONT MESS WITH THE MAN UTD PERRY BOYS PAL!
LETS FACE IT, IT NEVER WENT AWAY
EEEEGHH! LOOK!
IF WE ALL CLOSE OUR EYES TOGETHER WE WILL SEE WHERE WE COME FROM!
HES BEEN VERY DEPRESSED RECENTLY
OKAY DONT GET UPTIGHT BILBO, LOOK WHAT GANDALF'S GOT IN HIS BAG
GET IT ON FREAK
ROLLING
© Wigan (detail)

I don't know that they ever say anything important or if it matters. "His poser-packed drawings immortalise the murky menagerie of late-night London hipsterdom" © NME

His cartoons are hung at the Garbanzo Coffee house for a month.

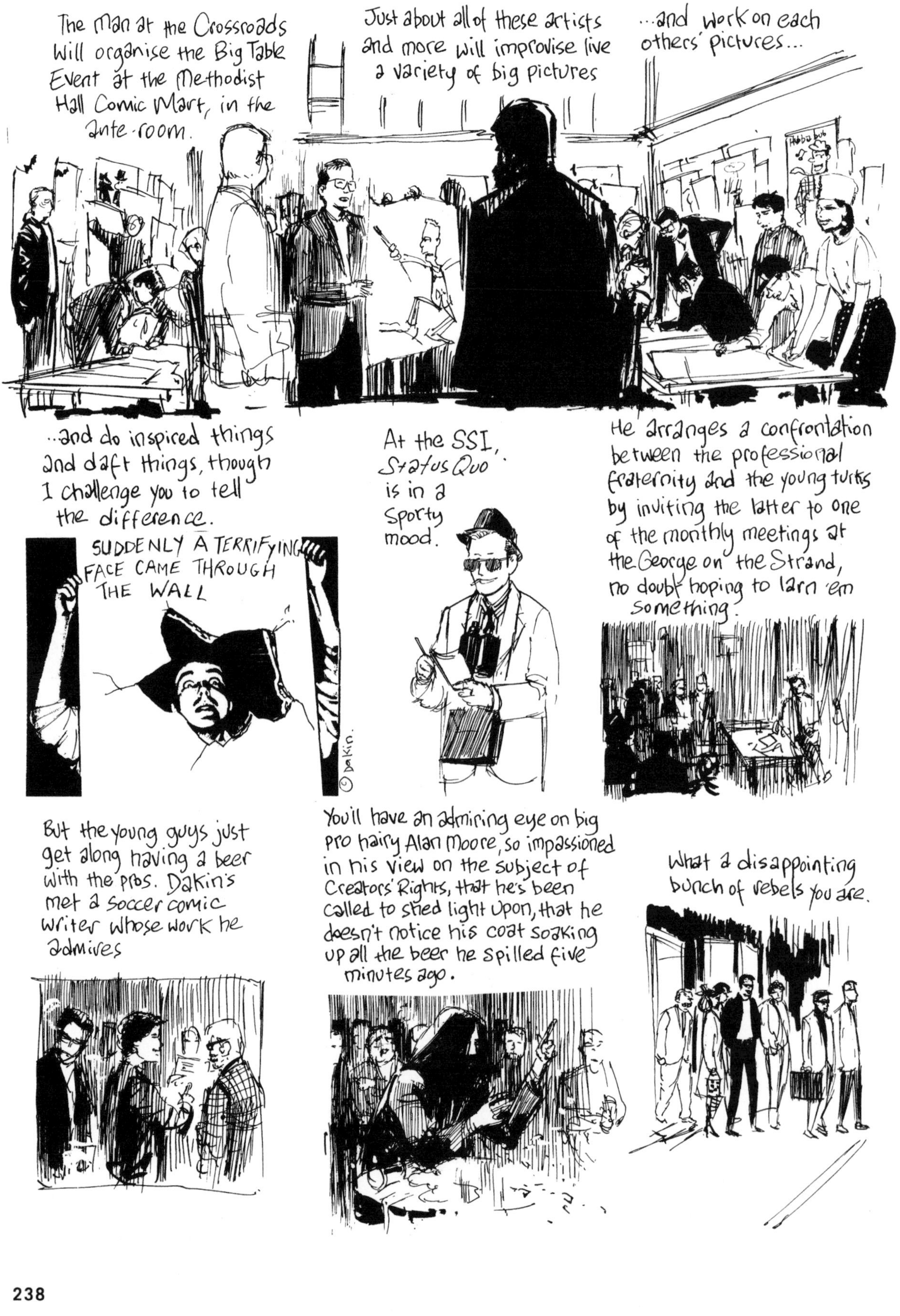
The Man at the Crossroads will organise the Big Table Event at the Methodist Hall Comic Mart, in the ante-room.
Just about all of these artists and more will improvise live a variety of big pictures
...and work on each others' pictures...
...and do inspired things and daft things, though I challenge you to tell the difference.
SUDDENLY A TERRIFYING FACE CAME THROUGH THE WALL
© Dakin.
At the SSI, Status Quo is in a sporty mood.
He arranges a confrontation between the professional fraternity and the young turks by inviting the latter to one of the monthly meetings at the George on the Strand, no doubt hoping to larn 'em something.
But the young guys just get along having a beer with the pros. Dakin's met a soccer comic writer whose work he admires
You'll have an admiring eye on big pro hairy Alan Moore, so impassioned in his view on the subject of Creators' Rights, that he's been called to shed light upon, that he doesn't notice his coat soaking up all the beer he spilled five minutes ago.
What a disappointing bunch of rebels you are.

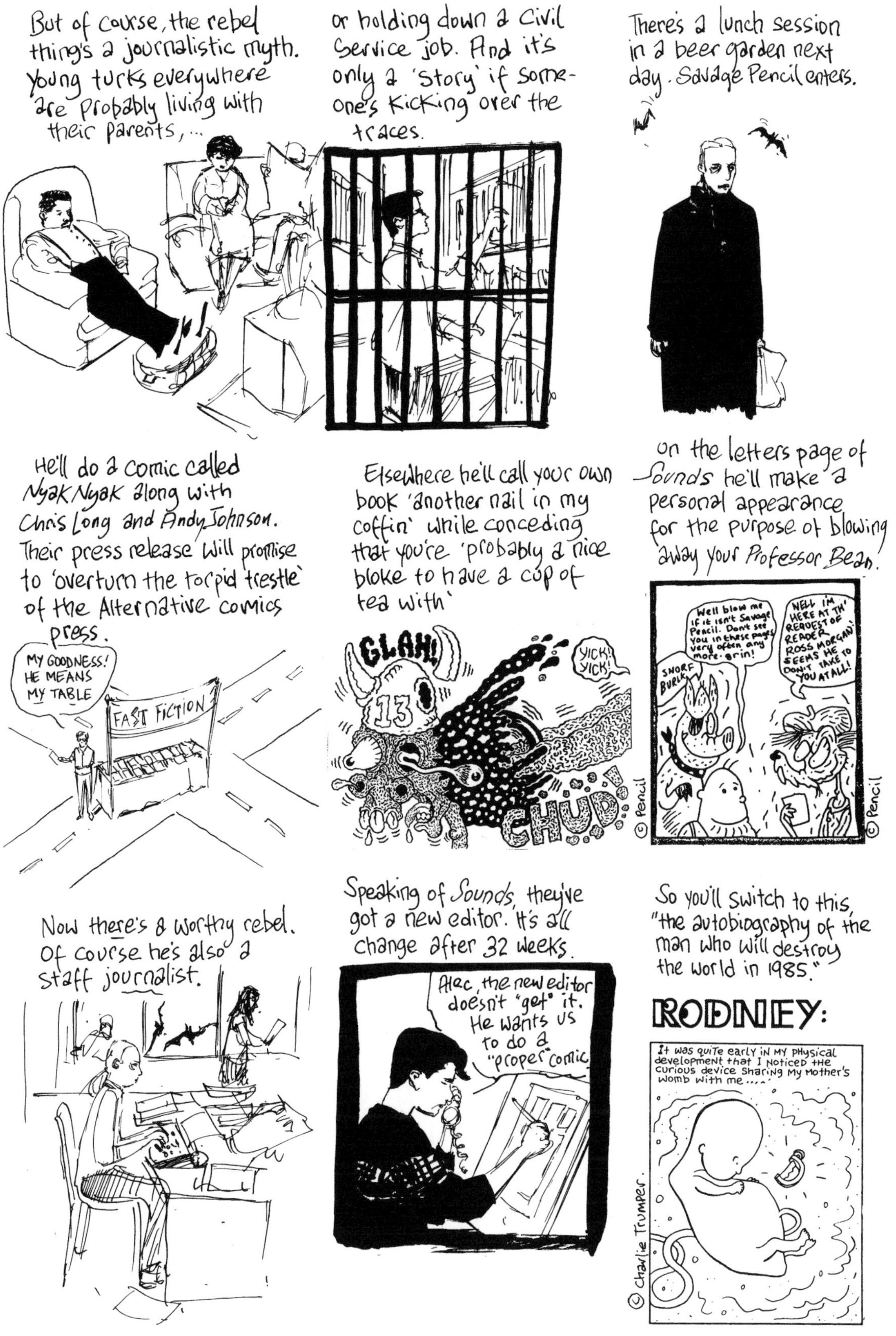
But of course, the rebel thing's a journalistic myth. Young turks everywhere are probably living with their parents, ...
or holding down a Civil Service job. And it's only a 'story' if someone's kicking over the traces.
There's a lunch session in a beer garden next day. Savage Pencil enters.
He'll do a comic called *Nyak Nyak* along with Chris Long and Andy Johnson. Their press release will promise to 'overturn the torpid trestle' of the Alternative comics press.
MY GOODNESS! HE MEANS MY TABLE
FAST FICTION
Elsewhere he'll call your own book 'another nail in my coffin' while conceding that you're 'probably a nice bloke to have a cup of tea with'
GLAH!
13
YICK! YICK!
CHUD!
© Pencil
On the letters page of *Sounds* he'll make a personal appearance for the purpose of blowing away your *Professor Bean*.
Well blow me if it isn't Savage Pencil. Don't see you in these pages very often any more. grin!
SNORF BURLK
WELL I'M HERE AT TH' REQUEST OF READER ROSS MORGAN! SEEMS HE DON'T TAKE TO YOU AT ALL!
© Pencil
Now there's a worthy rebel. Of course he's also a staff journalist.
Speaking of *Sounds*, they've got a new editor. It's all change after 32 weeks.
Alec, the new editor doesn't "get" it. He wants us to do a "proper" comic.
So you'll switch to this, "the autobiography of the man who will destroy the world in 1985."
RODNEY:
It was quite early in my physical development that I noticed the curious device sharing my mother's womb with me....
© Charlie Trumper.

And you'll do real rebellious stuff like having peoples arses exploding.
© Charlie Trumper.
You'll even start to influence your peers.
BLARRAMPH
Curry Kills
Don't Do It
© Cooper.
You and Annie will sneak down to the Registry Office without telling anyone.
You don't think this hair's a mistake?
You'll stop a stranger to take the wedding photos. Annie's mother won't talk to her for a year and a half.
YEH...look the doohickey. just there
Well, it's either that or go to Australia and stand up and recite the usual nonsense.
You rebel, you.
more tea, darl?
certainly, dear.
Then you'll tour the country in your wee car, dining with your pals along the way.
Card from Dakin:
I hear Alec's getting married to some australian lass
Dont tell me— he met her at a Eurythmics concert—
BUT MY DEAR KRAZY — WHY SHOULD I KNOW ANYTHING ABOUT THE MARRIAGE? WHY "I" I ASK?
S'FUNNY IGNATZ WAS SO SHOO YOU WOOD...
JOE'S STORK
Love from GLENN
© Dakin.
Homage à Herriman
Krazy Kat © King Features.

Chapter Six

The cycle of renewal in Art is pedalled by the periodic influx of stuff from somewhere else. That's why you need a Man at the Crossroads.

HITHER
YON
INFLUENCE

For three years he'll have been jabbering about what's going on in FRANCE. "La Ligne Claire" and all that.

One day they stop looking at all those *Druillet* monstrosities...

MINING ROBOTS! BUT CAN THEY STILL BE FUNCTIONING ?

© Druillet.

And decide that *Hergé's* the man to be with after all.

WOOU-HOUW-OU-OU-OU-WOOUUH!
!
!
?

Herge 1948
©Editions Casterman

The Man at the Crossroads conveys it to Elliott and Elliott spends the rest of his life drawing 'Clearlines'.

PERICLES.THE PUNK WAS THROWING OUR PRECIOUS PORK PIES AT THE FLYING FISH~
PLOP
PLOP!

© Elliott '85

Serge Clerc will be one of the new French crop. In fact the NME will have been importing his little illustrations quite early.

NME
WE POSE THE QUESTIONS AND QUESTION THE POSERS.

©clerc.

However, if you can read French, none of it is saying anything profound or memorable or even endearingly amusing on the level of Laurel and Hardy. It's just the next fashion.

The exception to the preceding, of course, is Claire Bretecher, who was translated in the *Sunday Times* magazine for a long while and has a page in *Cosmo* for a year.

if only I could get pregnant without meaning to
BRETECHER
Bretecher '84

The French government uses comics at the forefront of its cultural exchange abroad. Thus it will transpire that they've got an exhibition of French comics and a day long seminar at the *Institut Francais* in Queensberry Place and there's a private cocktail party at the apartments of the Cultural counsellor to the French Embassy. You're invited, Alec.

Druillet will be there in the flesh.

And Claude Moliterni. Now that will be interesting, bumping into him at this stage.

As a wee laddie of only fifteen, on your first time in London, you'll have stumbled on a book.

A History of the Comic Strip with Pierre Couperie, Maurice Horn and Claude Moliterni sorting out the chapters between them.

It was originally published as *Bande Dessinee et Figuration Narrative* and released to accompany an exhibition of comic art at the *Louvre* in 1968 with panels blown up huge.

The Pop Art movement had put a spotlight on comics and it was inevitable that the history of the form would be reviewed and revised.

-R-R-R
-R-RING!!
Lichtenstein, oil, 2ft high. 1961

Such things tend to be in the water a long time before bobbing to the surface.
THOR
The idea of artistic worth residing in the comics will have arisen naturally in the minds of some who made them and, more importantly, of a good number of the kid's who read them
As a ten year old you could sort out all the different uncredited artists even when there was more than one fiddling about in the same pictures, which was the norm.
Far from it being a faceless industrial product, the comic book will have been to you a collective popular art not unlike jazz music used to be.
In a shop called *Bookends*, in a heady atmosphere of eclectica and esoterica, you will have discovered a remote shelf devoted to the literature that will have been growing around the subject.
Others will have been haunting this spot you probably pass them going in and out...
...each drawing from the implications his own conclusions, forming his own plan...
...to create a monumental kind of comic strip and add his own chapter to the story in these days when you will still have believed art to be a continuous narrative.

Between the French book and the *Penguin Book of Comics* by Perry and Aldridge and a whole slew of histories and collections that followed them onto that particular shelf in *Bookends of Camden*, you will have discovered the heroes of the next phase of your artistic life:

the grand old men of the newspaper comic strip: most of them dead by this time.

George Herriman

HEH ?
Y'CAN GET A COUPLE OF PRETTY FAIR SODIES AT SCHNIEDER'S DRUG STORE FOR A DIME, JOE. WUTCHASAY ?

1922 © King Features.

Milton Caniff.

BUT I CAN'T TOUCH THAT GUN — I'M A CORRESPONDENT — A CIVILIAN!
MISTER, YOU'LL CORRESPOND TO A SIEVE IF YOU DON'T START POURIN' STEEL!

©Trib-News Syndicate. 1943.

Tad Dorgan

GANS

is BATTLING NELSON BITING OFF MORE THAN HE CAN CHEW

1906

Noel Sickles

ME PACK? — GEE I NEVER OWNED MORE'N ONE DRESS IN M' LIFE! — GIT YER GOGGLES ON FELLERS — TH' CINDERELLA O' TH' NORTH WOODS WANTS HER COACH!
OKAY! — THIS WAY, MILADY! — BUT IT'S A FLYING CARPET — AND WE'RE BOUND FOR BAGDAD ON THE SUBWAY — WHERE PRINCESSES GET IN AT TWELVE O'CLOCK — THE NEXT DAY!
NOEL SICKLES

© A.P. 1936.

Winsor McCay

I NEVER DID LIKE YOU!!!
THAT GOES BOTH WAYS! I WAS CRAZY WHEN I MARRIED YOU!

©N.Y. Herald. 1909

Clare Briggs.

YOU'RE ONE OF THE SLOWEST WORKERS I EVER SAW -- MY ARMS ARE ABOUT READY TO BREAK

1926

Rube Goldberg.

IT'S A LONG TIME SINCE I HAD MY FACE MEASURED FOR A LAUGH
THAT'S ODD — A MAN LAUGHING IN BROOKLYN — HE MUST BE A STRANGER
THE INHABITANTS OF BROOKLYN SMILED FOR THE FIRST TIME IN SIXTEEN YEARS.
BROOKLYN, N.Y.

1919

Cliff Sterrett

GUESS WHAT! MLLE. MODESTE HAS WROTE PAW A LETTER SAYIN' YOU AN' ME CAN'T HAVE ANY MORE CLOTHES TILL OUR BILL IS PAID!
GOOD NIGHT! DID HE HAVE A FIT?

© King Features. 1927

Roy Crane

WHY DO YOU TAKE THESE BACK ROADS INSTEAD OF THE HIGHWAYS, CHUCK?
OH.... YOU MISS THE CROWDS, AND THE SCENERY'S BETTER.
© 1956, King Features Syndicate, Inc. World rights reserved

© King Features. 1956

John Striebel

I HAVE SOME WONDERFUL NEWS!

1929

Harold Gray

CHARITY, EH- CHARITY!!! IF I WAS AS FULL OF CHARITY AS YOU ARE I'D BE THE MOST SUCCESSFUL MORTGAGE-LOAN SHARK OUTSIDE OF SING SING-

© Trib-News Synd. 1924

Fred Opper

FLENCHMEN VELLY HUNGLEE ME GETTEE 'EM SOME SOUP!
HELP! I FAMISH
I WISH TO RETURN INSTANTLY TO THAT DEAR PATERSON, N.J.
I STARVE
4

© King Features. 1906

Alex Kotsky

I'M SORRY... I MUST HAVE LOST IT!

1972

Billy Debeck.

ALL OUR TROUBLES ARE OVER NOW, SWEET WOMAN - I GOTTA RACE HOSS!
SPARK PLUG
DEBECK
—Copyright 1922

1922

Jimmy Swinnerton

7
'OH, DE GLORY'S IN DE SKY! SING HO FO' DE LITTLE 'POSSUM!'

© King Features. 1904

Stan Drake

GOOD NIGHT!
SLAM
GOOD NIGHT, GRADY.

© King Features. 1959

George McManus

WELL · SAY YOU SHOULD HAVE SEEN KID HEAD CHEESE KNOCK THE BLOCK OFF SLANT HEAD MORRIS LAST NIGHT · LOOK · HE STOOD LIKE THIS ·

©King Features. 1912

Elzie Segar.

LAUGH, EMMA, LAUGH!
I CAN'T SEE ANYTHING FUNNY ABOUT A MAN WITH HIS NOSE IN A VASE
11

©King Features. 1929

Walt Kelly

Honor Sick an' Davey Criss-Cross, MacTruloff said to me, Tutor Killduffs Anna Pottage inner Pair threes.
THAT'S HOW IT GOES... AN' NONE TOO SOON.
GIVE HIM A HAND... WHAT GOOD'S A PAIR OF THREES?

1967

Bud Fisher

YOU'RE A CLASSY LITTLE CHICKEN
FEEL HOW COLD MY HAND IS
THE PLACE

© King Feat. 1908

Frank King

THAT'S RIGHT, PAL, YOU'LL PROTECT ME, WON'T YOU!
GO AWAY PAL! I WANT TO BEAT HER UP.

© Trib-News Synd. 1929

Leonard Starr

...WHAT DID HARDING DO THAT WAS SO BAD ANYWAY?...
FORGET HIM. A LOT OF MEN VOTED FOR HIM TOO. WE HAVE A CONTEMPORARY PROBLEM... THERE'S SOMETHING WRONG WITH OUR ACCOUNTS...

© Trib-News Synd. 1968

R.F. Outcault.

1896

Jules Feiffer.

THIS PARTY IS FOR THE BIRDS. LET'S CUT OUT.
BRING OUR WINE BOTTLE. I HEAR ANOTHER ONE UPSTAIRS
8.

© Feiffer. 1956

Once the French guys get hold of a thing, it becomes in their essays a high and serious Art. They did this with the movies in their *Cahiers du Cinema* away back when.

So now it's the 'funnies'. Horn takes *Flash Gordon* (in his intro to one of the Nostalgia Press volumes) and compares and contrasts the 'drang und sturm' of Raymond's middle period with the classicism of his late, the panels ordered 'like French gardens'.

MING, PREPARED AGAINST A RESCUE ATTEMPT BY FLASH, BANQUETS WITH THE UNHAPPY DALE—"IF I KNOW FLASH," SAYS MING, "AND I THINK I DO—IF I CAN JUDGE BY PAST PERFORMANCES, HE'LL COME SOON—AND WHEN HE DOES---"
Copr. 1940, King Features Syndicate, Inc., World rights reserved.
6-8-40.

© 1940 King Features. Raymond

All of this kind of appeals to you at first and then one day you're looking back at Moliterni's dissection of *Hogarth's* narrative technique on *Tarzan*.

NAH

He's got "narrative technique" divided up into types, like 'parallel' and 'accelerated'. You decide it's all cuckoo and razor the pages out. I mean, *Tarzan*, I ask you!

TARZAN WHEELED TO AVOID THE TRAP. THEN, FROM THE OPPOSITE SIDE, ANOTHER GROUP CONVERGED.
Copr. 1950, by Edgar Rice Burroughs, Inc.—Tm. Reg. U. S. Pat. Off.
DISTRIBUTED BY UNITED FEATURE SYNDICATE, INC.

Once you've done that, the book swiftly dismantles itself and you end up filing a couple of pages and losing the rest.

© 1950 United Features. Hogarth.

A remark of Henry Miller's in *The Air-Conditioned Nightmare* just about closes the matter. Seeing a 'funny sheet' on the ground while 'taking a promenade along the rim of the Grand Canyon' ('Prince Valiant was what caught my eye')

"YOU MEN WANTED A FIGHT, NOW YOU'LL HAVE IT! A STRANGE SHIP IS PURSUING US, SO FOLLOW MY ORDERS CLOSELY AND WE'LL RID THE SEAS OF ANOTHER PIRATE!"

© 1941 King Features. Foster

He writes: "What can possibly appear more futile, sterile and insignificant in the presence of such a vast and mysterious spectacle"?"

God.

Anyway, all this will be running through your noggin while Claude's over there, sipping his Pernod.

You will be arguing with yourself that no matter where one's head has gone in the meantime, one should take the opportunity to acknowledge the receipt of influence at an earlier date and you will proceed forthwith:

Bonjour

He'll seem quite pleased to be recognized in a foreign place for a book published 16 years back.

The small, independent comics publishers are here, too; Knockabout, for instance, at this time right in the middle of another prosecution.

The police are trying an interesting new trick by getting them under the Obscenity law for books about drugs.

Attempt to widen obscene books act fails

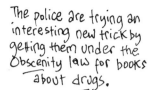

The jury won't know what to make of it and the Knockabouts will go home happy but harrassed. They'll have just published a neat big fundraiser to cover legal costs.

KNOCKABOUT
SPECIAL
1984

They'll cheerfully get along like this forever. The tea-leaves show them fourteen years from here jumping out of an aeroplane to raise funds to fight an umpteenth prosecution.

The Escape boys are here, taking the opportunity to mooch an invitation to the big comics festival in Angoulême.

And the third English independent publisher, *Titan*, who will only ever put out collections of stuff that's already successful. Take chances, us?

If that's your mighty three-pronged cake-fork assault on the world of culture, you might as well go home and go to sleep. Wait! You've just seen Posy Simmonds hiding behind the rubber plant.

ALEC. HAVE YOU MET POSY.

Her weekly half-page in *the Guardian* is a treasure.

How much I want to **spit** on your basket-weave!...
CRUNCH
CRUNCH
© Posy Simmonds 1984

Time to go. The Escape boys will have got what they want and will be slipping out just ahead of you.
Wait. Manners. Shake the host's mitt, mumble something in o-level French.
Moliterni's mitt will get in the way. You'll shake it again cheerily. You wouldn't have thought reading his book would be such a big deal. And you cutting it all up like that too.
Kiss the hostess in the French manner
It's been a wonderful time. I thank you, m'am
Then the Cultural Counsellor to the French Embassy's wife will say:
You must come again.
And you'll light out of there before anyone can contradict the sweet lady.
A good night's work.
A good night's work, indeed.
MR SMITH! QUICK! WAKE UP!
NOEL SICKLES
"Noel Sickles - 'Scorchy Smith' © 1935 - A.P. Syndicate
Addendum:
From Pat Rogers' editorial intro to The Oxford Illustrated History of English Literature, a must for us who don't mind a lot of pictorial documentation with our reading:
"Is literary history necessary? It is possible... to write great literature with little or no sense of one's place in a great tradition Shakespeare would have had very little idea of his historical bearings. The truth is that literary history is a modern invention and so is the automatic sense which a modern writer must have of his location in the flow of literary time (whether or not he cares about it)."

Chapter Seven

The map of the history of Art is like any other map. There are main roads and side streets; old masters and lesser masters

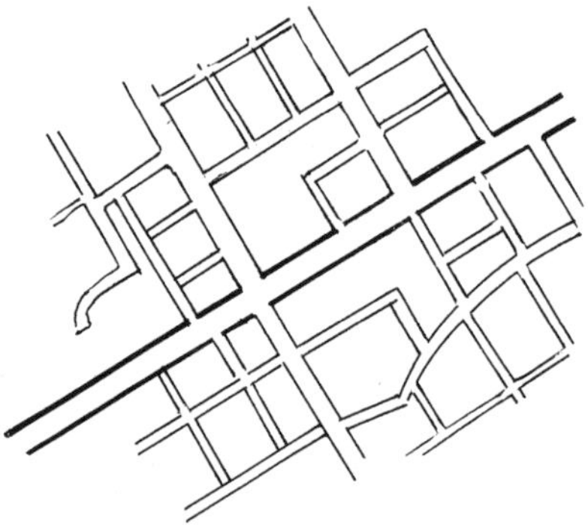

But there are also back yards, middens, coal bunkers and rhubarb patches; artisans so minor that their names will never be retrieved from the debris in the vacant lot.

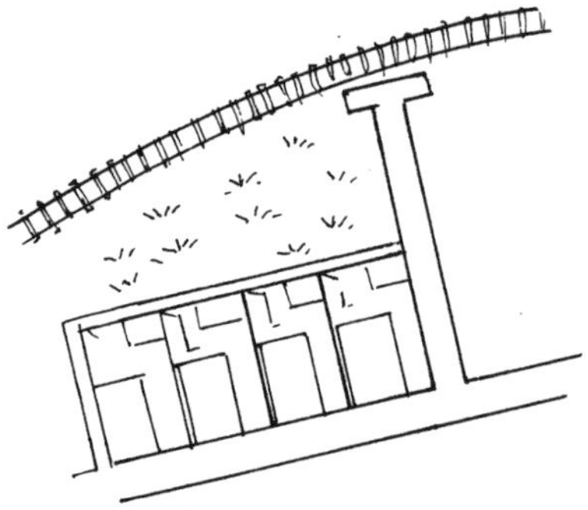

Lovers of old art may speculate on whether the *Housebook Master* is the same bloke as the *Master of the Amsterdam Print-room* or whether the *Circumcision in Aachen* may be given to the *Master of the Tucher Altarpiece*.

1450

It may sound like moving old dust around to some, but the joy of spending time with those works is to you like a grand meal with a fine wine.

No doubt that's lost on many also. To them, eating and drinking is but refuelling. Keep a pump in the kitchen and top up three times a day.

UNLEADED
OIL CHANGE ?

No the fine things speak across physical and temporal distances. A song, a tale, a cartoon, a chair.

Oh gie me a lass wi' a dowry, the nice yellow guineas for Meeeee
Burns, 1790s

However, the pleasantly naive among us may think that the measure of art is that it "has passed the test of time". No map remains for long an accurate representation of the locale.

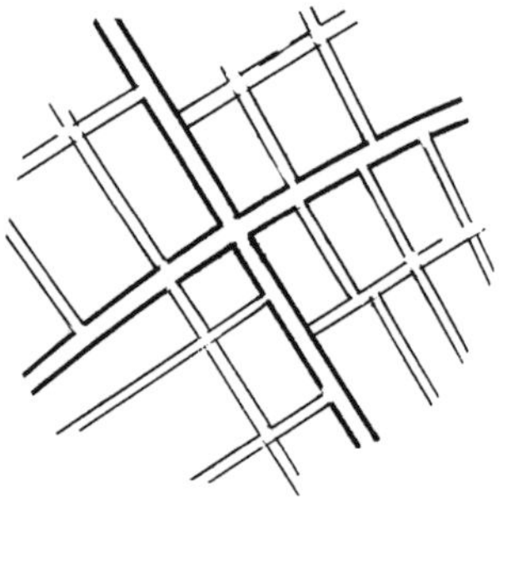

Favour ebbs and flows. The crossroads is turned into a flyover, an underpass. The disused road was once a thoroughfare. The Via Roman underneath it all is nowhere indicated.

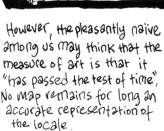

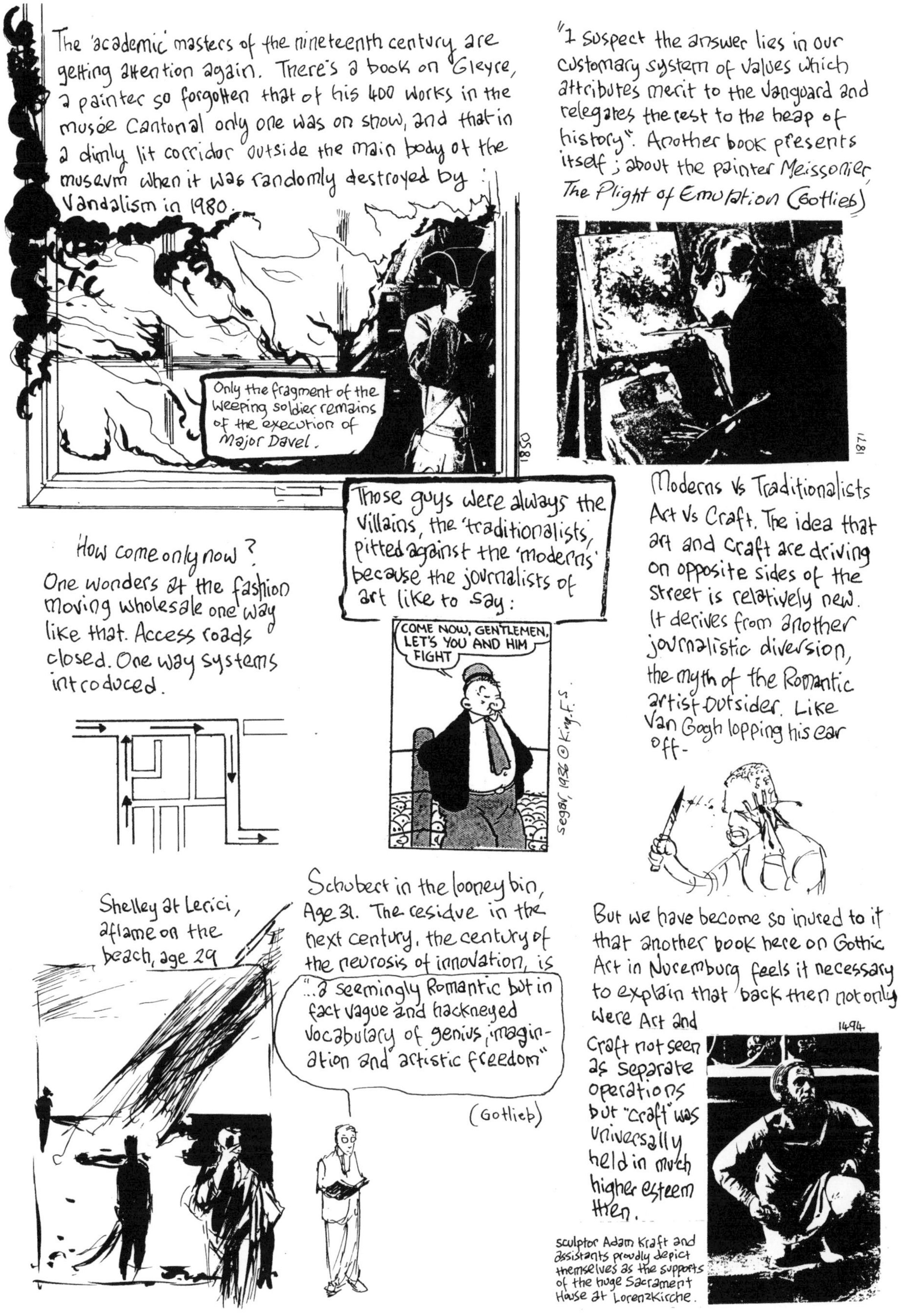
The 'academic' masters of the nineteenth century are getting attention again. There's a book on Gleyre, a painter so forgotten that of his 400 works in the musée Cantonal only one was on show, and that in a dimly lit corridor outside the main body of the museum when it was randomly destroyed by vandalism in 1980.
Only the fragment of the weeping soldier remains of the execution of Major Davel.
1850
"I suspect the answer lies in our customary system of values which attributes merit to the vanguard and relegates the rest to the heap of history". Another book presents itself; about the painter Meissonier, The Plight of Emulation (Gotlieb)
1871
How come only now? One wonders at the fashion moving wholesale one way like that. Access roads closed. One way systems introduced.
Those guys were always the villains, the 'traditionalists', pitted against the 'moderns' because the journalists of art like to say:
COME NOW, GENTLEMEN, LET'S YOU AND HIM FIGHT
Segar, 1936 © King F.S.
Moderns vs Traditionalists Art vs Craft. The idea that art and craft are driving on opposite sides of the street is relatively new. It derives from another journalistic diversion, the myth of the Romantic artist-outsider. Like Van Gogh lopping his ear off.
Shelley at Lerici, aflame on the beach, age 29
Schubert in the looney bin, Age 31. The residue in the next century, the century of the neurosis of innovation, is
"...a seemingly Romantic but in fact vague and hackneyed vocabulary of genius, imagination and artistic freedom"
(Gotlieb)
But we have become so inured to it that another book here on Gothic Art in Nuremburg feels it necessary to explain that back then not only were Art and Craft not seen as separate operations but "craft" was universally held in much higher esteem then.
1494
Sculptor Adam Kraft and assistants proudly depict themselves as the supports of the huge Sacrament House at Lorenzkirche.

The same book, discussing the anonymity of 15th Century Masters, explains it as though we can no longer revive a tribal memory of how it used to be, even though anonymous works of art flicker past our gaze daily among TV commercials.

And it is careful to advise that just because an altarpiece happens to bear a master's signature doesn't mean he made the whole thing with his own two hands.

Strange that this has to be explained in a century when Disney signs all his movies and Ford signs all his autos.

Ford
Next!

The personal touch of the master. Another journalistic myth. They're everywhere.

RED! THERE!

The daydream is still in currency that one may labour obscurely in a garret in one's life and strut proudly down the mainstreet of the Map of Art in an artistic afterlife.

I would rather achieve immortality by not dying.

The adventure of fame is a separate one from the adventure of Art, though one may be used to further the other.

Self Portrait Warhol - 1970s

And cartography is a separate discipline altogether: "This is the true spirit of history, which fulfils its real purpose in making men prudent and showing them how to live, apart from the pleasure it brings in presenting past events as if they were in the present" (Vasari, Lives of the Artists 1568)

Self portrait

The true history of humour may never be written. It defies that kind of organisation. It is the interlude, the relief, graffiti, the half-hidden gesture, the barnacle, the midden, the rhubarb patch.

Print by Kuniyoshi: "Graffiti on a storehouse wall" - 1847, Japan.
(one presumes the artist is 'mugging' rather than reporting)

It's Shakespeare's clown, Will Kemp, Morris-dancing his way from London to Norwich as a stunt in 1600 and writing a book about it.

It takes you by surprise in reproductions from illuminated manuscripts. Sometimes it's ribald and obvious

Sometimes the subject isn't meant to be funny but you know from a certain feeling of kinship that the satirical monk got this job because the pious one had the flu that week.

15th C

Galen lecturing on the application of enemas

It's in ancient Greek terracotta statuettes of everyday life.

Bosch

1490s

Chinese guy with bear on a pole.

a Japanese official

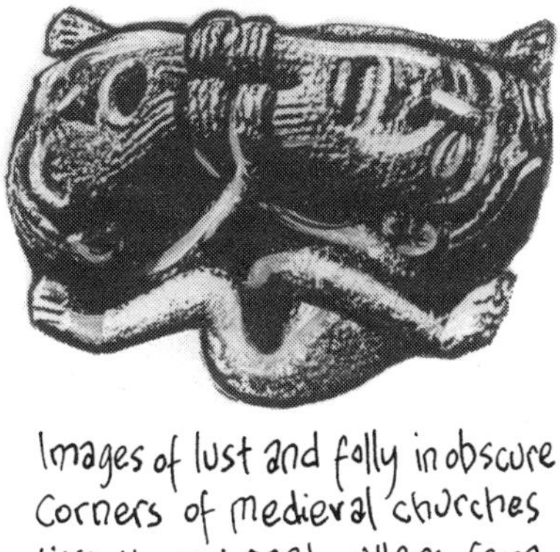

Images of lust and folly in obscure corners of medieval churches like these beard-pullers from France.

It's sweet and gentle in Erasmus' *Praise of Folly*.

Clap your hands, live well, and drink

Ms. Folly descends from the pulpit on the last page, from Hans Holbein's own hand-illustrated copy c 1515

English entertainer Charles Mathews in 1820's New York reported the following dialogue from a black production of *Hamlet*.

To be or not to be, dat is him question, whether him nobler in de mind to suffer or lift up him arms against one sea of hubble-bubble and by oppossum, end 'em.
Poss
Possum up a gum tree!
Possum up a gum tree
SING POSSUM
Poss
Possum up a gum tree

(cast and audience break into song: Possum up a gum tree, up he go, up he go)

It's vitriolic in the Reformation pamphlet war.

The Pope is crowned in the jaws of Hell c1545

Native American face-masks.

Iroquois, late 19th c

It's Bernini's party-trick caricatures.

c 1640

It's banana skins.

Feet-ticklers.

the fart in the public library.

Chapter Eight
While some guy's jabbering about ART, you'll be moving house, Alec MacGarry.
It's the Australian, you see. They come from a big open place and they can never be happy again.
I need more space
It's a country with nothing as far as the eye can see. You must go and see it for yourself (as an Australian once exhorted me to do).
HUH?
Never one to waste time on these projects, you'll grab the first place you hear about
we've got to move out by the weekend.
Come again.
KILL
There will come a phase in your life when you move in and out of flats so fast you're already measuring them up for a nostalgic effect on your way in.
The landlady sports a sprig of broccoli in her front teeth. Surely she must notice.
It's an awful place. You'll sit on the front stoop and wonder what the hell you've gone and done.
The attraction was the Georgian bedroom doors big enough to drive a car through.
WOW!

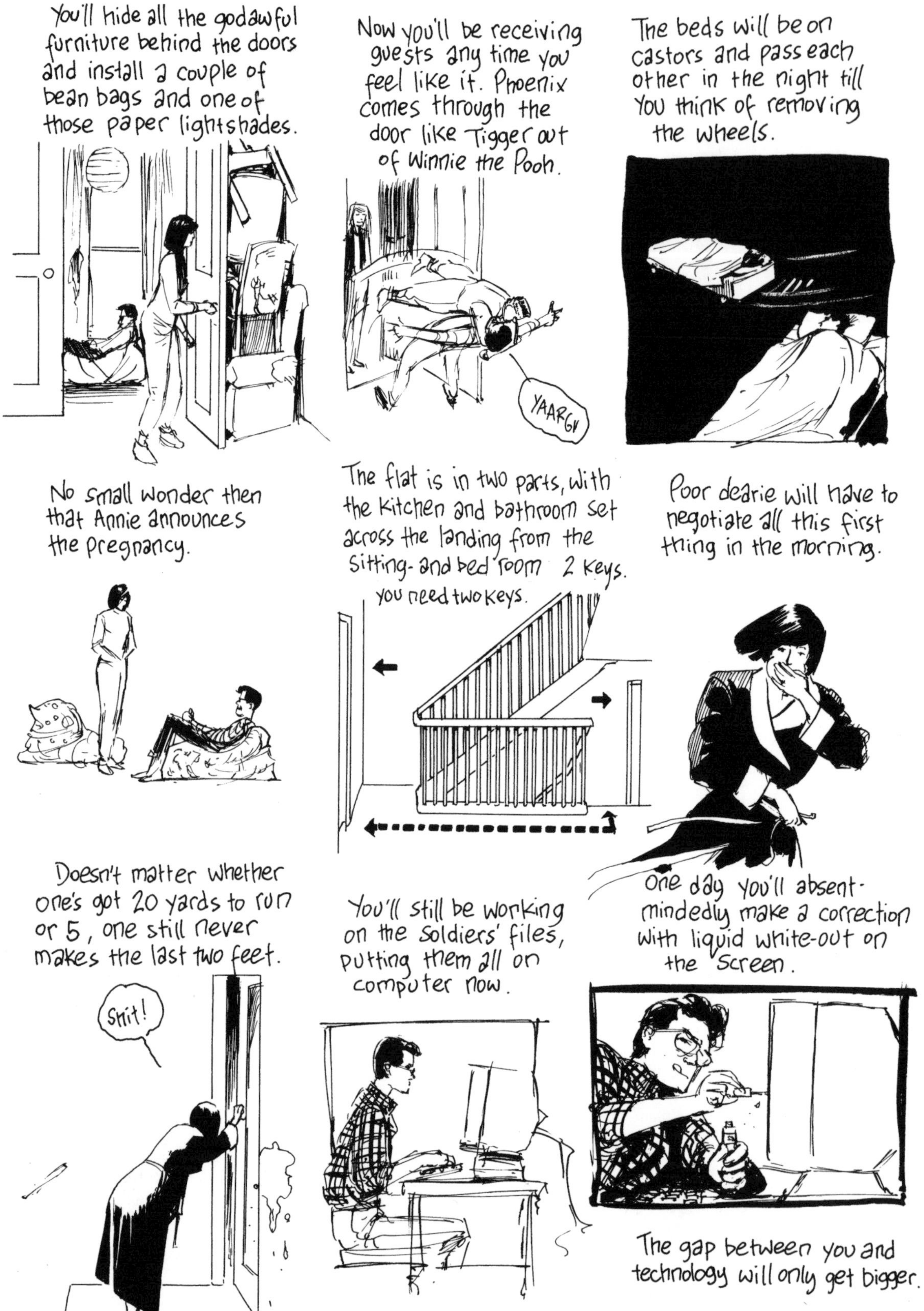
You'll hide all the godawful furniture behind the doors and install a couple of bean bags and one of those paper lightshades.
Now you'll be receiving guests any time you feel like it. Phoenix comes through the door like Tigger out of Winnie the Pooh.
YAARGH
The beds will be on castors and pass each other in the night till you think of removing the wheels.
No small wonder then that Annie announces the pregnancy.
The flat is in two parts, with the kitchen and bathroom set across the landing from the sitting- and bed room 2 keys.
you need two keys.
Poor dearie will have to negotiate all this first thing in the morning.
Doesn't matter whether one's got 20 yards to run or 5, one still never makes the last two feet.
Shit!
You'll still be working on the soldiers' files, putting them all on computer now.
One day you'll absent-mindedly make a correction with liquid white-out on the screen.
The gap between you and technology will only get bigger.

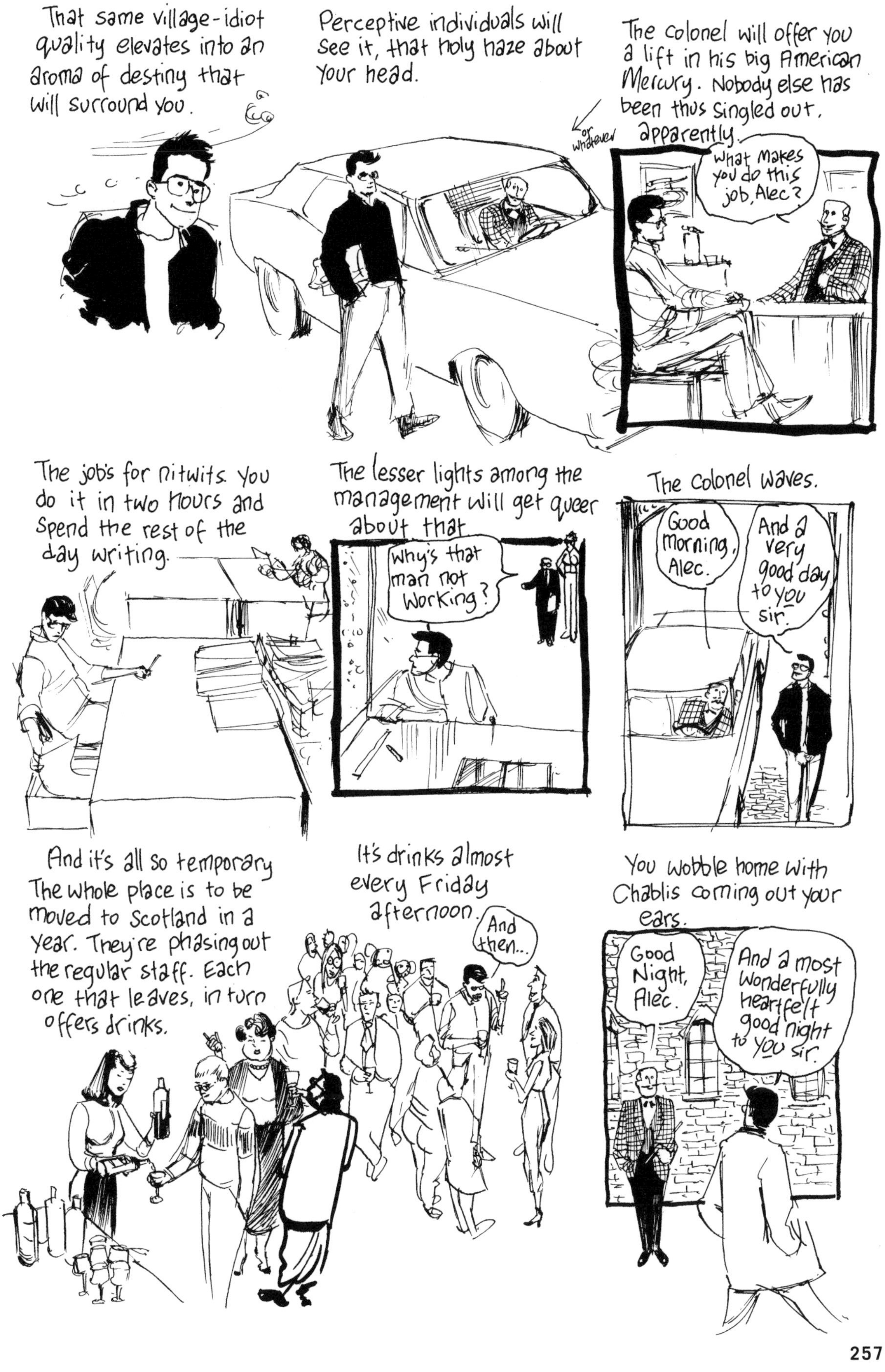
That same village-idiot quality elevates into an aroma of destiny that will surround you.
Perceptive individuals will see it, that holy haze about your head.
The colonel will offer you a lift in his big American Mercury. Nobody else has been thus singled out, apparently.
or whatever
What makes you do this job, Alec?
The job's for nitwits. You do it in two hours and spend the rest of the day writing.
The lesser lights among the management will get queer about that
Why's that man not working?
The colonel waves.
Good morning, Alec.
And a very good day to you sir.
And it's all so temporary The whole place is to be moved to Scotland in a year. They're phasing out the regular staff. Each one that leaves, in turn offers drinks.
It's drinks almost every Friday afternoon.
And then...
You wobble home with Chablis coming out your ears.
Good Night, Alec.
And a most wonderfully heartfelt good night to you sir.

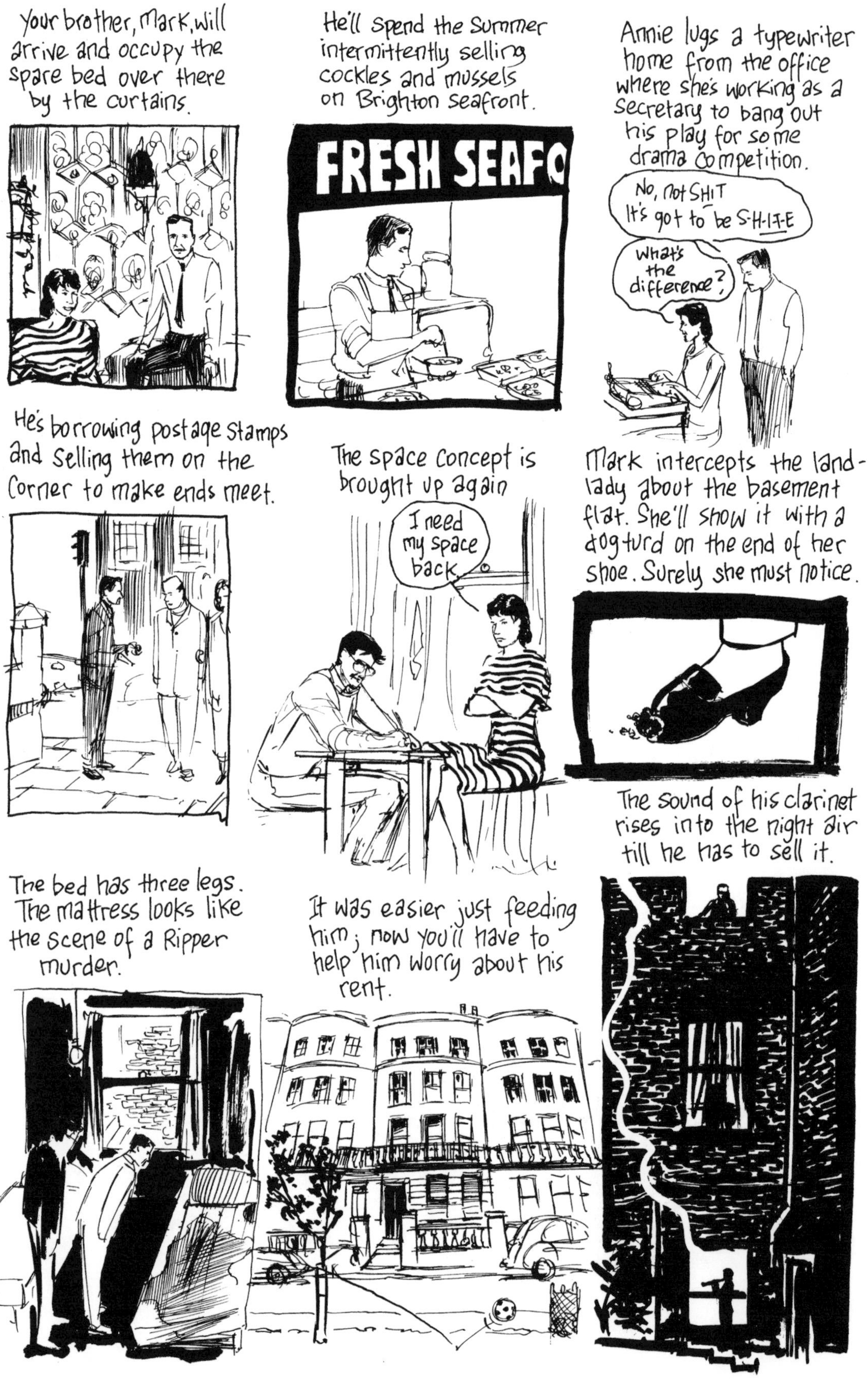
Your brother, Mark, will arrive and occupy the spare bed over there by the curtains.
He'll spend the Summer intermittently selling cockles and mussels on Brighton seafront.
FRESH SEAFO
Annie lugs a typewriter home from the office where she's working as a secretary to bang out his play for some drama competition.
No, not SHIT It's got to be S-H-I-T-E
What's the difference?
He's borrowing postage stamps and selling them on the Corner to make ends meet.
The space concept is brought up again
I need my space back.
Mark intercepts the landlady about the basement flat. She'll show it with a dog turd on the end of her shoe. Surely she must notice.
The sound of his clarinet rises into the night air till he has to sell it.
The bed has three legs. The mattress looks like the scene of a Ripper murder.
It was easier just feeding him; now you'll have to help him worry about his rent.

You'll draw into the wee hours, originality and skill in inverse proportion, as always, as everywhere, reaching towards the moment when they change places.
When are you coming to bed, honey?
On Sunday mornings there will often be a traveller on the spare bed over there by the curtains with holes big enough to pass a watermelon through.
Maybe tall Jenny from Canada.
Dakin with his guitar
Trevvy Trevs and Charmaine.
GOTCHA!
Everybody will be full of unfulfillable promise in the cheery winesodden Friday afternoon of your life when you feel an unbearable nostalgia for events less than a day after they happen. You just see if I'm not wrong, Alec MacGarry. Just see if the Monday morning of your life don't arrive like a broken elevator.

Letter from Phoenix. His visit to you will have galvanized him into dropping both the Town Planning course and the day job plan in exchange for being an artist complete and whole.
You'll wonder why you have this effect on your fellows. It's not like you've given up your own day job.
Elliott will have dropped his job right at the onset, just after you met him. Surely you wouldn't have known him long enough to be such a bad influence.
You'll take a holiday down to Devon with the Elliotts. Phil needs to have it all arranged in advance to allay all fears.
He's in convulsions of terror in case they misplace his booking and when he gets there nobody will know who he is.
GUEST HOUSE
we're all right
He cooks a midday meal and then enjoys his repose.
Now I'll have my scrumpy, dear.
You come up with a bunch of comic strip ideas to sell to "subject" magazines, like computer mags and medical journals etc.
HAVE YOU BEEN HAVING FLATULENCE?
WHAT DOES THAT MEAN?
OH NO... IT MUST HAVE BEEN ONE OF YOU!
© Campbell - Elliott '85
Eventually you'll realize it's only keeping you both from your important work.
START WITHOUT ME
NOT FUNNY

The second part of your graphic novel will have come out a year after the first to hardly any notice whatsoever.
The 'media' thrives only on novelties, but you knew that, didn't you?
LOVE AND BEERGLASSES
ALEC
MORE EPISODES FROM THE LIFE OF ALEC MacGARRY
ESCAPE
Campbell © 85
The trouble is; you'll feel that your second volume is definitely not as arresting as the first.
You'll determine to cure the problem with the opening to your third.
"A funny notion occurred to me while I was drowning..."
..."I saw humanity all pasted together with semen..."
The thing about hitting the mark with ideas is that you'll rarely know at the time when one has opened a door.
Usually you won't be aiming to kick a door in, just create a lively piece of humour
"It was dripping off the ends of noses."
One door's already banging in the wind. A comic called GAG lands in somebody's hands in California.
Deadline
GAG
One of Elliott and Dakin's bright ideas, all the parties involved will have chucked in fifteen quid and got 200 copies to dispose of.
!GAG!
steve way
ed pinsent • trevs phoenix
eddie campbell • phil elliott
russell christian • glenn dakin
Dakin © 84

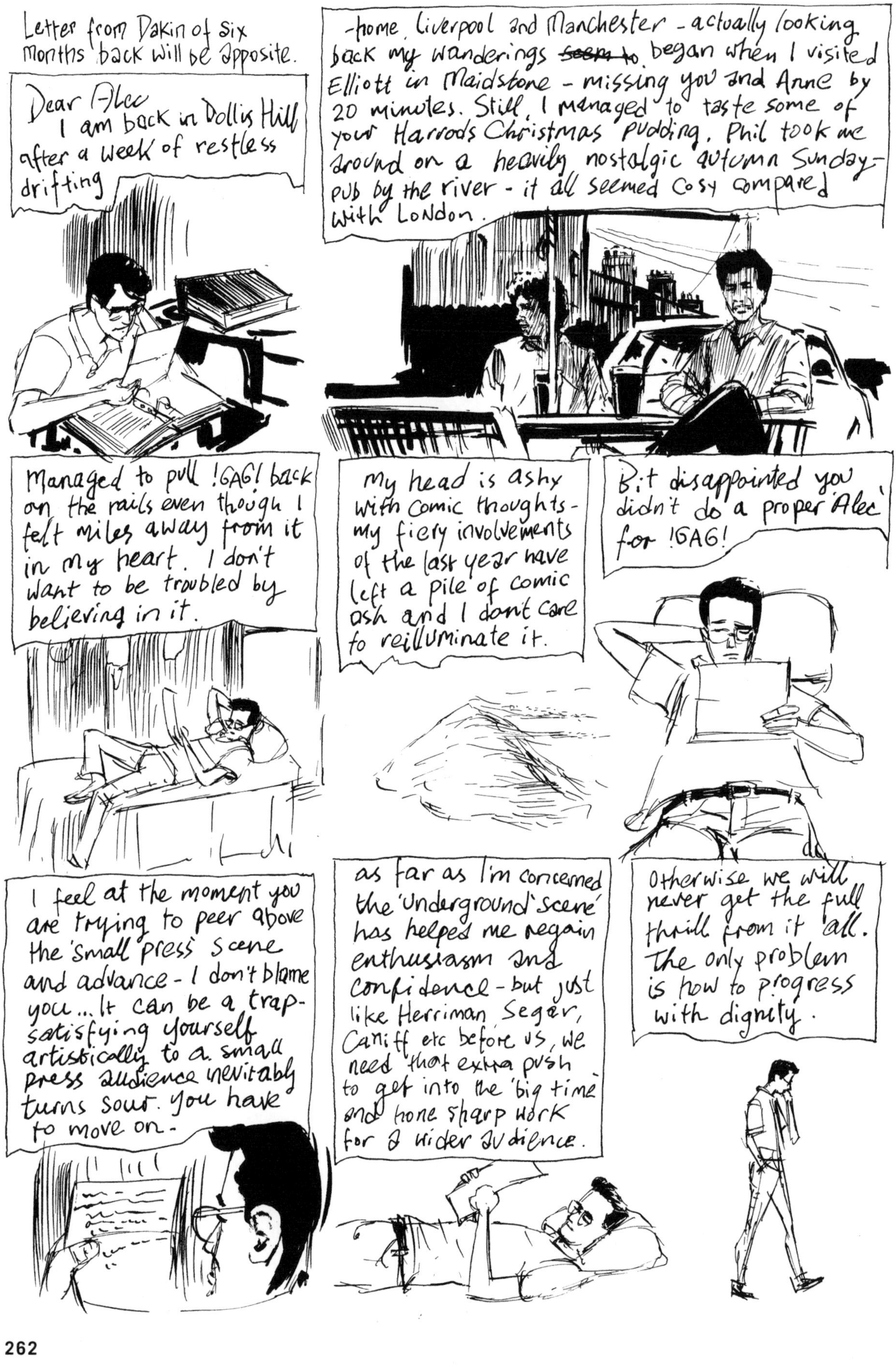

Letter from Dakin of six months back will be apposite.
Dear Alec
I am back in Dollis Hill after a week of restless drifting
-home, Liverpool and Manchester - actually looking back my wanderings seem to began when I visited Elliott in Maidstone - missing you and Anne by 20 minutes. Still, I managed to taste some of your Harrods Christmas pudding. Phil took me around on a heavily nostalgic autumn Sunday - pub by the river - it all seemed cosy compared with London.
Managed to pull !GAG! back on the rails even though I felt miles away from it in my heart. I don't want to be troubled by believing in it.
My head is ashy with comic thoughts - my fiery involvements of the last year have left a pile of comic ash and I don't care to reilluminate it.
Bit disappointed you didn't do a proper 'Alec' for !GAG!
I feel at the moment you are trying to peer above the 'small press' scene and advance - I don't blame you... It can be a trap - satisfying yourself artistically to a small press audience inevitably turns sour. You have to move on.
as far as I'm concerned the 'underground' scene has helped me regain enthusiasm and confidence - but just like Herriman, Segar, Caniff etc before us, we need that extra push to get into the 'big time' and hone sharp work for a wider audience.
Otherwise we will never get the full thrill from it all. The only problem is how to progress with dignity.

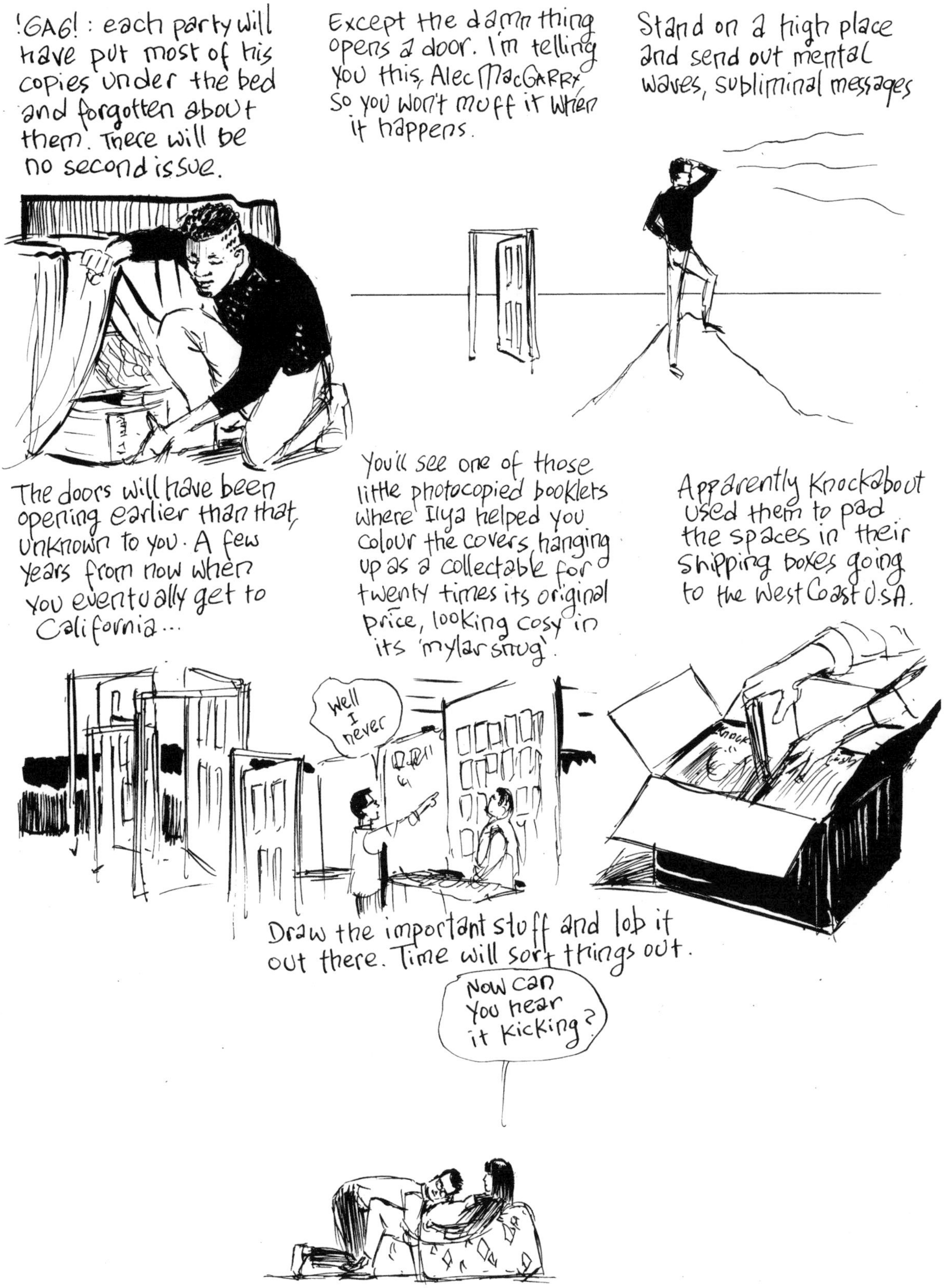
!GAG! : each party will have put most of his copies under the bed and forgotten about them. There will be no second issue.
Except the damn thing opens a door. I'm telling you this, Alec MacGARRY, so you won't muff it when it happens.
Stand on a high place and send out mental waves, subliminal messages
The doors will have been opening earlier than that, unknown to you. A few years from now when you eventually get to California...
You'll see one of those little photocopied booklets where Ilya helped you colour the covers hanging up as a collectable for twenty times its original price, looking cosy in its 'mylar snug'.
Apparently Knockabout used them to pad the spaces in their shipping boxes going to the West Coast U.S.A.
Well I never
Draw the important stuff and lob it out there. Time will sort things out.
Now can you hear it kicking?

Chapter Nine

The first indication that serious critical acclaim is to visit the world of the comics will be Art Spiegelman's nomination for the National Book Critics Circle Award in biography for his *Maus*.

I WANT TO TELL YOUR STORY, THE WAY IT REALLY HAPPENED.
Spiegelman © '80 '86

The first sign that there's any money in it will be Alan Moore's white suit.

New York is the center of this particular world. There will always be a center and you can depend on it being away over somewhere else. New Yorker Spiegelman imagined it would be France

Success will eventually demand of you an expedition.

Big hairy Alan Moore's stirring up a storm with the muck monster monthly so the company flies him into the Big Apple for a publicity jaunt. Safely back in Northampton, he gives Escape an article about it.

"I find I'm only able to sleep about 3 hours a night. There's an airconditioning unit which takes me two days to realise I can switch off and there is a little notice informing me that I should keep the door double-locked and always look through the peephole before answering in case it's a bag-lady with a meat cleaver and a shopping bag full of index fingers."

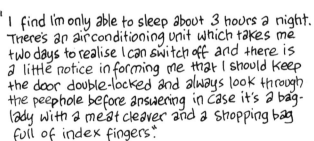

"Julie orders me a corned beef sandwich that consists of two slices of bread with a mound of beef between approximately the size of Mickey Rooney"

We'll all think he's joking and pay no attention to the signs, which include a narrative in Knockabout titled Globetrotting for Agoraphobics, which he'll get you to illustrate.
Moore's U.S. artistic collaborators on the muck monster, horror maniac Bissette, and Totleben, and their wives, will be over for the London Convention.
Come and spend your last night with us and we'll get you to Gatwick airport.
At first they won't be too sure about it, but you'll get to play host with your big bedroom doors and assorted mattresses.
A million years from now when you own a house with more than two rooms you'll wonder at everyone enjoying this ramshackle hospitality.
As an afterthought, you'll show your Australian crime piece, The Pyjama Girl, or at least, the photocopy you had the sense to keep.
And in the morning Annie will drive you all around looking for an English castle
The best you can find is Roedean girls' school. Bissette loves it.
MY GOD WHAT A CHILLY PLACE
You won't even be aware at the time of the importance of this friendship you'll have struck up.
© D.C Comics
To EDDIE & ANNIE - SRBISSETTE 7/85
Live well and toast the gods, Alec MacGarry. Fate is minding the wheel

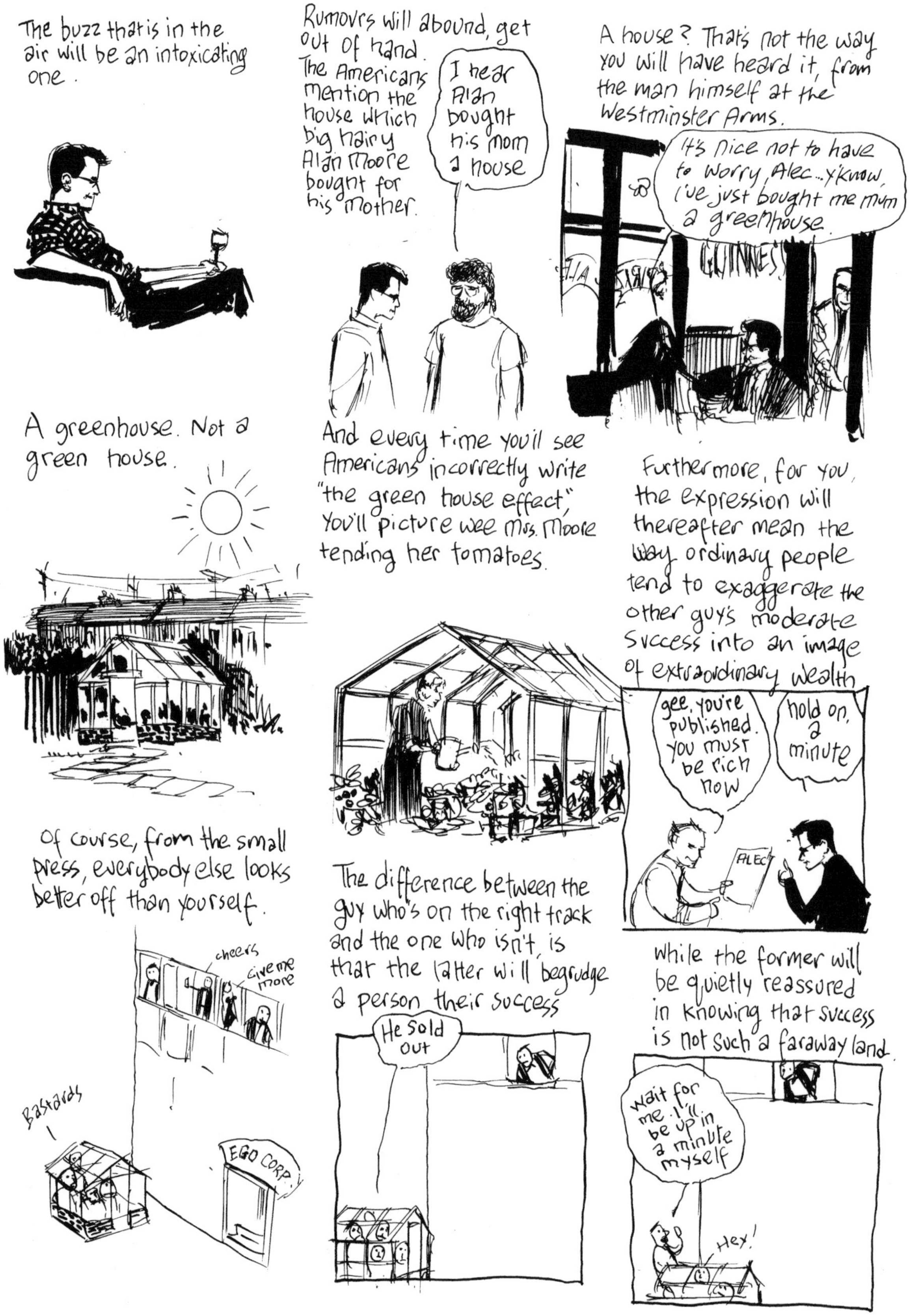
The buzz that is in the air will be an intoxicating one.
Rumours will abound, get out of hand. The Americans mention the house which big hairy Alan Moore bought for his mother.
I hear Alan bought his mom a house
A house? That's not the way you will have heard it, from the man himself at the Westminster Arms.
It's nice not to have to worry, Alec... y'know, i've just bought me mum a greenhouse.
GUINNESS
A greenhouse. Not a green house.
And every time you'll see Americans incorrectly write "the green house effect", you'll picture wee Mrs. Moore tending her tomatoes.
Furthermore, for you, the expression will thereafter mean the way ordinary people tend to exaggerate the other guy's moderate success into an image of extraordinary wealth
gee, you're published. you must be rich now
hold on, a minute
ALEC
Of course, from the small press, everybody else looks better off than yourself.
cheers
give me more
Bastards
EGO CORP.
The difference between the guy who's on the right track and the one who isn't, is that the latter will begrudge a person their success
He sold out
While the former will be quietly reassured in knowing that success is not such a faraway land.
Wait for me. I'll be up in a minute myself
Hey!

Big hairy Alan Moore will be on the verge of becoming a celebrity.

Fate will move mountains to accommodate the man of destiny.
Ha! You mean even a slate falling off a roof will contrive to miss him?

He's already examining from a whole bunch of viewpoints the theme of a person's control of life and history in his first drafts of the script for the Watchmen, soon to be his first huge graphic novel success.

You'll be watching Danny Grey's alsatian having pups on a cold winter night. They're all coming out dead.

He'll have buried a couple before succeeding in getting the vet round.

AW

The vet takes the third dead pup and does extraordinary violence to it.

Well, waddaye know? At times like this the difference between all and nothing can seem close to random.

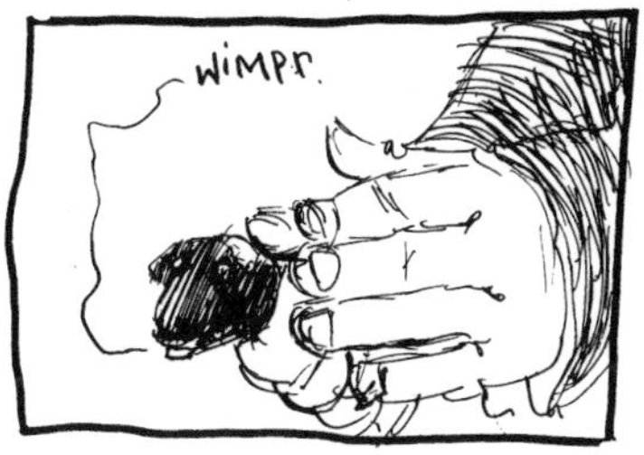
WIMPR

As an agent of Fate Danny Grey will find himself wanting. Make sure your account is in the black.

Alec, I think I killed the other two.

The reminders will be everywhere. Annie will slip on the ice, carrying the baby.

OH SHIT

And you, carrying the new china dinner set. no damage.

In the collective noodle of history, or at least, that obscure corner of the car-boot of history where comics are remembered at all, it will be the age, or the phase, of the 'graphic novel'.

COMIC STRIP
COMIC BOOK
graphic novel

Really, all the man in the street will remember of comics will be the icons like Batman and Superman, Charlie Brown, Popeye.

But the bookish fraternity will have it divided up in phases, three in fact:
1. The newspaper comic-strip, which thrived in the first half of the 20th century,

HAW HAW!

But of course it was still around during:
2. The heyday of the comic book, the 40s and 50s, with occasional revivals after that.

And both survived to see the final great fireburst expiration of the art in its final phase, that of 3. the graphic novel.

"Graphic Novel". Will Eisner invented the term. He'd already had a career, as a young man, at the onset of the previous phase. You'll always get oddbodies that won't stay in their proper categories.

I'd like to show you something different... it's a... uh... novel. you might say a, uh... graphic novel..
BANTAM BOOKS

A Contract With God, in 1978, was the book. The idea of a big damn serious event of a comic dealing with stuff worth thinking and talking about was already fermenting in various heads:

This isn't quite it, but who'd've thought Eisner..

Of his next two, appearing in parts over the following eight years, *Life on Another Planet* will seem a step backwards but *A Life Force* will be the goods.

YOU HAVEN'T CHANGED AT ALL! I RECOGNIZED YOU AT ONCE..
OH, JACOB, I'M AN OLD LADY NOW!
'85 © Will Eisner. A Life Force

There can be displays of sentimentality and melodrama in Eisner's 'serious' works that would be at home in a reconstruction of Dickens but sit uncomfortably in the 1980s. However his best book waits down the track...

?

So he invented it and then it got hijacked by the moneyspiders and the bullshitters issuing their foolish masquerades as 'graphic novels' so that we'd just as soon go back to calling the real McCoy just 'comics'
It wasn't clear when Moore's first significant big work was coming out in parts in Warrior that it was a 'graphic novel'. Far from the 'center', it got lost in the confusion of publisher-collapse and acrimony.
FASCIST BRITAIN 1997. EVERYONE KNOWS YOU CAN'T BEAT THE SYSTEM ...EVERYONE BUT V.
© D.C. Comics. Art: Leach.
And it won't get finished until after his second big work will be a roaring success.
© D.C. Comics. Art: Gibbons.
In between these he churns out the muck monster for four years. The graphic novel is the mountain peak on a solid core of bread and butter.
TYPITTY TYPE TYPITTY TYPE
Maus comes out in parts in RAW while Spiegelman edits bubblegum novelties. He doesn't like 'graphic novel'. Finds it genteel and unnecessary.
YOU WILL TAKE AN UNEXPECTED TRIP!
DOWN A MANHOLE!
© Topps Bubblegum. Art: Lynch.
1986. It's funny how a whole mess of things will happen all at once.
Comicbook scribblers will become fashion plates
HAVE YOU SEEN BILLY THE SINK?
The media will be gathering on the phone wires.
Alec! My waters have broken
oh Jeezis oh fuck oh.

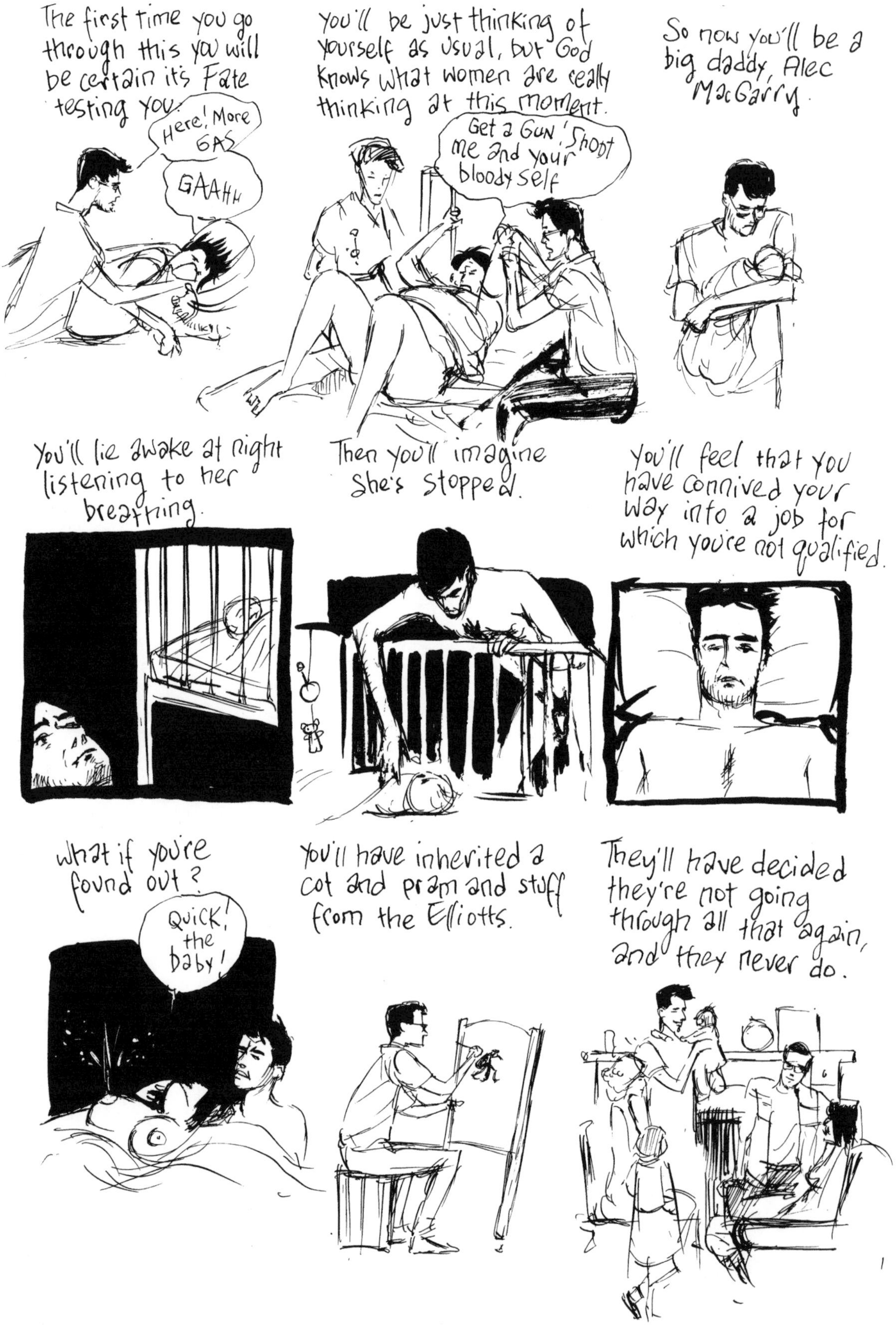
The first time you go through this you will be certain it's Fate testing you.
Here! More GAS
GAAHH
You'll be just thinking of yourself as usual, but God knows what women are really thinking at this moment.
Get a Gun! Shoot me and your bloody self
So now you'll be a big daddy, Alec MacGarry.
You'll lie awake at night listening to her breathing.
Then you'll imagine she's stopped.
You'll feel that you have connived your way into a job for which you're not qualified.
what if you're found out?
Quick! the baby!
You'll have inherited a cot and pram and stuff from the Elliotts.
They'll have decided they're not going through all that again, and they never do.

Annie's parents will be staying at the time the baby arrives.
Her dad will be waiting outside the Cricketers for you every night on your way home from the office.
One night you'll forget to go home for dinner
After you, Jack
Coward.
He's the shire Chairman of the County of Hinchinbrook in tropical North Queensland which is like the country version of the mayor.
He'll come armed with a document of introduction with which to present himself to British dignitaries.
Meeting no dignitaries he'll give it to the barman of the Cricketers
You're the only important person I've met so far
Gee
Then they'll fly off leaving behind them a bad case of homesickness
That's all you need

Chapter Ten
Fate taketh and Fate giveth away
A month after becoming a father you'll finish your day-job. You won't know it then, of course, but it's the last one you'll ever have.
That won't be so bad; it's on the cards. But the very same day you'll lose your art job, the weekly SOUNDS thing.
"For some time I've had misgivings about your strip cartoon...
Exactly one night later there'll be a foreign voice asking if you were to be invited on an all-expenses paid trip to Switzerland, would you accept?
You have to go, darling; don't worry about me.
The Man at the Crossroads will explain:
It's the comics festival in the little Alpine town of Sierre. Each year they have a different guest country. Last year it was China, next it's India. I'm coming with you, at my own expense.
So a committee of people in the know will have selected five representatives of British Comic Art, to show the broadest spectrum, and you'll be in it, for your isolated and ambitious use of autobiography.
You'll think it odd, being wined and dined in the Alps at a time when you're completely out of work, but these things are to be expected. Trust me.
DEPARTURES
Tell you what though; you never realized they got 40° heat up there.

Brian Bolland's another invitee. You first knew him 12 years ago during your wasted year at Art School in London.
It's a pity we don't meet these days, Alec. We seem to be in separate camps.
He'll have been the first in a growing wave of British talent moving in on American comic books, a phenomenon he represents like this:
cover Comics Journal 1987 © BOLLAND
retouched from the colour by Campbell
Kevin O'Neill's here too. He's an agreeable oddity. With writer Pat Mills he does a thing full of the wicked satire of a rejected Catholic upbringing.
NEED THE WORDS OF TORQUEMADA! BE PURE...! BE VIGILANT...!
BEHAVE!
© IPC 1981 - Nemesis by Mills e O'Neil
We're met in Geneva by an expat Liverpudlian named Gordon and it's up into the Tobleroney Alps...
BD 86
...Always another one behind the one you see.
Fendant and *dôle* wines at a street-table café all paid for by the festival. You're concerned on behalf of the show about their money being chucked about so merrily. Maybe you should get out more often, Alec MacGarry.
hey, you're the guest.
You'll never have the run of an expense account like that. and will remain unsure as to whether you enjoy being on either side of this indirect line to the owners money.
I've been escorting Don Lawrence and his wife around for 2 days. this is nothing
Gordon's a volunteer at the festival, immediately assigned to *British liaison*. His own work is his small bar in the hills, a tourist thing. In the off-season (now) he buys up novelties to sell:
such as ski-poles with hollowed hand-grips to hold a few nips of cognac.
also, I'm importing this thing called a 'reflex'
a what?

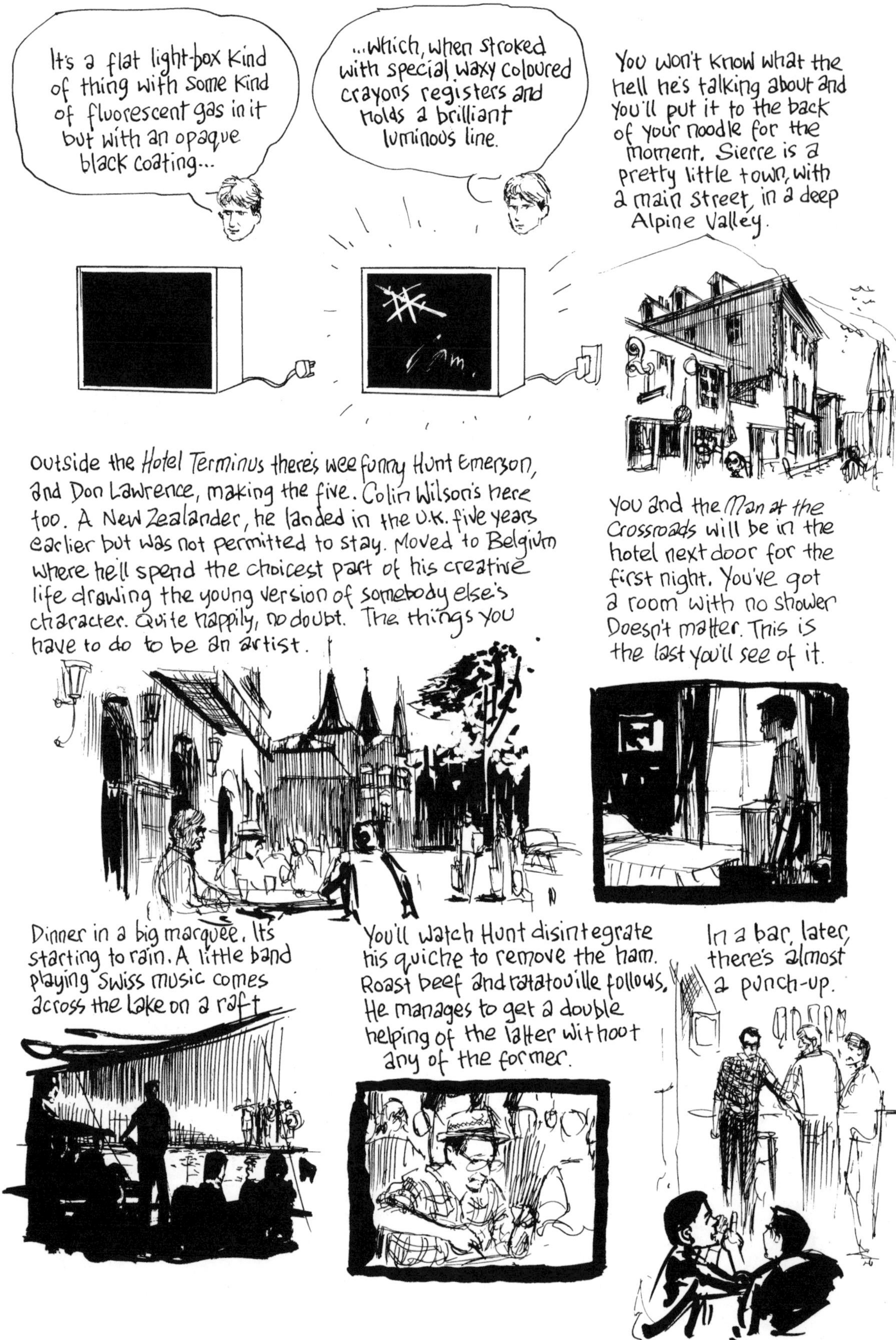

It's a flat light-box kind of thing with some kind of fluorescent gas in it but with an opaque black coating...
...which, when stroked with special waxy coloured crayons registers and holds a brilliant luminous line.
You won't know what the hell he's talking about and you'll put it to the back of your noodle for the moment. Sierre is a pretty little town, with a main street, in a deep Alpine Valley.
Outside the *Hotel Terminus* there's wee funny Hunt Emerson, and Don Lawrence, making the five. Colin Wilson's here too. A New Zealander, he landed in the U.K. five years earlier but was not permitted to stay. Moved to Belgium where he'll spend the choicest part of his creative life drawing the young version of somebody else's character. Quite happily, no doubt. The things you have to do to be an artist.
You and the *Man at the Crossroads* will be in the hotel next door for the first night. You've got a room with no shower Doesn't matter. This is the last you'll see of it.
Dinner in a big marquee. It's starting to rain. A little band playing Swiss music comes across the lake on a raft
You'll watch Hunt disintegrate his quiche to remove the ham. Roast beef and ratatouille follows. He manages to get a double helping of the latter withoot any of the former.
In a bar, later, there's almost a punch-up.

Two young wankers are trying to wind you up. Don Lawrence stops you from mixing it
come away, Alec - You've got no Health insurance here.
Ah yes. Age brings experience and the ability to keep one's emotions under control.
Don's an English comics artist from way back, now doing all his work for a Dutch publisher. There's a whole generation of artists in this business with a heap of disgruntlement from being ripped off by the business people.
I KNOW WHERE TO GET MILLIONS OF CREDITS...
... BUT IT WILL TAKE TIME!
STORM by LAWRENCE-© '80
That's an inevitable side of Art. It's not necessarily in the artistic temperament to be good at business or to care to think about it, so there's potential in the business department for taking advantage of the situation.
Over the next few days, sitting near Lawrence doing signings, you'll notice he always does his sketches in pencil and if possible on a coloured endpaper.
dédicace?
JE DETESTE LE TRAVAIL
makes reproduction more difficult, you see. But you won't make this observation till later, till after the events of the final night.
ah, yes.
You're locked out of the hotel. This won't strike you as unusual till you've travelled a bit more in your life. Don throws a stone at a window where it happens Hunt can't get to sleep.
Here's a picture of Hunt asleep, by himself, though actually he'll have brought his sweetie along on this trip.
knockabout
©'81 Emerson by Emerson
As for you, you're sleeping with an Alsatian dog in Gordon's mountain chalet.

You wake up on the mountain and you're supposed to be in the valley
They're hanging about outside the hotel when you get there, with Nadine and Benedicte who are looking after us.
You're back in the original hotel. Crossroads has put your unopened suitcase in your room. This is the first time you've seen an electronic key. You have to get someone up to open the door for you. But there's still no shower. Use the one in the corridor.
You're too late for breakfast. You order a cappuccino, which Gordon indicates is to be put on the slate.
Now here's the British exhibit at the town hall. 38 current artists represented. A fine coming together of the various denominations of the comics scene.
Old pros like Embleton and Lawrence next to new-wavey photocopy guys like Fiewitt and Pinsent, even newspapery stuff like Posy Simmonds. and there's that daft bugger Alec MacGarry, still asleep at the turnpike.
In the next gallery, a sampling of Dennis Gifford's collection of old British original art pages. Gifford's here too to make sure nobody spills anything on them.
Gifford will have had a number of posh-looking books out from various publishers. They're mainly an excuse to show the world his prodigious collection of old comics.
An artist himself, his claim to fame was the *Classics Illustrated Baron Munchausen*, created for the English editions and the only one ever done in a cartoony style.
CLASSICS Illustrated
Featuring Stories by the World's Greatest Authors
146 1'3
© Gilberton '60 ? art by Gifford.

It's a funny old world, the world of arT (with a capital T). In its back alleys you'll find all kinds of old junk dropped out of windows.
And speaking of junk, in the Town Hall the president of the festival has had a signing area done up in a way he considers 'English', which is to say, like Madame Tussaud's.
There's a lump of turf he had the presence of mind to lift from Hyde Park, and a very grey looking flag, but not the one from the Charge of the *Light Brigade* which looks more like a fishing net now and hangs in St Paul's.
At some point over the weekend Hunt mops up a beer with it.
The main marquee's alive. All the European publishers are arranged neatly with their latest "albums" advantageously displayed. None of your jumble sale British comic marts here.
FLUIDE GLACIAL
It puts us all in perspective, eh?
You're here for the local T.V. *The Man at the Crossroads* does all the translating, but it's a shambles. The fact is, MacGarry, you won't be crossing that language barrier now or later.
sierre
Canal 9
You're driven to a hotel for the publisher's dinner. You intend to take away a copy of the specially printed menu to show Annie but you'll forget.
It's chicken breast with a vegetable stuffing. You wonder what Hunt's going to do to it.

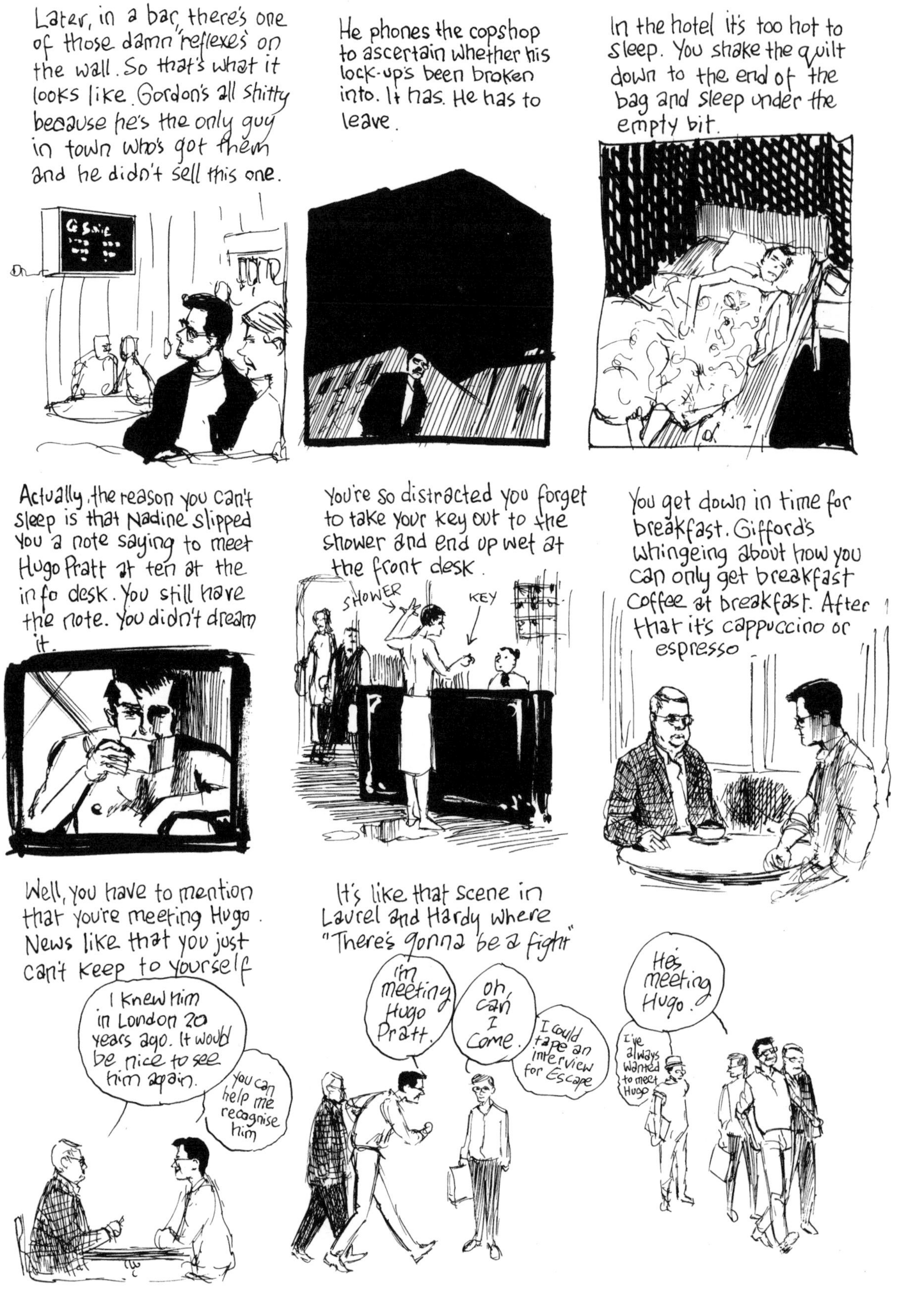
Later, in a bar, there's one of those damn "reflexes" on the wall. So that's what it looks like. Gordon's all shitty because he's the only guy in town who's got them and he didn't sell this one.
He phones the copshop to ascertain whether his lock-ups been broken into. It has. He has to leave.
In the hotel it's too hot to sleep. You shake the quilt down to the end of the bag and sleep under the empty bit.
Actually, the reason you can't sleep is that Nadine slipped you a note saying to meet Hugo Pratt at ten at the info desk. You still have the note. You didn't dream it.
You're so distracted you forget to take your key out to the shower and end up wet at the front desk.
SHOWER
KEY
You get down in time for breakfast. Gifford's whingeing about how you can only get breakfast coffee at breakfast. After that it's cappuccino or espresso.
Well, you have to mention that you're meeting Hugo. News like that you just can't keep to yourself
I knew him in London 20 years ago. It would be nice to see him again.
You can help me recognise him
It's like that scene in Laurel and Hardy where "There's gonna be a fight"
I'm meeting Hugo Pratt.
Oh, can I come.
I could tape an interview for Escape
He's meeting Hugo.
I've always wanted to meet Hugo

Majestic Hugo Pratt is one of the few famous people you'll meet who won't fail to impress. From Italy to Ethiopia to Argentina to England to France to Switzerland. Author of Corto Maltese.
JAVA, SEND THIS TO MILNER THE LAWYER.
'70 © Casterman - Hugo Pratt
Corto Maltese
Gifford will get him talking about the old days and Crossroads will tape it. Presumably nothing great will be said because you will not notice the chat published anywhere, so we're reading some words from an older interview with the mighty fellow who will no longer be with us when this document goes public
I once wrote a kind of an autobiography where I talked about people, and through them, about myself. Everyone said it was a wonderfully funny autobiography.
Whereas I thought I'd written a very sad book. Scary, in fact. It was the end of my youth, the evocation of people who have died, who have disappeared. No one noticed the poetic touches.
Corto Maltese
You'll have to go and do a signing at the Town Hall and it will occur to you that you never discovered what Hugo wanted to see you about
uh... dedicass?
But later that day, you'll be passing the exhibits, running late for another scheduled event and there will be Hugo, with the Man at the Crossroads talking up a storm. They're standing before your own work
You'll pass just close enough to hear Hugo ask a question:
Tell me, how does he do that with the little dots?

Lovely Switzerland with its cheese salads and cowbells in the mountains. There's Somebody tumbling out of a doorway here.
Don Lawrence is doing an appearance on a German-Swiss Television channel.
The M.C. kicks off with a leading question: Isn't it odd, a wee hick town like Sierre trying to do a big International festival (roughly translated)
Don declines to discuss his hosts in such terms. A French-Swiss butts in on his behalf.
The big German-Swiss pops the little French-Swiss on the beak. Don tries to break it up but he's all wired for sound -
Ah, yes. One day, when you're older, Alec MacGARRY, you'll be so cool as to break up other people's fights and not get into any of your own.
Later, a girl will ask Don to do a sketch on her back, which gives the Reuter's photog. an idea.
He'll find a willing pretty girl and with Lawrence and Emerson and Gifford you'll cover her with cartoon characters. It'll go out on the wire. You might find it in your local paper.
You worked with Don Lawrence!? What on?
A young Lady's back.

Now it's dinner in the Chateau de Venthône.
(13th Century)
Another specially printed menu. You'll remember to take this one away to show Annie, but then leave it in a bar while walking back to your hotel with Bolland.
Next Morning. Sunday. It's quiet. You're drawing pictures of each other.
HUNT EMERSON
Sierre BD86.
A lot of guys in this game have their own little worked-out presentation sketch which they repeat every time but Hunt always creates one anew...
Spinning out his improvisations like a jazz soloist.
©86 Emerson (Max Zillion)
The whole show closes down and beer and wine appear. We're doing sketches all the way back up the street for people who've just managed to get out of bed.
You'll use the bath in Crossroad's room.
Then all the takings will be spent on a slap-up meal, which is a bummer. You'd kind of hoped to take some home.
The wine'll be all kind of bitter everywhere you go, all Fendant and dôle. You'll have a word with Gordon and he'll phone ahead to another place to put some Muscat in the chiller.

You'll read somewhere that Muscat is the only grape that when vinified still tastes like grapes. What an astonishing thought.
You thought there was just red, white and Thompson Seedless. You make a mental note to investigate this wine thing at greater length. There's obviously a lot more to it
Anyway we arrive at Café Muscat, and the denouement of this adventure.
Here's Ash. I've been saving him till now. He's Nadine's husband; one of those blokes that seeks to impress by doing psychological analyses of everyone present.
Hunt, you're a small fellow. You got by as a child by making everybody laugh. The camera is turned upon you and you feel obliged to be funny.
Don is hiding in fantasy. But his feelings are tempestuous, and not too far under the surface
My own story is very interesting and one day I shall tell it. Now there's a thought. Nobody is doing their own experiences in comics.
well actually, thats what Alec's doing
Truly? what do you do when you catch up to today? Do you run out of material?
ARGGH. WHAT A HORRID THOUGHT! That my life's work should end here with me listening to HIM... Gotta get away—
Now, Gordon will be in the middle of selling one of his Reflex things to the landlord. He must have brought it in the boot of his car.

A splendid notion forms itself in your bean and you call Hunt over.
Well, naturally, he improvises a bit of business without needing to be asked.
And then everybody's adding to it; Don, Bolland, Barrie, Arthur, O'Neill, Jewelz. It's quite a collectable object
picture it on your mantelpiece.
Meanwhile, Ash is still psychoanalyzing. The bitter wine is obviously less dense than the sweet because it's coming to the surface, all acidity and sucked-in cheeks.
Apparently Ash and Nadine got sacked by the festival for going way over budget in the U.K. department. But to his annoyance, silver-tongued Gordon came out of it smelling of roses.
HA
Cough
HA
Splutter
HA
(yes, laugh you may)
So now he's poisoning Don's ear with an analysis of Gordon.
He's a hustler and a con-man. You wait and see. He'll be selling his Reflexes with your pictures reproduced on them, profiting from your work
The night's finishing. Going out you see the Reflex. But all the graphic delights have been erased.
Up yours Gordon!
Alec!
It's Don. He's waiting outside the door for Gordon to appear so he can punch his lights out. Ah yes.
Don't wipe it!

For God's sake man the things are worth more without our drunken scribbles all over them.
get your facts right Alec.
It ends in a shouting match. Oh well, at least you wiped the inflammatory remark. Written offence is harder to forget than alcoholic ranting on the morning after.
People are funny monkeys. Morning: You've left your toothbrush in Crossroads' room.
You'll phone Gordon and he'll come down with the big alsatian dog. Everybody makes up over breakfast. The president of the festival gets train tickets sorted.
Thanks for wiping that, Alec.
HA! I owed you one
Geneva
ENTHUSIASM
ENTHUSIASM
ENTHUSIASM
London
I have a sudden desire to eat some leeks.
I think we may have some in the fridge.
Brighton
I'm ho-wome
What in God's name have you been eating?

Chapter Eleven
You're down off the mountain, Alec MacGarry. Now what do you do?
On top of the world one day, fretting about money the next. But it's not like things aren't developing fast...
The Man at the Crossroads will call you up to London to help present a slide-show and talk at the Royal College of Art.
...to accompany a small exhibition of the new comics in the cafeteria organized by small press man Caspar Williams.
ELLIOTT
Elliott will be there too but will vapourize just before going in.
Hey, where's Phil?
Whaddaya know - He's gone again.
You mean he's done this before?
AARG
That'll be just one of Crossroads' endeavours. Between that and publishing Escape magazine and its offshoots (including your books, Alec MacGarry), he'll be writing articles for mags all over the place on the subject of "the new comics".

He'll be ruling connecting lines across a firmament of artists, from the hip Hernandez brothers in California.

WE STUMBLED AROUND SMALL TALK. SHE SEEMED REALLY IMPRESSED WITH MY, ER, ACADEMIC STANDING, EVEN IF SHE KEPT FORGETTING MY NAME. BUT I WAS USED TO THAT.
© Beto Hernandez '85

To the surreal Bob Burden in Georgia.

Peter Pronto
© Bob Burden '84

The mad and sensitive visions of Chester Brown in Canada.

HMN... CAN'T SEEM TO STOP.
CWDB 85
© Chester Brown © 85

The acute ear of Susan Catherine in Seattle.

"Trudy got her body down to nothing but it still looks like she's storing nuts in those cheeks."
© Susan Catherine '86

Pekar in Cleveland, the original autobiographer, who on the wave of comic book popularity finds himself on the David Letterman show and returns for two rematches.

AMERICAN SPLENDOR
ALL STORIES BY HARVEY PEKAR
INSIDE TV
STARS
©Harvey Pekar '87

The older Raymond Briggs, children's-book illustrator in England, arrives at the graphic novel from a different angle from the rest of us, and sticks with the form. His *When the Wind Blows* of '82 is made into a celebrated animated movie.

The Cruelty Man is going to do Legal Proceedings to me if it's not up, and the Planning Man is going to prosicute me if it's not down.
Then there's the Muni-pical Authorities up the Rec. and the Sums from the Man in the Yellow Hat.
© Raymond Briggs '82

It's not often that a coherent movement springs up spontaneously in a lot of different countries like this. Crossroads will introduce you to the work of Lat, of Malaysia.

The media is suddenly interested; Crossroads will expand his pieces out of the afficionado publications like *Cahiers de la Bande Dessinée* into art journals like *Illustrators*

and then to full-blown colour pieces for news-stand youth and style magazines; 6 pages in Jamming, 11 in I-D magazine

© Lat '87

COMIC KRAZED
i-D
bumper annual 87!

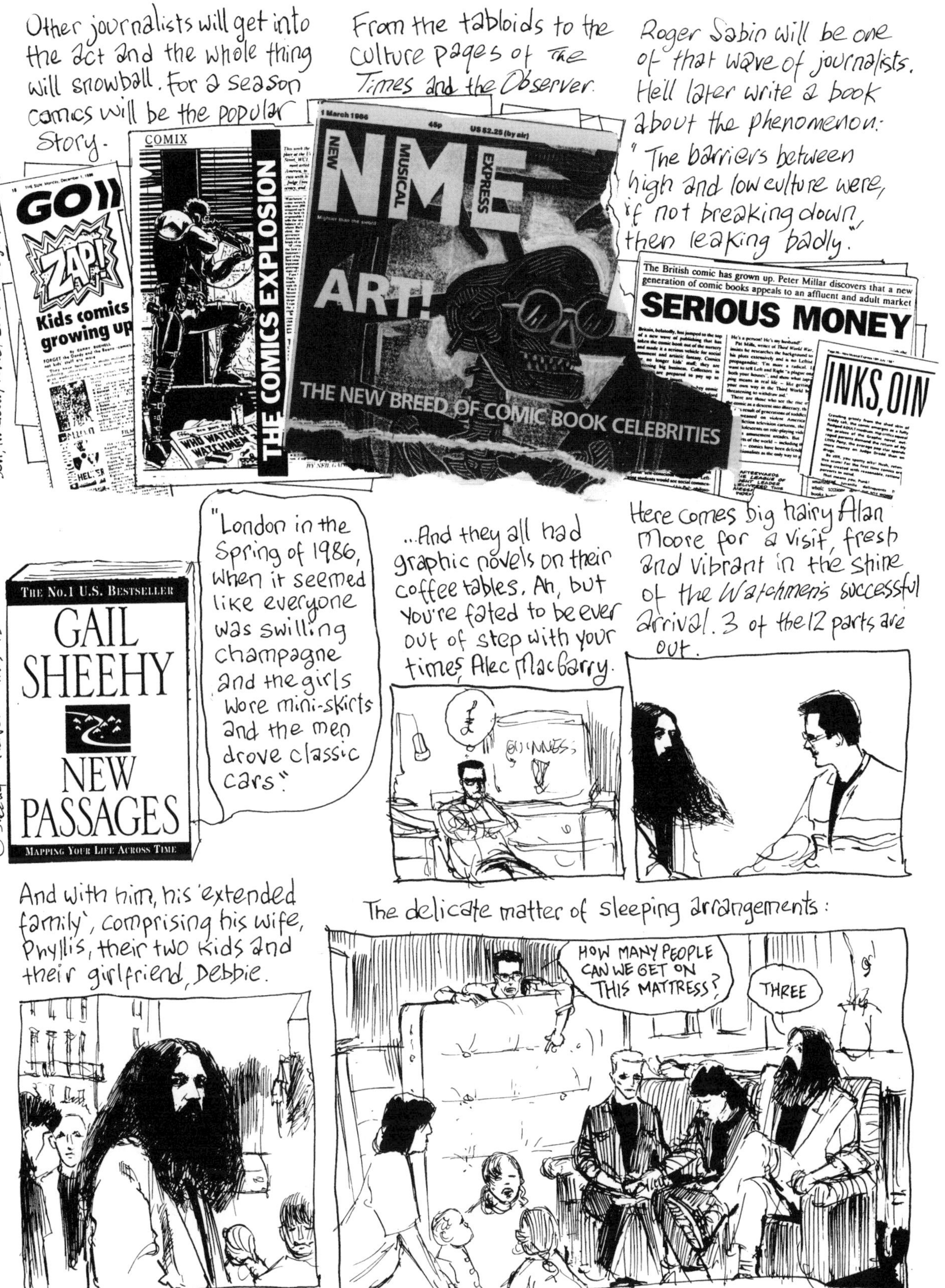
Other journalists will get into the act and the whole thing will snowball. For a season comics will be the popular story.
From the tabloids to the culture pages of The Times and the Observer.
Roger Sabin will be one of that wave of journalists. He'll later write a book about the phenomenon: "The barriers between high and low culture were, if not breaking down, then leaking badly."
Sun, TimeOut, NME, Sunday Telegraph, NME
THE SUN Monday, December 1, 1986
GO!!
ZAP!
Kids comics growing up
By GARRY BUSHELL
FORGET the Dandy and the Beano - comics are not kids' stuff any more
COMIX
WHO WATCHES THE WATCHMEN
THE COMICS EXPLOSION
1 March 1986
45p
US $2.25 (by air)
NEW MUSICAL EXPRESS
NME
ART!
THE NEW BREED OF COMIC BOOK CELEBRITIES
BY NEIL GAIMAN
The British comic has grown up. Peter Millar discovers that a new generation of comic books appeals to an affluent and adult market
SERIOUS MONEY
INKS, OIN
© Sheehy - Harper-Collins '95
THE No.1 U.S. BESTSELLER
GAIL SHEEHY
NEW PASSAGES
MAPPING YOUR LIFE ACROSS TIME
"London in the Spring of 1986, when it seemed like everyone was swilling champagne and the girls wore mini-skirts and the men drove classic cars."
...And they all had graphic novels on their coffee tables. Ah, but you're fated to be ever out of step with your times, Alec MacGarry.
£
GUINNESS
Here comes big hairy Alan Moore for a visit, fresh and vibrant in the shine of the Watchmen's successful arrival. 3 of the 12 parts are out.
And with him, his 'extended family', comprising his wife, Phyllis, their two kids and their girlfriend, Debbie.
The delicate matter of sleeping arrangements:
HOW MANY PEOPLE CAN WE GET ON THIS MATTRESS?
THREE

The Watchmen by Alan Moore and Dave Gibbons will be one of the successes of the season, with the 12 parts wrapped up by mid '87 and the whole then issued in a single 500 page volume.

YES, I HAVE. I THINK PERHAPS I'LL CREATE SOME.
JON, WAIT, BEFORE YOU LEAVE...
GOODBYE, ADRIAN.
I DID THE RIGHT THING, DIDN'T I? IT ALL WORKED OUT IN THE END.

© D.C Comics '87. Moore · Gibbons.

The other two, for the media will eagerly boil it down to "THE BIG THREE" will be Maus, the first half of it out as a 160 page book.

PUT ASIDE ALL YOUR PRECONCEPTIONS.
THIS IS NO TOM AND JERRY CARTOON.
THIS IS A NEW KIND OF LITERATURE.
MAUS
A remarkable work at one and the same time a novel, a documentary, a memoir and a comic book. Brilliant, just brilliant' Jules Feiffer
'A very moving book about a subject so terrible it is almost impossible to comprehend. A great achievement' Raymond Briggs
art spiegelman
A SURVIVOR'S TALE
Now in paperback £5.95 Penguin Books

© '86. Spiegelman

And The Dark Knight, Frank Miller's dramatic revision of Batman, in four 48-page parts collected.

BATMAN
THE DARK KNIGHT RETURNS
FRANK MILLER
KLAUS JANSON
LYNN VARLEY
INTRODUCTION BY ALAN MOORE

© D.C Comics '87. Miller.

Batman. Well, of course, the whole plot has already gone to fuck as you can see right there. But it's too late. It's in the hands of the PR Yuppies

comics 35 interview
© 1986 DC COMICS, INC.

© D.C Comics · Miller

The Watchmen and The Dark Knight will both be published in British editions by Titan. They'll get in a whiz kid named Igor Goldkind.

"There was a marketing opportunity. My job was to develop a semantic the general public and the book trade could understand."

"Literature for the post-literate generation" will be one of the phrases befuddling our ears.

Watchmen. Moore · Gibbons © DC.

Techically American in origin, all three will be on the best seller lists on both sides of the Atlantic, Dark Knight in Britain for as long as 40 weeks.

Frank Miller, left, is th
American artist whose
"graphic novel" sold
millions. Now, ROB RY
reveals, Fleetway's cha
could bring British stri
US-style status at home

IMAGINE Ian Fleming, having written Casino Royale, being told by the publisher that he did not own his James Bond character; furthermo Bond could be given t

portrayed in the stri
In June this
Baxendale finally st
receive more of his money
future re-prints, film rights or
merchandising deals.
Unlikely? In the book world
perhaps, but practices such as

observer Dec '87

Moore will be a celebrity, his white suit everywhere.

THE OBSERVER

WEEKEND

EDITED

Shazam! The hero breaks down

The neurotic super-hero has arrived. Today's comics, writes DON WATSON, deal with real problems.

ALTHOUGH comics have long been regarded as a respectable art form on the Continent, something to be read by an adult on the Metro sans embarrassment, in Britain the ghosts of Dennis the Menace and Gnasher, Desperate Dan's cow pie and the pre-pubescent gratification of endless amounts of grub are difficult to dispel.

It is a prejudice that finally seems to be on the way out. Two writers, Frank Miller (American) and Alan Moore (British), have revolutionised the way mainstream comics are seen in this country. The response is already remarkable, and comic shops around the country now find that titles by either Miller or Moore are selling out within days. Collections of both men's work are planned in novel form, and film options have already been taken out on their comic book creations. They admire each other, but have only met briefly.

Alan Moore's fearsome appearance (over six foot tall, shoulder-length hair and beard) belies a character of gentleness and restless intelligence. Despite the fact that the title that made his name, Swamp Thing monthly, is set in the rotting opulence of the American South, he himself still resides in his native Northampton. 'I was invited to visit the South,' he says, 'but the letter made mention of carnivorous spiders, and I don't have to deal with that in Northampton High Street.'

Moore, 32, has made his name as a writer capable of treating the most controversial subjects — incest, menstruation, nuclear power — with great sensitivity. Lisa Tuttle, editor of the 'Encyclopedia of Feminism,' has commented on his ability to formulate independent female figures, a rare skill ... world of ...

Alan Moore won feminist approval for Halo Jones (top). Above: Frank ...

director of "Nosferatu," were other innovation.

everyday space travel as real and tangible because it touched people's dreams, so Moore and Miller have taken the creaking institution of ...

actually having to learn how to do a close-up.

The first innovation, Miller's, was to redefine the timing and construction ...

emotional sensitivity into comics. Hence the hero Daredevil was, as a child, blinded after coming into contact with radioactive mat-

September 1985 with societal tab ing menstruat radically rewritin lycanthropy (we woman in mid-

observer - '87.

(96)

The comics companies are collecting every old nonsense from their published inventories into "graphic novels". Nevertheless it's possible to trace a line of progress. Take Violent Cases by Neil Gaiman and Dave McKean.

VIOLENT CASES
ESCAPE

© Gaiman · McKean. Escape · Titan Nov '87

Gaiman will be the most perceptive of the journalists arriving on the scene in '86; will write some articles on comics, including a review of the third Alec yearly part in Knave magazine —

ALEC
I'M ON GUARD
ESCAPE
© Campbell. Escape '86

Will host a panel with Moore and Gibbons at the '86 London convention.

And with McKean will talk on his own account on an '87 TV. production which will also have Myra and Gibbons.

It's an incredibly exciting time to be in comics.

Spiegelman, with the critical success of *Maus*, resents giving up his career as an artist for one as an interview subject.

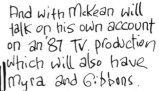

is the recipient of a Guggenheim award and gets back to work on the second half of his masterpiece. He starts by reflecting upon the horrors of public attention that followed the publication of the first half.

If your book was about ISRAELI Jews, what kind of animal would you draw?
I have no idea. ...porcupines?
Excuse me...
© Spiegelman '88

Published in parts for six years by Spiegelman in *RAW*, *Maus* goes with Random House for the 'book market'. (PENGUIN IN THE U.K.)

art spiegelman
PANTHEON BOOKS NEW YORK

So now all the "book" publishers will want a piece of the pie. Kyle Baker's experience is not untypical:

around the time the *Dark Knight* and *Maus* came out in the book market, Doubleday thought that comics would be the next big thing, so they published any cartoons they could find. I said I had some.

With no "reservoir" the book companies will have to cast about and commission new works. Alas, foolish novelties will be the order of the day. Or is that just a bunch of sour grapes, Alec MacGarry?

And that's where it will fall apart. Most of the people making the decisions will not have any real grasp of the situation. But it will be a mad couple of years for those caught in it.

BLOODY HELL
ALAN MOORE
© Q magazine. Oct '86

Chapter Twelve
Alec MacGARRY, don't go saying yes to the emotional demands of a woman in the afterwash of childbirth. No! Don't!
I want to go home to Australia and if you don't want to come I'm going anyway.
Well... I guess there's no champagne or classic cars keeping me here.
say ma ma ma ma
blg
Too late. Oh well, at least you'll have a plan. A plan of compromise.
It'll be four years since you danced out of the pointless dead-end job.
That won't seem a long time to cling to an ideal in retrospect, in the way that Odysseus' nineteen years away from Ithaca, while Penelope waits for him, seem impossible to to a young bloke but not so to an old one.
The plan: an improbable success in the States, titled *The Teenage Mutant Ninja Turtles* will have opened up a lucrative opportunity for enthusiatic amateurish comics. Elliott is the first in.
I just got advance orders of 13,000. You should give it a try too.
All kinds of successes will be published out of back bedrooms, looking cheap as blazes.
It's too easy. I'll make a bundle.
The hypothesis of the intelligent comic book novel is accepted and then the next dog out of the traps is a wave of daft juvenilia.
GOT ANY BEER?
© Eastman + Laird '85

So you'll need money and come up with some badly drawn American-style comic-books. Don't worry. The world will forget.
Dead
Meanwhile, the life you lead inside your head will follow its own course.
You keep all your cuttings and correspondence in loose leaf files
That way you change the order of it. Reshuffle it, extend a branch, prune another. History shapes up differently every time.
The artist is given a different role in each version. Sometimes he fails his own audition altogether.
I'm just a wanker compared to Caniff. Can't you see?
...on a day of dark despair.
I need a theme!
A bigger subject!
The world needs one!
One pantheon steps down and lets another step up.
Caspar, come and take these old comics off me
Nothings fixed.
They're even worse wankers than me compared to Caniff, Tad, Clare Briggs..
Who?
Immortality isn't forever.
If the greats are already forgotten, what chance do any of us have?

It's your duty to your art, you argue, to go out there and have a few global adventures.
You edit your files, your cuttings, your 'power battery', down to what will fit in this old trunk and leave the rest with friends. You give away your two jackets. Won't be needing them now.
They'll all be seeing you off. Danny Greys there.
And your brother, Mark, will lug you to the exit gate, while your Mother sheds a tear.
OCH!
How can they be so silly
SOB
Then you're on the plane and there's no more thinking about it.
You'll be living for a year rent-free on a tropical beach in Annie's parents' house in Little Italy, mailing off your comic-book falsities.
Plus some 'funny pages' to a bunch of new-wave humour mags. That's the door that Gag opened.
Until this whole end of the market will suffer what it is bound to suffer when tens of thousands of collectors speculate wildly on amateur enthusiasm.

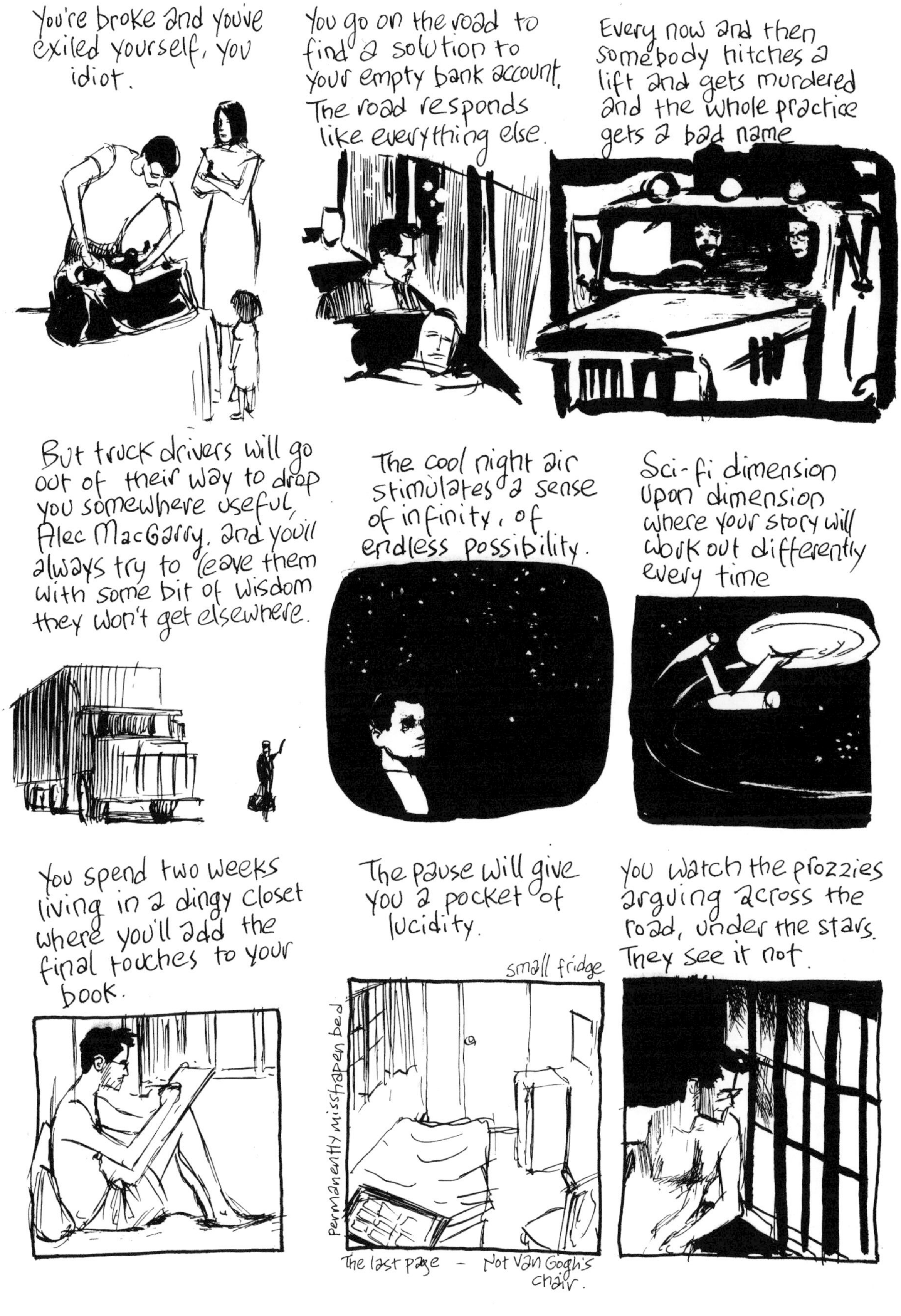
You're broke and you've exiled yourself, you idiot.
You go on the road to find a solution to your empty bank account. The road responds like everything else.
Every now and then somebody hitches a lift and gets murdered and the whole practice gets a bad name
But truck drivers will go out of their way to drop you somewhere useful, Alec MacGarry, and you'll always try to leave them with some bit of wisdom they won't get elsewhere.
The cool night air stimulates a sense of infinity, of endless possibility.
Sci-fi dimension upon dimension where your story will work out differently every time
You spend two weeks living in a dingy closet where you'll add the final touches to your book.
The pause will give you a pocket of lucidity.
small fridge
permanently misshapen bed
The last page - Not Van Gogh's chair.
You watch the prozzies arguing across the road, under the stars. They see it not.

After three annual showings, the fourth and final part of your graphic novel will have already failed to appear.
The Man at the Crossroads will hawk the complete thing around the book publishers but with no success, and this in the YEAR of the graphic novel
Penguin Books Ltd
Dear Paul
I am afraid
Alec
With best wishes.
Yours sincerely
You'll get him to send you back the few hundred £ pounds £ with which you had earlier shored up the project at a time when the Escape boys needed backing more than anything.
TIKKA
TIKKA
The cash will be as though from heaven. Here's to Bacchus.
It will dawn on you that you have apparently made your third and final lapse of faith in the bargain you struck with Fate.
when did it happen?
You will imagine that you have murdered your muse.
Maybe you want too much. You'll have had a notion of an art that would be the inevitability of all that preceded it. The culmination of the comic strip.
Its last hooray before draining the glass and retiring into the night.

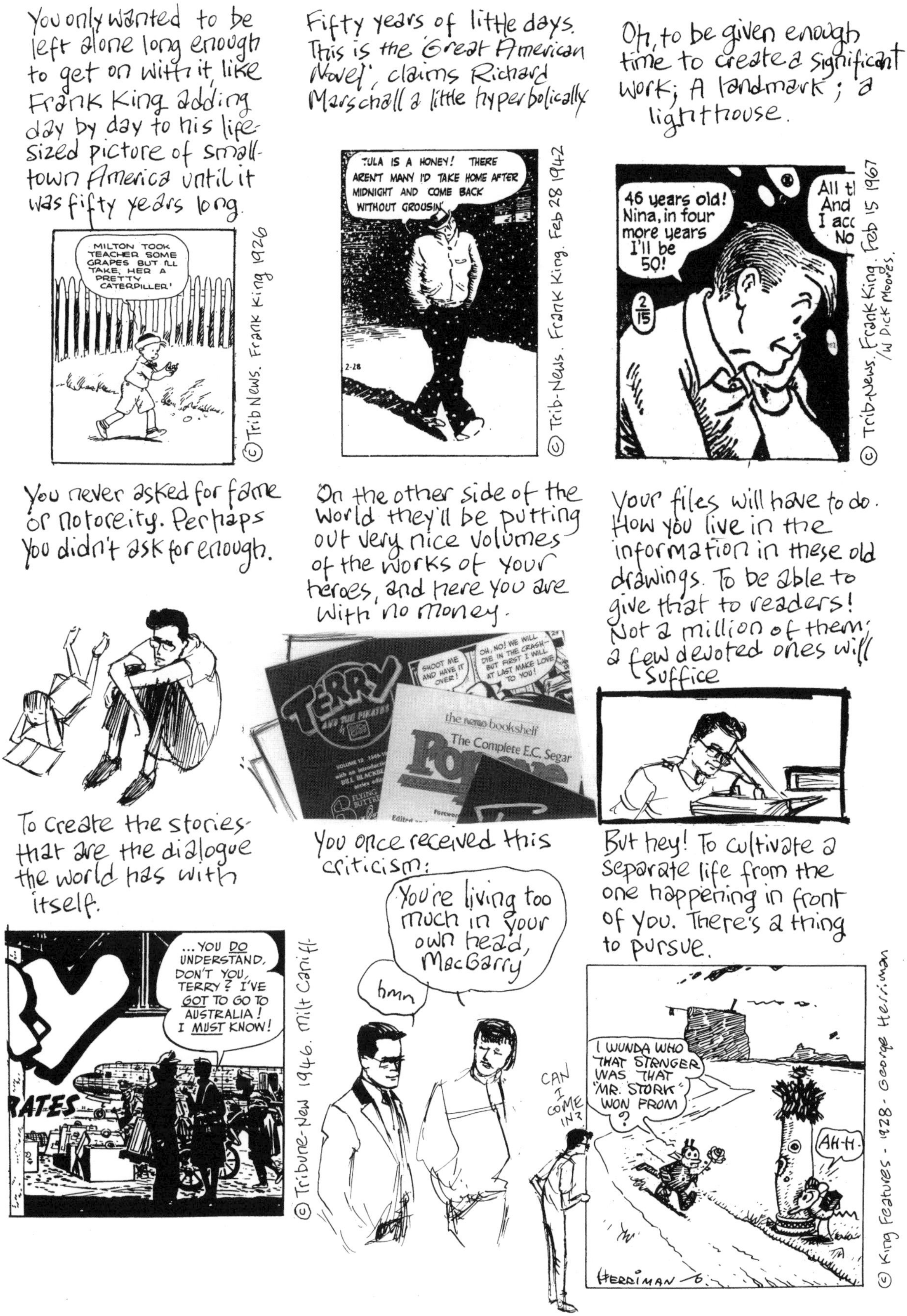
You only wanted to be left alone long enough to get on with it, like Frank King adding day by day to his life-sized picture of small-town America until it was fifty years long.
MILTON TOOK TEACHER SOME GRAPES BUT I'LL TAKE HER A PRETTY CATERPILLER!
© Trib News. Frank King 1926
Fifty years of little days. This is the 'Great American Novel', claims Richard Marschall a little hyperbolically
TULA IS A HONEY! THERE AREN'T MANY I'D TAKE HOME AFTER MIDNIGHT AND COME BACK WITHOUT GROUSIN'
2-28
© Trib-News. Frank King. Feb 28 1942
Oh, to be given enough time to create a significant work; A landmark; a lighthouse.
46 years old! Nina, in four more years I'll be 50!
2/15
© Trib-News. Frank King. Feb 15 1967 /w Dick Moores.
You never asked for fame or notoreity. Perhaps you didn't ask for enough.
On the other side of the world they'll be putting out very nice volumes of the works of your heroes, and here you are with no money.
Your files will have to do. How you live in the information in these old drawings. To be able to give that to readers! Not a million of them; a few devoted ones will suffice
SHOOT ME AND HAVE IT OVER!
OH, NO! WE WILL DIE IN THE CRASH— BUT FIRST I WILL AT LAST MAKE LOVE TO YOU!
TERRY AND THE PIRATES
the nemo bookshelf
The Complete E.C. Segar
To create the stories that are the dialogue the world has with itself.
You once received this criticism:
You're living too much in your own head, MacGarry
hmn
But hey! To cultivate a separate life from the one happening in front of you. There's a thing to pursue.
...YOU DO UNDERSTAND, DON'T YOU, TERRY? I'VE GOT TO GO TO AUSTRALIA! I MUST KNOW!
© Tribune-New 1946. Milt Caniff.
CAN I COME IN?
I WUNDA WHO THAT STRNGER WAS THAT "MR. STORK" WON FROM ?
AH-H.
HERRIMAN
© King Features - 1928 - George Herriman

An inside life, where Fate talks to you, sometimes in the charming tones of a girl singer with old Jazz bands.
when you consider The highest bidder can't buy the dream in your eye
You're a lucky guy
Othertimes in a naive wee voice in which all things are still possible.
Eh?
Go for it.
Conceit is no criticism here in the realm of the spirit as it is in real time where your heroes are long gone.
TERRY AND THE PIRATES
On an airfield in China, Terry Lee is still kissing Jane Allen goodbye.
© Tribune/News. Dec 29 1946 Milt Caniff.
In Gasoline Alley, Skeezix is having his midlife crisis.
All those years! And what have I accomplished? Not much!
You own a garage and we have a nice home, Skeezix!
© Trib News, Frank King Feb '67
In a vast silent Arizona desert, a Coconino moon pours out molten silver.
© 1928 King Features - George Herriman
It drips on Alec MacGarry, asleep at the turnpike.

That's Fate taking another voice, painting a new picture in your head...
...of the road you will follow when you awake.
And follow it you will, but after this drama is done. Take your seats, ladies and gentlemen, for the final act.

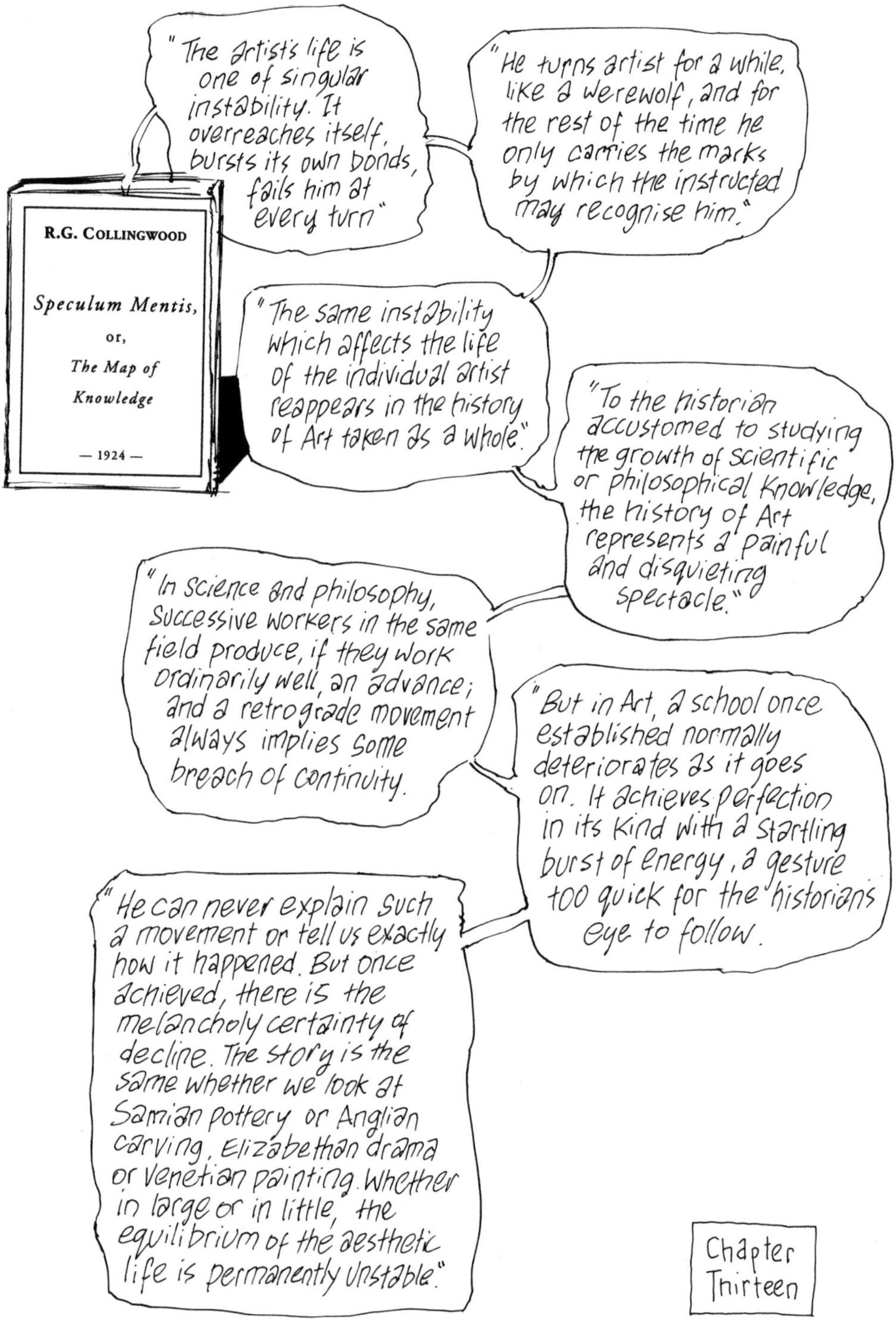
R.G. COLLINGWOOD
Speculum Mentis, or, The Map of Knowledge
— 1924 —
"The artist's life is one of singular instability. It overreaches itself, bursts its own bonds, fails him at every turn"
"He turns artist for a while, like a werewolf, and for the rest of the time he only carries the marks by which the instructed may recognise him."
"The same instability which affects the life of the individual artist reappears in the history of Art taken as a whole."
"To the historian accustomed to studying the growth of scientific or philosophical knowledge, the history of Art represents a painful and disquieting spectacle."
"In science and philosophy, successive workers in the same field produce, if they work ordinarily well, an advance; and a retrograde movement always implies some breach of continuity.
"But in Art, a school once established normally deteriorates as it goes on. It achieves perfection in its kind with a startling burst of energy, a gesture too quick for the historians eye to follow.
"He can never explain such a movement or tell us exactly how it happened. But once achieved, there is the melancholy certainty of decline. The story is the same whether we look at Samian pottery or Anglian carving, Elizabethan drama or Venetian painting. Whether in large or in little, the equilibrium of the aesthetic life is permanently unstable."
Chapter Thirteen

The artist carried off by the madness of 20th century commercialism. At first he will enjoy the novelty.
"We've written and drawn the comic. We've helped design the badges and approved the wristwatches."
"We've discussed the film and the role-playing game and given a nod to the t-shirt..."
"We've done the British tour and the American press interviews"
"We've done the photo session where they asked us to pose as Adam West and Burt Ward walking sideways up a wall on our bat-rope."
I don't think so
"We've signed so many books that we're thinking of swapping names just to relieve the tedium"
"and every time we see that stupid, jaundiced face with the red blood splash we get a crippling migraine"
ART: GIBBONS © D.C.COMICS 1987
There will be, much later, an article entitled: "Whatever happened to Alan Moore?" by one Nick Hasted: "In 1987 the comic book seemed the most exciting medium in existence"
THE COMICS JOURNAL
"And Alan Moore had helped that happen, with Watchmen's clockwork precision, depth and density."
"IN THE END"?
NOTHING ENDS, ADRIAN. NOTHING EVER ENDS.
JON? WAIT! WHAT DO YOU MEAN BY...
ART: GIBBONS © D.C.COMICS 1987
"When he arrived onstage at the U.K. con that year, the cheer was for a star; the comic book moment when pop and art merged."

At that same show there will be a panel discussion on the subject of The Future of Comics, with all the key people present, from the point of view of this thesis.
the Man at the Crossroads
Elliott (unvapourised)
Dakin
Eisner
Big hairy Alan Moore
Spiegelmaus
Billy the Sink
new area of specialty: making the catalogues for a number of gallery exhibitions with comics links. Escape now a flash magazine
Just done a travel comic, small press
Just out with The Dreamer, an autobiographical subject, the artist as a young man in 1939 at the beginning of the comic book era
SO...YOU'RE VINCENT'S NEW GENIUS...HAVE A DRINK!
THANKS ...DON'T MIND IF I DO... AHEM
© Will Eisner 1986
"I've had to reinvent the alphabet for everything I do"
Graphic virtuoso. illustrated a couple of Frank Miller books and is now about to test the boundaries of intelligibility with his own graphic novel in 4 parts, Stray Toasters.
© Bill Sienkiewicz. 1988
And didn't that future look quite rosy. Moore's memory of the day, however, will sound a note of despair
"I was just held pressed up against a stairwell for almost the entire convention."
"I arrived at one panel late, the only one I was on, and for the rest of the time I was hiding in the hospitality room. I couldn't get out of the door."
The last straw may well go down as apocryphal.

Sick of it all, the big hairy one will cease appearing at conventions, except a couple of foreign ones then that's the end of it.

Furthermore, at the end of the year he will fall out irrevocably with WATCHMEN publisher DC over impending censorship impositions brought about due to the sudden public spotlight on the medium.

Next, he will announce his intention to self-publish, using the funds of his success to set up his independent imprint, MAD LOVE. Under this banner he will create works of a more serious nature.

ENTRE
Angoulême

"They would surrender to the book-burners"

We were caught on the Main Street of Culture wearing our underpants outside of our suits.
MAD LOVE

It's Dave Sim of Canada that will put him up to it. Sim has his own story, which touches this one but briefly. At the centre of it is the politics of distribution in the comics market, and the balance of rewards.

He'll call together the leading creative figures to a "summit" on self-publishing, a message of empowerment which he is disseminating with holy zeal.

For about as long as an afternoon, they'll be referred to as "the gang of 12" and by this device Sim will place himself in our view...

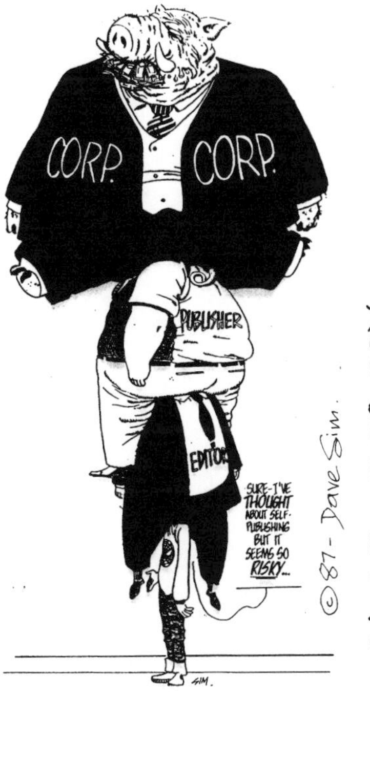
CORP.
CORP.
PUBLISHER
EDITOR
SURE-I'VE THOUGHT ABOUT SELF-PUBLISHING BUT IT SEEMS SO RISKY...
SIM.

© '87 - Dave Sim.

DAVE SIM HOSTS TORONTO "SUMMIT"

Guests at the summit. Left to right: Laird, Eastman, Sim, Murphy, Totleben, Bissette, Kneeling: Zulli.

Dave Sim hosted a "summit conference" with six other comics professionals who self-publish or ar- con-sid-ring self-publishing the ... '8 to June ...

Several other items of business were announced or decided at the meeting. Sim announced that he would be -olving ...

© Comics Journal '88.

... though he belongs there anyway. Having already gathered his ten years of work into four volumes, he commences a fifth, but this time with an integrated structure and meaning from the outset. This will be JAKA'S STORY which he'll collect in 1990.

I DON'T GET IT
FIRST IT'S A BIG DEAL THAT I CLEAN OUT THE CLOSETS
AND THEN IT'S A BIG DEAL THAT I COME OVER HERE
WOMEN DEAR BOY ARE UNFATHOMABLE
IT'S THE REASON THEY'RE SO COMPLETELY SELF-
THEY SPEND ALL OF THEIR LIVES PLUMBING THEIR OWN DEPTHS WITHOUT EVER
SO TO SPEAK
TOUCHING BOTTOM.

© '88 - Dave Sim / Gerhard

In assembling this 'gang', Sim will get the big name guys caught in the censorship row: Brits Moore and Gibbons, Yanks Miller and Billy the Sink and then Bissette of muck monster fame.
Then the guys in his own distribution fight, and the *Turtles* guys, which brings us to the daftest curiosity of all.
Borrowing 2000 bucks from an uncle, these two, Eastman and Laird, between '85 and '89, without finacial savvy or any particular common sense, parlay it, with an enthusiastic amateurism, into a fortune.
© Bissette '88
© Laird/Eastman '88
"We're not millionaires yet, but we may be by the end of the year."
We just wanted to not have to do stupid kitchen jobs.
Strange bedfellows these unabashed boy hobbyists, catapulted to loony fame, and Moore, with his highflown seriousness as he announces his most ambitious work, in collaboration with virtuoso illustrator Billy the Sink.
Indeed it will be the most ambitious comic ever conceived, to be titled *The Mandelbrot Set*, until mathematician Mandelbrot will request that his name be removed.
You see, I'm having a hard enough time getting my ideas accepted without my name being the title of a comic.
I completely understand.
Benoit Mandelbrot
"The vocabulary is being created now by the different people who are working, like Alan Moore and Frank Miller. We're making it up as we go along."
ink adapted from photos of Mitch Jenkins
↑ Now they're doing rock-star photo-shoots! →
Big Numbers it will be then, using a metaphor sprung from the mysteries of fractal maths and chaos theory.
"It's a medium that still hasn't produced its *Citizen Kane* of comics, or its *Mona Lisa* or its *Swann's Way*, but that's not to say it isn't capable."

Moore clarifies two principles of his new-found autonomy: that he will sink or swim as an Independent, and that fellow independents will hang together to avoid hanging separately
Big Hairy Alan Moore
Muck Monster
Horror maniac Bissette
Bissette will establish his own imprint, Spiderbaby and under this will launch a quarterly anthology entitled TABOO. Prolific, as ever, Moore offers his next big book for serialization in here
SPIDERBABY GRAFIX & PUBLICATIONS/TABOO
Suddenly you'll get a call and they'll be enlisting you to draw it. This comes completely out of the blue, though your Pyjama Girl, a story of murder, is the obvious connection.
For all your friendship, you will thus far have felt yourself and Moore to be in mutually exclusive camps. It comes as a shock to see that you've met somewhere in the middle.
You won't have realised you've drifted so far off your original course.
Furthermore, I will only lie in the service of TRUTH
Long ago you imagined the adventure of art was Monet in his houseboat. Now it's Odysseus all at sea for ten years.
Strapped to the mast so he can't get where the action is.
FAILURE
COMPROMISE
WATCHMEN, with its formal complexities and its swan song of the superhero, is a novel of modern America, a work of Art even, using comic-domain archetypes the way that Maus does.
SENSIBLE MOVE. MAKE FINAL APPROACH LOW, BENEATH RADAR.
I DON'T THINK WE'VE GOT MUCH CHOICE. YOU FEEL THAT SORT OF KICKING IN THE ENGINE, LIKE IT'S ABOUT TO SEIZE?
"ICE. SHIT, I BET IT'S ICE..."
Now you're drawing Jack the Ripper, perennial standard of cheap horror literature as a symbolic midwife of the twentieth century.

Around the same time, in a bold move, Gaiman and McKean land a serialized graphic novel in style magazine *The FACE*.

There is a sense of achievement that comes with finishing something that is unlike anything else I know.
It's about people, I suppose.

© Gaiman/McKean 1989

Signal to Noise, like *Big Numbers*, will employ a technological conceit with open graphic possibilities.

"We're still working out the vocabulary"

Following that lead, Morrison and Yeowell will launch the splendid *New Adventures of Hitler* in Scottish style mag, *CUT*. The staff object and start walking out.

Bastards.

© Morrison/Yeowell. 1989

THE COMICS JOURNAL
"It is no more acceptable to toy with the profane than with the sacred"

(observes critic Rob Rodi.)

It'll be relaunched a year later in new colour comic mag *CRISIS*, but by then time will be running out.

CRISIS
Mr Hitler's Holiday

© Morrison/Yeowell 1990

It's '90 and all the promise of '88 is in danger of fizzing out, with no work of substance ready enough to follow *Maus* and *WATCHMEN* into the bigger book market. The window of opportunity is blowing shut.

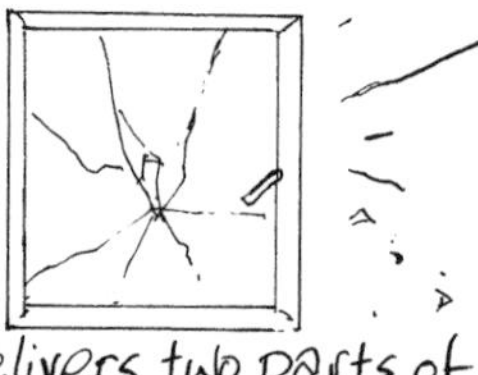

Billy the Sink turns this way and that, to show a flourish of caricature cards here.

a colourful adaptation of *Moby Dick* there, and takes a bow.

GENERAL JORGE RAFAEL VIDELA
GENERAL FRANCISCO FRANCO
JOHN FITZGERALD KENNEDY
MARILYN MONROE
LEE HARVEY OSWALD
Right-
so named because it is easy to kill and full of oil.

© Eclipse. Art: Sinkiewicz 1990

Art: Sinkiewicz

He delivers two parts of the promised twelve of *BIG NUMBERS* over a too-long wait before the project runs aground and Moore falls out with him

Big numbers
1
ALAN MOORE
BILL SIENKIEWICZ

© Moore/Sinkiewicz 1990

The *Citizen Kane* of comics, in pieces on the cutting room floor; the *Mona Lisa*, ripped from its frame, and everybody's still working out the vocabulary.

© Moore/Sienkiewicz 1991 from the legendary lost third vol.

Movie, TV, toys, etc. The *TURTLES* boys reportedly take in 50 million in the two years 90-91.

Turtle Eastman takes his fortune and creates a publishing house called *TUNDRA*, founded upon the finest principles of artistic freedom, to be remembered as "the biggest and most absurd catastrophe in the history of comics" Groth, Comics Journal

TUNDRA

oh that woolly mammoth.

One of his first endeavours is to take over the publishing of *BIG NUMBERS*. Billy the Sink's ex-assistant *Al Columbia* will draw in a continuation of Billy's style.

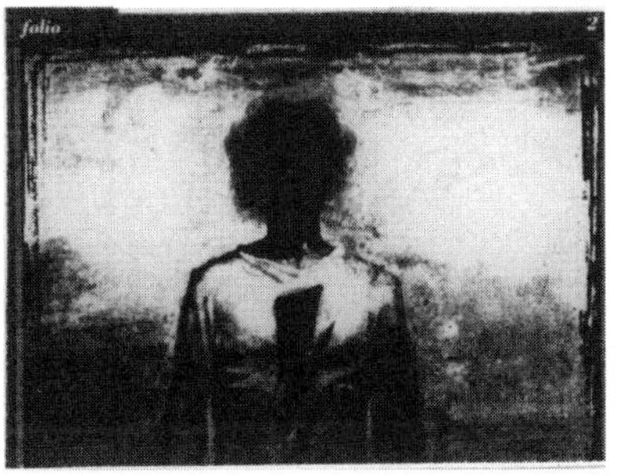
folio
2

© Al Columbia - 1993

Let's step aside for a moment. How to be an artist, indeed! Here is the bright-eyed young hopeful just out of high school

Little wee AL
So you want to be a cartoonist I can help you.

Following the chance encounter with a photocopier rep who will have sold a machine to Stan Drake, Al gets to meet some real professionals.

Stan, I brought this young guy into town to meet you.

Billy the sink will at this time have studio space next to Drake's. Little wee Al will have imagined these mighty ones working in 'opulent dens' and lunching on 'a sea-side deck'

© King Features. Juliet Jones by Stan Drake 1958

Oh, but they're in "tiny closets". Never mind, Little wee Al can hardly believe his luck, getting to meet his idol, Billy the Sink.

Bill. There's a guy here wants to meet you.

"Bill seemed eight feet tall, even though he was smaller than me", Al will later say.

Come on in. Let's hang out

With such ease are dreams realised; Little wee AL shows his Portfolio, mostly imitations of Bill, and three weeks later he gets a call to come up to town and be Bill's assistant.
Hey. I could use someone like you
Of course, at first AL will just be sweeping and running errands, but Bill will have promised Little Wee AL a chance to work on his big new project, Big Numbers
"He paid me five dollars an hour. I think this was more out of kindness at first, because I was no help at all. I'd spend five hours painting a teapot.
WELL, I'M NO NEARER.
SHE DOES 'AVE MILK IN 'ER TEA STILL, DON'T SHE?
©Alan Moore-Bill Sienkiewicz '90
"But we would stay up long hours together; sometimes we'd goof around and have fun, rubber cement our lips to our noses, gossip, tell jokes"
"Bill and his girlfriend, Betty, became like an uncle and aunt to me."
© Betty: Archie comic pubs Inc.
"I imitated his mannerisms, dressed like him, even wore his fancy suit-jackets into town on errands."
Bill will have started to feel uneasy about Al's imitations. He'll have seen the lad becoming him before his eyes.
!
"When Big Numbers #1 saw Print I was excited to see Bill had thanked me. When #2 was released, I was irritated to see no mention of me, even though that was the one where I helped the most".
"Journalists would come and there would be photo sessions, but most of the articles on Big Numbers focussed on Alan Moore, barely mentioning Bill".

Billy the Sink will have been hired to illustrate a set of political 'trading cards' with a writer named Veronica, sister-in-law of the publisher of same.
© Veronica: Archie Comics Pubs.
Some people will have thought they're having an affair. Betty will have thought AL would know and grilled him over the phone while Bill's out of the studio.
"I was in no position to tell her anything and was certainly not going to betray Bill."
Little Wee AL will allege: "Betty got hold of Bill, apparently to bluff him, and told him that I had ratted him out which wasn't true."
According to AL, Billy the Sink will have admitted to Betty that he had begun an affair with Veronica. Betty then tells the publisher's brother.
Bill will have been distraught at what this revelation could mean to the trading card project.
oh fuck!
AL will accuse: "In order to salvage his professional relationship with the publisher, he threw me to the wolves. He kicked me aside like a dead cat."
We can get this thing back on track
"He continued with Veronica, wrote a check to Betty for a chunk of cash and gave me two hundred dollars severance pay."
It's at this juncture that Billy will have left Big Numbers in the lurch and Tundra approaches the novice to ask him to take over.
We can get this thing back on track
Wow Me?

"I half expected Bill would give me his blessing", the young Al will say, "Instead he informed everyone that I was deranged".
Are you kidding? The guy's a nut!
Tundra editor Jenkins will say: "Bill told us this kid is a menace, a lunatic who's not right in the head, but we only gave him half an ear. Here was Bill, dropping the ball and complaining about somebody else's ability at the same time"
TUNDRA
"The enormous tectonic plates of Alan Moore, Billy the Sink, Kevin Eastman and a potload of money would have ground pretty much any other young cartoonist to paste," a sensitive observer will later note.
Kim Thompson, 2000.
THE COMICS JOURNAL
Labouring under this betrayal, the sensitive and confused young artist will come to see his work as a "replicant abomination"
"This is a fraudulent use of my skills"
Around the world, there are kids going to their beds dreaming of being comic artists. Three of them will be in the tableau below.
Unfair! He's stealing my thunder
You want a fuckin Sink clone - you don't want fuckin AL
But, AL, that's why we brought you in. You agreed to it!
The fourth volume is complete. AL surveys his handiwork.
I'll deliver it in the morning. I'll just paste over this figure
That's great, AL
Paid in full for the job, Little wee AL destroys it and disappears
a small cut out figure on the floor of the studio rented for AL is all that is ever found of BIG NUMBERS #4
Big hairy Alan Moore will close the book and never speak of it again.
Fuckadoodledo.

Bissette will manage to get his quarterly anthology out once a year
Mark my words, in 'undred years there'll still be cunts like 'im, wrapping these killings up in supernatural twaddle. Making a living out of murder, Godley...
© Moore/Campbell: 1992
His plans and his visions will expand inside his cranium, each pushing the other out of the way.
one book isn't enough to contain it all
His visions and his plans and his plans and his visions. It'll be a stalemate. Every thing will freeze after six years.
He'll get his head clear and start over with the biography of a dinosaur. A singular idea.
THERE
ONK
ONK
ONK
ONK
ONK
© Bissette 1994
He'll go visit the capable and stable Sim in Canada and work out a 15-year plan of bi-monthly issues.
Now... wearing your publishers hat for a minute
hmm
He'll get four of them out in five years in this grand adventure of self-empowerment.
Time folds in on itself 5 different ways like Mexican food and maybe in a corner of the back of his head he still thinks things are getting done.
The angle poise lamp burns away into the wee hours.
If only the industry wasn't in such a lousy state
Alan Moore's fourth big graphic novel will take ten years to get done and Odysseus ain't home yet.
This is the one that I didn't finish, isn't it?
© Moore/Campbell 1992

Turtle Eastman will take up the slack at year four. He's expanding his Tundra empire like crazy, funded by the Turtles.
They'll fly you into London for the opening of the U.K. division, Alec MacGarry.
That's great, Alec
The first thing they'll do is rent a big office and fill it with furniture.
They'll have a big party at the Natural History Museum, pretty girls on every arm, and the champagne flowing.
oh that woolly mammoth again
And they're getting their underpants forwarded by Fedex from hotels after leaving conventions in a squiffy cloud of intoxication.
GRAVY
In two years Eastman will gloriously squander fourteen million dollars on artistic follies, with genuine quality only an occasional accident.
I've advanced so many artists large amounts of money and they've taken advantage of me.
He will get rid of the whole mess by buying a half-interest in struggling Kitchen Sink Press for two million and selling him Tundra's inventory for a buck fifty.
Can you change a five?
No hurry, Denis. You can owe me.
Will still manage to go out of business himself five years later
You'll be in town again and there are not so many girlies and no champagne whatsoever.
"If graphic novels are the literature of the future, then howcome nobody's reading them?"
NEW MUSICAL EXPRESS
NME
Big hairy Alan Moore's marriage will have crashed and broken and the white suit is nowhere to be seen. The tiles are all over the place and nobody's putting them back now.
IDEA!
...You know what,... I think I'll become a magician!

In his obituary of the comic-book great Harvey Kurtzman, Moore will recall an incident.
YEAH... 'IF'!... 'IF'! NOT MUCH OF A WORD! A LITTLE WORD! BUT LOTS OF MEANING!
© E.C. Comics 1952
Halfway through what he will describe as "the lousiest week" of his life, He'll find himself at the Grenoble Comics festival
TWELVE TWENTY-SEVEN! IF ONLY IT HAD WAITED TILL TWELVE TWENTY-EIGHT! IF ONLY...! IF... IF... IF!
Written and drawn by Kurtzman
And while there, up an alp, he'll spend time with fellow guest, Kurtzman.
YAAAH... WHAT'S THE USE OF SAYIN' 'IF'! THERE WOULDN'T HAVE BEEN IF'S, IF THE OLD MAN HADN'T DECIDED WE SHOULD GO ON RECONNAISSANCE THIS MORNING... AT OH-NINE-HUNDRED!
"Big If."
Harvey, suffering from the debilitating effects of Parkinson's disease, will be bundled up warm on an already warm day, drinking cocoa.
I've lost the copyright to my two most successful books. But we press on merrily. With the total folly of youth we assume that we'll have an inexhaustible supply of good ideas
That's true what you said about assuming you'll always have ideas. That's very true.
How about another cocoa, Harve?
No. Better not. I might start something.
Eldorado

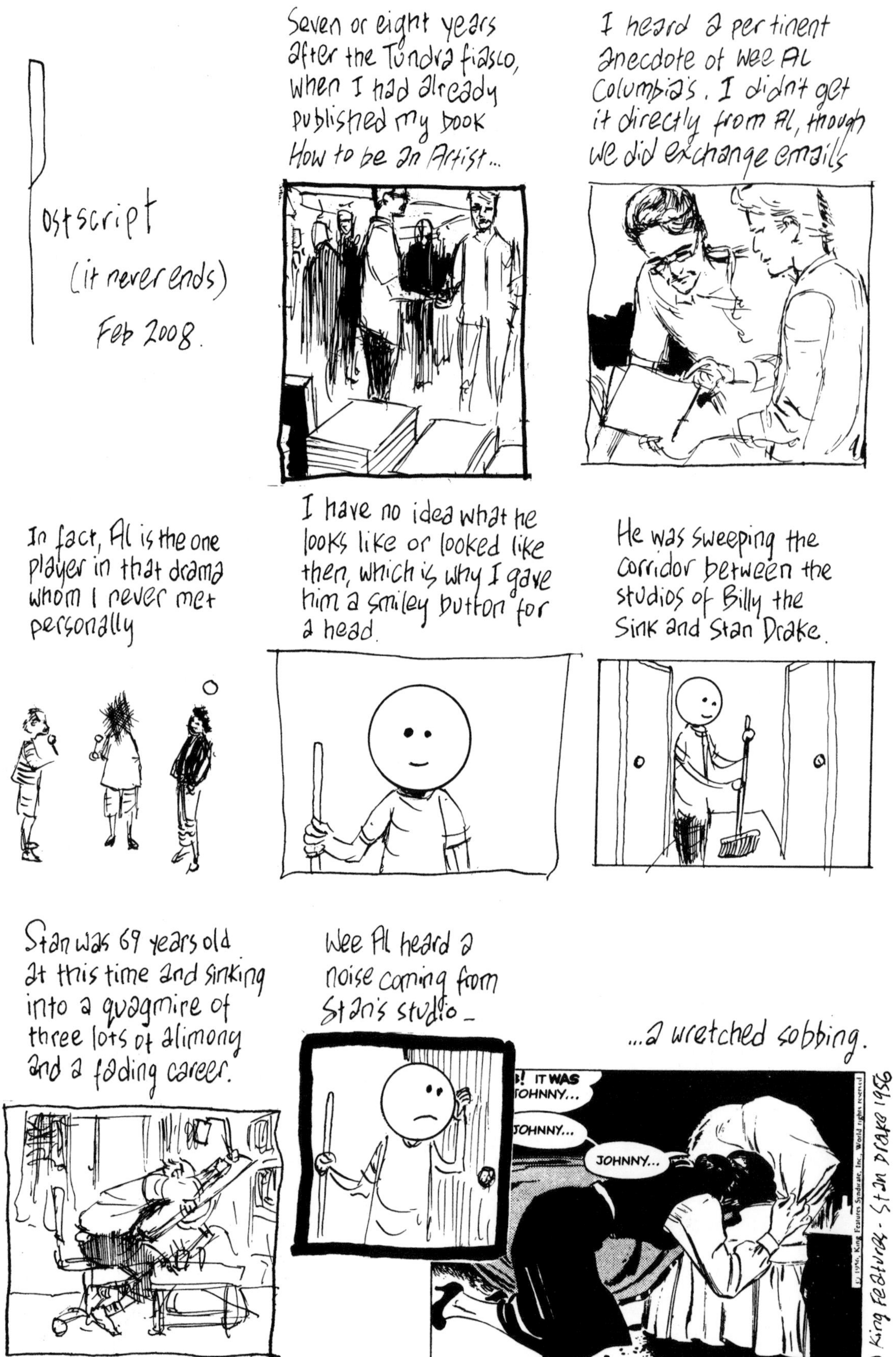
Postscript
(it never ends)
Feb 2008.
Seven or eight years after the Tundra fiasco, when I had already published my book How to be an Artist...
I heard a pertinent anecdote of Wee Al Columbia's. I didn't get it directly from Al, though we did exchange emails
In fact, Al is the one player in that drama whom I never met personally
I have no idea what he looks like or looked like then, which is why I gave him a smiley button for a head.
He was sweeping the corridor between the studios of Billy the Sink and Stan Drake.
Stan was 69 years old at this time and sinking into a quagmire of three lots of alimony and a fading career.
Wee Al heard a noise coming from Stan's studio _
...a wretched sobbing.
B! IT WAS JOHNNY...
JOHNNY...
JOHNNY...
© King Features - Stan Drake 1956

Stan Drake died six years after and the Comics Journal printed a two-page obituary.
It included a representative panel of his art, except that it wasn't a Drake drawing, nor apparently from any series he ever worked on,
© King F. Drake.
VETERAN CARTOONIST STAN DRAKE DIES AT 75
LONGTIME BLONDIE ARTIST BEST KNOWN FOR WORK ON THE HEART OF JULIET JONES
Veteran strip cartoonist Stan Drake, who earned his fame with The Heart of Juliet Jones before leaving the strip in 1989 to draw Blondie, died following a long illness on March 10 at the age of 75 in Norwalk, Conn. Drake — "one of the masters," according to King Features Editor Jay Kennedy — was renowned amongst his peers for his skill and versatility. The National Society of Cartoonists named him cartoonist of the year three times for his work on Juliet Jones (a popular soap opera strip that had its heyday in the 1970s), and Drake's slick style and technique served as a seminal influence in the art of Neal Adams. And while the bulk of Drake's career was spent on Juliet Jones, the cartoonist worked in a variety of styles and disciplines — ranging from paintings to technical drawings for golf magazines
WE'RE GOING TO CHICAGO TOGETHER, STEVEN? THAT'S WONDERFUL! BUT--
GRANT'LL BE HOME AFTER I SCARF SOME OF GENA'S CHOW.
CIAO.
From Drake's award-winning work on Juliet Jones.
But drawing eventually won out over Hollywood and the PGA, and Drake enrolled in New York City's Art Students League. There, Drake
career interrupted by World War II. In 1941, he was drafted and served in the army for about four years. Drake then returned back to New York in 1946
His skills were once envied and widely imitated, but now the organ of serious commentary in this field can't even recognize them.
— eh?
When the Journal ran their 'best-of-century' list, I questioned their competence, since they couldn't tell the difference between one artist and another.
Dear Comics Jou
And I quoted the Drake obit, the first attention that had been drawn to it in the three years since its appearance.
You are a bunch
When the smoke cleared, somebody asked: "Well if it wasn't Drake who drew the panel in Comics Journal #194, Then who was it?
of clots.
As it was known that Billy the sink had worked in proximity to Drake, one of the guys at the mag thought to fax him a copy of the disputed panel...
I'm sending now, Bill - It's a real mystery.
...to enlist his expertise in identifying its author.
Just coming through now.
Is this some kind of JOKE? That's not from the Heart of Juliet Jones - It's from one of my old Moon Knight comic books!!
The End.

Little Italy

XXXX

There are two different kinds of books in this collection. The first is the through-composed narrative written some time after the fact, of which I know how it ends before I start (like the one you've just read). The second consists of brief moments captured, thoughts expressed immediately, and anecdotes illustrated the day after hearing them (I had found a small market for single-page humorous pieces). *Little Italy* fits the second category. A few pages have been edited out for this showing, since they contain either material which describes incidents better described in one of the other books, or stuff which I now consider irrelevant, for that is in the nature of pages written on the run. The book represents a year in which I lived in a grand house on a tropical beach, and chronologically this and the two following it are busy catching up to the point where *How to be an Artist* concluded.

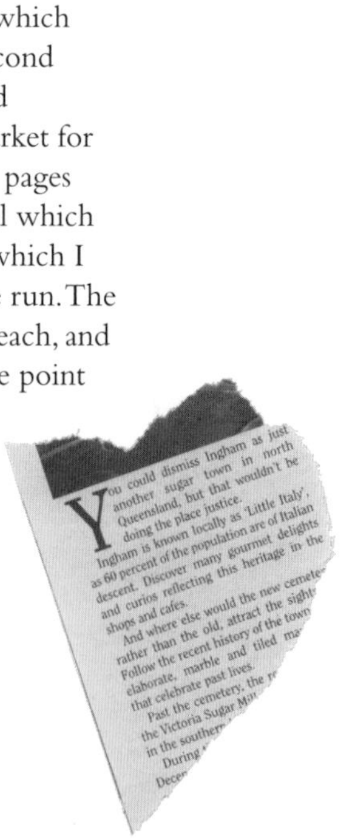

You could dismiss Ingham as just another sugar town in north Queensland, but that wouldn't be doing the place justice.
Ingham is known locally as 'Little Italy', as 60 percent of the population are of Italian descent. Discover many gourmet delights and curios reflecting this heritage in the shops and cafes.
And where else would the new cemete rather than the old, attract the sight Follow the recent history of the town elaborate, marble and tiled ma that celebrate past lives.
Past the cemetery, the r the Victoria Sugar Mi in the southern
During
Dece

thE cartoons iN this buK wer dron by the old fella during three stops in tropical North Australia, once for 3 months, once for a whol yere and once just for Christmas. He aloodid to this buk in his other buk The Dead Mouse calling it his famis 'Lost' buK because he inventid the idee of sellinge off the artworks befoor it ad evern bin publiged. The currant volyum is put together theroffer curtzy of a bunch of photocopies he had the good sens to salt away...

I'M SENDING THIS IN FROM THE HACIENDA- WHAT AM I DOING HERE?

I'M WATCHING TERESA KALACHOFF
OPEN A COCONUT FOR ME.

I AM BEING WATCHED
BY TERMITE MOUNDS.

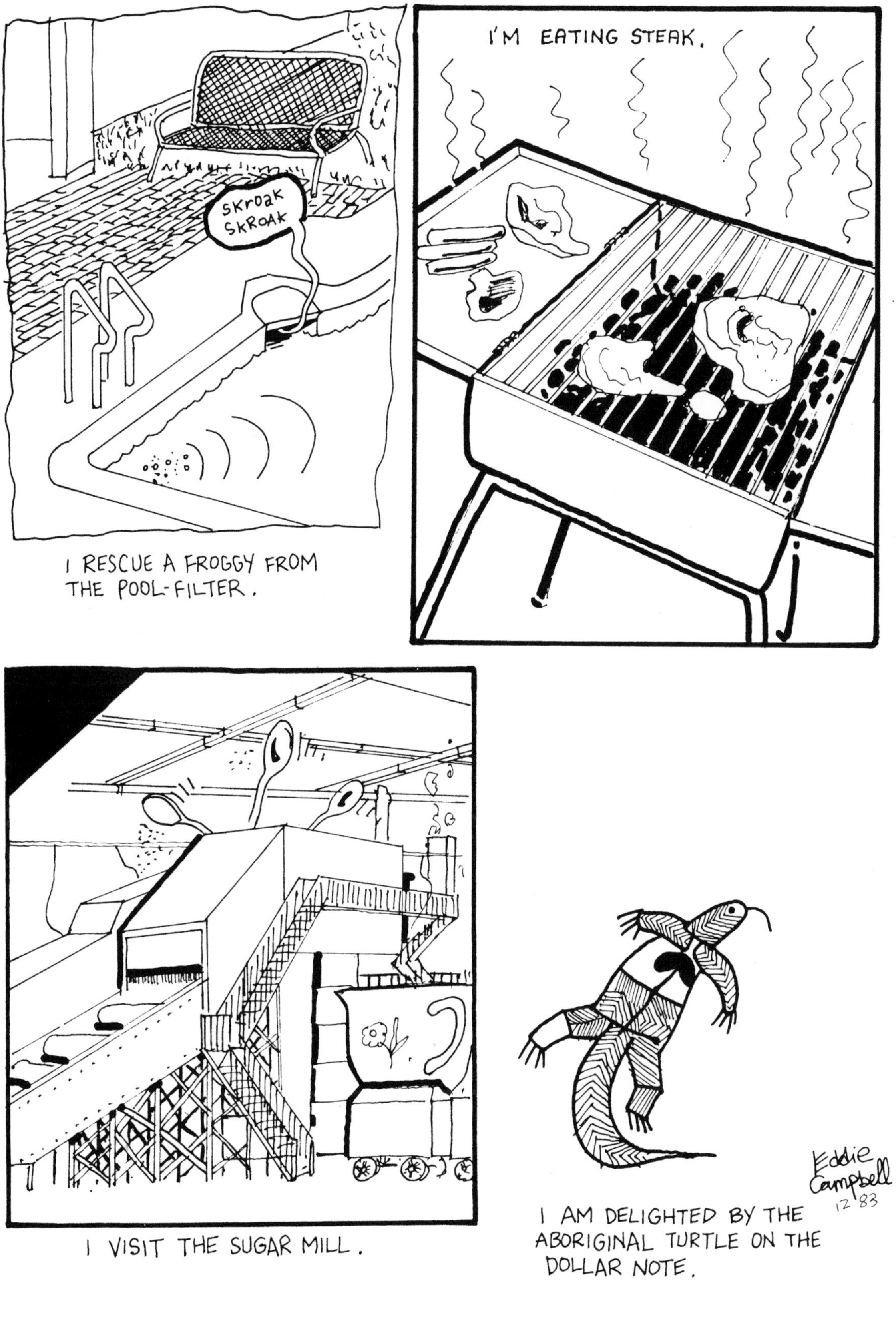
SKROAK SKROAK
I RESCUE A FROGGY FROM THE POOL-FILTER.
I'M EATING STEAK.
I VISIT THE SUGAR MILL.
I AM DELIGHTED BY THE ABORIGINAL TURTLE ON THE DOLLAR NOTE.
Eddie Campbell 12 '83

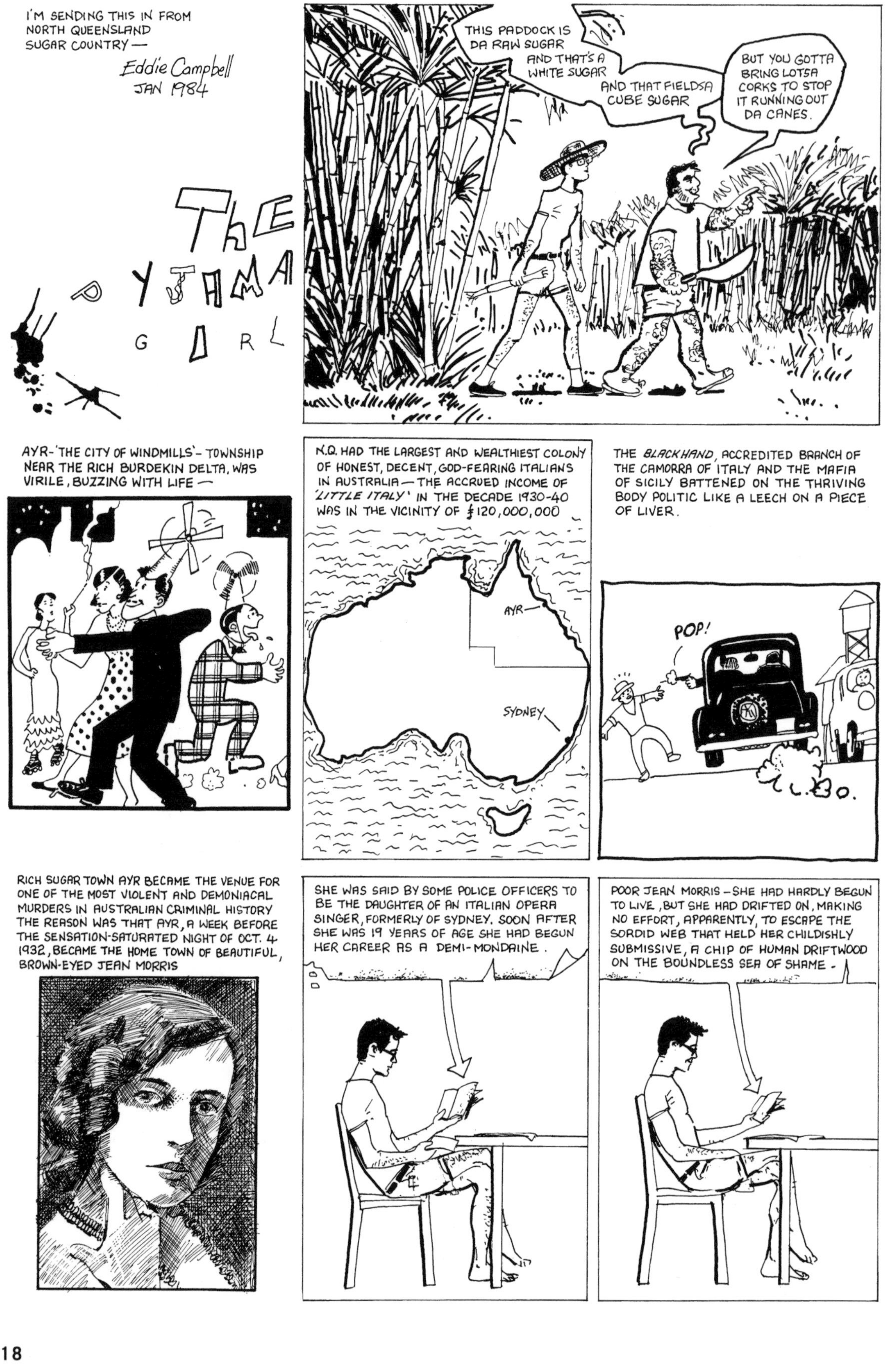
I'M SENDING THIS IN FROM NORTH QUEENSLAND SUGAR COUNTRY —
Eddie Campbell
JAN 1984
THE PYJAMA GIRL
THIS PADDOCK IS DA RAW SUGAR
AND THAT'S A WHITE SUGAR
AND THAT FIELDSA CUBE SUGAR
BUT YOU GOTTA BRING LOTSA CORKS TO STOP IT RUNNING OUT DA CANES.
AYR-'THE CITY OF WINDMILLS'- TOWNSHIP NEAR THE RICH BURDEKIN DELTA, WAS VIRILE, BUZZING WITH LIFE —
N.Q. HAD THE LARGEST AND WEALTHIEST COLONY OF HONEST, DECENT, GOD-FEARING ITALIANS IN AUSTRALIA — THE ACCRUED INCOME OF 'LITTLE ITALY' IN THE DECADE 1930-40 WAS IN THE VICINITY OF £120,000,000
AYR
SYDNEY
THE BLACKHAND, ACCREDITED BRANCH OF THE CAMORRA OF ITALY AND THE MAFIA OF SICILY BATTENED ON THE THRIVING BODY POLITIC LIKE A LEECH ON A PIECE OF LIVER.
POP!
RICH SUGAR TOWN AYR BECAME THE VENUE FOR ONE OF THE MOST VIOLENT AND DEMONIACAL MURDERS IN AUSTRALIAN CRIMINAL HISTORY THE REASON WAS THAT AYR, A WEEK BEFORE THE SENSATION-SATURATED NIGHT OF OCT. 4 1932, BECAME THE HOME TOWN OF BEAUTIFUL, BROWN-EYED JEAN MORRIS
SHE WAS SAID BY SOME POLICE OFFICERS TO BE THE DAUGHTER OF AN ITALIAN OPERA SINGER, FORMERLY OF SYDNEY. SOON AFTER SHE WAS 19 YEARS OF AGE SHE HAD BEGUN HER CAREER AS A DEMI-MONDAINE.
POOR JEAN MORRIS - SHE HAD HARDLY BEGUN TO LIVE, BUT SHE HAD DRIFTED ON, MAKING NO EFFORT, APPARENTLY, TO ESCAPE THE SORDID WEB THAT HELD HER CHILDISHLY SUBMISSIVE, A CHIP OF HUMAN DRIFTWOOD ON THE BOUNDLESS SEA OF SHAME.

DURING VISITS OF JEAN MORRIS TO INNISFAIL, N.Q., DETECTIVES HAD BEEN INTRIGUED TO NOTE SHE WAS ON FRIENDLY TERMS WITH VINCENZO DAGOSTINO AND FRANCESCO FEMIO, ACCREDITED MAFIA LEADERS.
ON 2 O'CLOCK ON THE MORNING OF OCTOBER 4, 1932, THERE STOLE INTO THE TINY HOME OF JEAN MORRIS A FANATICAL ASSASSIN WHO HAS NEVER BEEN IDENTIFIED
WHAT COLOUR WAS HER HAIR, GREG?
BLACK, MATE
Her abundant black hair cascaded across the pillow. Her arms were stretched straight out at her sides. Her body lay fully extended down the centre of the bed. clack clack clack
clack.
THE GROTESQUELY SLASHED BEDCLOTHES AND THE BLOOD-DRENCHED MATTRESS WERE POINTERS TO THE LETHAL FEROCITY WHICH THE KILLER MUST HAVE EXHIBITED WHILE HE WAS MAKING SURE THAT HIS VICTIM WAS REALLY DEAD
THE AUTHORITIES WERE CONVINCED THAT A BLACK HAND GANGSTER WAS RESPONSIBLE. THE STORY GOES THAT HE WAS SMUGGLED OUT OF THE COUNTRY AND PLACED ABOARD AN ITALIAN STEAMER BOUND FOR NAPLES. HE DISEMBARKED AT PORT SAID.
FOLLOWING ARREST IN PORT SAID BY TURKISH AUTHORITIES, DEPORTATION TO ITALY, COMMUNICATION BETWEEN QUEENSLAND POLICE AND ITALIAN POLICE, THE MAN BELIEVED TO BE THE KILLER HANGED HIMSELF IN AN ITALIAN PRISON
VIVACIOUS JEAN MORRIS, STABBED 35 TIMES BY A SATANIC MURDERER AT AYR, BECAME THE PRINCIPAL IN AUSTRALIA'S MOST AMAZING IDENTITY RIDDLE WHEN HER DEATH WAS LINKED WITH THAT OF THE ALBURY 'PYJAMA GIRL' -
ON THE MORNING OF SEPTEMBER 4 1934 THERE WAS FOUND IN A CULVERT ON THE HOWLONG ROAD, ALBURY, THE BATTERED, PARTLY-BURNED, ALMOST UNRECOGNISABLE BODY OF A YOUNG WOMAN CLAD IN SILK PYJAMAS OF CHINESE DESIGN.
HALF NAKED GIRL
EXTRA
MURDER
THE BODY WAS PRESERVED IN A FORMALIN BATH IN THE SYDNEY UNIVERSITY. POLICE APPEALED THROUGH THE NEWSPAPERS IN THEIR NEVER-CEASING EFFORT TO ESTABLISH IDENTITY. A FILM WAS PRODUCED AND SCREENED THROUGHOUT AUSTRALIA -

IT SEEMED INCREDIBLE THAT NOBODY WAS ABLE TO IDENTIFY THE 'PYJAMA GIRL'. IT JUST DIDN'T SEEM POSSIBLE THAT YEAR AFTER YEAR SHE COULD REMAIN SOAKING IN THE FORMALIN, WITHOUT ANYONE COMING FORWARD TO SAY THEY KNEW HER.

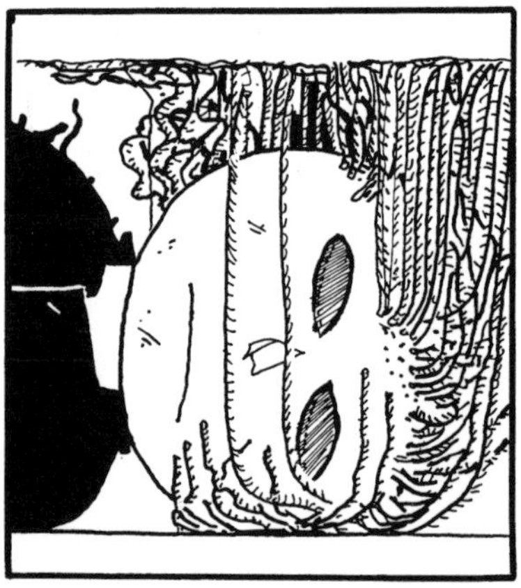

AND SO, INTO THIS STRANGE STORY, ON MAY 11, 1937 STEPPED MRS. JEANETTE CONSTANCE ROUTLEDGE, OF MARRICKVILLE, SYDNEY. IT SEEMS THAT HER DAUGHTER ANNA PHILOMENA VANISHED FROM HER HOME SOME YEARS PREVIOUSLY AND MRS. ROUTLEDGE THOUGHT SHE MAY BE THE 'PYJAMA GIRL'.

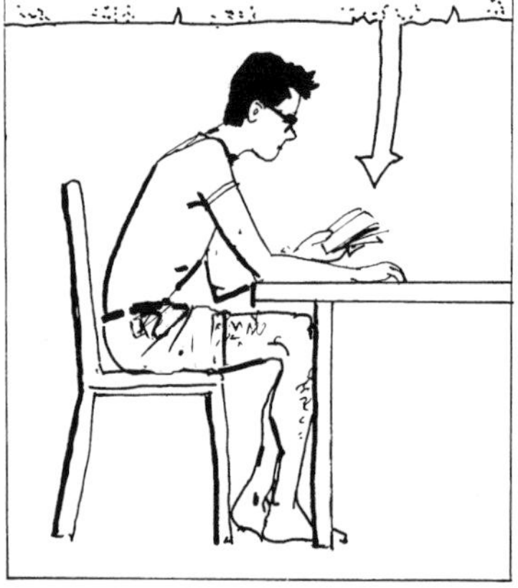

YET SHE SUBSEQUENTLY ADMITTED IN A SWORN AFFIDAVIT- "THE BODY WAS HOOKED OUT OF THE LIQUID IN MY PRESENCE. I LOOKED ON THE FACE WHICH WAS BATTERED AND HIDEOUSLY MANGLED AND I WAS TOO OVERCOME TO INSPECT IT. I HAD A DESIRE TO GET OUT OF THE ROOM"—

SHE IS NOT MY DAUGHTER

HOWEVER, AFTER HEARING 'CERTAIN THINGS', MRS. ROUTLEDGE WENT BACK TO THE SYDNEY UNIVERSITY IN SEPTEMBER 1940. SHE LOOKED AGAIN AT THE BODY RAKED OUT OF THE FORMALIN BATH AND THIS TIME SHE SAID IT WAS HER MISSING DAUGHTER, ANNA PHILOMENA MORGAN.

THAT CLAIM CREATED A PROFOUND SENSATION, FOR SOME MEMBERS OF THE POLICE FORCE HAD BEEN CONVINCED THAT MRS. ROUTLEDGE'S MISSING DAUGHTER WAS NOT IN FACT THE 'PYJAMA GIRL' BUT THE GIRL MURDERED AT AYR. THE POLICE OF NEW SOUTH WALES AND QUEENSLAND WERE SENT INTO A WELTER OF FEVERISH ACTIVITY

THEN BECAME APPARENT AN UNHAPPY OVERSIGHT. DURING THE ORIGINAL INVESTIGATION - A CASUAL PHOTOGRAPHER HAD BEEN ASKED TO MAKE A CAMERA RECORD OF THE SCENE OF THE MURDER BUT DUE TO A MISUNDERSTANDING REGARDING THE ISSUING OF INSTRUCTIONS, THE BODY OF JEAN MORRIS HAD NOT BEEN PHOTOGRAPHED BEFORE BEING BURIED

JEAN MORRIS
1932

IT WAS CLAIMED THAT A FURTHER BLUNDER OCCURRED EITHER IN BRISBANE OR SYDNEY CONCERNING THE PHOTO PUBLISHED IN THE *POLICE GAZETTE* PURPORTING TO BE THE LIKENESS OF JEAN MORRIS, FOR IT WAS SAID THAT THE PHOTO WHICH APPEARED IN SOUTHERN ISSUES WAS NOT THAT OF JEAN MORRIS!

azette
RRIS
JEAN MORRIS, MURDERED
AYR

THE QUEENSLAND POLICE WORKED HARD RE-INTERVIEWING ITALIANS WHO HAD KNOWN JEAN MORRIS BOTH IN SYDNEY AND IN NORTH QUEENSLAND

NO UNDERSTAND

THE POLICE, HAVING DECIDED THAT THE TASK OF IDENTIFYING THE 'PYJAMA GIRL' WAS A HOPELESS ONE INTENDED, THEREFORE, TO HAVE THE BODY BURIED AS THAT OF AN 'UNKNOWN WOMAN'. IT WAS THEN THAT MRS. ROUTLEDGE MADE HER SENSATIONAL, LEGALLY-UNIQUE MOVE.

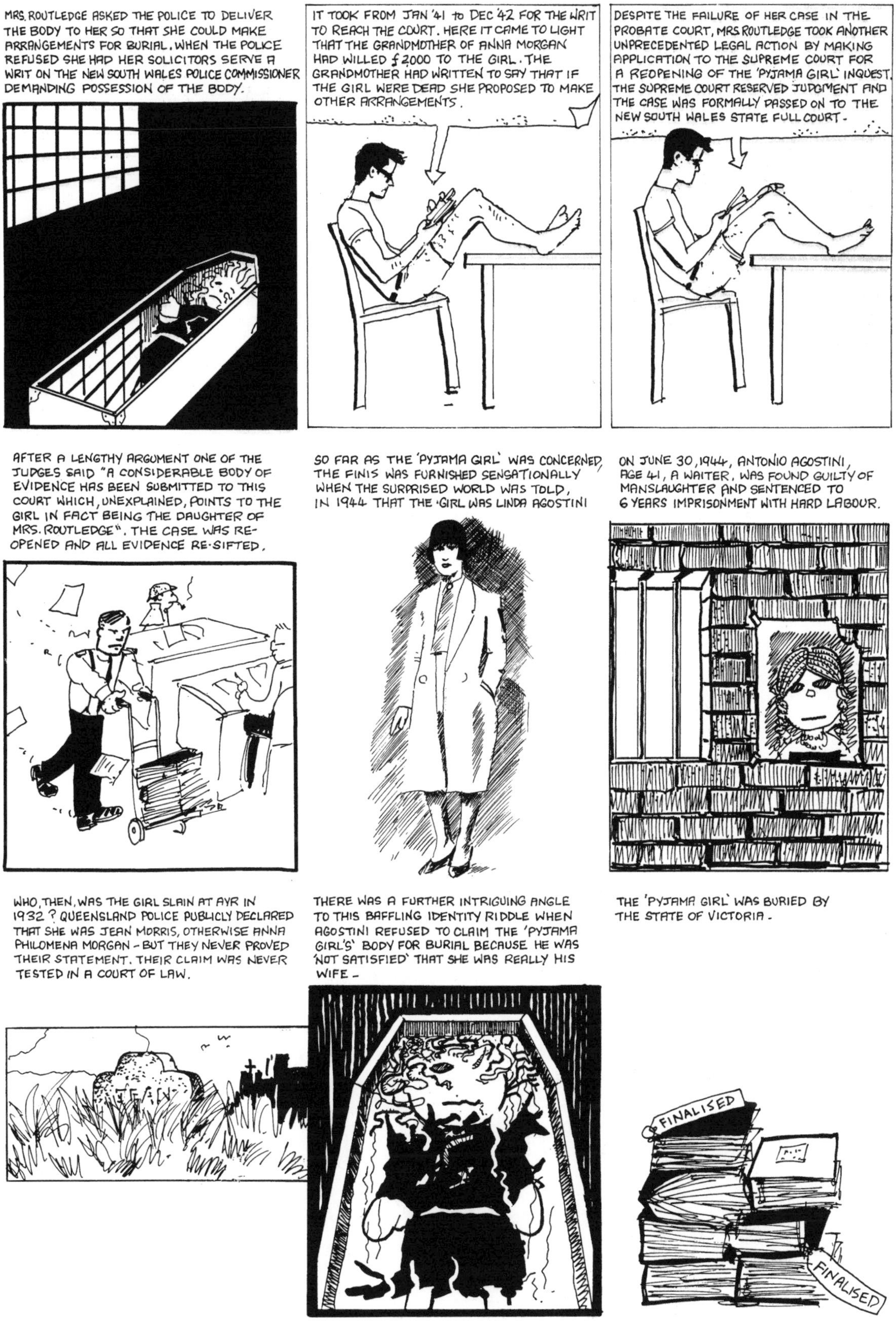
MRS. ROUTLEDGE ASKED THE POLICE TO DELIVER THE BODY TO HER SO THAT SHE COULD MAKE ARRANGEMENTS FOR BURIAL. WHEN THE POLICE REFUSED SHE HAD HER SOLICITORS SERVE A WRIT ON THE NEW SOUTH WALES POLICE COMMISSIONER DEMANDING POSSESSION OF THE BODY.
IT TOOK FROM JAN '41 TO DEC '42 FOR THE WRIT TO REACH THE COURT. HERE IT CAME TO LIGHT THAT THE GRANDMOTHER OF ANNA MORGAN HAD WILLED £2000 TO THE GIRL. THE GRANDMOTHER HAD WRITTEN TO SAY THAT IF THE GIRL WERE DEAD SHE PROPOSED TO MAKE OTHER ARRANGEMENTS.
DESPITE THE FAILURE OF HER CASE IN THE PROBATE COURT, MRS. ROUTLEDGE TOOK ANOTHER UNPRECEDENTED LEGAL ACTION BY MAKING APPLICATION TO THE SUPREME COURT FOR A REOPENING OF THE 'PYJAMA GIRL' INQUEST. THE SUPREME COURT RESERVED JUDGMENT AND THE CASE WAS FORMALLY PASSED ON TO THE NEW SOUTH WALES STATE FULL COURT.
AFTER A LENGTHY ARGUMENT ONE OF THE JUDGES SAID "A CONSIDERABLE BODY OF EVIDENCE HAS BEEN SUBMITTED TO THIS COURT WHICH, UNEXPLAINED, POINTS TO THE GIRL IN FACT BEING THE DAUGHTER OF MRS. ROUTLEDGE". THE CASE WAS RE-OPENED AND ALL EVIDENCE RE-SIFTED.
SO FAR AS THE 'PYJAMA GIRL' WAS CONCERNED, THE FINIS WAS FURNISHED SENSATIONALLY WHEN THE SURPRISED WORLD WAS TOLD, IN 1944 THAT THE 'GIRL WAS LINDA AGOSTINI
ON JUNE 30, 1944, ANTONIO AGOSTINI, AGE 41, A WAITER, WAS FOUND GUILTY OF MANSLAUGHTER AND SENTENCED TO 6 YEARS IMPRISONMENT WITH HARD LABOUR.
WHO, THEN, WAS THE GIRL SLAIN AT AYR IN 1932? QUEENSLAND POLICE PUBLICLY DECLARED THAT SHE WAS JEAN MORRIS, OTHERWISE ANNA PHILOMENA MORGAN - BUT THEY NEVER PROVED THEIR STATEMENT. THEIR CLAIM WAS NEVER TESTED IN A COURT OF LAW.
THERE WAS A FURTHER INTRIGUING ANGLE TO THIS BAFFLING IDENTITY RIDDLE WHEN AGOSTINI REFUSED TO CLAIM THE 'PYJAMA GIRL'S' BODY FOR BURIAL BECAUSE HE WAS 'NOT SATISFIED' THAT SHE WAS REALLY HIS WIFE -
THE 'PYJAMA GIRL' WAS BURIED BY THE STATE OF VICTORIA -
FINALISED
FINALISED

JACK Takes iT eASY.
BUZZZZ
DAMN THING
BZZSHH
CAN YOU SEE THIS O.K., DAD
i'm not really watching it Darling
WOZZSHH
WOZZSHH
PRANG
BLOZZZ
HEH HEH HEH
86 Eddie Campbell

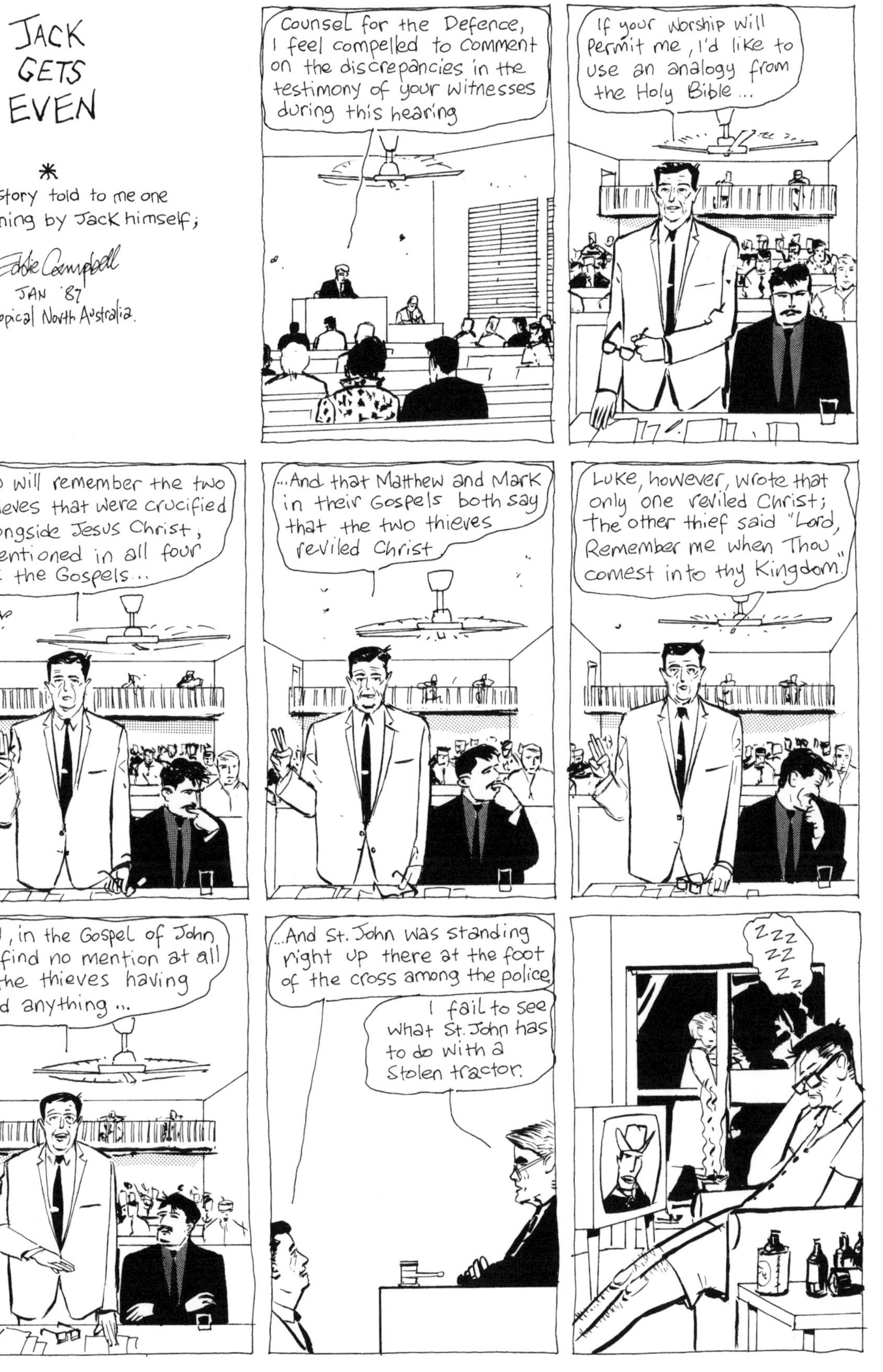
JACK GETS EVEN
a story told to me one evening by Jack himself;
Eddie Campbell
JAN '87
tropical North Australia.
Counsel for the Defence, I feel compelled to comment on the discrepancies in the testimony of your witnesses during this hearing
If your worship will permit me, I'd like to use an analogy from the Holy Bible...
You will remember the two thieves that were crucified alongside Jesus Christ, mentioned in all four of the Gospels...
...And that Matthew and Mark in their Gospels both say that the two thieves reviled Christ
Luke, however, wrote that only one reviled Christ; the other thief said "Lord, Remember me when Thou comest into thy Kingdom"
Now, in the Gospel of John we find no mention at all of the thieves having said anything...
...And St. John was standing right up there at the foot of the cross among the police
I fail to see what St. John has to do with a stolen tractor.
ZZZ ZZ Z Z

RING RING
O.K, I'LL see him on my way to the office
Dash it! forgot to tell Joy. oh, never mind.
APITOL BUILDING
POLIC
COSTA FIORELL
He killed and stole this beast, Williams
That remains to be seen, murphy.
POO
SALT
He's all yours.
Wait a minute!
I can't talk to my client when he's caged up like an animal. Open this door, Murphy!!
O.K. you can sit in with him
Don't go too far away now.
CRONK

PITOL BUIL
COSTA
Frosty Mangoes getta ya Frosty Mangoes here.
MURPHY! I'm finished here. You can let me out now !! MURPHY!!
MRS. Williams. your husband hasn't arrived today. I have appointments booked all morning for him. You don't Know where he is ?
PITOL BUIL
COSTA
Watamelonie Watamelonie No Sweeta No pay
ZZZZ
ZZZZ
The Defence wishes to apply for a formal hearing of its case,
The case will be brought before this court therefore on the ...uh, 29th of this Month,
And the defence wishes to apply, furthermore, for all evidence to be held until the formal hearing of its case.
granted.
I can't Keep that rotten meat for three weeks, Williams, and you Know it!

SALT
Williams! I have no Police Force this Morning!! You gotta let me get rid of this carcass!!!
oh, alright, Murphy... Go ahead and bury it.
Harry, I think you better get down to the police station.
But Williams said it's O.K.
I'm saying it's NOT O.K. - get that beast out of the hole.
Williams. I've had that meat for four days. It's a healt' hazard. I need your written consent!
DRINK XXXX
See me in work time
Hey, Williams!! nobody'll let me keep that carcass in their freezer.. you gotta let me —
I'm busy, murphy.
AWARD
Aw, Jack, come on, please...

oh, alright, Murphy. I'll get one of the girls to type it up. call by this afternoon.
Gina ... can you do this for me next.
I'll be out fishing for the rest of the day Have a nice weekend.
MR S.J. Williams
PITOL BU
COSTA
No squeeza the banana. Squeeza the coconut
Hello, Gina. Mr. Williams will have left a letter for me. can I take that now?
Mr. S.J. Williams
Oh, I'm sorry, Mr. Murphy.. I've posted all the mail. my boss didn't specify that yours was to be collected.
Mr. S.J. Williams
B-But there's no post delivery now till Monday Morning. my..ah!!
WILLIAMS!!
I'll chuck the pick out here, Jack
Then we'll follow the advice of St. Paul in his first epistle to Timothy: "Remember to take a little wine for thy Stomach's sake"
Eddie Campbell '87

THINGS I LEARNED AT COLLEGE
by Eddie Campbell JAN '87
Everybody else lost their virginity. All you lost was your common sense
Lots of mosquitos down here at the beach, babby. Y'gotta wear this repellant
You idiot !! She's only going to put her hands in her mouth now !!
I never thought of that !
RID
DA
Get some soap and water, quick !
You so-called Educated people. You're so clever but you don't know how to scratch your bum!
Agg!! We're locked out !!
It SLIDES, for heavens sake !!
I had to go to college to learn about these things. but you take my father-in-law...
We're very impressed with your proposals, Mr. Williams. We'll sleep on this and discuss it again tomorrow.
hold on

...I've just come several hundred miles !!... I was to go back tonight.
I'm sorry. It's the best we can do.
I'LL need some basic survival equip— Agg
JOCKEY SHORTS
SHIRTS
34 36
38 40
42 44
Joy.. what size underpants do I take?
Why don't you look at the label on the ones you're wearing.
I never thought of that
LATER-
ugh... Ak..grrr
You'd think they'd have standard sizes for butter packs. this doesn't fit in the bloody dish!!
give it to me!
I never thought of that
Isn't that amazing! and I never even went to college — I'm a self-made man.
Campbell

LITTLE ITALY
by Eddie Campbell
1. 2. 87
Today the rain started.
It's late. For a month everyone's been watching the clouds gather on the hill.
I think of the rain in ONE HUNDRED YEARS OF SOLITUDE by Gabriel Márquez, which lasted, I think, four years and brought a relentless erosion of everything.
Aureliano, Help me get the washing in.
I'm in staunch Catholic country here... But I know better than to argue about religion, so let's watch these idiots doing it.
Through fear and ignorance.
...Christians have kept half mankind slaves to a pseudo-intellectual religion for 2,000 years
What has Christianity given us apart from Inquisitions, Holy Wars.. Witch-hunts?
You can't blame all that stuff on Christ-He preached the most beautiful ideal of humility the world has ever known.
For instance he said "If thou wilt be perfect, sell all you have and give to the poor."
Yeh, and how many of his followers followed that.?!
He said "Judge not lest you be judged."
Better still, let's watch these other guys playing a game called Murra.
Quatro!
Cinque.!
drrrr

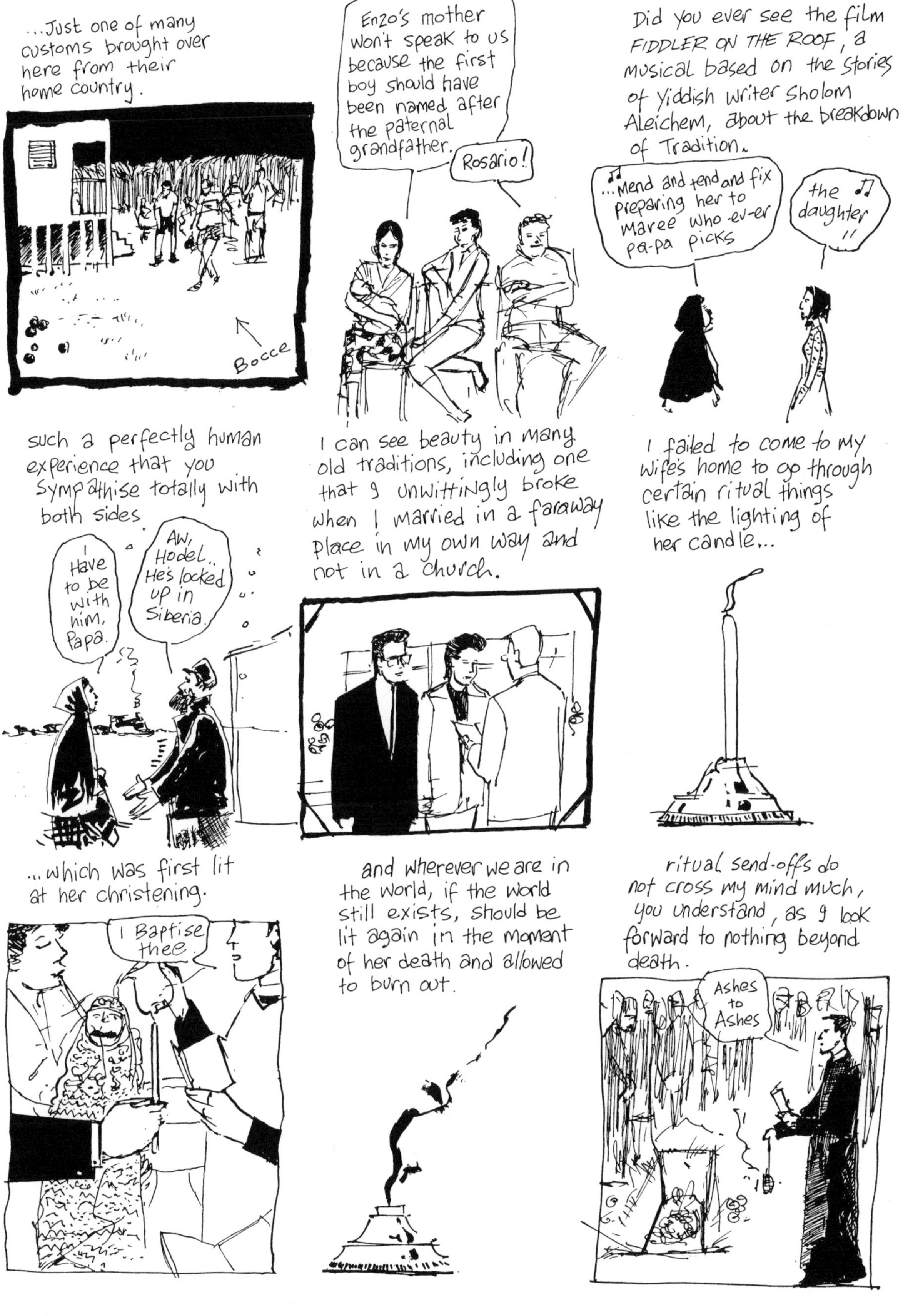
...Just one of many customs brought over here from their home country.
Bocce
Enzo's mother won't speak to us because the first boy should have been named after the paternal grandfather.
Rosario!
Did you ever see the film FIDDLER ON THE ROOF, a musical based on the stories of Yiddish writer Sholom Aleichem, about the breakdown of Tradition.
...Mend and tend and fix preparing her to maree who-ev-er pa-pa picks
the daughter
such a perfectly human experience that you sympathise totally with both sides.
I have to be with him, Papa.
Aw, Hodel.. He's locked up in Siberia.
I can see beauty in many old traditions, including one that I unwittingly broke when I married in a faraway place in my own way and not in a church.
I failed to come to my wife's home to go through certain ritual things like the lighting of her candle...
...which was first lit at her christening.
I Baptise thee.
and wherever we are in the world, if the world still exists, should be lit again in the moment of her death and allowed to burn out.
ritual send-offs do not cross my mind much, you understand, as I look forward to nothing beyond death.
Ashes to Ashes

The thing I can't get along with is the frightening pride that Faith arouses in some.
How can Anyone look at those stars and say God doesn't exist?
Well, around all those stars are planets bigger than ours, maybe with people.
I don't believe there are people out there.
In Genesis It says God created the firmament. It doesn't say anything about him putting people in it.
If you think there are people up there, explain why they have never contacted us.
There are people in the next street who have never contacted us!!
I'm browsing in a Woman's Magazine. This is the actor Mel Gibson's father talking. Surely the most presumptious nonsense I've come across today.
"The greatest benefit anyone can have is to be a Catholic - you have the lifelong satisfaction of being right."
Midnight, New Year's Day, my baby bird died I'd kept him going for five days. It had become important to me.
Baby Minah (fell out of a coconut tree)
I looked in his little gasping face and I knew he was on the out.
He pushed my hand away to concentrate entirely on the task of dying.
I burned his little body in its box on my mother-in-law's compost heap.
Ashes

She spreads the ashes all around her plants.
Mythology is full of beings rising out of ashes. Can you picture a man made of ashes standing up in the wind.?
Well I worked in a night club where I'd sometimes get stuck with the job of washing up the ash-trays.
And the resultant mulch, I am telling you, is the base constituent of everything.
You could build an ashman out of this stuff and trees could grow on him... trees of the most exotic variety.
Frangipani
Fan-palm
silky-Oak.
Rain Tree.
etc
etc
etc
Amen.

THE AUTHOR DISCOVERS ARTEFACTS OF LOST CIVILISATION IN A DREAM.
by Eddie Campbell 3 - 2 - 87.
ME
E.C.

THIS HAPPENED LAST NIGHT
To Eddie Campbell 11 Feb 87
I woke up with a dread fear.
A nauseating conviction actually.
The certainty that I will fail my final exams.
I have not studied a jot.
I will have to face my parents with my failure.
I will have to leave school and work in a factory.
I will be on the human scrap-heap
Then I remember that I left school 12 years ago.
Eddie, can you get Bubba this time
Wah
Eddie

THE AUTHOR IS COERCED INTO DOING 'REAL' WORK, LIKE THEY USED TO DO IN OLDEN TIMES.
by Eddie Campbell
14 th March '87.
STOP doing that wimpy stuff and go out there and mow the lawn !!
as long as we're staying here, you can do the heavy jobs around the place - look! My mother's doing it !! Dad'll go ape
This is the age of equal opportunity
If you worked at it you could just about make equal !!
Why don't you go out there and do some man's work for a change.
MOOMPH MOOMPH
Hey, you go and water the pot-plants or sew doileys or something.
BRUP BRUP BRUP
MANLY SHOULDERS
VRRUMMM

VRUMM
VRUMM
SPLAT
SKROAK
SKROAK
"Wee sleekit cowrin' tim'rous beastie," *
BRUP BRUP
"O what a panic's in thy breastie. thou need na start away so hasty."
BRUP BRUP
BRUP BRUP
BRUP BRUP
VRUMM
* Footnote
From the Great Scots poet Robert Burns when he turned up a mouse's nest with his plough in winter 1785.
"Still thou art blest compared with me. the present only touches thee".
'SKWEEK'
Eddie

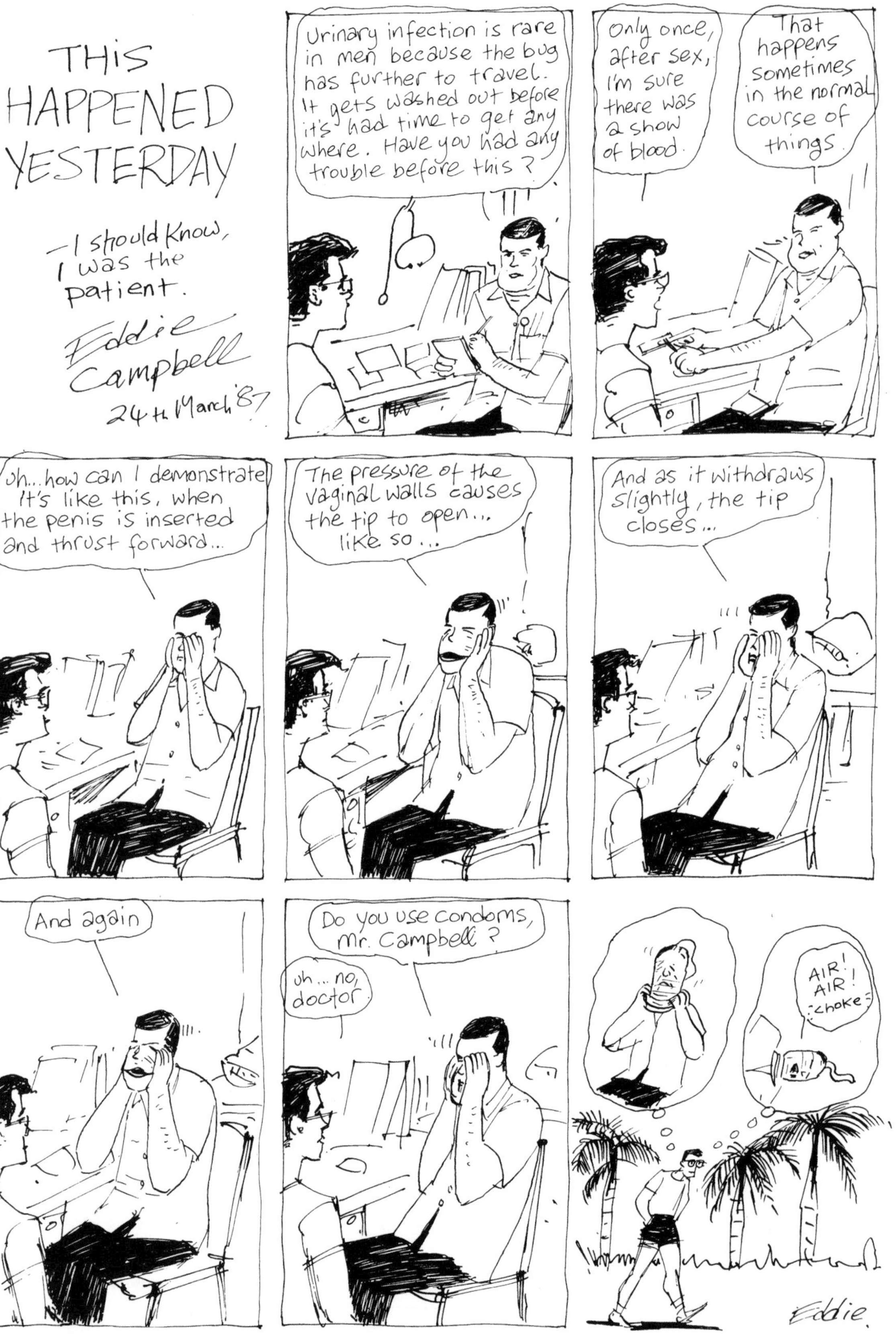
THIS HAPPENED YESTERDAY
—I should know, I was the patient.
Eddie Campbell
24th March '87
Urinary infection is rare in men because the bug has further to travel. It gets washed out before it's had time to get any where. Have you had any trouble before this?
Only once, after sex, I'm sure there was a show of blood.
That happens sometimes in the normal course of things.
oh... how can I demonstrate It's like this, when the penis is inserted and thrust forward...
The pressure of the vaginal walls causes the tip to open... like so...
And as it withdraws slightly, the tip closes...
And again
Do you use condoms, Mr. Campbell?
uh... no, doctor
AIR! AIR! choke
Eddie.

BARGAINING WITH MEDICAL SCIENCE
by Eddie Campbell
25th March '87
And Sam, no ALcohol
O.K. Doc
That will be twenty dollars consultation fee, Mr. Russo.
RECEPTION.
$ 20
AHHH
XXXX
Doc, if you don't let me have one beer a day, I'm going to another Doc.
O.K. Sam just one beer.
a ten-ounce of Four-x, Angela
Sure Sam.
gulp
What the Hell, if one beer do me no harm.
Give me another, Angela.
That's what we're here for, Sam
Eddie

YARN HEARD IN AUSTRALIAN PUB

by Eddie Campbell

3 April 87

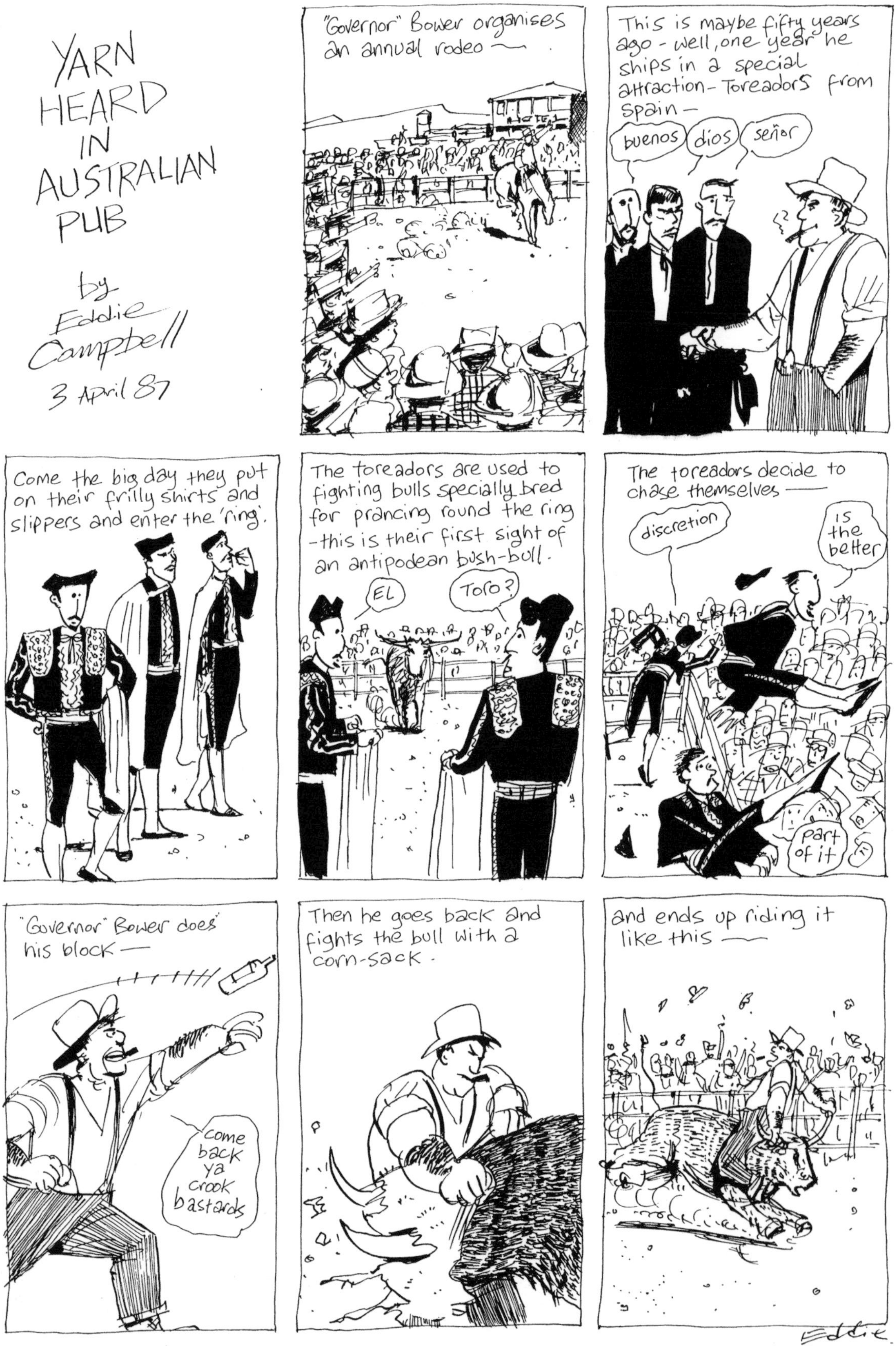

"Governor" Bower organises an annual rodeo —
This is maybe fifty years ago - well, one year he ships in a special attraction - Toreadors from Spain —
buenos
dios
señor
Come the big day they put on their frilly shirts and slippers and enter the 'ring'.
The toreadors are used to fighting bulls specially bred for prancing round the ring - this is their first sight of an antipodean bush-bull.
EL
TORO?
The toreadors decide to chase themselves —
discretion
is the better
part of it
"Governor" Bower does his block —
come back ya crook bastards
Then he goes back and fights the bull with a corn-sack.
and ends up riding it like this —
Eddie

AH THOSE OLD HORROR COMICS OF THE 1950's
a not-so-old cutting from the archives of.. Eddie Campbell 4th April '87 and a glossy magazine article
Bloodied waters
CANBERRA health officials said yesterday
Unlike the sprawling early development of Sydney and Melbourne, Canberra is a dream come true.
The dreamer, or, more fittingly, the planner, was the young U.S. architect, Walter Burley Griffin.
that blood and human remains
have been quietly flowing into the ornamental lake
in the centre of Australia's capital for the last 30 years.
In the early 1900s Burley Griffin's design won the contest organised by the Australian Government and his dream city became the National Capital
For the people who live in the dream city, life is truly Idyllic
one of the city's main attractions is Lake Burley Griffin
Refuse washed from the city's morgue after post-mortems
has flowed down drains wrongly connected to a storm water system.
—Reuter. (Feb 4th 1986)
with its carillon that plays Australian English and Scottish airs,
And its Water Jet, which sends a column of water
nearly 500 feet into the air

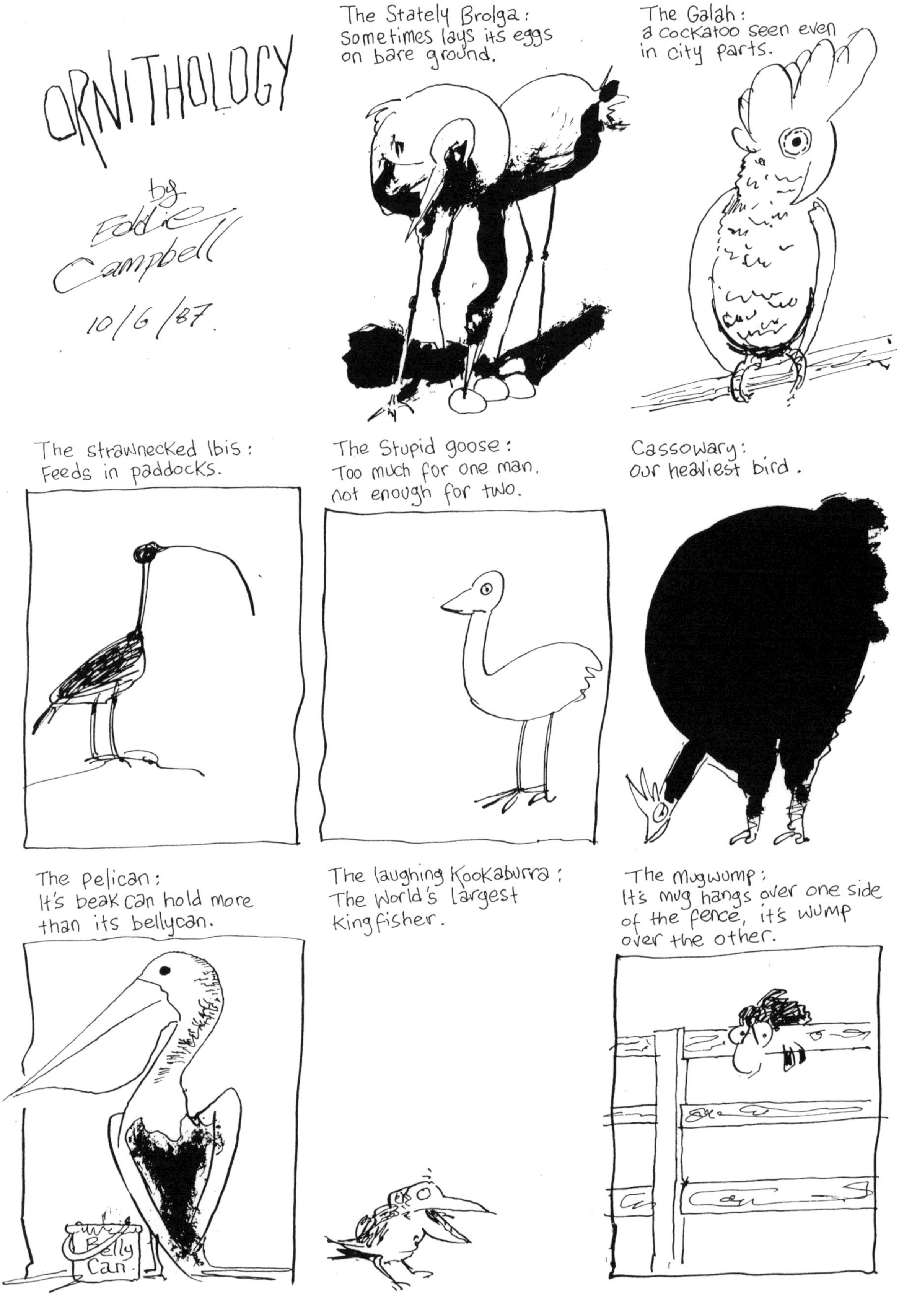
ORNITHOLOGY
by Eddie Campbell
10/6/87.
The Stately Brolga: Sometimes lays its eggs on bare ground.
The Galah: a cockatoo seen even in city parts.
The strawnecked Ibis: Feeds in paddocks.
The Stupid goose: Too much for one man, not enough for two.
Cassowary: our heaviest bird.
The Pelican: It's beak can hold more than its bellycan.
Belly Can
The laughing Kookaburra: The World's Largest Kingfisher.
The Mugwump: It's mug hangs over one side of the fence, it's wump over the other.

I HAD A RINGSIDE SEAT.
Eddie Campbell 11/10/87
Opening of the Kelly Memorial theatre -There's a cranking behind the curtain - I thought they were lowering the singer in by crane.
But he's just a little bloke — they've brought in the great Joe Sorbello and a first class pianist —
They've wheeled in the baby grand presented by the COLONIAL SUGAR REFINERIES = From where I'm sitting I can see hand-prints all over it —
Flinga Flinga Flinga Flinga
Listen, you can keep all your fine sophisticated discussions insights and critiques -
O sole Ay Mee oh
You can blow all your boloney about form and colour and expression and the existenlial basis of Art's perpetual self reevaluation out of your nose.
la Daw Na Ay mo bee lay
Just give me the simple charm of Joe singing di Capua, Puccini, Spolianski, Cordillo, Rossini, Verdi and Tauber's "My Heart and I"
"If you should say goodbye then we should surely die ~
And in particular John Colwill the pianist raising a knowing eyebrow in the middle of Chopin's Fantasie Impromptu and having everyone in the first six rows laugh with joy —
FINI — Joe gives the applause to John and John gives it to the piano —
Ed.

MORE ADVENTURES OF THE FAMOUS PYJAMA GIRL
by
Eddie Campbell
THE PYJAMA GIRL'S BIG NIGHT OUT
LINDA AGOSTINI WORKED AS AN USHERETTE IN THE OLD HOYT'S DE LUXE THEATRE IN GEORGE ST. SYDNEY. SHE HAD A DRINKING HABIT WHICH HER HUSBAND APPEARED TO FIND EMBARRASSING.
ON OR ABOUT THE NIGHT OF AUG 26 1934 HE BASHED IN ONE SIDE OF HER HEAD WITH SOMETHING HEAVY AND PUT A .25 BULLET IN THE OTHER.
HE TOOK HER PYJAMA CLAD BODY TO THE HOWLONG RD. NEAR ALBURY AND TRIED TO BURN IT IN A CULVERT. WHEN IT WAS FOUND FOUR DAYS LATER IT WAS BEYOND ALL POSSIBILITY OF IDENTIFICATION.
SHE WAS TAKEN TO SYDNEY AND PLACED IN FORMALIN AND KEPT AT THE MEDICAL SHOOL OF THE UNIVERSITY. A REWARD WAS OFFERED FOR A CLUE LEADING TO IDENTIFICATION.
IN THE FOLLOWING YEARS THOUSANDS OF PEOPLE WHO CLAIMED THEY COULD IDENTIFY HER WERE TAKEN TO SEE THE PYJAMA GIRL. MANY WENT OUT OF MORBID CURIOSITY.
THE UNIVERSITY ASKED FOR THE BODY TO BE REMOVED AND IN 1942, EIGHT YEARS AFTER HER DEATH, THE PYJAMA GIRL WAS TRANSFERRED TO POLICE H.Q.
IN MARCH 1944 INFORMATION WAS RECEIVED BY COMMISSIONER OF POLICE MR. McKAY WHICH PROMPTED HIM TO HAVE ANTONIO AGOSTINI BROUGHT IN FOR AN INTERVIEW.
SIXTEEN MEN AND WOMEN WHO KNEW THE AGOSTINIS IN SYDNEY WERE ASKED BY DETECTIVES TO COME TO A SPECIALLY ARRANGED INSPECTION OF THE BODY.

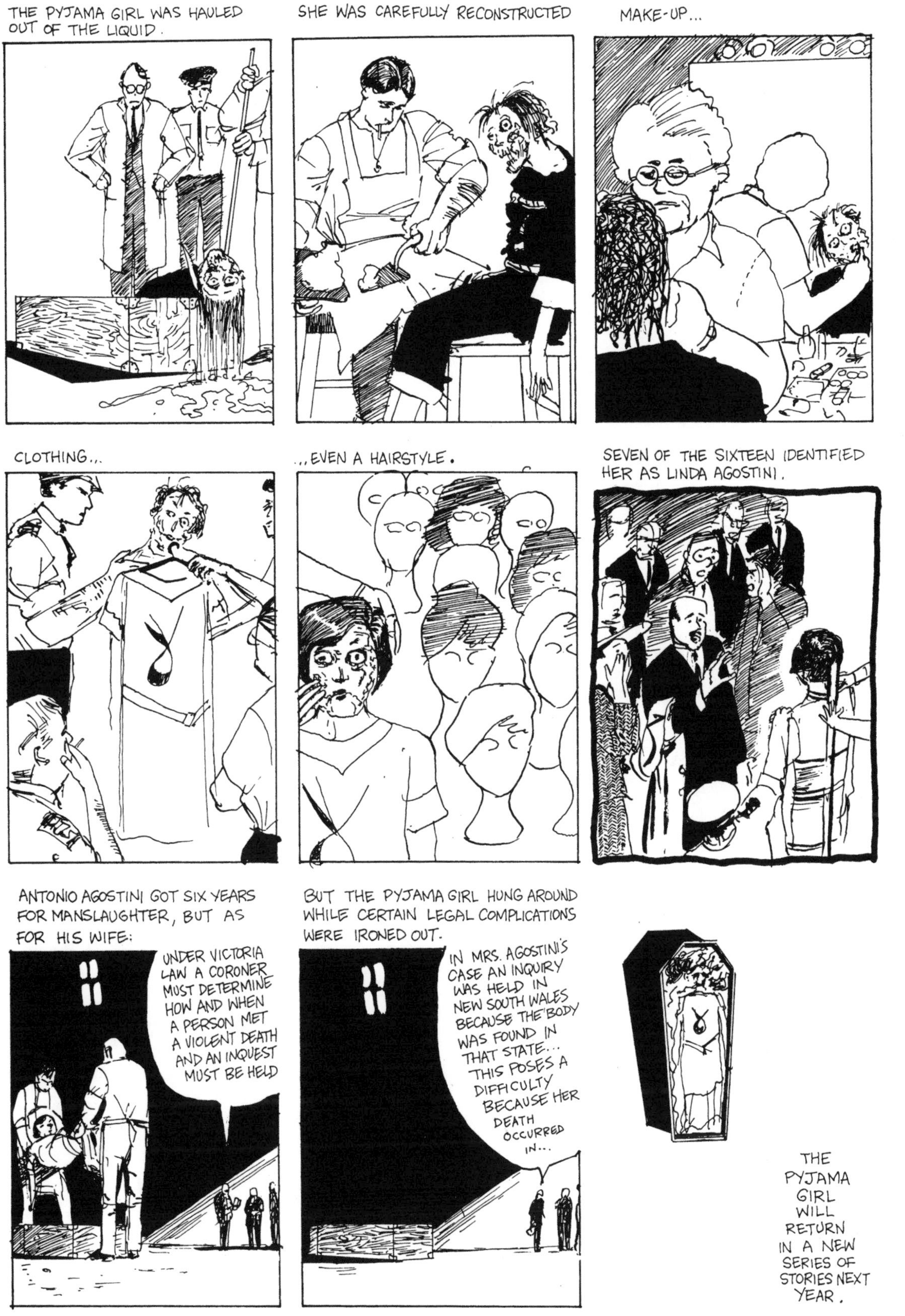
THE PYJAMA GIRL WAS HAULED OUT OF THE LIQUID.
SHE WAS CAREFULLY RECONSTRUCTED
MAKE-UP...
CLOTHING...
...EVEN A HAIRSTYLE.
SEVEN OF THE SIXTEEN IDENTIFIED HER AS LINDA AGOSTINI.
ANTONIO AGOSTINI GOT SIX YEARS FOR MANSLAUGHTER, BUT AS FOR HIS WIFE:
UNDER VICTORIA LAW A CORONER MUST DETERMINE HOW AND WHEN A PERSON MET A VIOLENT DEATH AND AN INQUEST MUST BE HELD
BUT THE PYJAMA GIRL HUNG AROUND WHILE CERTAIN LEGAL COMPLICATIONS WERE IRONED OUT.
IN MRS. AGOSTINI'S CASE AN INQUIRY WAS HELD IN NEW SOUTH WALES BECAUSE THE BODY WAS FOUND IN THAT STATE... THIS POSES A DIFFICULTY BECAUSE HER DEATH OCCURRED IN...
THE PYJAMA GIRL WILL RETURN IN A NEW SERIES OF STORIES NEXT YEAR.

MY LITTLE GIRL

Eddie Campbell
24 10 87

You pour it down the toilet- that's a good girl
Now put it back in the seat.
KLONK
We'll have to turn it this way- go on- turn it round
Aw, that's wonderful.
Now, if you lift up the little bowl..
And bring it round to this side.
Almost there, honey.. All you've got to do now is press it down down.. press!
PRESS
FLUSH
Ed

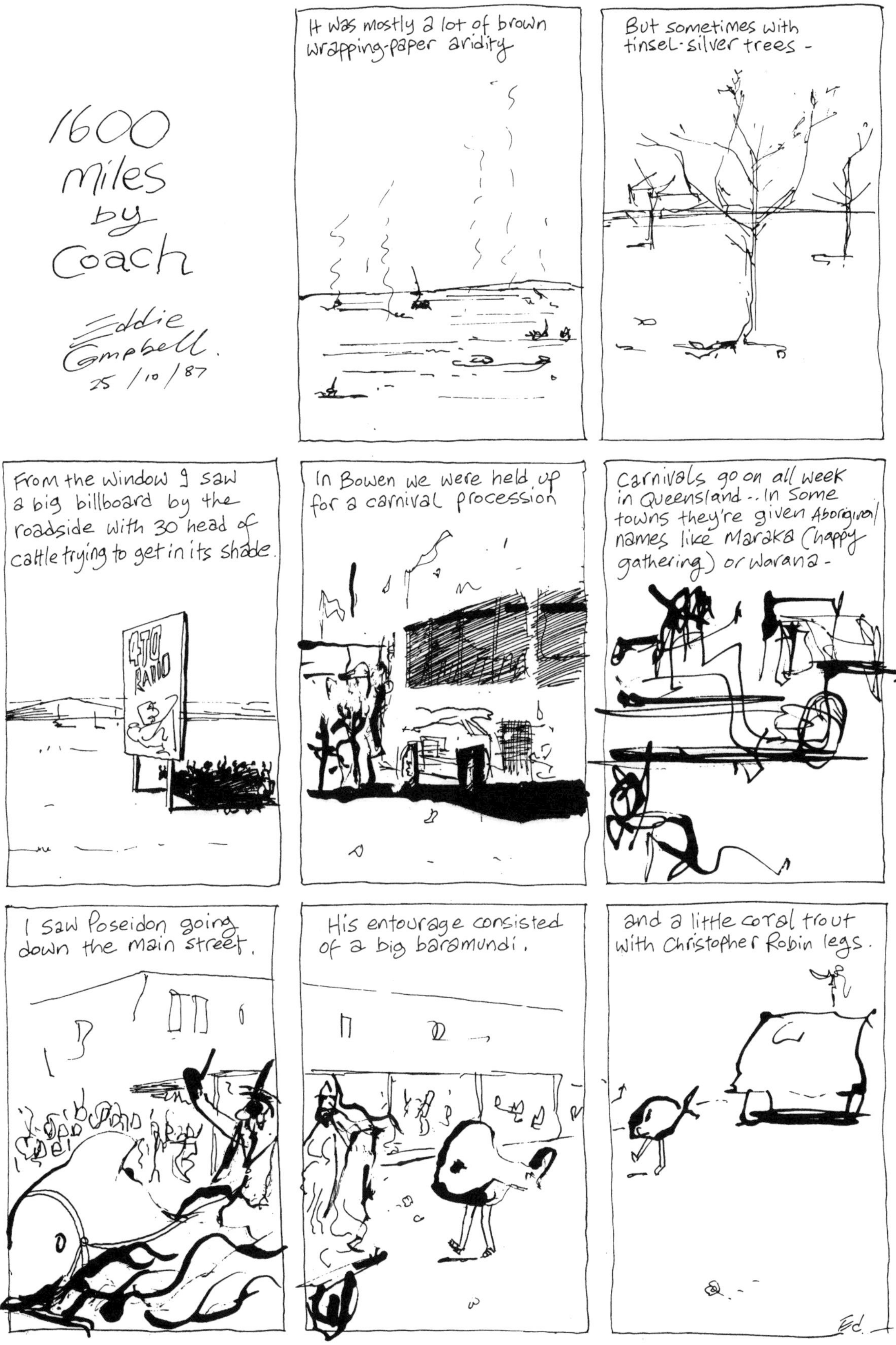
1600 miles by Coach
Eddie Campbell. 25/10/87
It was mostly a lot of brown wrapping-paper aridity
But sometimes with tinsel-silver trees -
From the window I saw a big billboard by the roadside with 30 head of cattle trying to get in its shade.
4TO RADIO
In Bowen we were held up for a carnival procession
Carnivals go on all week in Queensland -. In some towns they're given Aboriginal names like Maraka (happy gathering) or Warana -
I saw Poseidon going down the main street.
His entourage consisted of a big baramundi.
and a little coral trout with Christopher Robin legs.
Ed.

wel that's about the lot of it. we had to move for some reesin ... the old fella daydreamed his way to the big smoko and we followed later. I mis l'il itly. But sumtimes we go bak ther like for Christmas or somethin
WHITE PAGES
YELLOW PAGES
Is Eddie there..., hello ?... hello ?...

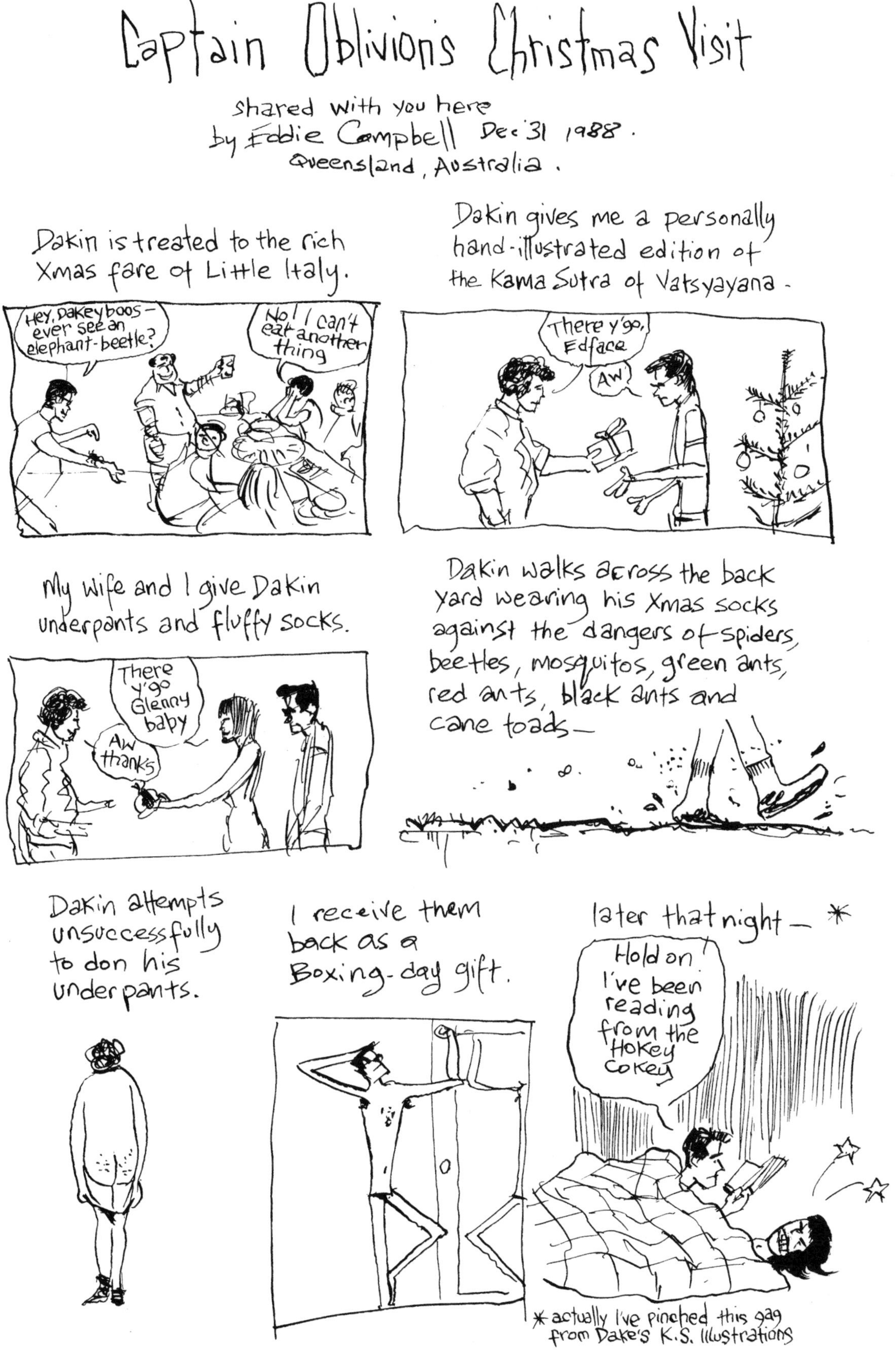
Captain Oblivion's Christmas Visit
shared with you here
by Eddie Campbell Dec 31 1988.
Queensland, Australia.
Dakin is treated to the rich Xmas fare of Little Italy.
Hey, Dakey boos — ever see an elephant-beetle?
No! I can't eat another thing
Dakin gives me a personally hand-illustrated edition of the Kama Sutra of Vatsyayana –
There y'go, Edface
AW
My wife and I give Dakin underpants and fluffy socks.
There y'go Glenny baby
Aw thanks
Dakin walks across the back yard wearing his Xmas socks against the dangers of spiders, beetles, mosquitos, green ants, red ants, black ants and cane toads –
Dakin attempts unsuccessfully to don his underpants.
I receive them back as a Boxing-day gift.
later that night – *
Hold on! I've been reading from the Hokey Cokey
* actually I've pinched this gag from Dake's K.S. illustrations

The Dead Muse

In *The Dead Muse* I introduced the work of fellow artists who wandered across my field of view, so bear in mind when reading it that those parts are now missing. There's never been any question of the whole thing being reprintable, so it has lain unseen for nineteen years. Another thing about *The Dead Muse* is that it takes off exactly where *Little Italy* ends. The trip being undertaken in the page titled *1600 Miles by Coach* is the same one that's happening on the first page of the *Muse*. These two, *Italy* and *Muse*, were drawn before *Graffiti Kitchen* and *How to be an Artist*; things are arranged, in this compendium, according to a chronology of events. The tailpiece to *Muse* is a portion of Glenn Dakin's sketch session at my house in 1988.

LOOK AT THIS. WOULDN'T YOU LIKE TO STAY HERE ?!
WE'RE here, but we're stuck out on the balcony with a cask of wine. The *Kiddie* has locked us OUT
While the women negotiate with the *Kiddie*, my mind muddles off back a year and a half or so....
I was putting together a regular comic-book called *DEADFACE* and before even the third one was out it was obvious to everyone except me that financially it was a non-starter.
The lack of money had become such an excruciating embarrassment to wifey that it was mutually agreed that our one-year tropical interlude was over and that we should go and seek material stability.
Thus, I trundle down to Melbourne, my first time in that city, to connect with my pal Phil Bentley, who's been keeping me abreast of developments while I was lost among the palm-trees.
HARRIER COMICS™ PRESENTS
DEADFACE
No.2
THE EYEBALL KID
He's involved in running a comics specialty shop down there – I'd forgotten how mindnumbingly disappointing a massed display of comic books can be –
You see, I have often amorously dallied with a tenth muse – the one who inspires some fools to make Art out of the comic-strip.
I say belated because it was a long while before I accepted that she had truly heaved off, and I persevered with my mission as though all were hunky dory
And it is with great sadness that today I write her belated obituary
Anyway Bentley
someone

Bentley is a thoughtful host - I start by losing his umbrella on the tram-
Eddie.. No, you take it.. It might rain
To console him I give him a page of original art from my portfolio —
uh, leeb ip ober derr.
While he's at work I think it will be a nice surprise if I put it in the place of some daft thing he already has framed on his wall.
I break the glass
Hmm..
CRACK
I accidentally turn the fridge off
He takes me to a soiree at Lazarus Dobelski's place to meet the mob who surround a remarkable little comics-anthology called Fox Comics, which comes out of this city — Laz is a lawyer with fine tastes —
Bentley buys five originals of my TROPICAL SET of pages to help defray my travel costs. They haven't even been published yet. Phil now owns more Campbell originals than anyone else.
Then he 'takes ill' and goes back to live with his parents. I'm in the shower when the announcement comes through -
I have to go now.
I have the flat all to Myself
One of the FOX mob, Maria Pena, is an artist at an ad agency - I go see her there and she gives me pointers on breaking into that game —
you could do storyboards easily, but you'll need some colour samples
Maria came over from El Salvador and illustrated Bentley's story just coming up.......

I confer with wifey. she'd rather sink her tent-pole in Brisbane and the thought of movement being mistaken for progress appeals to me—
In case you don't know— I'm talking 24 HOURS of this—
In Bris. I launch myself off the train, have a shower, set up a job interview for a freight-clerk, try another one for a barman-
GENT.S
I impose on my Brother-in-law's family just as I did on the southward trip two weeks previously.
I shoot through for another 24 hours and am reunited with my love of loves at the coolabah motel
I send Glenn Dakin a cutting from the paper bath-mat.
My little girl doesn't recognise me.
ah home—
Two weeks, I'm off again - the Kiddie realizes what's coming off this time - they'll join me in Brisbane...
I arrive at my brother-in-law's joint all set to make an impression on the AD business—two more of my TROPICAL originals take a nose-dive when I convert them into colour samples— a sorry fate for that great unpublished book—
I blow fifty bucks on some of those markers the slick guys use
I even improvise some handsome business cards

I trudge the rounds daily in searing November heat. It's clear to me that I can break into this business, but it'll need a long campaign of action and I'm running out of time at a hundred miles per hour—
ON THIS SITE
Wifey and Kiddie are staying with another brother of hers across town— these guys are all lawyers and accountants, by the way. Us?— We meet up and take our last cent out of the bank.
The lawyers and accountants all get together for a meeting to discuss my future. We're all supposed to sit around the table for this—
You're kidding.
It's time you faced up to your responsibilities
I put my walking shoes on.
Wifey's on the floor in tears— one of the women's got all the kids out in the back yard.
Come back here
I've nowhere to go— I come back that night and weep me heart out. Brother-in-law attempts to console me—
Well, I'm now in a flea-pit rooming house in the red-light district. I've got a telephone-sales job that pays commission only. I work for two days and don't make any money. I figure I only need 35 bucks for the rent and another 35 for food.
You meet a range of types in this kind of job— semi-nut-cases, out-of-work actors.. There are two holidaying Irish girls and this guy here who says he does a course of lectures on how to get what you want from life but he's doing this just for the mental exercise—
Well I had to get out of jail so I did my techniques
In the middle of this confusion the clouds clear and I am suddenly elevated. It happens in the street— A passing Hare Krishna recognises my spiritual moment and gives me a book— right on cue.—
It was like the muse had left me some inspiration in her will. The guy on the next page is jealous, but since he comes from the pen of New Zealand's Dylan Horrocks, another Fox regular, he'll see better days—
Coming...

Now I'm back with everloving wifey. She's got a little place in the inner suburbs and a good job. A package of Deadface #4 arrives with four different addresses crossed out on the envelope..
I write to every publisher who still owes me money and a couple of cheques trickle in, - but Hell, if I don't then go and lose the phone job.
Come and see me when you've finished that one
I make a few bucks delivering leaflets at 5 in the morning before Annie leaves for work.
NO JUNK MAIL
My old pal Danny Grey visits from England — via Raffles in Singapore and other places of romantic interest
We seem completely out of tune and I guess he's dismayed to see me all day pushing a kiddie carriage around.
And no doubt he's bored out of his brain hearing about all my wee domestic worries -
On my first day as a househusband I was convinced the garbage bin had been stolen...
Eddie, why don't you give up this comics nonsense!
We take a long drive westward just to drink in any obscure pub and watch the trucks go by.
(actually, HE drives — I still haven't learned.)
We finish with a 14 hour session and he gets on the plane 3 hours later in the same clothes for a thirty-hour flight —
After he goes I feel desperately empty and totally incapable of saving myself.
bloonk
plotz
For God's sake, who's on next?

The previous was drawn by NIGEL GURNEY who turns up on our doorstep totally out of the blue — He's just finished doing a 9-month run of his comic, 'Brigid Bolt' in the Sun-Herald in Sydney.
BRIGID BOLT FREEDOM FIGHTER
after and copyright N. Gurney © '88.
He says the Sydney Guys love Deadface and shows me a small-press review of it —
Hey!
POUNDING TALES
He's surprised to see me working on the Kitchen table -
I thought you'd have a big professional draughtsman's table
Developing a severe fondness
We kill a cask of wine, and here's the coincidence - three days prior to his appearance I discovered his work among a pile of stuff a Brisbane pal was showing me — and wrote to tell him I love it — The letter is unopened in his P.O. Box when he appears -
I think Gurney got my number from Paul Gravett in England - Paul is the 'Man at the Crossroads' of the world's crisscross network of small press, Art Press, obscure Press comics-publishing, that melee of tangents where the muse was last seen hitchhiking
Here's a letter from a fellow named Lindsay Arnold down in Tasmania ...
Dear Eddie, Paul Gravett has been very insistent that I should write to you. He says he's "Sure Eddie would love to hear from a fellow cartoonist in Australia especially because you both draw on autobiographical experiences ~ ..
It's Arnold who draws my attention to the possibility that Gurney is related to the great Australian strip-cartoonist ALEX GURNEY who drew 'BLUEY AND CURLEY'. Nigel confirms he's a grandson.
S'FUNNY, ... WE MUSTA HAD BULLY-BEEF AGAIN!
?
Arnold himself starts turning up in Fantagrothics magazines and other things out of the West Coast of the U.S.A. such as Kominsky-Crumb's WEIRDO and he's only been drawing since '86...
Arnold during his acting career, seen here as MAD MORRIE with patented clip-on beer belly (wharfie size) fabricated by the actor's then wife
But this guy's 49 and goes way back to the sixties with a musical career, which is the milieu of the following — ...

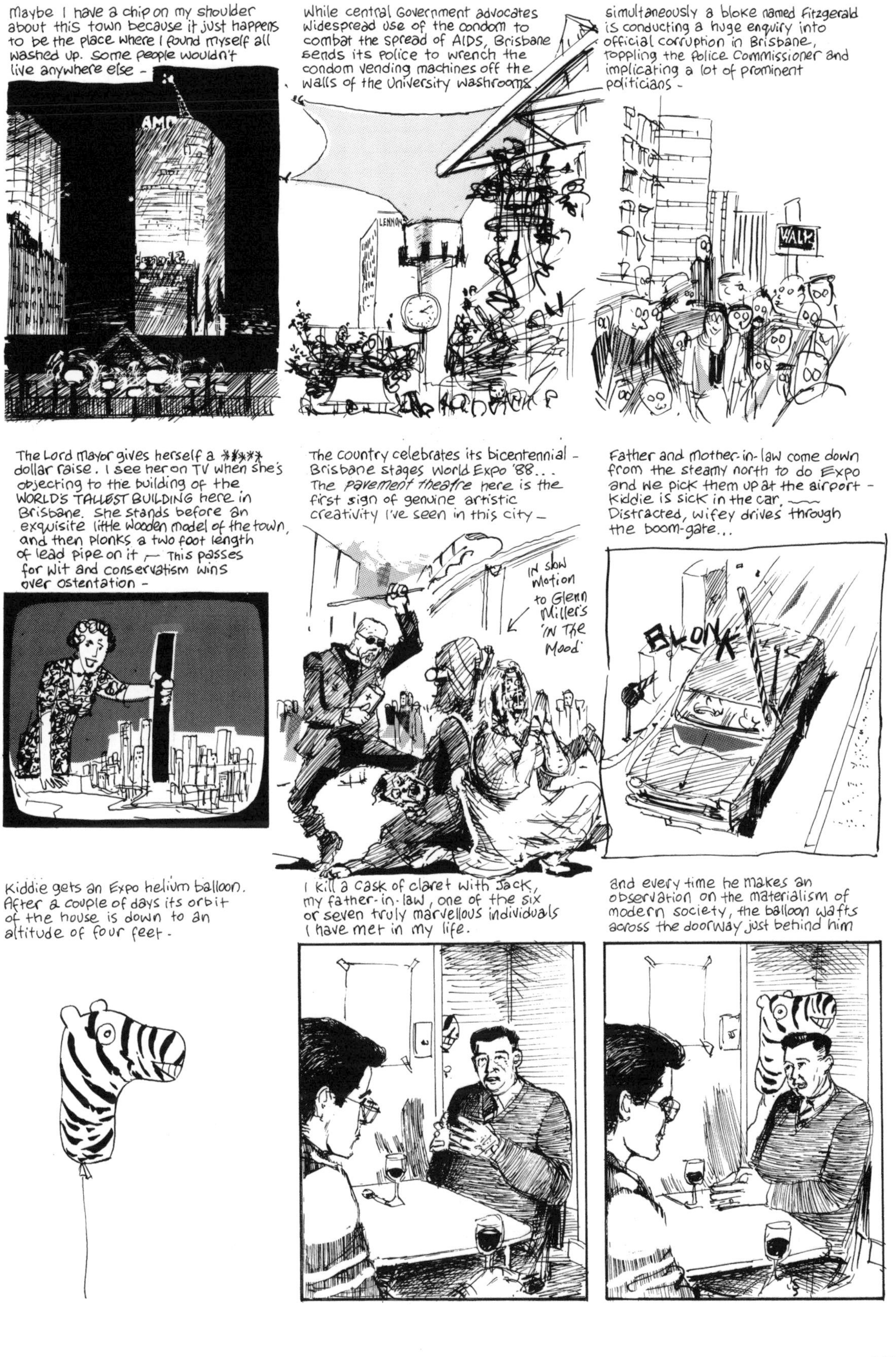
Maybe I have a chip on my shoulder about this town because it just happens to be the place where I found myself all washed up. Some people wouldn't live anywhere else -
While central Government advocates widespread use of the condom to combat the spread of AIDS, Brisbane sends its police to wrench the condom vending machines off the walls of the University washrooms
LENNON
simultaneously a bloke named Fitzgerald is conducting a huge enquiry into official corruption in Brisbane, toppling the Police Commissioner and implicating a lot of prominent politicians -
WALK
The Lord Mayor gives herself a ***** dollar raise. I see her on TV when she's objecting to the building of the WORLD'S TALLEST BUILDING here in Brisbane. She stands before an exquisite little wooden model of the town, and then plonks a two foot length of lead pipe on it, — This passes for wit and conservatism wins over ostentation -
The country celebrates its bicentennial - Brisbane stages World Expo '88... The *pavement theatre* here is the first sign of genuine artistic creativity I've seen in this city -
IN slow motion to Glenn Miller's 'IN The Mood'
Father and mother-in-law come down from the steamy north to do Expo and we pick them up at the airport - Kiddie is sick in the car. —— Distracted, wifey drives through the boom-gate...
BLONK
Kiddie gets an Expo helium balloon. After a couple of days its orbit of the house is down to an altitude of four feet -
I kill a cask of claret with Jack, my father-in-law, one of the six or seven truly marvellous individuals I have met in my life.
and every time he makes an observation on the materialism of modern society, the balloon wafts across the doorway just behind him

The nation is suffering from a bad case of self-importance, or covering up a rampant inferiority complex ——— The TV ads play on it like crazy –
Are you hungry for the flavour, of those burgers from Australia
The Australian Company working for Australia.
The Lucky Country
The helpful Queenslander.
Stick by yer Mates
Expo – we showed the world
true blue
There's no comics industry in this country to speak of. The papers are full of the usual American Syndicated stuff. An astounding number of citizens actually think that Garfield and Peanuts are 'true blue' Aussie products like Coca Cola and Kelloggs Corn Flakes –
When some enterprising young guy does get a little comics publication on its feet he invariably sticks 'All Australian' on the cover – Even the Fox down in Melbourne –
198
FOX
COMICS
TWENTY-ONE
AUSTRALIA'S INTERNATIONAL COMICS MAGAZINE –
after and Copyright © '88 D. Horrocks
Of course, since the Death of the Muse it's pretty rare to find the Spirit of Art inhabiting or informing the comics that do occasionally surface –
ALL AUSTRALIAN Serious ASPIRATIONS TO mediocrity
The PHANTOM
IMITATION Japanese Robots from Australia
The Dingaroo
Phantom reprints
Downunder wasted punk energy
One day I'm coming back from Play-Group after helping all the other mothers clear up the usual debris when I come across a comic on the stands with a Brisbane address –
ALL AUSTRALIAN Eureka
MITTY MOUSE
Eureka subsequently runs for three issues and the best thing in it is a serial called *Verity Aloeha*, which I take to be a neat play on Aloe Vera, that herbal panacea –
after and © copyright M. Dutkiewicz '89.
I get to thinking that there's a great deal of struggling stuff in this country, most of it probably forgettable because it's not a society that challenges and encourages the creative –
MITTY MOUSE
What good work there is exists in total isolation, because of the vast distances between urban centres, enhancing its peculiarities more than would happen in Britain where there is a busy exchange of ideas and where the population of London alone is about equivalent to that of this whole continent.
Mike Dutkiewicz is the guy behind *Verity Aloeha* – I track him down in Adelaide where he has a fourth part half-finished and unpublished and I bag it for here ———
Daddy, where are we going?

The car starts to be a problem one night when we have a flat tyre. I change a wheel for the first time in my life.

The following week another one goes — and this time there's no spare.

I have to carry the wheel to the garage in Kiddie's push-chair.

It never looks quite the same again —

We sell the car

LIFE GOES ON.....
many commentators assert that the artist is losing weight —

There's only one side to you

I instruct Kiddie in the rudiments of debate —

Ants!
Bees!
Ants!
Bees!
Ants!
Bees!
Ants!
Bees!
Bread!
uh... cake!

Other games we play:
① What does Nana drink?

What does Bacchus drink?
Wed Wine!
What does Grandad drink?
Four-X beer!
What does Nana drink?
Tea!
and what does she put in it?
Sugar!
Milk!
a spoon!
tea-bags!

② Find Ned Kelly —

BANK OF A
In Deh
TTER,

Another old pal comes over from England - Glenn Dakin the demon cartoonist. He swiftly notices the absence of the muse -
TAXI
One night he sits at my kitchen table and fills page after page not with doodles but with completely formed ideas -
He finishes as abruptly as he started.
The tank's empty
Dakin goes down the coast to Sydney where he stays with Tim Piggott, Gurney's sometime collaborator who according to my vague memory of a glimpsed photo may look like this.
Dakes phones me and says I should be down there instead of mouldering in Brisbane.
He goes to Melbourne and stays with 'The Body' Vodicka, the geezer who puts Fox Comics together - The Body gets Dakes on his radio show for five minutes between the discs -
since the British 'small Press Scene' was apparently the inspiration for Fox, the Body asks him to talk about that. Dakes dismisses any notions of a 'café society'...
..And regales the audience with an anecdote about the tea and the cucumber sandwiches served at the first official meeting of Escape Magazine —
I suppose I have to laugh: I was there too. But here's his treatment of me, which arrives in the post from Melbourne —
JUNK MAIL

Dakes returns in time for a 24-hour ride up north for a tropical Christmas. Wifey and Kiddie take the plane.
jeez, look at all these trees
There goes a man who doesn't get out much.
CARPET WAREHOUSE
We stop at Rockhampton where he introduces me to the pleasures of youth-hostelling. It's supposed to refresh us for the second half of the trip but we fall in with two half mad veterans of the Army Catering Corps.
Your friend's been sick all over the place. What are you going to do about it, eh? What?
The heat and humidity are getting him down — Dakes reckons this is what killed off the muse — Not a climate to inspire poetry he says
Grandad would disagree, singing Alice Blue Gown to the Kiddie in the paw-paw sweet cool of evening with the cicadas and frogs on rhythm and base —
The 24 hours back is the most pleasant spell of travelling I have undertaken —
Dakes gets on a 30 hour plane flight after only a 7-hour break and I'm not sure how he ever pulls himself together again — I greet the New Year in my dreams —
April never got to meet Dakin. She comes in just where he goes out. She originates in Los Angeles and is expressing similar misgivings to my own —
This town has no soul.
She starts turning her artistic skills to the comics page and lands her first one in Canadian Dave Sim's guest page in his Cerebus reprint series.
even gets unusual gig doing a mural in a local take-away café
Meanwhile, here I am watching her arrive home at two in the morning to her small rented room to chuck out all her daughter's pals, who had unofficially convened there, so to speak.

Well I finally give Deadface away after EIGHT issues and things are on the up again.
DEADFACE
Alan Moore, whom I haven't spoken to for two years, gets my number, probably from the Man at the Crossroads, phones me and asks if I want to illustrate his proposed series about Jack the Ripper.
So what else is new? My brother-in-law gives me a great big desk that he doesn't need –
No more butter stains on the artwork
Wifey gets a new job that will give her a raise in pay greater than the total amount I made last year –
How do I look?
To celebrate we spend a few days in this luxurious hotel on Stradbroke Island. This is where you came in.... Wifey indicates that she could get accustomed to such extravagance –
Maybe you will.
Kookaburras
and my little girl gets a new role-model –
I finish Jackarippy now.. I go to bed.
LUX SOAP
Cottees CORDIAL
and the Lord Mayor gives herself another raise.
Kiss
As for the muse..
Is Anybody there?

ABE
by Glenn Dakin

Glenn Dakin, 1988

The Dance of Lifey Death

You may have noticed a growing sense of mortality as we tear through the years. I don't think I'm morbid. On the contrary, I'm quite fond of life and I think I'd miss it terribly. But I don't think I thought half as much about the inevitability of our eventual doom until I started making a comfortable living as an artist, twenty years ago in 1989, as described at the beginning of *The Dance of Lifey Death*. It might have something to do with my expanding family, who by the end of this book have all climbed aboard and made their presence felt. My prediction, on the final page, as to how they would look as adults, was a little challenge I set myself and has never been retouched or amended in any way.

A thank you to Diana Schutz, who first edited this book for Dark Horse Comics of Portland, Oregon.

AROUND THE WORLD IN EIGHTY FRAMES

Eddie Campbell. MAR '91.

Frame 1; Brisbane, Australia.

Good-bye, house. See you in six weeks.
DADDY

I hate travelling. I never even meant to leave home fifteen years ago. It was my parents who left home. I mean, they moved house and I hung about for the sake of keeping a job.

I never meant to live on the other side of the world either. I married an Australian girl who then insisted on going home. I've had eleven addresses in ten years, and I can explain them all like that. My insides heave in anxious turmoil at the mere mention of the subject of moving house.

You'll be all right when you get up there, honey.

Frame 4; 60,000 feet over the Pacific. In-flight movie: *The Accidental Tourist*, William Hurt, Kathleen Turner.

Something else I loathe is "business". In the perfect state, life, work, and reward should be bound up so tight that one is indistinguishable from the others. But to keep things simple, I tell people that this is a "business" trip. I even make up a bunch of "business" cards.

Alec MacGarry 80 Oxford Tce.

I have to go to San Diego. It turns out I can go to London, too, for just a little bit extra dosh, so the challenging proposition of circumnavigating the globe raises its head.

It IS round!!

Frame 7; Honolulu, Hawaii. The atmosphere is 19% Oxygen and 81% vapourised pineapple. Rather coincidentally, my pal Doc Nodule is on the same plane.

No, Alec. Let me get them.

He's more at home in "business" than I am. I make a mental note to get the Doc to help me with my tax return. The doc makes an ink note in his book.

Let's see... "entertaining artist, two beers, one cocktail" "$7.50 U.S."

Frame 9; My old pal Doxy meets me at L.A.X. I haven't seen him since we sat together in Art class twenty years ago in Scotland.

brothers of the brush

Now he lives in Santa Monica. He draws Conan the Barbarian, and I draw us walking up Wilshire Boulevard with a mop and a squeegee.

ditto

Frame 11; Greyhound to San Diego a day early because I don't have a hotel booking. I find the place and get a room without any trouble because my guardian angel is an old pro. I'm beginning to warm to the travelling.

TREAT YOURSELF TO CHAMPAGNE BREAKFAST.
It's a busy week. You're lucky that other guy just checked out 3 days early.
Someone always does.
WHAT HAPPENS IF...?
You need medical care and you've run out of money.
SWIM IN OUR 82 DEGREE CRYSTAL BLUE WATER HEATED POOL

Von Stroheim's *GREED* is on the cable. I decide to write off the rest of the day to watch it, but Frank turns up. I'd left a message for him at the front.

Tod's in the bar. See you there in five, Alec.
SNAP YOUR PICTURE IN THE CLASSIC WHITE BENTLEY OUT FRONT.

I'm doing my laundry one night; the little Mexican woman is pretty but morose. You walk into all kinds of racial tensions, or maybe just workaday tensions.

LAST WASH 7.30
SOAP

HEY! STOP!

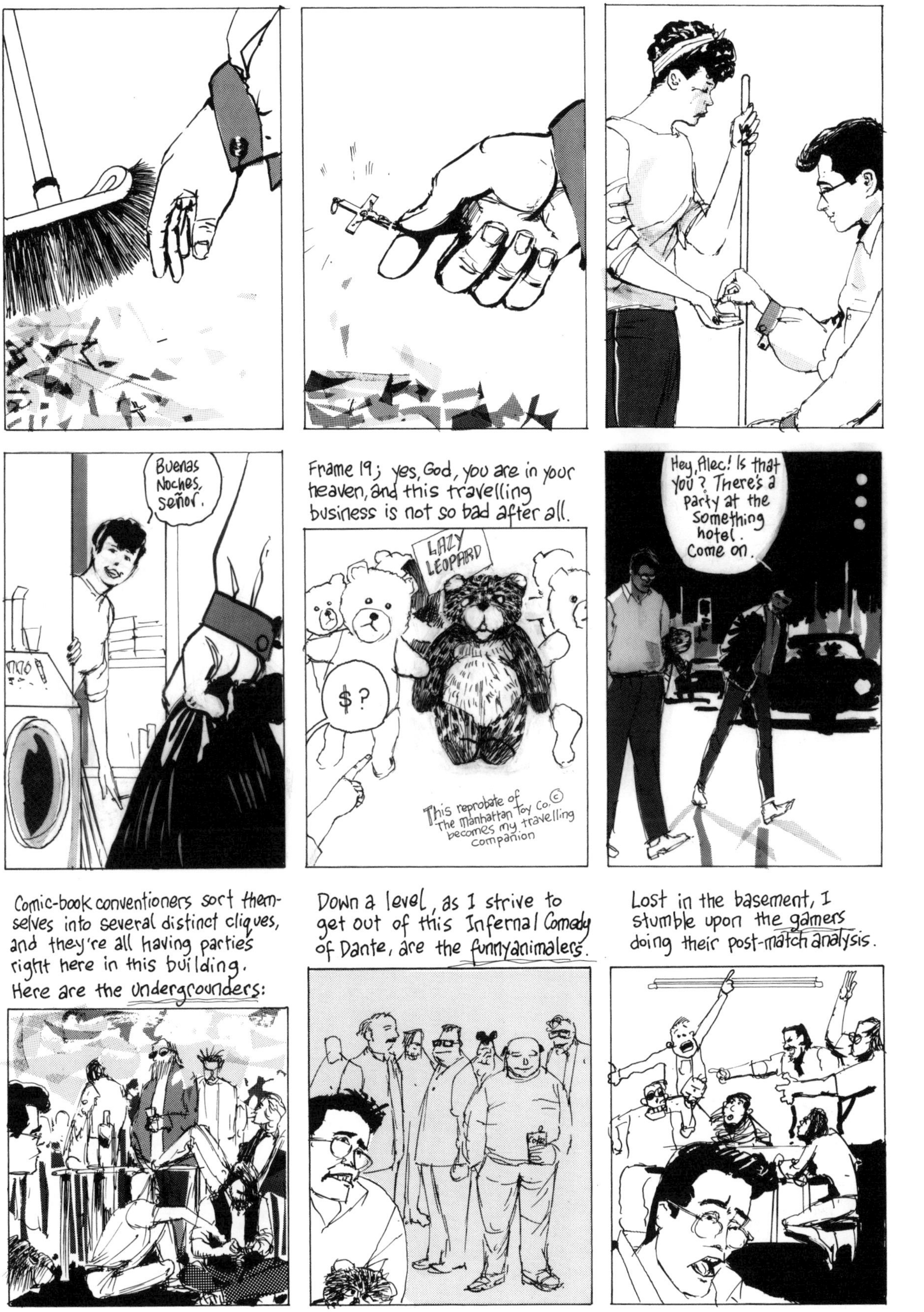

Buenas Noches, señor.
Frame 19; yes, God, you are in your heaven, and this travelling business is not so bad after all.
LAZY LEOPARD
$?
This reprobate of The Manhattan Toy Co.© becomes my travelling companion
Hey, Alec! Is that you? There's a party at the something hotel. Come on.
Comic-book conventioners sort themselves into several distinct cliques, and they're all having parties right here in this building. Here are the undergrounders:
Down a level, as I strive to get out of this Infernal Comedy of Dante, are the funnyanimalers.
Lost in the basement, I stumble upon the gamers doing their post-match analysis.

Frame 24; I tear out of there the following morning. Greyhound is great. You put your bags in early, and everything gets taken care of. By a magical process the bag is put on the right bus.

GREYHOUND GL
4650
MONICA CA 04
PLEASE RETAIN THIS COUPON AS IT, OR A PHOTOCOPY THEREOF MUST BE SUBMITTED WITH ANY CLAIM FOR BAGGAGE LOSS OR DAMAGE. © 1985 Greyhound Lines

Problem this time is that ye artist gets on the wrong bus, and he's expressing to Santa Barbara before he knows it.

excuse me, is this bound for Santa Monica?
Qué?

Normally he opens his mouth and unleashes the poodles of Confusion, but today says the right thing.

Well, whose fault is that then?
mine— I'm stupid.

The driver goes eight miles out of his way to drop me at a service station where I can intercept the right bus.

Hopefully he'll have left my bag in lock-up at my correct destination back down the line. An hour and a half passes.

No, sir. Santa Monica was closed—I had to leave it at Oxnard.
I wondered what happened to you.

I fall in with a drunk. Always the best thing to do in the circumstances.

Ah, Ximenez tortilla paco bombazullo, eh, amigo?

When my bag went, so did all my fret and worry. What a whining malcontent I must have been. You fear the worst until it happens; then you're free as a bird.

TRAVEL, HA!

Two hours later here's the bus going the other way. I try to get back on using the same weary ticket and succeed only because the drunk's a bigger nuisance than me.

You're not getting on, and that's final.
WHAT HA
Your credit ca
PPENS IF ...?
-ds, wallet, passport
or tickets are
stolen
or lost.

Frame 32; Oxnard – I've got all these drivers going to the wrong stops –
STAFF ONLY
My case!
Joe, what are you doing here?
But no one will do Santa Monica for me. I have to wait till 5 A.M. I find a bar. There's a little old lady at the back doing tacos and coffee. I forget to say no sugar. A girl waves, and I inadvertently wave back.
Then she starts to get up, and I panic.
Uh...
No! Stay away.
She's all offended now. Shit, that's all I need.
That's a bit presumptuous...
look, I just thought you might need directions somewhere.
Aw, forgive me. I've had a rough night... may I join you?
El Mariachi Nuevo Guadalajara
del Charro Rangel
PARA FIESTAS · MATRIMONIOS · BAUTISMOS
DIAS DE CAMPO · CUMPLEANOS
JESUS RANGEL
REPRESENTATIVE
1621 W. BIRCH ST
OXNARD, CA
Señor – More cervezas, por favor.
I'll get them this time.
We can give you a lift to a very late restaurant. My car's just around the corner.
Ha-ha – look, I've gotta go.

Frame 41; back at the bus stop.

Frame 42; Santa Monica.

Where the hell have you been?

Frame 43; Newark airport. I dread tackling the problem of going into New York. I freeze.

Frame 44; New Jersey Turnpike. A big funnel to Hell—and not Dante's poetical, satirical version.

Frame 45; draggin' that damn case full of books and artwork to Penn Station. I swear I will never travel this heavy again. Almost wish I never got it back.

EAT
In America you always see the farts coming out of the manholes

Frame 46; train to Springfield, Mass. Friend picks me up there. I have a bath.

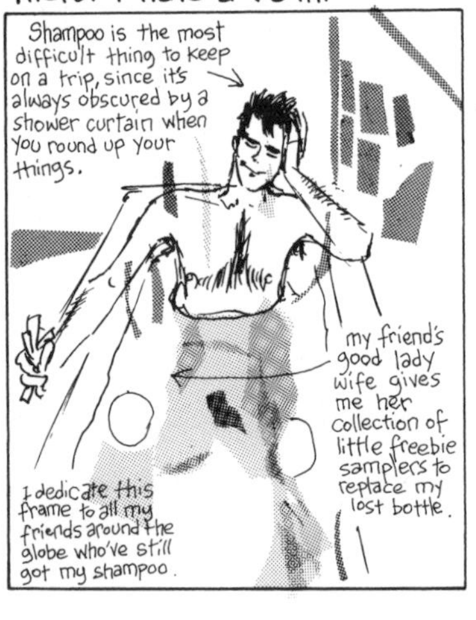
Shampoo is the most difficult thing to keep on a trip, since it's always obscured by a shower curtain when you round up your things.
my friend's good lady wife gives me her collection of little freebie samplers to replace my lost bottle.
I dedicate this frame to all my friends around the globe who've still got my shampoo.

Frame 47; car to Vermont.

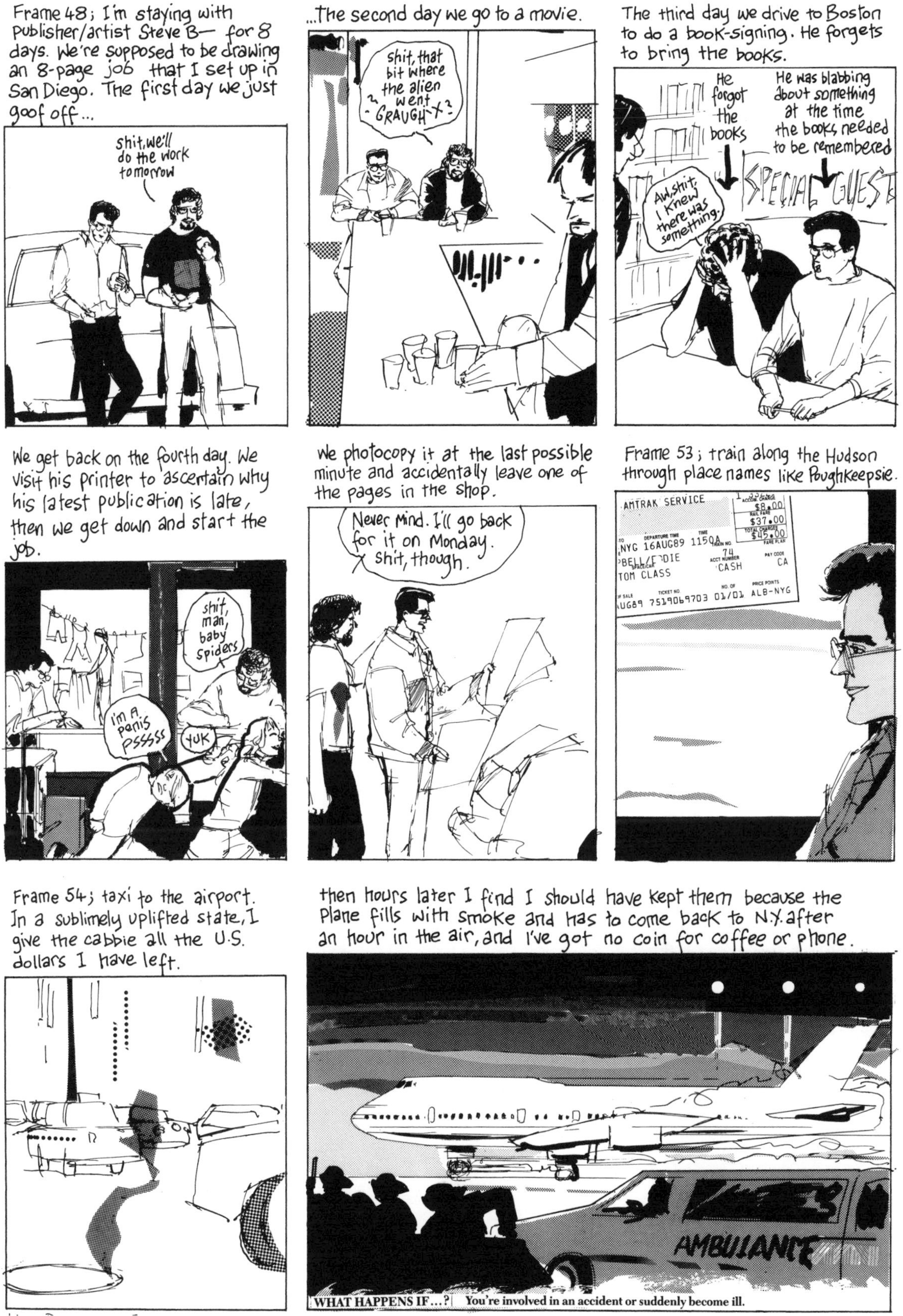
Frame 48; I'm staying with publisher/artist Steve B— for 8 days. We're supposed to be drawing an 8-page job that I set up in San Diego. The first day we just goof off...
shit, we'll do the work tomorrow
...The second day we go to a movie.
shit, that bit where the alien went "GRAUGH-X"?
The third day we drive to Boston to do a book-signing. He forgets to bring the books.
He forgot the books
He was blabbing about something at the time the books needed to be remembered
SPECIAL GUEST
Aw, shit, I knew there was something.
We get back on the fourth day. We visit his printer to ascertain why his latest publication is late, then we get down and start the job.
shit, man, baby spiders
I'm a penis pssssss
YUK
We photocopy it at the last possible minute and accidentally leave one of the pages in the shop.
Never mind. I'll go back for it on Monday. Shit, though.
Frame 53; train along the Hudson through place names like Poughkeepsie.
AMTRAK SERVICE
$8.00
$37.00
$45.00
NYG 16AUG89 1150A
74
TOM CLASS
CASH
CA
7519069703 01/01 ALB-NYG
Frame 54; taxi to the airport. In a sublimely uplifted state, I give the cabbie all the U.S. dollars I have left.
then hours later I find I should have kept them because the plane fills with smoke and has to come back to N.Y. after an hour in the air, and I've got no coin for coffee or phone.
AMBULANCE
WHAT HAPPENS IF...? You're involved in an accident or suddenly become ill.

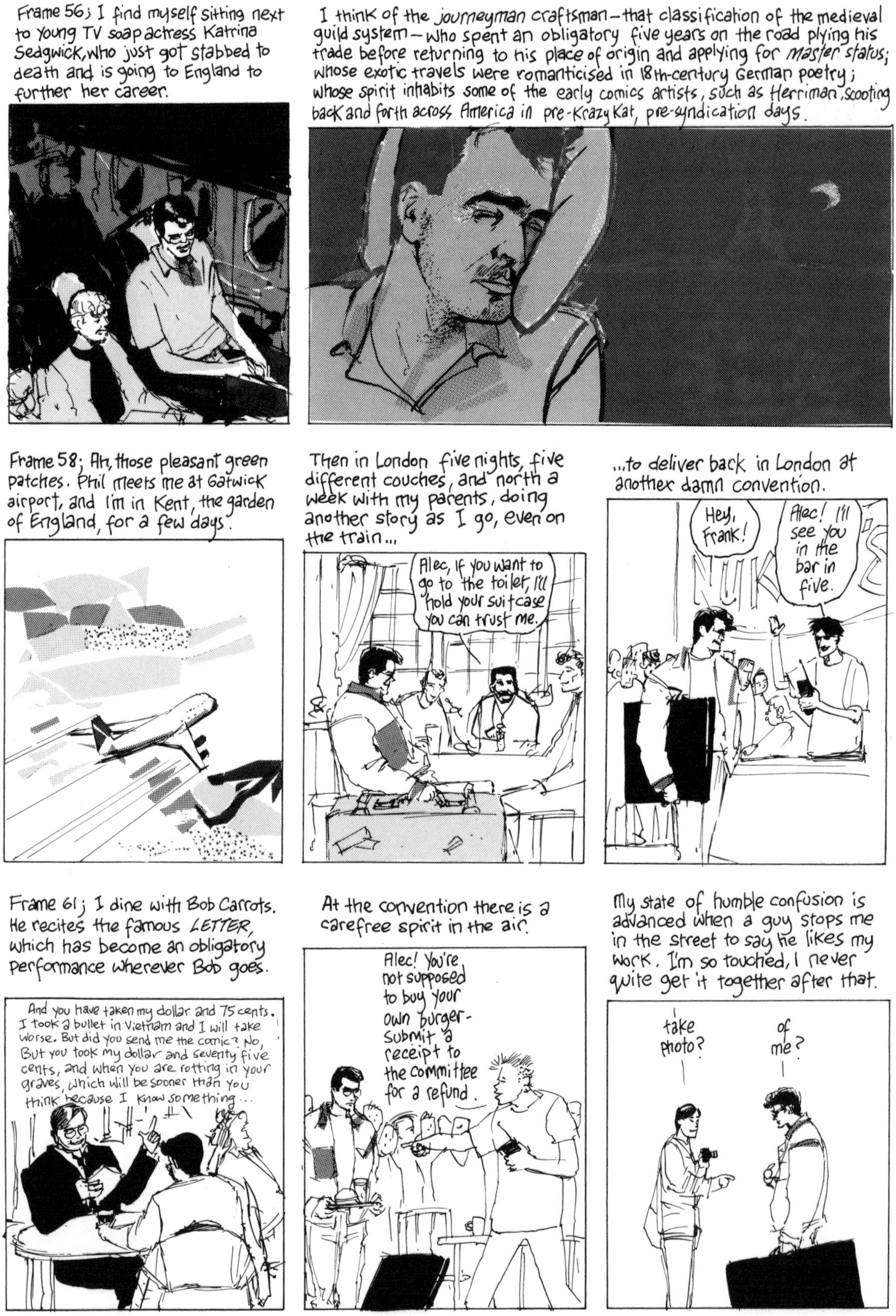
Frame 56; I find myself sitting next to young TV soap actress Katrina Sedgwick, who just got stabbed to death and is going to England to further her career.
I think of the *journeyman* craftsman—that classification of the medieval guild system—who spent an obligatory five years on the road plying his trade before returning to his place of origin and applying for *master status*; whose exotic travels were romanticised in 18th-century German poetry; whose spirit inhabits some of the early comics artists, such as Herriman, scooting back and forth across America in pre-Krazy Kat, pre-syndication days.
Frame 58; Ah, those pleasant green patches. Phil meets me at Gatwick airport, and I'm in Kent, the garden of England, for a few days.
Then in London five nights, five different couches, and north a week with my parents, doing another story as I go, even on the train...
Alec, if you want to go to the toilet, I'll hold your suitcase you can trust me.
...to deliver back in London at another damn convention.
Hey, Frank!
Alec! I'll see you in the bar in five.
Frame 61; I dine with Bob Carrots. He recites the famous *LETTER*, which has become an obligatory performance wherever Bob goes.
And you have taken my dollar and 75 cents. I took a bullet in Vietnam and I will take worse. But did you send me the comic? No, But you took my dollar and seventy five cents, and when you are rotting in your graves, which will be sooner than you think because I know something...
At the convention there is a carefree spirit in the air.
Alec! You're not supposed to buy your own burger- Submit a receipt to the committee for a refund.
My state of humble confusion is advanced when a guy stops me in the street to say he likes my work. I'm so touched, I never quite get it together after that.
I take photo?
of me?

Frame 64; Monday morning, and I see the grey September fog coming in my window, and in the streets the grey faces going to their "business".
OMIC ART CONVENTION
VAL DATE 09/08
ROOM
443
I'm supposed to be in England another week, but I get on the phone and spend 70 bucks in half an hour, changing the plan.
09/11 16.03
09/11 .40
09/11 .70
09/11 1.60
09/11 .40
09/11 .40
09/11 1.00
09/11 .40
Can I bring my flight forward...? today.
ROOM GROUP RATE 3 NIGHTS %
907 TELEPHONE
920 TELEPHONE
1014 TELEPHONE
1025 TELEPHONE
1029 TELEPHONE
1033 TELEPHONE
Anne... I'm coming home.
Wait. We've got a new address.
MPERIAL HOTEL
Russell Square
I Moved Us.
Why?
You know I've wanted to for ages and you wouldn't be in it, so I did it while you're away.
WHAT HAPPENS IF...?
Evacuation back to Australia is necessary.
eek that ust out early.
Someone usually does.
Frame 70; I make more calls from Heathrow airport.
Frank, I hope you get this message, but I can't make it this after-noon, and I'm off the team for tomorrow.
that afternoon in a bar
I don't think he's coming, Frank.
I'll give him another five minutes.
Hey, Ed! I'm getting out... I won't be able to see you.
Like shit you won't! When's the flight? Look, we'll be there in twenty.

Frame 73 ; Bye-bye, England.
Frame 74 ; Bye-bye, Lucerne.
Frame 75 ; Bye-bye, Addis Ababa.
Frame 76 ; Bye-bye, Singapore. I've landed here six times and never gone out of the airport lounge. One day...
Frame 77 ; Melbourne. I arrive back in the middle of a pilots' strike. I get onto waiting lists for vaguely hopeful flights. I need sleep but must stay alert.
Only a direc
unfair directive
domestic airlines, is standing in the way
The need for reform is clear.
The time for reform is now.
Frame 78 ; Sydney. My wife's duty-free Opium™ is leaking from a faulty nozzle. I'm wafting through the airport in a cloud of fragrant Eastern promise.
EVENTS FOR WHICH WE WILL NOT PAY
Claims under any Section of this policy involving:
1. War like activities, insurrection, nuclear reaction, contamination by nuclear weapons material or radioactivity.
2. Any illegal or unlawful act by you or confiscation, detention, destruction by customs or other authorities.
3. Any breach of any prohibition or regulation of, any Government.
4. You not taking reasonable precautions to avoid a claim under the policy following the warning of any intended strike, riot, commotion, through or by general mass
Loss of cash, bank notes
Frame 79 ; this last leg of the trip has taken 38 hours.
Frame 80 ; Brisbane.
DADDY
Hello, house. It's good to be home.

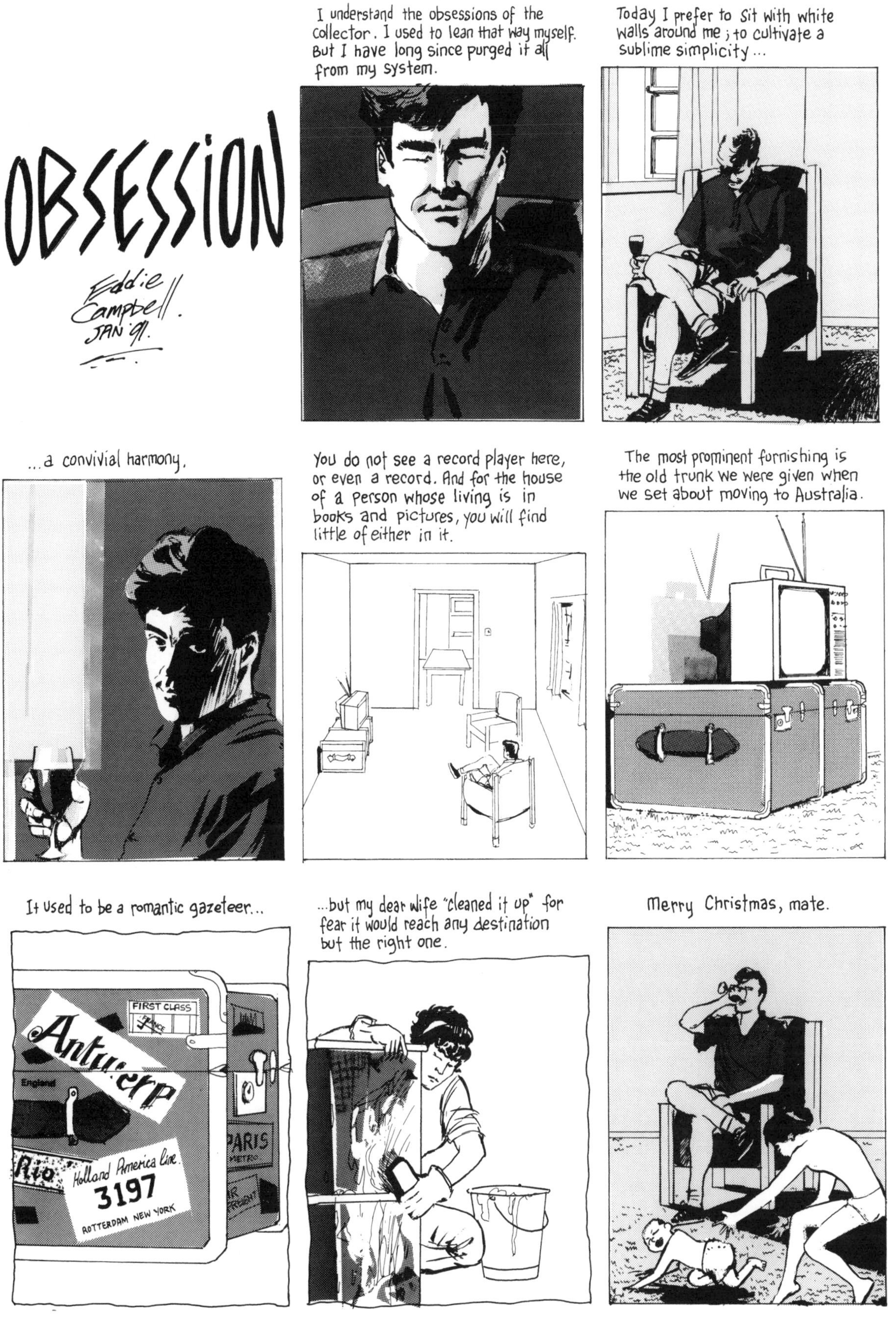
OBSESSION
Eddie Campbell. JAN '91.
I understand the obsessions of the collector. I used to lean that way myself. But I have long since purged it all from my system.
Today I prefer to sit with white walls around me; to cultivate a sublime simplicity...
...a convivial harmony.
You do not see a record player here, or even a record. And for the house of a person whose living is in books and pictures, you will find little of either in it.
The most prominent furnishing is the old trunk we were given when we set about moving to Australia.
It used to be a romantic gazeteer...
FIRST CLASS
England
PARIS
METRO
Rio
Holland America Line
3197
ROTTERDAM NEW YORK
...but my dear wife "cleaned it up" for fear it would reach any destination but the right one.
Merry Christmas, mate.

On the other hand, I can enjoy a proliferation of keepable *objets* in a purely vicarious way, from a position of detached amusement.

Have you got the spare nappies, Alec?
yup

Thus it is with relish that I arrive at Doctor Nodule's place, to spend this Christmas.

I was bemused when I first learned that in his professional capacity the Doc owns five surgeries.

I was furthermore stupefied to know that he owns four comic-book shops, merely as a hobbyist.

I never cease to be overwhelmed with wonder upon viewing his three sports cars, including an old MG.

And I marvel at his pool, surely the deepest of domestic pools. The Doc swam in the Munich Olympics, but that has nothing to do with the story.

Nowadays he sails his catamaran and his canoes and boats forth and back.

PHOENIX CAT

His latest acquisition greets us in the hall.

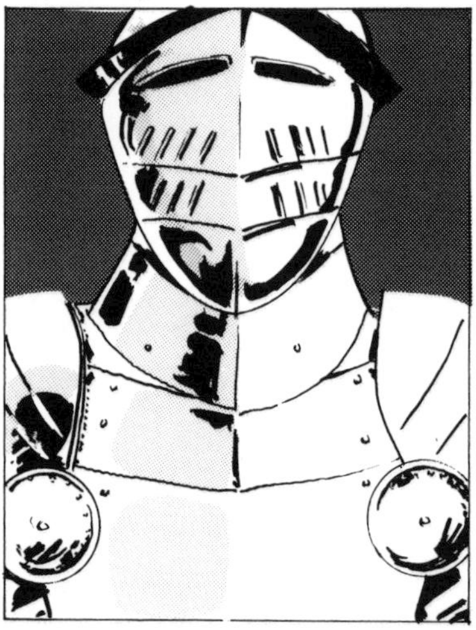

He was obsessed with the notion of owning one.

He just had to have it, you know.

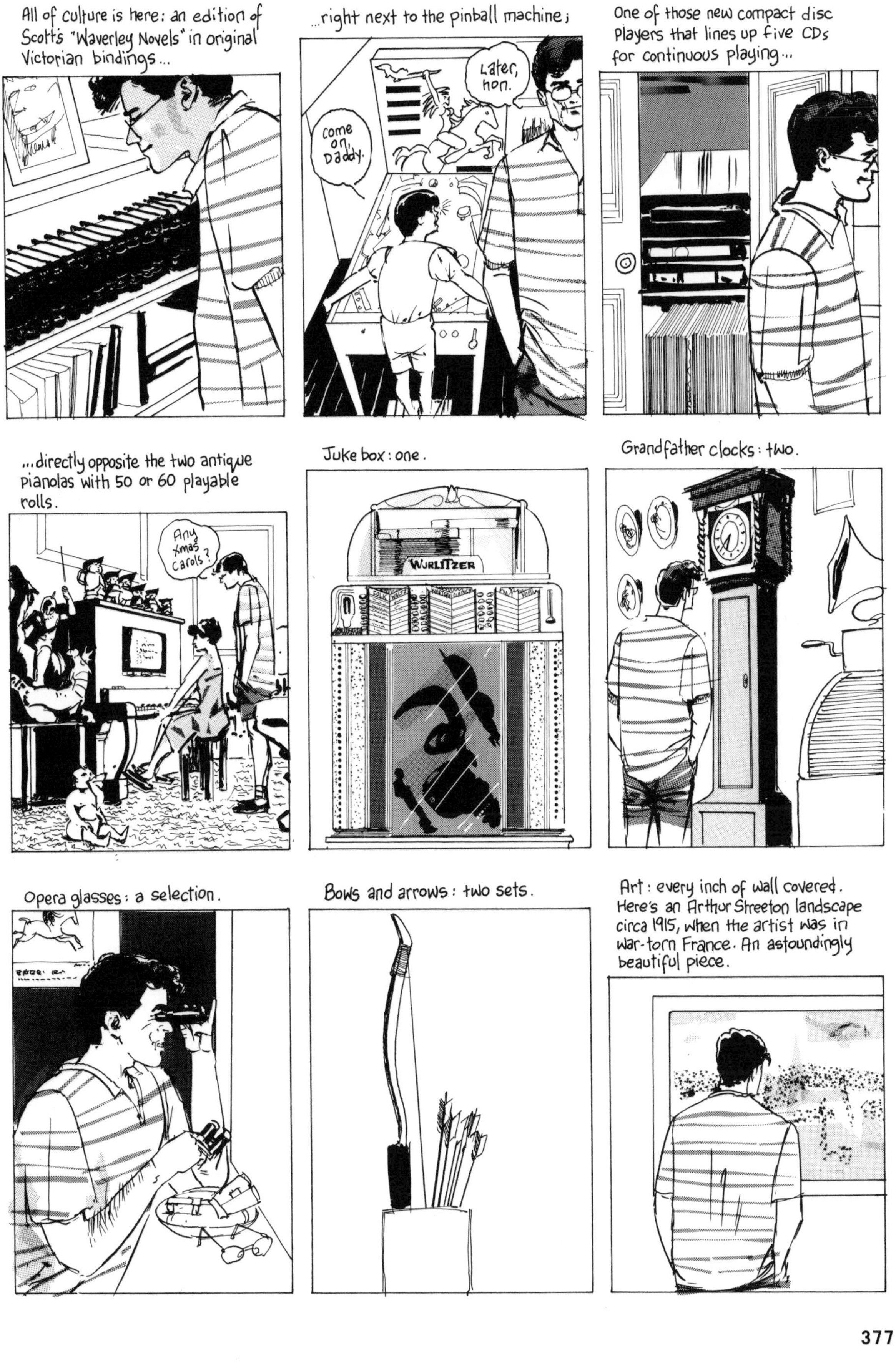
All of culture is here: an edition of Scott's "Waverley Novels" in original Victorian bindings...
...right next to the pinball machine;
Later, hon.
come on, Daddy.
One of those new compact disc players that lines up five CDs for continuous playing...
...directly opposite the two antique pianolas with 50 or 60 playable rolls.
Any xmas carols?
Juke box: one.
WURLITZER
Grandfather clocks: two.
Opera glasses: a selection.
Bows and arrows: two sets.
Art: every inch of wall covered. Here's an Arthur Streeton landscape circa 1915, when the artist was in war-torn France. An astoundingly beautiful piece.

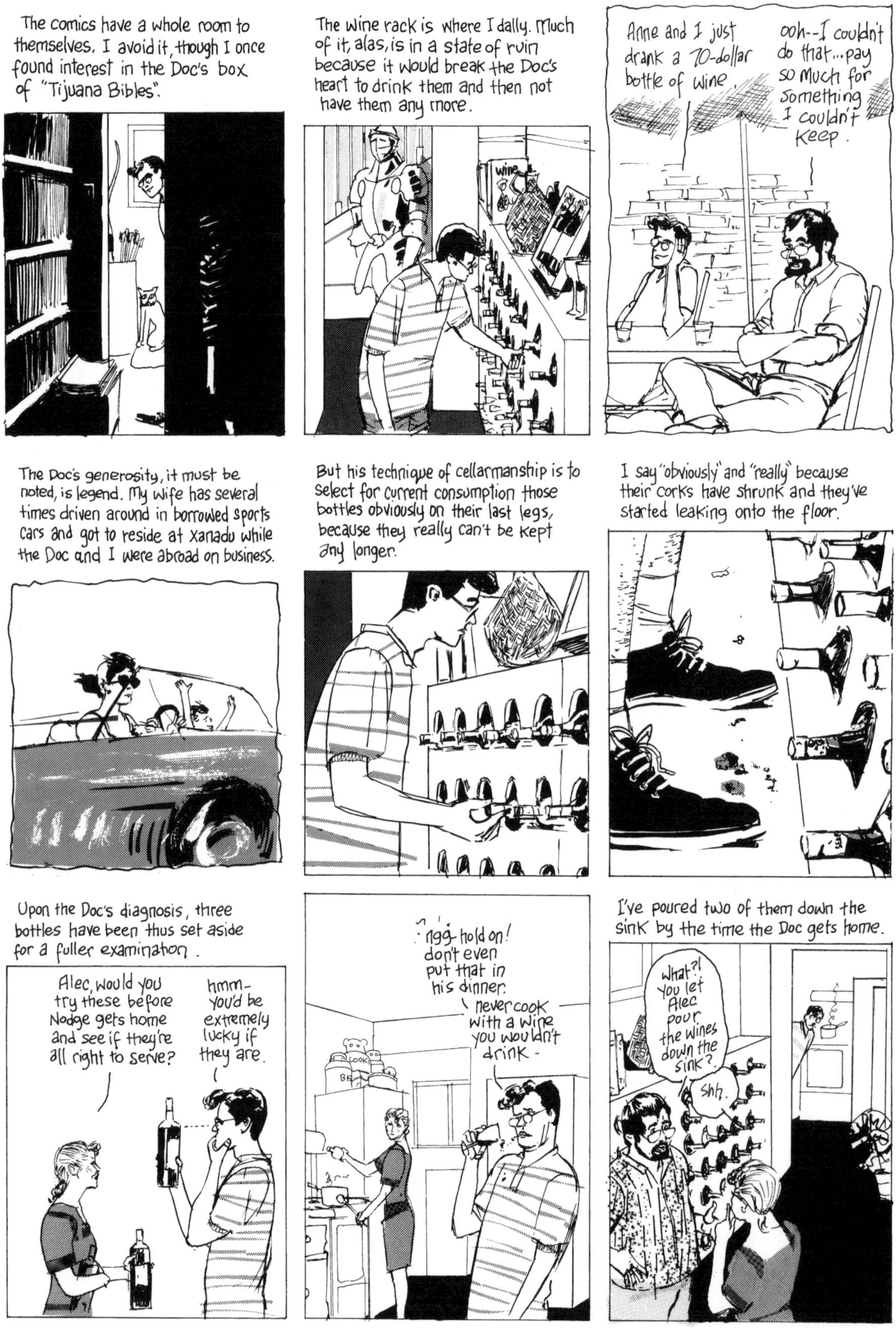
The comics have a whole room to themselves. I avoid it, though I once found interest in the Doc's box of "Tijuana Bibles".
The wine rack is where I dally. Much of it, alas, is in a state of ruin because it would break the Doc's heart to drink them and then not have them any more.
Anne and I just drank a 70-dollar bottle of wine.
ooh--I couldn't do that... pay so much for something I couldn't keep.
The Doc's generosity, it must be noted, is legend. My wife has several times driven around in borrowed sports cars and got to reside at Xanadu while the Doc and I were abroad on business.
But his technique of cellarmanship is to select for current consumption those bottles obviously on their last legs, because they really can't be kept any longer.
I say "obviously" and "really" because their corks have shrunk and they've started leaking onto the floor.
Upon the Doc's diagnosis, three bottles have been thus set aside for a fuller examination.
Alec, would you try these before Nodge gets home and see if they're all right to serve?
hmm- you'd be extremely lucky if they are.
ngg- hold on! don't even put that in his dinner.
never cook with a wine you wouldn't drink-
I've poured two of them down the sink by the time the Doc gets home.
What?! You let Alec pour the wines down the sink?
Shh.

Later, while the Doc's opening all the crackers to insert extra surprises and goodies, I tarry once more. And here's the rub...

Hey, Doc, did you know you've got a '68 Grange Hermitage in here?

I will have to digress for a page to explain, for the benefit of the post-convivial generation, the *Auteur* theory of winemaking (so to speak)...

Making wine is an art, and like all the other arts it has its Acme, its Biederbecke, its Krazy Kat, its Citizen Kane.

In 1949, a time when Australia was steeped in the making of fortified wines, young grapesmith Max Schubert was sent to Spain to study Sherry-making.

As an afterthought, he was allowed to follow the harvest northward and in Bordeaux gained several insights that inspired him to create, in the early '50s, a great wine which for many years foxed the wine world as to exactly how it was made.

Like many new ideas in the other arts, Grange Hermitage was not readily accepted. Penfold's Wines PTY LTD., Schubert's employer, curtailed his experiments, in particular regarding the crucial use of (expensive) new American oak casks.

But the '60s brought Show Prizes for the earlier, now mature, wine, especially the '55, and an end to the "cycle of indifference". Penfold's Grange Hermitage has come to hold a distinct place in the affections of Australian wine lovers and indeed in the bigger World of Wine.

It's also Australia's most expensive table wine. Some people suffer from the obsession to own Granges at almost any price...

159

...and sometimes even to drink it.

The problem, of course, is that the new release isn't ready for drinking, and your impatient author is incapable of keeping a bottle, or anything else, for five or more years.
I didn't even know it was there, Alec.
I'll tell you what... let's open it for Xmas... Just for us.
Aw, no, Doc... please eh... seriously? Doctor Nodule... your aura has acquired a saintly tinge... On the strength of this I'll do a painting for you.
Great! I'll put this in the fridge for tomorrow, then.
Fr--? No, hold on— It's a full bodi--red-- you ca—
Now I think I'll go and wrap some extra Xmas presents in case of unscheduled visitors—
·gnn·
The night passes like eighteen months in American oak puncheons.
I get up once and go visit the Grange. I let it in from the cold and gaze upon its comely features.
It was the '80 Grange that my wife and I drank that time: my most thrilling vinous adventure.
dry throat.
drink five pints of water.

On the morrow, all the Doc's relatives are there for present-giving and a buffet lunch. Nobody ever seems certain how to conduct the obligatory hot Christmas dinner in the Southern hemisphere.
I open an "unwooded" Marsanne that I brought. It stimulates my taste buds in anticipation of things to come.
And later a light, crisp-style Chardonnay I also brought livens my palate in readiness for the grand consummation.
And now it's time- no wait! - the Doc has another dodgy bottle that must be dealt with before we can get to the Grange: a wine whose label slipped off in embarrassment years ago.
I wonder what it is...
I plead.
Must be another one for the sink, Doc.
SSPP
SWW
I get red in the face, but I cannot persuade my host to deviate from his prescriptions.
But Jesus said drink the Good wine first.
uh ...John Chapt. 2
uh... verse 10
Jubble Jubble
He finishes his autopsy and gives the patient a clean bill of health.
It's a '78 Shiraz
And smooth, at that.
Then he skips upstairs to select from his immense collection of board games for the evening's amusements.
grab a glass and come on.
I seethe.
I boil.

In the end I play sociable.
Comeon, Alec - I was only Kidding, You can have the ship this time, and I'LL take the old boot.
Then I go to bed with murder in my heart.
What in God's name is the matter with YOU?
The Grange has found its way back into the fridge again. I let it in from the cold. Its poor label is sagging from the weight of condensation.
Well, I made such a fuss over the damn thing that the doc gives it to me as a Christmas present.
AW
I buy a decanter.
SSWARE
POST XMAS SALE
That'll do.
I let the bottle stand for 12 hours.
Kublick, get over here - I've got a '68 Grange!
I get it to exactly the right temperature.
It's well ullaged - add another ten years.
40% chance it's drinkable, I'd say.
It's on its deathbed, and its last words are barely audible.
Can I eat the cheese now?
Da
But no matter, for the true goal of the obsessed is very modest, as you Know. They only want to get some sleep soon.
Zzzz

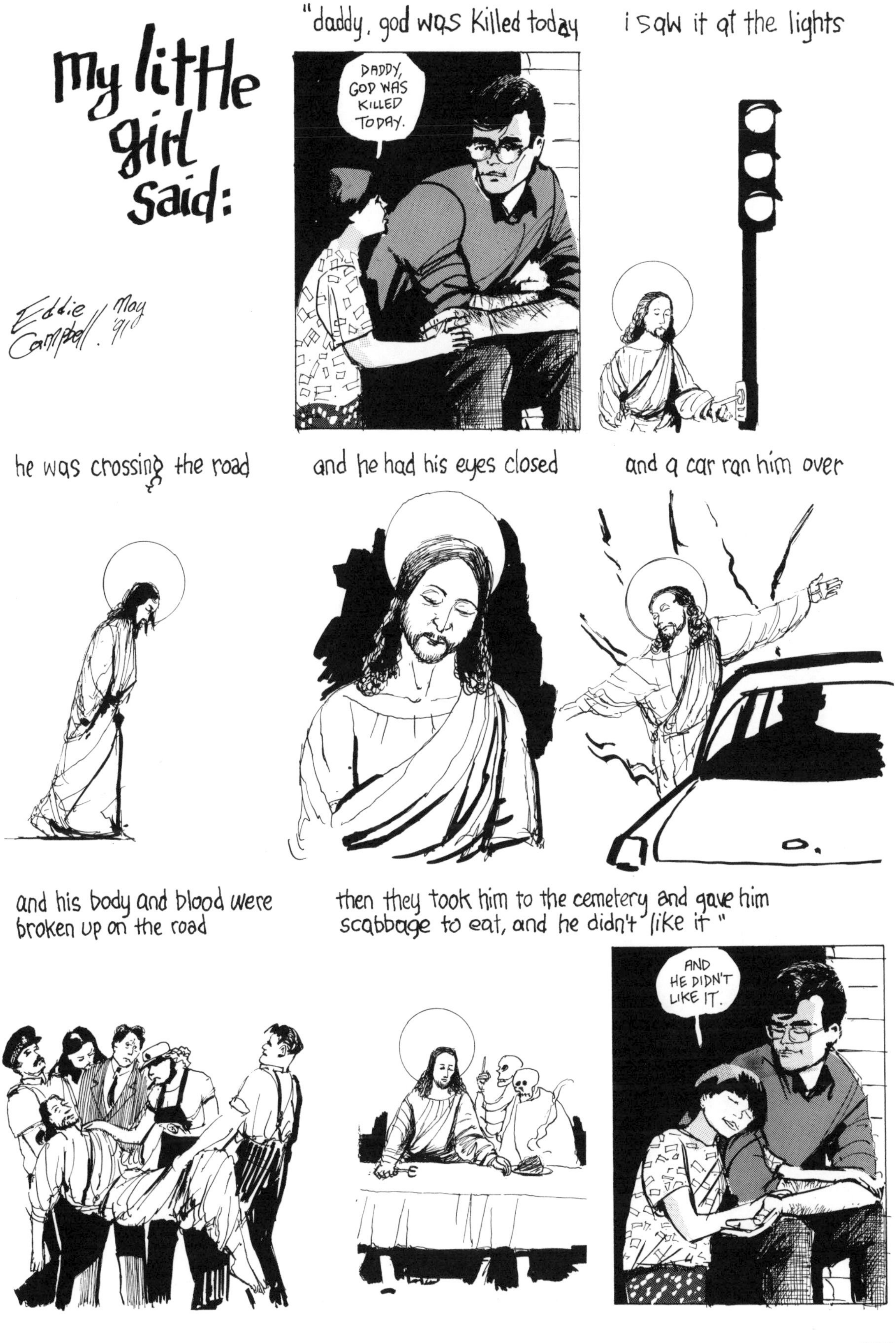
my little girl said:
Eddie Campbell. May '91
"daddy, god was Killed today
DADDY, GOD WAS KILLED TODAY.
i saw it at the lights
he was crossing the road
and he had his eyes closed
and a car ran him over
and his body and blood were broken up on the road
then they took him to the cemetery and gave him scabbage to eat, and he didn't like it"
AND HE DIDN'T LIKE IT.

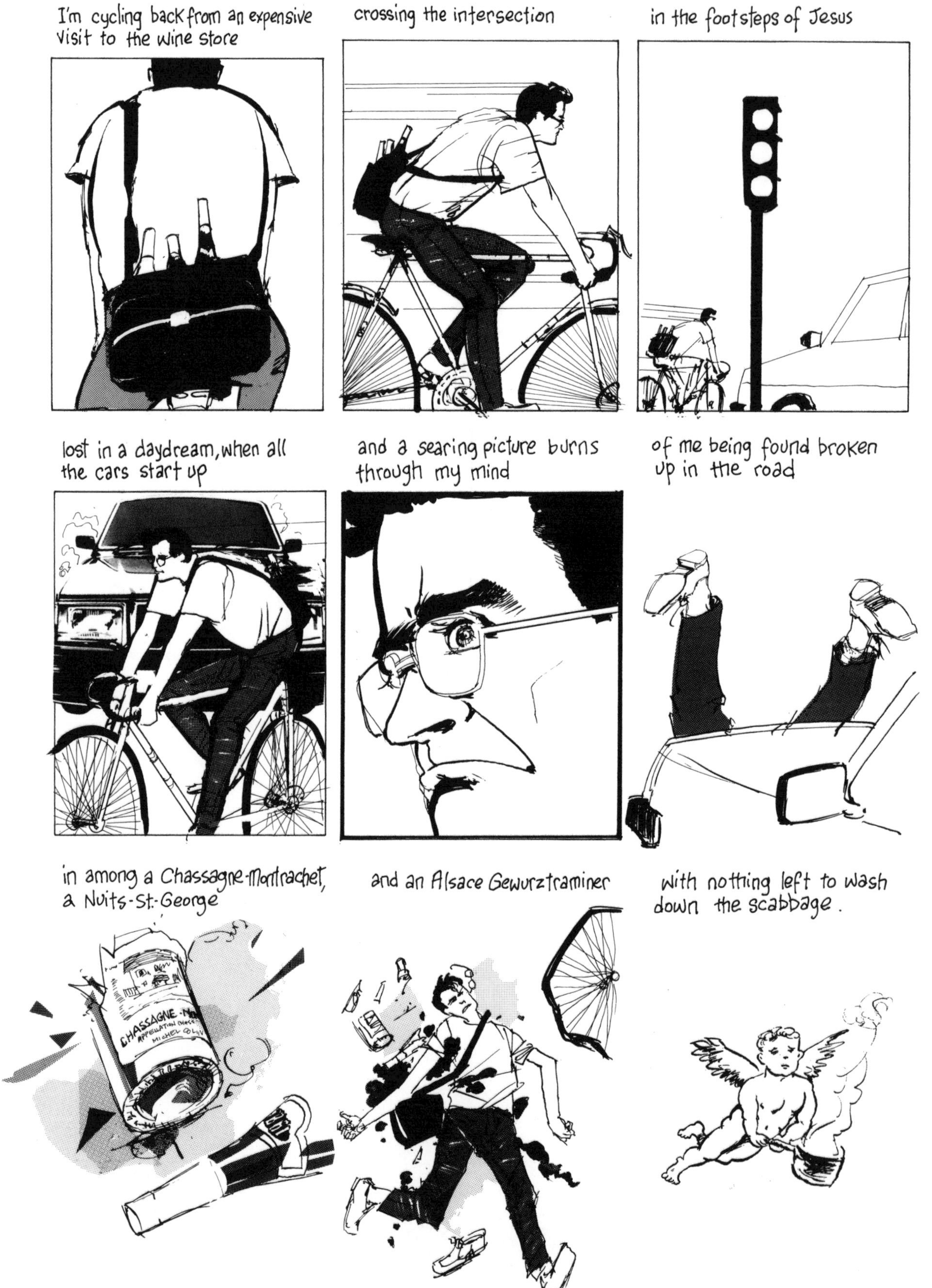
I'm cycling back from an expensive visit to the wine store
crossing the intersection
in the footsteps of Jesus
lost in a daydream, when all the cars start up
and a searing picture burns through my mind
of me being found broken up in the road
in among a Chassagne-Montrachet, a Nuits-St.-George
and an Alsace Gewurztraminer
with nothing left to wash down the scabbage.

GENETIC DEFECTS
Eddie Campbell. July '91.
i say to my dad:
Daddy, Daniel, one of the kids in my class, is cross-eyed.
he says:
PEOPLE CAN'T HELP HOW THEY LOOK. IT ALL GETS PASSED DOWN FROM YOUR PARENTS.
and he adds:
YOU WON'T SAY ANYTHING ABOUT IT TO HIM, WILL YOU, OR HE MIGHT BE SAD.
and my dad should know because he comes home sad from the pub
and says:
I'M NOT GOING BACK THERE. IT BRINGS OUT THE STUPID IN ME.
Mum cheers him up again...
...but then she's in a poo because he won't tell her what was so stupid he had to fall out with himself.
Let's hope the stupid isn't being passed down.
ECampbell.

Ah kids, don't ya just love 'em

Eddie Campbell.
July '91.

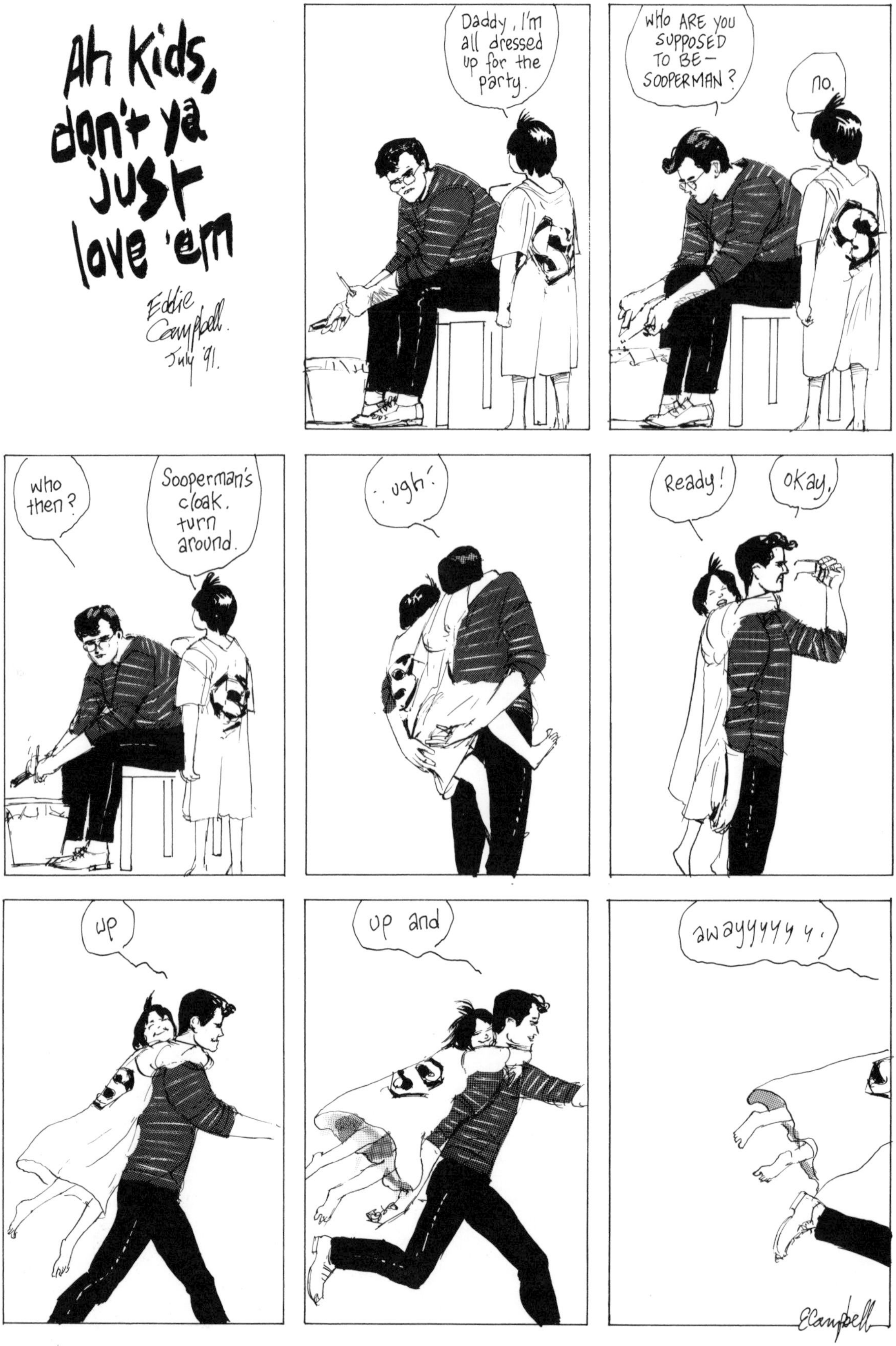

Daddy, I'm all dressed up for the party.
WHO ARE YOU SUPPOSED TO BE— SOOPERMAN?
no.
who then?
Sooperman's cloak. turn around.
: ugh!
Ready!
okay.
up
up and
awayyyyyy.
ECampbell

The remarkable history of the NULLARBOR Nymph
Eddie Campbell July '91.
I've just been reading in the newspaper about some blokes out at Eucla in Western Australia, twenty years back, spinning a yarn one night in the pub—
yeah, mate... the wild nymph o' the bush... fair dinkum.
bloody oath.
The guy listening to it is one Geoff Pearce, a travelling reporter who has to phone in some copy the next morning—
oh, sh— ... what can I do? What was that yarn again about the girl runnin' wild with the wallabies?
Two days later—
Hey, you blokes, me editor loved the one about the Kangaroo-girl! ya gotta help me get a photo.
One of the blokes, Laurie Scott, goes and gets his girlfriend
Ginny! Get ya gear off, an' get this roo-skin aroun' ya.
oh, yeh?
They photograph Geneice like this, with half a dozen live silver roos they'd caught
GREAT!
Within days of this photo appearing in print, the story spreads like wildfire, and the legend of "The Nullarbor Nymph" grabs worldwide attention.
By the start of 1972 the Nymph is known around the world, with stories appearing in Time and Newsweek and on the BBC and CBS networks, and all the time she's serving tea and coffee in Eucla—
Some more toast, Ginny!
comin' up.
We've come to try and spot the famous "nymph."
This cartoon serves to show, dear reader, what happens when professional scribes try to fill up space with someone else's story.
E Campbell

An old Australian Yarn
found in the writings of Walter James and paraphrased here by the less eminent Eddie Campbell Aug '91.
It has been said that Governor MacQuarie's wife used to keep a herd of cows to provide her daily milk bath...
...which, made all the better by her having been in it...
...would then be run off for the nourishment of the poor convicts.
A good many years later and in another part of Australia, a celebrated actress is visiting some wine cellars and is invited to fulfill her ambition of bathing in Champagne.
A bath is filled using a hundred bottles of the frothing wine...
...which, made all the better by her having been in it...
...is then put back into the hundred bottles by a stingy cellarman...
...who finds that there is enough wine to fill an extra bottle.
?
E Campbell

OBSESSION
REVISITED
Eddie Campbell
JUN '93
My pal Dakin arrives in the country, Coincidentally on the same weekend as auntie Ella
So we've got to entertain everybody at once. The only solution is to take them for a visit to the eccentric Doc Nodule.
I've never met a doctor before. Socially, I mean.
The Doc won 30,000 bucks on the lottery. The guys in the pub have been whingeing about how there is no fairness in the universe.
Ya gotta laff.
The Doc used the dosh to buy himself an old 1940s Jaguar. I do not see it parked with his other cars, such as the REO Flying Cloud.
He doesn't see it much either. One of the Doc's peculiarities, you see, after his pathological need to be always buying things, is that he likes to cut corners, so he's got a mechanic pal fixing the car up in his spare time, which means Saturday mornings, so the thing never really gets done.
Another peculiarity of the Doc is that he rates quantity over quality, so he's bought all these broken, antique tin toys, rather than pool all the dosh and get a really good one.
So in we go. His latest acquisition greets us in the hall.
He just had to have another one.
oh my Goodness.

The Doc serves apéritifs from his ecclesiastical pulpit, and a bottle of something is deemed to be off and heads down the sink.
Is this a real pulpit?
We check out his big Norman Lindsay Illustration to Gargantua, with its authentic burnt corner deriving from the calamitous destruction of the artist's best work at Scranton railway station.
Pity about the damage.
In 1940 the work was taken out of Australia for safekeeping. It was being railfreighted in the car just behind the engine when the crates caught fire. They offloaded the stuff in a hurry onto the platform, but when the good citizens got a look at Lindsay's nudes, they did their duty and restarted the blaze.
Now let me tell you about the oddest of Doc Nodule's recent acquisitions. He's at one of those contents-of-house auctions and manages to come away with the staircase.
He takes it home like this.
It stands out behind the house for a while till he gets time to bring it in.
Inside, it leans against a wall, much like the imaginary stairs in the song from my favourite movie, FIDDLER ON THE ROOF.
In the song, Tevye the milkman's nutty idea of being rich is having two separate stairways, one for going up and one for coming down...
...And a third stairway going nowhere, just for show.
Is he going to knock the wall through?

MEMENTO VITA

by

Eddie Campbell

JUN '93

...in which I am visited by one of those moments of unearthly clarity that strike sometimes, but only once, and never leave guidelines for a reconstruction on paper, so that this one may be applesauce.

We go for an adventure down to the Hunter Valley and back with my pal Dakes. It's about 2 days getting there, 2 there, 3 back.

Wanna stay in Motel.

The kids love the novelty of staying in motels.

LOOK, DAD. THEY've got another one of those books.

One place has got a spare bed curtained off. The kids put on a show.

The old man loses himself in the wineries.

McWilliams
9671

We try to drive over the Barrington Tops and are enchanted by the sounds of the Bellbird which fends off predators by imitating the squeak of an axle and emitting the smell of burning rubber, according to Dakin, who has a way with the concepts of nature.

Dakes and I step out for a beer at Port MacQuarie but can't find a bar.

So we hop in a cab and say:

Take us to the best bar in town.
Well, you've got a choice between the R.S.L. and the such'n'such hotel.
TAXI

So we say: deposit us before the such'n'such hotel.
The front window of the bar is on the sidewalk.
Inside, there's shredded cabbage everywhere.
The place has got a decent stout on tap, and after two or three of those we get to thinking a visit to the Returned Servicemen's League clubhouse and a chat with some crusty, weathered, old geezers might leave us with a fine spiritual memento of this country...
...but we get in the joint and we're the oldest people there. The League has run out of returned soldiers, I deduce, and is renting its clubhalls out for teen-age discos.
I bet Dakes that most of these kids don't even know what R.S.L. stands for.
Oh, you'd be totally correct, I'm sure.
And I try it on one of them just for the record.
We're foreign here. Like, what does R.S.L. mean?
Oh, that's just what they call it.
In a place further north, the businesses on the main street have persuaded the local council to have the War Memorial moved to the back of town so they can have more parking spaces out front.
And in a wise old book it says, "Remove not the ancient landmark which thy fathers have set." (Prov. ch.22 v.28)
But nobody's reading; nobody's listening.

It's as though Death belongs on another planet, and we can beam all the Death stuff up there...
... instead of it being one of the team.
We go through life with our eye fixed on something or other.
And in life's forward progress the ground beneath our feet falls back as we plough ahead. We overlook it.
But one day a door swings open at the end of all those engagements that keep our heads facing forward.
You peep through it and nothing's there.
Out in the night a guy's putting the finishing touches on a new window, and the cabbage husk is in the middle of the road. It must have been a monster to be still so big after festooning the such'n'such hotel's bar.
I pick it up to remind me of this moment of insight, and we football it back to the motel.
Honey, where did that lettuce come from?
Eh? Dakin said it was a cabbage.

A pub far away
Eddie Campbell July '91.
(TOURING AUSTRALIA)
Well, here we are.
Say that again, mate.
We're here.
Are you blokes British?
uh...
Hey, Johnno, a couple of poms!
Come here!
Are you gay?
AW FAK!
Hey, Johnno. what's up, mate?
Aw, look, I'm sorry, you blokes. I really didn't mean it. I buried me nan this mornin'. Y'know how it is.
Aw, shit, I upset those blokes.
Did Johnno upset ya?
Him and his mouth! I'll sort it out!
!! !!
What's goin' on? Ya want me to come over there?
Well, here we are.
Shh.
ECampbell

William Tell
by Eddie Campbell 30 May '92.
Dad, let me put this apple on your head and shoot it off.
Are you supposed to be William Tell?
Who's William Tell?
He's a legendary hero of Switzerland, and the story goes like this...
The Duke of Austria's men ordered all the peasants to salute the Duke's hat, and they all did, except William Tell.
No Way
So he was sentenced to death unless he could shoot an arrow off his son's head from way back over there.
He held two arrows in his hand but succeeded with the first.
If you'd missed and killed the kid, what good was the second arrow?
That one was for you.
He was arrested again but escaped, and later led an uprising that freed Switzerland from being bossed around.
Wm. TELL and son from the statue by Kissling in Altdorf
That's bad, eh, Dad... wasting food like that.
Yup... and that's why you've got to go and eat your apple.
Old Jokes revival dept.: definition of an intellectual: person who can hear the William Tell overture by Rossini without thinking of the Lone Ranger.

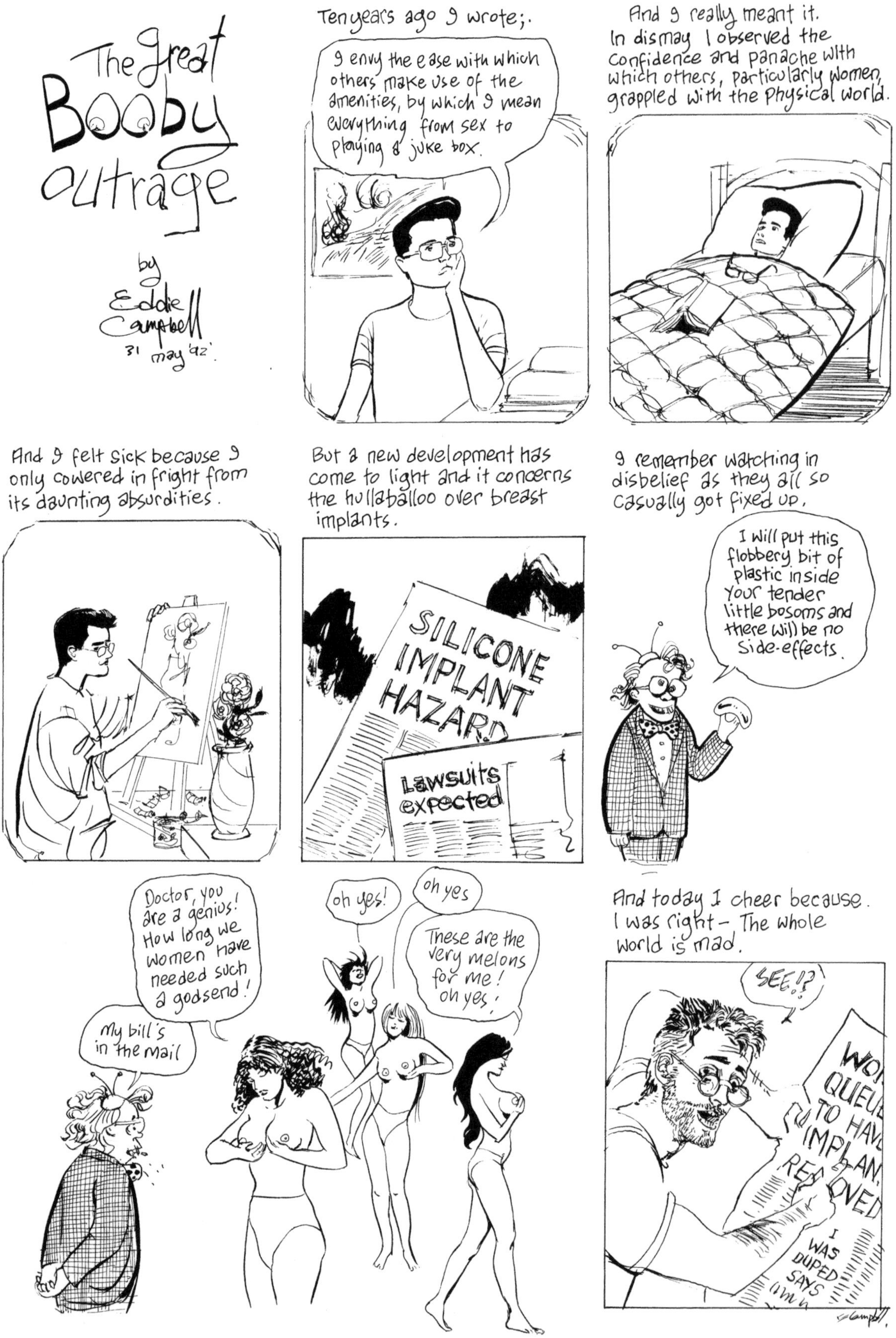
The Great Booby outrage
by Eddie Campbell
31 may '92.
Ten years ago I wrote;.
I envy the ease with which others make use of the amenities, by which I mean everything from sex to playing a juke box.
And I really meant it. In dismay I observed the confidence and panache with which others, particularly women, grappled with the physical world.
And I felt sick because I only cowered in fright from its daunting absurdities.
But a new development has come to light and it concerns the hullaballoo over breast implants.
SILICONE IMPLANT HAZARD
LAWSUITS expected
I remember watching in disbelief as they all so casually got fixed up.
I will put this flobbery bit of plastic inside your tender little bosoms and there will be no side-effects.
Doctor, you are a genius! How long we women have needed such a godsend!
My bill's in the mail
oh yes!
oh yes
These are the very melons for me! oh yes!
And today I cheer because. I was right – The whole world is mad.
SEE!?
WO
QUEUE
TO HAV
IMPLAN
RE OVED
I WAS DUPED SAYS
Campbell

This is your lunch
Eddie Campbell 5 JUN 92
HEY! Get out of there!
Bawbaw moonk
You can't spend your whole life drinking milk - this is your lunch here.
Bawbaw moonk
Look - lovely quiche... mmm...
Bawbaw moonk
...and carrots. numnum carrots.
Bawbaw moonk
Look! celery! You'll love it. come on!
Bawbaw moonk
oh, give her a bottle of milk.
Bawbaw moonk
For a quiet life, eh? okay, here.
Bawbaw moonk
This was a public service allegory. Go out there and get yer bawbaw.
EC.

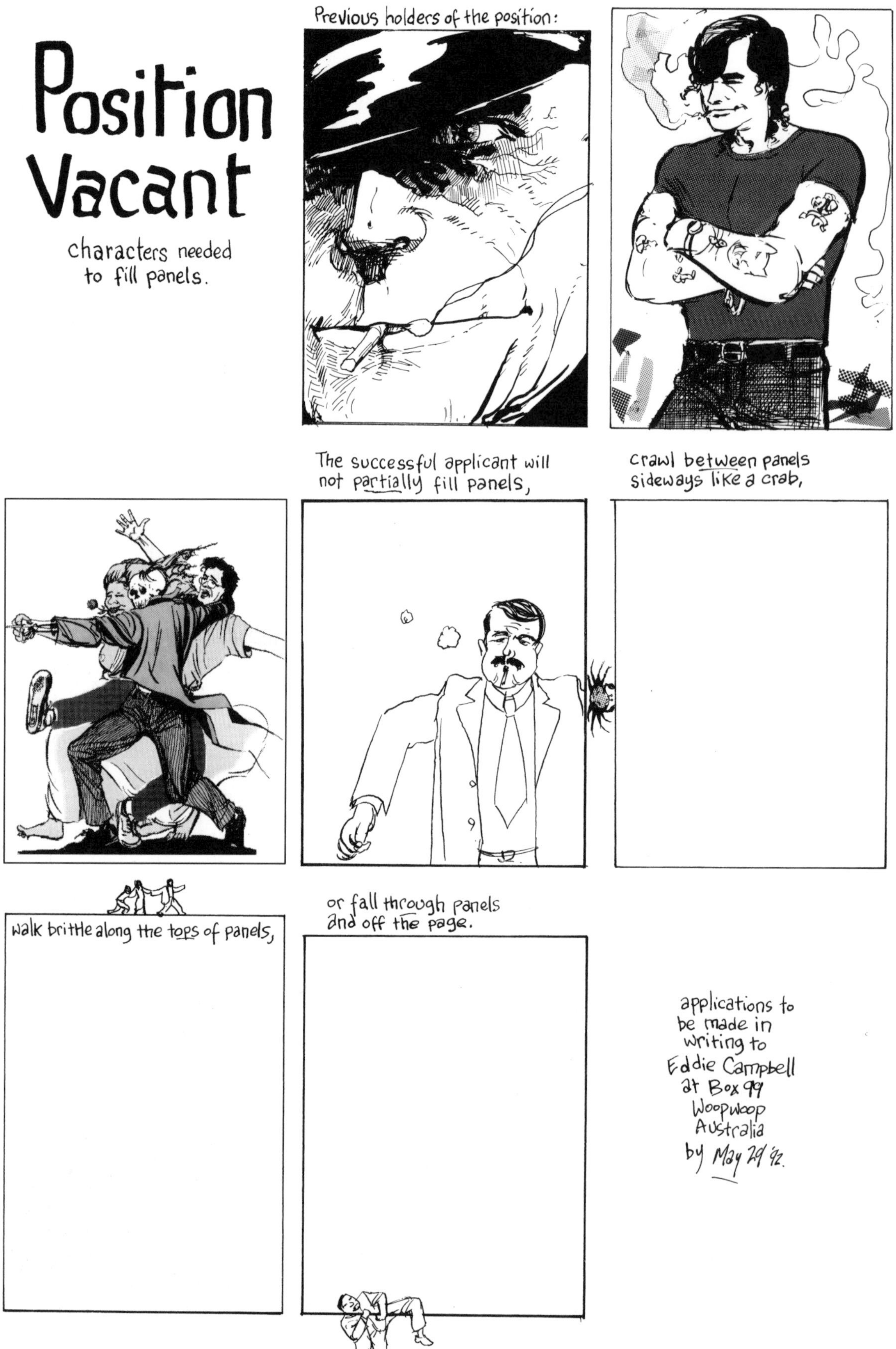
Position Vacant
characters needed to fill panels.
Previous holders of the position:
The successful applicant will not partially fill panels,
crawl between panels sideways like a crab,
walk brittle along the tops of panels,
or fall through panels and off the page.
applications to be made in writing to Eddie Campbell at Box 99 Woopwoop Australia by May 29 '92.

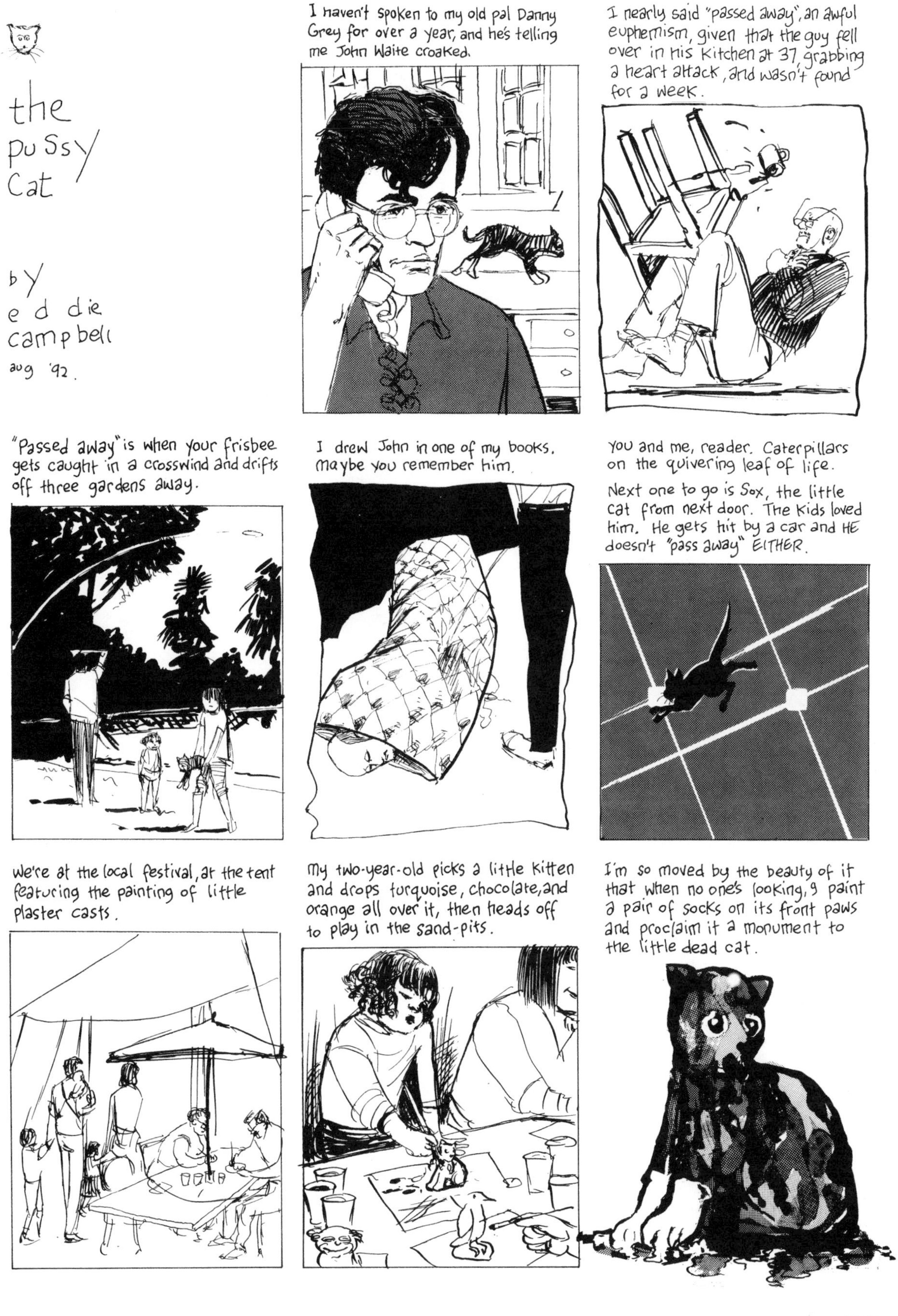
the pussy cat
by eddie campbell aug '92.
I haven't spoken to my old pal Danny Grey for over a year, and he's telling me John Waite croaked.
I nearly said "passed away", an awful euphemism, given that the guy fell over in his kitchen at 37, grabbing a heart attack, and wasn't found for a week.
"Passed away" is when your frisbee gets caught in a crosswind and drifts off three gardens away.
I drew John in one of my books. Maybe you remember him.
You and me, reader. Caterpillars on the quivering leaf of life.
Next one to go is Sox, the little cat from next door. The kids loved him. He gets hit by a car and HE doesn't "pass away" EITHER.
We're at the local festival, at the tent featuring the painting of little plaster casts.
My two-year-old picks a little kitten and drops turquoise, chocolate, and orange all over it, then heads off to play in the sand-pits.
I'm so moved by the beauty of it that when no one's looking, I paint a pair of socks on its front paws and proclaim it a monument to the little dead cat.

I gently carry the object home, but the paint is all too thick to dry properly. The Kiddy takes a dislike to my interferences and casually smears off the socks.
I'm so angry I send everyone to bed early, even my wife.
And under the ghostly fluorescent tube in the dark night, I mix my tints.
Next day I'm paying the rent and broach the subject of how the landlady might feel, were we to acquire a pet of the feline species.
You mean a cat? Well, they urinate all over my lawn.
And you've got another baby now, and this cat would only get killed too, but you'll have to talk to my son—he owns the house.
Yes, I'll talk to him.
Well, before I get a chance to talk to him, another corpse turns up. A full-size dead cat on the pavement in front of our house. Same injuries.
No I.D. on this guy, and he's already stiff. Things move quickly in this heat. So do I.
Can you get me a box, luvvy?
Who should drive past right now but the landlady and her son, making me feel just a little foolish.
I borrow a shovel and bury the body under the house.

Poor wee pussycat.
Hey, Alec, if you don't get back up here soon, your assistant will have rewritten the script.
Oh, blow. I nearly forgot.
How are we doing, April?
No problems.
Where Gull holds up her cervix, you had it looking like a lima bean, but I fixed it.
Oh my God.
Two days later, wifey voices her concern.
Alec, the burial mound's no good under the house.
Oh, it'll be al right there, darling. Don't worry about it.
I have trouble getting to sleep.
MEOW!
I check the mound.
Funny thing—my pal Kublick says the same thing as wifey.
You need to go down at least two or three feet to keep the possums out.

The angels talk to me in my sleep.
You haven't dug the hole deep enough.
So, in the dim light of morning, I dig up the body and move him to another hole down at the end of the garden.
I still can't get it deep enough because it's all rock and rubble after 1½ feet down.
I spy a big rock:
Aw, we'll just bung that on the top, and it'll keep the dogs and possums out.
While my mind wanders for a minute, the rock is brought over:
How the hell did you lift that, luvvy ?
In my curiosity I hit it with the shovel, and thousands of ants start running all over the place.
It was a bloody anthill.
Hoo
I walk back to the house for breakfast, and when I trudge down there a half hour later, the area is crawling with big lizards feasting on ants.
The angels talk to me in my sleep...
You're goin' mad.
...and I hear them scratching on the metal roof with their fingernails.
E Campbell

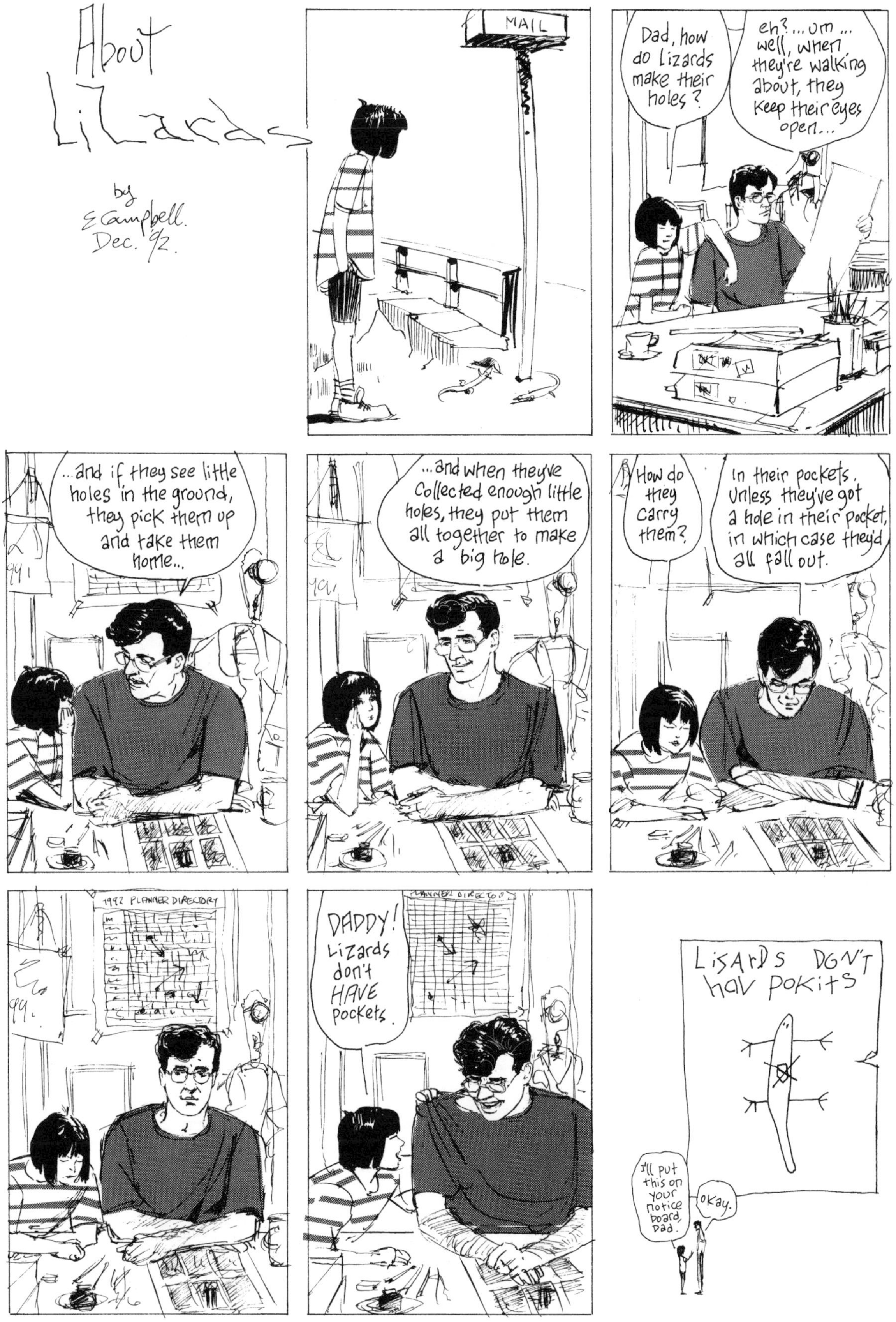
About Lizards
by E Campbell. Dec. '92.
MAIL
Dad, how do Lizards make their holes?
eh? ... um ... well, when they're walking about, they keep their eyes open...
...and if they see little holes in the ground, they pick them up and take them home...
...and when they've collected enough little holes, they put them all together to make a big hole.
How do they carry them?
In their pockets. Unless they've got a hole in their pocket, in which case they'd all fall out.
1992 PLANNER DIRECTORY
DADDY! Lizards don't HAVE pockets.
LISARDS DON'T HAV POKITS
I'll put this on your notice board, Dad.
Okay.

Nature's Way
by
Eddie green fingers
Apr. 93.
The little orange tree in our garden gave us thirty-three oranges last year.
But this year it just dropped its eight puny offerings on the ground, then died.
I come from Scotland. It never occurred to me to water it. I always presumed that trees look after themselves.
It's funny how fickle nature can be... abandoning the poor wee sprout like that...
...while heaping its ample bounty upon the ferns under the house...
...which gather themselves under the leaky water-heater.
E Campbell.

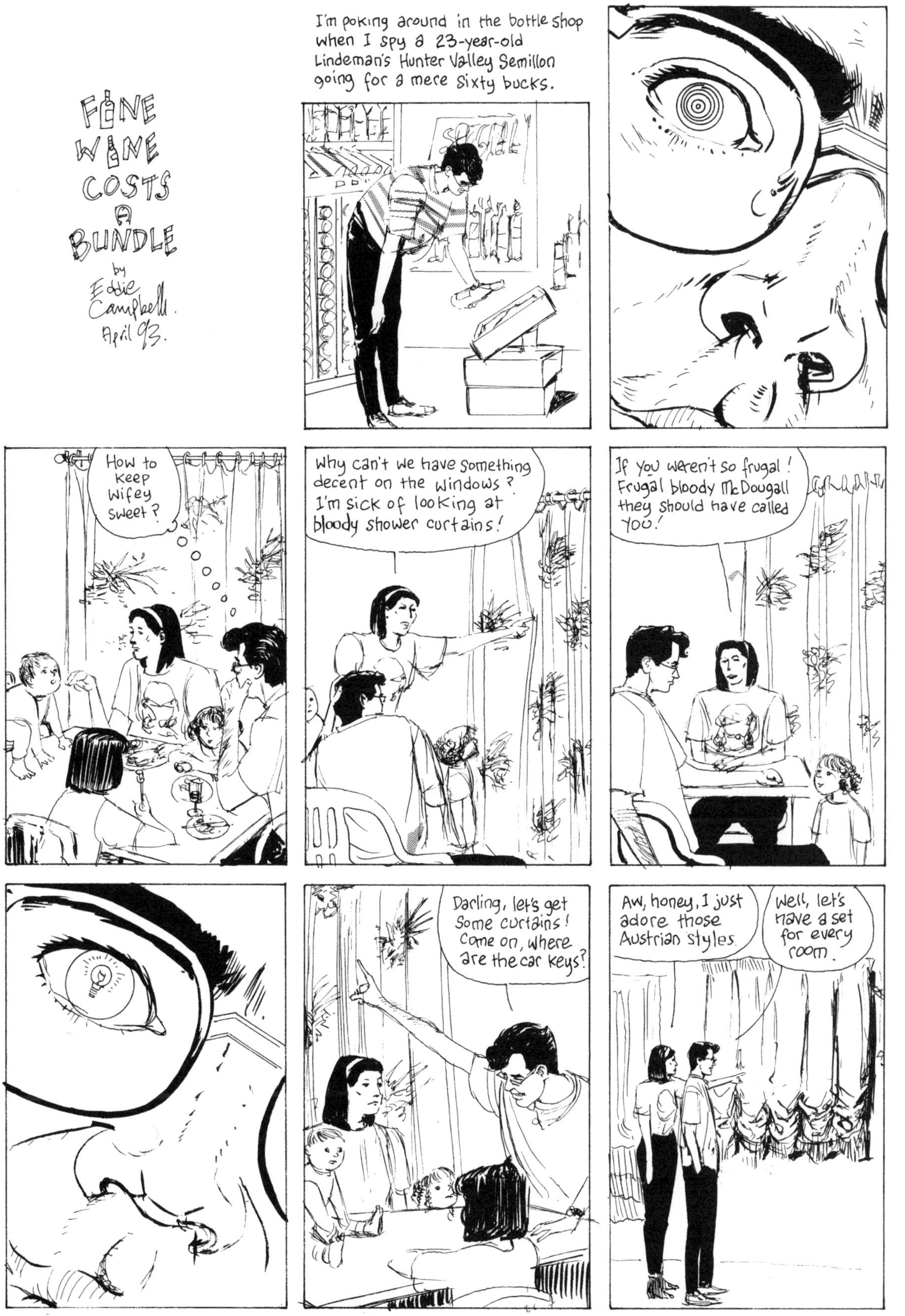

FINE WINE COSTS A BUNDLE
by Eddie Campbell. April 93.
I'm poking around in the bottle shop when I spy a 23-year-old Lindeman's Hunter Valley Semillon going for a mere sixty bucks.
SPECIAL
How to keep wifey sweet?
Why can't we have something decent on the windows? I'm sick of looking at bloody shower curtains!
If you weren't so frugal! Frugal bloody McDougall they should have called YOU!
Darling, let's get some curtains! Come on, where are the car keys?
Aw, honey, I just adore those Austrian styles.
Well, let's have a set for every room.

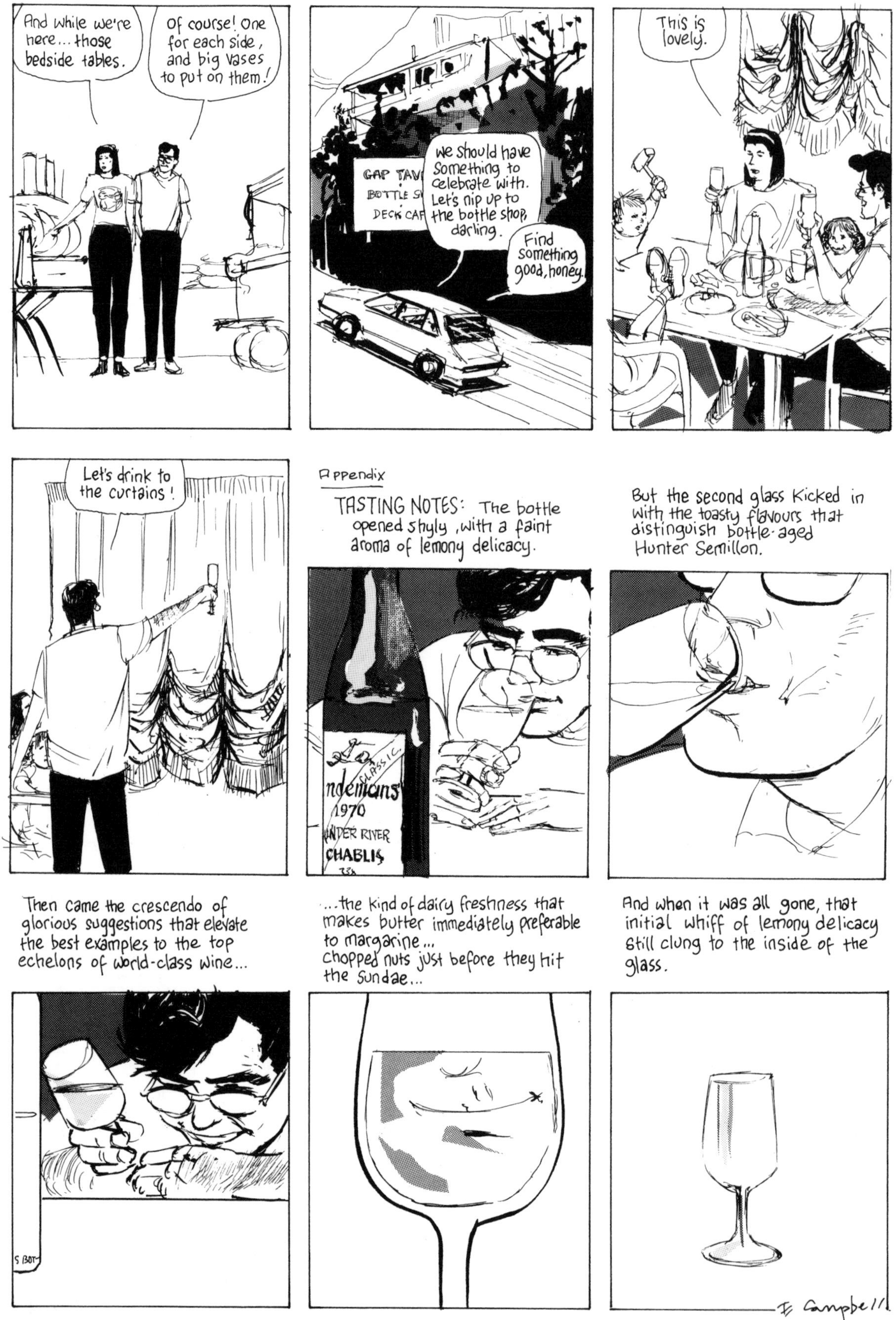
And while we're here... those bedside tables.
Of course! One for each side, and big vases to put on them!
We should have something to celebrate with. Let's nip up to the bottle shop, darling.
Find something good, honey.
This is lovely.
Let's drink to the curtains!
Appendix
TASTING NOTES: The bottle opened shyly, with a faint aroma of lemony delicacy.
1970
CHABLIS
CLASSIC
But the second glass kicked in with the toasty flavours that distinguish bottle-aged Hunter Semillon.
Then came the crescendo of glorious suggestions that elevate the best examples to the top echelons of world-class wine...
...the kind of dairy freshness that makes butter immediately preferable to margarine...
Chopped nuts just before they hit the sundae...
And when it was all gone, that initial whiff of lemony delicacy still clung to the inside of the glass.
I Campbell

FLYING NEIL GAIMAN IN
by Eddie Campbell. AUSTRALIA. May '93.
Hey, Doc, I've got a fax from Neil. He says thanks for the new schedule.
Okay, Alec. my people at the shop will fix up the signing, but what about the chat-show?
We'll have to forget the chat-show.
But you said you'd organise it.
No, I said I'd "host" it. I haven't got time to organise stuff like that.
The university wants us to do it there, so all i'll have to do is show up and blether with him.
Can't I persuade you to do a second one in the evening?
No way.
Okay, then,... the dinner... I've booked a table at Chez Nous B.Y.O. French Restaurant.
Waitaminnit! Bring Your Own Booze? No way, man! I don't want you bringing any of your lousy wines!
Let's negotiate then.
Um... lessee... Chateauneuf du Pape '85.
Alright, Neil comes in on Tuesday night, we do the Uni Weds Morning then the signing, Chez Nous for dinner... now... sleeping arrangements...
ECampbell

Some People Have to WORK for a Living

by Eddie Campbell, July 93.

Let's have one more wine!
...and then I lunged like this, and the sunlight glittered on my chain mail.

Hey, look at the time! We better get back to work!
I'll clear up here later. First I'll take these cheques to the bank and do the accounts.
Okay, honey!
That one ready for inking yet?

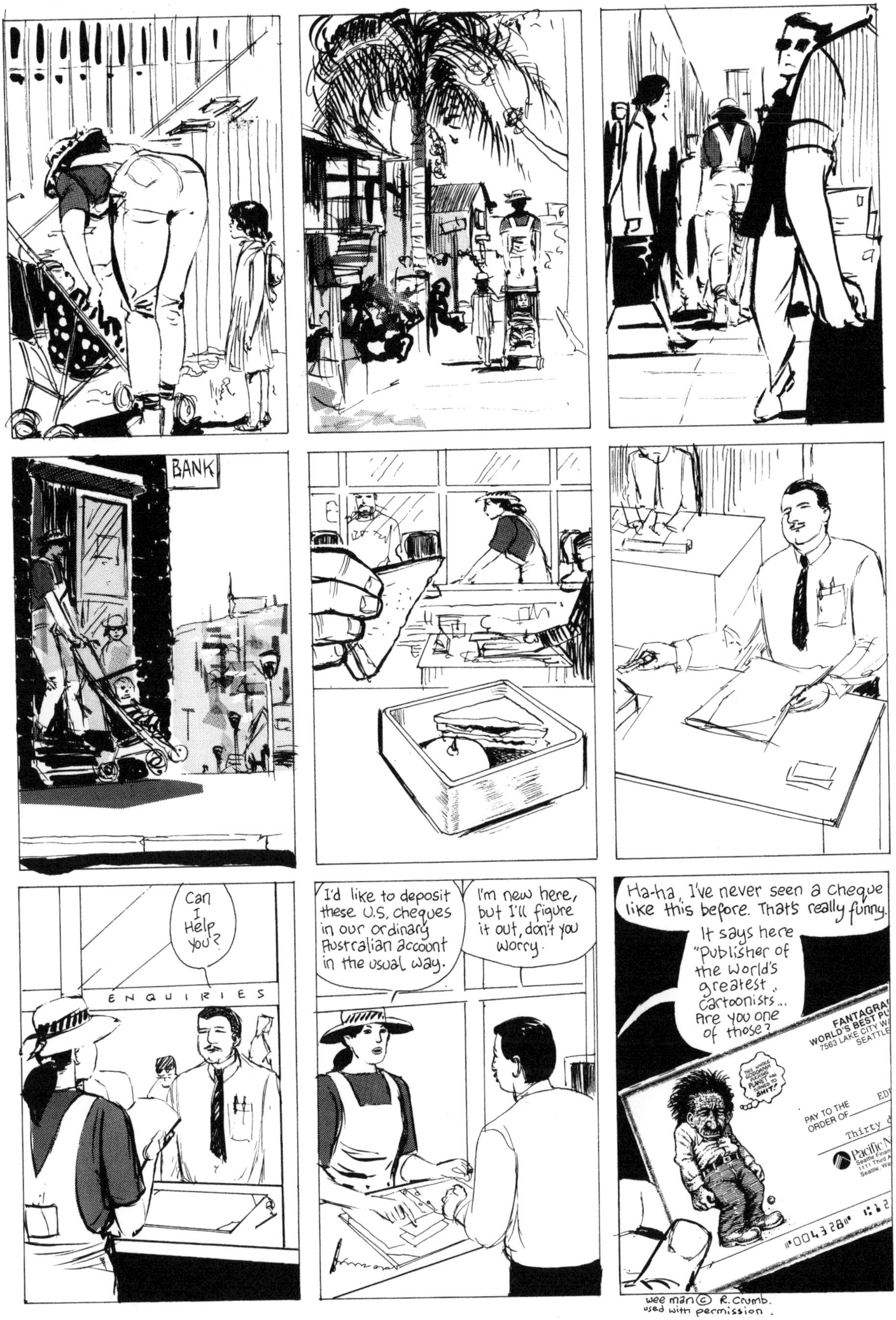
BANK
ENQUIRIES
Can I Help you?
I'd like to deposit these U.S. cheques in our ordinary Australian account in the usual way.
I'm new here, but I'll figure it out, don't you worry.
Ha-ha, I've never seen a cheque like this before. That's really funny.
It says here "Publisher of the World's greatest cartoonists"... Are you one of those?
PAY TO THE ORDER OF

wee man © R. Crumb. used with permission.

It's my husband's cheque, actually. He's the artist. I handle all the paperwork.
Aw, that must be the life, eh, to sit at home and draw pictures all day?
ENQUIRIES
It's not quite how you imagine it, I'm sure.
Well, uh... I'm not certain of the routine with this, so I'll just go in the back room and ask someone.
ENQUIRIES
Oh my God! I don't know what to do!
I've been asking questions all morning, and everybody's fed up with me... oh, what am I going to do? Please, God, take me away from here ...
Don't fret, young earthling. Just come over here to DIMENSION X, and we'll look after you.
Seriously?
Yes, just step through the dimensional doorway.
Somebody tell me what's going on in there! That guy's been gone fifteen minutes !!
Eddie Campbell

The dance of Life's death
by Eddie Campbell. may '93.
incorporating part of "The Jumblies" by Edward Lear (1812-1888)
I'm having my Thursday Night Guinness with Kublick.
The sky is dark and sparkly.
They're Killing each other in Bosnia.
Nature's Killing them in Somalia.
They're Killing themselves in Waco.
And the interviewers are addressing the survivors as though they're any loonier than the rest of us.
I wish I died with the others.
You're Kidding!
I have another Guinness with Kublick.

One day it comes to all of us...
Fortysomething, thirtysomething, twentysomething...
Boo
Graugh
AAH
OH MY GOD
The Newsreader...
Boo
GKK
The computer programmer...
The cold, clammy hand of... and a hot sweaty one.
The comic-book artist...
OH SHIT BLAZES AGH.
YEE HAH
YEE HAH
The Entrepreneur...
The Unemployable...
pussycats...
Yow
you.
Me?

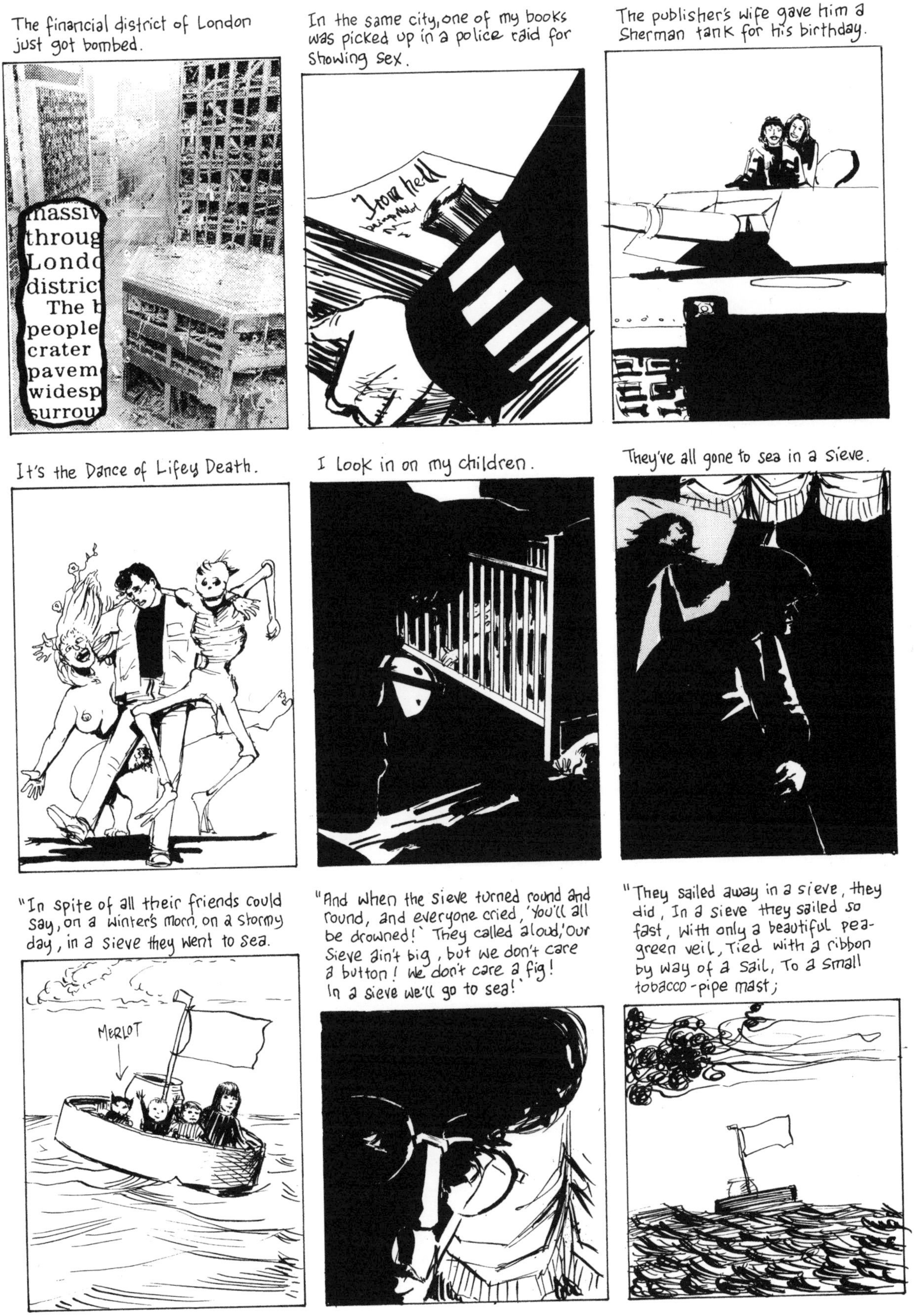
The financial district of London just got bombed.
massiv
throug
Londo
district
The b
people
crater
pavem
widesp
surrou
In the same city, one of my books was picked up in a police raid for showing sex.
The publisher's wife gave him a Sherman tank for his birthday.
It's the Dance of Lifey Death.
I look in on my children.
They've all gone to sea in a sieve.
"In spite of all their friends could say, on a winter's morn, on a stormy day, in a sieve they went to sea.
MERLOT
"And when the sieve turned round and round, and everyone cried, 'You'll all be drowned!' They called aloud, 'Our sieve ain't big, but we don't care a button! We don't care a fig! In a sieve we'll go to sea!'
"They sailed away in a sieve, they did, In a sieve they sailed so fast, With only a beautiful pea-green veil, Tied with a ribbon by way of a sail, To a small tobacco-pipe mast;

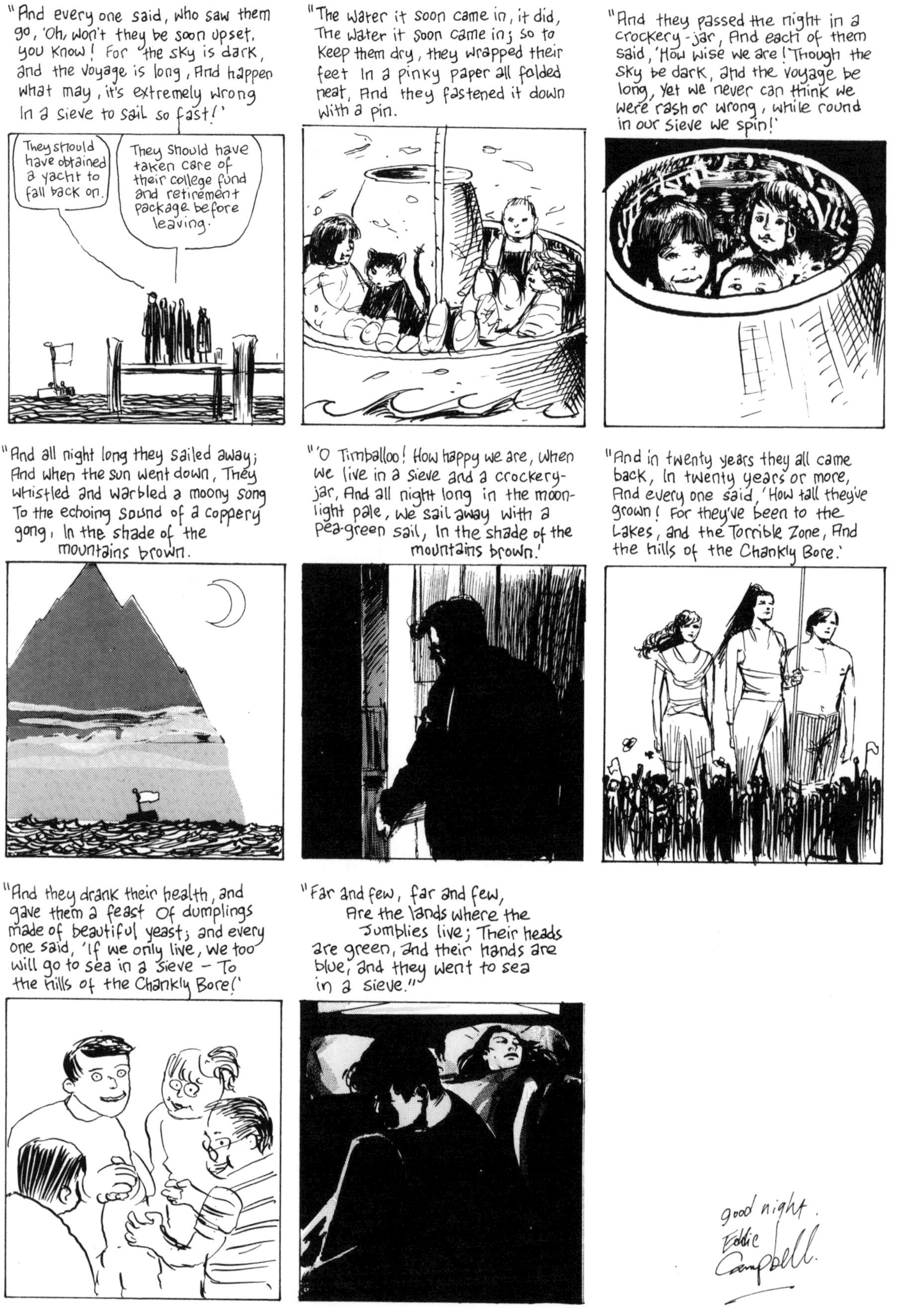
"And every one said, who saw them go, 'Oh, won't they be soon upset, you know! For the sky is dark, and the voyage is long, And happen what may, it's extremely wrong In a sieve to sail so fast!'
They should have obtained a yacht to fall back on.
They should have taken care of their college fund and retirement package before leaving.
"The water it soon came in, it did, The water it soon came in; so to keep them dry, they wrapped their feet In a pinky paper all folded neat, And they fastened it down with a pin.
"And they passed the night in a crockery-jar, And each of them said, 'How wise we are! Though the sky be dark, and the voyage be long, Yet we never can think we were rash or wrong, while round in our sieve we spin!'
"And all night long they sailed away; And when the sun went down, They whistled and warbled a moony song To the echoing sound of a coppery gong, In the shade of the mountains brown.
"'O Timballoo! How happy we are, when we live in a sieve and a crockery-jar, And all night long in the moonlight pale, We sail away with a pea-green sail, In the shade of the mountains brown.'
"And in twenty years they all came back, In twenty years or more, And every one said, 'How tall they've grown! For they've been to the Lakes, and the Torrible Zone, And the hills of the Chankly Bore.'
"And they drank their health, and gave them a feast Of dumplings made of beautiful yeast; and every one said, 'If we only live, We too will go to sea in a sieve - To the hills of the Chankly Bore!'
"Far and few, far and few, Are the lands where the Jumblies live; Their heads are green, and their hands are blue, and they went to sea in a sieve."
good night.
Eddie Campbell.

after the Snooter

After the Snooter was constructed in quite a different way from the through-composed *How to be an Artist*, or the simply collected consecutive units of *Little Italy*. With the *Snooter*, the pages were originally published in the order of their making; as soon as they were drawn they went into the next issue of my *Bacchus* monthly. But their order, when collected in one book, was quite different and the reader who saw it the first way would have been taken aback by the rearrangement. In the making of a large pictorial composition, an artist does not normally start at the top left and work across and down as in writing; he works on all the parts simultaneously. As always, the signature dates are left in place.

My favourite theme here, the recollection of childhood, was sparked by an invitation to draw a page, as an ex-pat looking homeward, for the national Scottish paper *The Herald*, significantly my father's paper of habit all through my childhood, when it was called the *Glasgow Herald*. I cunningly planned *The Forriners* so that it would fit both full broadside format as well as three comic book pages. I had to phone Auntie Ella, the only rellie I still knew in Scotland, and ask her to walk out of the retirement village in the snow and pick up a copy for me. She was uncertain about it, but obliged. When she realised I gave her a big hello on the newspaper page, she went back out and bought all the copies in the shop.

DVD era readers looking for 'out-takes' and 'deleted scenes' may note that two pages here were not included in the original printing of the book (567-568). In particular, *Bastards under the Sea* was the last thing I planned for the *Snooter*, before the late-hour addition of the final, closing page used up all available space. Surplus to requirements, *Bastards* remained lettered but only partially pencilled until now and appears in print for the first time.

These years were the best, so maybe life really does begin at forty. But alas so do faulty eyesight, and the tendency to tell a story to the same person several times, as American humorist Helen Rowland once observed.

A tale of horror by Eddie Campbell Feb 95
The Snooter buffers in on a humid night.
I am cleaning my empty bottle collection...
...like they were doing in the galley of the *Marie Celeste*
...on that dark and doleful day.
They too saw the sign.
BZONK
KDINK
KDUNK
I too fail to take heed...
...and feel only sympathy for the creature.

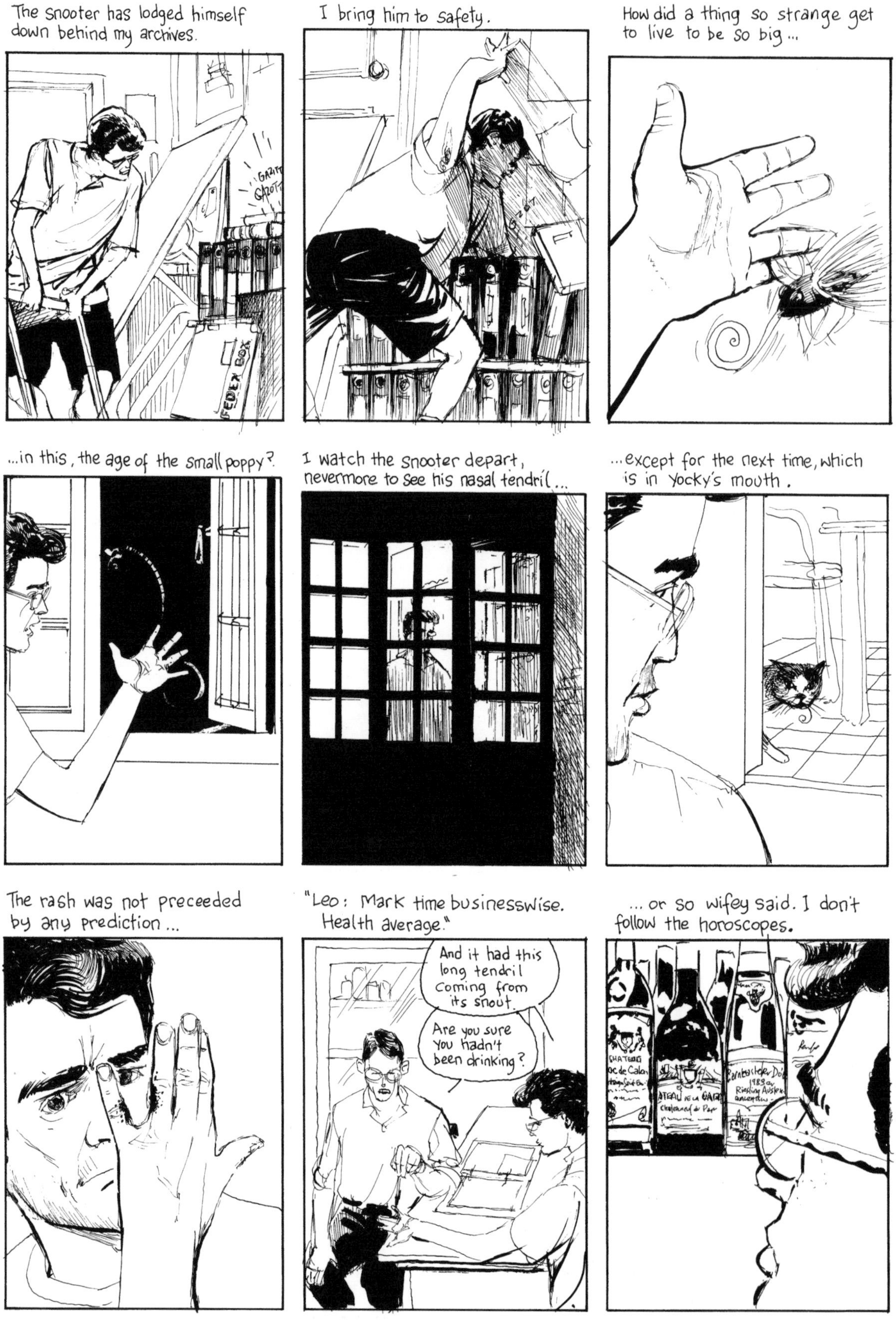
The snooter has lodged himself down behind my archives.
FEDEX BOX
I bring him to safety.
How did a thing so strange get to live to be so big...
...in this, the age of the small poppy?
I watch the snooter depart, nevermore to see his nasal tendril...
...except for the next time, which is in Yocky's mouth.
The rash was not preceeded by any prediction...
"Leo: Mark time businesswise. Health average."
And it had this long tendril coming from its snout.
Are you sure you hadn't been drinking?
...or so wifey said. I don't follow the horoscopes.

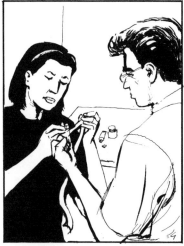

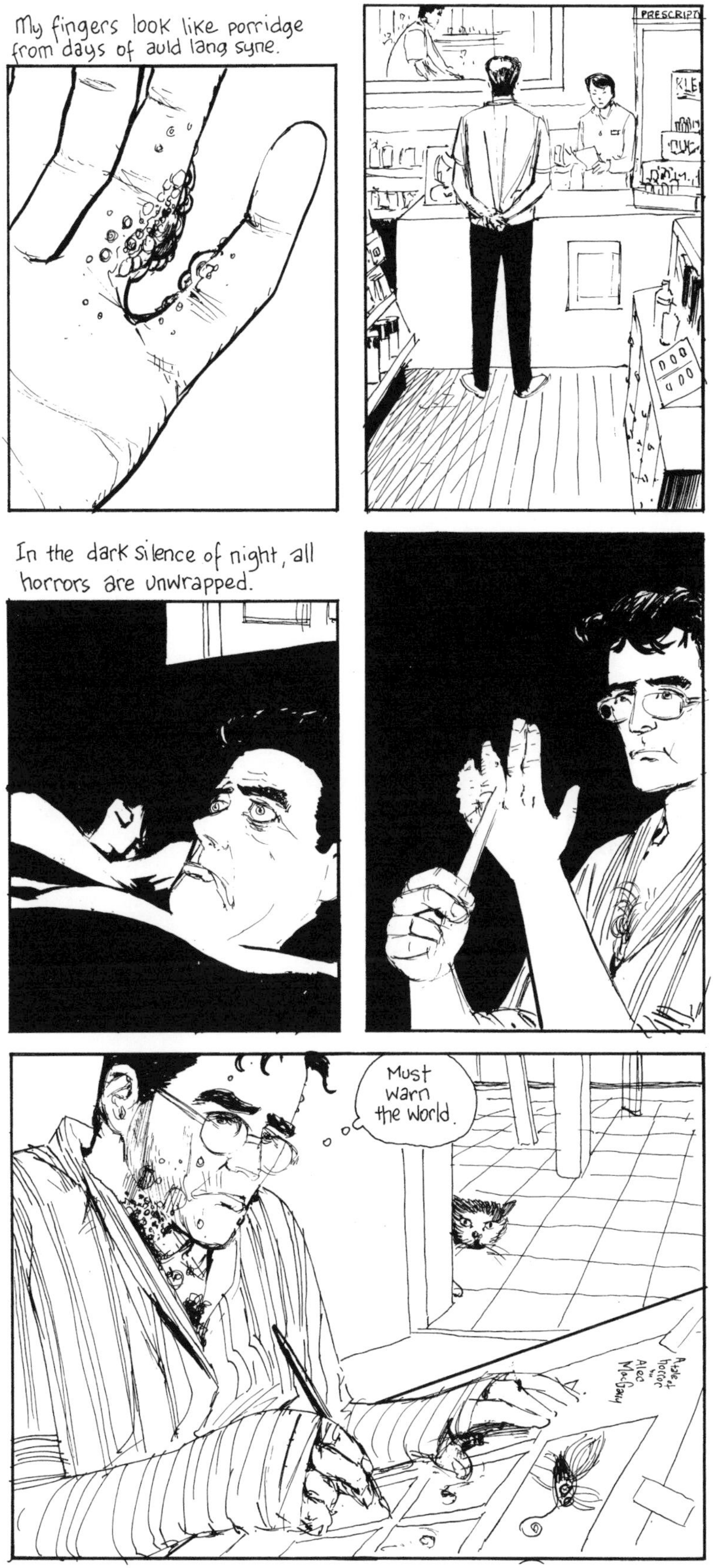
My fingers look like porridge from days of auld lang syne.
I have not been sleeping well for years.
In the dark silence of night, all horrors are unwrapped.
Must warn the world.

Beware the Snooter
Eddie Campbell 10.00
The Snooter next visits the Cat-man. He was a University Professor till one day he looked in the mirror and saw the Snooter.
He went down the road and set up house on a bench.
He licked himself while his family moved away and the house sat empty.
Months became years.
Once, the city council removed the bench, but there was a local murmur of complaint on the cat-man's behalf.
The cat-man got a new bench.
One Father's Day Sunday he was gone.
On Monday morning he returned.

Onward it flies, on its dark mission, the Snooter.
Many years ago, a couple wanted to go back to England but their kids didn't like the idea.
They'd already sold up the house and were in a hotel *en route* to flying out when they changed their minds and decided to stay.
They returned to their country town and rented a house on the street where they had lived.
Eventually their old house came up for sale and they bought it again.
SOLD
The daughter's course through life was not marred by any untoward event; worked as a secretary for a local small business for twenty five years after leaving school, married for twenty years, chose to have no children.
One Tuesday evening while driving to visit her parents at 6.30, as she had done every Tuesday evening, she saw a strange shadow in a dark side street.
She went home and hung herself in the bathroom.

After the Snooter...
11/4/94
Eddie Campbell
...everything is different. Not necessarily chronologically, like "before and after" pictures of cellulite, but I look back and realize that somewhere around that time, before or after, I became another person.
It's one of Ms. Sheehy's life "passages" I suspect. Everyone starts glancing sideways to see if one's fellows are alongside, or ahead, or behind.
Richard said he met a man yesterday of his own age, who has three real estate investment properties and it made him assess what he's achieved with his life so far.
The information comes to me like that, indirectly. Nobody will tell me straight either because they don't talk straight at all or because they think I'm a piss-taker and I'll put it in a comic and laugh at it.
Ha ha ha! and that's his idea of what's important?
I notice that suddenly I'm open to suggestions
I wake up in the awful dark with the terrors of the infinite upon me.
Have you thought of giving up the drink?
And sensitive to comments
Dad. Millhous's hair's going grey just like yours. starting at the back
MILLY MOOMOO
I find myself, unusually, looking back down the road all the way to school. The new music teacher favoured me for some reason. I was not great at music, or any other subject, except for art of course.
I played the violin. Never with enthusiasm. And was uncomfortable about the un-coolness of it. Of course nobody ever said 'cool' except Ice Cool on West Side Story.
Go Cooly coo boy
There were outings to the opera. I had nothing in common with the other guys here. But then, I didn't have much in common with anyone.

My anti-social adolescence manifests itself in the solitariness of artistic pursuit.
Anthony, you're up here on your own too much. Why don't you come and watch TV with us?
Later, mum.
It's difficult to be objective, of course, but in memory's mirror I see a good-looking kid, painfully shy, but with a surprising certainty about his destination in life.
One evening I turn up for one of those operatic outings to find I'm the only boy there. The school music teacher's taking me to the opera.
It happened more than once.
Thanx.
I sympathised with his anguish as the jackals of 4B(2) routinely tore pieces off him and he didn't appear to have any kind of survival instinct.
Yes, well sometimes popular music can be good. The crooners for instance...
Fuckin' crooners Ha Ha!
He took his frustration out on me once and I could see his immediate and painful regret.
Oh ED-WARD YOO-HOO.
Edward.
I presume the pack explained away to themselves his slip of familiarity as resulting from being a family friend or something like that, otherwise they'd have been shredding me up too.
For a bookworm I seem to have garnered an odd amount of jackal-respect, without ever being mentally present enough to care about seeking jackal-favour.
Let me nick it for ya.
I think you would too
I just bought myself a violin.
What? We've been together fifteen years and I didn't even know you could read music.

First there was the Shooter and then there is Sim. The Silver Surfer and Galactus. The Canadian's in this part of the world for a show in Sydney and comes up for a big hello.
You're planting your seeds all over the place like Little Johnny Appleseed. It would be okay if somebody was watering them.
No. He's been sent here. The show is irrelevant. The agent sent from the other side usually knows what his business is. He's delivering a package of information.
You've just got to rechannel all your energy and I'll tell you how.
To repeat the information here of course would be foolish. It comes encrypted in language so simple that I spend five days laughing.
We're in a hotel suite for that time ostensibly doing a little throwaway collaboration.
The Fire hose reel
FIRE HOSE REEL
He ends on an odd note:
And one last thing, Johnny Appleseed... Never bore your god.
Later he gets religion. I don't know who delivers his package.
I leave him to recuperate and catch his plane out. Back home my confidence dissipates with Sim's smoke after I open my bag.
I run it past my father when I'm in England.
I'm thinking of becoming my own publisher.
Isn't that a bit risky, son?
Well, how am I making my living now? I say. I make up stories then get on the phone and try to sell them. I mention my plan to one of my American editors
I'm thinking of becoming my own publisher.
Surely this is a bad time, the way the market's going.
A couple of months later, a brain tumor is diagnosed and within the year the poor guy's dead. What is risk? By that time I'm already my own publisher. I should have done it ten years ago.

New Year's Eve I'm sitting on the veranda with Annie and a bottle of Champagne. The kids're asleep.
We call Little old Nell over to have a glass with us. But after ten minutes she spies a more interesting proposition up the road. Even little old ladies have got better places to be. I'm crestfallen
What I need is a new gang.
So I dig out the mail I've been getting for my magazine, the local ones.
There's this guy who gift-wrapped a bottle of Speckled Hen and left it for me at the comic shop. Then there's this guy... "Campbell you're a fuckin' amateur... give me a call on..."
I arrange to meet them all at a pub at the same time. It goes off without a hitch. I introduce everybody to everybody else. instant gang.
A crowd for Saturday afternoon beers, New Year's Eve singalongs, 'dambusters' (a game in which you clench coins in your buttocks)
Dress balls with Pride of Erin and all that.
My 40th Birthday party.
And I still wake in the dark night with the Snooter staring down at me. I stare right back at the bastard.
Now, what else needs changing?

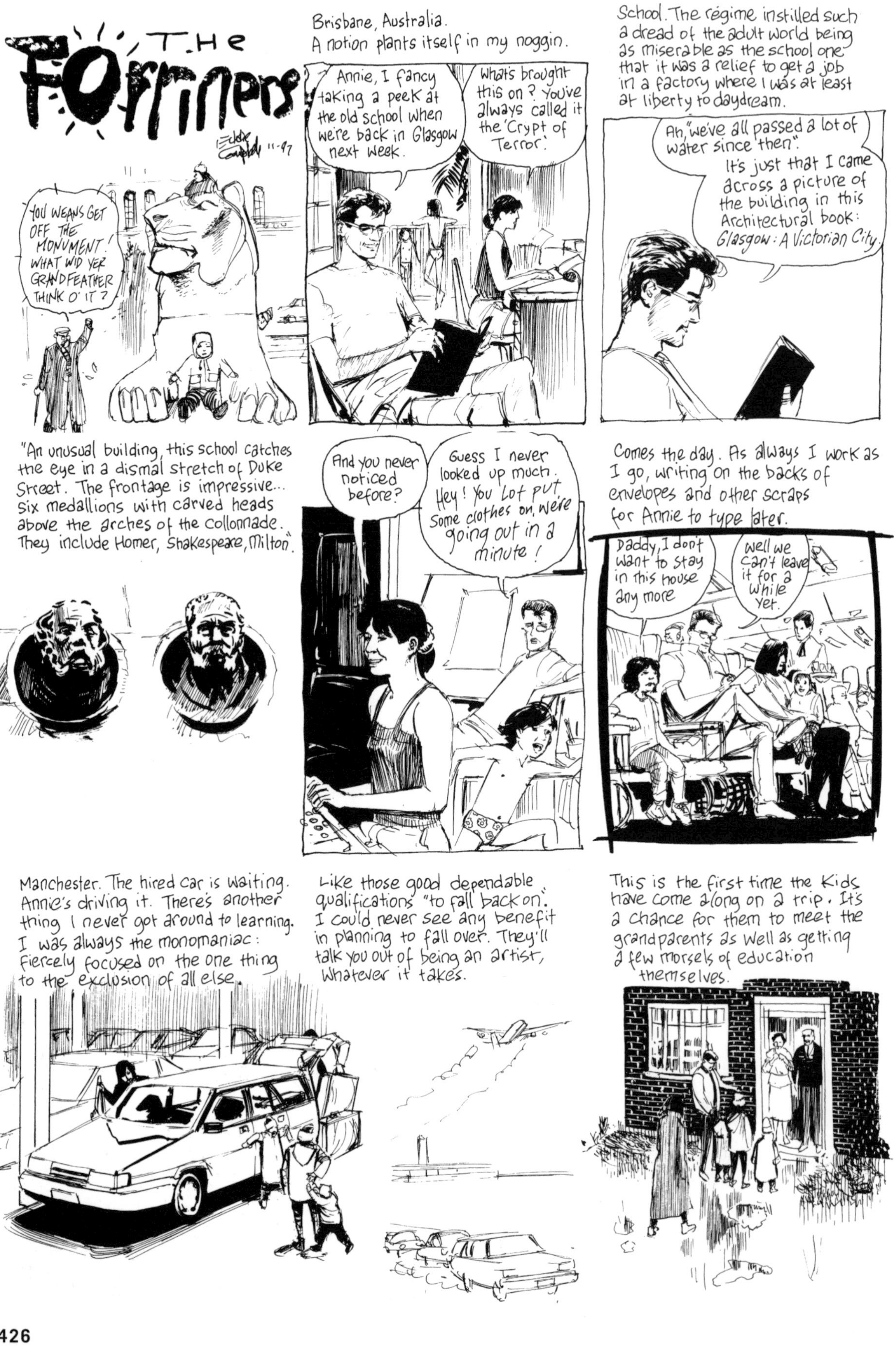
The Forriners
Eddie Campbell 11-97
YOU WEANS GET OFF THE MONUMENT! WHAT WID YER GRANDFEATHER THINK O' IT?
Brisbane, Australia.
A notion plants itself in my noggin.
Annie, I fancy taking a peek at the old school when we're back in Glasgow next week.
What's brought this on? You've always called it the 'Crypt of Terror'.
School. The régime instilled such a dread of the adult world being as miserable as the school one that it was a relief to get a job in a factory where I was at least at liberty to daydream.
Ah, "we've all passed a lot of water since then".
It's just that I came across a picture of the building in this Architectural book: Glasgow: A Victorian City.
"An unusual building, this school catches the eye in a dismal stretch of Duke Street. The frontage is impressive... six medallions with carved heads above the arches of the collonnade. They include Homer, Shakespeare, Milton".
And you never noticed before?
Guess I never looked up much. Hey! You lot put some clothes on, we're going out in a minute!
Comes the day. As always I work as I go, writing on the backs of envelopes and other scraps for Annie to type later.
Daddy, I don't want to stay in this house any more
Well we can't leave it for a while yet.
Manchester. The hired car is waiting. Annie's driving it. There's another thing I never got around to learning. I was always the monomaniac: fiercely focused on the one thing to the exclusion of all else.
Like those good dependable qualifications "to fall back on". I could never see any benefit in planning to fall over. They'll talk you out of being an artist, whatever it takes.
This is the first time the kids have come along on a trip. It's a chance for them to meet the grandparents as well as getting a few morsels of education themselves.

① Foreign languages
How's your yarm now, Grampar?
Aw yer a wee treasure you warm the cockles o'yer auld grand pas heart. It disny bother me at a' now.
Mummy Grampar does funny torks.
② Other climates
Wow! Where's that stuff coming from?
Weird. Do they just leave it lying around?
③ exotic cuisine
Now, you see, the beans make a wee lumpy lake on top of the pie.
once you bite the crust you have to eat quickly
My God, that's feral
Festy
Can we go now?
Hold on. I've just had another idea.
We check into the Copthorne on George Square
It was meant to be two connecting rooms.
I'm afraid we can't do anything about it at this late stage, sir.
I'm in town for a trade show and to hook up with some editorial people from the U.S.
Script? It's still at the pencil stage.
That's okay. I'd like to see it any way.
They're asleep. Your turn in twenty minutes.
The kids, safe in their room, wake up and go looking for the other room.
You hold the door
Okey

oh no! the door!
If mum finds out she'll have a spak attack Do you think that man will dob us in?
Dear Granmar Old men yell at us ol the time in Glasger
Missus, Don't let the weans wander all over the place like tha'. It's no safe fer godsake
SUKKY HALL STREET?
Aye, look. There it is up there S.A.U.C.H...
There it is. See what you think and I'll get it back tomorrow.
413
It's a few days before I remember to see the old Alma Mater.
Come on, kids. We're going to see Dad's school
TAXi
A feeling of unease grips me as we cross High street into Duke, just as it always did long ago
Twenty-five years have not softened the severity of those chiselled features under judgemental white wigs. I hear their voices; Homer, Aristotle, Michelangelo and the rest.
Submissions must be in neat double-spaced type.
Do the Art in your own time. Get Academic qualifications to fall back on.
You will not wear the combat jacket in my class again boy
brrr. Alright, let's go to Pizza Hut
Good onyer, Dad!
Eddie Campbell

On the Street Where I lived
SUBURBIA. ST
Wee Eddie Campbell 6/99.
There was a big woods behind the houses. Well, it seemed big to him when he lived there.
He had a recurring heroic half-dream where he was in a flat box go-cart, a wheeled wardrobe, I suppose, with mounted guns, hurtling down the slope, taking out the jerries, or teddy boys, or proddies...
BUDDA BUDDA
...whoever they were. Something to do with Rangers versus Celtic, he guessed, but it bewildered him later that nobody knew what he was talking about and neither did he.
FENIANS!
Proddy dogs
He became more introverted as he proceeded, watching the world go by from the dormer window of another house in another street.
dreaming of glugging wine in the Café Guerbois with the Impressionists.
making oil painting after oil painting, hundreds of them. He's scumbling down Cadmium street, brushing up against his heroes, greeting them with impasto.
Bong Zhoor M'sieu Campbell
The paintings pile up. He's cataloguing them in the certainty that a historian will be travelling back this way.
Then he throws them all in the bin one day when the bubble bursts.
Aw, no...and those ones of Grandma too?

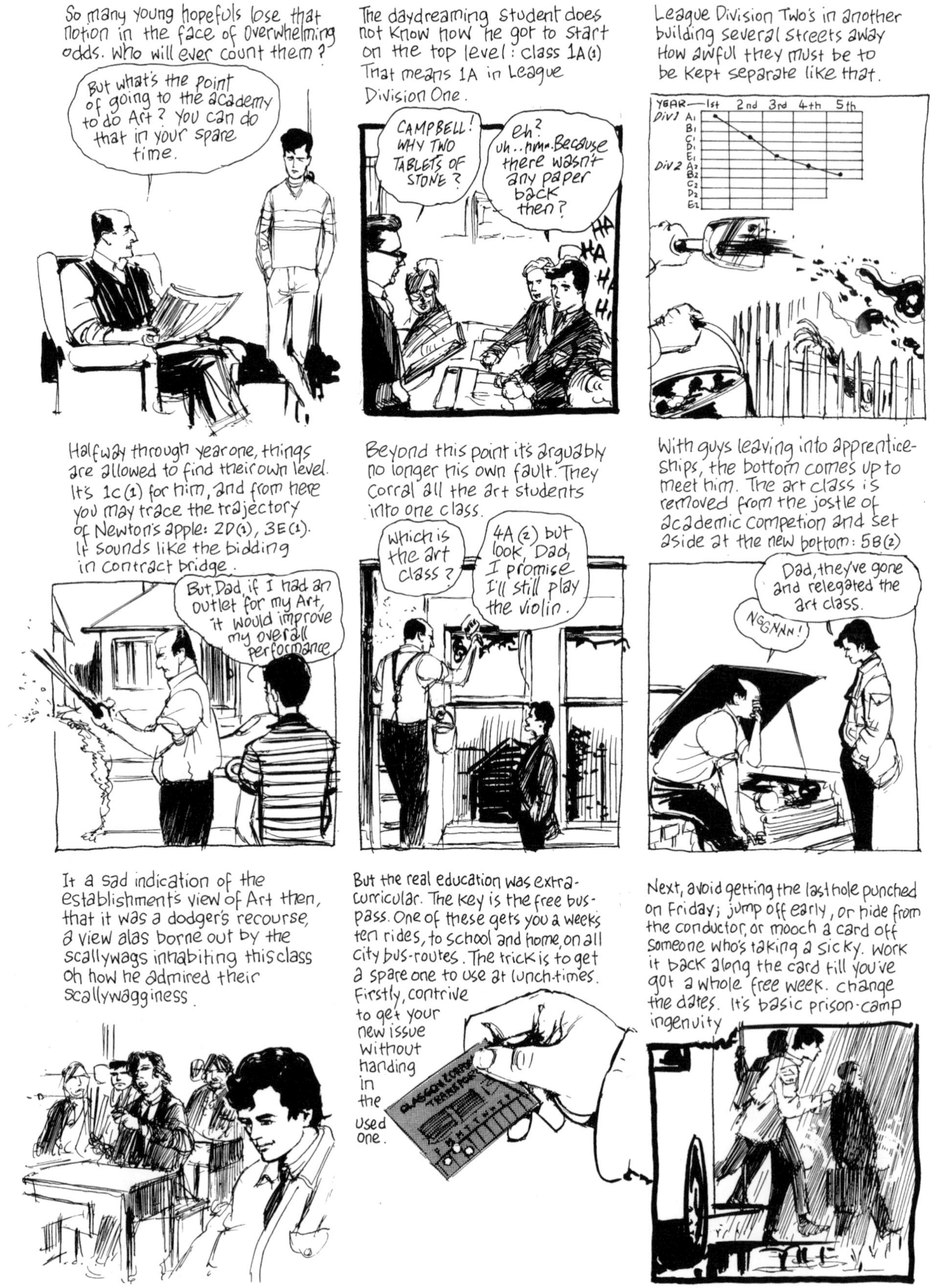
So many young hopefuls lose that notion in the face of overwhelming odds. Who will ever count them?
But what's the point of going to the academy to do Art? You can do that in your spare time.
The daydreaming student does not know how he got to start on the top level: class 1A(1) That means 1A in League Division One.
CAMPBELL! WHY TWO TABLETS OF STONE?
eh? uh..hm..Because there wasn't any paper back then?
HA HA HA HA
League Division Two's in another building several streets away How awful they must be to be kept separate like that.
YEAR 1st 2nd 3rd 4th 5th
DIV 1 A1 B1 C1 D1 E1
DIV 2 A2 B2 C2 D2 E2
Halfway through year one, things are allowed to find their own level. It's 1C(1) for him, and from here you may trace the trajectory of Newton's apple: 2D(1), 3E(1). It sounds like the bidding in contract bridge.
But, Dad, if I had an outlet for my Art, it would improve my overall performance
Beyond this point it's arguably no longer his own fault. They corral all the art students into one class.
Which is the art class?
4A(2) but look, Dad, I promise I'll still play the violin.
With guys leaving into apprenticeships, the bottom comes up to meet him. The art class is removed from the jostle of academic competion and set aside at the new bottom: 5B(2)
Dad, they've gone and relegated the art class.
NGGNNN!
It a sad indication of the establishment's view of Art then, that it was a dodger's recourse, a view alas borne out by the scallywags inhabiting this class oh how he admired their scallywagginess.
But the real education was extra-curricular. The key is the free bus-pass. One of these gets you a week's ten rides, to school and home, on all city bus-routes. The trick is to get a spare one to use at lunch-times.
Firstly, contrive to get your new issue without handing in the used one.
Next, avoid getting the last hole punched on Friday; jump off early, or hide from the conductor, or mooch a card off someone who's taking a sicky. Work it back along the card till you've got a whole free week. Change the dates. It's basic prison-camp ingenuity

Starting a week with two blank cards, he'll be jumping on and off buses, tearing around the city with his accumulated lunch money, learning a million things; second-hand books, Comics, Art gallery, the hunger for information outrunning the hunger for a ham sandwich.
The river, fish market veg market, the starlings in George' Square, the damn peculiar smell trapped under the Argyll Street bridge in this whisky-bottling city.
And in the street where he lives, in his head, it's all on the same street, all the information, conceptualization and reek and one reminds him of the other.
Monet and Renoir are painting boats. Susan Sontag's telling passersby about "a vision of the world in terms of style"
In the Coffee-a-go-go, Lee and Kirby's Bernard the poet is reading his phone bill
While in the Silver Spoon, Gwen and Mary Jane are dancing to the juke box. How he wishes he could be in their world.
Marshall McLuhan's having a massage. Picasso's passing off another parsimonious cheque for his lunch, knowing it will never get cashed.
SSAGE
RLOUR
Wee Eddie, since age 11, has the old '50s BATMAN ghost-artists down pat without knowing their names. "artist D" won't be "Lew Schwartz" for another 30 years.
BATMAN
He can't be snobby about Art after failing so triumphantly in order to get there.
Anthony! Come in for your tea!
Cat no. 228.

The move to
STRAIGHT STREET
Eddie Campbell. 6-00
Forty and still picking up his books from his parents' house.
What's this? Some of these oil paintings survived the purge.
Anthony
A world in the smell of paint.
Of turpentine.
LINSEED OIL
and smoky late afternoon associations.
Of sand and time.
The dead serious face in the mirror.
An old scrapbook filled with tiny ruled lines of lettering and not a single mistake. The entire nineteenth century of French painting.
Jesus
18

Then he had to move to Straight Street where the dreams get paved over.
Even wearing eyeglasses he can make no sense of the signs.
Succeed with caution
Get A-levels, get a career, get a driving license, 'get laid'.
Now he's got a girl friend. He meets her on the train when she's carrying an art portfolio.
He's feeling her bosoms in the park. He's coming in his trousers.
They're filling their time with daffy nonsense.
...in a fanciful shared place of the imagination that ends one day with a sulk.
He never knew why, just walked away.
Still, it was a mistake to make a pass at the sister on the way out.

He's not sure how he got into art school after doing a joke picture for the exam.
He doesn't last long there anyway. What was he thinking? That he could make a living pouring the stuff in his head out onto paper.
Despite efforts by his supervisors to improve his standa
and the attention drawn to his shortcomings, Mr Campbell
displays an apathetic lack of interest, his output is
disappointing, there are too many omissions and his erro
rate is not acceptable.
Because of his general lethargy I cannot see that he
improve and can only report that I am not
the post of clerical
Another lot goes in the bin. All the comics with which he imagined he would astonish the world.
What a wanker! I'm going to punch him in the back of the head
No! You'll see it differently in a few years.
Yes! He needs a wake-up call!
BOF!
URG
WHA—?
Bastid!
It's a strange winter of the mind
where self-cancelled people notice each other on Straight Street.
It happens once in Paris. He's not sure if it's bad or good, a fight or what?

And he remembers that strange punch on the back of the head.
But which way to the Café Guerbois?
REPUBLIQUE
And what's he doing here anyway? and with all these condoms?.
Why were you taking Sharon to Paris? I dont think you even like her. Her mothers been phoning here...
Mum! I'm not even in the door.
Monday Morning. His heart sinks in the factory gloom.
And yet there's a calm here. A quiet respite. No pressure. Time to work things out.
Explain it to me. He had his chance at Art School, then he had a civil service job only an idiot could lose. What's the matter with him?
I'm worried.
Och, the boy's head's in the clouds.
SUNDAY TELEGRA
Eddie Campbell

Give us a hug then!
Eddie Campbell 6/99
There was a news item recently where Doctor Spock's son came out and said:
My father was supposed to be the expert in child rearing. His was THE book on the subject
It says it there see
But I'll tell you.. he never once hugged us.
What a bunch of fuckin' Pansies we have all become.
My daddy never hugged me and now I'm all fucked up
Boo hoo
You make me sick, the lot of you! You're a failure so you blame it on the old man? Give me a break!
My brother tried that one:
My therapist says it's all because you never hugged me.
Aw, so help ma boab.
But it's not too late to start.
Eddy, maybe it wouldn't hurt to give it a try
Och, am off to watch the fitbaw.

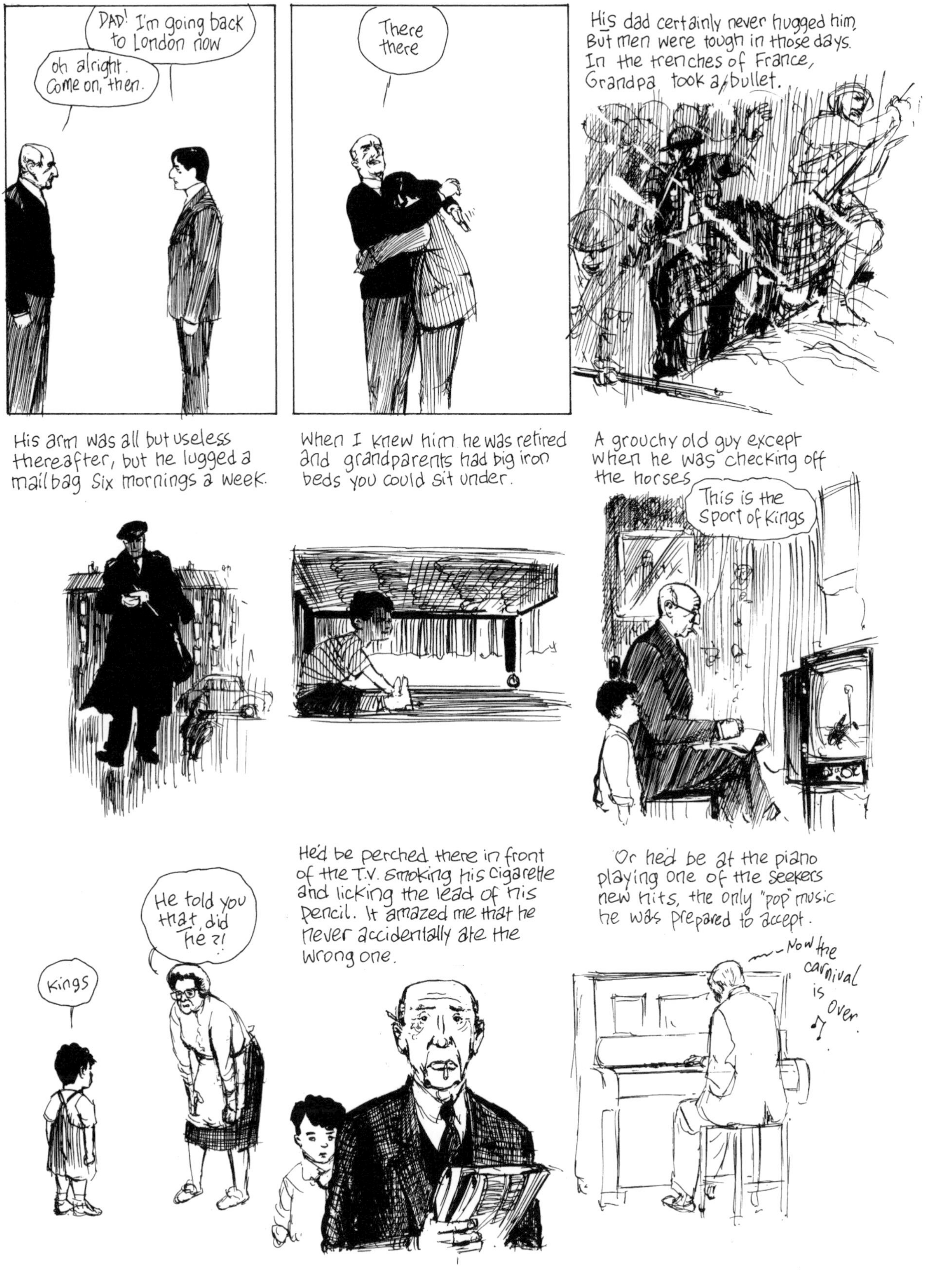
DAD! I'm going back to London now
oh alright. Come on, then.
There there
His dad certainly never hugged him, But men were tough in those days. In the trenches of France, Grandpa took a bullet.
His arm was all but useless thereafter, but he lugged a mailbag six mornings a week.
When I knew him he was retired and grandparents had big iron beds you could sit under.
A grouchy old guy except when he was checking off the horses
This is the Sport of Kings
Kings
He told you that, did he?!
He'd be perched there in front of the T.V. smoking his cigarette and licking the lead of his pencil. It amazed me that he never accidentally ate the wrong one.
Or he'd be at the piano playing one of the seekers new hits, the only "pop" music he was prepared to accept.
Now the carnival is over

I don't remember any kind of contact ever, even when I had to be hauled out of somewhere.
Ella! get the boy out of there.
AYE, DA
Dad was telling a story the other day:
It was the day you got hit by a car, when you were seven... I was on my way to the hospital, waiting at the bus stop when...
Waitaminnit. I've been run over and you're taking a bus to the hospital... DAD!
I've been drawing him with a broken arm. This is how that happened:
So there you go. I changed the cheque for you and there's the other—
A
AA
DAD! Are you all right down there?
Aye, I'll just be up in a minute.
Are you sure?
Aye.
So help ma boab.

The Magus is house-proud

by Eddie Campbell

30. 12. 98.

"I'm buying a house, Eddie. I have to come out of all this with something"

And of course, there is the basement.

ah! a basement...

So while we're in Britain we visit the *Magus*. He meets us at the *Red Lion*, with Melinda. A guy named *Fred* appears to be filling the role of chauffeur.

Fiery Fred is celebrated in the *Magus'* first novel, not published yet at the time of my visit. A man "...with the courage and fines of his convictions, both outstanding." He "was handling the door the night Iain Sinclair and... Brian Catling did their reading at the Holy Sepulchre"

Halfway through; an interruption. ("poetry hooligan".) Two teeth knocked out, blood everywhere.

The poets are gleeful at this real-life fracas. Read the book.

A lot of stuff has changed since I last saw the *Magus* only 3 years ago for a quick beer in London. I got held up that day because of a body on the tracks. His grim view of the world starts to get to you when you fall within his orbit. He's waiting down the line. You just have to get past a dead body.

I observe the changing cast of characters in his life as though they are the characters in his books, by the analysis of whom we may understand the authorial method.

Did *From Hell* open the door to a new reputation or vice versa. From comic book guru to well known English oddball, requested for sometime TV appearances, once (an anecdote in the intro to one of the Magus' books) by Sinclair whom he notices characterized on the schedule as:

"Freak wrangler"
HEH HEH

They pop up in each other's books. (Sinclair): "When we turned up (to photograph Christ Church) the building was filled with smoke...

"A documentary was being shot in which Alan Moore realized the Church and its fellow East End leviathans according to some dangerous occult prescription. (Christ Church) had willingly rented itself out as a set for Clive Barker's history of horror."

In his own recollection of the night, *I Keep Coming Back*, he's in the Ten Bells afterwards, a crucial site in *From Hell*. "I don't mean to do it. It just happens. Write about a place and you're cemented to it." Geographical locations become significant in his work.

In another pub, in his home town, he's painted on the ceiling in the company of 19th century poet, John Clare. His grand subject narrows till it becomes this town; its presence, its history.

NOT PAINTED ON ANY CEILING EXCEPT IN HIS OWN HEAD

The Magus places the town of Northampton at the point in England furthest from any sea and characterizes it as a black hole: "Nothing that gets out of here is not pulled back in"

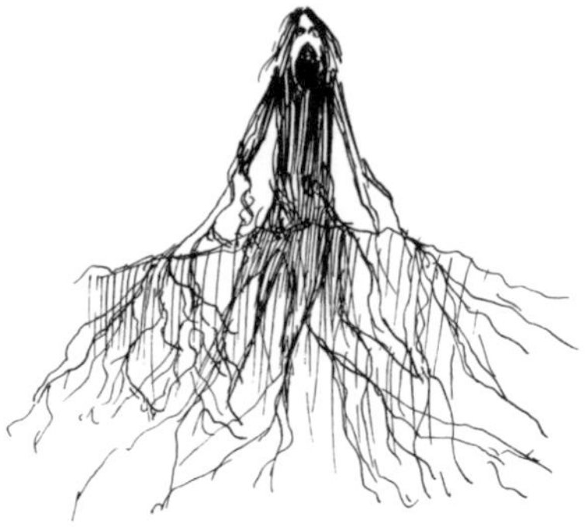

An idealistic image from one of his earlier comics comes back to me: the Parliament of Trees: "Lived too long and grown too wise for the distractions of the world".

"... so much that I had not imagined in the unmappable continent of their mind"

Perhaps our home town shapes us more than we'd like to think: Glasgow as a big river city with ships taking people somewhere else.

Each book takes the magus closer to home. The one we share is about London: "The pictorial aspect" (wrote Sinclair) "proved very seductive to the Hollywood dealmakers, who increasingly want product served neat."

Yes, Hollywood wants to turn From Hell into a movie. Somewhere, a green light is turned on.
He has an alchemical touch; not only the ability to create saleable ideas at the drop of a hat but also to turn the humdrum into something magical. This would be the magus' third foray into moviedom, but with not a scrap of celluloid to show for it.
A house, yes, with the rest of the money going out its windows in delicious clouds of fragrant smoke.
The magus has an idea to convert his house into a moorish palace.
Fancy glazed screens are installed, with order on one side and chaos encroaching upon the other.
The bathroom is developed under the enterprise of Fred, builder. He and his mates fashion the stainedglass porthole, depicting Asmoday, after a sketch made by the magus following his audience with the grand duke.
The magus sacrifices to his patron, the snake god, Glycon. Being a vegetarian, he burns only a cherished possession, a letter, a photo, its essence now removed to 'idea-space'.
Rats, some dozen cheery pets, live happily in his daughters room in a bank of cages, free from any threat.
What do you think of all those rats then?
Dad, they weren't all rats! there were five rats, four mice, one hamster, a snake and a chombywomby.
chinchilla?

"The bed is comfortable and the big attic room serene, another Fred conversion."
As everyone knows, the joy of home ownership lies in being able to bang nails in the wall anytime you feel like it, without asking anyone's permission. One day the basement is dug out into an enormous dark cavern.
Anyone who has dabbled in renovations, or any creative endeavour for that matter, knows the difficulty of escorting one's original vision all the way through to a concrete reality.
It gets so far and has a tendency to stay like that. The magus turns to consider a delicate phrase for about four years or so.
"The smile might be mistaken for a friendly one...
"...were it not for the cold, sardonic and unwavering superiority always apparent in Gull's eyes."
"To him, everyone else is a particularly amusing strain of paramecium"
Why, it seems like only yesterday that he converted his basement into the gaping maw of Hell.
Even if I get it finished, I'm here forever. I can never sell it...
Anybody who'd want a moorish palace wouldn't want it on Canal Street.

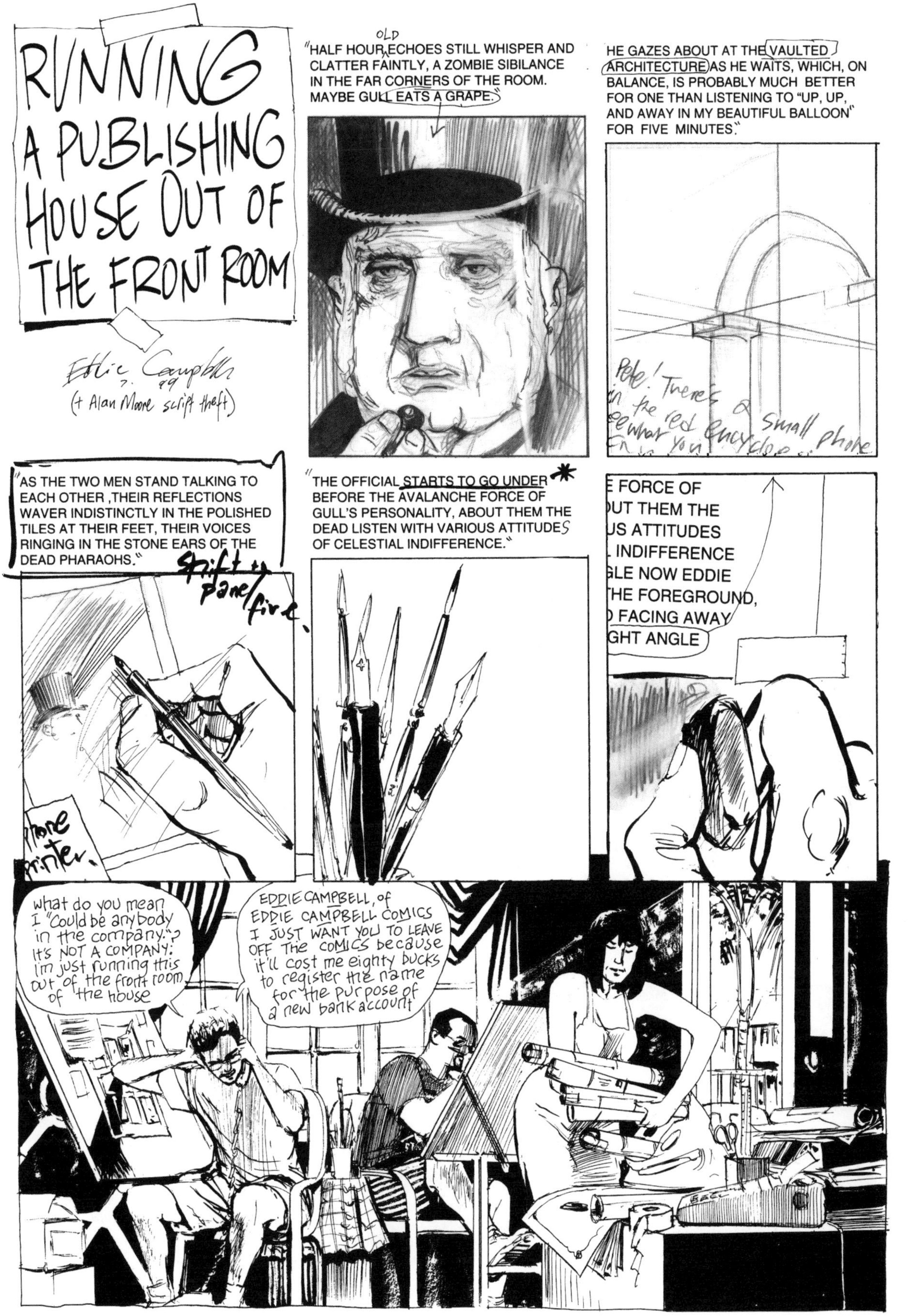
RUNNING A PUBLISHING HOUSE OUT OF THE FRONT ROOM
Eddie Campbell 7. 99
(+ Alan Moore script theft)
"HALF HOUR OLD ECHOES STILL WHISPER AND CLATTER FAINTLY, A ZOMBIE SIBILANCE IN THE FAR CORNERS OF THE ROOM. MAYBE GULL EATS A GRAPE."
HE GAZES ABOUT AT THE VAULTED ARCHITECTURE AS HE WAITS, WHICH, ON BALANCE, IS PROBABLY MUCH BETTER FOR ONE THAN LISTENING TO "UP, UP, AND AWAY IN MY BEAUTIFUL BALLOON" FOR FIVE MINUTES."
Pete! There's a
small phone
"AS THE TWO MEN STAND TALKING TO EACH OTHER ,THEIR REFLECTIONS WAVER INDISTINCTLY IN THE POLISHED TILES AT THEIR FEET, THEIR VOICES RINGING IN THE STONE EARS OF THE DEAD PHARAOHS."
shift to panel five.
"THE OFFICIAL STARTS TO GO UNDER* BEFORE THE AVALANCHE FORCE OF GULL'S PERSONALITY, ABOUT THEM THE DEAD LISTEN WITH VARIOUS ATTITUDES OF CELESTIAL INDIFFERENCE."
E FORCE OF
UT THEM THE
US ATTITUDES
INDIFFERENCE
GLE NOW EDDIE
THE FOREGROUND,
FACING AWAY
GHT ANGLE
phone printer.
what do you mean I "could be anybody in the company."? it's NOT A COMPANY: I'm just running this out of the front room of the house
EDDIE CAMPBELL, of EDDIE CAMPBELL COMICS I JUST WANT YOU TO LEAVE OFF the COMICS because it'll cost me eighty bucks to register the name for the purpose of a new bank account

MAIL
MAIL
my, aren't we all busy little elves
Mick! Just in time for coffee.
You're such a fuckin' amateur, Campbell, but I got it into photoshop and cleaned up your awful mess. Now it's as flash as a rat with a gold tooth. It's shmicko!
Don't get too technical. You know Eddie doesn't like that.
Now, I traded off some typesetting for the scans, but it'll cost us a carton of beer for the negs. 'mates rates'
I can't hang about here all day with you wankers
wey hey.
Marcus!
well look who's here
Just get your page here by Thurs day.
You know the ad on the TV... the mint made for mouths. I've just had an idea.. What if they made mints for your arse?!
An arse-mint! brilliant.
Don't the Japanese already have them?
If you're not using it, that would fit nicely into the current Bacchus story.
I thought so too.
why don't you put the kettle on.

Wouldn't it be easier to just buy the paper at A3 size ?
Eddie reckons we can save twenty bucks this way.
Marcus. Can you turn off the CD as you pass. His jazz music's giving me a headache
I'll do the mail and bank and then we'll have lunch
Eddie! Chris here. There's another box smashed up in California. Why don't you get your printer in Canada to double-box all the books.
But that would cost extra.
I had an idea for the cover. Here's a sketch.
a sketch?
Hi, Dad
Hey Pete. Don't fill in the blacks. Leave something for Anne to do.
Hello Pete
Sorry - I got carried away
"Hey, Pete! Let's eat more meat"

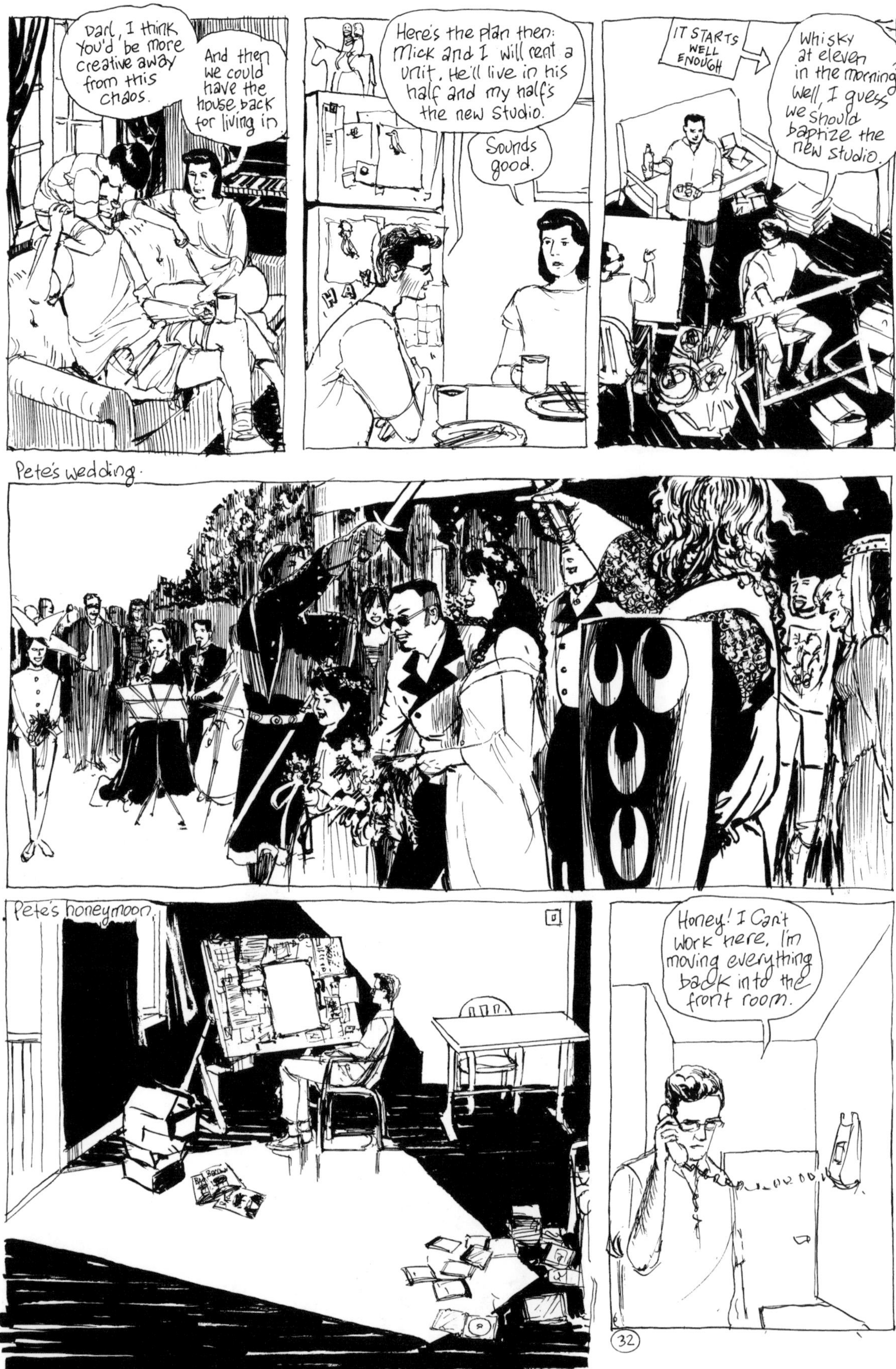
Darl, I think you'd be more creative away from this chaos.
And then we could have the house back for living in
Here's the plan then: Mick and I will rent a unit. He'll live in his half and my half's the new studio.
Sounds good.
IT STARTS WELL ENOUGH
Whisky at eleven in the morning? Well, I guess we should baptize the new studio.
Pete's wedding.
Pete's honeymoon.
Honey! I can't work here, I'm moving everything back into the front room.
32

MAIL
cor, what's that supposed to be, Dad?
Eddie, this is Chalky. About that guy who wants cartoons for his new magazine. I saw him today...
Nice painting, Pete. Dad should get you to do them all.
Hey, Pete! Look at this cool thing I found.
Half a bloody hour it took just to bank a foreign cheque, so the xeroxes will have to wait till tomorrow
FED EX! you have a package for me?
FedEx
Federal Express
What's Marcus doing asleep on the couch?
Oh, jeezis! I forgot about him.
DAD! you said you'd take the fax out of my bed room!
Eddie Campbell.

Another sleepless night

...but then, of course, Herrmann scored Citizen Kane too
That would explain it.
I'll see you Monday then
I might come on the bike if it's not too hot and I'm not too lazy
All-you-can-eat salad bar... or fish'n'chips?
FISH AND CHIPS
Puss
FISH LOVERS
The cat with the broken miaow
Goodnight darling.
G'Night Daddy

No more, honey
Whuzzr

!
Oh my goodness! Isn't that something. It's not even touching the carpet.
You want to go out, don't you.
There you go
Sigh
Aw Shit

Bacchus?
Have a glass of milk.
Make it a snifter of brandy
The Snooter?

Can't sleep again, eh?
It's the damn cats. And the bloody traffic out there. We're at the bottom of a hill, just before a roundabout, so cars are either braking or changing gear outside my window.
Once I'm awake I can't help but hear my bike being stolen, ...the vegetables my children didn't eat, decomposing in the dustbin...
At night when the traffic subsides, they're dismantling the welfare system.
They turn the clock of time faster at night when we're not paying attention.
The precepts we thought engraved in stone are being sanded down.
They're putting illusions in their places. By the time sun comes up you can't tell.
HAVE YOU THOUGHT OF GIVING UP THE DRINK ?

What has that got to do with it?
Drink has got to do with everything that goes wrong in you.
"Although moderate drinking will not kill irreplaceable brain cells, as once argued, alcohol use can interfere with sleep, with memory and with cognition.
How much would you have to pour down your gullet to qualify for that?
Well, how much do you drink?
I'm hardly a heavy drinker; a glass of white wine with my salad lunch, a gin and tonic in the late afternoon watching the sun go down from my verandah... a couple of glasses of wine with dinner... a wee nightcap with wifey while we review the events of our day...
SWOON
I shall start from the beginning.
A. Allergies: Alcohol is only one ingredient of alcoholic beverages. Others include grains, yeast, fruit, malt, molasses, spices, colouring agents and preservatives, all of which may produce allergic reactions in susceptible individuals.
B. Birth Defects: The Journal of the American Medical Association has reported: having just one or two drinks daily while pregnant is associated with a substantially increased risk of producing a growth-retarded infant.
C. Cancer: "After cigarettes, alcohol is probably one of the most important environmental influences on cancer." According to William Bennett of the Harvard Medical School Health Letter.
"Excess alcohol intake clearly raises the risk of developing cancer in the liver, mouth and esophagus. Many other cancers in the lung, pancreas, intestines, prostate and recently breast have also been related to alcohol."
D. Digestion: Alcohol irritates the stomach lining—
NO MORE! STOP!

– the story behind this one?
Ah! The Doctor. The Elector of Trier, in 1360, seriously ill and fed up with his physicians, drank himself back to health. The vineyard was duly dubbed 'the doctor'.
The various proprietors of the famous *Doctor* vineyard have been in a position to charge like a bull for their wine ever since a British King expressed a fondness for it.
...while the neighbouring vineyards, it is said, have been justifiably miffed since their wine is just as good but sells for considerably less.
Didn't think you'd fall for that old label hype
I had to know for myself. We'd just got the down-payment for the movie rights.
We sped out in the car and spent 300 bucks on a handful of bottles of wine. It was a heady moment.
Look, darl! A furniture sale! We need a coffee table
Stop the car. We'll shove one in the back.
And the other one you're holding; the *Colares*; a fellow in Portugal sent me that after I did the story about you and the vines curled up in bunches on the ground to keep them low out of the Atlantic winds.
He couldn't have known this ten year old red was vintaged in the year Annie and I got married. We drank it on our anniversary. It's so easy to forget that every empty bottle up here is a treasure. Only the special ones make it of course.
Each one was a place and a time captured in a bottle and another place and time in the glass. Almost every wine-making country in the world is represented here

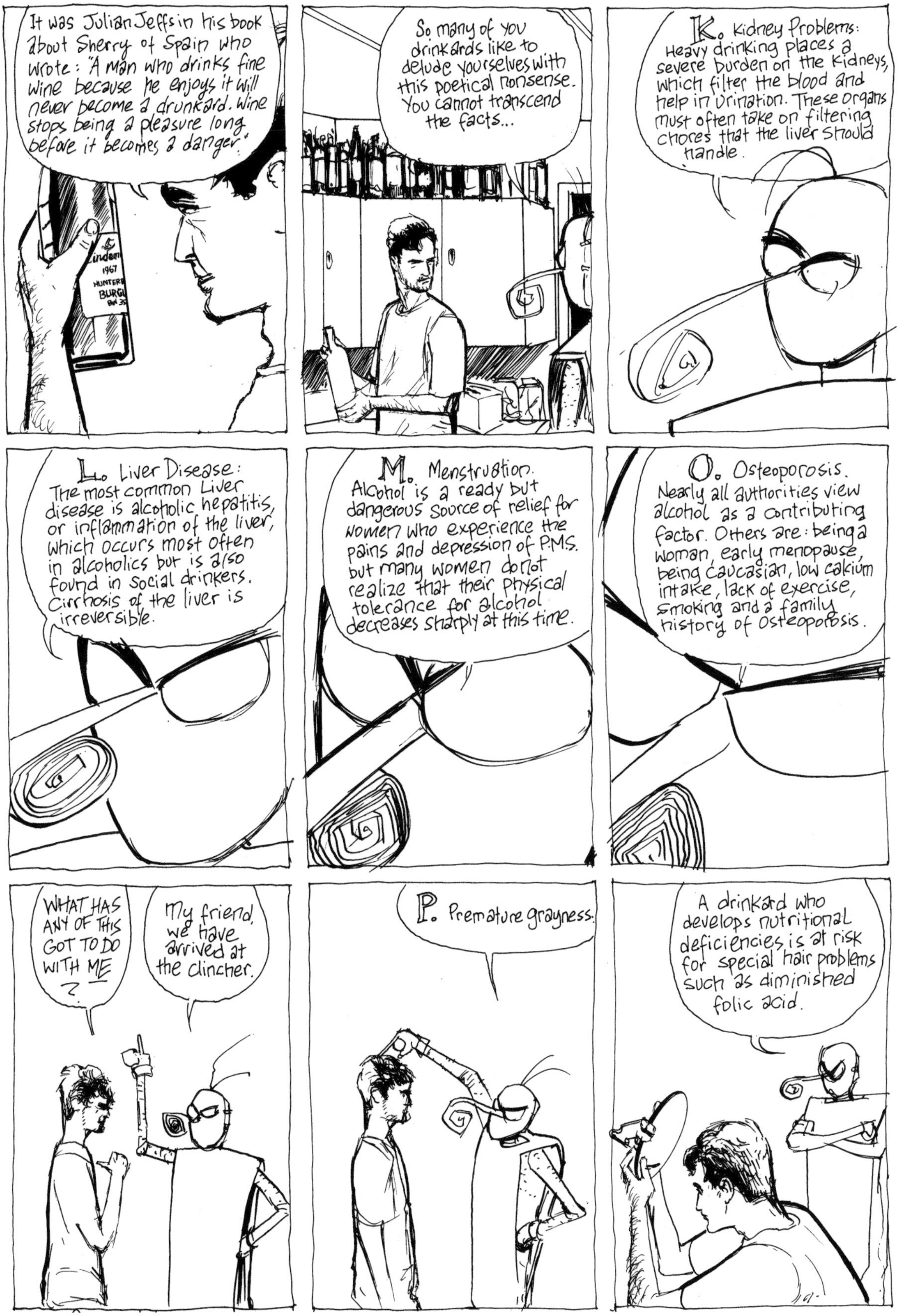
It was Julian Jeffs in his book about Sherry of Spain who wrote: "A man who drinks fine wine because he enjoys it will never become a drunkard. Wine stops being a pleasure long before it becomes a danger."
So many of you drinkards like to delude yourselves with this poetical nonsense. You cannot transcend the facts...
K. Kidney Problems: Heavy drinking places a severe burden on the kidneys, which filter the blood and help in urination. These organs must often take on filtering chores that the liver should handle.
L. Liver Disease: The most common liver disease is alcoholic hepatitis, or inflammation of the liver, which occurs most often in alcoholics but is also found in social drinkers. Cirrhosis of the liver is irreversible.
M. Menstruation. Alcohol is a ready but dangerous source of relief for women who experience the pains and depression of P.M.S. but many women do not realize that their physical tolerance for alcohol decreases sharply at this time.
O. Osteoporosis. Nearly all authorities view alcohol as a contributing factor. Others are: being a woman, early menopause, being caucasian, low calcium intake, lack of exercise, smoking and a family history of osteoporosis.
WHAT HAS ANY OF THIS GOT TO DO WITH ME?
My friend, we have arrived at the clincher.
P. Premature grayness.
A drinkard who develops nutritional deficiencies is at risk for special hair problems such as diminished folic acid.

Wait a minute! A drinkard?
Take off the mask!
Ugnh
Just as I thought: MR. DRY!
I wondered when you'd notice.
Of course! How could I be so stupid? The Snooter symbolizes the dark encroaching terrors of the night...
...while Mr. Dry represents that part of human society which presumes to know what is best for its fellows.
You are the Wowser, the killjoy. You have no poetry in your soul and cannot recognise it in others.
My old pal Simpson used to recite a poem by Robert Herrick... lemme see if I can recall it... "Born was I to be old...
"And for to die here. After that, in the mould, Long for to lye here...

"But before that day comes, Still I be bousing For I Know in the tombs There's no Carousing."
You get yourself back to bed. I'll see this buzzard off the premises!
MILK
You want back in? Make up your mind.
CLICK
That means the Snooter is still out there... in the dark... watching... waiting.
Bring on the morning! Roll all the demons up inside the curtains
A bright new day!
Daddy, if you gave food to your bottom, would it come out your mouth?
Of course it would, darling
Campbell

Eddie Campbell.
3/00
VISITATION
"Look at them tracing their desperation, the makers of strong images.
Look at their ink clotting brown and black on the parchment skin
Look: they render us down there limb from limb."
© Neil Gaiman Angels and Visitations.
Neil Gaiman comes for a visit while he's down this side of the planet doing an appearance in Adelaide
It was a sci-fi con. A lovely lady named Helen organized my appearance and looked after me.
He came out of the same small-publishing milieu as I did, just after I left Britain and then he burst onto the international scene.
This would be the first time I'd really gotten together with him not counting a few brushes at convention parties (when the business still flourished enough for that sort of thing)...
...and a fragmentary communication I had with him on his answering machine when I was passing near Little Nutley and he still lived there.
Eddie, I was in the garden. If you phone again...
Determined to pin him down for a proper conversation, I've arranged to take up an open invite at the university to present a talk. This way, at least, we won't be interrupted
We omit to discuss the subject until the very last minute.
We'll just wing our way through the history of comics
and I haven't really got the hang of talking on this scale yet, but it goes down well enough.
There are three things that distinguish the medium of comics. Thing one:
Actually, that's the opening of another speech on another occasion, but what the hey!
And they write us cheques there and then for $150 each.

So I pick up some fine wines, we have dinner and everybody gets to meet Neil.
I've got two or three Australian wines here I want to tell you about.
Two or three ?..
Hayley's wearing Neil's famous jacket, a period piece which he reckons is made from buffalo or elephant hide or some other impenetrable beastie.
Chalky White's being belligerent about President Clinton's impending impeachment.
A politician's only skill is his good name and reputation. If he stuffs that up he's lost the reason he's there!
I'm not saying I vote for the guy, but if he does his job well enough, shouldn't we just be thankful and not make an issue of his private life?
At last we get some time alone.
No, it's not the drink, it's something about this phase of life, I think.
Or maybe it's just me. Things get easier, but it's all a veneer.
The Beasts of cancer and catastrophe lurk behind the phony curtain of daylight, with its cheery, gibbering distractions.
This is for you, Neil

oh, this is wonderful. I can use this when I side with the dwarfs in the beleaguering of Angband.
And I will turn the tide of battle as I pick off the Balrogs, shooting them slap-bang upon their hairy bottoms.
But it's only a stick.
This "stick"... shall have pride of place in my luggage.
Denis Kitchen asked me to write a Spirit story: I want you to draw it.
Will Eisner's SPIRIT! hoo hah!
I'll call you.
Darl, if money weren't a worry, what wine would you drink tonight?
eh? Money's always a worry. One of our distributors just went bankrupt.
we just had a party. Now it's back to work.
It's always either a feast or a famine with you

Anne, where's my striped shirt?
I'll talk to you later
I threw it out.
You didn't!
When I was a kid, no shirt ever got thrown out! My mother used to turn them into painting smocks.
The collars would be frayed from my Dad's stubble but she'd cut them off and sew a tidy edge around.
I thought they were real cool, like olde worlde shirts when collars used to be separate.
I remember her looking horrified when she found me wearing one at the shops.
Hi Mum
Oh my God, you're a sight.
Of course, the paint stains were another matter altogether.
But I'm an artist! I'm entitled to have paint all over me.
Sigh... give me a hand with these spuds
But not Bolognese Sauce!
RING
I'LL GET IT!
Okay. Keep your shirt on.
HEH HEH
RING

you've been working hard, darl. You deserve a better wine than that. What are the good ones?
You know I'm holding a tight rein on things right now, honey.
MORRIS
Yes, but if you weren't so bloody Scottish...
Is that your secret friend again?
What's going on?
How am I supposed to have my own life with you around the house all the time?
I bloody work here! I'm saving money by working at home!
What the hell are you up to? Skulking around on the phone!
All RIGHT! I'll tell you! It was supposed to be a surprise!

Neil sent his cheque for $150 to Helen in Adelaide and asked her to get you a bottle of wine with it. It's my job to find out what one you'd like.
But you don't deserve it!
And you don't deserve a friend like Neil! WAHHHH
Let me see... She could get a '79 Grange Hermitage and still have enough left for packaging...
Not as grand as the celebrated 1980, but my oh my...
Note from my Dad
I confess I crammed the events of two separate, five-year apart Neil visits into this one narrative, but memory is a big plate of soup in this book.
£13,200 wine
Adelaide: A bottle of 1951 Penfolds Grange Hermitage wine fetched an Australian record of A$33,660 (about £13,200) at auction. It was bought by an anonymous collector from Queensland. There are fewer than 100 bottles left in the world. (AP)

The accOuntant
LIBERTY
1998
CHALKY WHITE
You can't drink that! It's your future.
Eddie Campbell 8.00
It's quite simple, really. What you do is: set up an excluded superannuation fund, say the Bacchus Super Fund, with the Campbell family as the sole beneficiaries.
Then you buy an off-the-shelf company and transfer a single share each to you and Anne.
You and Anne then appoint yourselves as directors and as directors you agree to act as corporate trustee for the Bacchus Super fund.
You then make tax deductable contributions into the fund until you reach your specific age-determined maximum, therefore considerably reducing your assessable income.
The contributions are taxed as they enter the Super Fund but that doesn't matter because, as a regulated Super Fund, tax is only payable at 15%.
Then, as corporate trustee, you determine that the investment strategy of the Bacchus Super Fund will be to invest in Fine Wine.
You spend all of the money on Grange Hermitage. You do a proper job and keep the wine cellared for ten to fifteen years and then sell it off at a considerable profit.
That's bloody brilliant! Okay, what do I have to do?
First you lodge form FD450-X74
Babble

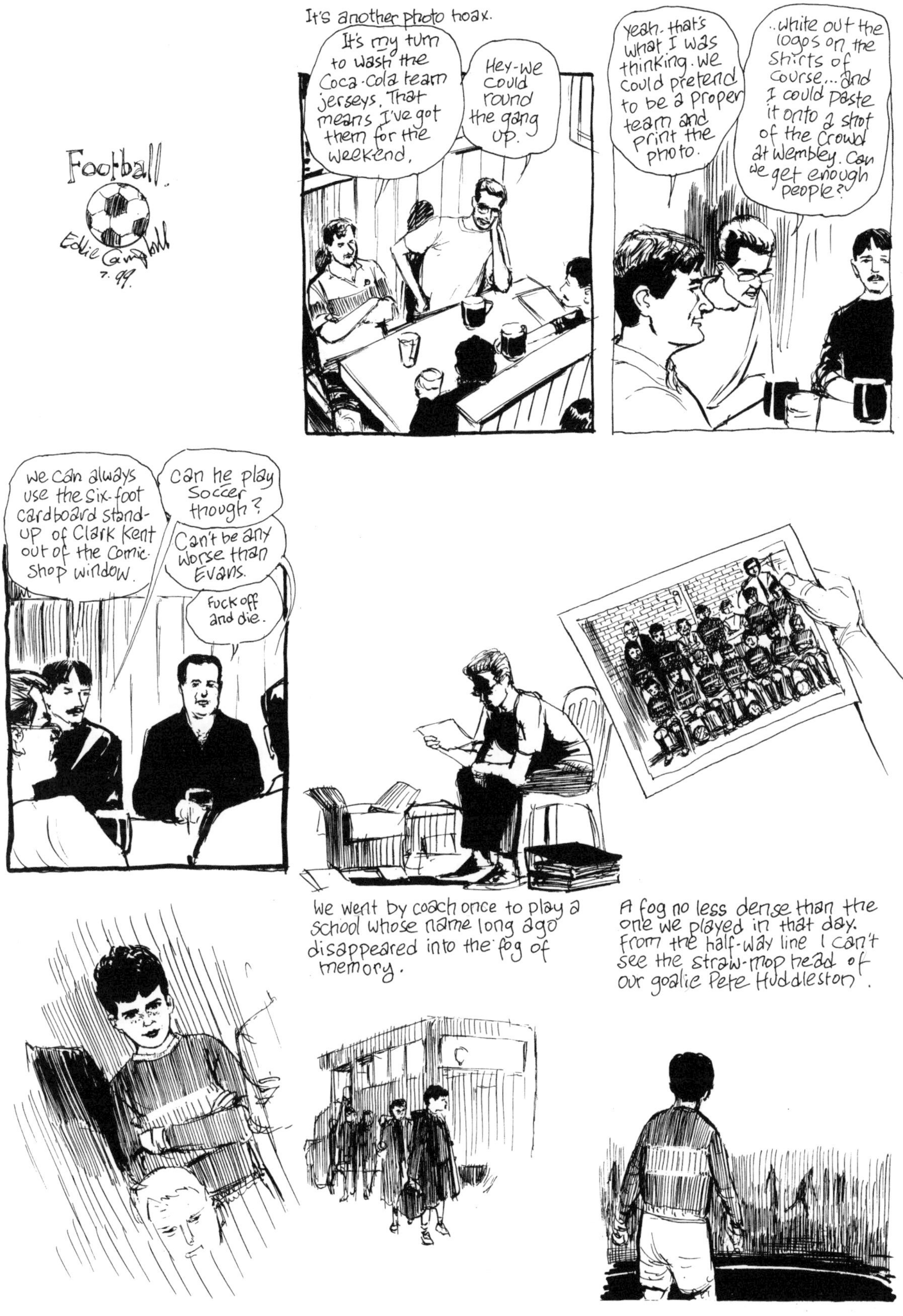
Football.
Eddie Campbell 7.99.
It's another photo hoax.
It's my turn to wash the Coca-Cola team jerseys. That means I've got them for the weekend.
Hey-we could round the gang up.
Yeah. that's what I was thinking. We could pretend to be a proper team and print the photo.
..white out the logos on the shirts of course... And I could paste it onto a shot of the crowd at Wembley. Can we get enough people?
We can always use the six-foot cardboard stand-up of Clark Kent out of the comic shop window.
Can he play soccer though?
Can't be any worse than Evans.
Fuck off and die.
We went by coach once to play a school whose name long ago disappeared into the fog of memory.
A fog no less dense than the one we played in that day. From the half-way line I can't see the straw-mop head of our goalie Pete Huddleston.

A pro. match would have been cancelled in these conditions. Willie Callahan's rubbing his hands gleefully, glad to be out of the office. He's taken the day off work to see his boys in action.
Nobody knew him before he'd been brought in, a friend of a teacher's son, to shape this team, drilling it in the ways of intelligent team-play.
You can always tell complete amateurs by the way they all chase the ball around.
Wankers
Yeh
I DIDN'T HEAR THAT
Now we're climbing up the league, game by game, and a bit of mist is nothing to us. Our home pitch is on a 15° slope.
Shuggy MacDonald comes out of the fog and goes back in; lapping waves and the horn of a coast-bound trawler.
Movement at the inside-left position. That'll be Jim Ireland. Looks more Jack the Ripper.
Sound of Stephen Patterson thrashing about in the middle. Ball's coming forward!
"Trust the instruments!" shouted Captain Biggles.
"Everybody will be where they're supposed to be when you come out of the clouds, flying low."
I skim it across to the right. Yup. Wee John Murphy's got it.

What's happening over there? Is he dribbling it around in circles again? Oh! It's back!
It's up to me! It's all noise and my heart's in my throat. The goal's in front of me!
I'm in slow motion. I'm halfway toward it.
Now I'm half of that distance.
To regular eyes I'm not moving, like the wee man on top of the trophy.
If I went back to that pitch today I'd still be on it, frozen in time forever. Prehistoric ice-boy.
You're always taking pictures of yourselves. You never take any of us girls
Yes, but this is a jest on a collossal scale
Wear the jumper, Callum. You're supposed to be the ball boy!
No!
I've brought some funny hats
I brought my netball trophies like you asked. I hope you're not going to break them.
Where's Slattery? He said he'd be here.

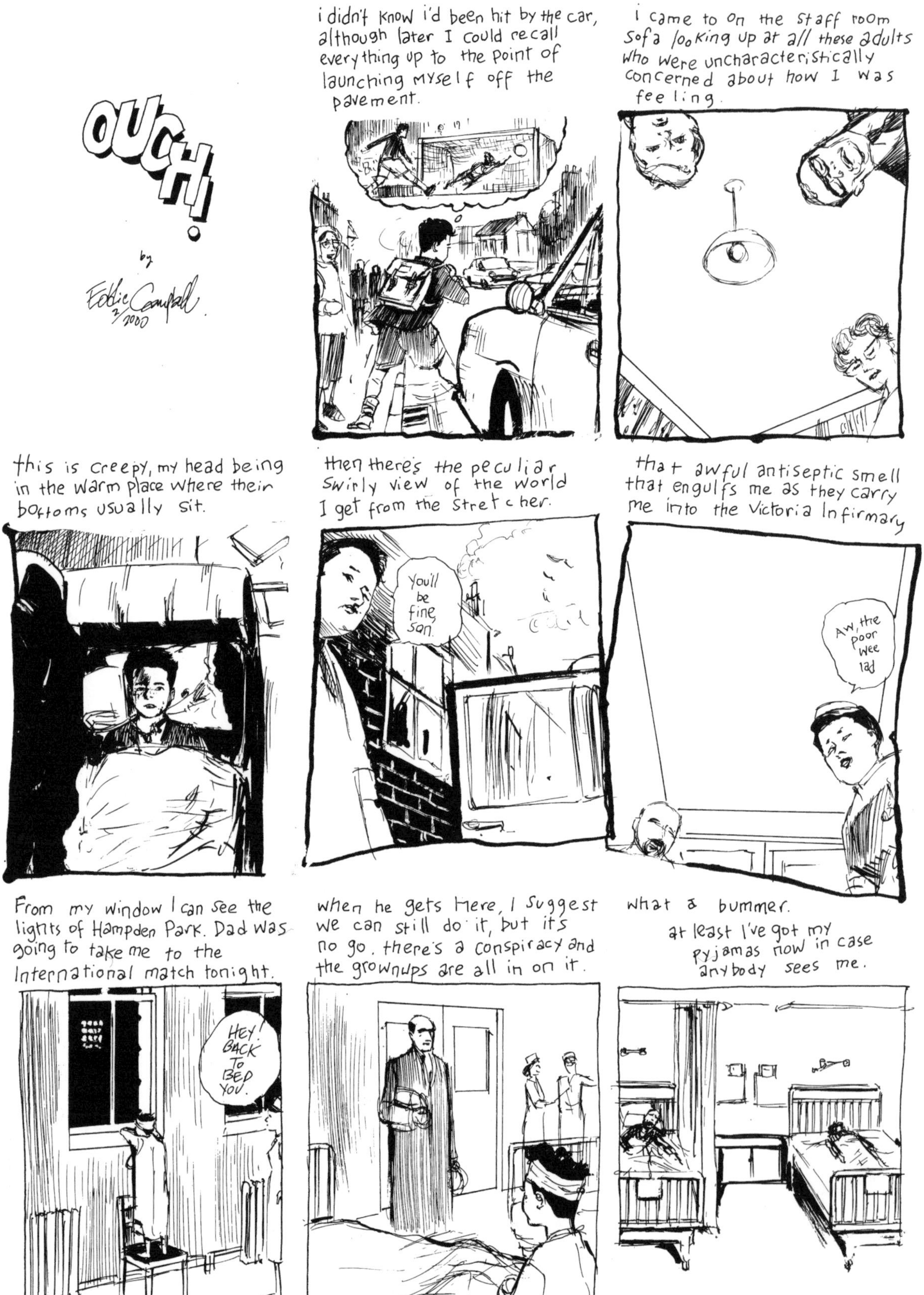
OUCH!
by Eddie Campbell 2/2000
i didn't know i'd been hit by the car, although later I could recall everything up to the point of launching myself off the pavement.
i came to on the staff room sofa looking up at all these adults who were uncharacteristically concerned about how I was feeling.
this is creepy, my head being in the warm place where their bottoms usually sit.
then there's the peculiar swirly view of the world I get from the stretcher.
You'll be fine, son.
that awful antiseptic smell that engulfs me as they carry me into the Victoria Infirmary
Aw, the poor wee lad
From my window I can see the lights of Hampden Park. Dad was going to take me to the International match tonight.
HEY! BACK TO BED YOU.
when he gets here, I suggest we can still do it, but it's no go. there's a conspiracy and the grownups are all in on it.
what a bummer.
at least I've got my pyjamas now in case anybody sees me.

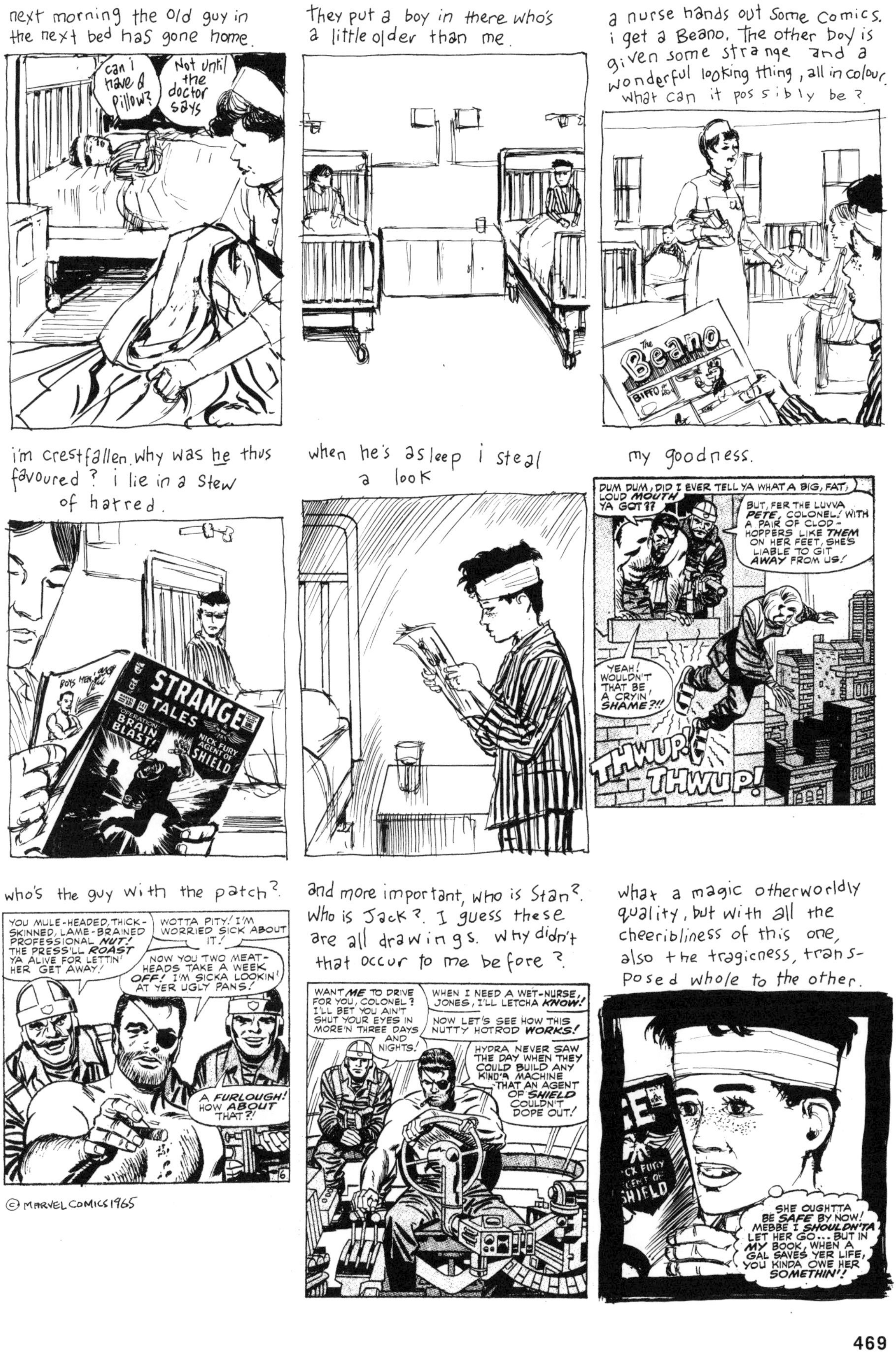

next morning the old guy in the next bed has gone home.
can i have a pillow?
Not until the doctor says
they put a boy in there who's a little older than me.
a nurse hands out some comics. i get a Beano. The other boy is given some strange and a wonderful looking thing, all in colour. what can it possibly be?
The Beano
BIFFO
i'm crestfallen. why was he thus favoured? i lie in a stew of hatred.
STRANGE TALES
OPERATION: BRAIN BLAST!
NICK FURY AGENT OF SHIELD
when he's asleep i steal a look
my goodness.
DUM DUM, DID I EVER TELL YA WHAT A BIG, FAT, LOUD MOUTH YA GOT?!
BUT, FER THE LUVVA PETE, COLONEL! WITH A PAIR OF CLOD-HOPPERS LIKE THEM ON HER FEET, SHE'S LIABLE TO GIT AWAY FROM US!
YEAH! WOULDN'T THAT BE A CRYIN' SHAME?!!
THWUP! THWUP!
who's the guy with the patch?
YOU MULE-HEADED, THICK-SKINNED, LAME-BRAINED PROFESSIONAL NUT! THE PRESS'LL ROAST YA ALIVE FOR LETTIN' HER GET AWAY!
WOTTA PITY! I'M WORRIED SICK ABOUT IT!
NOW YOU TWO MEAT-HEADS TAKE A WEEK OFF! I'M SICKA LOOKIN' AT YER UGLY PANS!
A FURLOUGH! HOW ABOUT THAT?!
© MARVEL COMICS 1965
and more important, who is Stan? Who is Jack? I guess these are all drawings. why didn't that occur to me before?
WANT ME TO DRIVE FOR YOU, COLONEL? I'LL BET YOU AIN'T SHUT YOUR EYES IN MORE'N THREE DAYS AND NIGHTS!
WHEN I NEED A WET-NURSE, JONES, I'LL LETCHA KNOW!
NOW LET'S SEE HOW THIS NUTTY HOTROD WORKS!
HYDRA NEVER SAW THE DAY WHEN THEY COULD BUILD ANY KIND'A MACHINE THAT AN AGENT OF SHIELD COULDN'T DOPE OUT!
what a magic otherworldly quality, but with all the cheeribliness of this one, also the tragicness, transposed whole to the other.
SHE OUGHTTA BE SAFE BY NOW! MEBBE I SHOULDN'TA LET HER GO... BUT IN MY BOOK, WHEN A GAL SAVES YER LIFE, YOU KINDA OWE HER SOMETHIN'!

if only i could take it home. but such a treasure would surely be missed. they would come to get it back.
where do you find these? the local newsagent's got a rack. I always thought i wasn't allowed to look at these
Playboy
PENTHOUSE
KNAVE
Fantastic Four... Tales to Astonish.
my goodness. nobody stopped me from buying it.
here's another newsagent. now. why are these all different issues from the other shop? i can start to piece together narratives where the missing portions are even more special than the ones i have.
The mighty Thor.
strange, obscure shops which i imagine will be unchanged so many years from now, in spite of the closed and condemned one with a Green Lantern in the window with only the blue not yet faded
That guy on the cover, Tomar-Re, looks like a cockatoo
it's a mystery. No two shops ever get the same selection. i know they're not always old ones that have been lying around for months because i get to open the bundles at one place
it doesn't really occur to me that there should be a system. i half believe that they deliberately print them in such a higgledy piggledy order.
? This should be a year old!
THE WORLD'S GREATEST COMIC MAGAZINE!
Fantastic Four
12¢
SILVER SURFER!
except that the letters pages are mailed from a happy land where you don't have to even wait till January to get the January issues, never mind look for them all over town.
excelsior!
i'm traveling further and further afield, in great secrecy. Oh no! i forgot to ding the bell and i've missed my stop. i'll be late home. i'll be found out.

i must risk a jump.
BUS STOP
ouch!
oh my goodness!!
hell's bells! i'm going to have to wear my bag back to front from now on, and hide it in my room.
At least Marvel Collectors' Item Classics didn't get wrecked.
One day i try to draw like Jack.
Now that you can draw comics yourself, you won't need to buy them any more.
Eh?
How dare you! the men who draw these don't breathe the same air as you and me.
the comics still bear the smells of the happy land far far away.
i'm not sure which is the more magical, the incredible hulk and the fantastic four, nick fury, or Stan, jack, Steranko, will Eisner
FLEEING FROM BLOODTHIRSTY BANDITS, BRUCE BANNER AND MAJOR GLEN TALBOT FALL FROM A HIGH CLIFF IN EASTERN MONGOLIA--PLUNGING TOWARDS CERTAIN DOOM! BUT, THE SHOCK OF THE FALL CAUSES THE DESPERATE BANNER TO UNDERGO THE MOST SPECTACULAR CHANGE EVER RECORDED, AS HE ONCE AGAIN BECOMES-- THE HULK!
STORY AND ART BY MARVEL'S MODERN MASTERS: STAN LEE and JACK KIRBY
INKING: MICKEY DEMEO
LETTERING: ARTIE SIMEK
i squint my eyes and look into one of those dimensions you get in comics where maybe Stan and Jack are just Mr. Lee and mr. Kirby like ordinary adults
and not nearly as famous as the beatles.
go and buy a 'masterworks' volume so they don't string me up for using the pictures
Eddie

The Fan
Wee Eddie Campbell.
12-98
Meeting your heroes is always daunting.
Oh, my God! It's really him.
At the San Diego Comic Convention I'm on a panel with Will Eisner where the subject is: Comics about real life. It would be 1989 or '90
It's Sunday Morning. Not too many people have got out of bed to hear comic artists seriously talking about real life.
came all the way from Poughkeepsie to ask a question.
Kim Thompson
Klingons
z
hasn't been to bed yet
This guy's always at the front.
After, I tell Will who I am.
You must send me your book
You bet.
Inevitably, it all looks different when I get home.
Ah, Will's too busy. He doesn't want to be bothered reading my silly little book.
I never send it.
But Sometimes after a few beers I picture Will at home in Florida...
...after these past eight years, going down to his mail box...
Still no book from Eddie.
US MAIL
campbell

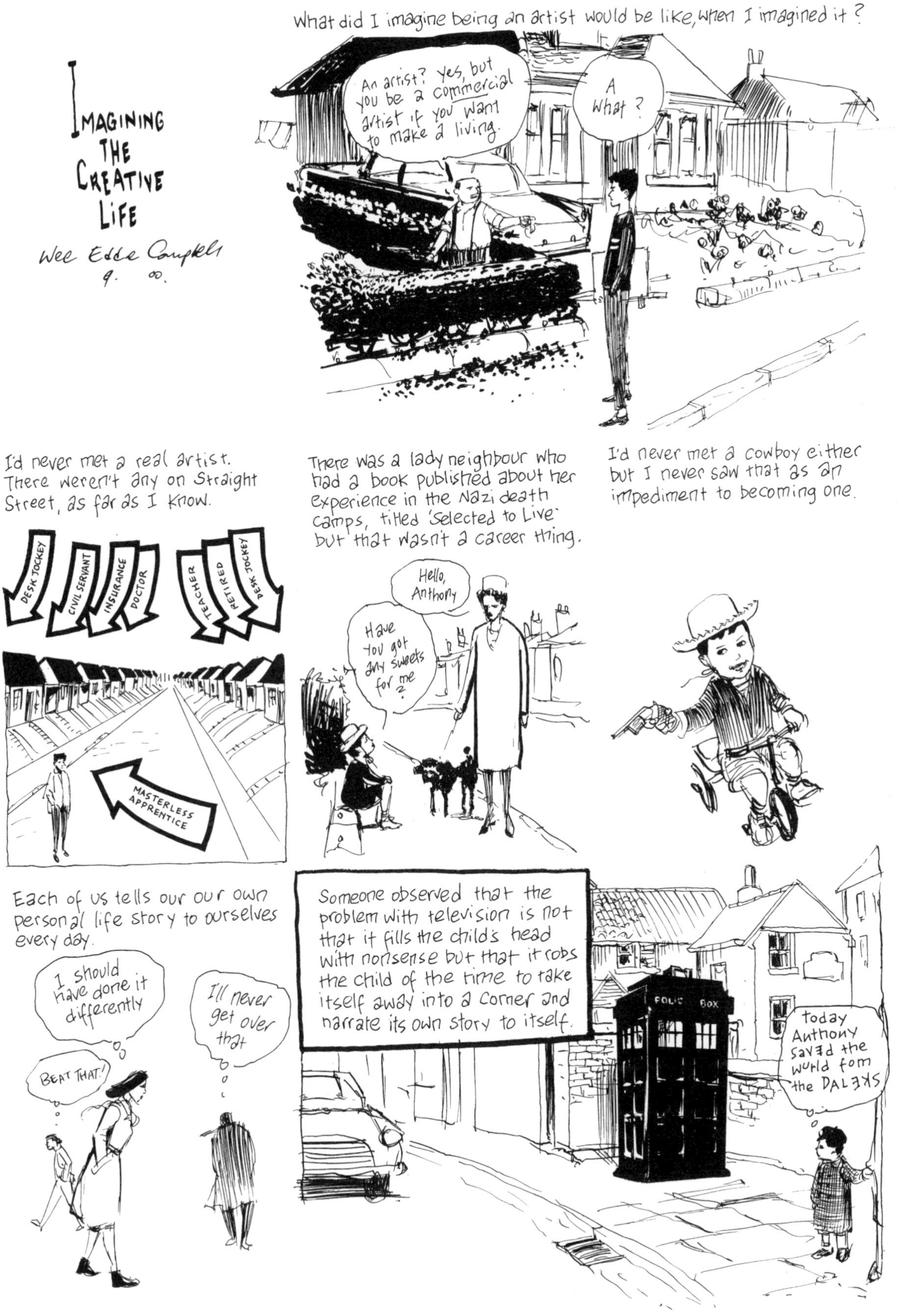
IMAGINING THE CREATIVE LIFE
Wee Eddie Campbell 9. 00.
What did I imagine being an artist would be like, when I imagined it?
An artist? Yes, but you be a commercial artist if you want to make a living.
A what?
I'd never met a real artist. There weren't any on Straight Street, as far as I know.
DESK JOCKEY
CIVIL SERVANT
INSURANCE
DOCTOR
TEACHER
RETIRED
DESK JOCKEY
MASTERLESS APPRENTICE
There was a lady neighbour who had a book published about her experience in the Nazi death camps, titled 'Selected to Live' but that wasn't a career thing.
Hello, Anthony
Have you got any sweets for me?
I'd never met a cowboy either but I never saw that as an impediment to becoming one.
Each of us tells our our own personal life story to ourselves every day.
I should have done it differently
I'll never get over that
BEAT THAT!
Someone observed that the problem with television is not that it fills the child's head with nonsense but that it robs the child of the time to take itself away into a corner and narrate its own story to itself.
POLICE BOX
Today Anthony saved the world fom the DALEKS

Eddie Campbell, the conquering artist.
Claude Monet said that to paint a picture you must first see it in your head.
DAMN!
Let's say that it works the same way with a "life".
Get a life, Eddie
OKay
A Life
Off the peg, sir, or to measure?
I could think of no reason why I wasn't already a real artist except that the real business of art would appear to consist of fighting to establish a new idea in the world.
An idea!
Oh, for an idea!
The heroic myth of the conquering artist.
You'll do
ACME NOVELTY
I'm next
When Art narrates its own story it tells itself that it is dead.
Pop Art blew a raspberry at my funeral.
The idea of Art as a continuum goes out the window.
It's absurd to still think of Art that way
How can you say that? there will always be Art.
The picture in my head goes too.
You're an educated bloke. Why do you do this job?
I don't know

It took years to replace it with another picture of the creative life.
Ah yes, the creative life.
Now, let me see..., we'll move everything from column A to here. Then if I revise the way I do the bookkeeping...
...So that spare cash shows up earlier over here... hmm... Ah yes! - the illusion of wealth. I'm a magician!
Then, by the day of reckoning, invoice 405 should come in...
But 407 arriving early would be a safer bet.
I'M HO-OME, DARL.
Oh shit
Working hard?
Yes, darling.
SKETCH SKETCH

The Creative Life

Eddie Campbell
JAN 96.

F*** the bloody creative life
Spend 70% of yer creative energy figgerin' ways to get overdue cheques
Annie, can you take a letter?
Okay, what do you want?
1946 JANUARY
Right..."you Bastard."
You can't say that.
1946 JANUARY
Why not?
Well, you have to start with "dear" and then the person's name.
eh?...oh alright then.
Dear Aubrey...
...you are a cockroach.

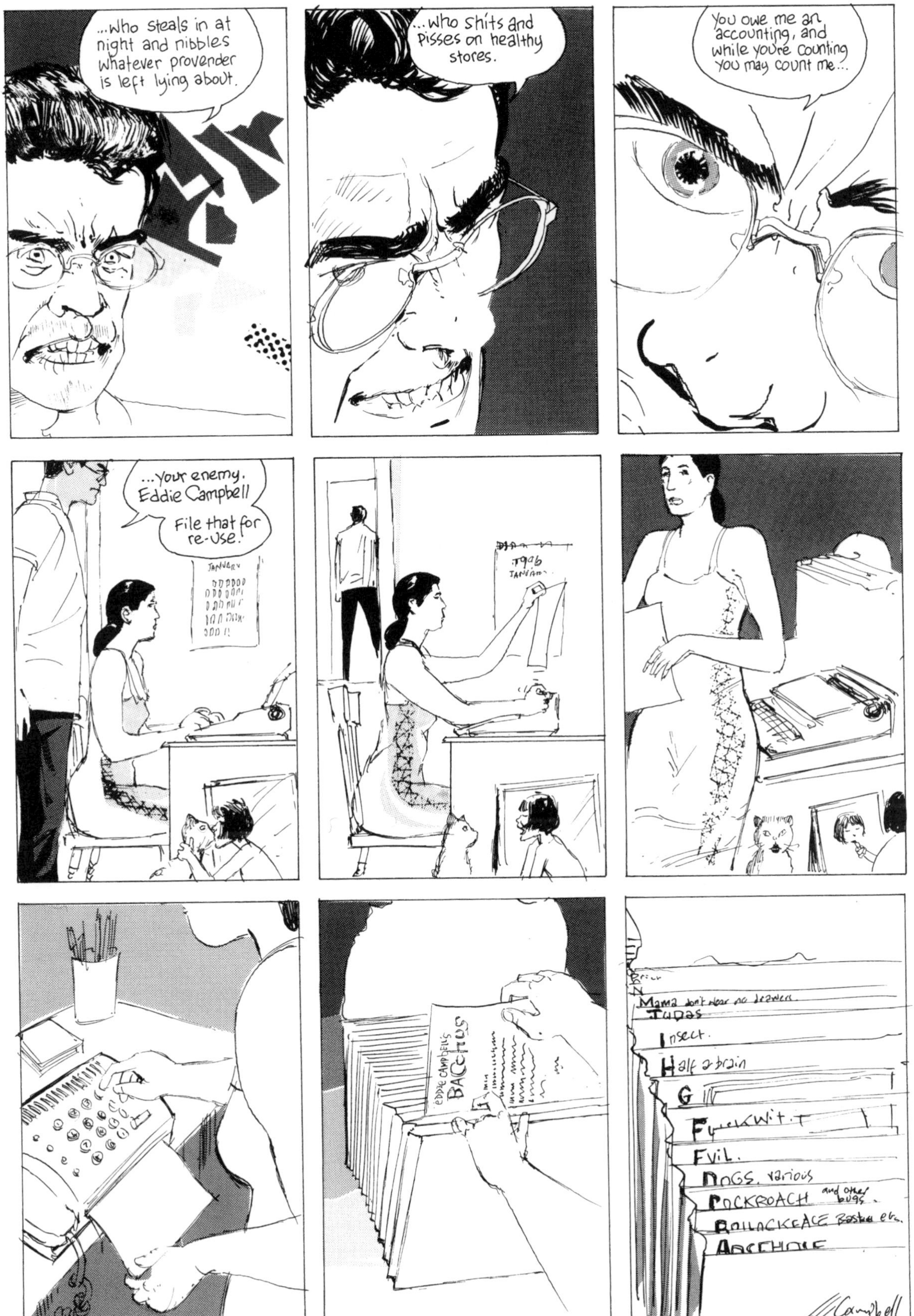
...Who steals in at night and nibbles whatever provender is left lying about.
...Who shits and pisses on healthy stores.
You owe me an accounting, and while you're counting you may count me...
...Your enemy. Eddie Campbell
File that for re-use.
JANUARY
1996
EDDIE CAMPBELL'S BACCHUS
Mama don't wear no drawers.
Judas
Insect.
Half a brain
G
Campbell

Used car dealers are human too.

Eddie Campbell 11/99

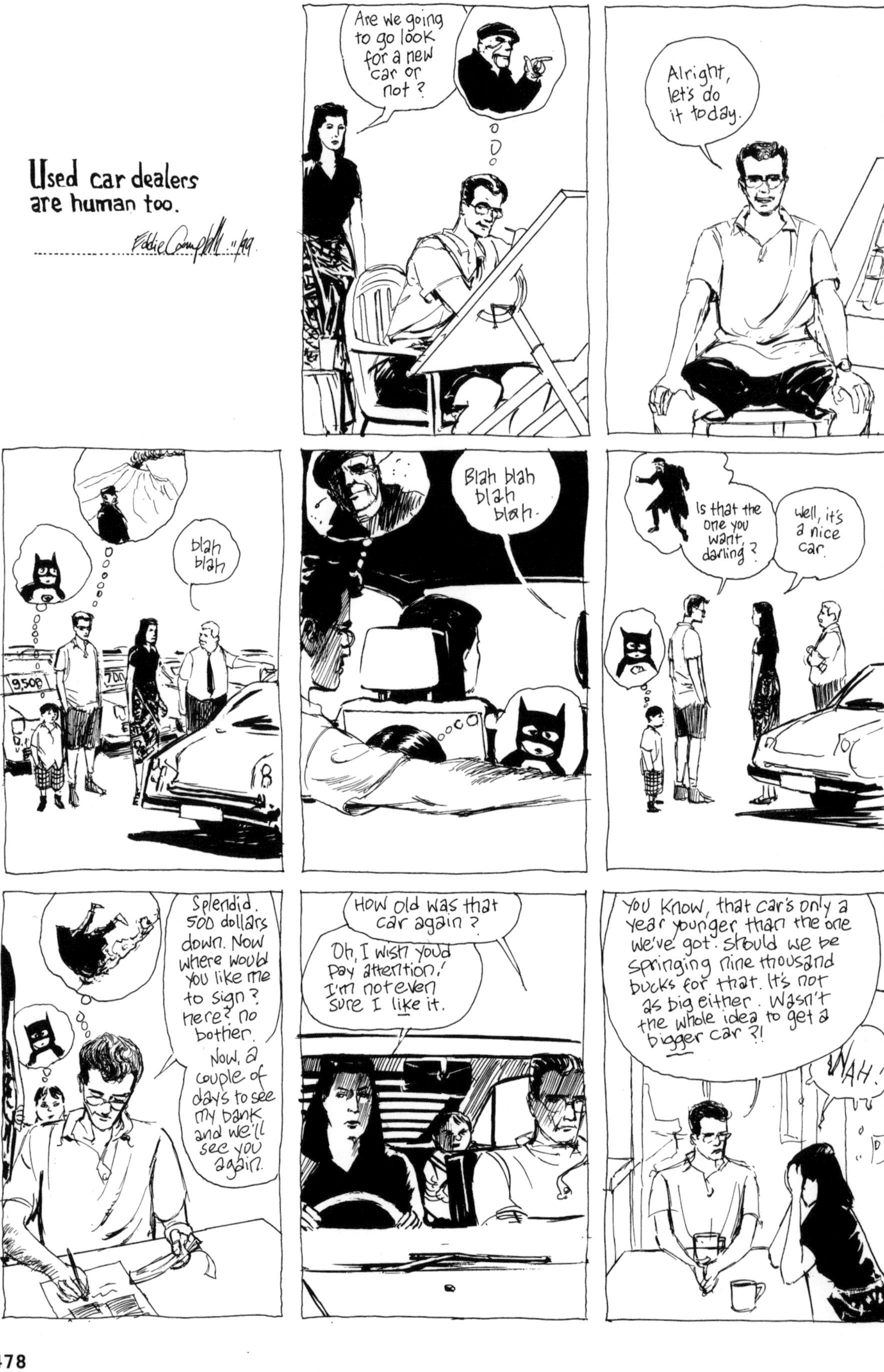
Are we going to go look for a new car or not ?
Alright, let's do it today.
blah blah
9,500
Blah blah blah blah.
Is that the one you want, darling ?
Well, it's a nice car.
Splendid. 500 dollars down. Now where would you like me to sign ? here? no bother. Now, a couple of days to see my bank and we'll see you again.
How old was that car again ?
Oh, I wish you'd pay attention! I'm not even sure I like it.
You know, that car's only a year younger than the one we've got. Should we be springing nine thousand bucks for that. It's not as big either. Wasn't the whole idea to get a bigger car ?!
WAH!

John, another hypothetical: a friend of mine signed a contract to buy a car... hmm yep... yes,... hum. okay given all that... how many legs does he have to stand on: a) Two b) one c) less than one.
Tell your friend he's fucked. These car people get out of bed earlier than you... I mean your friend.
Jesus suffering fuck.
ZZZ
Right then! I have girt my loins for battle.
You've got your plan of attack all worked out.
YUP
Now, regarding the automobile which I have purchased...
SALE
I have been a silly boy and I would like you to let me off lightly here. You have my deposit. I'd like you to keep that and permit me to renege on the rest of our agreement.
I see, Mr. Campbell. This is most irregular. Do you feel that we have coerced or otherwise imposed upon you?
Good heavens, no. I have only myself to blame.
sigh.
BIG SALE
Mr. Campbell, we like the gentlemanly way you have gone about this, and we want to give you your deposit back.
Why, thank you, sir.
CHEERS
MOTORS
E Campbell

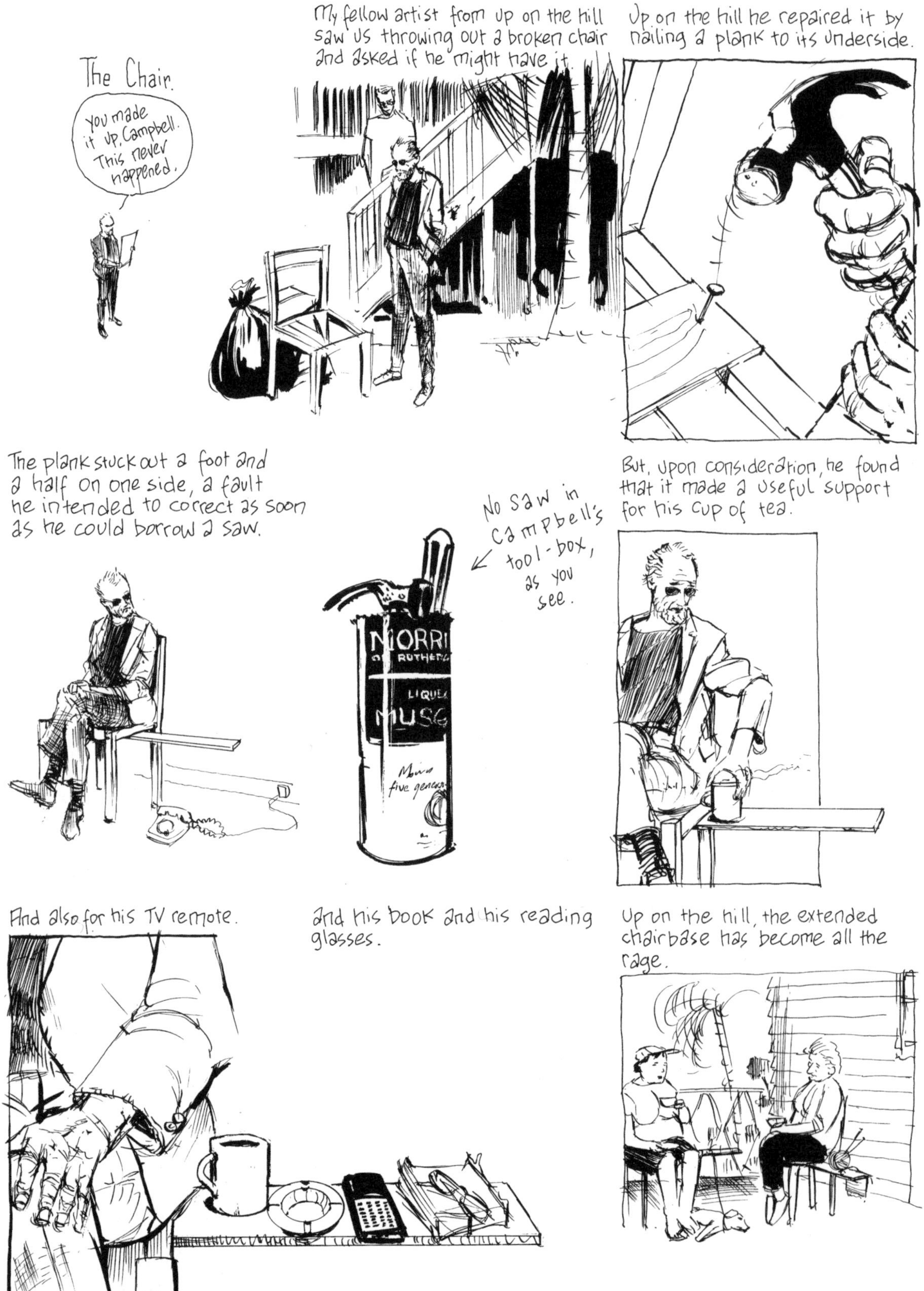
The Chair.
You made it up, Campbell. This never happened.
My fellow artist from up on the hill saw us throwing out a broken chair and asked if he might have it.
Up on the hill he repaired it by nailing a plank to its underside.
The plank stuck out a foot and a half on one side, a fault he intended to correct as soon as he could borrow a saw.
No saw in Campbell's tool-box, as you see.
But, upon consideration, he found that it made a useful support for his cup of tea.
And also for his TV remote.
and his book and his reading glasses.
Up on the hill, the extended chairbase has become all the rage.
Eddie.

Sexy
by Eddie Campbell
13. 9. 98.
Wilt thou come with me sweet Tibbie Dunbar
Wilt thou ride on a horse or be drawn by a car.
Aw darlin, you look sexy in that dress
MUM
This old thing?
well, if you think it's sexy— YOU WEAR IT
OKAY
GIVE IT HERE THEN
Roast beef yum.
my Dad wears mum's dress

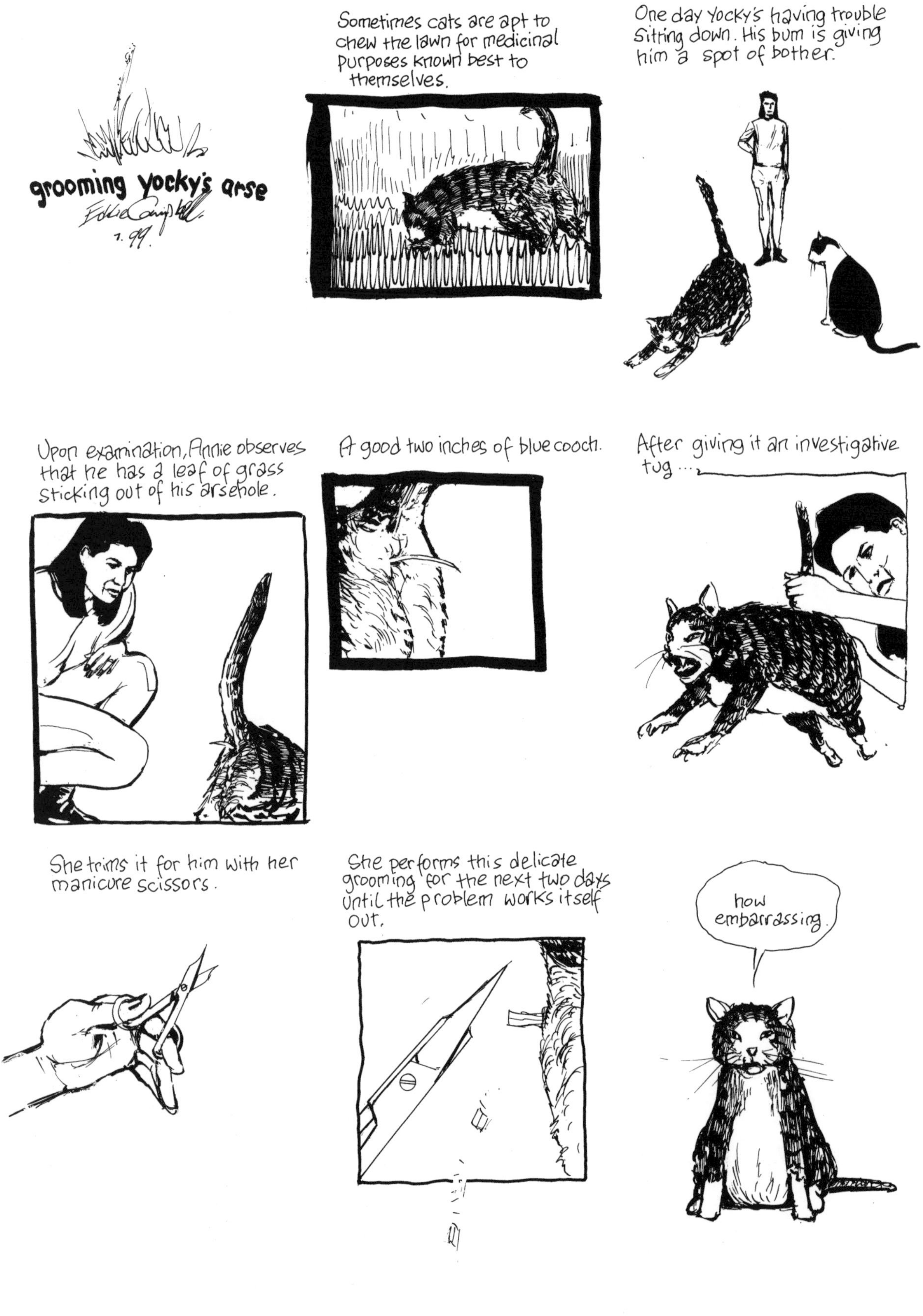
grooming yocky's arse
Eddie Campbell
7.99.
Sometimes cats are apt to chew the lawn for medicinal purposes known best to themselves.
One day Yocky's having trouble sitting down. His bum is giving him a spot of bother.
Upon examination, Annie observes that he has a leaf of grass sticking out of his arsehole.
A good two inches of blue cooch.
After giving it an investigative tug ...
She trims it for him with her manicure scissors.
She performs this delicate grooming for the next two days until the problem works itself out.
how embarrassing.

PETS
by
Puss was found out in the country by our next door neighbour, left to fend for herself with her brother.
She decided to jump the fence and live with us instead. We named her by committee.
Merlot
No! Puss
Puss
Ps
Sox came from across the road. He also got renamed by the lowest common denominator.
Mummy, why won't our cat live with us any more?
Yocks!
Rosie was a lost peach-faced lovebird that landed in our patch and was being menaced by Puss.
WOUNDED
We bought a cage to keep her safe. One day she got out.
Tweet!
Then we got a pair of lovebirds to put in the cage and named them Bill and Coo. One did a flyer and the other got birdie-cancer in its wing and was put down.
exeunt
Dad, why don't we catch him up there and put him in the empty cage
Aw leave him be. He's happy
Yeh, but he's not doing anything.
69

Confiscation
Eddie Campbell 6/99.
Die, Vader, die!
Mum! Make him stop that.
Give me the stick! Give it to me NOW!
But why?
Because it too easily turns into a weapon
Mum! Mum! Can I have the stick that turns into a weapon?

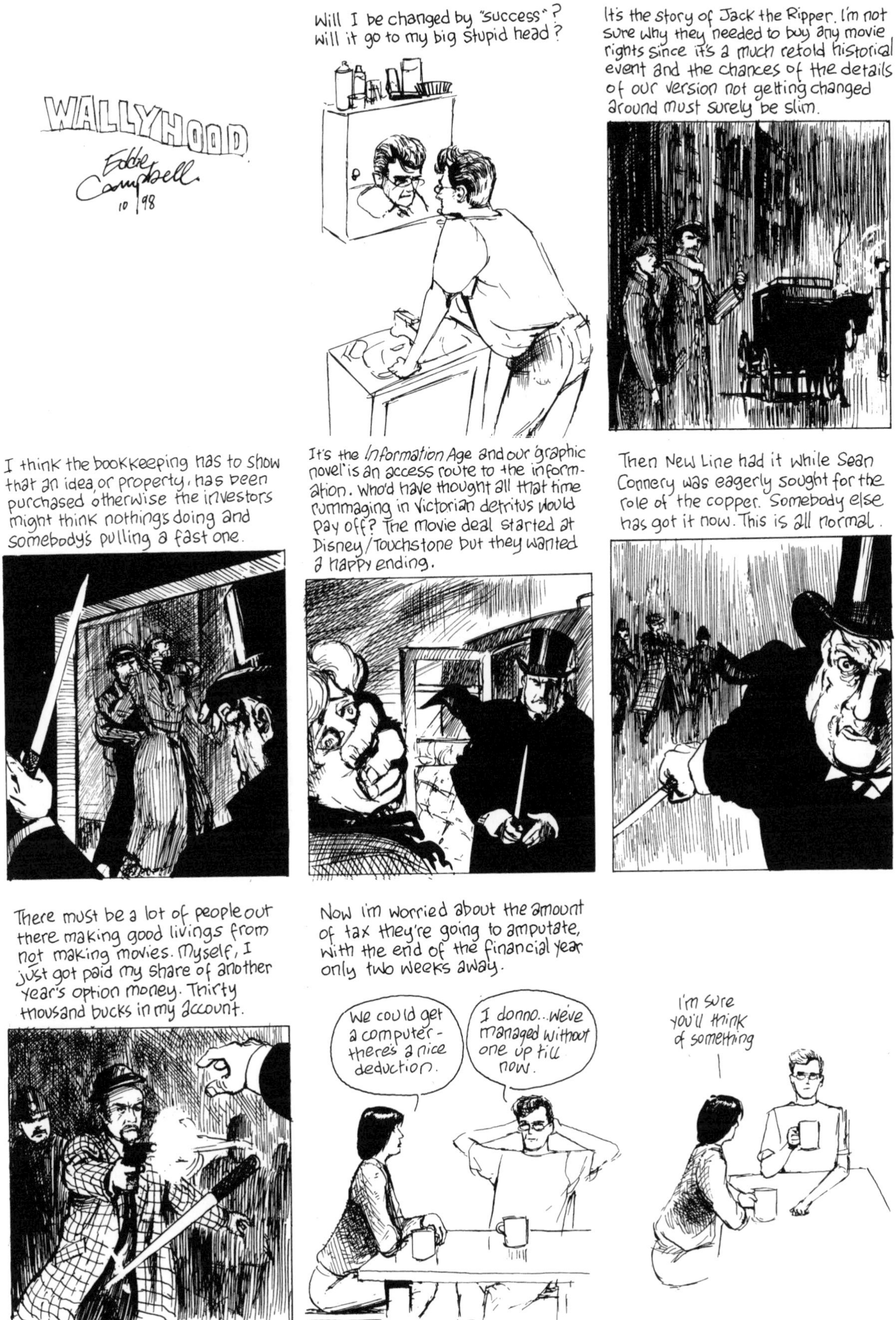
WALLYHOOD
Eddie Campbell 10 98
Will I be changed by "success"? will it go to my big stupid head?
It's the story of Jack the Ripper. I'm not sure why they needed to buy any movie rights since it's a much retold historical event and the chances of the details of our version not getting changed around must surely be slim.
I think the bookkeeping has to show that an idea, or property, has been purchased otherwise the investors might think nothing's doing and somebody's pulling a fast one.
It's the Information Age and our 'graphic novel' is an access route to the information. Who'd have thought all that time rummaging in Victorian detritus would pay off? The movie deal started at Disney/Touchstone but they wanted a happy ending.
Then New Line had it while Sean Connery was eagerly sought for the role of the copper. Somebody else has got it now. This is all normal.
There must be a lot of people out there making good livings from not making movies. Myself, I just got paid my share of another year's option money. Thirty thousand bucks in my account.
Now I'm worried about the amount of tax they're going to amputate, with the end of the financial year only two weeks away.
We could get a computer - there's a nice deduction.
I donno... we've managed without one up till now.
I'm sure you'll think of something

The way is hard the night is dark but I don't mind cause a happy lark will be sing-ing at the end of the road.
BOOKS
SECOND HAND
FINE BOOKS
ANTIQUARIAN
AND
RARE
!
ART
TOPOGRAPHY
I can't help noticing you've got some old volumes of PUNCH back there.
Have a look by all means. I'm still sorting them.
WINES
Ah, these old Richard Doyle drawings! It's a shame there's no current collection of his work.
JACOBS CREEK CLARET
Oh, I have to tell you he's not selling those individually. You'd have to take them all
What do you mean, "ALL"?
It's a set - the first fifty years - very nice condition, - too. all in 25 books
1841-1891.!
How much is he asking then?
Five thousand. If you want to haggle you'll have to come back when he's here.
BOOKS

(Doyle spot-illo, Punch, c.1849)

scheme Scheme
I can negotiate him down to maybe three Five... but what to do about my parsimony?
Hey! Are you With us?
I've changed my mind! Let's get a Computer.
?
YAY
YAY
Yes, and we'll need a scanner of course, and a printer! No doubt about it! and throw in some extra ram of megs
WINDOWS 95
HEY GEROFFA ME
HAVE THEY GOT ANY SUPA REAROES
You know, I have another potential deduction: uh... a wee library of books.
You'd better go for it then, darling.
How much is it? Five Hundred?
blub blub blub.
WHAT?
Thirty-five hundred, cash.

Now here's how the bedroom used to look.
That was before I found this great plan chest.
Well, you'll have to put a patterned sheet over it.
Where do you intend to keep all these books?
I'm just going out for some stuff for my trip.
Don't forget underpants!
Well, we do have the Calvin Klein.
Yeah, they'll do. Three of them, and throw in a t-shirt.
The one I love will be waiting at the end of the road.
WHAT? 105 bucks? You idiot! give them to me. I'm taking them back.
What a rigmarole. In the old days you'd have said to the antique dealer; "Put the books in the car, and while you're about it, throw in a stuffed partridge."

The Court Sketcher
Eddie Campbell 3/98.
Are you staring at me?
Just tell me — what's that written on your forehead?
How did I get into court-sketching for the T.V. News? It was Mullins.
Pete's been working with me since I got the idea about eight years ago of running my show along the lines of an old fashioned workshop.
How's that going to get us anywhere?
Look, I'll show you.
So I'd have an assistant or two doing backgrounds and stuff and Annie running the "office", supplying cut paper, cleaning and dispatching finished art, putting on lunch, etc., with everybody paid by the hour.
This was just ahead of my start in self-publishing. Pete Mullins grew out of it after three or four years but still puts in an occasional day for the social value.
His main gig these days is with Channel 7 News, freelancing the animated weather charts and other odd-job stuff like sketching at the trials.
Now there's something I wouldn't mind trying at least once in my life.
I've always found it an attractive concept, that of the artist as journalist. It's honest and down-to-earth.
It's a job that all but disappeared with the nineteenth century when they figured out an economic way of printing photos.
(Winslow Homer covers the Civil War for Harper's. He also sketched in court at least once but clearly didn't enjoy it)
The man on the spot would do his sketch, then get it back to the art-room in a finished state to be hand-engraved on wood by a craftsman working to a tight deadline. A big picture would be sawn into smaller blocks which would be worked on simultaneously by a team and then bolted back together. You can usually see the joins if you look.

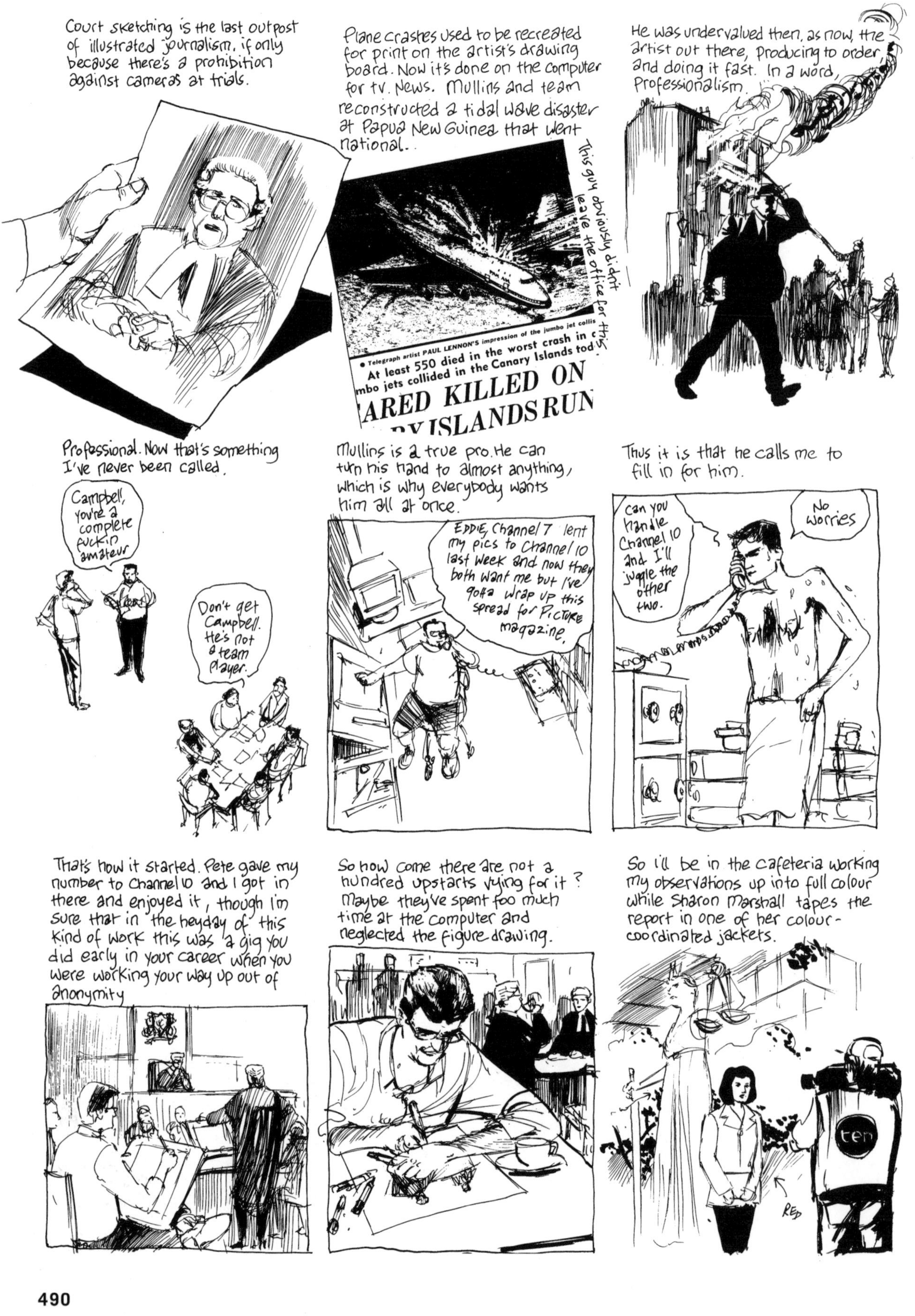
Court sketching is the last outpost of illustrated journalism, if only because there's a prohibition against cameras at trials.
Plane crashes used to be recreated for print on the artist's drawing board. Now it's done on the computer for tv. News. Mullins and team reconstructed a tidal wave disaster at Papua New Guinea that went national..
This guy obviously didn't leave the office for this.
• Telegraph artist PAUL LENNON'S impression of the jumbo jet collis
At least 550 died in the worst crash in c
mbo jets collided in the Canary Islands tod
ARED KILLED ON
RY ISLANDS RUN
He was undervalued then, as now, the artist out there, producing to order, and doing it fast. In a word, Professionalism.
Professional. Now that's something I've never been called.
Campbell, you're a complete fuckin amateur
Don't get Campbell. He's not a team player.
Mullins is a true pro. He can turn his hand to almost anything, which is why everybody wants him all at once.
EDDIE, Channel 7 lent my pics to Channel 10 last week and now they both want me but I've gotta wrap up this spread for PICTURE magazine.
Thus it is that he calls me to fill in for him.
Can you handle Channel 10 and I'll juggle the other two.
No worries
That's how it started. Pete gave my number to Channel 10 and I got in there and enjoyed it, though I'm sure that in the heyday of this kind of work this was a gig you did early in your career when you were working your way up out of anonymity
So how come there are not a hundred upstarts vying for it? Maybe they've spent too much time at the computer and neglected the figure drawing.
So I'll be in the cafeteria working my observations up into full colour while Sharon Marshall tapes the report in one of her colour-coordinated jackets.
ten
RED

It gets me out of the house and into the mainstream of life for perhaps a couple of mornings in a month. And my God, there's heaps going on out there. Here's the blackguard who abducted a boy for sex.
Here's the prison breakout team
This pair set fire to a vagrant
This girl survived a double suicide and had to carry the can for her more successful boyfriend. The judge dealt with her very sensitively.
Once I get a bit of unexpected recognition:
This bloke shot his wife because he thought she was having an affair.
Unnerving the jury by writing down their names during the selection process.
Eddie! I saw you do a talk once at Ozcon!
I'm looking forward to the FROM HELL collection
Another time I find myself sitting next to Mullins. It's like we've just moved the whole studio up to the Supreme Court, borrowing each others' pencils and all.
Pete had sat in the empty jury box for a good angle on the accused. I presumed he had permission and joined him. Then they moved us. Very embarrassing.
And being on the TV news is kind of cool because everybody knows about it. They think I'm suddenly getting somewhere even though publishing a monthly comic is significantly more complicated and also more lucrative.

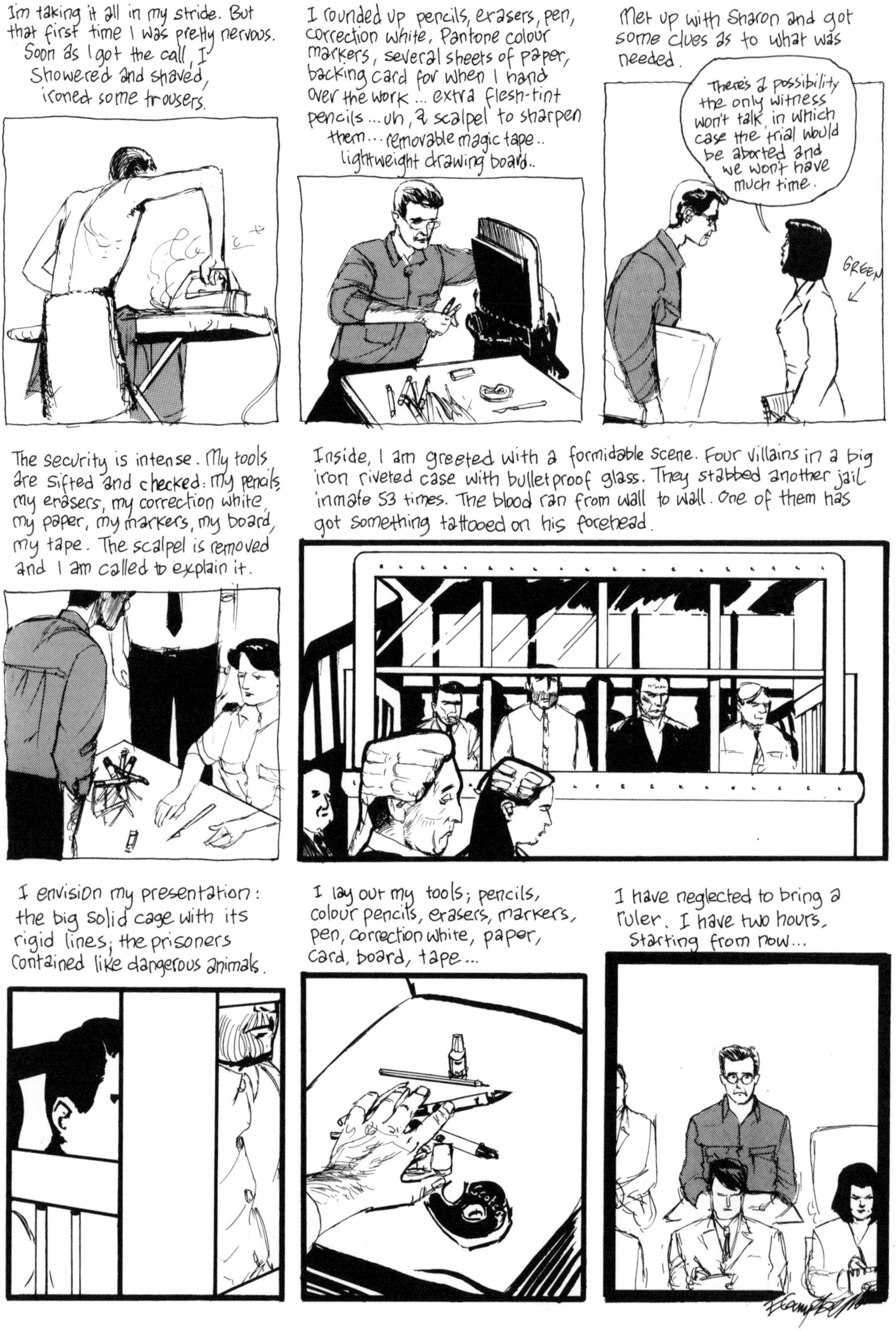
I'm taking it all in my stride. But that first time I was pretty nervous. Soon as I got the call, I showered and shaved, ironed some trousers.
I rounded up pencils, erasers, pen, correction white, Pantone colour markers, several sheets of paper, backing card for when I hand over the work ... extra flesh-tint pencils ... uh, a scalpel to sharpen them ... removable magic tape .. lightweight drawing board ..
Met up with Sharon and got some clues as to what was needed.
There's a possibility the only witness won't talk, in which case the trial would be aborted and we won't have much time.
GREEN
The security is intense. My tools are sifted and checked: my pencils, my erasers, my correction white, my paper, my markers, my board, my tape. The scalpel is removed and I am called to explain it.
Inside, I am greeted with a formidable scene. Four villains in a big iron riveted case with bulletproof glass. They stabbed another jail inmate 53 times. The blood ran from wall to wall. One of them has got something tattooed on his forehead.
I envision my presentation: the big solid cage with its rigid lines; the prisoners contained like dangerous animals.
I lay out my tools; pencils, colour pencils, erasers, markers, pen, correction white, paper, card, board, tape ...
Scotch
I have neglected to bring a ruler. I have two hours, starting from now ...

Metamorphosis
12.00
For the benefit of the jury...
Please describe the events in their precise sequence
I was sitting by my open window contemplating the annoying complacency of people...
I need a symbolic form, by which to strike fear into their hearts.
That's it... I shall become a hideous insect of the sleepless humid night.
I shall remind them of their childhood terrors... of snakes under the bed and beast droolings in the dark that make you afraid to put your bare foot on the floor.

I set about my transformation
that very night.

g'night cal
mumble

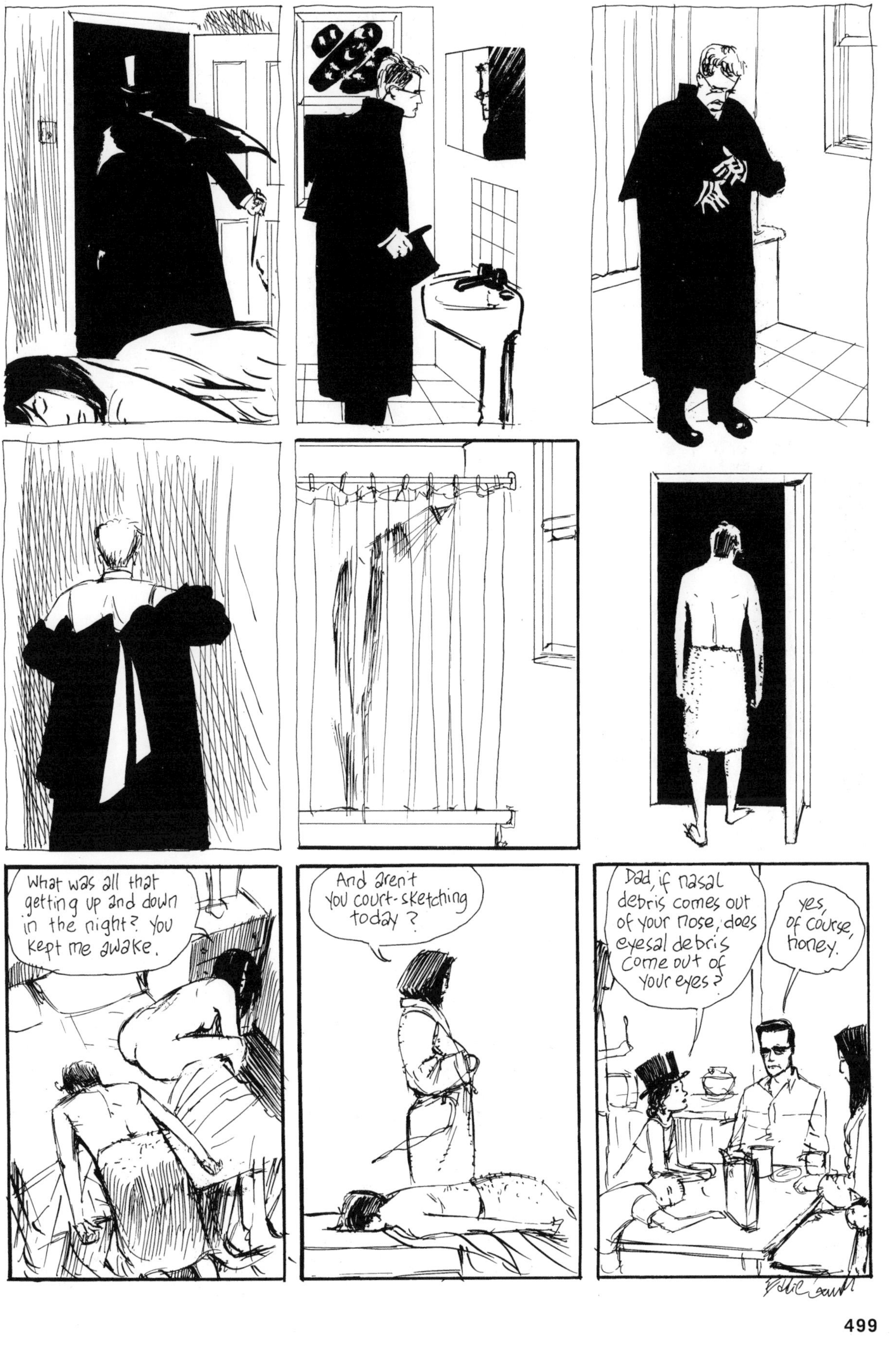
What was all that getting up and down in the night? You kept me awake.
And aren't you court-sketching today?
Dad, if nasal debris comes out of your nose, does eyesal debris come out of your eyes?
yes, of course, honey.

The House that Jack Bought
by Eddie Campbell 5/00
yes
yes, you're right. Nice pension, nice perks, nice expensive residence near the sea-front at Bournemouth.
Didn't do bad out of it, did I?
umm... look, perhaps I should be heading home myself.
No, no, I insist. You've walked me all this way, you'll come in for a nightcap, surely. After all Mr. Lees, this is the very place...
This is the house that Jack built.
Thus ended the prologue of From Hell, twelve years ago when it was to be a modest serial of twelve eight-page parts.
Five years into this ten-year tale of intrigue and conspiracy theory, two publishers have gone broke. It will eventually be three.
It's a jinx I tell you.
It's only a coincidence.
Suddenly there comes a nibble from Hollywood.
KEVIN B. EASTMAN
Northampton, Massachusetts 01060 U.S.A.
Feb 11, 1994
Dear Alan and Eddie:
I've got some really weird news to share with you both, and I hope you find it as exciting as I do!
I just hung up the telephone from speaking with a gentleman from Oliver Stone's office. It seems some of the pass around copies of the Tundra Kitchen Sink books we forwarded to Limelight Productions found their wa to Stone's office. To use their words (Mr. Stone's I guess) they a "extremely" interested in talking about moving this project into the featu film area.
It seems they feel, as you both did, that even though so much has been and done on the subject of Jack the Ripper, the way you approach matter finally works and is truly unique.
Mark my words. In 'undred years some cunt'll be wrapping these murders up in supernatural twaddle. Making a living out of murder, Godley. That's our job!
TAB
Do you think they'll make this movie?
Can they get Tom and Nicole?
Yes, darling, and when the cheque comes in, you go out and buy a house.
But take your time, my darling. You find one you like.

It is an observable effect in the world of movies that whatever stimulus gave rise to the idea of a Jack the Ripper movie in one domain is quite likely to have repeated itself across town.
Thus we hear there is to be a second, concurrent, "Ripper movie," with Anthony Hopkins in the lead role (fresh from playing Hannibal Lecter) This one's to be based on the recently discovered Diary of the Ripper.
Our movie is dropped due to a lack of interest at the top levels of New Line Cinema and the other one is dropped because the "diary" proves to be a hoax.
Ripper Diary Hoax
Touchstone/Disney take a notion to grab one of these floating Ripper properties, but which to go for? The comic book or the hoax?
OR
THE HOAX?
THE COMIC?
The comic book comes in just ahead of the hoax, so now the movie's with Touchstone. And then it's with another Mob.
Every time I pull it from the back of my noggin it reels out in a different sequence.
FedEx letter
Suddenly it's all a goer and signatures are put on big fat cheques.
There it is, my honeybee. now you take this cheque and find a big house.
But look, my love, you take all the time you need. Make comparisons, find one that you like.

I must state here that I've never cared for the idea of owning a house. I just don't get it.
In fact I've always favoured a good and simple rental arrangement.
Is this new concrete driveway to your liking, my good tenant?
Why, it is splendid my fine landlord.
But money paid in rent is wasted money.
How so? Show me the figures.
Look, It just is. Everybody Knows that.
Me, I would sooner do business with a fellow human being than with a big faceless banking corporation.
may I plant you some more trees, my good tenant?
No, thanks, but if you would move that one so wifey can get her car out...
So this rigmarole becomes a standing joke over a number of years.
When the dosh arrives, then you must go out and find us...
...a house!
But don't just pick the first one you see, my sweet. The one for us is out there somewhere...
Will you bloody shut up!
The speculation is at an end. The cheque is banked.
The house is sought -
i've found the very house for meee
eh? You only just started looking!
Well, what do you think?

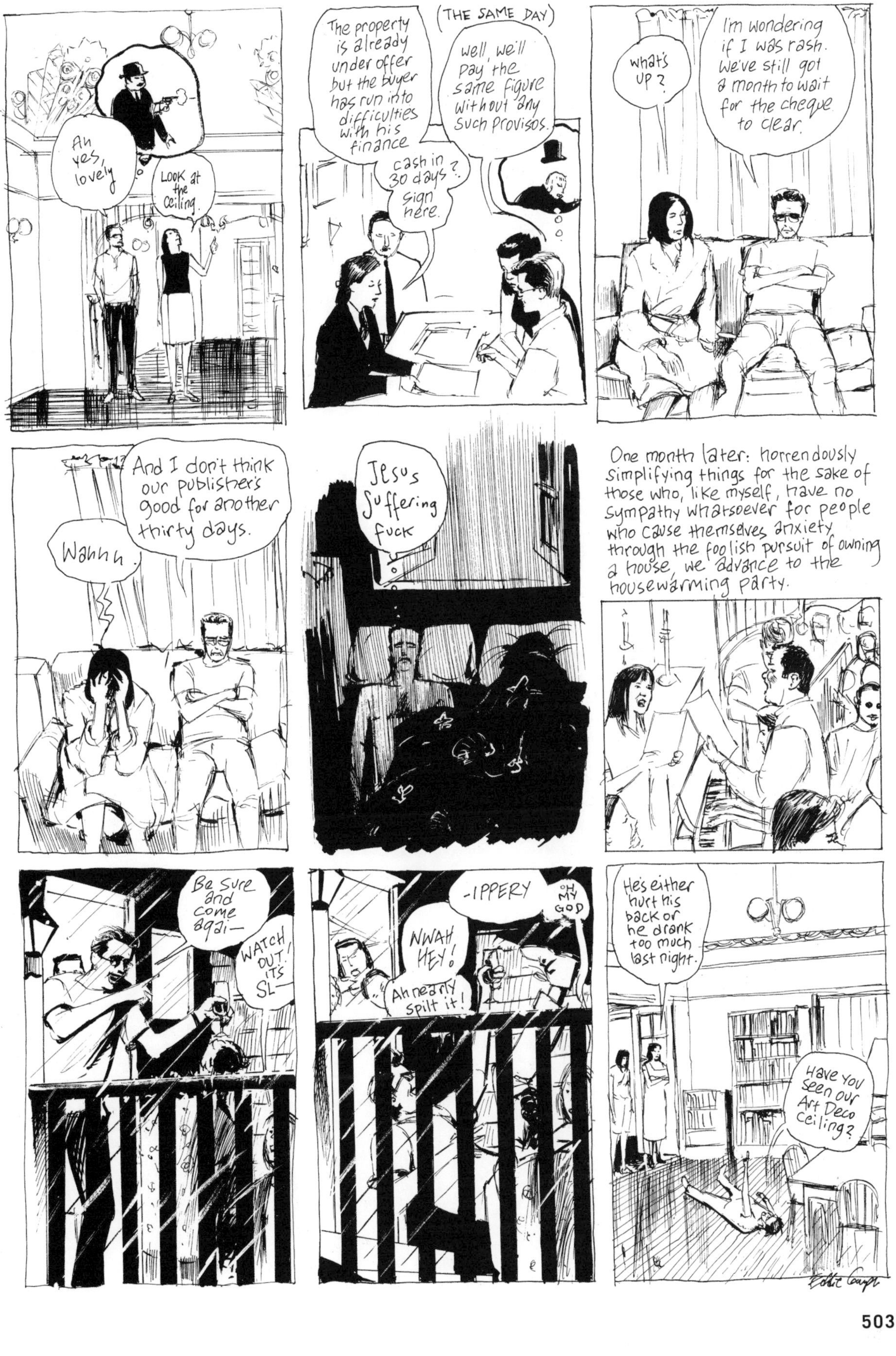
Ah yes, lovely
Look at the ceiling.
(THE SAME DAY)
The property is already under offer but the buyer has run into difficulties with his finance
Well, we'll pay the same figure without any such provisos.
cash in 30 days?.. sign here.
What's up?
I'm wondering if I was rash. We've still got a month to wait for the cheque to clear.
And I don't think our publisher's good for another thirty days.
Wahhh.
Jesus Suffering fuck
One month later: horrendously simplifying things for the sake of those who, like myself, have no sympathy whatsoever for people who cause themselves anxiety through the foolish pursuit of owning a house, we advance to the housewarming party.
Be sure and come agai—
WATCH OUT! IT'S SL
-IPPERY
OH MY GOD
NWAH HEY!
Ah nearly spilt it!
He's either hurt his back or he drank too much last night.
Have you seen our Art Deco ceiling?

Voodoo.

Eddie Campbell 4.01.

YAWN
What's up?
Aw bloody hell! Kitchen's just gone bust owing us fifteen thousand bucks
Eddie Campbell

The Fan
sigh
Eddie Campbell 18. 12. 98.
When I get to the Irish Club for the show, Paul Furey's leaning on the bar.
So I go through the obligatory muddle:
That can't be him. What's he doing standing out here?
I should say something but maybe he just wants a quiet drink before the show.
Aw, I'm such a fuck-up.
The Fureys are maybe the best pub-band in the world.
After the show he's back at the bar.
Great show! You know, I was standing next to you earlier and didn't know who you were!
Well, I didn't know who you were either.
Ha Ha.
gloom
I stood at that bar and nobody knew who I was. My life has been for nothing.
Campbell

MONEY
Eddie Campbell. 29.8.98
Dad, can I have my pocket money ?
Yeah. Sure. There you go.
Thanx
Dad... How do you get the money ?
Well... let's see. I draw my stories on these sheets of big paper, see.
Then I send them all to Mr. Printer in Canada in one of those boxes.
FedEx
And he makes it into lots of comic books like this, thousands all the same, and sends them to Mr. Distributor.
BACchus
Mr. Distributor, now he's in America and he sends the comics to all the shops and every time some wee person comes in and buys one, some of the money comes back to me.
Yeah, right, Dad
HA HA HA

Hey. I'm trying to get some work done

Eddie Campbell 11 9 98.

Gaaah. Gaaah.
Look, Dad, the mabonyible Snowman's biting you!
Hey, Dad, what's that under his foot?
That tells you where it was made
Yeah, but what does it say?
Let me see it says: "made in China"
Giner... That's what girls have.
How come everything's always made in Giner?

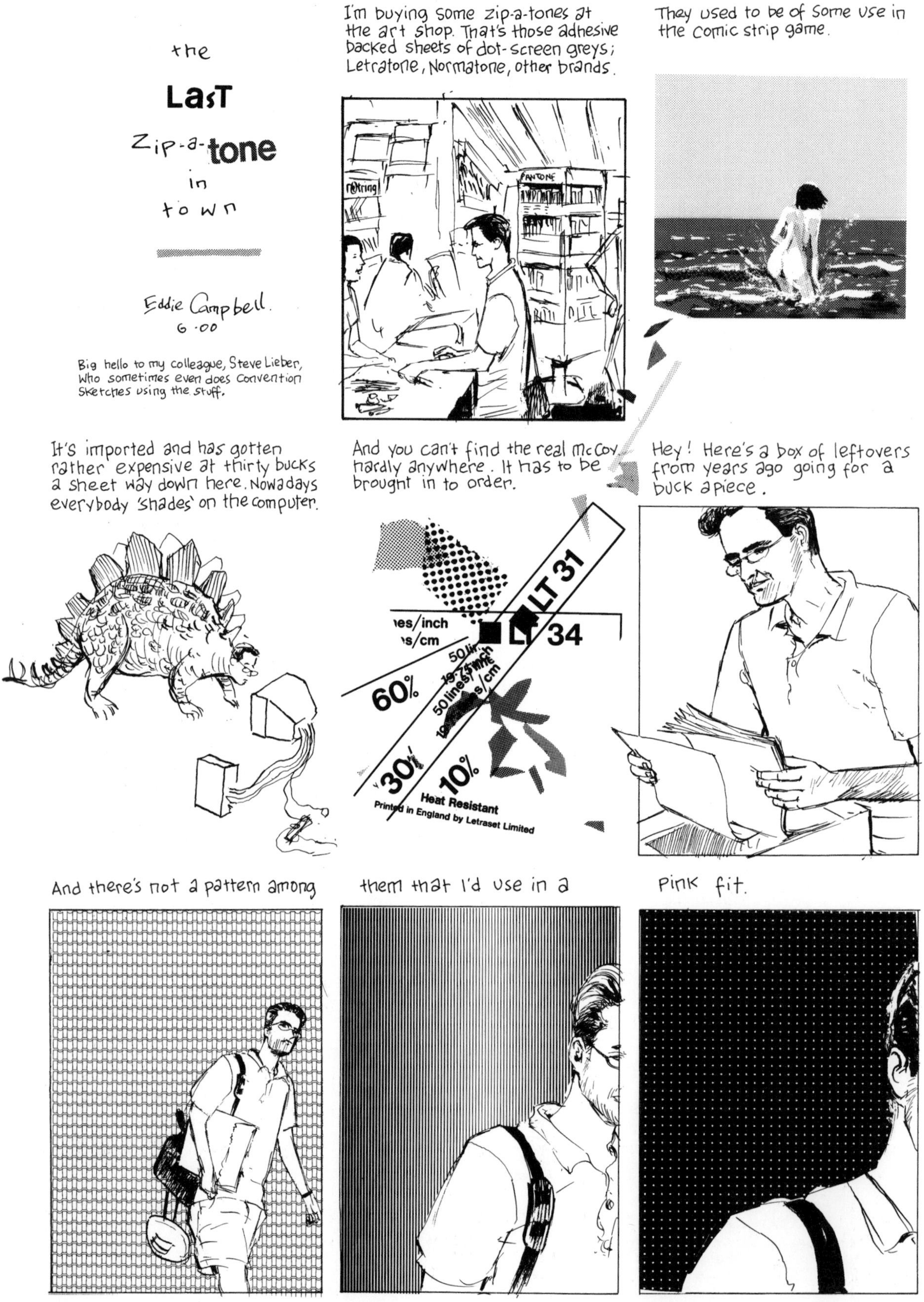
the Last Zip-a-tone in town
Eddie Campbell. 6·00
Big hello to my colleague, Steve Lieber, Who sometimes even does Convention Sketches using the stuff.
I'm buying some zip-a-tones at the art shop. That's those adhesive backed sheets of dot-screen greys; Letratone, Normatone, other brands.
PANTONE
They used to be of some use in the comic strip game.
It's imported and has gotten rather expensive at thirty bucks a sheet way down here. Nowadays everybody 'shades' on the computer.
And you can't find the real McCoy hardly anywhere. It has to be brought in to order.
LT 31
LT 34
60%
30%
10%
Heat Resistant
Printed in England by Letraset Limited
Hey! Here's a box of leftovers from years ago going for a buck apiece.
And there's not a pattern among
them that I'd use in a
pink fit.

The Court Sketcher
Eddie Campbell
13 12 98
Here's the "postcard bandit": a likeable rogue, a Robin Hood.
Massive security operation gree
A prison escapee, he was on the run a long time, supposedly taunting the Police by sending them photo-postcards of himself in famous tourist locations and posing in front of police stations.
POLICE
He was a master of disguise; he'd do the armed hold-up, run down the street into public toilets where he'd shave off his moustache.
He had a plane seat next to Jana Wendt, famous hard-nosed TV journalist and she didn't recognise him with his hair cut short.
MILE-HIGH FLUB: Jana and Brendon Abbott
Scoop came, Wendt
JANA Wendt missed the scoop interview of the year when she didn't recognise Australia's most wanted criminal sitting next to her on a plane.
The ABC spent $1.1 million sending Wendt around the world for interviews for her Uncensored series, but her big chance came when armed robber Brendon Abbott joined her in the first-class cabin on a flight to Melbourne.
At the time, a nationwide hunt was on for Abbott, who led the mass break-out from Brisbane's Sir David Longland maximum-security prison last November.
The ABC confirmed the encounter. Wendt did not recognise Abbott, a known master of disguise.
Now they've nabbed him up north and they're flying him down for processing at the city courthouse.
The streets are crowded. Everybody is out to get a look. But where is the Court sketcher?
POLICE
He was supposed to be on stand-by but he's standing at a bar. He misunderstood the brief. All he can say in his defence is at least he was only drinking a shandy.
And anyway, it's only the postcard bandit. It's not like it's the kissing bandit or the Wet bandits.
Campbell

SLIDING DOORS
Eddie Campbell
7 / 99.
Have you got any dosh? I need a twenty.
What on Earth do you do with it all ?!
We've been spending more than we earn for a year and a half - First it's the —
STOP! I don't want to hear it. Go and get your ink!
BOOKS
CD's
Haven't you got any cheap, bogus ink?
No sir, and with an Epson printer you should use Epson ink.
Aw, Bugger that
Review: Eddie Campbell is a genius. Buy his comic.
MYER CENTRE
Dad, can we eat out tonight
Now, there's a wonderful thought. Let's go to Sizzler.
Look, Real Daddy's caught behind the sliding doors.
Campbell

Questions
Alright, you lot! You've had a big night and it's School tomorrow. ?hic!.
into bed!
Dad, can I take my barbecue beer-bottle tops in for show-and-tell?
hmm...I'll have to think about that one
Goodnight, honey. I'll see you in your dreams.
Dad... do the King and Queen know each other.
why, yes, of course, because every night before he goes to sleep he leans over and kisses her and says, "Good night, my fine feathered friend"
Dad, why does he call her that?
Why, because they're the King and queen of the Cockatoos.
Nighty night.

The Court-Sketcher
by Eddie Campbell. 5.4.99.
They found Mr. Sillitoe Killed in his cell.
Objection!
We do not know that Mr. Sillitoe was "Killed"
What exactly do you mean, Mr. Cuthbert?
There are other ways to die, your honour, apart from "being Killed." One may, for instance, take one's own life.
hmm. Objection sustained
Yes... when Mr. Sillitoe was found dead in his cell, strangled by the electrical cord from the television in a way that I shall demonstr—
Your honour, if I may interject at this point.
I am concerned about a news "Sketch" artist representing my client as being in a cage.
your client is in a cage, Mr. Johnson.
For his own Protection.
Indeed he is, your honour and I fear that should the public see him thus depicted, it would result in a widespread prejudice against our case.

Does the public not have a right to see things as they are, Mr. Johnson.
Obviously, I have no objection to the...uh..."sketching" of my client per se
hmm... and do we have such a "sketcher" in the court today?
Here.
The learned gentleman is clearly familiar with my work, but I would like to reassure him...
...that I drew that thing once and have no intention of tackling it again.
Is that assurance satisfactory to you, Mr. Johnson?
Yes, Certainly your honour
Please proceed Mr. Humber.
...strangled by the cord of the television—
Objection!
"Sketched" by "E.Campbell"

Dr. Doolittle
by
Eddie Campbell
4. 00.
Chook Chook Chook Chookie
I'm a chook magnet!
Chook Chook Chookie
Chook
Pig!
gronk
Pig!
gronk
Pig!
gronk
merrrr, Prince Ludwig
merr
Where to next?
Merrrr
merrrr.
Gus, you're a bandit.
mmrrgh
mmrrgh
Daddy, I can't get along with any of the girls in my life-skills class. They're all bitches.
hmm. yeah.

Boojers! Get out of there. Silly toad.
Yock-eee Yock-ee puss! puss!
Aeeoooo
Shmighh.
Aeoooo
Shmighh.
7.00 Seinfeld. (G)(R). George li
about his profession to impress a
mer classmate. 340203
7.30 Friends. (PG)(S). The gu
their feminine side. 341932
8.00 Spin City. (PG)(S)
sends Michael and C
counselling. 348845
8.30 The Melbourne Comedy Festi
val. (MI). Hosted by Lano and Woodley,
from Melbourne's Regent Theatre.
137086
10.30 The Sopranos. (AVlv). Tony wel-
comes Furio. 701425
11.30 Nightline. 359086
12.00 Hyperion Bay. (PG). 504568
5207723
I haven't got a life.
HAHAHAHAH HAHAHA

Eat your vegies.
— YES DAD
Eddie Campbell 10.00
CALLY! COME and get your dinner!
Can't you do that later?
It'll just take a minute.
CARROTS! Bloody hell! There's two-week-old vegetables under here.
Sit down and eat your dinner for heaven's sake.
Aw, geez! What's this black gunk?
That's disgusting
Get back here this minute!
Smack him

Bastards I have been called.
You're such a sullen bastard when you're sober
You self-important, patronising bastard.
YOU'RE A SUPERCILIOUS BASTARD, CAMPBELL
UGh
That mischievous bastard over there!
That opinionated bastard at the head of the table
you thin lipped, disapproving Scot.
well that was a bit tactless, don't you think!?
WAH
You lanky streak of piss!
WRAUGGHNNBSTARD.
?
AND THAT'S JUST THE PEOPLE WHO LIKE ME

MINDSWEEPING.
Eddie Campbell 10.00
Let me see, I have half an hour. I shall undertake an ontological review of my weltanschauung.
Get a proper helmet you dickhead!
Campbell raids Evans' brain for ideas to pass off as his own.
Have another beer
What do you think of gambling, as a concept?
Isn't it based on the assumption that one can get rich by accident? As a system of belief, I can see no profit in it.
The classification of stuff.
1. Money.
Getting by.
We will help you pay off your mortgage quicker so you can stretch your social status by two and a half inches.
Get knotted
Anomaly: the money going into third world countries as aid is a fraction of that coming out as national debt repayment.
Getting rich.
There are five accredited systems, listed here in descending order
1. by inheritance.
2. by imagination.
WHAT THE CHAMBER MAID SAW.

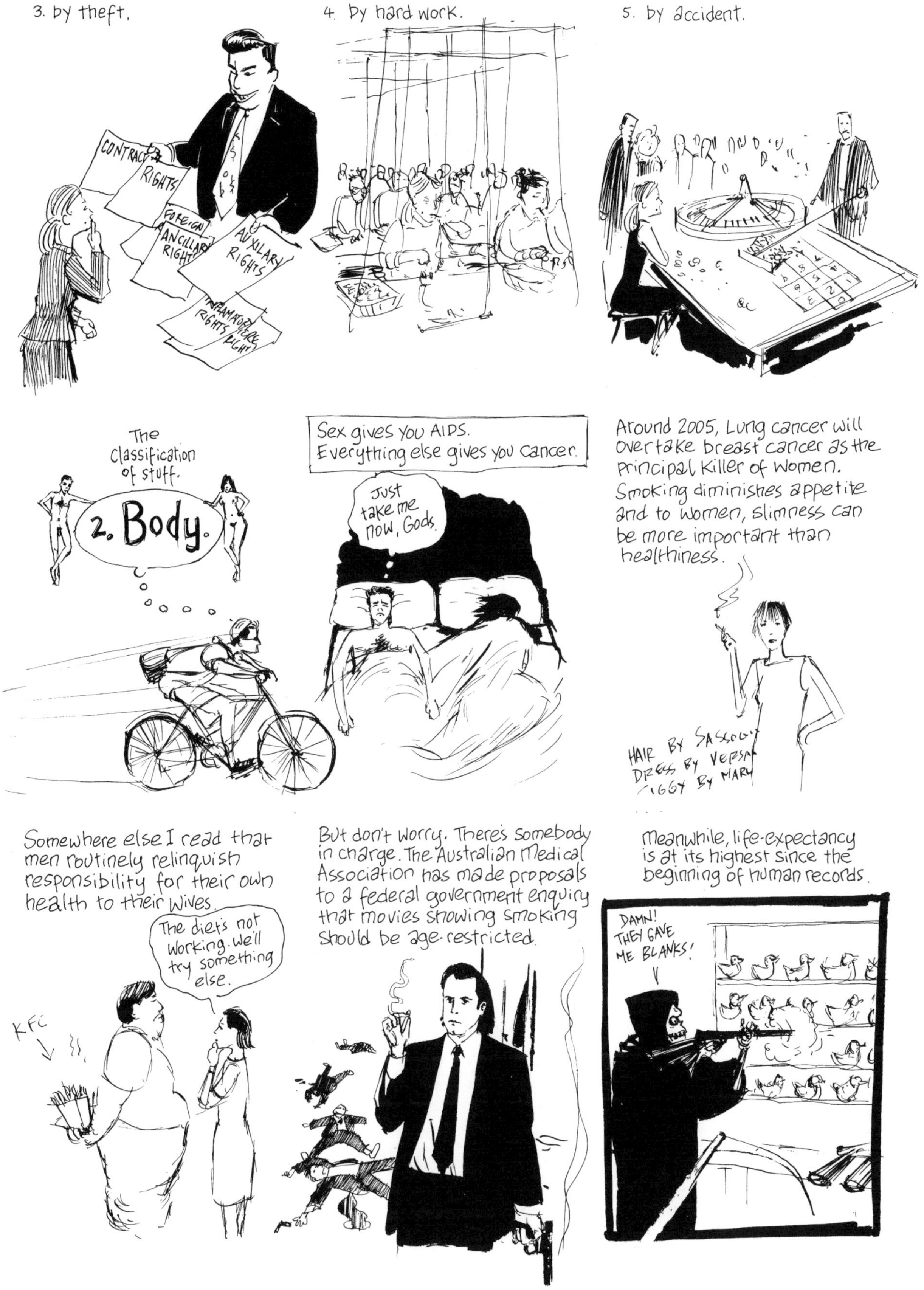
3. by theft.
CONTRACT
RIGHTS
FOREIGN
ANCILLARY RIGHTS
AUXILARY RIGHTS
4. by hard work.
5. by accident.
The Classification of stuff.
2. Body.
Sex gives you AIDS.
Everything else gives you cancer.
Just take me now, Gods.
Around 2005, Lung cancer will overtake breast cancer as the principal killer of women. Smoking diminishes appetite and to women, slimness can be more important than healthiness.
Somewhere else I read that men routinely relinquish responsibility for their own health to their wives.
KFC
The diet's not working. We'll try something else.
But don't worry. There's somebody in charge. The Australian Medical Association has made proposals to a federal government enquiry that movies showing smoking should be age-restricted.
Meanwhile, life-expectancy is at its highest since the beginning of human records.
DAMN! THEY GAVE ME BLANKS!

The classification of stuff.
3. Nation.
I am confronted by the proposition, made in all seriousness by one who flies the flag over his front lawn, that, after living here fourteen years, I should by now think of myself as Australian
with all respect, get knotted
The country is awash with national spirit, and also, more anomalies. On the TV news, juxtaposed but no similarity noted, WW II veterans visit sites in Japan and petition for an apology from that government. At home, the Aboriginal community demands an apology from its own government for the 'lost generation' and is rebuffed.
As in so many other places in a modern world where the boundaries of nation disintegrate, a reactionary group arises to reclaim some old imagined dignity.
National Front, Neo National Socialist and other "demagogues wrapping themselves in the flag." Here, it's the One Nation Party. The world watches to see if this country is about to embarrass itself.
But no, One Nation fails to get enough votes and in addition is in trouble for electoral fraud.
FIRST THING THE JACK ACID SOCIETY SHOULD DO IS GET RID OF ALL THE BUSYBODIES... ALL THE JOHNNY-COME-LATELIES.
© Kelly - Pogo
The great Walt Kelly in the 1950s
In my naivete, when I lettered the above caption, I didn't realise she had literally done it. (From photo on their website)
August 18 1999
One Nation leaders facing fraud charges after
AAP -- Fraud charges may be laid against the One Nation including the ruling trio of Pauline Hanson, David Oldfiel Ettridge, Queensland Premier Peter Beattie said.
Mr Beattie also said the Queensland Electoral Commission action to recover up to $500,000 in public funding the party following last year's state election.
"The Electoral Commission is currently seeking legal advice fro Law as to whether any person should be prosecuted under the Ele for making false and misleading statements," the Premier said.
The members start bickering and the organisation splinters after only three years. HA! The Monster Raving Loony Party in England has been thriving for three decades
My Goodness, even after Sutch popped off?
And when its leader Screaming Lord Sutch died recently, they replaced him with another human and a cat.
JOINT PARTY LEADER
ALAN HOWLING LAUD' HOPE
JOINT PARTY LEADER
CAT-MANDU
PARTY CHAIRMAN
T.C.OWEN
PARTY SECRETARY
MAD COW-GIRL
From their website.
But Australia opens the door to a new era with the High Court's Mabo decision of 1992, regarding land rights, which destroyed the legal doctrine of terra nullius. It stands as a bright example, attracting from overseas both admiration and delegates to study all the moves for their own benefit.
Eddie Mabo with his lawyers, Murray Island 92.

In the 1940s one Sacheverell Sitwell wrote: "compared to us, the aboriginals are like the muses crowned with flowers... they take part in their ceremonies, we merely sit and gape."
The passage as a whole reeks too much of "the noble savage," but that last bit has lodged itself in my noggin as a biting criticism of modern man.
That reeks a little.
Yes, it does, but... "We merely sit and gape"
The Classification of Stuff
4. Worship.
There are two theories: the Evolution theory and the God Theory
Send twenty five dollars for your free prophecy bible!!
zz
As Hazlitt observed, Netley, "The Gods have gone further off."
On the whole, if you need a god, you could do worse than worship cats.
In 522 b.c., the King of Persia, Cambyses II, defeated the Egyptians at Pelusium. Capturing several cats, he used them as shields. The Egyptians, reluctant to wound their sacred cats, surrendered the city.
The magus, he picked a snake.
"If I'm going to adopt a god, I'd rather start out knowing that it was a glove-puppet."
"my imaginary pal"
"It's a fiction. All gods are fiction. It's just that I happen to think fictions are real. Everything around us was once fiction. Before there was the table, there was the idea of the table".

"If I'm going to be dealing in totally imaginary territory, it struck me that it would be useful to have a native as a guide"
magic:
I had to seek his advice when I took on a short gig writing a magic character. I had no business being in it, of course.
But I concocted the notion of sending Joe Magic off on an occult, binding circle around the world.
Finally, Nemesis or, just retribution for overconfidence.
The Classification of Stuff.
The 5. Millennium.
That's the state of play as we enter into the new century.
I shall follow Joe Magic in his circle around the planet
I shall tie a bow on the millennium.
Put that in your Weltanschauung and smoke it.
Get knotted

The Millennium World Tour
of
Eddie Campbell.
9.00
PART ONE: HE SETS OUT.
The only difficult part of going round the world is in getting out of the house.
Hurry up or you'll miss the plane
AAARGH
It doesn't matter whether I packed this morning or the night before, I still run out the door five minutes later than I should have, get in the car and realise I've forgotten something important.
You'll be all right once you're upstairs. You always are.
I'm up for only an hour when the plane has engine trouble and has to come back.
There won't be another flight till tomorrow.
Let me have my suitcase back then.
I'll see what I can do.
I cheerfully go home.
Yeehah! I live to die another day
Aha! I've caught her at it! The sad and awful day has come. Betrayed!
You're not supposed to be back!
She's filled the kitchen with new furniture and I've only been away two hours.
HEY!!
Hi, Eddie

The Millennium World Tour of Eddie Campbell 7.99!
Singapore.
or
PART TWO: HE SETS OUT AGAIN
A Singapore Sling in Raffles Hotel.
It was created there in 1915 by Chinese bartender Ngaim Tong Boon: ½ measure gin, ¼ measure cherry Brandy, ¼ mixed fruit juices (orange, lime, pineapple) a few drops Cointreau and Benedictine, a dash of Angostura Bitters, top with cherry and pineapple.
EIGHTEEN BUCKS! But if you go to Singapore, you have to go to Raffles, and you can't go to Raffles without having a Singapore Sling. It would be bad manners.
Pretend you're with Somerset Maugham and Noel Coward.
I say, who is this insufferable man?
I thought he was your bit of rough
In the hotel where I'm staying, the bar has a six-piece Filipino band. They're good. I don't understand why I'm the only customer.
They're chatting with me. We're having a rare old time.
What shall we play next, Edee?
Beer is nine bucks.
Tiger
I don't see any drunks.
O inscrutable orient.
Campbell.

The Millennium World Tour of Eddie Campbell. 1999. People I don't go for in a big way.
The guy visiting town who gets me caught up in a conversation and then has to cut out to go look off the bridge or something; just when I'm getting up a head of steam.
oh yes, pointing no fingers
Because he's only here once and has to go and be a tourist and all that.
when he could have been drinking a beer with me. And he's only going to meet me once probably.
Take it for a fact, even. If I see him coming I'll be crossing to the other side.
I went to Australia. Beautiful country. I had a beer with Eddie Campbell
What did you see there?
Apart from Eddie? hmm.
In the bar of the Excelsior, I get into a conversation with a retired cop who shows me photos of his twelve children. We talk into the wee hours.
you have Tiger, isn't it?
His name is David. He calls me Goliath.
E Campbell

The Millennium World Tour of Eddie Campbell. 7-99.
MADRID.
(nothing works in Spain)
The baggage carousel takes an hour to start.
When it starts, the first thing out is a shampoo bottle
David Macho's been waiting ages to pick me up. The police have taken his car away.
*#!!#
Big Jim Hudnall's bags don't come off the carousel at all. Lesson: always wear your best clothes on the plane.
Dave Gibbons is here, amused to still be signing copies of the eleven-year-old WATCHMEN as though it's just out. With Jaime Delano we go through the PRADO composing dialogue for the characters in the paintings.
(and the modern museum too)
Hugo, our official translator, works overtime.
tell her she has pretty eyes
Edee, I wish to sleep.
On the second evening in the hotel I find that all the soap's been removed from my room.
Where's my soap gone?
Que?

Do you have someone who talks English?
Can I Help you sir?
i've got no soap in my room. I need two bars as soon as possible.
Have you got me some soap yet?
oh look i'm coming DOWN THERE!
Eddie
Later
Now. I need: TWO BARS OF SOAP.
yes, sir, I'll phone room service now.
It's just coming. There you are, sir.
Not SOUP ...SOAP!
Sopa?
Campbell's Soup

The Millennium World Tour of Eddie Campbell, one of several foreign guests in Madrid.
8-99
David Macho's telling me:
You'll be at the awards ceremony, of course you will. It's at a disco.
Discos are not my scene.
You'll love it. We've got a stripper and transvestites on stilts.
transvestites on stilts.
Publi
It's in Tres Cantos, a concrete New Town satellite of Madrid.
Everywhere I go on the planet, Kurt Busiek's there ahead of me getting an award. He's wearing spanking new white trainers that look like big baby-bootees under the disco lights.
Then they give some plaques and certificates to people I've never heard of while I'm getting a round of gins and tonics. And finally, there's the lifetime achievement award for an old cartoonist in his eighties.
He's a local hero who fought by Castro's side in Cuba. A hum of awe goes round the place: standing ovation.
He's shakily getting off the stage when the transvestites arrive.
And the smoke bombs go off.
Eddie Campbell.

The Millennium World Tour of Eddie Campbell. 9-99 in transit.
I was sitting over there waiting for three hours! honest.
London Heathrow, British Midland lounge. The screen directs flyers to the right gates. It's telling me to "wait in this lounge". I imagine it will say "now boarding" when the time comes, but this does not happen and I fail to hear the loudspeakers call my flight.
Even when they call a bunch of names including Campbell, I think "gee, those guys are so cool they get a personal wake-up call. Only when I hear "Eddie Campbell" does the coincidence seem stretched.
I think you just called me. Eddie Campbell?
huh?
Mister, I've been calling you for ten minutes! where have you been?
Just over there!
Okay. when's the next one?
two hours.
hmm... my bag's on this one. Can I make sure somebody holds it for me in Manchester?
You're bags on this one?..oh.. hold on.
We really shouldn't be doing this!
HURRY
SAFETY
The captain wants to speak to you
Congratulations. for keeping us all late.
This is not funny, you know.
Campbell.

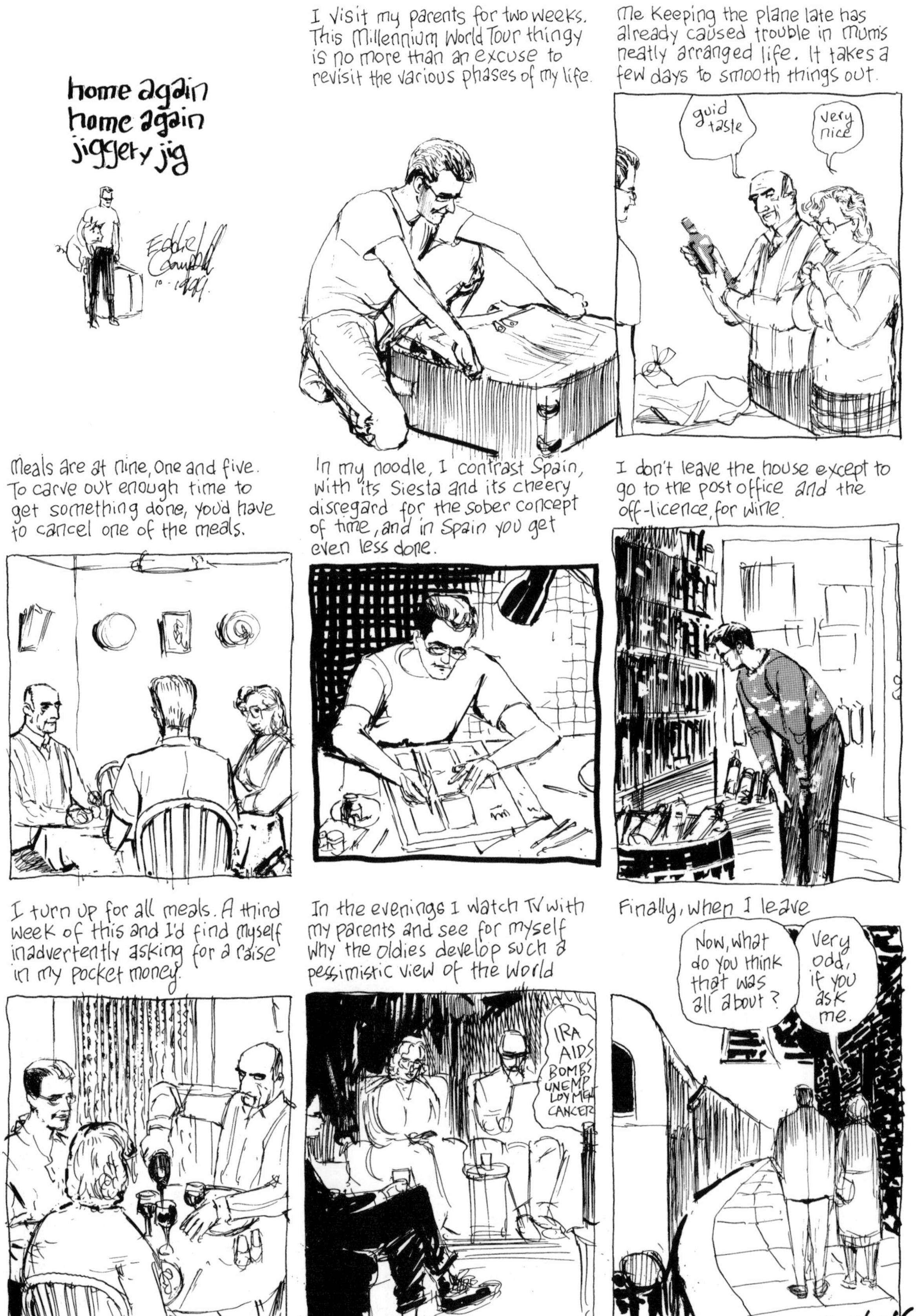
home again
home again
jiggery jig
I visit my parents for two weeks. This Millennium World Tour thingy is no more than an excuse to revisit the various phases of my life.
Me keeping the plane late has already caused trouble in Mum's neatly arranged life. It takes a few days to smooth things out.
guid taste
very nice
Meals are at nine, one and five. To carve out enough time to get something done, you'd have to cancel one of the meals.
In my noodle, I contrast Spain, with its siesta and its cheery disregard for the sober concept of time, and in Spain you get even less done.
I don't leave the house except to go to the post office and the off-licence, for wine.
I turn up for all meals. A third week of this and I'd find myself inadvertently asking for a raise in my pocket money.
In the evenings I watch TV with my parents and see for myself why the oldies develop such a pessimistic view of the world
IRA
AIDS
BOMBS
UNEMPLOYMENT
CANCER
Finally, when I leave
Now, what do you think that was all about?
Very odd, if you ask me.

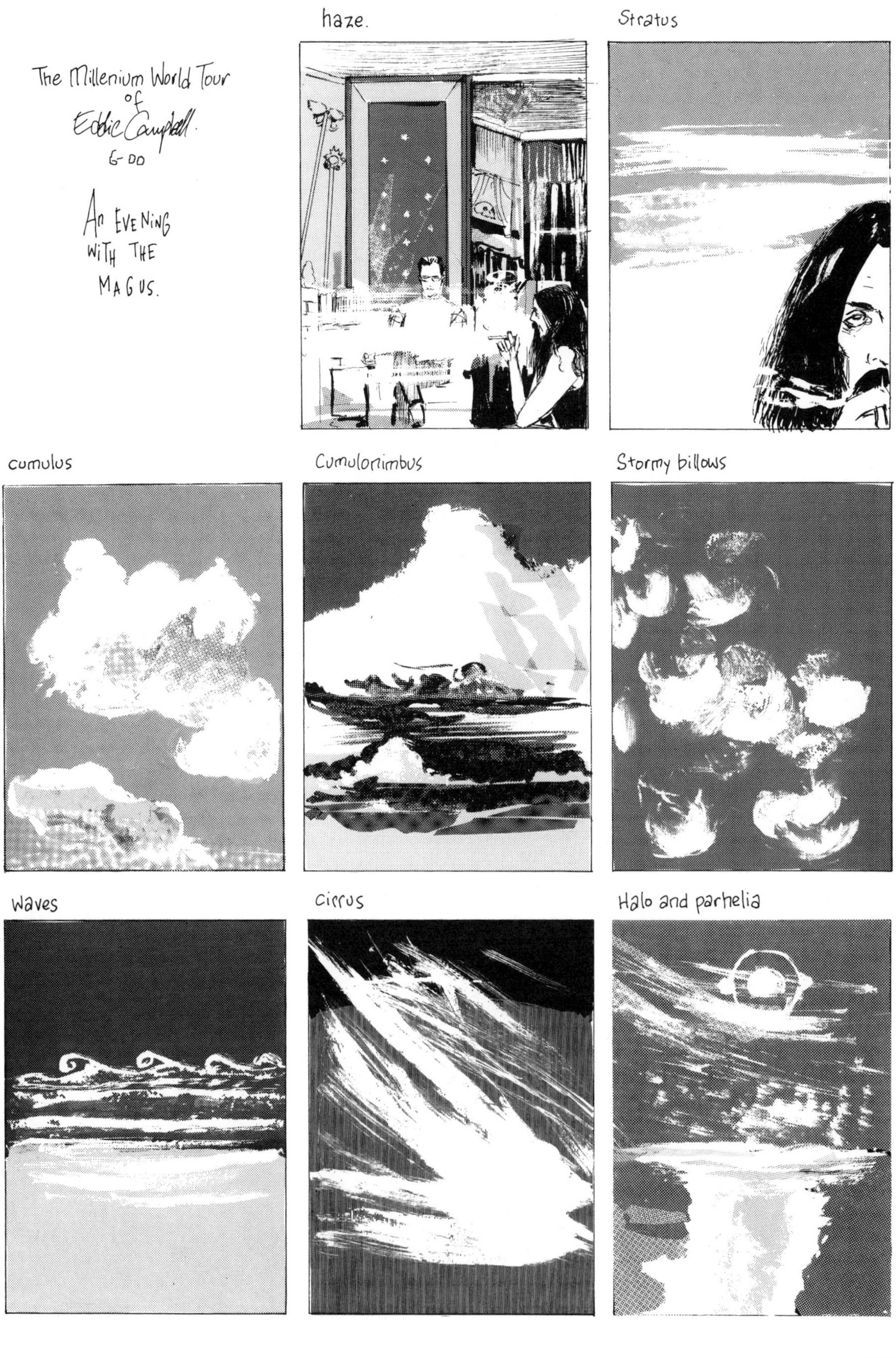
The Millenium World Tour
of
Eddie Campbell.
6-00
An Evening
with the
Magus.
haze.
Stratus
cumulus
Cumulonimbus
Stormy billows
Waves
Cirrus
Halo and parhelia

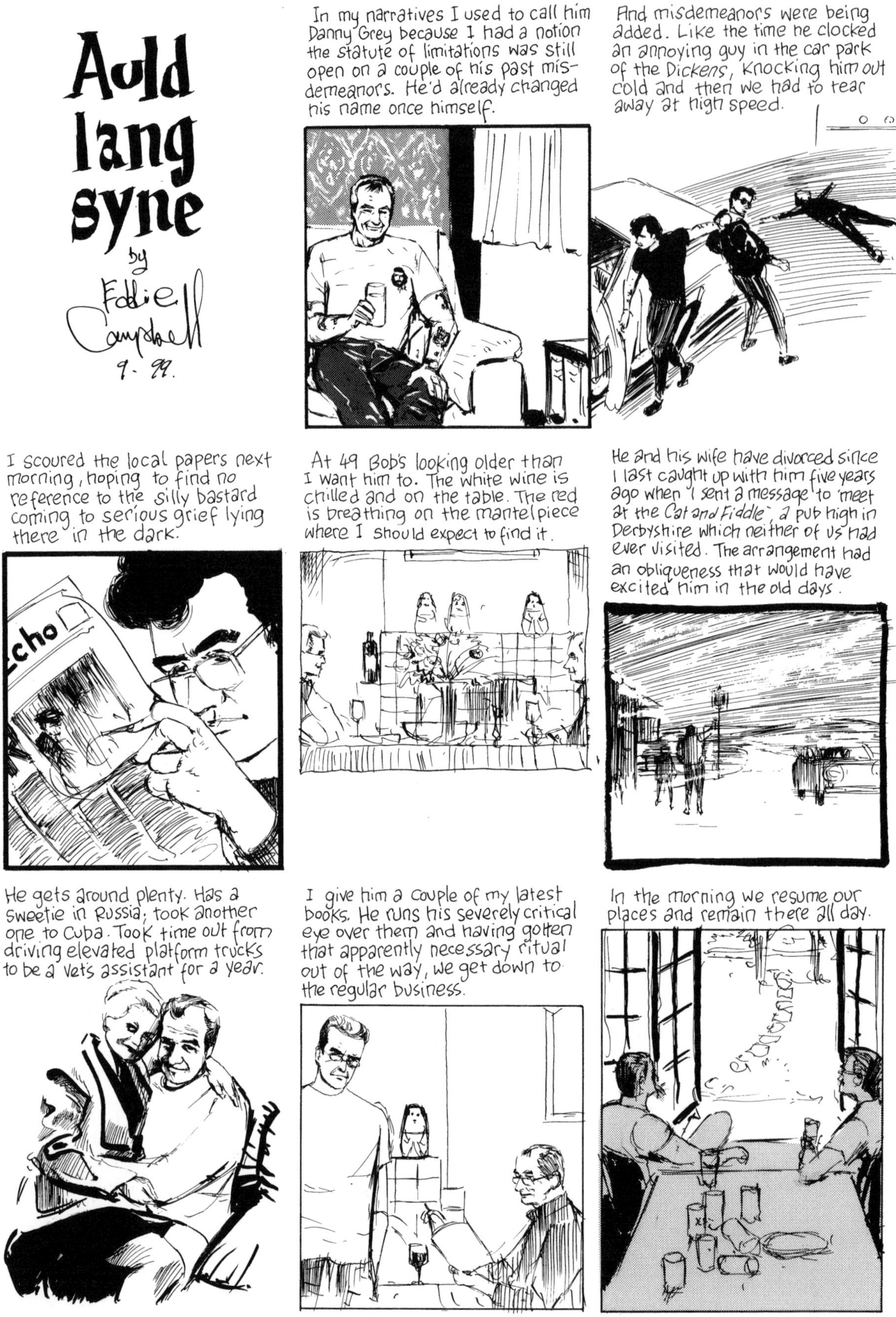
Auld lang syne
by
Eddie Campbell
9-99.
In my narratives I used to call him Danny Grey because I had a notion the statute of limitations was still open on a couple of his past misdemeanors. He'd already changed his name once himself.
And misdemeanors were being added. Like the time he clocked an annoying guy in the car park of the Dickens, knocking him out cold and then we had to tear away at high speed.
I scoured the local papers next morning, hoping to find no reference to the silly bastard coming to serious grief lying there in the dark.
Echo
At 49 Bob's looking older than I want him to. The white wine is chilled and on the table. The red is breathing on the mantelpiece where I should expect to find it.
He and his wife have divorced since I last caught up with him five years ago when I sent a message to 'meet at the Cat and Fiddle', a pub high in Derbyshire which neither of us had ever visited. The arrangement had an obliqueness that would have excited him in the old days.
He gets around plenty. Has a sweetie in Russia; took another one to Cuba. Took time out from driving elevated platform trucks to be a vet's assistant for a year.
I give him a couple of my latest books. He runs his severely critical eye over them and having gotten that apparently necessary ritual out of the way, we get down to the regular business.
In the morning we resume our places and remain there all day.

Wee Eddie would have lapped it up, imagining a day when the world might give him leave to be in stories instead of reading them in comics or watching them on the TV
The stories all connect with a riverside pub situated in the uncomplicated magic night. I called it the King Canute when my narrative technique was less certain.
camp, what the fuck have you been up to?
Everybody met everybody else at this King Canute. Bob met his wife there; I met Penny Moore. She met somebody else. By this time it had gotten complicated.
Penny Moore married our old pal, George Waite. I'm looking at the photographs.
They look happy. It lasted all of five months.
Next day we visit the old pub. It seems very sedate now.
In the car park I recall a car I bought for Penny: a Hilman Husky, for £35.00, which was less than half my week's wages. I had to get Bob to drive it to here for me, it sat outside the pub for months till we got complaints.
Apparently there was a problem with the cooling system. I got John Godfrey to look at it for me. He poured in two pints of water and watched it all come out of the exhaust pipe.
I've never driven a car myself except the one time I drove Bob home in his Mercury Marquis a big 7½ litre job, along the Southend Arterial Road. A Police vehicle even passed us.

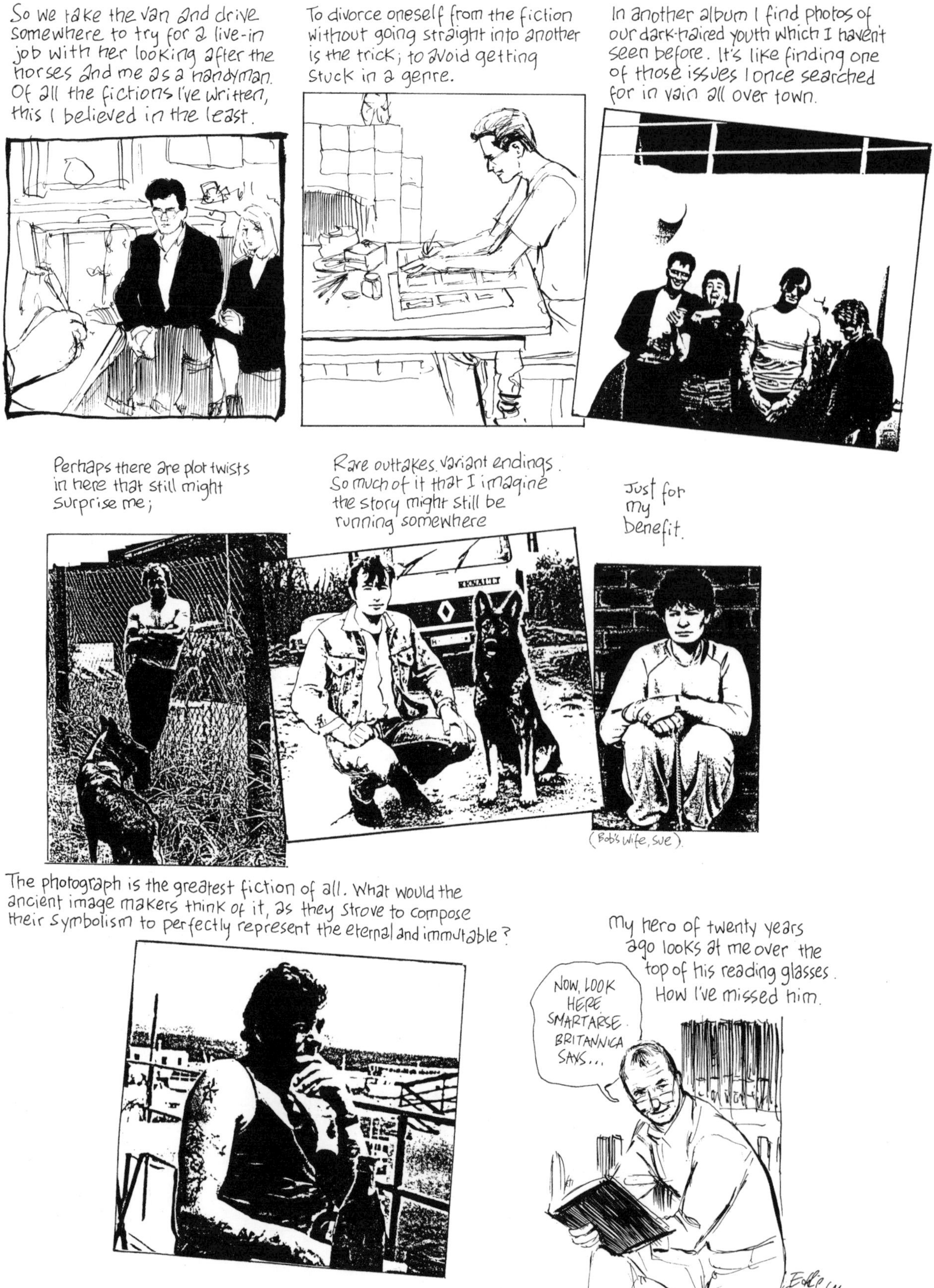
So we take the van and drive somewhere to try for a live-in job with her looking after the horses and me as a handyman. Of all the fictions I've written, this I believed in the least.
To divorce oneself from the fiction without going straight into another is the trick; to avoid getting stuck in a genre.
In another album I find photos of our dark-haired youth which I haven't seen before. It's like finding one of those issues I once searched for in vain all over town.
Perhaps there are plot twists in here that still might surprise me;
Rare outtakes, variant endings. So much of it that I imagine the story might still be running somewhere
Just for my benefit.
RENAULT
(Bob's Wife, Sue).
The photograph is the greatest fiction of all. What would the ancient image makers think of it, as they strove to compose their symbolism to perfectly represent the eternal and immutable?
My hero of twenty years ago looks at me over the top of his reading glasses. How I've missed him.
NOW, LOOK HERE SMARTARSE. BRITANNICA SAYS...
Eddie Campbell

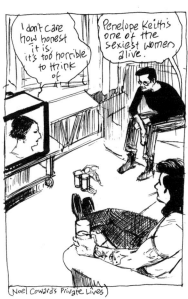

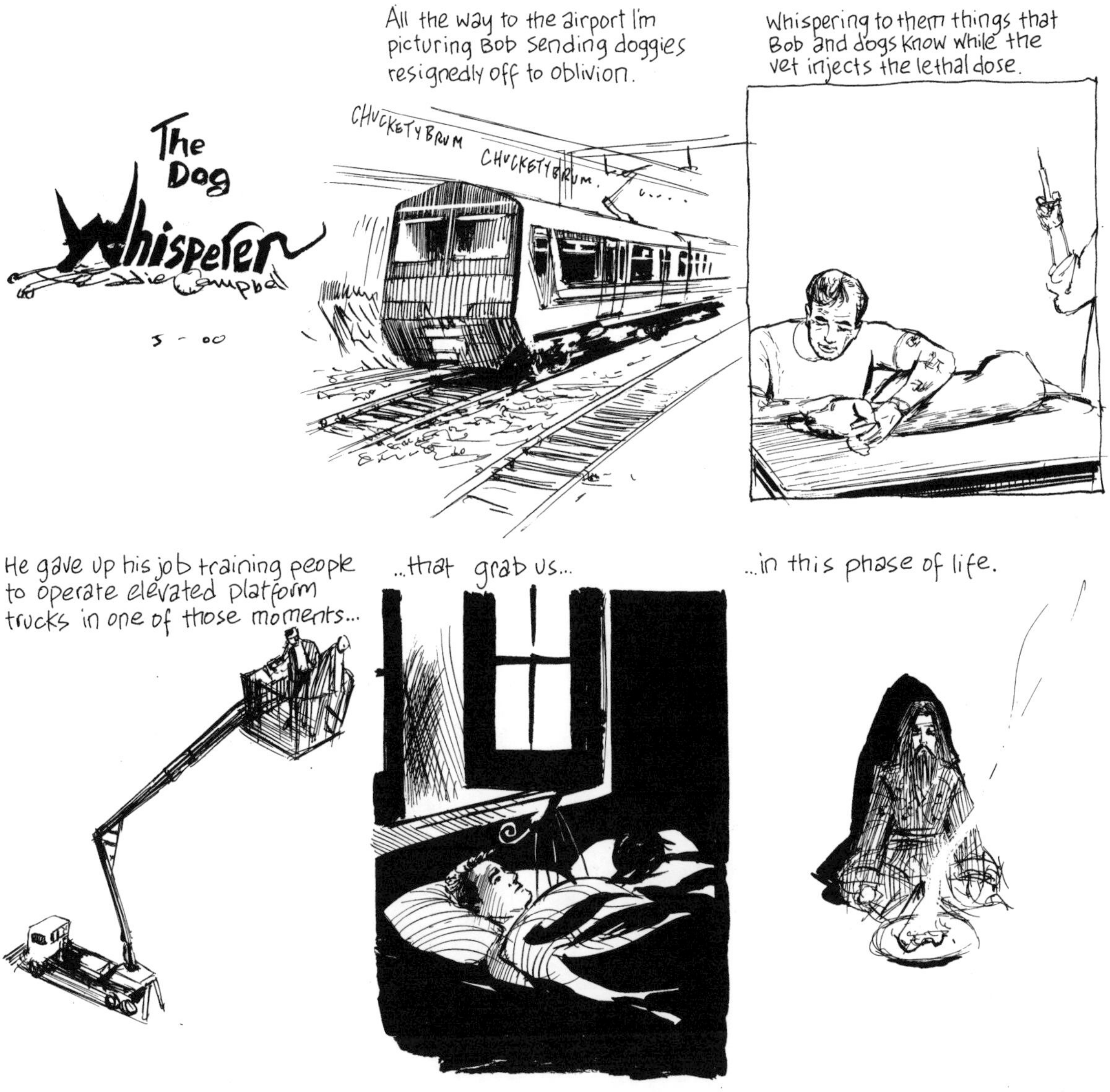
The Dog Whisperer
Eddie Campbell
5 - 00
All the way to the airport I'm picturing Bob sending doggies resignedly off to oblivion.
CHUCKETYBRUM
CHUCKETYBRUM...
Whispering to them things that Bob and dogs know while the vet injects the lethal dose.
He gave up his job training people to operate elevated platform trucks in one of those moments...
...that grab us...
...in this phase of life.
Then while taking one of his own dogs to the vet he cheerfully offered himself as a cheap assistant.
chucketybrum, chucketybrum. We're watching television one night twenty or so years ago.
I don't care how honest it is: it's too horrible to think of
Penelope Keith's one of the sexiest women alive.
(Noel Coward's Private Lives)

Let's be superficial and pity the poor philosophers. Let's blow trumpets and squeakers and enjoy the party like small quite idiotic school children. Come and kiss me, darling before your body rots and worms pop in and out of your eye sockets
Worms don't pop.
Isn't this so redolent of sex. But if it was a modern play, by now you'd see them on the setee with his spotty arse bobbing up and down
chucketybrum, chucketybrum. It's a long old ride out to Heathrow, but being permitted to sit and do nothing is such a luxury these days.
For three or four years Bob and I used to just mooch around wherever the whim took us. I made a book about it.
eddie campbell
alec the King Canute Crowd
I recall one night we took Beryl from the factory out to dinner in appreciation of all the apple pies she used to bake for us.
oh good Lord NO!

we're Not paying
If it's broken, let me see it
It's gone
Chucketybrum, chucketybrum. There's always been some kind of story trying to happen around Bob. I wistfully think about all the ones I've missed.

!
What's that clattering ?!
oh· oh ·
I think your days are numbered, Rab.
chucketybrum, chucketybrum.

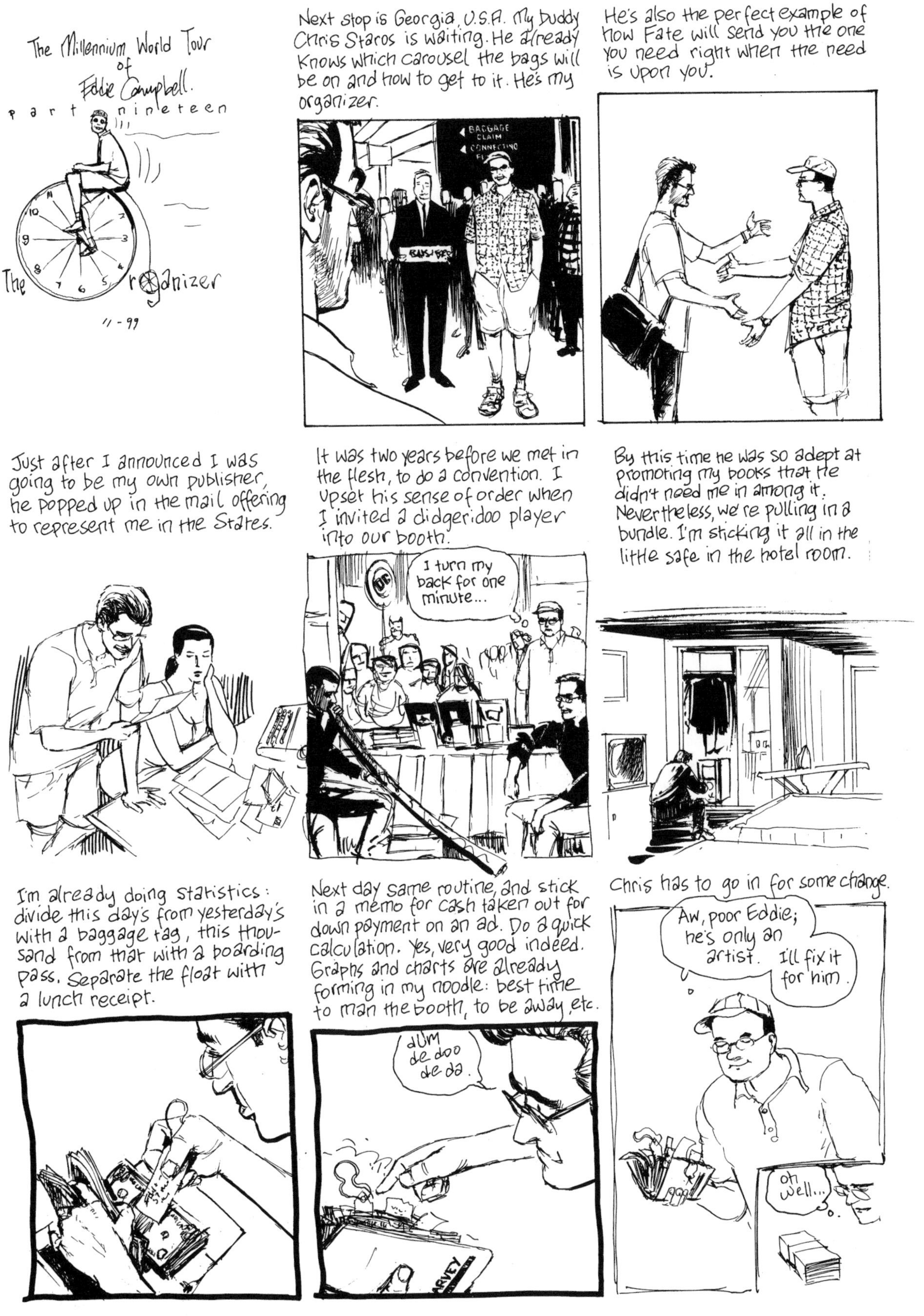
The Millennium World Tour of Eddie Campbell.
part nineteen
The Organizer
11-99
Next stop is Georgia, U.S.A. My buddy Chris Staros is waiting. He already knows which carousel the bags will be on and how to get to it. He's my organizer.
BAGGAGE CLAIM
CONNECTING
He's also the perfect example of how Fate will send you the one you need right when the need is upon you.
Just after I announced I was going to be my own publisher, he popped up in the mail offering to represent me in the States.
It was two years before we met in the flesh, to do a convention. I upset his sense of order when I invited a didgeridoo player into our booth.
I turn my back for one minute...
By this time he was so adept at promoting my books that he didn't need me in among it. Nevertheless, we're pulling in a bundle. I'm sticking it all in the little safe in the hotel room.
I'm already doing statistics: divide this day's from yesterday's with a baggage tag, this thousand from that with a boarding pass. Separate the float with a lunch receipt.
Next day same routine, and stick in a memo for cash taken out for down payment on an ad. Do a quick calculation. Yes, very good indeed. Graphs and charts are already forming in my noodle: best time to man the booth, to be away, etc.
dum de doo de da.
Chris has to go in for some change.
Aw, poor Eddie; he's only an artist.
Ill fix it for him.
oh well...

So now he's a partner in running a publishing operation called Topshelf. For his day job he's a manager at Lockheed. He used to be a heavy metal guitarist (I've seen the video)
Nita Staros has every corner of the house looking like a photo from Better Homes and Gardens.
Oh, what luxury. There are a zillion e-mails from my kids and other stuff. A magazine wants a phone interview. Time is arranged. Shop appearance in New York. Contents of a speech in Maryland to be discussed...
Staros gets me on my plane to N.Y.
Then by a mysterious sleight of hand he's waiting for me when I get there.
Gates
The schedule is all pinned down. In N.Y. I'm meeting all these Small Press guys. Sleeping bag days are here again.
It's strange revisiting smallpressdom this late in the day. The daft enthusiasm of it all. O me, where is the life I led?
(i'm leaving in the twin towers)
Way back in '76 I was in N.Y. with my first wee silly hand-made comic, too afraid to go in anywhere.
SONY
But how pleasing it is to go visiting when you're not selling anything. So we drop in on Superman, and Vertigo, and all that...

The big 600 page From Hell will be out for Christmas. I'm sure the lovely Karen Berger thinks Chris is the publisher. Nobody wants to believe that the illustrator can publish too.
But then, maybe it's because I got off the last plane deaf in one ear. I just came down Third Avenue like walking under water
Maybe I'm missing some of the conversation and Chris is holding up my end for me. Who knows what's going on out there?
It's like being sozzled. And the lovely Karen Berger could be the Queen of the bottom of the sea. We're showing pictures of our children.
All life has lately become a big daft stage. Nothing's real.
Next day we almost truly are walking under water. Hurricane Floyd is pissing up and down the coast.
We're stuck on an immobile train halfway to Washington D.C. Temporary suspension of the normal schedule can bring out the best in people.
Then we're all ushered off the train and onto a bus. Why, oh why did I pick up all those damn books at my parents' house? Forty Four and still going home for my things.
Bethesda, Maryland. Staros is sorting out the room bookings. He's got it so that the home team are paying for mine, except some wires have got crossed.
This first room should already be taken care of.

He's got it all ship-shape in no time.
ICAF will take care of the room as you're doing the speech. Greg and Joel have defrayed your travel expense to get you to SPX, so you give them a box of books...
Good idea
ICAF: International Cartoon Arts Festival.
SPX: Small Press Expo.
He's the emcee at the Ignatz awards:
Our next presenter has been creating graphic novels for a quarter of a century!
You don't look that old.
MY GOODNISS, IGNATZ
Nix with the quarter century.
YOU ARE DEWELOPING A KALF UPON ONE OF YOUR LIMBS
It's an actual brick!
Now I realize why you never sent the one I won two years ago.
We've still got it at the shop - I'll get it for you tomorrow.
ZING
THATS WHERE A BEE BIT ME, SILLY
While I'm relaxing in the glow of the moment, one Victor Cayro plonks himself next to me. I ran one of his drawings in a recent issue of my magazine.
You bitches don't even fuckin' know who this is! He taught us every thing.
He forgot to teach you some manners.
Cayro is gulping his way through all the stages of intoxication in one six-pack which he has smuggled into the function.
Now what were they again... verbose, jocose, bellicose, morose, lachrymose...
Next time I see him he's asleep in an armchair in the lobby.
Comatose!
Z
There's a genuine jolly old party upstairs with a jacuzzi-full of beer and cider.

Some wags have carried Cayro in his armchair into one of the elevators where he goes up and down all night.
Staros has got three rooms including this one and he's juggling all his artists in and out in different permutations.
Then in the morning he's away early.
I'm trying to remember why I booked my flight out so late in the day. Oh yes! The last time I woke up with a sore head and Chris had to reorganize my flights
He's flying out later than planned. Now, how long can he remain in the room before he's into another day's charges?
I have brunch with Connie, that delightful lady who happens to also be Quentin Tarantino's mom, and Neil. I've managed to catch up with just about everyone on this tour.
Then they're all off in a limo to watch Neil introduce the special preview showing of *Princess Mononoke*.
To Hell with it, I'll wait at the airport.
It's 73 lbs. sir. We will only take bags 70 and under. You're overweight.
I'll just have to take out the brick then
UNITED AIRLINES
UNITED AIRLINES
Nothing's real. Take a bow.
I'LL KREASE THAT KRAZY KARTOONIST'S KOKONUT

Eternity
It's a friendly, safe feeling, arriving home to a warm, humid place. Is it just familiarity, or a womb-thing? Or the memory of the anticipation of a hot-climate holiday.
INTERNATIONAL ARRIVALS
Dad, we forgot what you look like.
Why have you got a brick, Dad?
First order of the day is to get the huge *From Hell* off to the printer.
It's the dog's bollocks
There's a face missin here. How come w never notice that befor
There's another sleepless night while the finished books go out of Canada filling up an eighteen-wheeler.
campbell's bloody books
With a wholesale value higher than the cost of our house, it runs off the road.
It is hijacked and blown up on the order of the Freemasons.
It'll murder me.
I've decided to drink sensibly this party season.
SPECIAL XXXX
TOOHEYS NEW
MILLENNIUM COUNTDOWN

The usual big Dickensian Christmas dinner has a way of keeping the booze in its place.
We attempt the same strategy on New Year's Eve, taking the whole party to a restaurant that closes at eleven.
Then we drive up the mountain to watch the fireworks over the city. Mullins tells me the Pyrotechnicians have reset their computers to 1998 to outwit the 'Millennium bug'.
Now the countdown. There it goes. End of a millennium.
...well take a cup o' kindness yet, for the sake of Auld Lang Syne.
uh how does the rest go? we're here because we're here because...
Aw no, we've forgotten the words!!!? How did that happen? Annie and I usually photocopy the sheet music and hand it out.
We twa hae run aboot the braes and pulled the gowans fine
...fields and plucked the daisies...
Auld Lang
It's almost tragic. It's one of the three most popular songs in the English speaking world along with Happy Birthday and For He's a Felly Good Jollo (as we call it in our house).
We've wandered mony a weary foot Since Auld Lang Syne
Words by BURNS.
Not too slow.
Voice.
Piano.
mf
Robert Burns, dying at the age of 37 in 1796; Could he have imagined the celebrity of his verses?
We twa hae paidl'd in the burn, From morning sun till dine
...paddled in the stream
Carried in Romantic feeling to the corners of the English speaking world.
But seas between us braid hae roared Since Auld Lang Syne.
...broad have roared.

I feel like I've left a country I was quite fond of, the twentieth century, heading over Burns' broad roaring seas.
A stretch limo passes. There's a big trade in limo hire tonight. Surely the point is to be in the picture, not gaping at it through dark glass.
All the way down the mountain I'm thinking something's missing. Observances have not been made.
The night is descending into bathos. Mick has to urinate in the vicinity of the graveyard.
DON'T LET MICK BACK IN THE CAR! HE'S A ZOMBIE NOW
QUICK MUM! DRIVE!
Evans is one of those who are still insisting it's not even the one true millennium.
Do your sums! It's next year.
The date is arbitrary! Anyone who'd save a party for next year that they could have now is no devotee of Bacchus!
BACCHUS?! But you're just a disapproving, thinlipped Scot!
I had a notion the millennium night would be so good that it would entertain me instead of the other way around. Feeling I have let it down, I sit up into the wee hours watching the global television coverage. The sun is setting on Easter Island.
In New Orleans they're giving the old millennium a funeral
They re-show the Sydney bridge fireworks. A word burns itself on my retina, and perhaps on the retinae of two billion others.
Eternity
And therein lies a story: it was a message that Arthur Stace, reformed criminal and recovered alcoholic, chalked almost everywhere in Sydney between his rebirth into Christianity in 1930 and his death in 1967.

Given his medium, most of his work washed off within a few days, but one example remains inside the big bell at Sydney's Martin Place, where it appeared in 1963.
Sydney poet Douglas Stewart wrote:
"That shy, mysterious poet, Arthur Stace, whose work was just one single, mighty word, Worked in the utmost depths of time and space..."
The fireworks go off around the planet in the same order that I did: Singapore, Madrid, New York. There's a baptism at sunrise by the Jordan in a combined Catholic-Jordanian ceremony.
In Africa, Nelson Mandela lights a candle in the cell where he was incarcerated for twenty-five years, and passes it to the young generation.
In the Amazon jungle they dance to their anaconda god. It looks like a perfectly natural conga line.
It's too late for me to believe in anything enough to dance with such fervent abandon. And it's too late tonight to do anything symbolically significant.
But I'll be damned if I'm going to bed yet.
Ma, let's take ourselves under the trees by the creek and make love as the sun comes up.
Okay, Pa. Let's paddle in the burrn.
So we go over to the woods, which is a bird sanctuary, or so they told us when they sold us the house, and we take off all our clothes...
In full sight of the Kookaburra, the sulphur crested cockatoo, the tawny frogmouth owl, the galah, the lorikeet, a bird which in our house we call the booger bird and a bird who sings the first two bars of the can-can.
Eddie Campbell

Mick's Grave New World
Eddie Campbell 11-00
Two thousand A.D.! In the seventies we imagined it would be a future of bubble-shaped anti-gravity cars.
With sky-ways linking the tops of strange expressionist buildings that even Mies van der Rohe couldn't conceive.
We thought we'd be dressing in tin-foil clothes but instead I'm looking at fucking brown corduroy with elbow patches.
Here we are in two fucking thousand with more cunts walking about than in the nineteen seventies.
We were supposed to have replicants of ourselves to perform all our works while we bask in the glory.
Instead we've got third world countries turning out ugly sports training shoes.
No glittering spires; no end to global warming; no unified world economy; no cures for AIDS or cancer. no cryogenic immortality!
But. it's the silvery suits I miss the most.
Campbell
134

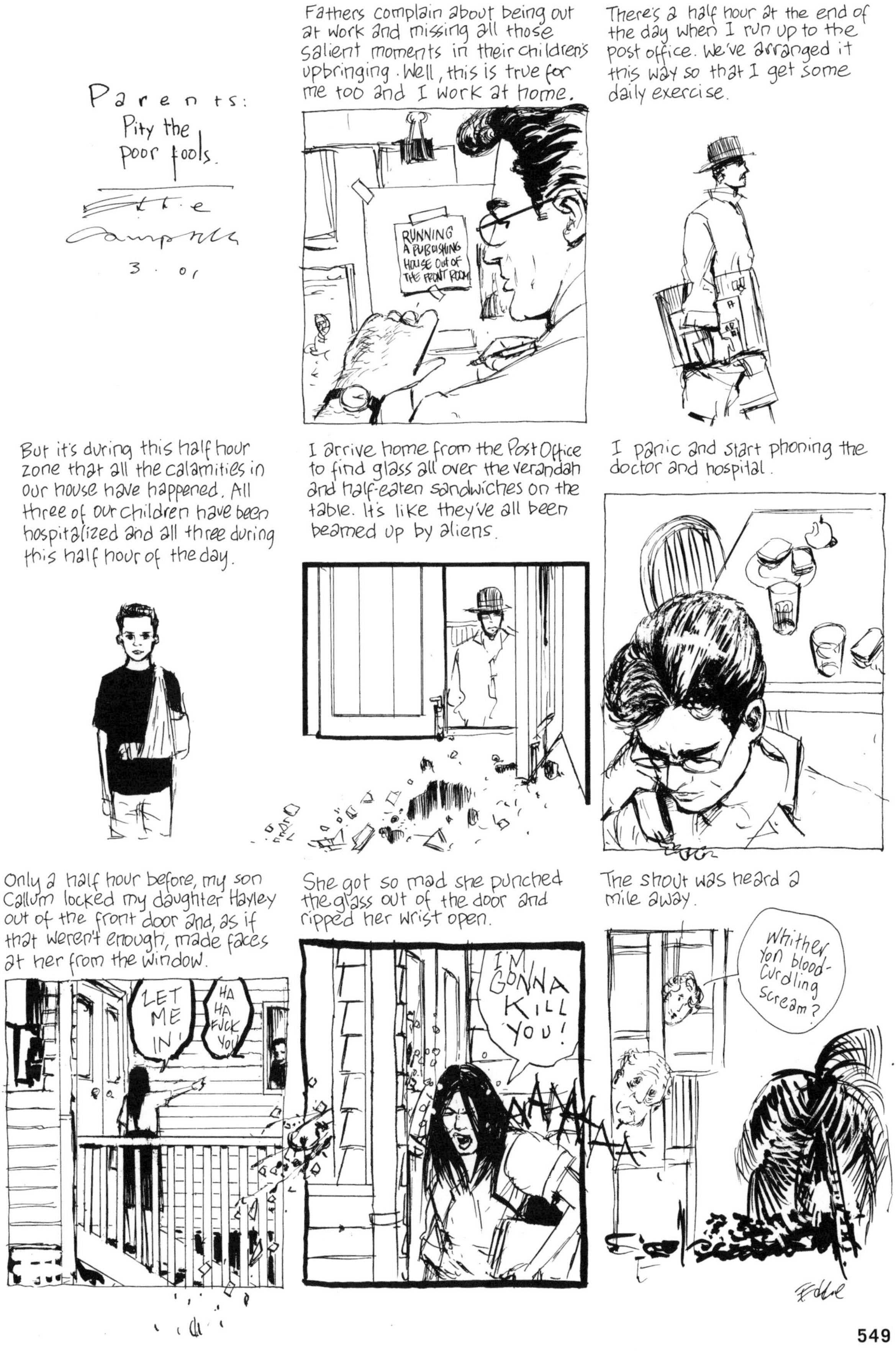
Parents: Pity the poor fools.
3 . 01
Fathers complain about being out at work and missing all those salient moments in their children's upbringing. Well, this is true for me too and I work at home.
RUNNING A PUBLISHING HOUSE OUT OF THE FRONT ROOM
There's a half hour at the end of the day when I run up to the post office. We've arranged it this way so that I get some daily exercise.
But it's during this half hour zone that all the calamities in our house have happened. All three of our children have been hospitalized and all three during this half hour of the day.
I arrive home from the Post Office to find glass all over the verandah and half-eaten sandwiches on the table. It's like they've all been beamed up by aliens.
I panic and start phoning the doctor and hospital.
Only a half hour before, my son Callum locked my daughter Hayley out of the front door and, as if that weren't enough, made faces at her from the window.
LET ME IN!
HA HA FUCK YOU
She got so mad she punched the glass out of the door and ripped her wrist open.
I'M GONNA KILL YOU!
AAAAAAAA
The shout was heard a mile away.
Whither yon blood-curdling scream?

I've got mail!
"Pay off your mortgage in five years.
Lose 15 pounds in a week...
Do you like hot sex?
Eddie Campbell 4.01
Hey, Erin! Look at this. It's vagina.com
Oh my God! that's disgusting
HOT CHILLI
Hee Hee
Tt.
Holee...
Ooon
Oh my God
Where's she putting that? Oh my god...
Tt.
WAH!
Hee Hee He
Ooo
HOT CHILLI
What's going on here? What's all the noise?
AAA! We're sprung!
It was him It wasn't me!
RUN!
HOT CHILLI
Eddie. This is serious. Look what they've been up to.
Amazing! How did they figure that out? You can take any word and put 'dotcom' after it.
That's awful. Can you go and have a talk to them?
Yes. We can't have this going on.
Tut tut.
hmm...
penis. com.
Eddie

Cider in Asturias
by Eddie Campbell 8.00
Here I am in Spain again. A suitcase falls off the baggage truck.
Spanair
How will they deal with it, I wonder. Ah yes, here comes a jeep chasing the truck.
BEEP BEEP
The truck driver can't hear a thing, so the jeep fetches the case.
And rides back, balancing it on the bonnet.
From Madrid to Asturias in Northern Spain. Here, cider (sidre) is the traditional drink. It's a particularly flat and cloudy variant of cider.
It is drunk, of course, in the Sidrerias.
Sidreria Cabranes
Very friendly little places indeed, Notice nobody is holding a glass. The same one gets passed around a group, with a new mouthful in the bottom of it, poured for each person. Any cider remaining in the glass after your mouthful should be tossed into the trough at the foot of the bar.
The cider must be poured from high up, or, more specifically, thrown. Presumably, this is to aerate and enliven it. No other method is acceptable.

It is to be chucked back immediately after pouring, as explained to me by my translator and drinking buddy for the week, Nino Ortea.
How do I order a refill?
Eddie, you ask for a 'culin', which means a um... "small bottom" but be careful...
I've been asked to do a front cover for the festival's journal. So I tape paper to the bathroom wall and paint myself practicing the throwing technique the way Nino says he learned as a kid.
We deliver the picture and go for more cider. It's all eat, drink and smoke here. And the rain in Spain falls mainly in this street.
At the pomologica, or cider research centre, out in the country, there are computers and test tubes everywhere, but I'm intrigued by a device on the wall of the recreation room for mechanically throwing the cider.
My host, Norman Fernandez
The week ends with a Sunday picnic where more cider is to be chucked. I'm up to my ankles in cider.
I dress knowing these things always end in a ball game.
and in Spain, the ritual embarrassing of the guests.
I thought I was just going to have to throw the cider
Then everybody sings an old sentimental song...
Adios con el corazon que con el alma no puedo.
as the coach takes away those guests bound by road for Madrid.
Al despedirme de ti al despedirme me muero.
Cider in Asturias - page 2
"Farewell with all my heart, because I can't say it with my soul. When I say goodbye to you, when I say goodbye to you, I feel like dying." or so Nino says, on the back of a handy coaster

THE TOPSHELF BOYS
We also have stickers, coasters, matchboxes and posters to help enhance Topshelf's presence in your store.
Eddie Campbell 8.00
I have to catch the next plane out. I don't think Nita's dad will see out the day.
Aw, we're all on a bus to shitsville, man.
Chris
Brett
So you're going to have to sell this to the retailers.
Hey, no sweat.
Now the package contains only our BEST SELLING GRAPHIC NOVELS, with a total retail value of FIVE... HUNDRED... DOLLARS. THEY only have to pay TWO-TWO-FIVE.
COOL.
That's 55% off!! FIFTY FIVE PER CENT!
Discount city, man.
We're even going to ship the books at our OWN expense
Awesome
They don't even have to pay for THIRTY DAYS! We'll invoice them.
Wow
And not only that, but any books they can't sell after ninety days we'll replace with anything else from the catalog of an equivalent value.
Have you got all that? Play it back to me.
Okay
Hey, dude! Here's the spiel on the deal...

IN WALLYHOOD
Eddie Campbell 8/00
In Wallyhood I audition for all kinds of roles.
Different lives.
Different deaths.
"LOOK, ma! Top of da WOILD! KA BOOM"
I'm eyeing off the leading ladies.
Check all the gear back into the costume dept. and start over
In this one, an exhibitionist.
In the next one, an inhibitionist.
Did I look stupid?
It was funny at first

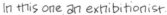

The script gets numerous rewrites.
I watch it all in the rushes.
oh no. oh no.
Oh Bloody blatherin' poo.
More lives.
More deaths.
"Not waving, but drowning"
(Death too reads for parts in Wallyhood.)
I grapple with my nemesis. over Reichenbach Falls
He gets me at the Alamo.
Then one day we all may wake up and find that we're stereotyped.
In Wallyhood the plot starts with a good idea and ends with a cliché.
STOP

Which cliché? How about the revenge scenario, in which, say, a great set-piece, a shoot-out on the stairs at Chicago's rail station, is superceded by a dumb finale on a rooftop.
The sadistic bastard goes off it. That's when I'm in *The Untouchables*. Where do they get this crap? Out of comic books? Don't laugh.
Another movie I can't watch to the end is *The Patriot*. It became a moot point with me, whether it buggered around too much with history...
When I absentmindedly wandered out of the cinema fifteen minutes from the end, having lost all interest in the futures of the characters.
It might as well have been Aliens, another movie I have to turn off early.
What is it with the revenge scenario? Why does the viewer desire to be manipulated in this way? Who are they getting vicarious revenge upon; themselves?
You idiots! Get outta here!
Have I become very moral? Indeed the greatest play in the English language was a 'revenge tragedy'. In taking his revenge, Hamlet must by all the rules be killed himself and probably go to Hell.
Die ya bastard. Garhhh. TAH!
In Wallyhood I have my cake and eat it too. The sadistic bastard must be shot by me and no other, and with the bullet made from the dead boy's lead soldier.
BOOM!
And then I go and marry Aunt Charlotte. At least, that's how it must end under the modern rules of play. And the rules are fixed. Nothing random here, thank God. It's all conspiracy theories and Wallyhood gossip and second endings.
The meter says more dumbness. Crank it up!
dumbmeter editomatic

Then all the poor dead people who were in the church when the sadistic bastard ordered the doors locked and the torch set upon it, they come out of their trailers for the wrap party.
The Snooter has to leave early for a location shoot in Prague
The triumph of Eddie Campbell.
Aw Fuck
Aw no.
Aw jeez.
'NN OH
GOD. AW
Cunt.
I read the previews.
Leo
July 24–August 23
These past seven days and those to come represent a period when what was once unchanging and unchangeable is utterly transformed—especially for those with a birthday on or near August 11. Tuesday's full moon falls in the relationship sector, so a partner requires extra understanding. But this also has the capacity reveal t
Scorpio
October 24–Novem
Are you enjoyi
roller-coaster ri
aspects range fro
great to the gha
could be soar
meting. No
same ma
it is non
if your
Nover
chan

Monty the dog
Eddie Campbell 3.01
When we moved into this house we found some attractive fixtures left for us, including the beautiful cream coloured curtains that make our bedroom look very bridal.
A dishwasher I hardly ever use because doing it by hand takes half the effort
And on the gate, a good example of one of the more inventive BEWARE OF THE DOG signs.
I can make the gate in six seconds. How fast are you?
I left it there for its attractiveness.
in conds fast you?
Later I found that it served the same purpose as a real dog.
Hallo!! Are you coming down?
Fed
That doesn't wash with the kids
But you said that one day...
Yeah sure. one day.
A year before the infernal day.
You can't keep putting off the decision.
We can put it off as long as we like.
Six months before the woeful decision.
You've no intention of buying a dog, have you!
You're just playing with our feelings.

One hour before the irreversible action.
Hey, Why don't we get a dog?
This is a wind-up, isn't it?
Do you mean it?
The brief window of opportunity during which my life might still go the way I planned it.
you've gone quiet.
Aw, you poor wee guy; you're lonely.
OWCH!
you bloody dog
Go
To
sleep
AAAA

We named him Monty after the character Monty Zoomer.
After Bunny
Created by my late friend, Bunny Wilson. My first choice was Herov, a dog character in the Wilson Universe, but the kids didn't get the joke.
Your trouble, Eddie, is that you still believe in the tooth fairy.
Monty was born the same week that Bunny died, a coincidence which only occurs to me as I write this.
WARF WARF WARF WARF
LEAVE THE CAT, YOU STUPID MUTT!
WARF WARF WARF
WARF WARF WARF WARF
Easy to fix, Mr. Campbell. I'll glue a piece of resin to the front there.
Be careful coming up, Dad. He bit the stair.
WARF WARF WARF WARF
He steals into my studio where I have artwork on the floor and snatches things from the waste-paper basket.
AH AH!

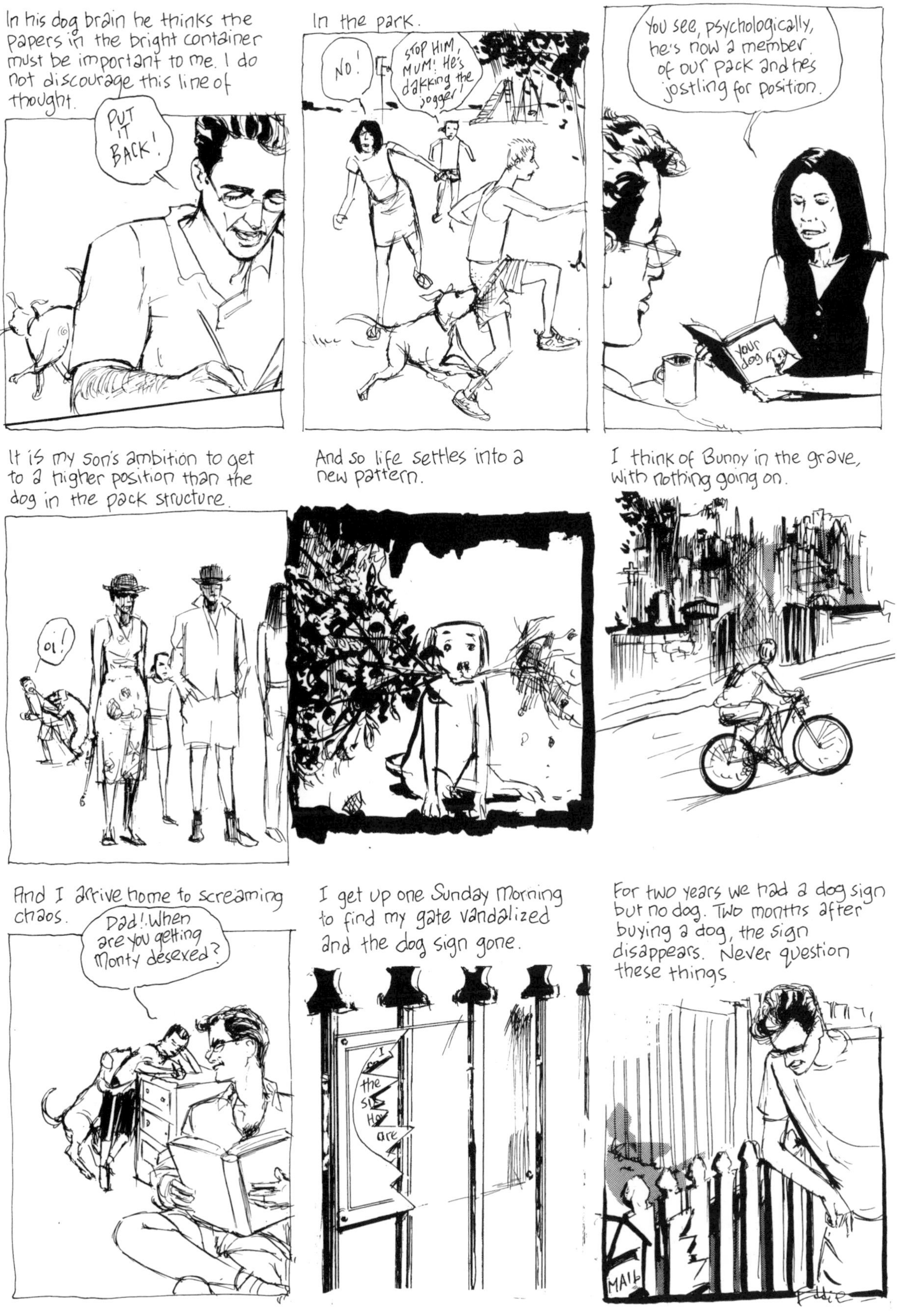
In his dog brain he thinks the papers in the bright container must be important to me. I do not discourage this line of thought.
PUT IT BACK!
In the park.
NO!
STOP HIM, MUM! He's dakking the jogger!
You see, psychologically, he's now a member of our pack and he's jostling for position.
Your dog
It is my son's ambition to get to a higher position than the dog in the pack structure.
OI!
And so life settles into a new pattern.
I think of Bunny in the grave, with nothing going on.
And I arrive home to screaming chaos.
Dad! When are you getting Monty desexed?
I get up one Sunday morning to find my gate vandalized and the dog sign gone.
For two years we had a dog sign but no dog. Two months after buying a dog, the sign disappears. Never question these things.
MAIL

This Enlightened Consumer age
Eddie Campbell 3.01.
We bought a border collie, but it was out of control in our small yard.
So we took it to the pound.
WARF WARF WARF WARF WARF WARF
Took it to the pound.
Took it to the pound.
The convenience of the consumer society. Everything can be returned to the store.
AAAAA! WHO LET THE DOG IN!?
WARF WARF
WARF WARF
The customer's always right.
WARF WARF WARF W
Trade in your old vacuum cleaner, car... your small breasts for big ones. your face for somebody else's.
WARF WARF WARF
Trade in your marriage for a divorce.
AAAAAAAA
WARF WARF
Your pregnancy for an abortion.
WARF W

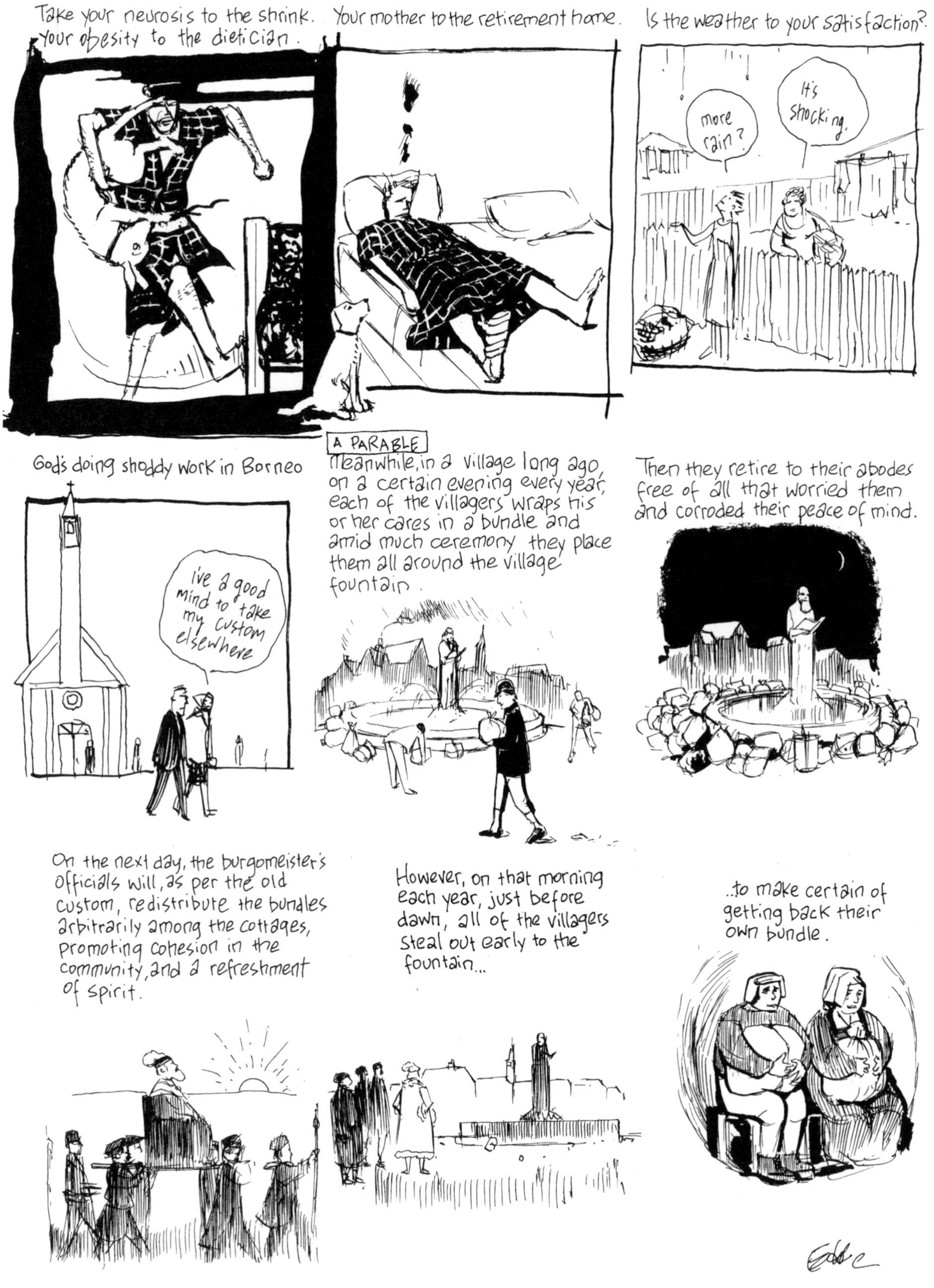
Take your neurosis to the shrink. Your obesity to the dietician.
Your mother to the retirement home.
Is the weather to your satisfaction?
more rain?
It's shocking.
God's doing shoddy work in Borneo
i've a good mind to take my custom elsewhere
A PARABLE
Meanwhile, in a village long ago, on a certain evening every year, each of the villagers wraps his or her cares in a bundle and amid much ceremony they place them all around the village fountain.
Then they retire to their abodes free of all that worried them and corroded their peace of mind.
On the next day, the burgomeister's officials will, as per the old custom, redistribute the bundles arbitrarily among the cottages, promoting cohesion in the community, and a refreshment of spirit.
However, on that morning each year, just before dawn, all of the villagers steal out early to the fountain...
..to make certain of getting back their own bundle.

Old Man's Town.
The fields of youth are filled with flowers
The wine of youth is strong.
What need have we to count the hours,
The summer days are long.
But soon we find to our dismay
That we are drifting down
The barren slopes that fall away
Towards the foothills grim and grey
That lead to Old Man's Town.
Banjo Patterson 1902.
4-01
We've worn him down with the pup. Now for the coup de grace.
We'll send in the Oldies
We mail the in-laws two plane tickets to come and visit for a fortnight.
They need a break. The world has been getting them down for so long. They carry their disappointment like a virus that they're trying to give to somebody else.
Take music for instance. No music can be just enjoyed without disparaging that other tuneless music which is presumably going on elsewhere, though I can't hear it
It's shocking what they play now.
Twas on the isle of Capri that I met her.

Now they're complaining about the exhibition that's in town, the Guillaume collection, Renoir to Picasso, a random assortment to be sure, but that's beside the point.
As for aboriginal art, what do you make of that, Eddie?
Well, they didn't paint it for you or me, Jack.
You see, Art creates the dialogue that a society has with itself.
Ah, you're talking nonsense.
It's all rubbish and you haven't the courage to say it
And furthermore, the dialogue that it has with its gods and with posterity.
Who said that?
Me.
That's rubbish! You people always say the artist meant this and that. He was just painting what he saw, with no thought of posterity.
It doesn't matter what he was thinking, the world takes it out of his hands.
That's rubbish what you said. The dictionary says: "Skill applied to imitation and—
DAMN THE DAMN Dictionary!
The music again. Old 1930s big band stuff.
And here comes the famous Bunny Berigan solo. You probably know it.
Marie
Ah, we had a guy in Ingham, Carl Hanson, he could knock spots off that. I can't hear any triple tonguing there
tri...
RIGHT! From here on it's the Sex Pistols
(an illustration of the earlier point: music as society's generational dialogue.)

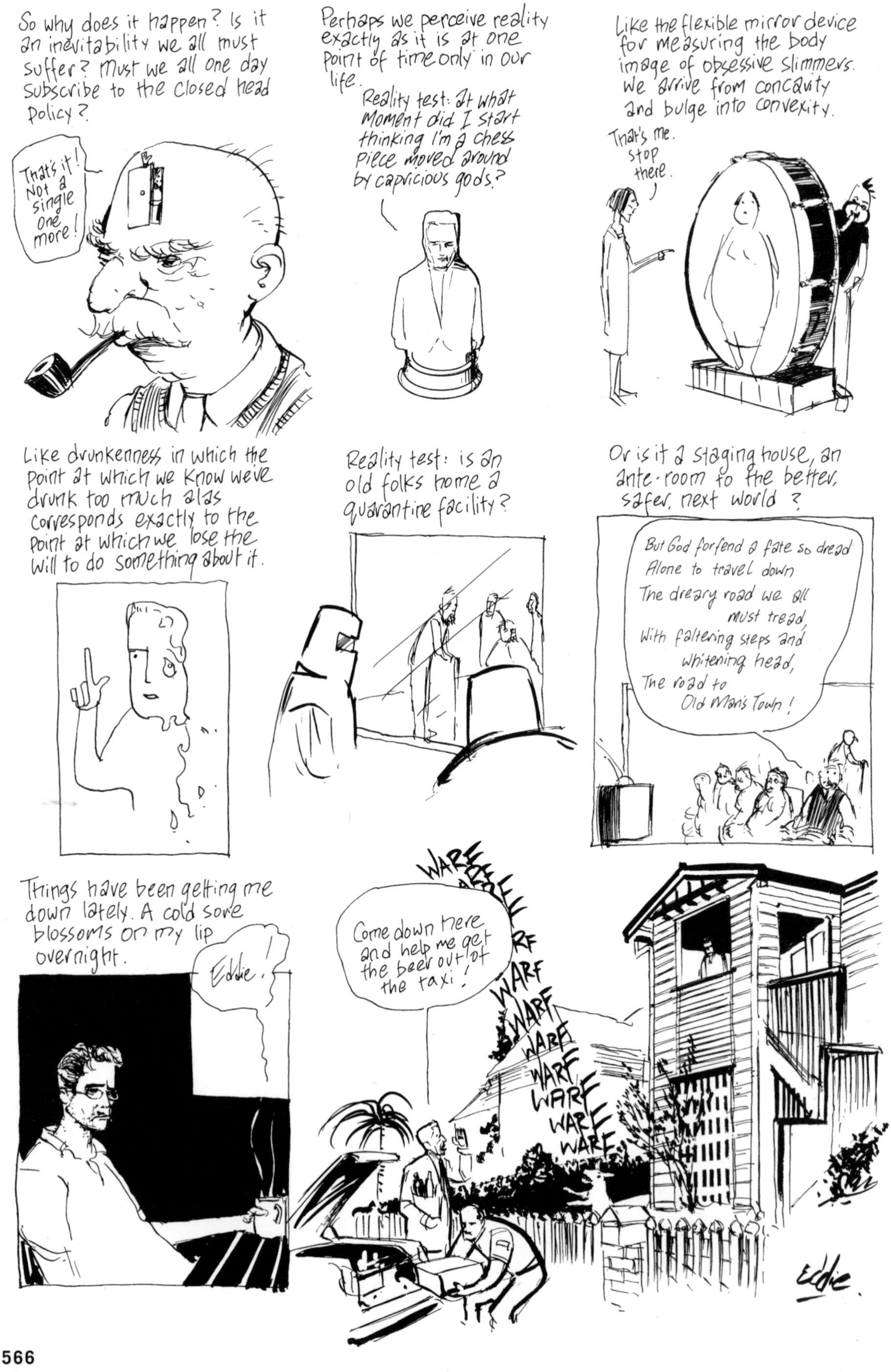
So why does it happen? Is it an inevitability we all must suffer? Must we all one day subscribe to the Closed Head Policy?
That's it! Not a single one more!
Perhaps we perceive reality exactly as it is at one point of time only in our life.
Reality test: at what moment did I start thinking I'm a chess piece moved around by capricious gods?
Like the flexible mirror device for measuring the body image of obsessive slimmers. We arrive from concavity and bulge into convexity.
That's me. Stop there.
Like drunkenness in which the point at which we know we've drunk too much alas corresponds exactly to the point at which we lose the will to do something about it.
Reality test: is an old folks home a quarantine facility?
Or is it a staging house, an ante-room to the better, safer, next world?
But God forfend a fate so dread
Alone to travel down
The dreary road we all must tread,
With faltering steps and whitening head,
The road to Old Man's Town!
Things have been getting me down lately. A cold sore blossoms on my lip overnight.
Eddie!
Come down here and help me get the beer out of the taxi!
WARF
WARF
WARF
WARF
WARF
WARF
WARF
WARF
WARF
Eddie.

Who Said 'Everyone's Entitled to their opinion' ?
not I
Eddie Campbell 5/01
Was it the oldies?
In my opinion, Modern art is the emperor's new clothes.
Was it the bigots?
In my opinion the Nazi holocaust never happened.
Was it the Pope?
In my opinion the Movie, The Exorcist is not appropriate viewing for Good Friday.
I love it. I've seen it twice
Was it Jack the Ripper?
In my opinion, people can't decide for themselves and From Hell should be banned from importation
Was it the guy stealing the Supermarket cart?
I buy my groceries there every week. Who's to say I'm not entitled to a cart now and then?
Was it the Snooter?
Well, everybody's entitled to their opinion
Whoever it was, in my opinion we should take him out behind the trees and beat the shit out of him!
IMHO this is definitely not fair.
MFF
Stick yer IMHO up yer arse!
We hope you have enjoyed your visit to the Eddie Campbell Police State. Do come again.
FUCK you too
Eddie

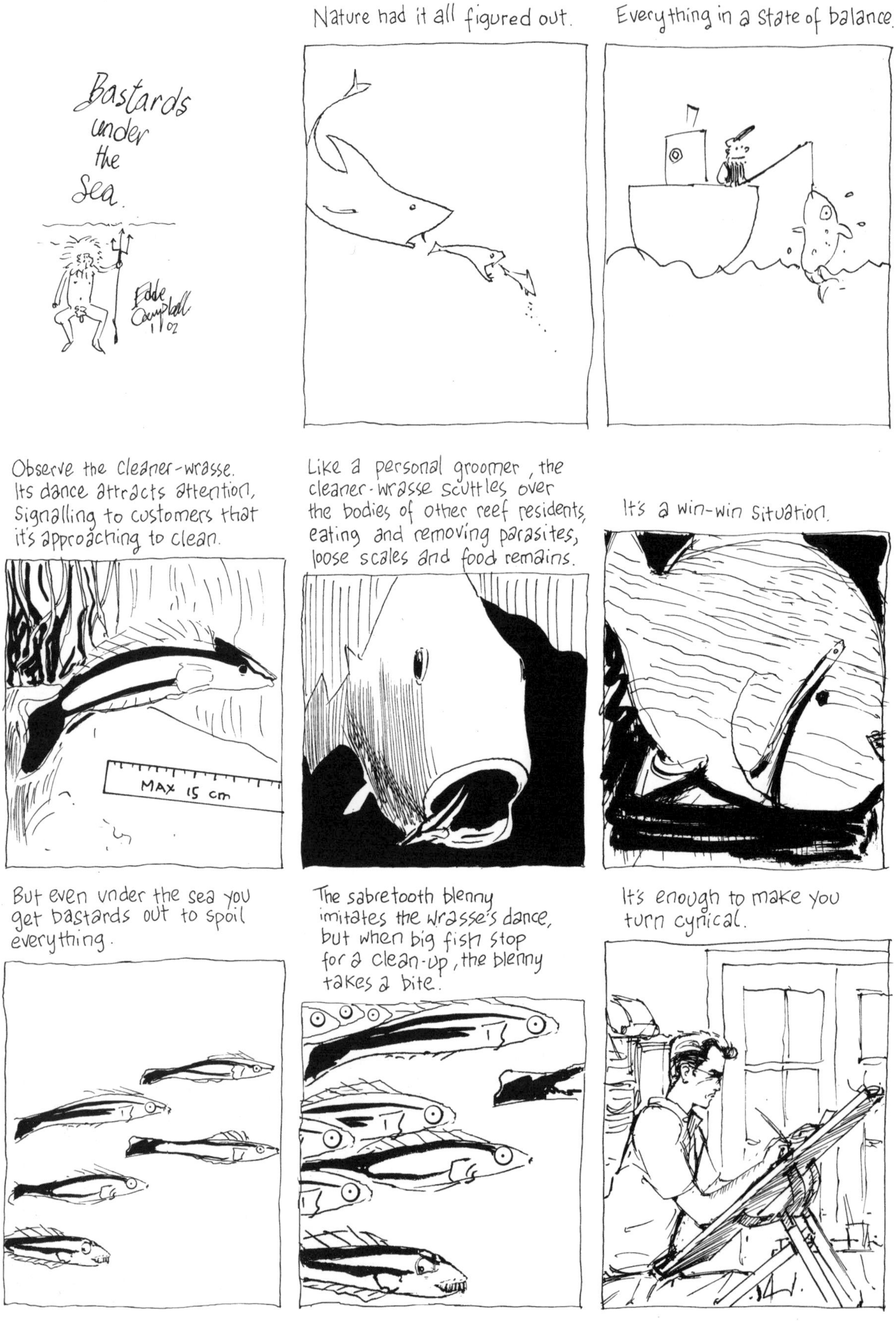
Bastards under the Sea.
Eddie Campbell 1/02
Nature had it all figured out.
Everything in a state of balance.
Observe the cleaner-wrasse. Its dance attracts attention, signalling to customers that it's approaching to clean.
MAX 15 cm
Like a personal groomer, the cleaner-wrasse scuttles over the bodies of other reef residents, eating and removing parasites, loose scales and food remains.
It's a win-win situation.
But even under the sea you get bastards out to spoil everything.
The sabretooth blenny imitates the wrasse's dance, but when big fish stop for a clean-up, the blenny takes a bite.
It's enough to make you turn cynical.

Nobody left at the Café Guerbois.
par Edouard Campbell '02.
In Paris we find ourselves in the Pere Lachaise cemetery.
At first it's just a cold big place where the dead people live.
And then it warms, becomes much more than that.
How could so much genius wind up in the same boneyard?
I feel at home.
LARCHER
Enjoying the posthumous company.
A HAHNEMANN FONDATEUR DE L'HOMŒOPATHIE
Chatting over "Fred" Chopin's nocturnes.
FRED CHOPIN
Tipping my chapeau to Theodore Gericault, lolling smugly on his stone.

I'll blow a big kiss to Oscar Wilde.
I'll prance around with Isadora, blow a couple of choruses with Mezz Mezzrow, whose primary skill, they say, was in getting hold of Marijuana.
APOLLINAIRE
APOLLINAIRE
Georges Bizet, I've been meaning to ask... how far back does that tango rhythm go anyway?
Georges Melies, pardon me for using the moon-face in Snakes and Ladders.
GEORGES MELIES
CREATEUR du SPECTACLE
Ah, Colette. L'Innocence Monstreuese' indeed.
COLETTE
Rest well, Abelard et Heloise, together toujours.
Au revoir, Honoré Daumier, Jacques Louis David, Eugene Delacroix.
FAMILLE PALANÇA
THOMAS COUTURE
Sisley and Pisarro, au revoir to you all.
Au revoir. I have a plane to catch.

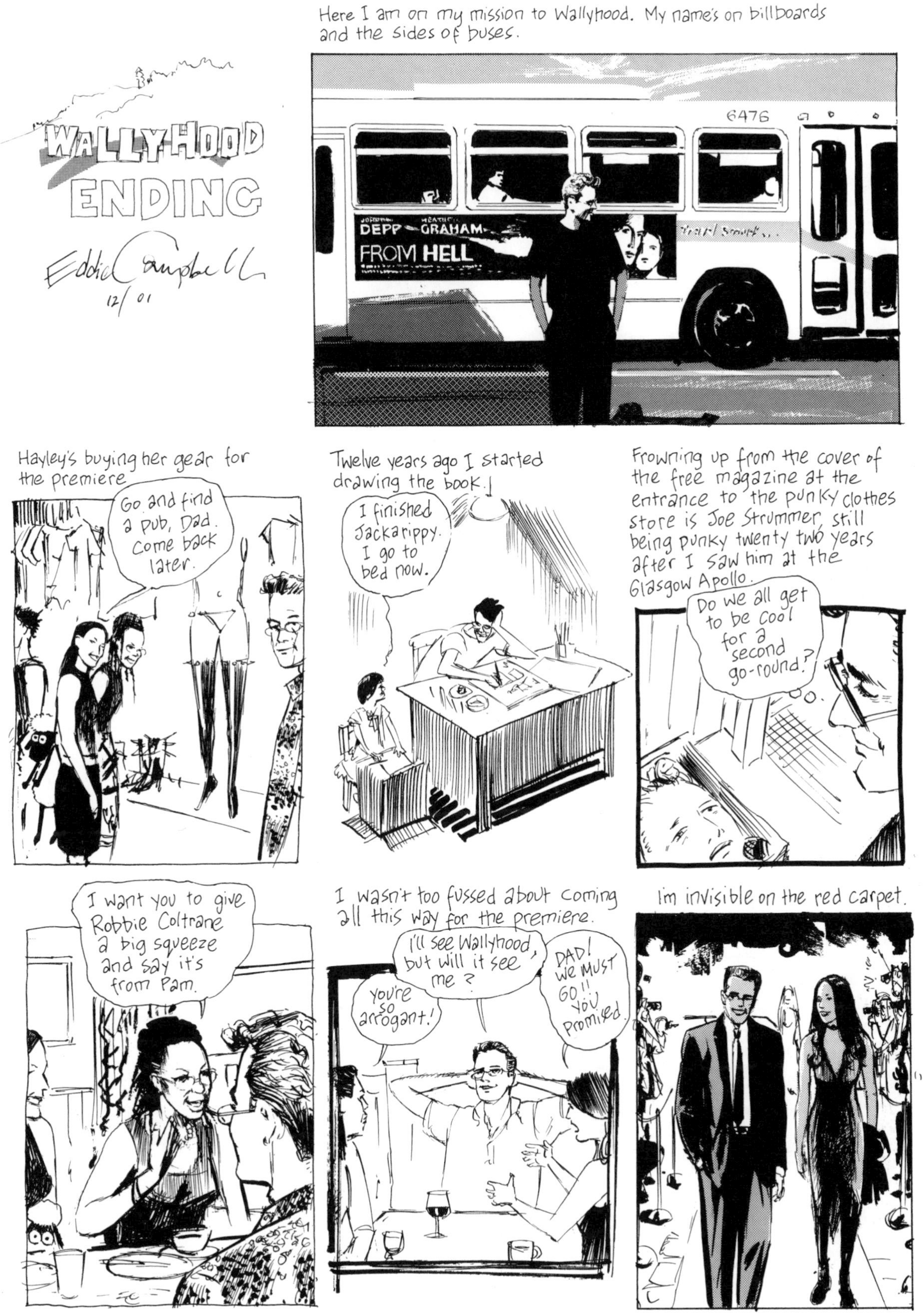

WALLYHOOD ENDING
Eddie Campbell 12/01
Here I am on my mission to Wallyhood. My name's on billboards and the sides of buses.
6476
DEPP GRAHAM
FROM HELL
Hayley's buying her gear for the premiere
Go and find a pub, Dad. Come back later.
Twelve years ago I started drawing the book.
I finished Jackarippy. I go to bed now.
Frowning up from the cover of the free magazine at the entrance to the punky clothes store is Joe Strummer, still being punky twenty two years after I saw him at the Glasgow Apollo.
Do we all get to be cool for a second go-round?
I want you to give Robbie Coltrane a big squeeze and say it's from Pam.
I wasn't too fussed about coming all this way for the premiere.
I'll see Wallyhood, but will it see me?
You're so arrogant!
DAD! We MUST GO!! You promised
I'm invisible on the red carpet.

I originally imagined I'd get a bunch of pals together for the gala party, but such is not to be in the aftermath of Osama Bin Laden's attack on New York.
It's all tight security and paranoia now.
FOX
WESTWOOD VILLAGE
FROM HELL JOHNNY DEPP HEATHER GRAHAM
Ah, but fictions everywhere! Lolita is sitting behind me.
Dad! There's the guy from 'Dude, Where's my Car?'
Eddie Campbell
Don Murphy
SP
Wait! Did I just see...?
Johnny kisses Heather for the photographers.
Then he scratches his head.
Then the showdown, with... !SPOILER!... Ian Holm as the villainous Dr. Gull.
No! It's a mask! It's... it's... My NEMESIS!
I'm Gary Cooper and it's High Noon.
Scene 58 ① Dramatic climax → SNOOTER REVEALED. (MUSIC) -
② PAN Right - chase starts -

I'm Humphrey Bogart in 'the Big Sleep'.
James Cagney in 'White Heat'.
John Wayne in 'True Grit'.
BANG
BANG
BANG
Top o' da woild, ma!
I've got a writ for you, rat. It's a rat writ, writ for a rat.
You know what he'll do when he comes back? Beat my teeth out and then kick me in the stomach for mumbling.
(3) c/u Eddie.
shoots in bg.
I've never held a gun in my life but my dreams are full of people shooting me and me shooting them back.
Help, Dad! He's taking me to Straight Street by way of Lobotomy Gardens!
Your armchair awaits...
WAL
BANG
BANG
(6)
(7)
Long shot. Chase
to HOLLYWOOD sign.
High angle.
(8) Eddie Pov. Snooter indicates the couch.
Think of it! You'll no more need to talk when you've got nothing to say.
...or drink when you're not thirsty.
It never looked so appealing before... Close down my head. Take it easy.
(9) med.sh. Snooter Pov.
(10) c/u Eddie, left Snooter persuades.
(11) Big c/u. Zoom in to eyes for reaction shot.

George Harrison dies at 58, perhaps the first of my generation's heroes to go in non-tragic circumstances.
And in a shop a particular bouquet of cheap newsprint transports me to a shop 35 years earlier.
Tomar-Re is saying something serious out of his funny beak.
I walk the dog just after the rain. Everything reminds me of something else.
All my friends advance a square in the big board game.
Two short TV spots taped in Paris.
I'm signing books in Madrid and Rome.
In Madrid I fall on my face.
I fall so hard I'm stunned

Deep breath
Deep breath
OUCH!
I'm still signing books on the Metro.
Then I find myself in a group photo.
What's up, honey?
I've lost the plot.
Oh my God... nyuhh n
Come here, let me fix it. there, there..
There there

Good night sweetheart
It's all for her.
Eddie Campbell
may 7 2002
Why did you stop darl?
I was suddenly taken with the certainty that I was doing it exactly the way my Dad did it...
Sigh.
...the night they conceived me.
"Aw, so help ma boab!"
Y'know, I'm worried about my violin being up there on top of the cupboard. It must be the hottest part of the house.
Why don't you move it down inside the cupboard then.
My old Punch books are in there. I'm worried about them too.
I don't know how you can sleep at night with so many important things to worry about.

The person 'Bunny Wilson' who appears on page 560 was a hoax that we perpetrated and kept going for a few years in the letters pages of the *Bacchus* and *Deevee* comic books. Above is his funeral, as it appeared in our mocked-up newspaper article. I still think it was something of an achievement to get all my pals to go to the cemetery in their best suits on a Sunday morning. Even their good ladies turned up.

FRAGMENTS

Eddie Campbell Aug '91

The History of Humour was an ambitious serial of which only three chapters were completed and published, in my own short-lived magazine, Egomania (2002). It was intended to be a sizeable book of around 160 pages and was composed in response to a challenge I inadvertently laid down in *How to be an Artist* (on page 252 herein). This is a reduced version (18 pages) of the existing material (30), but *"I have Lost my Sense of Humour,"* drawn for Diana Schutz' *Autobiographix* anthology and published by Dark Horse in 2003, gives it some closure. Note: My adaptation of O. Henry's *Confessions of a Humorist* now appears in *The Fate of the Artist* (First Second Books, 2006) and prior to that colourized version, was originally intended for this '*History*.'

'Graphic Novelist' is a term I no longer use, but as a guest at the Melbourne Writers' festival I knew I'd be expected to explain it. This piece, 'The Graphic Novelist,' was a full page I drew in colour for an interview article covering the event in *Melbourne Age*'s weekend magazine of 26 Aug 2007. Alas, it appears here only in black and white. I was hoping that, like *The Forriners* ten years before, the commission would inspire a new book, or at least a theme in a new book, but it remains isolated and I almost forgot to include it here.

In my files I found two 2-page lettered fragments from a project I was pitching for a season and a half in the late '90s titled *Eddie Campbell's Big Book of Drunks; a compendium of lushes, topers and sots*. I finished the drawings of one of them, 'The Demise of Robert Johnstone,' for this showing. I have my suspicion that the method of hanging depicted in the piece, the long drop, is anachronistic. I should have known to interrogate my source material more thoroughly.

The History of Humour
Chapter one
Them funny foreigners
I'm going to write the HISTORY OF HUMOUR.
Didn't you say in How to be an Artist that such a history would never be written because it defies that kind of organisation.
BOLLA
MOCK
I did write that, but I'm feeling up to the task now. I can stand far enough back to get it all into one frame.
You think so, do you?
MOCKERY
You see, a society builds all its noble, serious and dignified Art and shows it in a fine and expensive manner.
Athena clothed in gold mouldings in the Parthenon.
Praschniker's reconstruction.
God the Father and his angels over the front door of the cathedral.
Notre Dame, Paris.
Our gods are perfect in their heaven and we worship them piously. We glorify our war heroes and honour our ancestors.
That's on top.
Then there's the underside!

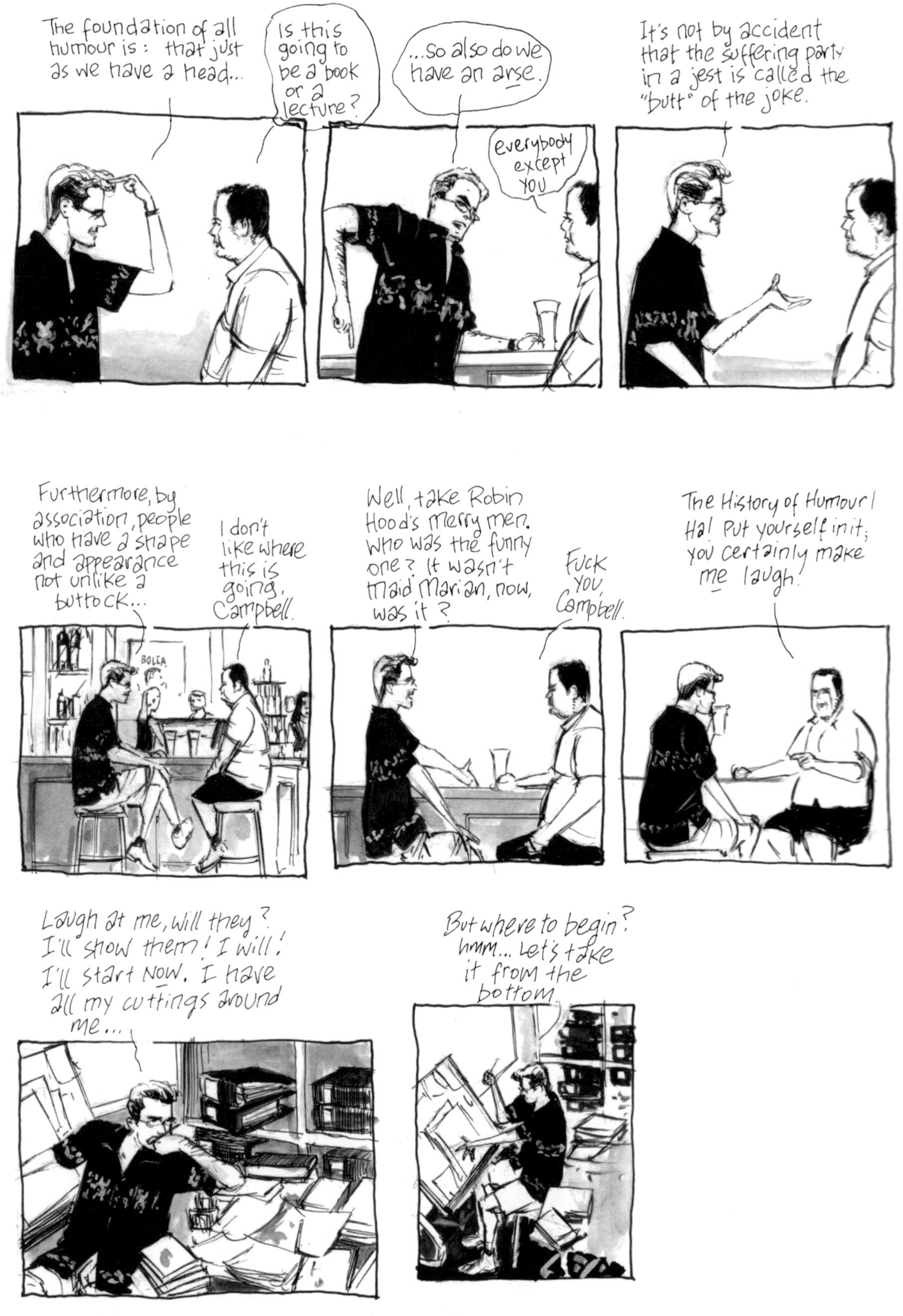
The foundation of all humour is: that just as we have a head...
Is this going to be a book or a lecture?
...so also do we have an arse.
everybody except you
It's not by accident that the suffering party in a jest is called the "butt" of the joke.
Furthermore, by association, people who have a shape and appearance not unlike a buttock...
I don't like where this is going, Campbell.
BOLLA
Well, take Robin Hood's merry men. Who was the funny one? It wasn't Maid Marian, now, was it?
Fuck you, Campbell.
The History of Humour! Ha! Put yourself in it; you certainly make me laugh.
Laugh at me, will they? I'll show them! I will! I'll start now. I have all my cuttings around me...
But where to begin? hmm... let's take it from the bottom.

The arse has always been the key element in the art of mockery. The movie, *BRAVEHEART* has some historically wayward moments, but its depiction of William Wallace and his Scottish warriors flashing their buttocks at the army of the English king rings true.

While St. James manages the main entrance of the gothic church in Brno, Czechoslovakia, this little chap shows his bottom over a side-door in a mockery of human folly.

While Prime Minister Walpole gets his official portrait painted in oils on canvas, his arse gets kissed in this print satirizing preferments.

Another English King gets the arse, this time from the French.

L'impudique Albion by Jean Veber in L'Assiette au Beurre 28 Sept 1901

IDOL-WORSHIP or The Way to Preferment
And Henry the KING made unto himself a great IDOL, the likeness of which was not in Heaven

English print, 1640 (George Bickham?)

Dante mocks Satan's retinue in the *Inferno*: (canto XXI)

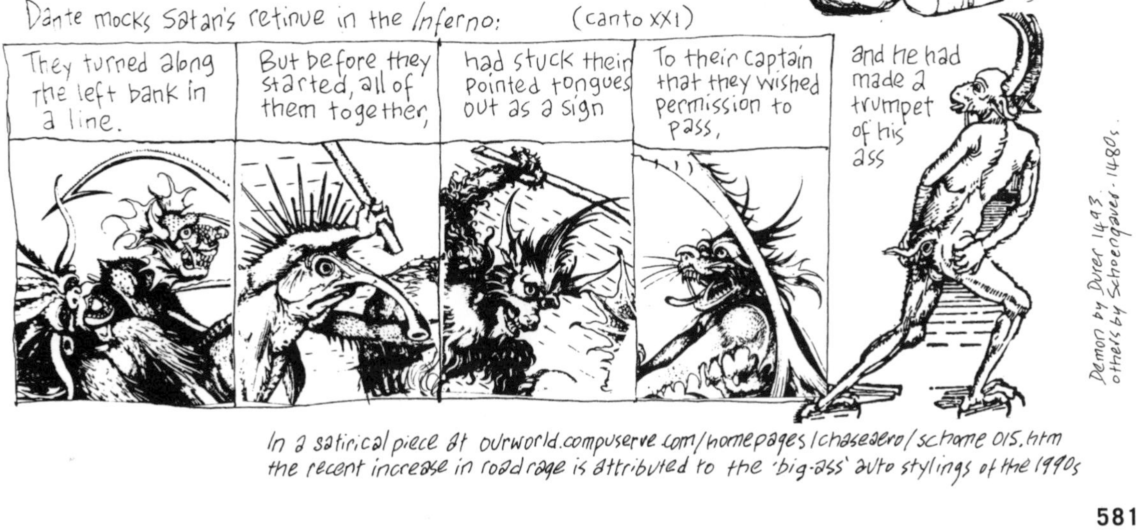
They turned along the left bank in a line.
But before they started, all of them together,
had stuck their pointed tongues out as a sign
To their captain that they wished permission to pass,
and he had made a trumpet of his ass

Demon by Durer 1493, others by Schoengauer, 1480s

In a satirical piece at ourworld.compuserve.com/homepages/chaseaero/schame 015.htm the recent increase in road rage is attributed to the 'big-ass' auto stylings of the 1990s

The bum has also been squeezed for its own innate funniness. The imagination may soar to distant heights of the universe but our bum makes us earthbound and eggbound

Hieronymus Bosch (detail St. Anthony – ca. 1500

Dutch Convenience. – the Lake.

'VENIENCES.

English Print – James Gillray – 1790s.

This illustration of Galen lecturing on the application of an enema is a comic masterpiece. The little dog makes it so. Whether the artist was instructed to include it as the loyal companion of the patient or as the iconographic attendant of the Humanist scholar, (on a line from Altichiero's Petrarch to Durer's St. Jerome), his placement of it with the students is unexpected.

Initial from illuminated ms. – 15th century

From an English print by Gillray on national conveniences. The English do it in the water closet, the Scotch in a bucket, the French in a commodité and the Dutch in the Lake.

A hairy arse sticks out of the window in *The Miller's Tale* by Chaucer, a situational farce of confused identities and body parts.

"This Nicholas anon let fle a fart,
As gret as it had been a thunder-dent
That with the strook he was almost yblent
And he was redy with his iron hoot
And Nicholas amydde the ers he smoot."

Geoffrey Chaucer – 1390–1400.

Mark Twain is perhaps mocking a strict upbringing and education in "1601", a short piece written for the amusement of himself and the Reverend Joseph Twichell and later published in fifty copies.

(In the court of Queen Elizabeth I)

O' God's name, who hath favoured us? Hath it come to pass that a fart shall fart itself? Not such a one as this, I trow.
Young master Beaumonte; but no, t'would have wafted him to heaven like down of goose's boddy. Twas not ye little lady Helen. nay, ne'er blush, my childe...
thou'lt tickle thy tender maidenhead with many a mousie squeak before thou learned to blow a harricane like this. was't thou, my learned Jonson?

Mark Twain – 1876.

E.C.

1601: complete text can be read at www.mbay.net/~jmd/1601.html
Bestiary for St. Jerome: animal symbolism in European religious art. H. Friedmann.

Mockery runs downhill in a society. The urbanite mocks the rustic.

Large Peasant holiday (detail) Sebald Beham 1535

The gainfully employed mocks the beggar

H. Cock after H. Bosch. 1550s

Everybody mocks the deformed.

Jacques Callot. 1622.

It takes a considerable act of defiance to turn it uphill as in this bronze statuette depicting the Roman emperor Caracalla as a dwarf distributing cakes.

c. 215 A.D.

Peasants, Warriors and Wives: Popular imagery in the Reformation - Keith Moxley - 1989.
Callot's Etchings - Dover 1974.

There is a tradition of saints using a defiant humility against their executioners.

St. Lawrence. St. Thomas More St. Maurus.

Turn me over so that thou may eat me well done.
Pray stay until I have removed my beard from the block as it hath committed no treason
It isn't hot enough
Let me feel that- AAGG!!

Reported by St. Ambrose.

'Thus with a mock he ended his life' witnessed by Edward Hall, Chronicles.

Related in The Name of the Rose by Umberto Eco.

Humour runs hot and cold like indoor plumbing.

George Grosz Blood is the best sauce - 1919

It can sneer cruelly like this war god.

Hawaiian statuette.

Or it can be the 'cold joke' of the tormentor. For instance it is recorded that at Auschwitz Jewish prisoner musicians were forced to play the tango and waltzes while graves were being dug

It may embrace empathy. We welcome that gregarious and generous humour that tells us we're all in this together.

NOUS. SOMMES. SEPT.

Engraving after a Picardian sculpture 13th c.

"We are seven" (Fools) But there are only six. You are the seventh.

This bloke is getting a hair-cut just like blokes still do.

Greek terracotta - 6 century b.c.

This cellarer monk gives in to temptation much as you or I would, given the cellar, the key, and nobody watching.

Illuminated initial - 13th century.

The 'cold joke': See Jonathan Glover: Humanity, a moral history of the twentieth century. 2001

Chapter two
The feast of topsy turvy
Momus is first mentioned by the Greek mythographer, Hesiod, around 800 b.c. He's the god of mockery, of laughter; the original pisstaker.
Aesop tells the story that Zeus, Athena and Poseidon were arguing over which of them could make the coolest thing
Zeus made man; Athena made a house; Poseidon made a bull; Momus was asked to judge
First Momus criticized man for not having a window into his heart so that his neighbour could peep through the curtains and see what he's planning
He put down the work of Poseidon, saying the bull's horns should have been placed below its eyes so it could see what it's aiming at.
Then he rubbished Athena's house because, despite having all the mod cons, it lacked wheels so that you can roll it away when the neighbourhood goes bad
In another tale, Momus wasn't a guy but instead a goddess, who was expelled from Olympus for her incessant mockery. She then started cross-dressing, to fool mortals, thus establishing the motif of reversal as a standard type of humour.
Are you a fruit bat?
No. I just woke up and remembered I'm in Australia.
Loony toons

Hesiod, Theogony. line 214. Momus usually translated as Blame.
Aesop, (Babrius 59) _collection of fables at AesopFables.com
third yarn probably a late carnival justification.

Four thousand years ago, or so, the Egyptians celebrated the rebirth of the sun for twelve days at the end of what we would call December.

Sacaea, or the annual renewal festival of the Babylonians was adopted by the Persians. One of the themes of the Sacaea was the temporary subversion of order.

Cat herds geese to market. Egyptian, 1300. b.c. another variant page 10.

In theory the old King had to die at the end of the year and accompany the god Marduk into the netherworld, battling at his side.

after a bas-relief in the British museum

But there came about the idea of a substitute or 'mock' King, which got the real one off the hook. A criminal or slave would be dressed in royal garb, given all homage and indulgence and permitted to rule for the duration.

Masquerades spilled into the streets. As the old year died, ordinary rules were relaxed.

Then, as soon as the mock King's reign was over, he was stripped of his royal trappings and slain.

The Romans believed in an ancient god of seed-time, Saturn, who had ruled their country ages before their own day, before he was overthrown by Jupiter. The Egyptian and Persian traditions merged in the Saturnalia.

Dion Chrysostom: "They take one of the prisoners condemned to death and seat him upon the King's throne and give him the King's raiment, and let him lord it and drink and run riot...

and use the King's concubines during these days and no man prevents him from doing what he pleases. But afterwards they strip and scourge and crucify him."

* parallel with passion of Christ, see Girard at www.execpc.com/~paulnue/year_b/th_passion.htm also Stecchini and Sammer, King and Mock King at www.Nazarenus.com.

For ordinary people the Saturnalia meant feasting, drinking, gift giving and role reversals.

Slaves and children were waited on for meals and participated in the revels as if they were parents and masters.

Another freedom was that of casual dress instead of the toga used for formal occasions such as sumptious dinners.

In which might be served sea-hedgehogs, sphondyli, glycimarides, becaficoes, sow's udder, boar's head, ducks, hares, fowls and Pontic pastry.

Showing similarities to the *Saturnalia* but otherwise unique and somewhat startling, was the medieval *Feast of Fools*. This took place on Jan 1st, or the feast of Christ's circumcision.

The whole community would enjoy the event, which was a rite of anti-structure. but it was principally clerical, centering on cathedrals and collegiate churches.

Rabbits hunt people c.1340. French. Romance of Alexander, MS in Oxford.

In what was essentially an exaltation of the virtue of humility, a 'boy bishop' would be elected and power, dignity and impunity would be conferred on him for a few hours

The feast was most popular in France between the 12th and 15th centuries and like so many things where humour gets the upper hand, we know about it mostly from letters of complaint.

The Faculty of Theology of the University of Paris decried some of the excesses taking place. Priests were apparently dancing in the aisles dressed as women and reading from upside down prayer books.

Most texts on the Feast of Fools lean on The Medieval Stage by E.K. Chambers 1903 Chambers spends 98 pages examining all the available evidence

"They eat black puddings at the altar while the celebrant is saying mass" continues the document, "They cense with stinking smoke from the soles of old shoes."

And during the mass a donkey may have been brought into the church and a braying chant introduced into the liturgy.

The ass was probably imported from another feast, the Feast of Asses, in which the story of Balaam would have been dramatized, with the player riding a wooden hobbyhorse.

The ass, mentioned a great deal in accounts of the Feast of Fools, is both a relic of ancient magical cults and the epitome of stupidity.

church carving, La Plaisance-sur-Gartempe c. 1100

The boy bishop would have been crowned with three buckets of water. (not more than this number as ruled by the Chapter of Sens, in an attempt to moderate the proceedings.)

After mass, the clergy may have careened through the town in a dung cart, pelting the people and making indecent gestures. In these ways did a humble and good-humoured tradition go wayward.

The celebrations were eroded by the Church authorities. For some reason the public shaving of the precentor's beard at Troyes was a bone of contention for a while.

But the Feast of Fools was finally forbidden under the very severest penalties by the Council of Basel in 1435 and supported by Paris in 1444.

cardinal-fool-woodcut circa 1530

European follies shifted to other days, such as *Mardi Gras*, *"... a shrewdly permitted license to the faithful on the eve of Lenten austerities."* * And Momus walked the earth again, as King Momus, the Carnival Lord of Misrule.

Drama and the Mass, see All the World's a Stage by Ronald Harwood 1984
Excesses, see Sex in History - G.R. Taylor - www.ourcivilisation.com/smartboard/shop/Taylorgr/sxhst/chap14/htm
* quoted from The Savage and Beautiful Country by Alan McGlashan 1967

It has been suggested also that some elements were transferred to April Fool's Day. The custom appears to have originated in France, where people traditionally exchanged New Year's gifts on April 1st.

In the modern reformed calendar, the start of the year was shifted from the end of March to Jan 1st. People being what they are, many did not shift with it.

These were considered fools and invites to non-existent parties and other practical jokes were played on them.

KICK ME

More rabbits - c. 1300 Flemish Psalter.

In Scotland the victim of the gag is referred to in the expression "hunting the gowk". The "gowk" is the cuckoo bird.

The 'kick me' gag was apparently invented one April Fool's day in Scotland and has never gone out of fashion.

In France the victim is the "poisson d'Avril". The fish of April are newly hatched and easy to catch.

Kick me

Today, the day of misrule still finds a place.

Hey, Dad. The year-12 girls came to school today in their brothers' clothes. They turned the duct on the roof of the science block into a huge dick, with balls, and the teachers couldn't do a thing because it's muck-up day. Funny, eh?

The title *Mardi Gras* has been incorrectly appropriated by Sydney's Gay parade. This year a guy dressed as the Pope distributed condoms from his float, which is appropriate enough.

And 'the world turned upside down' remains one of our basic humorosities. Here's the Wonderworks building in Orlando, Florida, left just the way Momus dropped it.

Can you get me a boiled icicle
Do you want a slice of lemon in it this time?

Chapter three
MARGINALIZED
These rabbits are funny, don't you think?
no, why?
Well, apart from having funny eyes, they're doing stuff that rabbits don't do. Human stuff.
Look. They're going to war.
It's not funny when humans do it. why should it be funny just because it's rabbits?
CONTRARINES
CONTRARNESS
And why are you obsessed with bunnies anyway? Didn't you have some in Chapter 2?
There are apes and other animals too. Perhaps the commonplace familiarity of the rabbit enabled this northern European artist to render them more vividly... these Mike and Ike lookalikes.

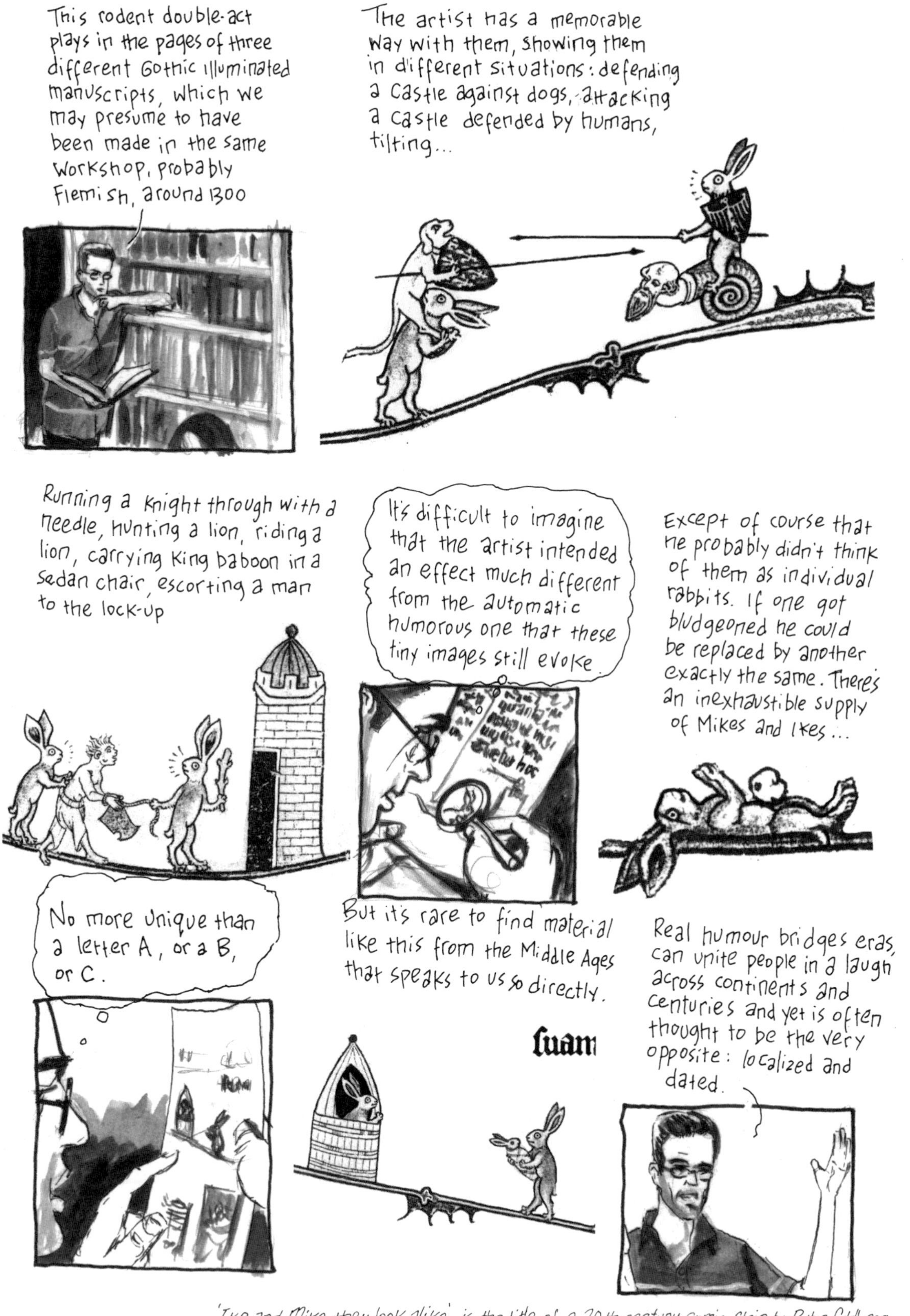
This rodent double-act plays in the pages of three different Gothic illuminated manuscripts, which we may presume to have been made in the same workshop, probably Flemish, around 1300
The artist has a memorable way with them, showing them in different situations: defending a castle against dogs, attacking a castle defended by humans, tilting...
Running a knight through with a needle, hunting a lion, riding a lion, carrying King baboon in a sedan chair, escorting a man to the lock-up
It's difficult to imagine that the artist intended an effect much different from the automatic humorous one that these tiny images still evoke.
Except of course that he probably didn't think of them as individual rabbits. If one got bludgeoned he could be replaced by another exactly the same. There's an inexhaustible supply of Mikes and Ikes...
No more unique than a letter A, or a B, or C.
But it's rare to find material like this from the Middle Ages that speaks to us so directly.
suam
Real humour bridges eras, can unite people in a laugh across continents and centuries and yet is often thought to be the very opposite: localized and dated.

'Ike and Mike, they look alike' is the title of a 20th century comic strip by Rube Goldberg
The rabbits are in: The Breviary of Marguerite de Bar, two parts, one in London (page 2 panels 2 and 7) one in Verdun (page 1 panel 6) and the Metz Pontifical in Cambridge (page 1 panel 2 page 2 panel 3) also probably in Metz ms 43, destroyed in 1944. All to be dated 1300-1310

At school I received an image of a medieval world that was savage and dangerous and had no familiarity with the concept of humour.

However, taking their cue from Aristotle's statement, 'no animal laughs save man', led many medieval scholars to "trawl the evangelists for such evidence of Christ's humanity."

The marriage at Cana has been cited as an example, in which Jesus is made to look slightly foolish by his mother. *

Jesus, they've run out of wine.
Woman, my time has not yet come.

Just do as he tells you.
John: 2.

Long before the church became tedious, the only thing that was more terrifying than being in it...

was being outside.

Sometimes I think that I can get a handle on medieval times by thinking back to my childhood, when my eye level was down around horse-poo and beasties.

Jack Frost was outside our window.

And Jack Daw would drink the top off the milk.

Mrs Stevenson says that back then we'd all be serfs, which means we'd belong to the manor and wouldn't be allowed to go into town.

* *Laughter at the Foot of the Cross*, M.A. Screech 1997 discussed in *On Humour*, Simon Critchley. 2002

All history was walking down our street at the same time. The Crusades were still considered a good idea. We all hoped to go on the next one.
That all happened hundreds of years ago!
Does that mean we're not going?
William Wallace was still fighting for freedom at Stirling Bridge. Mrs. Stevenson never mentioned the bare arses but I daresay it's the way we'd have dealt with it ourselves.
Except we'd never met any English. And she said nothing about Wallace skinning the bishop. The movie left out that part too.
We did get the whole 'hanged-drawn-and-quartered' routine and also Robert the Bruce murdering the 'Red' Comyn in the church.
You see, sacrilege was a big deal then. Joseph Fabiano went into the church and put on all the vestments and drank the wine. We'd never heard of such evil.
I don't remember seeing Joseph after that and I suspected he was hanged, drawn and quartered. It definitely wasn't the three buckets of water. I'd have heard about that.
Later, around 1530, Protestantism arrived, with its stern-faced iconoclasm.
Papist bastard! We don't want to see your face here again.
And three hundred years after that, Victorian prudery.
But oh, for those days when pictures ruled.
Rabelais and his World, M.M. Bakhtin, trans Iswolski 1965 effected a new way of thinking about humour in the Middle Ages' widely accepted with allowance for his Marxist point of view.

High up, in hardly visible corners of 11th and 12th century Romanesque churches, in France, England and Spain.
Many are within view of the people, but some are so high they can only be communicating with the beyond...
Conceptions of ugliness that may be classified with the caricatures of evil spirits discussed earlier...
Mouth-puller, Castletown, Dundalk, Ireland
Mouth-puller, Oloron-Sainte-Marie, France
Beast, Civray, France
And the ridiculing of human folly and wickedness in order to focus the minds of the congregation upon goodness.
Bestiality, sodomy and plain old fornication. These carvings have been largely incomprehensible to observers in later times, who have sometimes taken them to be remnants of pre-christian fertility cults.
And we should not exclude the Christian church's canny annexation of pagan practice.
Moneybags, Aulnay, France
Lust, Nieul-le-Virouil, France
Demon, St. Pierre, Aulnay, France
A part of the design of the whole building, the intention behind them was to give offence, in a certain way. But they were often executed with a sardonic humour
Bernard of Clairvaux didn't get the joke.
"What are the filthy apes doing there? If we are not ashamed by the absurdity, we should at least be concerned about the expense!"
What would Bernard have said a century later when the baboons came down off the walls into the prayer books?
Exhibitionist, Sainte Radegonde, Poitiers, Fr.
from letter of complaint to the abbot of St. Thierry
Chained apes, San Quirce, Spain.

Images of Lust and Folly on Medieval Churches: Weir and Jerman 1986
Gargoyles and Grotesques: Paganism in the Medieval Church: Sheridan, Ross 1975

It's impossible now to reach into the rationale and origins of these secondary carvings, playing their obscene obbligato to the holy and decorous main theme.
But their subsequent direction is clear. As architectural decoration in the Gothic period, 13th to 15th centuries, the monsters moved to the outside and became gargoyles (waterspouts).
Those erected inside became more humanized, whimsical and charming, such as the marvellous series of column capitals in the sculpturally lavish Wells Cathedral.
Acrobat, Saint-Servais, Brittany, France
Arsehole, Autun, France
Mouth-puller, Wells, England.
But they are always in a "realm of otherness at the edge of things." "The monster is a point of reference, an image at the edge," writes Michael Camille, "just as important as the signs at the centre."
And the edifice is not just the house of God but the concrete symbol of everything, with God at its centre and wickedness pushed to the outer limits.
It has been observed that these secondary figures have a vitality lacking in the primary images of Sanctity.
Dog-Man, St. Johns, Den Bosch, Netherlands
Face outside cloister, Oviedo, Spain
Mouth puller, York, England
In this respect we may refer to another letter of complaint, that "too much license" was given to artists, "by those who supervise such matters"
We should be careful to avoid exaggerating the freedom of the medieval craftsman...
But it does appear that he had some leeway in these, which would probably have been ordered by the job-lot while the primary sculptures would have been described contractually.
Nagging wife, Thaxted, England
Artisan working, monster reading, roof, St. Johns, Den Bosch, Netherlands.
Gothic. ed Rolf Toman. pub: Könemann, 1998 covers architecture without mentioning gargoyles
Holy Terrors by Janet Rebold Benton 1997, takes up the slack.

As for me, I was having breakfast at a convention recently with Sergio Aragonés, the cartoonist whose best known work has been the marginal gags he's drawn in MAD Magazine since 1963.
Sergio, I plan to write the HISTORY of HUMOUR!
Ah, you know, humour... eet's not selling any more.
We've come to think of humour as a genre, separated off onto it's own shelf, instead of being mixed up with the sacred essence of everything.
At least, when we consciously think of it at all. At heart maybe it just plays the same roles as always.
For one, keeping evil at bay. My wife's granny was upset as the boys marched off to World War II. Instead of singing the Romantic It's a Long Way to Tipperary, the ballad of World War I, they cried out:
We're off to see the wizard, the wonderful wizard of Oz
The official record of the World is written at the centre:
My first complaint concerns the lack of respect shown by...
The margin acquires a new cachet with the appeal of the anti-hero, the punk, and the elevation of snook-cocking and raspberry blowing to the status of admirable practices. Wee Eddie sits on the border with Jack Daw, Ike and Mike, Van Gogh before he was dead, the cabbage-arsed monster and all the other babooneries.

I have lost my sense of humour.
aw, the poor bloke. Somebody help him up.
It's funny
Throwing trash on the footpath isn't funny. Somebody might hurt himself. It could be me.
Now that would be truly hilarious.
Here's another example: boy's party invitation.
what shall I bring?
EMINEM
I am given to thinking that boys acquired nice manners and considerateness since I last paid attention, but then the twist:
Aaron said he'll bring the fart-gas.
There was a time when I would have easily built a whole page of comic dialogue around such a situation.
I try to run all the set-up variations through my noodle.
who's bringing the honey-puffs?
you just bring yourself.
But it ain't happening. nothin's doing.
GET YER GUN

I first noticed it right in the middle of publishing the opening parts of my ambitious new graphic novel, The History of Humour. In this huge masterwork, you would have espied me in the landscape of the soul...
prancing with Harlequin...
delivering pamphlets for Erasmus of Rotterdam.
chasing after the madcap Squire Mytton
Hey, Eddie! I've got some ass jokes for your new book.
Where did I go off the rails? Was it the talking endless pretentious rubbish to promote a Hollywood movie about Jack the Ripper and our book on which it was based?
The graphic novel has an opportunity to walk down the main street of culture
Only to find myself the fool who is invited to pontificate on screen against the next nitwit who claims to have unmasked Jack the Ripper.
Oy! That wasn't the point— oh, never mind.
Was it the discomfort I felt as all sorts people I once met found me via the internet.
I'm wondering if you're the same Eddie
I had counted on them never seeing their depictions in the books. (That's what we say in the trade..)
I was concerned when I created Daredevil that I might be giving offence to blind people
Don't worry, Stan. They'll never see it!

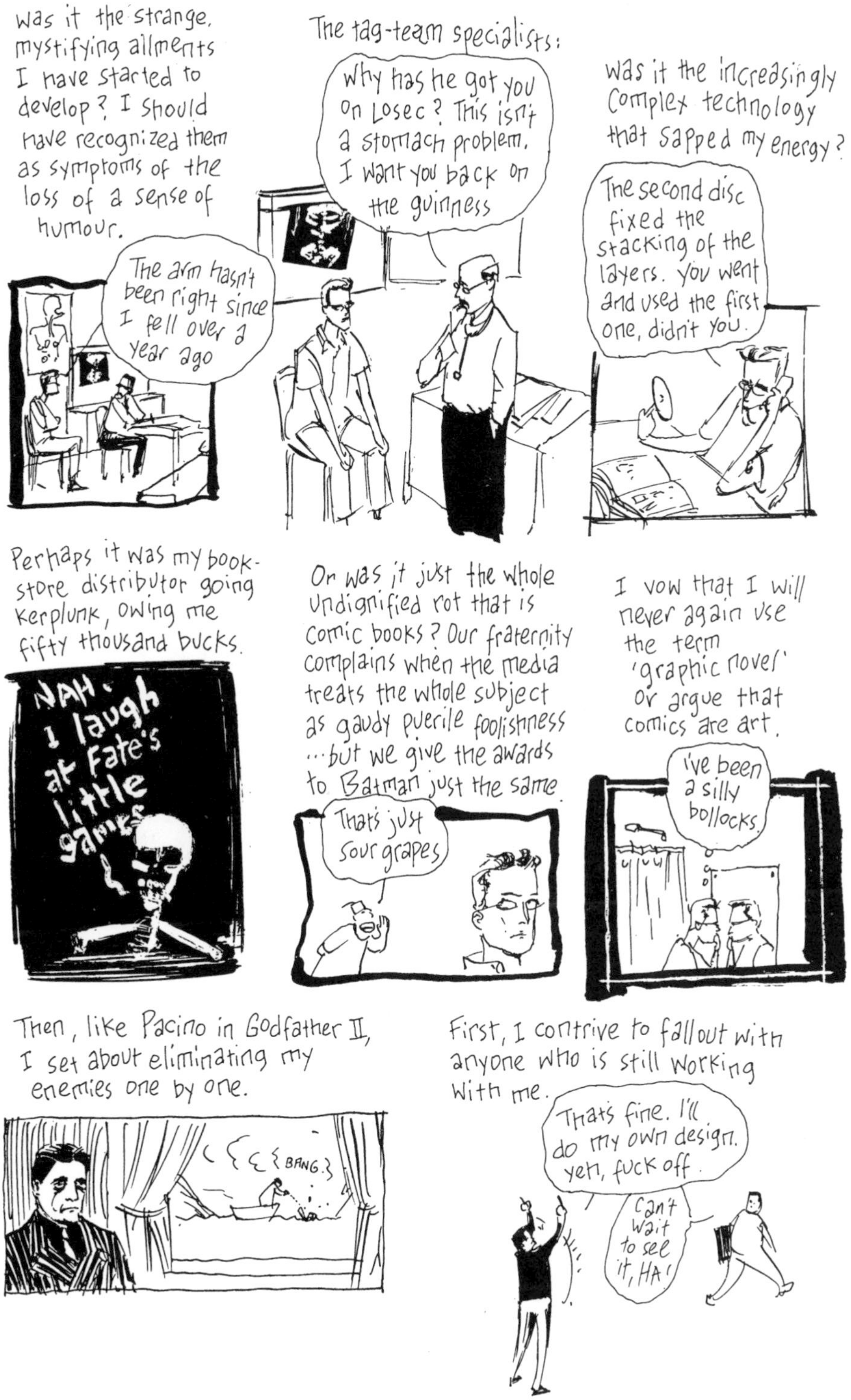

Was it the strange, mystifying ailments I have started to develop? I should have recognized them as symptoms of the loss of a sense of humour.
The arm hasn't been right since I fell over a year ago
The tag-team specialists:
Why has he got you on Losec? This isn't a stomach problem. I want you back on the guinness
Was it the increasingly complex technology that sapped my energy?
The second disc fixed the stacking of the layers. You went and used the first one, didn't you.
Perhaps it was my book-store distributor going kerplunk, owing me fifty thousand bucks.
NAH. I laugh at Fate's little games
Or was it just the whole undignified rot that is comic books? Our fraternity complains when the media treats the whole subject as gaudy puerile foolishness ...but we give the awards to Batman just the same.
That's just sour grapes
I vow that I will never again use the term 'graphic novel' or argue that comics are art.
I've been a silly bollocks.
Then, like Pacino in Godfather II, I set about eliminating my enemies one by one.
BANG
First, I contrive to fall out with anyone who is still working with me.
That's fine. I'll do my own design. yeh, fuck off.
Can't wait to see it, HA!

Next, I get Breach my website guy to announce the closing down of my publishing operation
does this mean I can go out and get a real job? I'm sick of this ramshackle business.
yes. on you go.
I decline to pay the renewal on my URL, effectively terminating the web page.
But why didn't you tell me? I'd have paid it myself to keep it alive.
I relinquish the key to my P.O. Box
I throw the telephone answering machine out the window.
Then I destroy the mouse.
Jesus! It's monkey versus robot!
Finally, I lock my studio door...
And move my barely essential gear onto the end of the dinner table.
I am once again master of all I survey...
fetch
Eddie Campbell Aug '03.

EDDIE CAMPBELL

the graphic novelist.

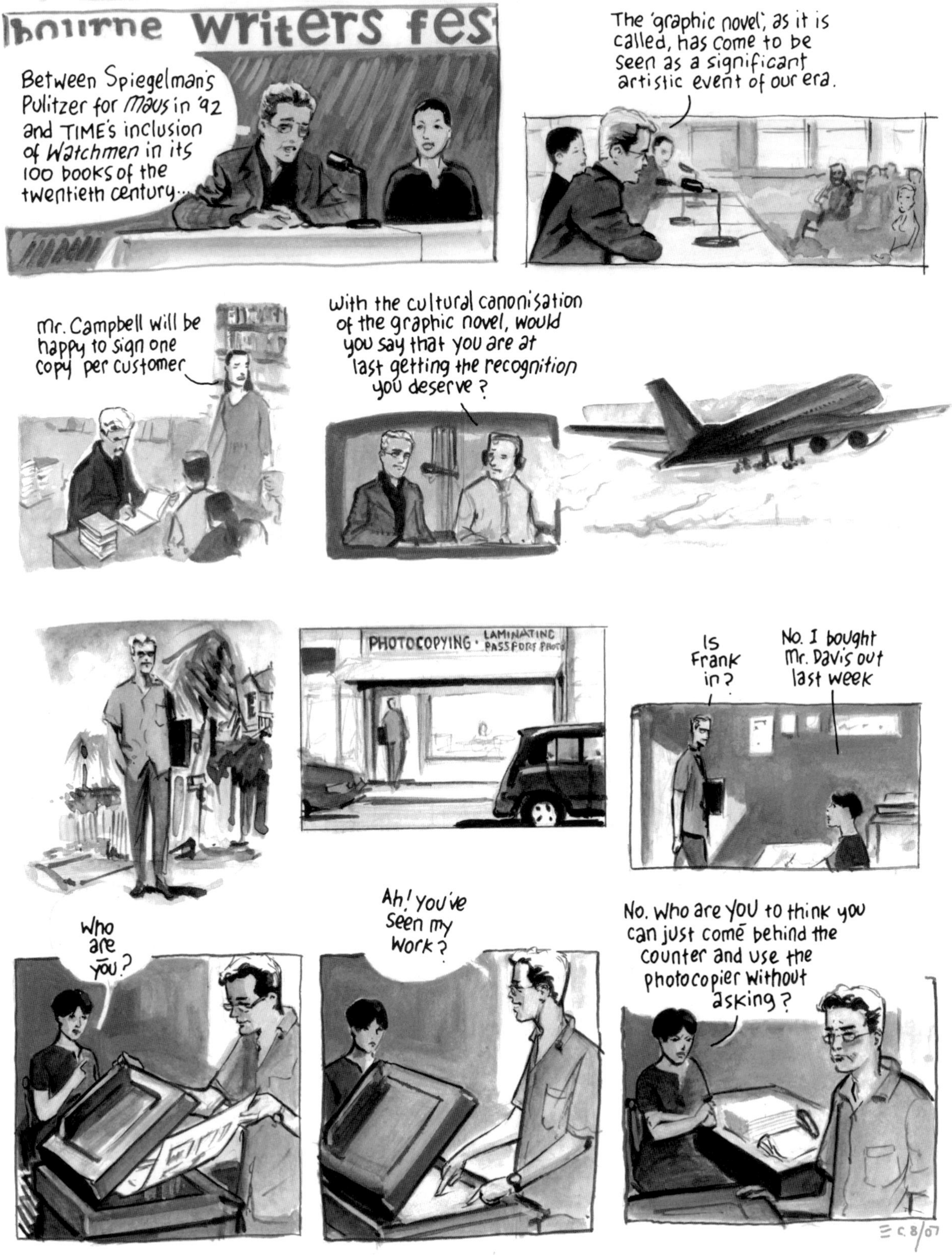

bourne writers fes
Between Spiegelman's Pulitzer for *Maus* in '92 and TIME's inclusion of *Watchmen* in its 100 books of the twentieth century...
The 'graphic novel', as it is called, has come to be seen as a significant artistic event of our era.
Mr. Campbell will be happy to sign one copy per customer
With the cultural canonisation of the graphic novel, would you say that you are at last getting the recognition you deserve?
PHOTOCOPYING · LAMINATING · PASSPORT PHOTO
Is Frank in?
No. I bought Mr. Davis out last week
Who are you?
Ah! You've seen my work?
No. Who are YOU to think you can just come behind the counter and use the photocopier without asking?
EC 8/07

The complicated demise of Robert Johnstone

by Eddie Campbell
2/2008

The real drunk is wrapped in an aura of chaos. Things will go awry around him even without his input, conscious or otherwise.
Edinburgh, 1818. Thirty-year-old Robert Johnstone stabs a man in a tavern altercation.

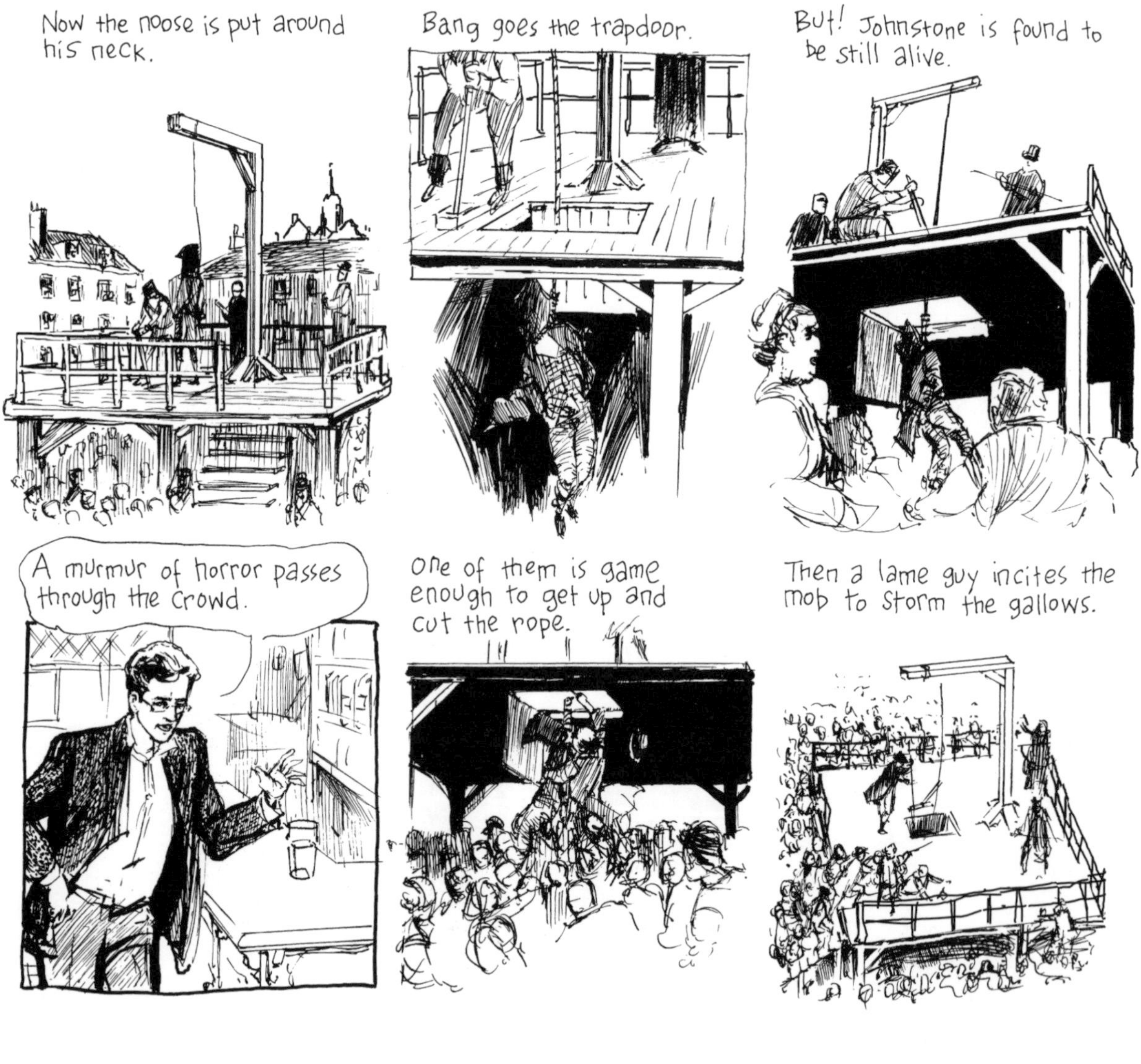

Now the noose is put around his neck.
Bang goes the trapdoor.
But! Johnstone is found to be still alive.
A murmur of horror passes through the crowd.
One of them is game enough to get up and cut the rope.
Then a lame guy incites the mob to storm the gallows.

Baillie Pattison leads his officials in a retreat to the castle to get military help.
But, by coincidence, while proceeding up Lawnmarket, they collide with the part of the crowd carrying Johnstone.
The crowd turns down the High Street.
But then clashes with a phalanx of constables.
When the dust clears, Johnstone is found lying on the cobbles.
They carry him into the police office to await the military detachment under major Graham.
The soldiers clear the streets.
And Johnstone is at last successfully "launched into eternity" as they used to euphemistically express it.

"The Years have Pants"

We can laugh about it now, but two hours ago it was tragic.

Once more Campbell imagines his own doom, above, introducing, at the end of this compendium, a brand new book of 35 pages, which was about the expected size of a book back at the beginning. It is made up of anecdotes spanning 27 years. Nothing in this one has previously appeared in print, though regular readers of my two-year-long daily blog may recognise a few anecdotal tidbits, albeit in a different form altogether. The blog was supposed to be a rehearsal for a proposed book, another Campbellian abandoned project, being a mystery about a blogger who goes off the rails. It would have been a puzzle that was to be read date-backwards, as is appropriate to a blog archive, with the comments box playing the role of the Greek chorus and the changing 'profile' being an evolving snapshot of the blogger's careening mental state. It would have been a complex of prose and picture and fictitious hyperlink, all telling a story, and probably a logical step forward from the formal hi-jinks of *The Fate of the Artist*. However, I got to enjoying blogging too much and feel disinclined to mine it for cheap fiction. Also, in the final analysis I reckoned that my readers would be more pleased with a book made along the lines of my ongoing material, and so here we are. I've given most of my favourite people a curtain call, and for old time's sake I fetched out the zip-a-tones, so that this compendium may finish in the stylistic manner in which it started.

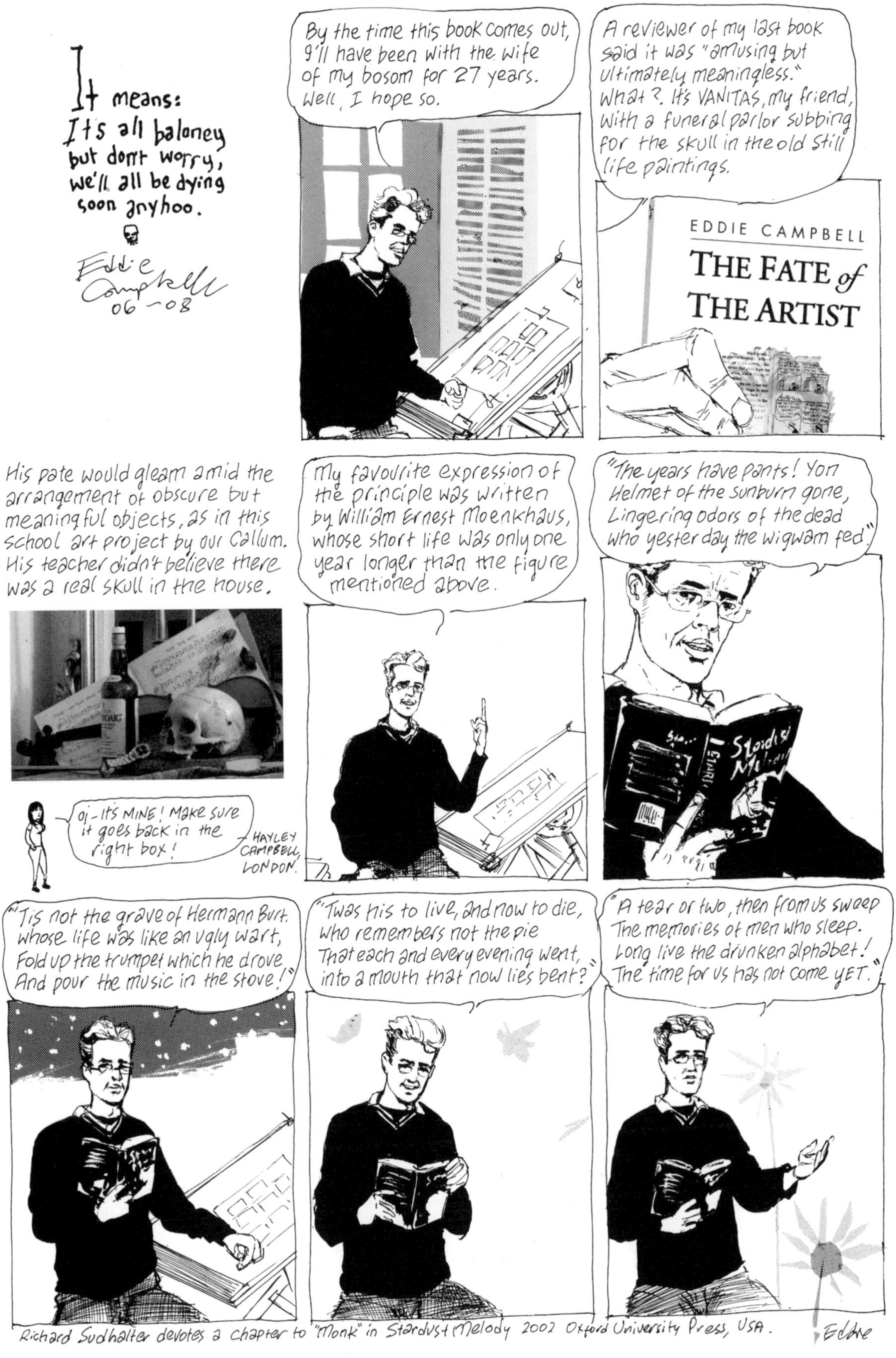
It means: It's all baloney but don't worry, we'll all be dying soon anyhoo.
Eddie Campbell 06-08
By the time this book comes out, I'll have been with the wife of my bosom for 27 years. Well, I hope so.
A reviewer of my last book said it was "amusing but ultimately meaningless." What? It's VANITAS, my friend, with a funeral parlor subbing for the skull in the old still life paintings.
EDDIE CAMPBELL
THE FATE of THE ARTIST
His pate would gleam amid the arrangement of obscure but meaningful objects, as in this school art project by our Callum. His teacher didn't believe there was a real skull in the house.
Oi - It's MINE! Make sure it goes back in the right box!
- HAYLEY CAMPBELL, LONDON.
My favourite expression of the principle was written by William Ernest Moenkhaus, whose short life was only one year longer than the figure mentioned above.
"The years have pants! Yon Helmet of the sunburn gone, Lingering odors of the dead who yester day the wigwam fed."
"'Tis not the grave of Hermann Burt. whose life was like an ugly wart, Fold up the trumpet which he drove And pour the music in the stove!"
"Twas his to live, and now to die, who remembers not the pie That each and every evening went, into a mouth that now lies bent?"
"A tear or two, then from us sweep The memories of men who sleep. Long live the drunken alphabet! The time for us has not come YET."
Richard Sudhalter devotes a chapter to "Monk" in Stardust Melody 2002 Oxford University Press, USA.
Eddie

On the Southend Arterial Road, somewhere between...
A127
I was on a coach after a weekend in London with the woman who would one day be the wife of my bosom. What if we could know such things?
NATIONAL EXPRESS
I was slouching home in the middle of a monday. It would take years to lose the guilty feeling of being out and about when others are working.
Suddenly, through the back window, I spot my old pal, Danny Grey.
He's still driving for Air Flo ducting and heating supplies. I haven't seen him in a year.
FIAT
We're on the Southend Arterial Road, somewhere between Graffiti Kitchen and How to be an Artist.
Trying to communicate from speeding compartments of laminated safety glass.
It was like visiting an old friend in jail and the speaking tube doesn't work.
FIAT
And now we're continents and ten years apart.

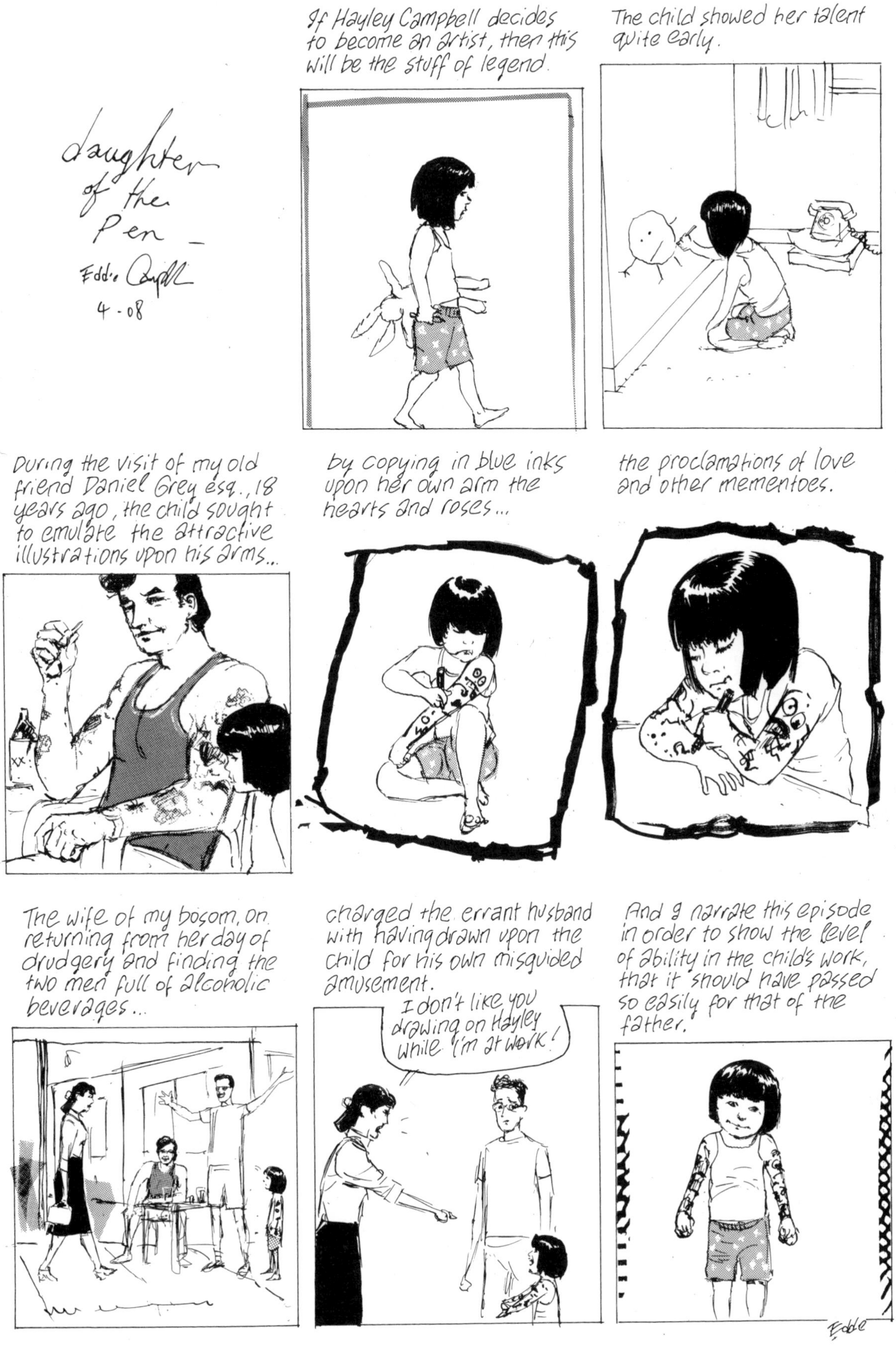
daughter of the Pen
Eddie Campbell 4-08
If Hayley Campbell decides to become an artist, then this will be the stuff of legend.
The child showed her talent quite early.
During the visit of my old friend Daniel Grey esq., 18 years ago, the child sought to emulate the attractive illustrations upon his arms...
by copying in blue inks upon her own arm the hearts and roses...
the proclamations of love and other mementoes.
The wife of my bosom, on returning from her day of drudgery and finding the two men full of alcoholic beverages...
charged the errant husband with having drawn upon the child for his own misguided amusement.
I don't like you drawing on Hayley while I'm at work!
And I narrate this episode in order to show the level of ability in the child's work, that it should have passed so easily for that of the father.
Eddie

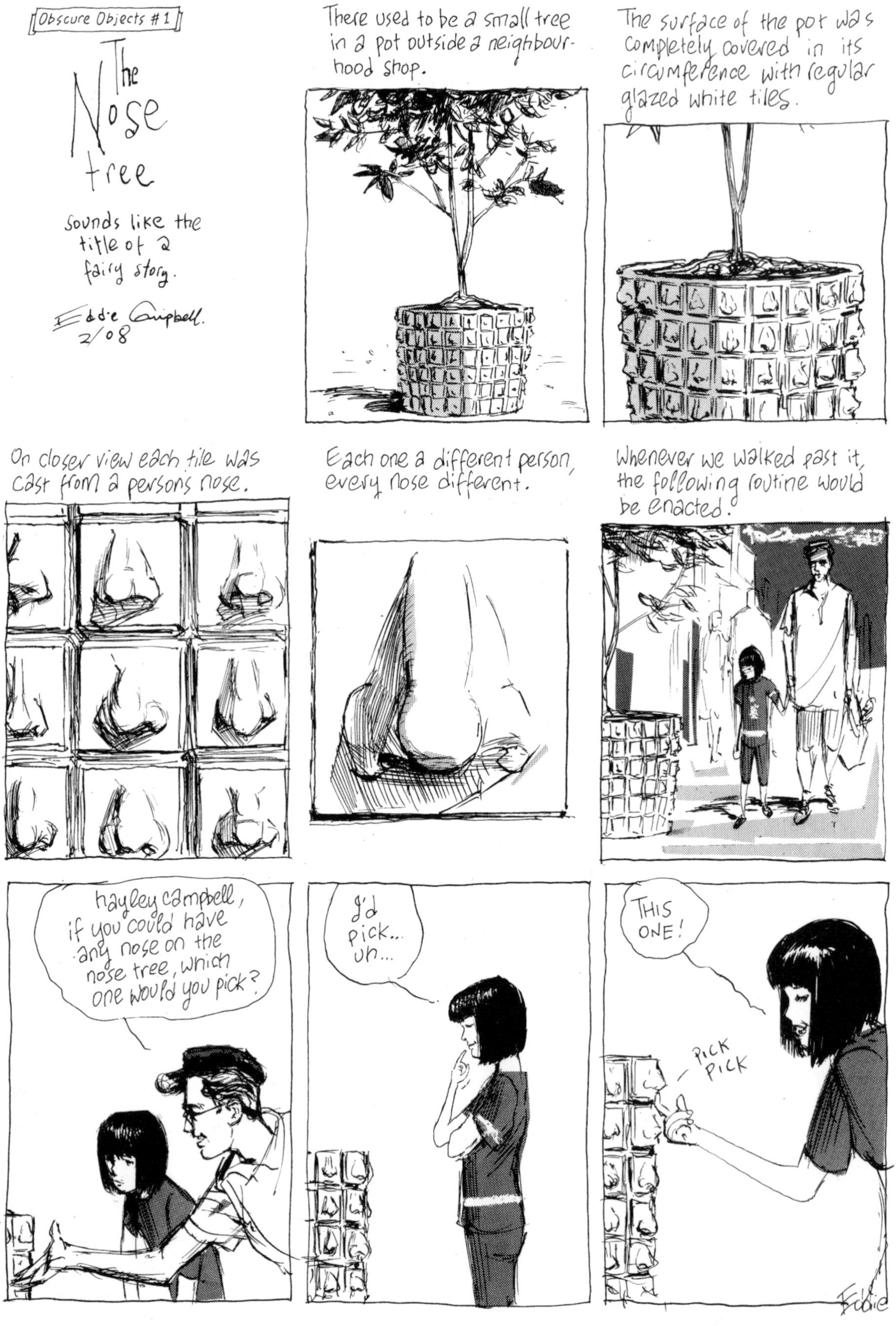
Obscure Objects #1
The Nose tree
sounds like the title of a fairy story.
Eddie Campbell. 2/08
There used to be a small tree in a pot outside a neighbourhood shop.
The surface of the pot was completely covered in its circumference with regular glazed white tiles.
On closer view each tile was cast from a person's nose.
Each one a different person, every nose different.
Whenever we walked past it, the following routine would be enacted.
hayley campbell, if you could have any nose on the nose tree, which one would you pick?
I'd pick... uh...
THIS ONE!
PICK PICK
Eddie

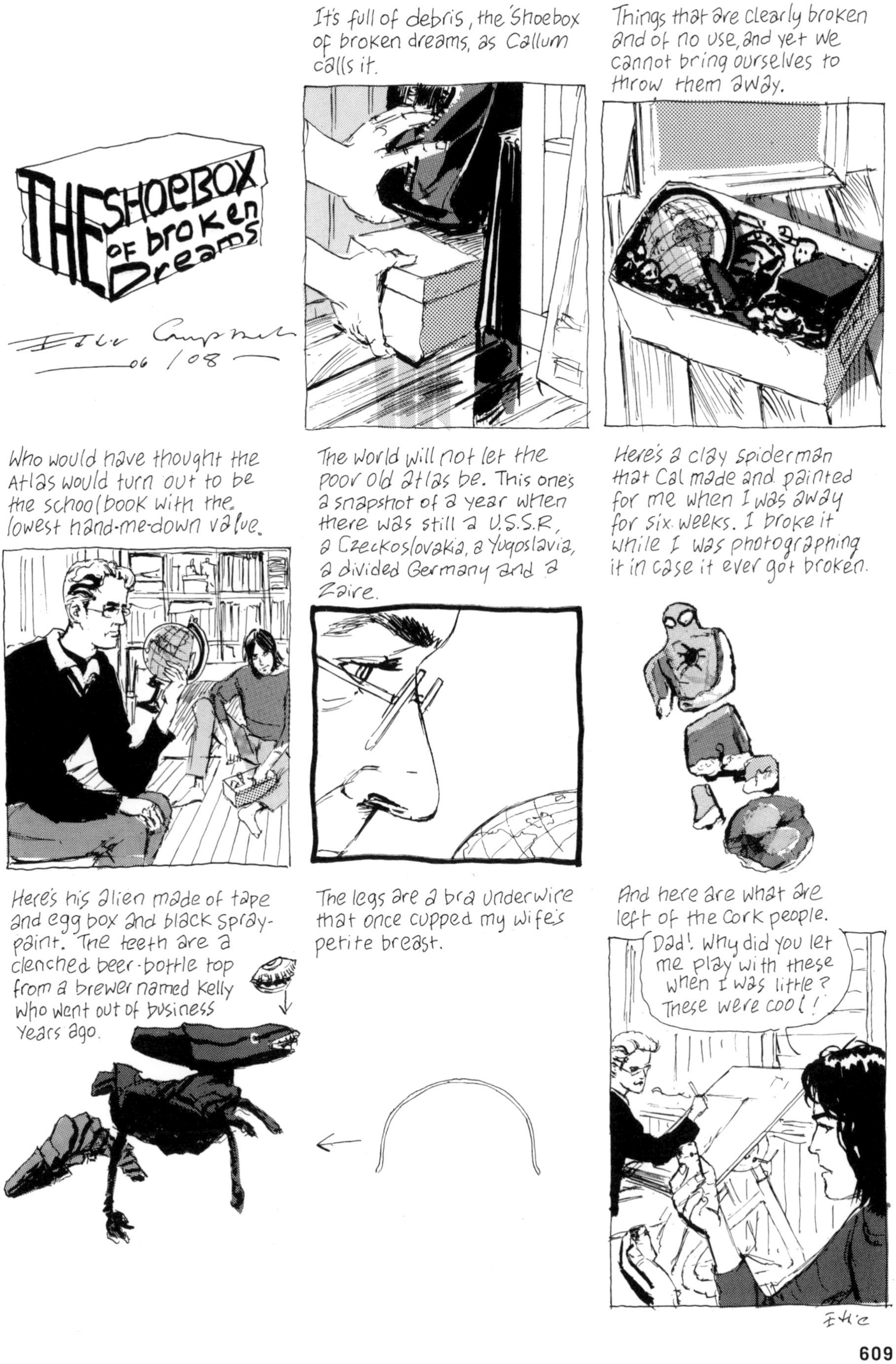
THE SHOEBOX OF broken Dreams
06/08
It's full of debris, the 'Shoebox of broken dreams,' as Callum calls it.
Things that are clearly broken and of no use, and yet we cannot bring ourselves to throw them away.
Who would have thought the Atlas would turn out to be the schoolbook with the lowest hand-me-down value.
The world will not let the poor old atlas be. This one's a snapshot of a year when there was still a U.S.S.R, a Czeckoslovakia, a Yugoslavia, a divided Germany and a Zaire.
Here's a clay spiderman that Cal made and painted for me when I was away for six weeks. I broke it while I was photographing it in case it ever got broken.
Here's his alien made of tape and egg box and black spray-paint. The teeth are a clenched beer-bottle top from a brewer named Kelly who went out of business years ago.
The legs are a bra underwire that once cupped my wife's petite breast.
And here are what are left of the cork people.
Dad! Why did you let me play with these when I was little? These were cool!

Obscure Objects # 2
Let me outta here
Eddie Campbell 06/08.
These are the cork people.
The fashioning of these little chaps owes something to the same impulse that guided Michelangelo: "freeing from the dead stone the beauty it imprisons."
Free me!
At the end of one of our christmas parties, I was picking the champagne cork off the floor when I was certain I saw my pal Pete Mullins in it.
Let me out!
So I immediately took to the cork with my scalpel and acrylics and in short order there he was on the table.
After that, every cork from a bottle of bubbly would be retrieved and one of those present, or not even present but dear to our funny bone, would ask to be let out.
YEE HA!
This tradition gave us a dozen cork men. I know this because Callum would put them in an egg carton for a bus. Standing room only. Once he took them to school for show and tell.
Looking at them now, the shine has gone off them and their paint has flaked, and only four remain. They once had necks, but champagne corks find their way back to cylinders.
CONAN the Barbarian
LIZ
Grampa
There's my father giving me a stern look. He doesn't know about this tradition.
So help ma boab
Eddie

Callum's Alan Moore anecdote
2/08
You'll dine out on that one day, son.
yeah, if you don't steal it first, Dad
When we were in England, you and mum had gone into the hotel to check us out, I think...
And you left me standing outside with Alan Moore.
He did that old trick with his hands:
Hey, look at this!
You know, the chopped off thumb gag.
Wait a minute! How did you do that?
good, eh?
Tell me how you Do that?
Can't... it's magic.
Eddie.

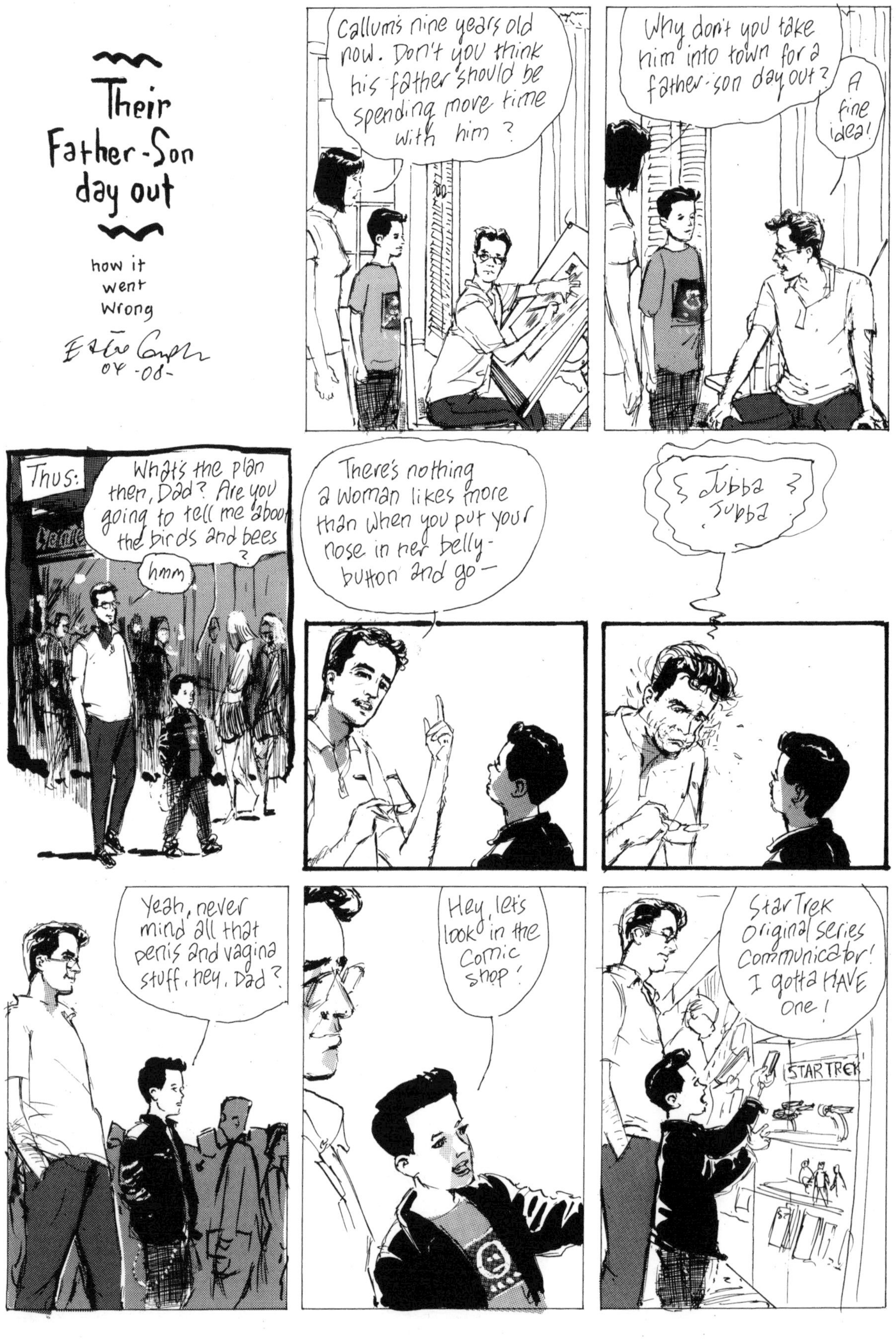
Their Father-Son day out
how it went wrong
04-08-
Callum's nine years old now. Don't you think his father should be spending more time with him?
Why don't you take him into town for a father-son day out?
A fine idea!
Thus:
What's the plan then, Dad? Are you going to tell me about the birds and bees?
hmm
There's nothing a woman likes more than when you put your nose in her belly-button and go—
Jubba Jubba
Yeah, never mind all that penis and vagina stuff, hey, Dad?
Hey, let's look in the comic shop!
Star Trek original series communicator! I gotta HAVE one!
STAR TREK

But this is a collector's piece. it's seventy dollars. That's a lot of—
But I've got my Christmas money!
~sigh~
It's battery operated. You can record a message.
Dad, You've got the Voice. Make it say 'Beam me up, Scotty!'
No, you're the one who says that. Scotty's up in the ship, on the other end...
eh?
Here we go— "Are ya reddy ta beam up noo, captin?"
"Are ya reddy
HA HA! That's brilliant
Now, before we go any further, you know this isn't real? you can't actually beam up with this...
You're funny, Dad.
Obscure Objects #3
Is Daren coming? And Mick too?
Yes, they'll be here after they knock off work. How about another coke?
Thus:
I'm hungry. Time we had dinner

Eating out with Chalky WHITE is fraught with difficulty
Tonight his argument is over the WRONG SAUCE served on his gourmet burger.
I asked for Cordon Bleu. This is Blue Cheese.
You've eaten most of it
He wants to see the manager.
I want to see the manager.
The chef-manager is busy and refuses to be seen.
Chalky instructs the waitress to tell the chef manager that if he wants to be paid, then he will find us
in the coffee house across the road
Thus.
Café
Café
Café
Police

What are these?
It's only talcum powder. It's not real. look
That's an original series Star Trek communicator, but it's not real.
I'm putting full payment for all meals consumed on the table here, okay?
Hey, Cal, see the rubber gloves; that's for when they have to stick their finger up your ass.
AW Dad no
Alright, it's sorted. Let's get out of here.

We should do this more often, hey, Dad?
Yeah. Hey, Callum - Look!
Imagine getting your head caught between THOSE thighs.
Blen
Oh - and one other thing - Not a word about this to the Mammy
I Know Nothing. HA HA.
Several Weeks Later.
- and it was all because he got cordon bleu sauce...
-instead of blue cheese.
Callum was there! And you made him keep it a secret from me?
Are ya reddy ta beam up, captin?
Let's Go, Scotty!
Eddie.

The Day I was mistaken for an author.
by Eddie Campbell 07-08.
Flying to Europe on Singapore Airlines I picked up a copy of THE STRAITS TIMES (NOV. 10, 2001 if you want to look for it)
SINGAPORE AIRLINES
And I found myself looking at my own photograph.
THE STRAITS TIMES
WALLYHOOP ENDING
With the FROM HELL movie being released around the world, I asked Liz to take a few publicity photos, and I was sending them out and about.
However, this interview is not with ME, but with Simon Winchester, author of The Surgeon of Crowthorne.
LIFE! • BOOKS
Time-traveller arrives
Alternative-reality Singapore
Note the serendipitous headline in the neighbouring book review, by a copy editor with science fiction on his mind.
Alternative-reality
FICTION
CRISIS IN THE STRAITS: MALAYSIA INVADES SINGAPORE
By Douglas Chua
Angsana/332 pages/$18
By CLARA CHOW
THE premise for Crisis In The Straits is controversial and exciting — going where politicians fear to tread. In an alternative-reality world, the Malaysian ambassador to Singapore is shot.
A breakdown in relations between the two countries ensues. But this is peanuts compared to the race for a mysterious document which can impinge on Singapore's sovereignty. The Malaysian minister for defence wants it,
CRISIS STRAITS
DOUGLAS CHUA
Only super-agent Alex Han, head of the fictional Central Intelligence Service of Singapore, holds the Missing Page, and can save the day.
When the same photo turned up a few weeks later with MY name under it, it would have confirmed the thought in many Asian minds that Westerners all look alike.
Lesser known history is rich ground for author Simon Winchester.
As for Simon Winchester, did he get a tearsheet from his publisher's publicity dept. and wonder who was that other bloke?
It must be that thing we do with the hand on the chin.

Obscure Objects #4
The Opening
Eddie Campbell
06/08
When they opened the From Hell movie here in Brisbane, the local newspaper was sponsor and they put their own guy up to introduce it.
He has just got to the part about it being based on my book. I'm in the audience, incognito.
CRINKLE CRINKLE
A guy across the aisle from me is noisily trying to open a packet of jaffas. (They're a chocolate-filled, orange-flavoured candy popular at the movies in Australia).
Jaffas
Give it here!
Some time later I'm waiting for a plane out of L.A. and a stranger comes up to me:
Are you Eddie Campbell?
Yes, that's me.
I was sitting right behind you that night in Brisbane when you opened that bloke's jaffas - that was the funniest thing.
Eddie

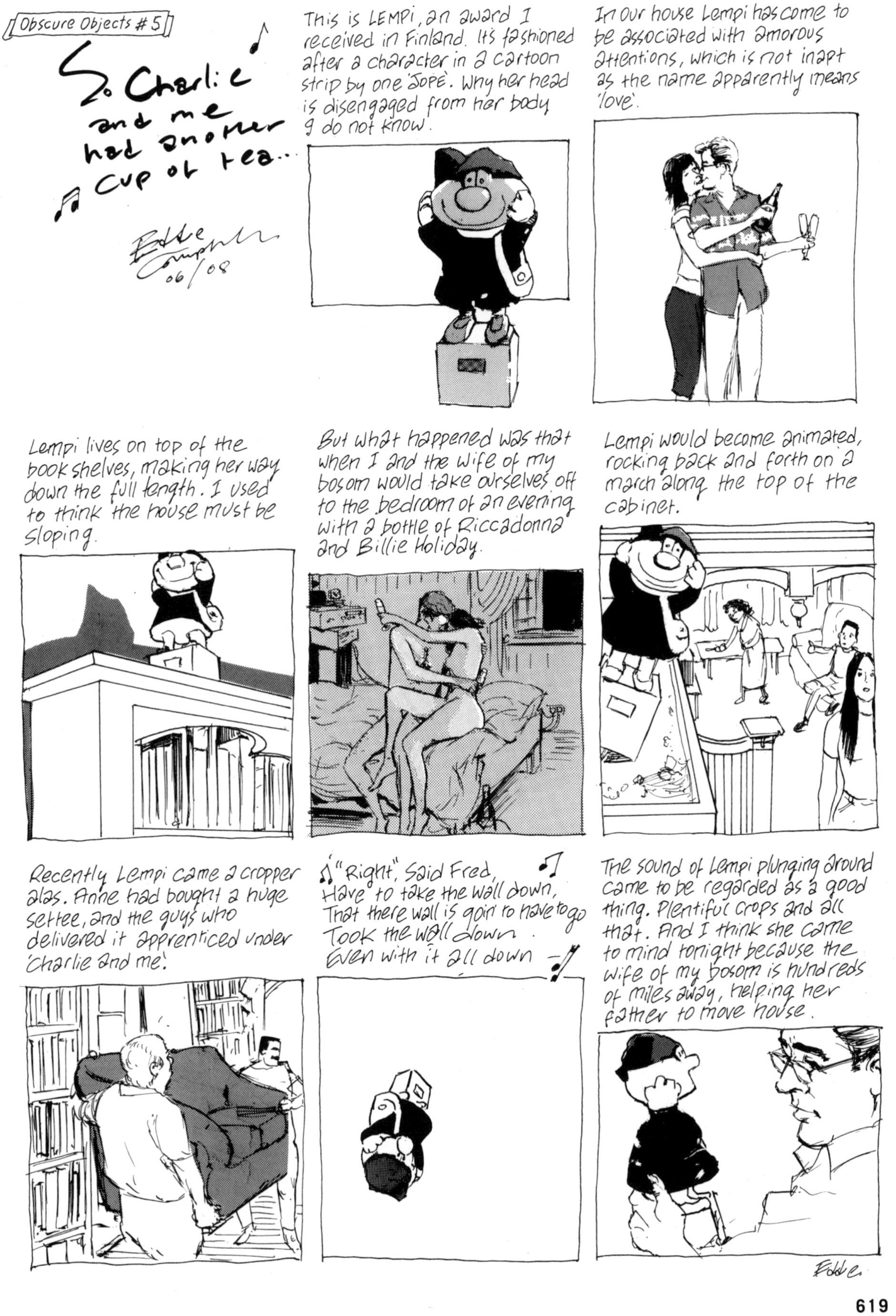

Obscure Objects #5
So Charlie and me had another cup of tea...
Eddie Campbell 06/08
This is LEMPI, an award I received in Finland. It's fashioned after a character in a cartoon strip by one 'JOPE'. Why her head is disengaged from her body I do not know.
In our house Lempi has come to be associated with amorous attentions, which is not inapt as the name apparently means 'love'.
Lempi lives on top of the book shelves, making her way down the full length. I used to think the house must be sloping.
But what happened was that when I and the wife of my bosom would take ourselves off to the bedroom of an evening with a bottle of Riccadonna and Billie Holiday.
Lempi would become animated, rocking back and forth on a march along the top of the cabinet.
Recently Lempi came a cropper alas. Anne had bought a huge settee, and the guys who delivered it apprenticed under 'Charlie and me'.
"Right", said Fred, Have to take the wall down, That there wall is goin' to have to go Took the wall down. Even with it all down –
The sound of Lempi plunging around came to be regarded as a good thing. Plentiful crops and all that. And I think she came to mind tonight because the wife of my bosom is hundreds of miles away, helping her father to move house.
Eddie.

Obscure Objects #6
These young 'uns today
Eddie Campbell 5-08
I want this place cleaned up before I collect my father from the airport!
Hayley, go next door and get that damn thing off Cynthia's wall - and do it without being seen!
We can no longer recall how it got there. I presume my daughter Erin, for it strikes me as her style, took it out of its box, soaked it in water, swung it around her head and tossed it out the kitchen window.
And for nothing more than gleeful mischief. Perhaps years ago.
It clings there, blossoming and compacting with the changing weather, exciting my perennial curiosity.
How can I get up there without breaking my neck? And anyway, surely grandad has seen one before.
Well, he's of that generation in which women didn't talk to men about such things, but he's a lawyer of fifty years experience. I'm sure in all that time he must have seen a tampon.
No, silly, I mean hasn't he seen one stuck to the side of a house before?
Eddie

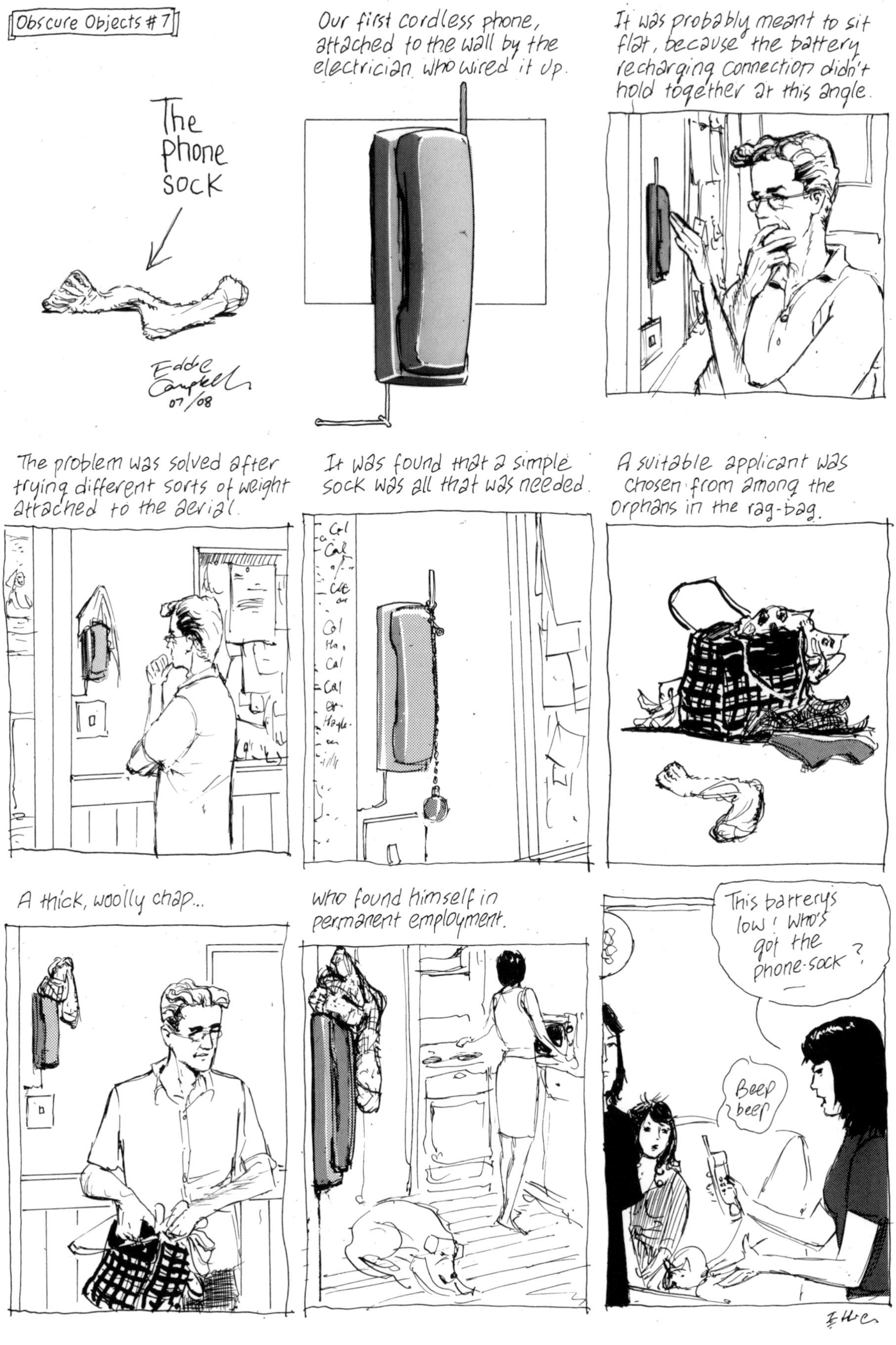

Obscure Objects #7
The phone sock
Eddie Campbell 07/08
Our first cordless phone, attached to the wall by the electrician who wired it up.
It was probably meant to sit flat, because the battery recharging connection didn't hold together at this angle.
The problem was solved after trying different sorts of weight attached to the aerial.
It was found that a simple sock was all that was needed.
A suitable applicant was chosen from among the orphans in the rag-bag.
A thick, woolly chap...
who found himself in permanent employment.
This battery's low! Who's got the phone-sock?
Beep beep

The Wife
from the keyboard of
The blogger.
8.08
21.9.11.
Labels: the wife
PERMALINK.
"I'm not quite the last person in the world you'd expect to start a blog, so there are still a few left, for those of you who have been thinking of getting one."
"Now, I have always liked the definite article in 'the wife', though wives do not tend to be fond of it. It has an unpossessive working class Britishness about it."
"It reminds me of an old TV show 'Meet the Wife', famously mentioned in a Beatles song, which we never missed in our house when I was a wee 'un."
"It reminds me too of 'The Mammy' of Irish usage, as celebrated in Brendan O'Carroll's book, when the Mammy wore kickarse boots and marched to the shops with a big bag in each hand."
BRENDAN O'CARROLL
The Mammy
"However, my story: my wife, (for I am a coward when all is said and done) Anne, has lately added a new word to the English lexicon."
"Caught on the phone during dinner, she yessed her way through a conversation while mentally rehearsing her exit line. 'thanks for ringing' - 'thanks for phoning', and when she found a break it came out as
Okay- thanks for roning.
In our house this is now the standard way of answering a call that's surplus to requirements.
Oy! Where do you think YOU'RE going? You haven't scooped the dogshit out of the yard
Yes, Dad. Thanks for roning
LET IT BE
"In the old days I'd have made a one-page 'Alec' out of this, but today we squander our narratives on a blog".
iMac

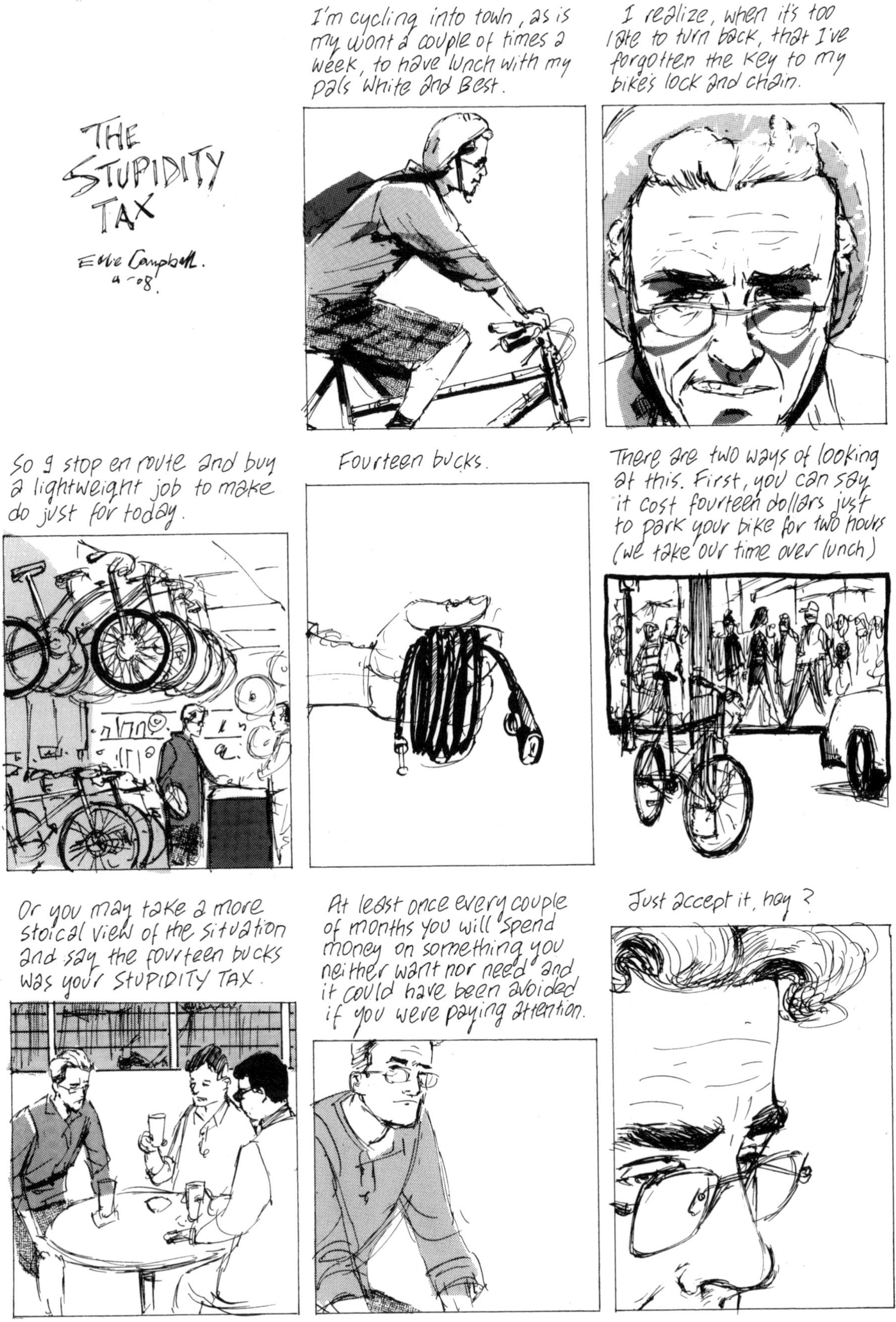
THE STUPIDITY TAX
Eddie Campbell. 4-08.
I'm cycling into town, as is my wont a couple of times a week, to have lunch with my pals White and Best.
I realize, when it's too late to turn back, that I've forgotten the key to my bike's lock and chain.
So I stop en route and buy a lightweight job to make do just for today.
Fourteen bucks.
There are two ways of looking at this. First, you can say it cost fourteen dollars just to park your bike for two hours (we take our time over lunch)
Or you may take a more stoical view of the situation and say the fourteen bucks was your STUPIDITY TAX.
At least once every couple of months you will spend money on something you neither want nor need and it could have been avoided if you were paying attention.
Just accept it, hey ?

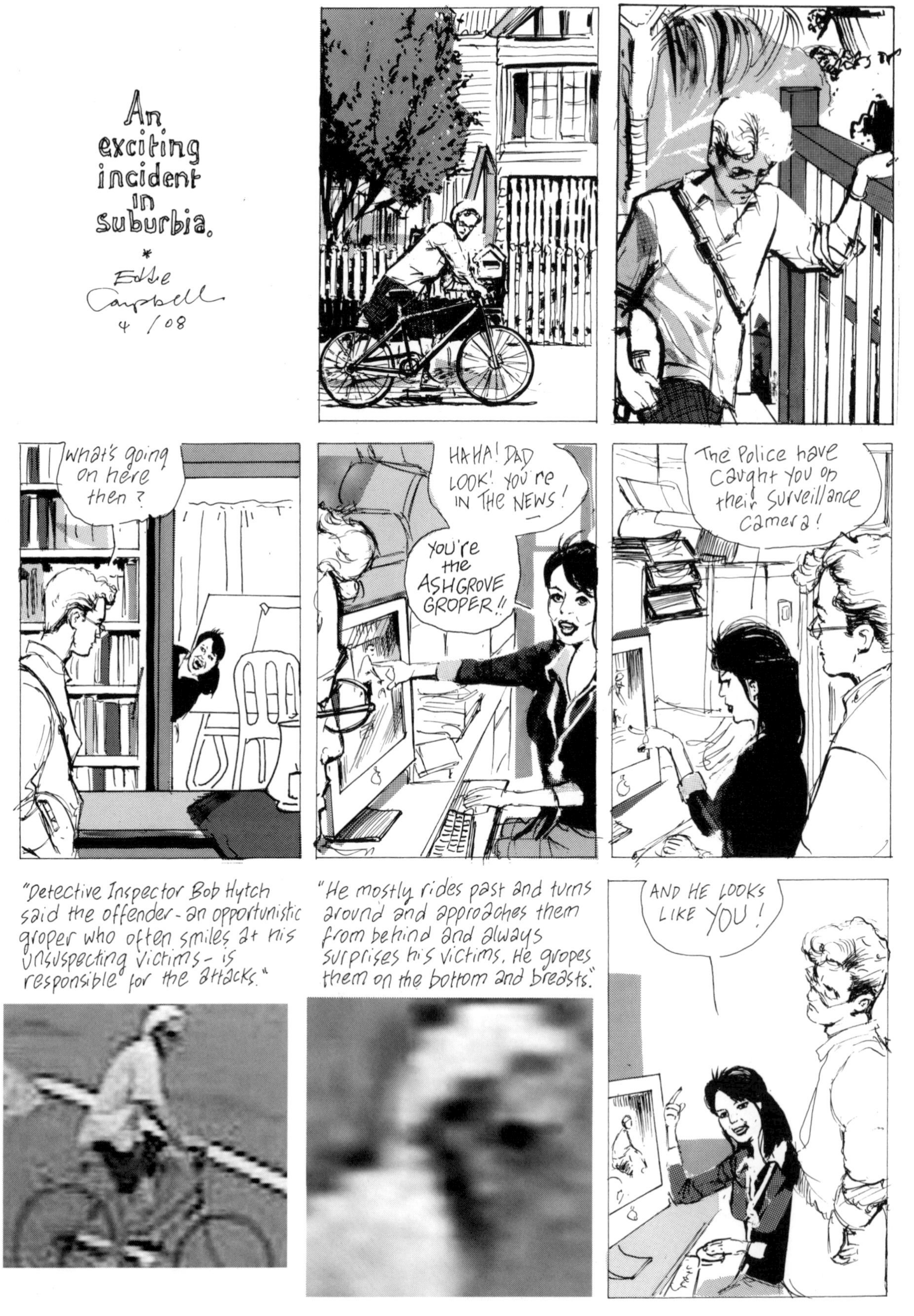
An exciting incident in suburbia.
*
Eddie Campbell
4/08
What's going on here then?
HA HA! DAD LOOK! YOU're IN THE NEWS!
YOU're the ASHGROVE GROPER!!
The Police have caught you on their surveillance camera!
"Detective Inspector Bob Hytch said the offender - an opportunistic groper who often smiles at his unsuspecting victims - is responsible for the attacks."
"He mostly rides past and turns around and approaches them from behind and always surprises his victims. He gropes them on the bottom and breasts."
AND HE LOOKS LIKE YOU!

But that's not my bike.
Yes, Dad, but it says: "The offender strikes in daytime, often using different types of bicycles, including a woman's bike."
That's when you're out and about, and remember you borrowed Mum's bike for a year after you broke your own.
He's wearing your blue shirt, Dad! And —
And look, he's got your esky on his head.
"Det. Insp. Hytch said the foam helmet worn by the offender was rare and not stocked in major cycling stores."
Obscure Objects #8
A groper? Well, you never know your luck in the big city.
I want to go to the police with my details, then they can 'eliminate me from their enquiries'.
DON'T YOU DARE!!

The local dog-walking crowd, a beloved loose society of the friends of man's best friend, are meeting in the park on a Friday evening.
The wife of my bosom will join us after finishing work.
I wait for her on the footpath to let her know we're meeting in a new place, hoping she hasn't gone the long way round.
I wait, while it darkens quickly.
I wait.
A Scream!
A damsel in distress? The groper?
I'M COMING!
"He rides past, then turns around and approaches his victim from behind."
MONTY

AAHHHHH
AAAAAAHHHHH
Anne?
TRUNdle Trundle
gee, I'm sorry. I stopped and turned and the lady panicked.
I stopped because I thought I'd hit your dog.
I didn't HAVE a dog!!
Nice bike.
Yes, it's got the new style gear-shift and

P.S. The 'Ashgrove groper' has never been identified — 15 May 2008

Monty's bath.
by Eddie Campbell 07/08.
We may have caught it in time. If you'd come a day later he'd have had to wear the lampshade.
Give him an anti-biotic twice a day with food, and a bath using this medical shampoo once a week for three weeks.
Y'know, it's a long time since you touched ME like that.
But you haven't got a horrible skin rash!
what are you laughing at?
Eddie.

Obscure Objects #9
Quasimodo's shirt
Eddie Campbell 07-08
Have you seen my thick denim shirt?
Didn't you wear it this week already?
Yeah
It should be on the line then. Callum hung the washing out for me this morning.
Okay
CALLUM!
He made a crap job of it. If you see him, give him a thump!
Okay
Eddie

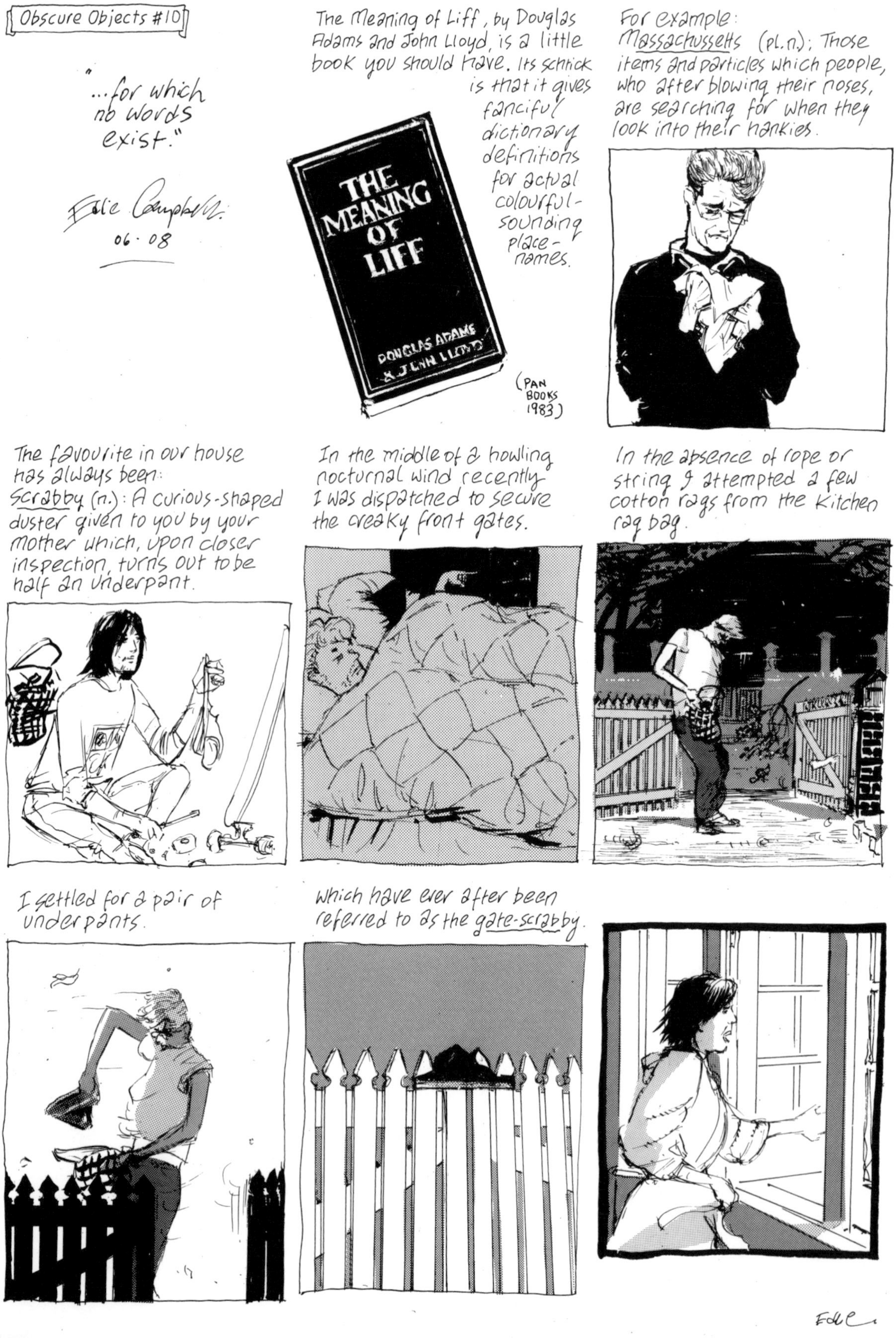
Obscure Objects #10
"...for which no words exist."
Eddie Campbell 06·08
The Meaning of Liff, by Douglas Adams and John Lloyd, is a little book you should have. Its schtick is that it gives fanciful dictionary definitions for actual colourful-sounding place-names.
THE MEANING OF LIFF
DOUGLAS ADAMS & JOHN LLOYD
(PAN BOOKS 1983)
For example: Massachussetts (pl.n.): Those items and particles which people, who after blowing their noses, are searching for when they look into their hankies.
The favourite in our house has always been: Scrabby (n.): A curious-shaped duster given to you by your mother which, upon closer inspection, turns out to be half an underpant.
In the middle of a howling nocturnal wind recently I was dispatched to secure the creaky front gates.
In the absence of rope or string I attempted a few cotton rags from the kitchen rag bag.
I settled for a pair of underpants.
Which have ever after been referred to as the gate-scrabby.
Eddie

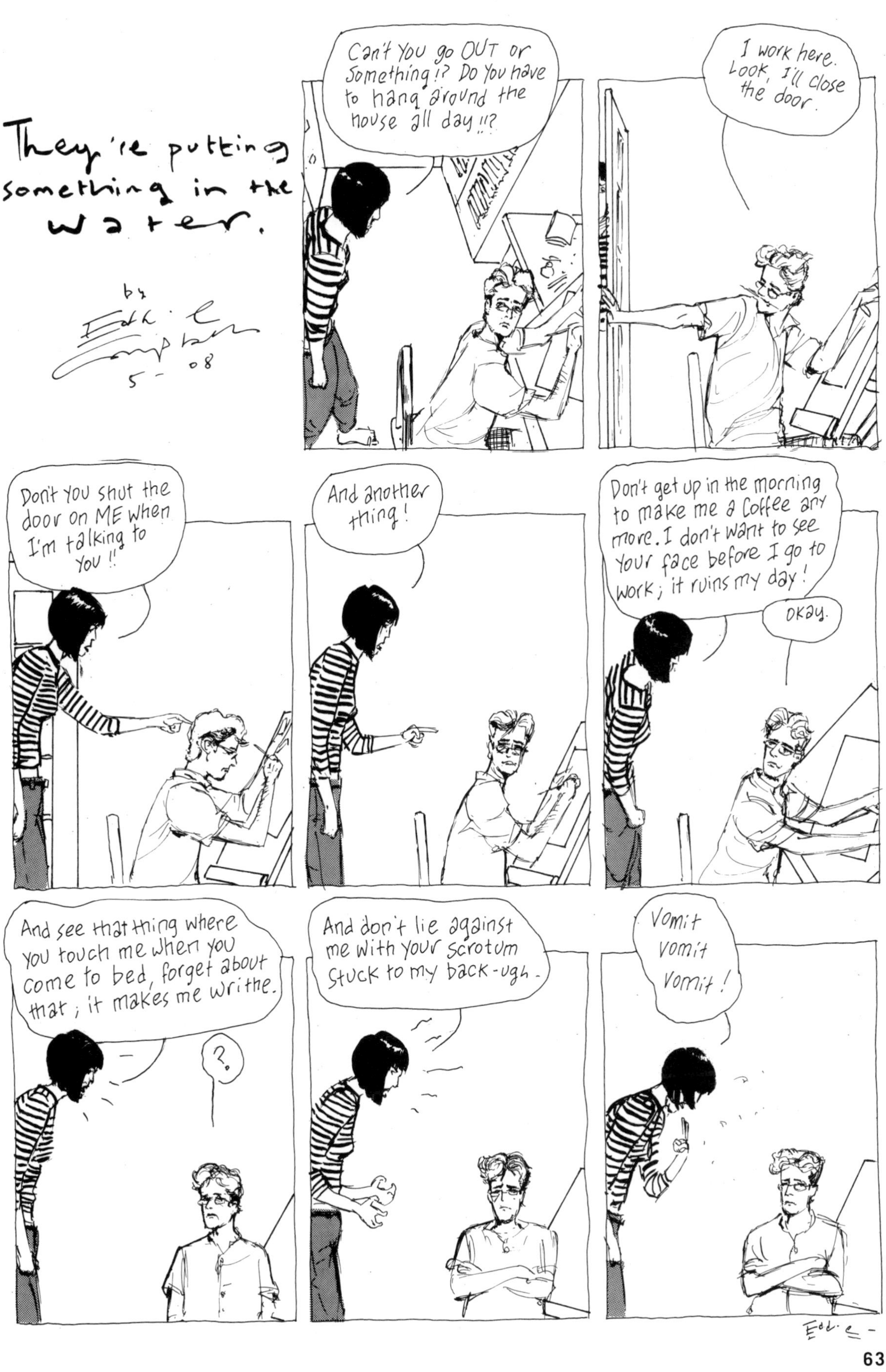
They're putting something in the water.
by Eddie Campbell 5-08
Can't you go OUT or something!? Do you have to hang around the house all day!!?
I work here. Look, I'll close the door.
Don't you shut the door on ME when I'm talking to you!!
And another thing!
Don't get up in the morning to make me a coffee any more. I don't want to see your face before I go to work; it ruins my day!
Okay.
And see that thing where you touch me when you come to bed, forget about that; it makes me writhe.
?
And don't lie against me with your scrotum stuck to my back-ugh.
Vomit vomit vomit!
Eddie

Lee Slattery's bucks night.
from the Keyboard of The blogger.
8 - 08
at 5.10
Labels: my pals. PERMALINK
"And tomorrow's post will be my FIFTIETH consecutive day of blogging! However, since I am now off to my pal Lee Slattery's bucks' afternoon..."
"(they start early here in Australia, but I hope to effect an exit well before my bedtime) do not expect it to be brilliant (like this sentence - but that's me out the door - too late!)"
iMac
iMac
your blog post published successfully
edit post create new post
"I managed to extricate myself from the boozy proceedings at a reasonable hour last night and so was not there to see the young husband lying in the gutter with his whole life before him..."
"and in closer proximity, his dinner."
iMac
"Since I wrote that before I got there, it may well have ended differently!"
iMac
save as draft
iMac

Big 50
*
from the keyboard of The blogger.
8 - 08
at 9.19.
Labels: birthdays
PERMALINK.
"my FIFTIETH day of consecutive blogging! I am reminded of another boozy night, my fiftieth birthday bash, which took place a couple of years ago."
"The photos were coming out looking all cold and harsh until I turned off the flash. With the longer shutter speed everything's out of focus now."
"Which is the way I remember it anyway, and the colours are all rich and fruity, except I don't remember my pal Mullins having a purple head on the night."
(click to enlarge)
"That's mr j and wee hayley Campbell at extreme right, chalky White in the red shirt, and I'm at the back acting like I've just scored a goal by getting to the end without anybody falling out."
"I can't see Best. Perhaps he 'extricated himself from the boozy proceedings' after his rendering of 'Meet me in the Alley, MacGarry', complete with additional verse and obscene epithet."
"And finally, a photo of me and the wife of my bosom. I seem to have lost my glasses, which I daresay is the reason everything is out of focus."
(click to enlarge)

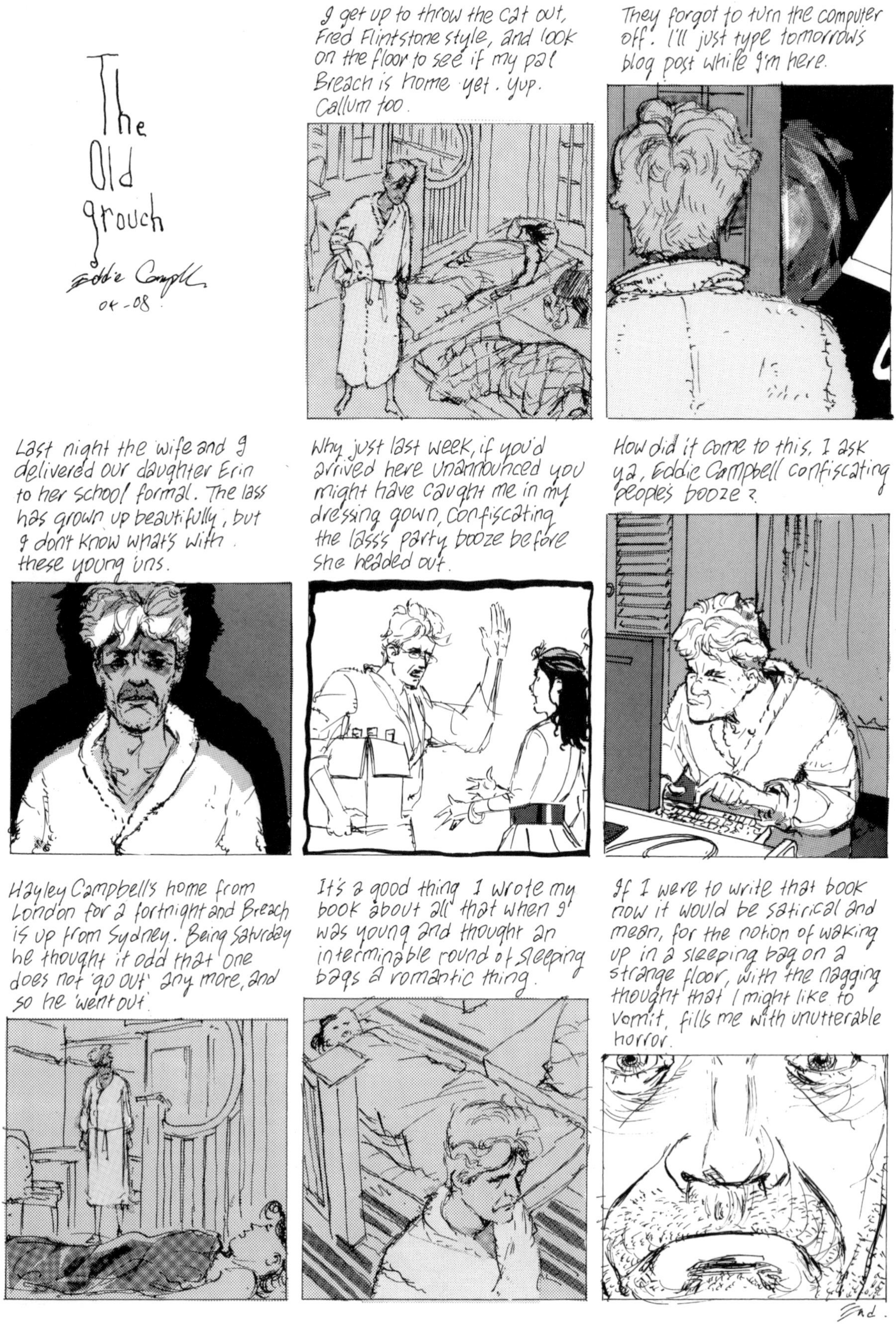
The Old grouch
Eddie Campbell
04-08.
I get up to throw the cat out, Fred Flintstone style, and look on the floor to see if my pal Breach is home yet. Yup. Callum too.
They forgot to turn the computer off. I'll just type tomorrow's blog post while I'm here.
Last night the wife and I delivered our daughter Erin to her school formal. The lass has grown up beautifully, but I don't know what's with these young uns.
Why just last week, if you'd arrived here unannounced you might have caught me in my dressing gown, confiscating the lass's party booze before she headed out.
How did it come to this, I ask ya, Eddie Campbell confiscating people's booze?
Hayley Campbell's home from London for a fortnight and Breach is up from Sydney. Being Saturday he thought it odd that one does not 'go out' any more, and so he 'went out'.
It's a good thing I wrote my book about all that when I was young and thought an interminable round of sleeping bags a romantic thing.
If I were to write that book now it would be satirical and mean, for the notion of waking up in a sleeping bag on a strange floor, with the nagging thought that I might like to vomit, fills me with unutterable horror.
End.

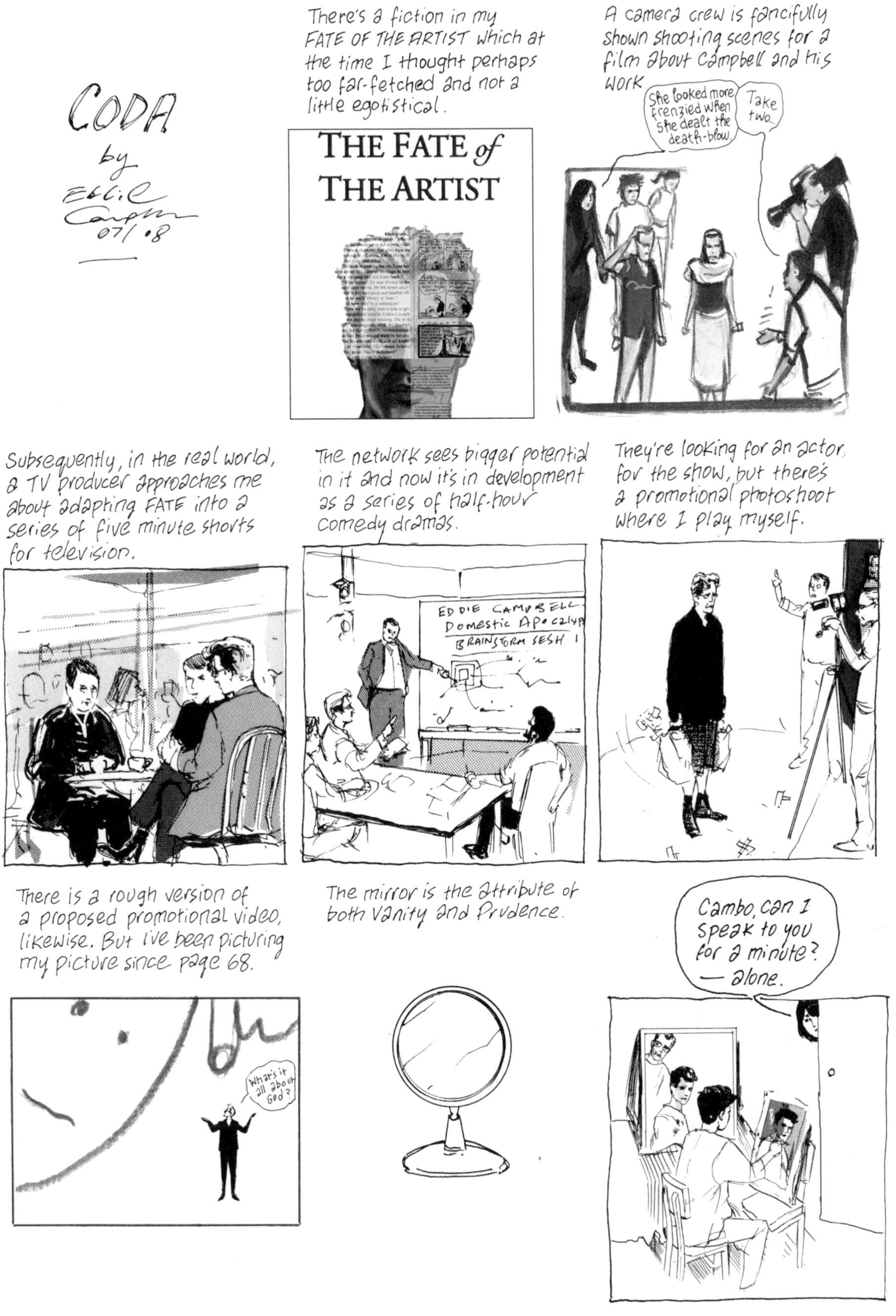
CODA
by
There's a fiction in my FATE OF THE ARTIST which at the time I thought perhaps too far-fetched and not a little egotistical.
THE FATE of THE ARTIST
A camera crew is fancifully shown shooting scenes for a film about Campbell and his work
She looked more frenzied when she dealt the death-blow.
Take two..
Subsequently, in the real world, a TV producer approaches me about adapting FATE into a series of five minute shorts for television.
The network sees bigger potential in it and now it's in development as a series of half-hour comedy dramas.
EDDIE CAMPBELL
Domestic Apocalyp
BRAINSTORM SESH 1
They're looking for an actor for the show, but there's a promotional photoshoot where I play myself.
There is a rough version of a proposed promotional video, likewise. But I've been picturing my picture since page 68.
What's it all about God?
The mirror is the attribute of both Vanity and Prudence.
Cambo, can I speak to you for a minute? — alone.

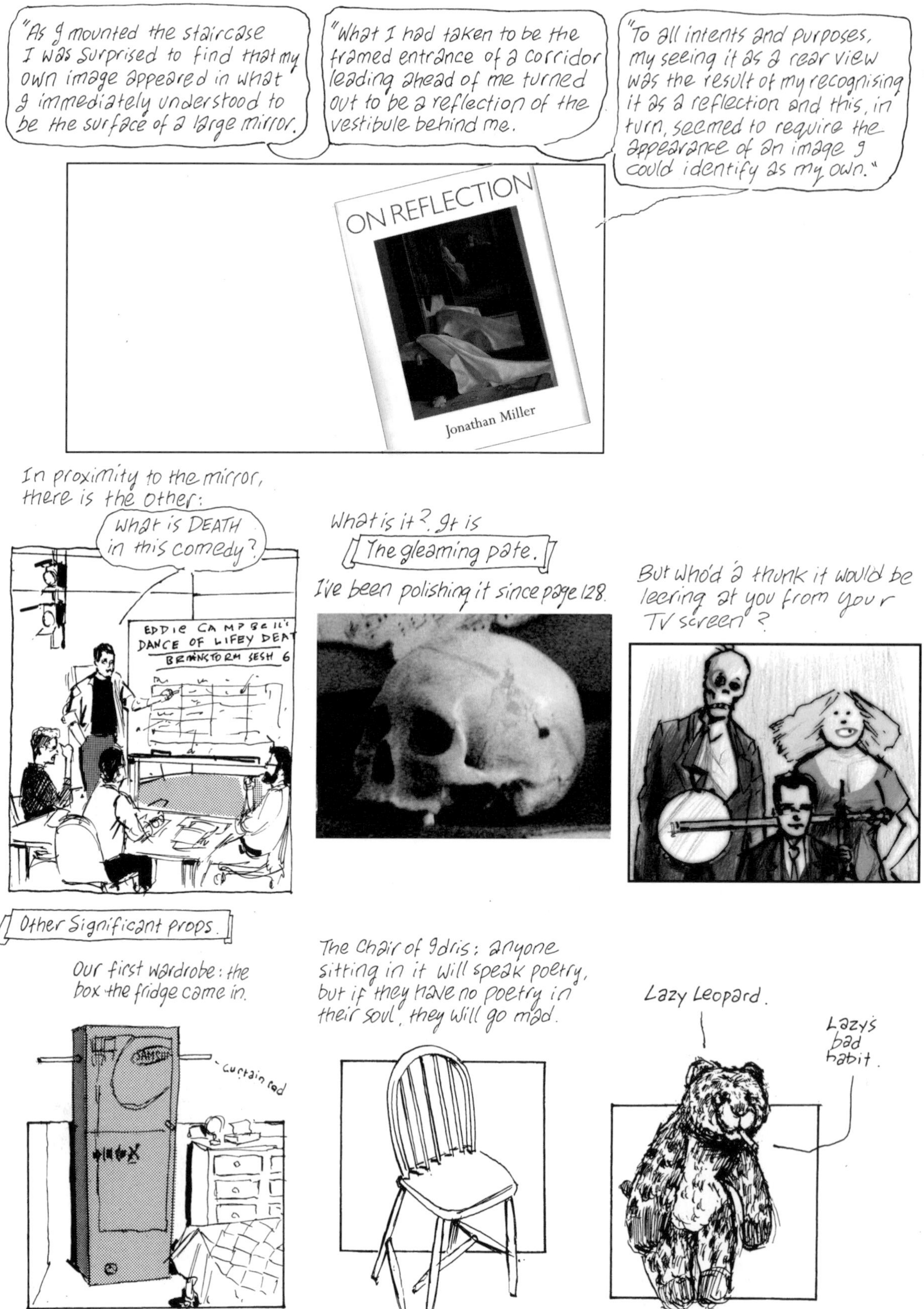
"As I mounted the staircase I was surprised to find that my own image appeared in what I immediately understood to be the surface of a large mirror.
"What I had taken to be the framed entrance of a corridor leading ahead of me turned out to be a reflection of the vestibule behind me.
"To all intents and purposes, my seeing it as a rear view was the result of my recognising it as a reflection and this, in turn, seemed to require the appearance of an image I could identify as my own."
ON REFLECTION
Jonathan Miller
In proximity to the mirror, there is the Other:
What is DEATH in this comedy?
EDDIE CAMPBELL'S
DANCE OF LIFEY DEAT
BRAINSTORM SESH 6
What is it? It is
The gleaming pate.
I've been polishing it since page 128.
But who'd 'a thunk it would be leering at you from your TV screen?
Other Significant props.
Our first wardrobe: the box the fridge came in.
curtain rod
The Chair of Idris: anyone sitting in it will speak poetry, but if they have no poetry in their soul, they will go mad.
Lazy Leopard.
Lazy's bad habit.

The two-way door-Knob.

Take the Knob through with you or you'll have to come back the long way round.

The key-ring souvenir, made in China, given to me innocently by my late mother-in-law, with a map of the Queensland coast, and all the place names misspelled.

Gravestones.

Puss
Yocky

Chloe.

What's left of the empty bottle collection, kept in the old trunk under the house.

They might need it for the SNOOTER sequence.

The Kangaroo-bound FROM HELL, a limited edition of nineteen copies, the most effective and straightforward bit of business I ever pulled off.

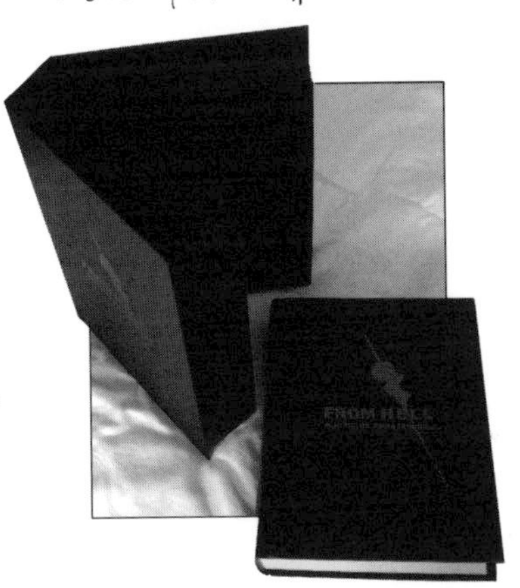

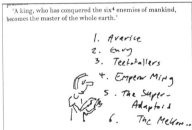

Dakin's Kama Sutra.

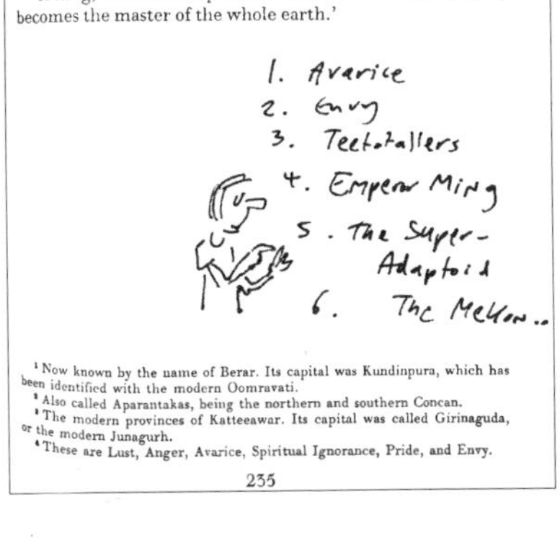

'A king, who has conquered the six[4] enemies of mankind, becomes the master of the whole earth.'

1. Avarice
2. Envy
3. Teetotallers
4. Emperor Ming
5. The Super-Adaptoid
6. The Mekon..

[1] Now known by the name of Berar. Its capital was Kundinpura, which has been identified with the modern Oomravati.
[2] Also called Aparantakas, being the northern and southern Concan.
[3] The modern provinces of Katteeawar. Its capital was called Girinaguda, or the modern Junagurh.
[4] These are Lust, Anger, Avarice, Spiritual Ignorance, Pride, and Envy.

235

The Party hat.

statue by Andrew Gallagher

The 'Meet me in the Alley, MacGarry' lyric sheet.

MULLINS' PART SONGS
Meet Me In The Alley, MacGarry
composed by
MR. M. MOORE & MR. D. WHITE
Sung by
The Three Tenners
At the
Magh Mell Ballroom
St. Patrick's Night
1996
CHORUS
So meet me in the alley, MacGarry.

The cutting of me, with White and Minty Moore (its authors) supposedly singing it at the "Magh Mell ballroom" in 1996.

Harry.

Harry's bad habit.

My Millennium medal, for my contribution to the Arts.

Hey, honeybee! While you were at work, they gave me a medal..

The tragic mask.

The gift-wrapped brick.

photo Phil Cross, 2007

Original publication information, chronologically

★Whenever I have been asked about influences, I seem to have always forgotten to mention that Danny Grey is named after the 'Danny' of Steinbeck's Tortilla Flat. Read the Wikipedia summary of that novel and you'll get my drift. The chapters beginning on pages 29, 56, 59, and 70 are modified versions of three and a half out of a set of five short stories, all originally five pages each, drawn in 10/80-1/81 that were an early attempt (not the first) to record the King Canute saga. Not having the heart to redo that much work, I incorporated them into the new chronological version even though there were stylistic incongruities. The first two books of *Alec: The King Canute Crowd* appeared in assorted small press photocopied pamphlets between 1981 and '85. While a large single collection was envisioned at the start, the logistics of making bigger packages was an evolutionary thing. It started with 32-page card-covered volumes. Three appeared from Escape Publishing in '84, '85, and '86. To these was added an unpublished fourth completed in '87 and the whole was released by Acme/Eclipse in '90, in both soft and hardcovers, erroneously titled *The Complete Alec.* I released my own edition of the same material in 2000. Note that the second of the four books has always been a problem for me. Initially it was really two books, 32 pages and 31 pages, that always needed to be tightened. The Escape print had the two boiled down to one at 30 story pages, while my own had 48. The current showing comes in at 40, but reinstates one page missing from the 48-page version. There are at least six pages that have still never been published anywhere, but they wouldn't improve the work.

★*Little Italy* was serialized mainly in the Australian anthology *Fox Comics* in '88 and '89, as well as Steve Bissette's *Taboo,* and collected as a 40-page book, in the same style as the Escape volumes, by Fantagraphics in '91. The current page count is 34.

★*The Dead Muse* was a 48-page anthology that I edited and which appeared from Fantagraphics in '90. All 12 of my own introductory pages are included here.

★Most of the parts of *The Dance of Lifey Death* appeared in various places between '90 and '92, and with 16 new pages was collected by Dark Horse in '94 as a 49-page comic book (including a story-page on the back cover.) My own edition of 48 pages was published in 11/'98. The whole pool is 52 pages, and every printing has had different exclusions.

★*Graffiti Kitchen* first appeared from Tundra in '93, and in my own edition in 2/'98.

★*Little Italy, Lifey Death* and *Graffiti Kitchen* were collected by me as *Alec: Three Piece Suit* in 6/'01.

★*How to be an Artist* was serialized in the fourteen issues of the Brisbane comic book anthology *Deevee* dated 6, 9, 12/'97; 1, 3, 5, 7, 9, 11/'98; 4,7,10/'99; 1,4/'00 and then collected by myself in 3/'01.

★*After the Snooter* appeared in parts between '95 and '01, mostly in issues of my own *Bacchus* monthly comic book. It was collected in my own edition in 6/'02 in what was, at 158 story pages, the largest book of my autobiographical material before this omnibus. Two more pages are added here.

★*The History of Humour* was serialized in the two issues of my own magazine, *Egomania*, in '02.

Sources of the 24 art pieces used as title pages and tailpieces

1- Preview sketch for cover of *Bacchus* #49, 12/'99, my millennium celebration, scanned from Diamond Distribution's colour catalogue; *2*-Drawn for this volume; *5*-Drawn for a French bookstore promotion, '06; *7*-My own photo, '79; *8*-Cover *Alec: The King Canute Crowd,* Eddie Campbell Comics edition, '00; *38*-Drawn for this volume; *79*-This was meant to be the cover of the Escape edition of *Alec* volume 3, *Doggie in the Window*, '86, but they gave me grief over it and preferred an inferior drawing. It was used there, as here, as a title page; *112*-From the cover of *Bacchus* #55, 9/'00; *139*-Photo, Paris '78; *140*-Based on a photo of 'Georgette' '81; *189*-Cover of *Flick* #3, 11/'81; *190*-Drawing for the '86 UKCAC convention booklet; *200*-Cover of *Bacchus* #56, 10/'00; *314*-Wraparound cover of *Fox Comics* #22, '88, shown here flipped; *350*-Cover of *The Dead Muse,* published by Fantagraphics books, '90; *363*-Sketch by Glenn Dakin, '88 (he also, by the way, drew the little angel on my page 384.); *364*-Cover of Eddie Campbell Comics edition of *The Dance of Lifey Death*, '98; *398*-A detail from the cover of the Dark Horse edition of *The Dance of Lifey Death,* 1/'94, has replaced the original panel 3 on this page; *415*-The cover of my own publication *Three Piece Suit,* '02; *416*-Drawing in pastels from cover of *Bacchus* #57, 11/'00; *577*-Photo from a mock newspaper report in *Bacchus* #56, 10/'00; *578*-Cover painted for *The Comics Journal* #145, '91; *604*-cover painted for *The Comics Journal* #273, 1/'06; *639*-Promo photo for tv show, '08, photographer Phil Cross; *640*-pencil drawing from cover of *Egomania* #1, '02.